BIOGRAPHICAL DICTIONARY OF JAPANESE HISTORY

Staff

Akio Yasuoka
Kenzō Tanji
Kōichi Fujimoto
Mitsumasa Yamamoto
Yoshiko Yamamoto
Mitsuo Fuse
Fumihiko Sueki
Yoshimitsu Iwakabe
Fumiko Umezawa
Mitsue Kuroda
Yoko Nakajima

BIOGRAPHICAL DICTIONARY OF JAPANESE HISTORY

supervising editor

Seiichi Iwao

translator

Burton Watson

Kodansha International Ltd.
in collaboration with the
International Society for Educational Information

Photo Credits

The compilers and publishers are grateful to the following institutions and individuals for permission to reproduce the photographs in this book: the Imperial Household Agency; the National Diet Library; Tokyo National Museum; the Institute for Compilation of Historiographical Materials of University of Tokyo; Kyodo News Service; Sanyo Photo; Daihikaku Senkō-ji; Yamazaki Fumiko; Kodansha, Ltd.; Jimyō-in; Kitano Temman-gū; Tōji-in; Kinkaku-ji; Jingo-ji; Kennin-ji; Nishi Hongan-ji; Seiken-in; Waseda University Library; Matsuura Shiryō Hakubutsukan; Tokyo Shisei Chōsakai; Shōrin-ji; Yōgen-in; Kyoto University Library; Manpuku-ji.

Distributed in the United States by Kodansha International/USA Ltd., through Harper & Row, Publishers, Inc., 10 East 53rd Street, New York, New York 10022, and in Japan by Kodansha International Ltd., 2–12–21 Otowa, Bunkyo-ku, Tokyo 112.

Published by Kodansha International Ltd., 2–12–21 Otowa, Bunkyo-ku, Tokyo 112 and Kodansha International/USA Ltd., 10 East 53rd Street, New York, New York 10022 and 44 Montgomery Street, San Francisco, California 94104 in collaboration with the International Society for Educational Information, Inc., 7–8 Shintomi 2-chome, Chuo-ku, Tokyo 104. Printed in Japan.

LCC 76–9359
ISBN 0–87011–274–0
JBC 1521–786265–2361

First edition, 1978

Contents

Foreword	7
Preface	9
Ancient Period	11
Medieval Period	75
Early Modern Period	147
Modern Period	287
Appendices	
Imperial Family Lineage	529
Fujiwara Family Lineage	532
Minamoto and Taira Family Lineages	533
Lineages of the Hōjō Regents and Ashikaga Shoguns	534
Lineage of the Tokugawa Shoguns	535
Buddhist Sects	536
Organization of the *Ritsuryō* Bureaucracy	541
Organization of the Kamakura and Muromachi Shogunates	542
Organization of the Tokugawa Shogunate	543
Organization of the Dajōkan Bureaucracy	544

Major Military Actions 546
Japanese Army Cliques 551
Japanese Navy Cliques 552
Major Right-Wing Organizations 553
Political Parties 555
Cabinets since 1885 558
Institutions and Terms 561
Maps 578
Bibliography 580
Index 619

Foreword

Since its establishment in 1958, the International Society for Educational Information has been working in various ways to insure that Japanese history and culture are better understood abroad. One aspect of its endeavor has been to examine the treatment of subjects pertaining to Japan in the textbooks and reference works of foreign countries. Where patent errors or misunderstandings were found in the written or visual material on Japan, notices have been sent to the authors or publishers so that corrections can be made in later editions. The response to these efforts has been highly favorable.

In addition to measures taken to correct errors in material already published, the Society has engaged in the compilation and publication of reference works that it hopes will help prevent future errors. Among these is a series of biographical dictionaries dealing with various aspects of Japanese life. The first volume in the series, the *Biographical Dictionary of Japanese Literature* edited by the late Professor Sen'ichi Hisamatsu, appeared in 1976 and has been warmly welcomed in Japan and abroad. The present volume, *Biographical Dictionary of Japanese History*, is a sequel to that work and deals with persons who have played outstanding roles in Japanese political, economic and social life. A third biographical dictionary now being compiled deals with figures historically important in the field of fine arts in Japan; such persons have not been included in the present volume.

Conceived more than ten years ago, much preparatory planning and research has gone into this project. The entries were written by a research staff composed of acknowledged Japanese historians; research and editing were coordinated and supervised by Dr. Seiichi Iwao, professor emeritus of Tokyo University and member of the Japan Academy.

The Society is highly indebted to all members of the editorial staff and to numerous others who have contributed both financial and moral support to this project. In particular, we would like to acknowledge the financial support provided by the Ministry of Foreign Affairs and the Commemorative Association for the 1970 Japan World Exposition.

Kodansha International has expressed its support of and enthusiasm for this project by designing, producing, and publishing the commercial editions of these dictionaries internationally in cooperation with the Society.

We believe that this comprehensive dictionary will assist those who desire an authoritative account of Japanese historical figures and that it will provide useful information to the English reading public for many years to come.

Michiko Kaya
Executive Director
International Society for Educational Information

Preface

After many years of planning and research, we are pleased to present this *Biographical Dictionary of Japanese History*, a volume that should prove of special value to all interested in the culture and history of the Far East.

It is an understatement to say that the effort put into this project has been ambitious. In the initial stages, a basic list of Japanese historical figures mentioned in foreign textbooks and reference works was compiled. This list was then expanded by the addition of carefully selected and screened names of persons of prominence in the political, social, religious, and scientific spheres of Japanese history. A biography of each figure was then composed, drawing upon the latest research data. Every effort was made to include the salient facts in the background and career of each personality and to convey the nature of the person's contribution to Japanese history and culture. Naturally, the amount of space devoted to each entry reflects the relative importance of the person, although some material required special explanation for the benefit of English readers. Portraits and visual material have been included when available, and a selected Bibliography is also provided.

The volume is divided into four chronological sections, with entries arranged alphabetically in each. In cases where a life spans two periods, the entry has been included in the period that witnessed the individual's most notable activity or contribution. The four periods reflect the major social and political transitions in Japanese history and represent the consensus of the scholarly community.

The first section, the "Ancient Period," includes the age of myth and legend and extends through the Asuka, Nara, and Heian periods. This period saw the ascendency of the nobility, centered on the emperor and his court, and the introduction of continental culture and thought, which exerted vast influence on the society.

The ensuing "Medieval Period" (1185–1572), including the Kamakura, Northern and Southern Courts, and Muromachi periods, was characterized by the establishment of the shogunate and a feudal society. The long period of strife between feudal lords at the end of this period set the stage for the unification of the country.

In the third historical division, herein called the "Early Modern

Period" (1572–1868), the feudal system continued, with the Tokugawa shogunate attaining undisputed control over a unified nation, and Japan entered a period of more than two and one-half centuries of peace. Domestic concerns became paramount, and learning and culture spread to the general populace. A vibrant, popular culture developed, and the foundations for the modern nation were gradually laid.

In the "Modern Period," the years following the Meiji Restoration in 1868 witnessed vigorous modernization in all spheres of political, economic, cultural, and social life. It was inevitable that this period should produce some of the outstanding personalities in Japanese history.

Appendices designed to clarify the social and political background of the biographical accounts have been included. These comprise genealogical tables, charts of the organization of political institutions, and explanations of institutions and terms. Maps showing the administrative divisions of Japan in past and present have also been provided so that the reader may have a clearer understanding of the geographical references in the biographies.

The editor and his associates hope that this volume will enable readers to gain a better understanding of Japanese history and that it will serve as a useful reference work in future studies of the subject.

Seiichi Iwao

ANCIENT PERIOD

Antoku Tennō

Ganjin

Daigo Tennō

Gembō

Fujiwara (Nakatomi) no Kamatari

Goshirakawa Tennō

Jimmu Tennō

Gyōki

Ichijō Tennō

Jingū Kōgō

Kammu Tennō

Minamoto no Yoshiie

Rōben

Saichō

Sakanoue no Tamuramaro

Seiwa Tennō

Shōmu Tennō

Shōtoku Taishi

Sugawara no Michizane

Taira no Masakado

Toneri Shinnō

Ancient Period

Abe no Hirafu 阿部比羅夫 (seventh century)

Military leader of the Asuka period. He was dispatched in 658 by Empress Saimei at the head of a force of 180 ships to proceed north and attack the Ezo people, who held power in northern Japan. The following year he is said to have crossed over to the China mainland to attack the Mishihase, or Sushen, state. This expedition represents the earliest recorded attempt by the Yamato court to extend control over the Tōhoku and Hokkaido regions. It is possible that the term Mishihase here does not refer to the actual Tungusic state on the China mainland whose name is read Mishihase in Japanese but to some group in Hokkaido.

In 662, when the state of Paekche on the Korean Peninsula was threatened with extinction by the combined forces of Silla and T'ang China, Abe no Hirafu was sent at the head of a Japanese relief force to attack Silla, but he was defeated in battle with the T'ang army in 663 at a place in Korea called Paek Ch'on River (Haku River). As a result, all vestiges of Japanese control on the Korean peninsula were brought to an end.

Abe no Sadatō 安倍貞任 (1019–1062)

Warrior of the middle Heian period. He was the son of Abe no Yoritoki and heir of the Abe clan, which controlled the area along the Kitakami River in the province of Mutsu. The members of the Abe clan worked together as a close-knit family group, Sadatō establishing his base in the *saku* (palisade) of Kuriyagawa in the Iwate district, possession of which he had received from his father. Able to exercise semiautonomous rule in the region, the members of the Abe clan often failed to render taxes to the central government or moved to extend their power over a still larger region, until the court finally dispatched Minamoto no Yoriyoshi and his son Yoshiie to suppress them. This led to the so-called Earlier Nine Years' War, which demonstrated how great was the power of Minamoto no Yoriyoshi and other warriors like him who drew their wealth from private manors and were beginning to come to prominence at this time. Initially Sadatō got the better of Yoriyoshi's forces, but he was defeated at the Koromogawa palisade and fled back to his base at the Kuriyagawa palisade, where he was once more defeated and killed.

Achi no Omi 阿知使主 (early fifth century)

Foreigner of the ancient period who settled in Japan. Achi no Omi, who settled in Japan in the time of Emperor Ōjin (third century), was said to have been the great grandson of Emperor Ling (A.D. 168–188) of the Later Han dynasty of China. Since he came to Japan at a time when the ruler of the Korean kingdom of Paekche was on close terms with Emperor Ōjin, it has been suggested that he was brought by Japanese generals on their return from the Korean peninsula.

He is said to have brought with him his family and followers and to have taken charge of the composition and handling of documents at the Japanese court. He is also supposed to have been sent on a mission to China and to have brought back four women who were skilled at weaving. He is representative of the persons who introduced various skills from Korea and China to the court of Emperor Ōjin. The family known as Yamato no Ayauji (倭漢氏 or 東漢氏), which looked to him as their ancestor, later became the hereditary handlers of documents at the Yamato court.

Amaterasu Ōmikami 天照大御神

Figure from Japanese mythology, also known as Ōhiru Memuchi. The central figure in the myths and legends recorded in the *Kojiki* and *Nihon Shoki*, she is the goddess considered to have been the ancestress of the Japanese imperial family and, as the deity enshrined in the Inner Shrine of the Grand Shrines of Ise, is accorded greater respect than any other deity in the Japanese pantheon.

The *Kojiki* and *Nihon Shoki* relate three theories concerning her birth:

1. She was born as child of the deities Izanagi and Izanami.
2. She was born when the deity Izanagi took into his hand a nickel mirror.

3. Izanagi returned from the underworld (Yominokuni) and was bathing to purify himself; she was born as he washed his left eye.

The myth also relates that Amaterasu had a brother, the god Susano-o, an unruly deity who committed an act of violence in Takamagahara (the Heavenly Plain, abode of the gods), thereby so enraging Amaterasu that she shut herself up in a cave, whereupon darkness covered the whole world. She is, thus, a kind of sun goddess also, and it seems likely that in this myth the imperial family, gradually building up the ancient Japanese state as agriculture developed, sought to relate its own ancestors to the sun—the farmer's greatest blessing—thereby giving itself a supreme position in its attempt to exert control over the other powerful families.

Antoku Tennō 安徳天皇 (1178–1185)

Emperor of the late Heian period. His father was Emperor Takakura and his mother the daughter of Taira no Kiyomori, Kenreimon-in Tokuko; he reigned from 1180 to 1185. By the time of his birth, the Heike, or Taira family, had reached the zenith of its power, and the high minister Taira no Kiyomori was thus able to place his grandson on the throne and handle all affairs of government in his name. Emperor Antoku was only an infant of three when he was made ruler, but soon after the Heike, suffering a series of defeats at the hands of their rivals, the Genji, or Minamoto, family, were forced to desert the capital and flee west, taking the child emperor with them. The final defeat of the Taira family took place at the naval battle of Dan-no-ura in the province of Nagato, present-day Yamaguchi Prefecture, when Emperor Antoku, then eight years old, was drowned along with the remaining members of his mother's family. The toys that the emperor played with have been preserved at the Itsukushima Shrine, the family shrine of the Heike.

Chōnen 奝然 (d. 1016)

Monk of the Sanron sect in the middle Heian period, he was born in Kyoto, the son of Fujiwara no Masatsura. He entered religious training at Tōdai-ji in Nara, studying Sanron doctrine under Kanri and Esoteric Buddhism under Gengō. From his early years he developed a strong desire to visit China, at this time under the rule of the Sung dynasty. In the eighth month of 983, he and his disciple Jōsan and others boarded a ship owned by the Chinese merchants Ch'en Jen-shuang and Hsü Jen-man, and in the tenth month sailed to China. Chōnen first paid a visit to the temple called K'ai-yüan-ssu in Yang-chou and then journeyed to the Sung capital at Pien (K'ai-feng), where he was received in audience by Emperor T'ai-tsung. The following year he visited the Buddhist temples at Mt. Wu-t'ai and then returned to the capital. He was generously treated by Emperor T'ai-tsung, who bestowed upon him a purple robe and the title Fa-chi Ta-shih (Hōsai Daishi). He returned to Japan in 986 on a ship belonging to a Chinese merchant named Cheng Jen-te, bringing with him a copy of the Tripitaka, a collection of Buddhist sacred texts, and a sandalwood image of the Buddha Śākyamuni. The Tripitaka had been completed in 983 and contained over five thousand volumes. The sandalwood image was a copy of an image housed in a temple called K'ai-pao-ssu in the Sung capital. The image was said to have come originally from India by way of Central Asia and to have been housed for a long time in K'ai-yüan-ssu in Yang-chou. Chōnen was given special permission to make a copy of it. When he returned to Japan, he intended to house the image in a hall in Saga in the western suburbs of Kyoto, but this plan met with opposition from the monks of Enryaku-ji on Mt. Hiei, and he was unable to carry it out. Only after his death was his disciple Jōsan, who had accompanied him to China, able to build the hall as Chōnen had planned. The hall and the statue remain in existence today at the temple known as Shōryō-ji in Saga. In 989 Chōnen became head of Tōdai-ji. He is said to have kept a diary of his trip to China entitled *Nissō nikki*, but it is no longer extant.

Daigo Tennō 醍醐天皇 (885–930)

Emperor of the early Heian period. The son of Emperor Uda, he ascended the throne in 897 to become the sixtieth ruler on the occasion of his father's abdication. By retiring, Emperor Uda had hoped to be able with greater freedom to join with his son and his advisers, Sugawara no Michizane and Fujiwara no Tokihira, in handling affairs of state, but in 901 Fujiwara no Tokihira suddenly contrived to have Sugawara no Michizane exiled and gathered all power into his own hands. Sugawara no Michizane died in exile, and when Fujiwara no Tokihira in turn died in 909, his death was believed to have been caused by the angry spirit of Michizane. In order to placate Michizane's spirit, he was given the title Tenjin and worshiped at various Shinto shrines.

Among Emperor Daigo's important political measures was a law promulgated in 902 that attempted to regulate the growth of *shōen* (private manors), and he took other steps to improve the financial situation of the government and correct defects in the *ritsuryō* system. He also commanded Ki no Tsurayuki and others to compile the *Kokin wakashū*, one of the most important anthologies of early Japanese court poetry.

In the summer of 930 the palace was struck by lightning, and Emperor Daigo, as a result of the shock, fell sick and died three months later. His father, Emperor Uda, died the following year.

The reign of Emperor Daigo, referred to by one of its era names, Engi, is often linked with that of Emperor Murakami (reigned 946–967), also referred to by one of its era names, Tenryaku, and historians speak of "the Engi-Tenryaku peace," meaning a time when the government was stable and orderly, a fit model for rulers of later times.

Dōkyō 道鏡 (d. 772)

Buddhist monk of the middle Nara period. Said to have come from Yuge, Shiki district in the province of Kawachi (present Osaka Prefecture), he is therefore also referred to as Yuge Dōkyō. He was a disciple of Gien, studying with him the doctrines of the Hossō sect of Buddhism. In 762 he attended retired Empress Kōken during an illness and won her confidence as a result, using it as a means to intervene personally in political matters. In 764, following the failure of an attempted coup d'état by Fujiwara no Nakamaro, he became *dajōdaijin zenshi* (prime minister priest), taking upon himself the supreme power in both the political and religious worlds. Then in 766 he was given the title of *hōō* (something akin to pope), thus embarking on a type of priestly government quite divorced from the legally established *ritsuryō* system, the centralized bureaucratic system of the day. However, despite his attempt to establish his own position as something conferred by divine authority, he was overthrown by the machinations of court nobles and others opposed to him, who claimed that he had gone against the divine oracle, and he was demoted to the Yakushi-ji temple in Shimotsuke (present Tochigi Prefecture), where he ended his days.

Dōshō 道昭 (629–700)

Monk of the Asuka period who introduced the Hossō sect of Buddhism to Japan. He was born in the province of Kawachi and in 653 went to China, at that time ruled by the T'ang dynasty. There he studied under the eminent monk Hsüan-tsang (d. 664). After returning to Japan, he built a cloister called Zen-in in the southeast corner of the grounds of Gangō-ji, where he devoted himself to teaching and religious practice. He also traveled about to various provinces devoting himself to works that would contribute to public welfare. In accordance with his instructions, his body was cremated when he died, the earliest known incidence of cremation in Japan. The Hossō sect, which he introduced to Japan, is based upon the *yuishiki* or "consciousness-only" doctrines of the Indian Buddhist philosopher Vasubandhu (ca. fifth century), which were transmitted to China and put into final form by Hsüan-tsang and his disciple K'uei-chi (632–682). Kōfuku-ji, one of the main temples of Nara, served as the chief center for the sect, which enjoyed great prominence during the Nara period. Recent researches, however, suggest that the sect of Buddhism introduced by Dōshō may not in fact have been the Hossō, but a similar sect known as Shōron. The Shōron sect bases its teachings upon the *Shōdaijōron*, a work by Asanga, the elder brother of Vasubandhu. It flourished in China somewhat earlier than the Hossō sect.

Eikan 永観 (1033–1111)

Monk of the Sanron sect in the late Heian period famous for his devotion to Pure Land teachings; his name may also be read Yōkan. He was a son of Minamoto no Tsunekuni. In 1043 he began the study of Buddhism under Jinkan of Zenrin-ji, a temple in Kyoto more popularly known as Eikan-dō. In 1044 he entered the clergy at Tōdai-ji in Nara; though officially a member of the Sanron sect, he became widely acquainted with many different schools of Buddhism. He was an excellent scholar and frequently took part in theological debates. From his early years he was greatly attracted to *nembutsu*, the ritual invocation of the name of the Buddha Amida. In 1064 he retired to a residence at Mt. Kōmyō south of Kyoto, but around 1072 returned to Zenrin-ji. For a brief period from 1100 to 1102 he served as *bettō*, or head of Tōdai-ji, but for the most part he remained aloof from worldly affairs, devoting himself to *nembutsu* practice and encouraging others to do likewise. Though there are various kinds of *nembutsu* practice, he advocated that known as *shōmyō nembutsu*, the recitation of the formula *Namu Amida Butsu*, and spoke of himself as a member of the Nembutsu sect. He was thus an important forerunner of Hōnen, who likewise stressed the importance of *nembutsu* and established Pure Land teachings as an independent school of Buddhism. Eikan's extant works include *Ōjō jūin* and *Ōjō kōshiki*, and a biography of him is found in the *Shūi ōjōden*.

Enchin 圓珍 (814–891)

Buddhist priest of the early Heian period. Born in the province of Sanuki in Shikoku, he entered the monastary of Mt. Hiei at the age of fifteen and became a monk of the Tendai sect. In 853 he journeyed to China and returned in 858, bringing back with him a thousand rolls of Buddhist scriptures. These he deposited in Onjō-ji (also called Mii-dera), a temple at the foot of Mt. Hiei on the shore of Lake Biwa, which had fallen into ruin but which Enchin proceeded to restore.

In 868 he became the fifth *zasu,* or leader of the Tendai sect; on his death he was given the posthumous title Chishō Daishi. The monks who carried on his teachings in time came to be known as the Jimon faction, centering around Onjō-ji and engaged in a protracted struggle for power within the Tendai sect with the so-called Sammon faction centered about Enryaku-ji on Mt. Hiei.

Ennin 圓仁 (794–864)

Buddhist priest of the early Heian period. Born in the province of Shimotsuke (Tochigi Prefecture), he became a monk in 802 under the guidance of the priest Kōchi. In 808 he journeyed to Mt. Hiei and became a disciple of Saichō, and after the latter's death in 822 he carried out his master's dying wish by working to promote the teachings of the Tendai sect, which Saichō had introduced to Japan. In 838 he journeyed to China, then under the rule of the T'ang dynasty, to continue the study and practice of Tendai Buddhism. He returned to Japan in 847 and in 854 became the third *zasu,* or leader of the Tendai sect.

The diary that Ennin kept of his ten-year sojourn in China, entitled *Nittō guhō junrei kōki,* is still extant and has been translated into English by Edwin O. Reischauer and published under the title *Ennin's Travels in T'ang China.* This work, while focusing mainly on Buddhism, also contains much data concerning T'ang society and folkways and the history and geography of the time. Written some four hundred years before Marco Polo's famous account, it constitutes one of the most valuable sources of information on China of the middle ages.

In 866, two years after his death, Ennin was honored with the posthumous title Jikaku Daishi. The monks who followed in his line came in time to be known as the Sammon or Enryaku-ji faction and engaged in a long and heated struggle for power within the Tendai sect with the members of the so-called Jimon or Onjō-ji faction, which centered around the followers of the priest Enchin.

En no Ozunu 役小角 (dates unknown)

Religious figure of the Nara period whose activities and practices were associated with mountains. He is also known as En no Gyōja or En no Ubasoku. According to the *Shoku Nihongi*, he lived on Mt. Katsuragi in the province of Yamato and was famous as a possessor of magical powers. But he was accused of deluding and leading men astray and in 699 was exiled to the island of Ōshima off Izu Peninsula. He had a disciple named Karakuni-no-muraji Hirotari and was said to have been able to command the gods to draw water and gather firewood for him. In later ages a great number of legends became associated with his name. Since the Kamakura period, when Shugendō,—the sect of Buddhism devoted to religious practices in mountain areas—became firmly established, he has been honored as the founder of the sect.

Fujiwara no Fuhito 藤原不比等 (659–720)

Court minister of the early Nara period. The second son of Fujiwara no Kamatari, he was ordered by Emperor Mommu to join with Prince Osakabe and others in compiling a *ritsuryō*, or code of laws modeled on those of China; on completion, the work was presented to Empress Gemmei and is known as the *Taihō ritsuryō* from the name of the era in which it was compiled. The *ritsuryō* comprises two kinds of laws, the *ritsu*, penal code laws, which deal with criminal offenses and punishments, and the *ryō*, civil code laws, which regulate the functioning of the type of centralized bureaucratic system of government at this time. Fuhito was chosen to participate in the compilation of the code because his father, Kamatari, along with Prince Naka no Ōe, had in 646 drawn up the Taika Reform Edict, which laid the foundation for the establishment of such a bureaucratic system of government. The code compiled at this time remained in effect until the Heian period. In 718 a group headed by Fuhito began working on a revision of the *Taihō ritsuryō*, but the work was suspended with Fuhito's death in 720 and was only brought to completion in 757 by Fuhito's grandson, Fujiwara no Nakamaro. The revised version of the code is known as the *Yōrō ritsuryō*.

Fuhito's oldest daughter married Emperor Mommu, and his third daughter married Emperor Shōmu to become Empress Kōmyō. His four sons all held high ranks and posts in the government, and the Fujiwaras thus established themselves in a position of great strength at court.

Fujiwara no Fuyutsugu 藤原冬嗣 (775–826)

Court official of the early Heian period. He was born into the so-called Hokke branch of the Fujiwara family at a time when the family had declined from its earlier position of power. He enjoyed the trust of Emperor Saga, and when the emperor in 810 set up the Kurōdodokoro, an office directly under the supervision of the ruler that was designed to handle confidential documents and other important matters of state, Fuyutsugu, along with Kose no Notari, was appointed to head it. Following this, he continued to advance in position until in 825, during the reign of Emperor Junna (reigned 823–833), he was appointed to the post of *sadaijin*, the most important in the government.

In addition to his state activities, Fuyutsugu founded the Kangaku-in, a private academy for the education of the sons of the Fujiwara family, set up facilities for medical treatment, and took other steps to provide for the welfare of the Fujiwaras. His descendants in time became the most important branch of the Fujiwara family at court.

Fujiwara no Hirotsugu 藤原廣嗣 (d. 740)

Courtier of the middle Nara period. He was the son of Fujiwara no Umakai and the grandson of Fujiwara no Fuhito, both powerful court ministers of the time. Perhaps as a result, he is said to have been inordinately proud of his family background and often willful and overbearing in behavior. In 737, when an outbreak of disease carried off his father and many of the other important ministers of the Fujiwara family, a new group of men headed by Kibi no Makibi and the Buddhist priest Gembō rose to prominence and began to introduce elements of Chinese culture, which they had become familiar with during visits to the continent. In 738 Fujiwara no Hirotsugu was suddenly assigned to a post in the Dazaifu (military governor's office) in Kyushu, an appointment that amounted to virtual banishment. In 740 Hirotsugu, declaring that Gembō and Makibi would bring about the ruin of Japan, raised the cry of revolt, but the court dispatched a force of some fifteen thousand troops against him, and he was killed.

Later, in 746, Gembō fell from power and was exiled to the Dazaifu, where he died. It is said that the people of the time attributed his death to the angry spirit of Hirotsugu.

Fujiwara (Nakatomi) no Kamatari 藤原(中臣)鎌足 (614–669)

Court official of the Asuka period. He was born into the Nakatomi family, a family of rather lowly status that served the Yamato court and had charge of affairs pertaining to the Shinto religion. From an early age he showed great fondness for learning and surpassed others in whatever he did. He studied under the Buddhist priest Min, who had been sent to China as a student and had remained there for over twenty years, and Min was said to have regarded him as a man of extraordinary ability. Even the most powerful minister of the time, Soga no Iruka, treated him with deference. Kamatari, angered at the excessive authority wielded by Soga no Iruka and at his lack of respect for Empress Kōgyoku, the ruler at the time, began to consider ways to overthrow him. He first became friendly with Prince Karu but later transferred his attentions to Prince Naka no Ōe, a person of superior ability, and together they plotted the downfall of the Soga family. In 645 they attacked and killed Soga no Iruka when he was in attendance at the palace and then succeeded in wiping out the other members of the family. It had earlier been agreed that Prince Naka no Ōe should be made ruler, but Kamatari persuaded him to give way to Prince Karu so as to avoid antagonizing the older factions at court, and the latter accordingly ascended the throne to become Emperor Kōtoku. He had no real power, however, all affairs of government being handled by Prince Naka no Ōe and Kamatari.

In 645, Taika, the first formal *nengō* (era name) to be used by the Japanese court, was adopted, and in 646 the so-called Taika Reform Edict was promulgated, setting forth the principles for a new system of government. The main characteristics of this system are as follows:

1. All land and persons were to become the property of the state.
2. In order to implement this goal, appropriate machinery for administration, communication, and military control was to be set up.
3. Population registers were to be drawn up and land alloted to the people in equal shares.
4. All taxes were fixed by law.

Kamatari and the others of his party thereby created the so-called *ritsuryō*, or penal and civil code system, a bureaucratic system designed to create strong centralized government with the emperor at its head, the kind of government that Min and others who had been to China had observed in operation there under the Sui and T'ang dynasties. The establishment of this new system of centralized government represents, along with the creation of the shogunate system by Minamoto no Yoritomo and the Meiji Restoration, one of the three most important political innovations in the history of the Japanese state.

In 653 Kamatari's eldest son, a Buddhist priest whose religious name was Jōe (born in 643), was sent to T'ang China as a student priest, ostensibly to study Buddhism but also to act as a hostage. At this time the T'ang dynasty was extending its power into the Korean peninsula, and eventually it conquered the state of Paekche, which had been strongly allied to Japan. Japan dispatched an army to go to the assistance of Paekche, but in 663 it was defeated, and all vestiges of Japanese control disappeared from the Korean peninsula. In order to guard the country from possible attack by Chinese or Korean forces, garrison troops known as *sakimori* were established along the coast of northern Kyushu. The T'ang government, however, only requested that Japan recognize its sovereignty over the Korean peninsula and did not attempt to send a military force against Japan. In 665 Jōe, who until then had remained in China as a hostage, was sent home, though the exact reason for this is unclear. On his return, he was poisoned by a man of Paekche who had taken refuge in Japan after the overthrow of his native country.

In 668 Prince Naka no Ōe ascended the throne to become Emperor Tenji. The following year, when Kamatari fell ill, the emperor came in person to visit him and inquire about his condition, whereupon Kamatari asked that he be given a modest burial that would not impose a burden upon the common people. The emperor, in recognition of his achievements, bestowed on him the surname Fujiwara, and on the sixteenth day of the tenth month, Kamatari died.

The Fujiwara family, which began with Kamatari, continued in later ages to be very closely associated with the imperial family, an association exemplified as recently as the time of the Second World War in the person of Prime Minister Konoe Fumimaro, the Konoe being a chief branch of the Fujiwara family.

Fujiwara no Michinaga 藤原道長 (966–1027)

Court official of the middle Heian period. He was born into the Fujiwara family, which earlier in the Heian period had produced the powerful ministers Fujiwara no Yoshifusa and Mototsune, and in 980 was given his first position at court. In 995 his elder brothers Michitaka and Michikane both died in an epidemic, and in the sixth month of the same year Michinaga was advanced to the post of *daijin*. He also held the position of *uji no chōja*, or head of the entire Fujiwara clan. In 996 his nephew Korechika, who up until this time had been an important rival for power, fell out of favor, and Michinaga advanced to a position of unprecedented authority. In 999 he married his daughter Fujiwara no Shōshi to Emperor Ichijō, and the sons of this union in time became Emperor Goichijō (reigned 1016–36) and Emperor Gosuzaku (reigned 1036–45) respectively. His second daughter, Kenshi, he married to Emperor Sanjō, and in 1016 he forced Emperor Sanjō to relinquish the throne so that he could set up his own grandson as Emperor Goichijō. The following year he turned over the position of *sesshō*, regent, to his son Yorimichi, while he himself assumed the highest of all ministerial ranks, that of *dajōdaijin*. At the zenith of his power, he described his life in a poem of the time as being like the full moon shining in the sky. He was troubled by frequent illness, however, and in 1019 he retired from government service, became a monk, and founded a temple, the Hōjō-ji. In 1027 he developed a swelling on his back that pained him greatly, and on the fourth day of the twelfth month he died. He is said to have been selfish and willful in behavior, and yet at the same time to have had a frank and forthright disposition. His diary written in his own hand is extant, the oldest Japanese diary to be preserved in the original. Known as the *Midō Kampaku ki*, it contains invaluable information on the politics and court life of the time and is regarded as one of the most important sources for the history of the period.

Fujiwara no Mototsune 藤原基經 (836–891)

Court official of the early Heian period. He was the son of Fujiwara no Nagayoshi but was adopted by his uncle Fujiwara no Yoshifusa and became the heir of the latter. When Emperor Yōzei came to the throne in 876, Mototsune was made *sesshō*, or regent, but he and the emperor did not get along well together, and because the emperor was a person of disorderly ways who was even rumored to have committed murder, Mototsune removed him from the throne and in 884 set up Emperor Kōkō in his place. When Emperor Kōkō died in 887, Mototsune selected Emperor Uda to be his successor. In return the emperor appointed Mototsune to the post of *kampaku*, sometimes translated as civil dictator, an office that empowered its holder to exercise complete control over all affairs of government.

FUJIWARA NO NAKAMARO (EMI NO OSHIKATSU) 藤原仲麻呂(恵美押勝) (706–764)

Court official of the middle Nara period. His political talents were first recognized by Empress Kōmyō, and in 749, when Empress Kōmyō's daughter ascended the throne to become Empress Kōken, Nakamaro became the most powerful minister of the Nara court. In 758 he made it possible for Emperor Junnin to ascend the throne, and the emperor in turn bestowed upon him the name Emi no Oshikatsu, meaning one who enjoys favor (*emi*), suppresses violence (*oshi*), and wins victory (*katsu*). After the death of Empress Kōmyō in 760, Empress Kōken began to bestow increasing favor on the Buddhist priest Dōkyō, who had nursed her through an illness, and the priest's power soon threatened to exceed that of Nakamaro. In 764 Nakamaro raised troops in an effort to overthrow Dōkyō, but the plot failed and he was killed while attempting to flee to the provinces.

He is said to have been fond of mathematics and historical studies and to have been a great admirer of Chinese culture.

FUJIWARA NO SHŌSHI 藤原彰子 (988–1074)

Empress of the middle Heian period. She was the daughter of Fujiwara no Michinaga. In 999 she married Emperor Ichijō and the following year she was named *kōgō*, empress. Emperor Ichijō already had an empress, Fujiwara no Teishi, but so great was Michinaga's power that he was able to induce the emperor to depart from custom and name a second empress. Shōshi bore two sons, who in time became Emperor Goichijō and Emperor Gosuzaku. She is also noted for the unusual quality of the ladies-in-waiting who attended her, among whom was Lady Murasaki, the author of *The Tale of Genji*, and Lady Izumi, author of the *Izumi Shikibu Diary*. Her rival, Empress Fujiwara no Teishi, was attended by Sei Shōnagon, author of the *Pillow Book*, this being the period when the women writers of the Heian were most active. In 1026 Empress Fujiwara no Shōshi was honored with the title Jōtōmon-in.

FUJIWARA NO SUMITOMO 藤原純友 (d. 941)

Official of the middle Heian period. Sometime around the Shōhei period (931–937) he became a local official in the province of Iyo, present-day

Ehime Prefecture. At that time the Inland Sea was beset by pirates, and the court accordingly dispatched Ki no Yoshito with orders to join Fujiwara no Sumitomo in suppressing them. This they set out to do, but when the term of Sumitomo's office came to an end, he made no move to leave Iyo, instead becoming a pirate himself. Before long he had made himself leader of the pirates and was roaming about the Inland Sea killing and plundering. In 940 the court sent Ono no Yoshifuru and others to apprehend him, and though he managed to evade them for some time, he was finally seized and put to death in 941.

At the same time this was going on, Taira no Masakado was leading a revolt in the Kantō area, and the court, believing that the two were acting in conjunction, was thrown into a state of terror. The two uprisings led by Taira no Masakado and Fujiwara no Sumitomo are often lumped together and referred to by the names of the eras in which they occurred—the Shōhei era mentioned above and the Tengyō era (938–949)—being called the Shōhei-Tengyō uprising.

Fujiwara no Yorimichi 藤原頼通 (992–1074)

Court official of the middle Heian period. The eldest son of Fujiwara no Michinaga, he was awarded high court rank and office at an early age. In 1017 his father turned over to him the post of *sesshō*, regent, and in 1019, when his father retired from official life to become a Buddhist monk, Yorimichi was made *kampaku*. The ruler at the time, Emperor Goichijō, was Yorimichi's nephew and a boy of eleven, and as a result all matters of government were disposed according to the wishes of Yorimichi. In 1025 a son was at last born to him, a boy named Michifusa in whom his father placed great hope, but he died in 1044, grieving Yorimichi so that he fell ill. In 1045, when Emperor Gosuzaku abdicated to make way for Emperor Goreizei, Prince Takahito, the future Emperor Gosanjō, was named heir apparent. Yorimichi opposed the selection because Prince Takahito was unrelated to the Fujiwara family, but since his daughter, Fujiwara no Kanshi, the empress of Emperor Goreizei, had given birth only to daughters, there was nothing he could do to block it. The year 1052, believed to be the 2001st anniversary of the death of the Buddha, ushered in the era known in Buddhist thought as Mappō, or the End of the Law, a time when it was believed that Buddhism would decline and the world would be filled with evil and disaster. Acceptance of this belief was widespread in Heian society, and Yorimichi, no exception, in this year converted his country home in Uji into a temple, calling it the Byōdō-in. The temple is still in existence and is constructed in such a way as to symbolize the Western Paradise, where souls of the faithful dwell after death. On the seventeenth day of the fourth month of 1068, two days before the death of Emperor Goreizei, Yorimichi gave up all government offices and retired to the Byōdō-in to live. In 1070 he built the Ikedono, the Pond Hall, close by the Byōdō-in and took up residence in it, and it was there that he died on the second day of the second month of 1074. It has long been a custom in the Fujiwara family to perform Buddhist memorial services each year on the anniversary of his death.

Because his father was a high minister, Yorimichi was able to succeed to high office without engaging in any protracted struggle for power. Perhaps as a result, he seems to have been a rather mild and simple-hearted man, though at the same time he was often short tempered and selfish. The time of Yorimichi and his father, Michinaga, marks the era of greatest power and affluence for the Fujiwara family in the Heian period.

Fujiwara no Yoshifusa 藤原良房 (804–872)

Court official of the early Heian period. The son of Fujiwara no Fuyutsugu, he became a court official at an early age. He arranged for his younger sister, Fujiwara no Junshi, to marry Emperor Nimmyō, and in the coup d'état known as the Jōwa disturbance in 842, he managed to have the son born of this union, Prince Michiyasu, declared heir apparent. In time the prince ascended the throne to become Empero Montoku. Yoshifusa then arranged for his own daughter to marry Emperor Montoku, and from this union was born the future Emperor Seiwa. With Emperor Montoku's death in 858, this boy came to the throne, though he was only eight at the time, while his grandfather handled the actual business of government. In 866, as a result of the coup d'état known as the Ōten Gate disturbance, Yoshifusa's opponents at court were removed from power, and in the same year he was formally named *sesshō*, regent, for the boy ruler, Emperor Seiwa. Though the title of regent had been in use before, as when Prince Shōtoku acted as regent for Empress Suiko, Fujiwara no Yoshifusa was the first commoner to hold it. Thus, as high minister and grandfather of the ruler, he laid the foundation for what was later to be called the *sekkan*, or *sesshō*-and-*kampaku* form of government.

Ganjin (Chien-chen) 鑑眞 (688–763)

Chinese Buddhist monk who came to Japan in the late Nara period. He was born in the Chiang-yang district of Yang-chou in eastern China in the time of the T'ang dynasty. He entered religious life at the age of thirteen and studied under the eminent monk Tao-an, receiving instruction in the *vinaya* (rules of religious discipline), known in Japanese as *ritsu.* He thereafter gained fame by traveling about China and lecturing on the *vinaya.*

In 742 he was urged by two Japanese monks studying in China, Eiei and Fushō, to journey to Japan. He attempted to do so, but was frustrated five times by storms and prohibitions imposed by the Chinese government. Meanwhile, an eye ailment deprived him of his sight. In 753, on his sixth attempt, he at last succeeded in making the journey, sailing in a ship carrying Japanese envoys on their way home from China. He landed in Kyushu, and, in the second month of 754, finally reached the capital at Nara. At this time he was sixty-six years old. He took up residence in Tōdai-ji, and at the command of Emperor Shōmu, set up a *kaidan* (ordination platform), where he transmitted the rules of discipline to the emperor, the empress, and a number of other distinguished personages.

As the first person to transmit the teachings on discipline to Japan, he is honored as the founder of the Ritsu sect of Buddhism in Japan. In 758 he was presented with the honorary title *daiwajō* and a mansion formerly belonging to Prince Niitabe. He took up residence there, and in time it became the temple known as Tōshōdai-ji.

In addition to founding the Ritsu sect in Japan, Ganjin brought with him a number of disciples and attendants who played an important role in introducing T'ang style sculpture and information on medicinal herbs to the Japanese of the time. The famous statue of Ganjin preserved in Tōshōdai-ji, which was said to have been made shortly before his death, is one of the oldest and finest examples of portrait sculpture in Japan.

Gembō 玄昉 (d. 746)

Buddhist priest of the middle Nara period. In 716 he was ordered to accompany the Kentōshi, the envoy to the T'ang court in China, where he studied Buddhism under the eminent monk Chih-chou and is said to have won the admiration of the T'ang emperor. In 735 he returned to Japan, bringing with him books to the amount of some five thousand scrolls as well as various Buddhist images. He was rewarded by the court with the high ecclesiastical rank of *sōjō*, and after curing Emperor Shōmu's mother of an illness, he came to enjoy the personal trust of the emperor. He acted as advisor to the powerful official Tachibana no Moroe and, along with Kibi no Makibi, wielded great authority in the government.

In 740 Fujiwara no Hirotsugu, disapproving of the way in which Gembō and the others of his party exercised power, began an uprising in an attempt to overthrow them, but he was defeated by the military forces of the court. Following this disturbance, Fujiwara no Nakamaro came to power and in 745 dispatched Gembō to northern Kyushu to supervise the building of the Kanzeon-ji, in effect a form of exile designed to strip him of his authority at court. He died the following year at his assigned post in Kyushu.

Gemmei Tennō 元明天皇 (661–721)

Empress of the Asuka period. The daughter of Emperor Tenji, she married Prince Kusakabe, the son of Emperor Temmu, but in 689 her husband died. In 697 Empress Jitō abdicated, turning over the throne to the son of Empress Gemmei, who became Emperor Mommu. He died in 707, however, and in accordance with his dying wish his mother ascended the throne to become Empress Gemmei, the forty-third ruler of Japan. During her reign, in 708, copper was for the first time mined in Japan and was used to mint the earliest Japanese currency, known as *Wado-kaichin*. In 710 she moved the capital to Heijō-kyō, on the site of the present-day city of Nara, where it remained until it was moved to Kyoto in 794; the interval from 710 to 794 is accordingly known as the Nara period. In 712 the *Kojiki*, the earliest work of Japanese mythology and history, was compiled and presented to her, and the following year she commanded the various provinces to compile *fudoki*, or local gazettes descriptive of their respective regions. In 715 she turned over the throne to her daughter, who became Empress Genshō, though she continued until her death to play an active part in politics, doing her best to maintain the *ritsuryō* system of government.

Genshin 源信 (942–1017)

Buddhist priest of the middle Heian period. He was born in the province of Yamato (Nara Prefecture). When his father died in 948, he carried out the latter's dying wish by entering the clergy, in 950 becoming a disciple of the priest Ryōgen of the Tendai sect.

He served for a time at court, taking charge of various ceremonies and religious affairs, but he had no desire for worldly fame and preferred to retire to Mt. Hiei and devote himself entirely to writing and religious practices. Among his numerous works, that which he wrote in 985, known as *Ojō yōshū*, "Essentials of Salvation," is the most famous. It is in three chapters and describes how the sincere believer may, after death, be reborn in the Pure Land of the Western Paradise. The book and its teachings spread among the aristocracy of the time, and such important and influential persons as the celebrated Fujiwara no Michinaga were counted among its followers. From these teachings concerning the Pure Land there eventually developed in the Kamakura period (1192–1333) the Jōdo or Pure Land sect of Hōnen and the Jōdo Shin or True Pure Land sect of Shinran, separate sects of Buddhism that gained a very wide following among the common people. Genshin's book was influential not only in Japan, but was taken to China as well, where it won great acclaim. So popular was it that numerous types of pictures illustrating its doctrines were produced, which circulated widely among the Chinese masses and were even imported to Japan, thus completing the cycle. Genshin is also known by the title Eshin Sōzu.

Gosanjō Tennō 後三條天皇 (1034–1073)

Emperor of the middle Heian period. He was the second son of Emperor Gosuzaku. When his elder brother ascended the throne in 1045 to become Emperor Goreizei, he was made heir apparent. The powerful court official Fujiwara no Yorimichi opposed the appointment because the future Emperor Gosanjō was not related to the Fujiwara family, but since none of his daughters whom he had married to the various emperors of the time had succeeded in producing a male heir, he was powerless to prevent it. The prince thus remained heir apparent until the death of Emperor Goreizei in 1068, when he became the seventy-first ruler. Because, unlike the previous rulers, he was not related to the Fujiwaras, he was able without undue encumbrance to embark on a new and independent course of political action. He set up an office called the *kirokujo* to examine the title deeds of the various *shōen*, or private manors, held by members of the Fujiwara family and temples and shrines, confiscating those manors that were of doubtful legality. In addition, he fixed the size of the measure by which taxes in rice were levied and took other steps to standardize prices and values. He also made efforts to draw men from various families into the bureaucracy instead of allowing the members of the Fujiwara family to monopolize government offices, as had been the practice in the past. However, after only four years of rule he fell ill and relinquished the throne to his son, Emperor Shirakawa. It was probably his intention to continue an active role in political affairs from the somewhat freer position of father of the emperor, but he died within half a year of his abdication.

GOSHIRAKAWA TENNŌ 後白河天皇 (1127–1192)

The seventy-seventh sovereign, he ascended the throne in 1155 at the age of twenty-eight and abdicated three years later, but continued until his death to exercise great power behind the scenes. He was the fourth son of Emperor Toba; his mother was Taikemmon-in Shōshi, the daughter of Fujiwara no Kinzane. His personal name was Masahito, and his Buddhist name Gyōshin.

In 1156, the year after he came to the throne, his father, Retired Emperor Toba, died, and his right to rule was challenged by Retired Emperor Sutoku and his supporters. Emperor Goshirakawa, aided by such powerful warriors as Minamoto no Yoshitomo and Taira no Kiyomori, emerged victorious in the struggle, which was known as the Hōgen uprising. After strengthening the position of the throne, he abdicated in favor of his son, Emperor Nijō, and established an *insei*, or office of cloistered emperor, from which he continued to exercise actual power of government. In 1159 a second civil disturbance broke out, known as the Heiji uprising. In it, Taira no Kiyomori defeated his former ally Minamoto no Yoshitomo and established himself as a central figure in the government. In 1167, Kiyomori became *dajōdaijin* (prime minister), and the Taira family approached the zenith of their power, the first time in Japanese history that a warrior family had dominated the government.

In 1169, Goshirakawa became a member of the Buddhist clergy, though he continued as before to maintain his cloistered government. In 1177, a number of his close supporters, angered at the dictatorial power of Taira no Kiyomori, gathered at a place called Shishigatani in Kyoto to plot the overthrow of the Taira clan. The plot came to light, and the conspirators were punished. As a result of the affair, Taira no Kiyomori became suspicious of Goshirakawa and in 1179 had him placed in confinement at the Toba Palace, thus temporarily ending the cloistered government.

After the death of Kiyomori in 1181, Goshirakawa reestablished his cloistered government and began actively plotting with the members of the Minamoto family to bring about the overthrow of the Tairas. In 1183, when an army headed by Minamoto no Yoshinaka marched on Kyoto, the Tairas fled west. They were finally wiped out in 1185 at the battle of Dan-no-ura, and Minamoto no Yoritomo emerged as the most powerful military leader. He received permission from Goshirakawa to establish constables (*shugo*) and stewards (*jitō*) in the provinces and estates throughout the country, thus helping to consolidate his power. But he was unable to persuade Goshirakawa to grant him the coveted title of shogun, the military leader of the nation. It was not until Goshirakawa's death in 1192 that he was able to receive the title of shogun and thus officially establish the shogunal government at Kamakura.

In addition to being an astute and tenacious wielder of political power, Goshirakawa was important as a patron and practitioner of the arts. With the funds from the numerous estates attached to the cloistered government, he financed the founding of Buddhist temples and commissioned works of religious art, as well as making elaborate pilgrimages to Mt. Kōya and Kumano on the Kii Peninsula. He was a skilled flute player and excelled in the types of singing known as *imayō*, *saibara*, and *rōei*. In addition to sponsoring musical recitals, he compiled an anthology of songs, the *Ryōjin hishō*, which holds a place of special importance in the history of Japanese songs and song lyrics. He is entombed at Hōju-ji in Kyoto.

Gyōki 行基 (668–749)

Buddhist priest of the middle Nara period. Born into the powerful Koshi family of the district of Ōtori in Kawachi Province (present-day Semboku-gun of Osaka Prefecture), he became a monk in 682 and began religious training as a disciple of Gien of the Yakushi-ji. Sometime later—the exact date is uncertain—he left the temple to continue his religious practices in the mountains and countryside, wandering from region to region spreading the teachings of Buddhism among the common people. In order to draw them to the faith, he is said in the course of his lifetime to have founded temples in forty-nine places. In addition, in the various places he visited, he constructed ponds, opened up and repaired rice paddies, built bridges and boat landings, and undertook other works of benefit to society. As a result of these activities, he gained a large following among the common people, who gathered around him in ever increasing numbers. The government, disturbed at this situation, in the fourth month of 717 issued an order forbidding Gyōki to continue his preaching, an order that was several times repeated during the period until 730. Eventually, however, the court was obliged to recognize the worth of his activities, and in 731 he was given official permission to preach the faith. When the court, implementing the plans of Emperor Shōmu, began construction of a giant Buddha image, the Great Buddha of Tōdai-ji, Gyōki and his disciples gave their full cooperation, going about among the common people to gather contributions and helping to bring the project to a successful conclusion. In 745, in recognition of his achievements, he was given the highest rank possible to a Buddhist monk.

After his death on the second day of the second month of 749, his body was cremated and the ashes placed in a bronze container inscribed with the story of his life, which was buried in the grounds of the Chikurin-ji in Yamato Province. Fragments of the container are still preserved today.

Himiko 卑彌呼 (third century)

Queen of the ancient period. According to the "Account of the People of Wa" in the *History of the Kingdom of Wei*, a section of the Chinese historical work entitled the *San-kuo-chih*, which deals with events of the late second and early third century, she was queen of a Japanese state called Yamatai. The account states that during the period around 170 to 180, Yamatai was beset by warfare, but after Himiko became ruler, the strife was brought to an end. She was a shaman who claimed to be following the instructions given to her by the gods in administering the government; she remained unmarried throughout her lifetime. In 239 she sent slaves and other articles of tribute to the Chinese state of Wei, acknowledging herself a subject of the Wei ruler. She is said to have died sometime between 240 and 248, and after her death the state was once more plagued by war. Scholars disagree as to the location of Yamatai, some placing it in Kyushu, others in the area around Nara; so far no way has been discovered to determine for certain which hypothesis is correct. The *Nihon Shoki*, a Japanese work that deals with the history of the early period, identifies Himiko with Empress Jingū, but such an identification involves a discrepancy in the dates customarily assigned to the two figures.

Hyekwan (Ekan) 慧灌 (seventh century)

Buddhist priest from the kingdom of Koguryŏ who transmitted the Sanron, or Three Treatise school, of Buddhism to Japan. According to the *Nihon Shoki*, he arrived in Japan in 625 and was given the ecclesiastical rank of *sōjō*. According to later tradition, in his youth he journeyed to China, at that time ruled by the Sui dynasty, and studied the teachings of the Three Treatise school under the Chinese priest Chi-tsang (549–623). The school bases its teachings upon three treatises, two of them attributed to the Indian Buddhist philosopher Nāgārjuna (ca. 150–ca. 250). It places great emphasis upon the concept of *śūnya* (Japanese: *kū*), often translated in English as "void" or "emptiness." Chi-tsang is said to have put the teachings of the sect into final form. Hyekwan took up residence in Gankō-ji, a temple in Asuka, and numbered among his disciples such men as Fukuryō and Chizō. Chizō in turn had such eminent disciples as Dōji, Chikō, and Raikō, who raised the Sanron school to a position of eminence during the Nara period.

Ichijō Tennō 一條天皇 (980–1011)

Emperor of the middle Heian period; sixty-sixth sovereign of Japan; son of Emperor En'yū and a daughter of Fujiwara no Kaneie. His reign, from 986 to 1011, saw the "Fujiwara culture," which centered around the person of Fujiwara no Michinaga, reach its zenith. The emperor himself had a taste for literature and gathered about him at his court such figures as Murasaki Shikibu, author of *The Tale of Genji*, and Sei Shōnagon, author of the celebrated *Pillow Book*. Politically, too, the reign is well known for the large number of able figures it produced. Personally, however, the emperor was politically ineffectual, since real power lay in the hands of his maternal grandfather, Kaneie, and his stepbrother Michinaga.

Jimmu Tennō 神武天皇

Legendary first emperor of Japan, who, according to traditional reckoning, reigned 660 to 585 B.C. His father was Hikonagisatake-ugayafukiaezu-no-mikoto and his mother was Tamayori-hime, the daughter of the god of the sea. His name was Sanu-no-mikoto, and he was also known as Kamuyamato-iwarehiko-no-mikoto. The posthumous name Jimmu was not given to him until the latter part of the eighth century. Accounts of him are preserved in the *Kojiki* and *Nihon Shoki*.

In his youth he lived in the Takachiho Palace in Hyūga in Kyushu, which had been established by his grandfather Ninigi-no-mikoto, the grandson of the Sun Goddess Amaterasu Ōmikami. He departed from Hyūga on an expedition to the east, passing through northern Kyushu and conquering the various regions of Aki and Kibi along the Inland Sea. Landing at Naniwa, the site of the present-day city of Osaka, he prepared to cross over Mt. Ikoma and invade the Yamato region when he was engaged in battle by a powerful local leader named Nagasune-hiko and driven back. He then turned southward and proceeded to the tip of the Kii Peninsula. There he made his way overland from Kumano to the mountains of Yoshino and thence to the southern part of the Yamato region. After regrouping his forces, he launched an attack on Nagasune-hiko. For a time he fared badly, but with the assistance of a golden bird of the variety known as a *tobi* (kite), he was finally able to gain victory. He thereupon pacified the remainder of the Yamato region and on the first day of the first lunar month of 660 B.C. ascended the throne at the Kashiwara Palace. This date has traditionally been regarded as the founding of the imperial line in Japan. In 1873, February 11, which corresponds to the lunar date above, was designated as Kigensetsu, a national holiday in celebration of the accession of Emperor Jimmu. It is now called Kenkoku Ki'nembi no Hi, or National Founding Day.

In the *Kojiki* and *Nihon Shoki*, the account of Jimmu Tennō appears at the end of the section dealing with the gods and the beginning of that dealing with human figures, serving as a bridge between the two. It is difficult to regard the account as historical, since Japan in the seventh century B.C. was still in the cultural phase known as Jōmon and could hardly have witnessed the establishment of a national state. The Yayoi culture, which replaced the Jōmon and was characterized by wet-rice agriculture and the use of metals, however, seems to have appeared first in Kyushu and thereafter to have spread rather rapidly to the east. It has been suggested, therefore, that Jimmu Tennō's eastern expedition is a mythicized reflection of that process. It has also been pointed out that the descriptive name Hatsu-kuni-shirasu-sumera-mikoto, "First Ruler of the Nation," is also applied to the tenth sovereign, Emperor Sujin. It appears possible, therefore, that accounts of Emperor Sujin may have influenced the legends associated with the figure of Jimmu Tennō.

Jingū Kōgō 神功皇后 (late fourth century)

Empress of the ancient period. She can best be regarded as a legendary figure. According to tradition, she was the empress of Emperor Chūai. The emperor set off on a campaign to wipe out the Kumaso people of Kyushu but died suddenly on the way. The empress, though already pregnant with the future Emperor Ōjin, in person led the forces in an attack on the Korean state of Silla, carrying it through to successful completion. From this time on Silla, as well as the other Korean states of Koguryŏ and Paekche, were said to have come under Japanese control. After the empress returned to Japan, she gave birth to the future Emperor Ōjin, but she continued until her death to exercise the power of rule and did not permit him to ascend the throne. The legend just recounted seems to have come into existence sometime around the fourth century and is believed to have been an attempt to explain, through the figure of Empress Jingū, the fact that Japanese forces at this time were sent to the Korean peninsula.

Kakuban 覺鑁 (1095–1143)

Buddhist priest of the late Heian period. He was born in the province of Bizen, the manor of Fujitsu, one of the manors belonging to the Ninna-ji temple in Kyoto. It is said that as a child he saw his father being mistreated by the tax officials and, vowing that he himself would never suffer such treatment but would become a man of high position, he entered the priesthood. At first he resided at the Ninna-ji, but later moved to Mt. Kōya to undergo religious training. Hoping to revive the teachings of Kūkai, the founder of the monastery of Mt. Kōya, he established a new temple called the Daidempō-in, and in 1134 he became its head and, with the backing of Retired Emperor Gotoba, gained control of all the temples on Mt. Kōya. There were many among the monks of Mt. Kōya, however, who opposed him in these moves, and in 1140 his enemies resorted to force and with weapons drove him and some seven hundred members of his faction from the mountain. With his followers he then went to Negoro in the province of Kii and founded a new temple, the Daidempō-in, or Negorodera, where he died. He was later given the posthumous title of Kōkyō Daishi.

Kammu Tennō 桓武天皇 (737–806)

Emperor of the early Heian period. The eldest son of Emperor Kōnin, he was made heir apparent in 773, and upon the death of his father in 781, ascended the throne to become the fiftieth ruler of Japan.

As soon as he came to the throne, Emperor Kammu set about working to free himself from the Buddhist clergy and other power groups that had dominated the Nara court. In order to facilitate his designs, he ordered Fujiwara no Tanetsugu to oversee the building of a new capital, and in 784 he accordingly moved from Heijō-kyō (Nara) to Nagaoka-kyō, just south of the present-day city of Kyoto. In 785, however, Fujiwara no Tanetsugu was assassinated and other difficulties were encountered in the building of the new capital; so, on the advice of Wake no Kiyomaro, the capital was moved once more in 794, this time to Heian-kyō, modern Kyoto. The period from this time until the founding of the Kamakura shogunate in 1192 thus came to be called the Heian period, and the city of Heian remained the residence of the emperor for over a thousand years until the capital was moved to Tokyo at the beginning of the Meiji period.

Emperor Kammu, as has been said, moved to a new capital in order to strengthen his rule. In addition he set out to conquer the Ezo people of the Tōhoku region, dispatching Sakanoue no Tamuramaro at the head of a force of forty thousand soldiers for this purpose. He also undertook numerous water control works, encouraged the opening up of new lands for cultivation, and endeavored to augment tax revenues. But the costs of the increased military activity and the construction of the new capital proved a heavy burden to the common people, and they began in growing numbers to desert their farming activities and turn to a life of vagrancy. In 805, therefore, on the advice of Fujiwara no Otsugu, he abandoned the military and construction activities that were proving so costly.

Emperor Kammu adopted various measures in an effort to correct and improve the *ritsuryō* system of government, but unfortunately he died before his plans could be carried to completion.

In later ages a number of warrior clans appeared in different parts of the country that claimed descent from Emperor Kammu, and one such group, the branch of the Taira family known as the Kammu Heiji, in time produced such famous men as Taira no Masakado, Taira no Kiyomori, and later Hōjō Tokimasa.

KANCHŌ 寛朝 (916–998)

Monk of the Shingon sect in the middle Heian period, founder of the Hirosawa branch of Shingon. He was a son of Imperial Prince Atsuzane and a grandson of Emperor Uda. He entered the clergy at the age of forty, and received *kanjō*, a ceremony in Esoteric Buddhism indicating the attainment of Buddhahood, from Kankū of Ninna-ji in Kyoto. He numbered among his religious followers Emperor En'yū and other members of the court. He served as head monk of Tō-ji and held the ecclesiastical rank of *daisōjō*. He founded a temple called Henjō-ji at Hirosawa in Saga, a suburb west of

Kyoto, and took up residence there. At the time, the Shingon sect was represented by two teaching lines, that descending from Yakushin, which enjoyed great prestige, and the less prestigious Shōbō line. Kanchō belonged to the former, which with him became clearly established as the Hirosawa branch of Shingon. The latter, represented by Ninkai, became known as the Ono branch, the Shingon sect thus splitting into two distinct groups. Kanchō's principal disciple was Saishin. He was well known for his mastery of *shōmyō*, the special type of chanting used in Buddhist ceremonies.

Kibi no Makibi 吉備眞備 (693–775)

Scholar and politician of the middle Nara period. Originally named Shimotsumichi Makibi, he was sent to T'ang China in 717, where he studied Confucianism, astronomy, and other subjects, returning to Japan in 735. Emperor Shōmu admired his learning greatly and appointed him tutor to his daughter, the future Empress Kōken. At the same time Makibi introduced to Japan new elements of Chinese culture that he had learned of during his long stay on the continent and, under the patronage of the powerful Tachibana no Moroe, joined with the monk Gembō in handling affairs of state. In 740 Fujiwara no Hirotsugu led an uprising and attempted to topple Makibi and Gembō from power, but his efforts ended in failure. In 746 Makibi was given the surname Kibi. When Fujiwara no Nakamaro came to power, Makibi was exiled to the provinces, but in 752 he was once more sent on a mission to China, returning in 754. After the failure of Fujiwara no Nakamaro's attempted coup d'état in 764, Makibi resumed a position in the government, becoming a *daijin* (minister of state) in 766.

Kimmei Tennō 欽明天皇 (510?–570?)

Emperor of the Yamato court period. He was the third son of Emperor Keitai. When his father died in 531, a struggle developed between Emperor Ankan and Emperor Senka, who were supported by Ōtomo no Kanamura, and Emperor Kimmei, who was supported by Soga no Iname, and for a time it is not certain who was actually ruler. Emperors Ankan and Senka, however, died in rapid succession, and Emperor Kimmei ascended the throne.

During Emperor Kimmei's reign Buddhism was first introduced to Japan through the efforts of King Syŏngmyŏng of the Korean state of Paekche (both 538 and 552 are given as the date of this event). When King Syŏngmyŏng's state was invaded by the armies of Silla, Emperor Kimmei sent troops to his assistance, but the king was killed in battle. In addition to Buddhism, knowledge pertaining to medicine, the calendar, and other subjects was introduced to Japan at this time from Paekche. In 562 the Japanese tributary state on the Korean peninsula known as Imna or Mimana was wiped out by the forces of Silla, and Emperor Kimmei accordingly expressed on his deathbed the hope that his successor would once more establish Japanese power on the Korean peninsula.

Kōken (Shōtoku) Tennō 孝謙天皇(稱徳) (718–770)

Empress of the middle Nara period. She was the daughter of Emperor Shōmu and Empress Kōmyō. In 749 her father turned over the throne to her, making her the forty-sixth ruler of Japan, though her mother, in conjunction with Fujiwara no Nakamaro, continued to exercise actual power. In 757 she removed Prince Funado from the position of heir apparent and replaced him with Prince Ōi, who enjoyed the backing of Fujiwara no Nakamaro. The move aroused considerable opposition at court and even led to plans for a coup d'état, but these were discovered before any decisive move could be made. Empress Kōken then relinquished the throne to Prince Ōi, who became Emperor Junnin. Fujiwara no Nakamaro originally enjoyed the trust of Empress Kōken and was able to exercise great power in affairs of state, but later he was replaced in the empress's favor by the Buddhist monk Dōkyō. In 764 he attempted to overthrow Dōkyō, but his efforts ended in failure. As a result, Emperor Junnin was obliged to abdicate, turning over the throne to the empress, who ascended it a second time, this time becoming known as Empress Shōtoku. She in turn prepared to turn over the throne to Dōkyō, but was opposed in this move by the ministers of the court. When she died in 770, Dōkyō was exiled to the province of Shimotsuke.

Kōmyō Kōgō 光明皇后 (701–760)

The consort of Emperor Shōmu, her personal name was Asukabe-hime or Kōmyōshi. Her father was Fujiwara no Fuhito, the son of Fujiwara no Nakatomi, the statesman who played a crucial role in the carrying out of the Taika Reforms. Her mother, Tachibana no Michiyo, was originally married to Prince Minu and bore him a son who later was named Tachibana no Moroe; subsequently she became the wife of Fujiwara no Fuhito.

Kōmyōshi became the consort of Emperor Shōmu while he was still heir apparent. She bore him a daughter, Princess Abe, who later reigned as Empress Kōken, and a son, Prince Motoi, who died in childhood. Emperor Shōmu came to the throne in 724, and in 729 Kōmyōshi was given the title of *kōgō* (empress). This was the first time that any woman other than a member of the imperial family had received this title, and the move aroused considerable opposition from members of the imperial family. It may be noted that the action took place just at the time when Prince Nagaya, who had previously dominated the government, fell from power and was replaced by the empress's brothers of the Fujiwara family. This marks the point where the reins of power were lost by the imperial family and taken up by the Fujiwara family.

The empress was said to have been a highly intelligent and cultured woman and an ardent Buddhist. In 730 she established Hiden-in and Seyaku-in, charitable institutions designed to dispense medicine and relieve poverty and famine among the common people. According to her biography in the *Shoku Nihongi*, it was her urging that prompted Emperor Shōmu to establish a government temple and nunnery in each province of the nation and set up the temple called Tōdai-ji in Nara to act as the head temple. The task of sutra-copying that was carried out by the Kōgō Gūshiki, a government office under the supervision of the empress, was later carried on by Tōdai-ji, and many copies of sutras made at the request of the empress remain in existence today.

In 749, Emperor Shōmu abdicated in favor of his daughter, Empress Kōken, and the Kōgō Gūshiki was given the Chinese style name Shibi Chūdai. At this time Empress Kōmyō's nephew Fujiwara no Nakamaro, later known as Emi no Oshikatsu, was appointed to head it, a move that led to his eventual rise to power. After the death of Emperor Shōmu in 756, Empress Kōmyō, now Empress Dowager, was said to have exercised the actual power of government in the name of her daughter, Empress Kōken. Empress Kōmyō was a skilled calligrapher, and examples of her calligraphy are preserved among the treasures of the Shōsō-in.

Kōtoku Tennō 孝徳天皇 (597–654)

Emperor of the Asuka period. His name was Imperial Prince Karu. In 645, after Imperial Prince Naka no Ōe, Nakatomi no Kamatari, and others of their party had assassinated Soga no Iruka and wiped out the Soga family, Empress Kōgyoku, who was the mother of Prince Naka no Ōe and the reigning sovereign at the time, turned over the throne to Prince Karu, making him the thirty-seventh ruler. As leader of the coup d'état against the Soga family, Prince Naka no Ōe should by rights have succeeded to the throne, but it was decided to make Prince Karu, the empress's younger brother, the ruler instead in order to avoid friction with the older and previously established elements within the government. As a result, the emperor in time became estranged from Prince Naka no Ōe and the other members of his powerful group.

Among the political acts carried out during his reign was the adoption in 645 of the *nengō* (era name) Taika, the first time that an era name had been formally assigned in Japanese history. 646 saw the promulgation of the so-called Taika Reforms, a set of new laws and institutional innovations designed to create a strong centralized government after the model of that of the T'ang dynasty of China, with the emperor as supreme ruler at its head. This, along with the establishment of the shogunate system by Minamoto no Yoritomo and the Meiji Restoration, constitutes one of the three most important social and political innovations in the history of Japan.

Kūkai (Kōbō Daishi) 空海(弘法大師) (773 or 774–835)

Buddhist monk of the early Heian period, founder of the Shingon sect in Japan; his posthumous title is Kōbō Daishi. He was born in the province of Sanuki in Shikoku; his father was of the Saeki family, his mother of the Atō family. Around 788 he went to Kyoto, where he studied first under his maternal uncle Atō no Ōtari and later entered the state university, specializing in Confucianism and the classics of Chinese literature. He also received instruction in the secret teachings pertaining to the Bodhisattva Ākāśagarbha (Japanese: Kokūzō). Strongly attracted to Buddhism, he returned to Shikoku to practice various religious austerities in the mountains there. In 797 he wrote a work entitled *Sangō shiiki* in which, employing the form of a literary debate, he compared the teachings of Confucianism, Taoism, and Buddhism, and argued in favor of the last. In 804 he went to China with the official Japanese embassy headed by Fujiwara no Kuzunomaro, traveling in the same ship as Tachibana no Hayanari. Saichō, another monk who was destined to become a leader of Japanese Buddhism, traveled in another ship. In 805, he received instruction in Esoteric Buddhism from Hui-kuo (746–805), head of the temple known as Ch'ing-lung-ssu in Ch'ang-an. Hui-kuo was a distinguished disciple of Amoghavajra (Japanese: Fukū), an Indian monk who played a major role in introducing Esoteric Buddhism to China.

Kūkai returned to Japan in 806 and, after staying for a while in Kyushu, made his way to the capital. He set about introducing the ceremonies and doctrines of Shingon, as Esoteric Buddhism was known, as well as the current fashions in Chinese poetry and calligraphy, gaining considerable prominence and establishing a close relationship with Emperor Saga. In 816 he founded a temple known as Kongōbu-ji on top of Mt. Kōya in the province of Kii, which was officially recognized as a training center for Shingon Buddhism. In 823 he was invited to the capital to head the newly founded Kyōō-gokoku-ji, popularly known as Tō-ji. These two temples in Kyoto and Mt. Kōya respectively served in the following centuries as the headquarters of the Shingon sect.

Kūkai's principal writings include *Himitsu mandara jūjūshinron*, *Hizō hōyaku*, *Sokushin jōbutsu-gi*, and *Shōji jissō-gi*. His teachings stressed that all the phenomena of the physical universe are manifestations of the cosmic Buddha Vairocana (Dainichi Nyorai), and that human beings, through mystic ceremonies and meditation, can attain unity with Vairocana. Kūkai also emphasized that Buddhahood is something that can be achieved in our present bodily form (*sokushin jōbutsu*). In addition to his importance as a religious thinker and leader, he contributed to other aspects of Japanese culture. He was a highly skilled writer of prose and verse in Chinese, as shown by his *Bunkyō hifuron*, a work on Chinese poetics and literary criticism, the *Shōryō-shū*, a collection of his prose and verse, and his verse preserved in the *Keikoku-shū*. He was celebrated as a calligrapher, being numbered among the Sampitsu, Three Masters of Calligraphy, of the period, the other two being Emperor Saga and Tachibana no Hayanari. The piece known as the *Fūshinchō* is a particularly renowned example of his skill as a calligrapher. Finally, he is important as the founder of the first private school in Japan, the Shugeishuchi-in, established in Kyoto in 828 to give instruction to sons of the common people. He also played an active part in flood control and other works designed to benefit society. After his death, a great many legends grew up about his name, and under his posthumous title Kōbō Daishi he has continued down to the present to be revered throughout Japan.

Kūya 空也 (903–972)

Monk of the middle Heian period who spread the teachings of Pure Land Buddhism among the populace; his name may also be read Kōya. Nothing is known for certain of his place of birth or background. In his youth he wandered about the country as an *ubasoku* or *shami*, a religious practitioner who has not received formal ordination as a monk. In his travels, he devoted himself to religious teaching and at the same time worked to build roads and bridges and perform other works of benefit to society. In 938 he went to Kyoto, where he labored to spread the practice of the *nembutsu,* or invocation of the name of the Buddha Amida, among the citizens. As a result, he came to be called Ichi-no-hijiri, "saint of the streets," or Amida-hijiri, "saint of Amida." In 948 he received formal ordination as a monk from Enshō of Mt. Hiei, taking the religious name Kōshō. He continued, however, to use the name Kūya, by which he had been known when he was a *shami.* He died at Saikō-ji, a temple that he founded in Kyoto and that was later renamed Rokuharamitsu-ji. He seems to have recited the *nembutsu* formula in a rapt and even ecstatic manner and to have urged others to do likewise. Because of the fervency with which he went about the streets of Kyoto reciting it, he has come to be regarded as an early practitioner of the so-called dancing *nembutsu,* a practice later advocated by Ippen. After his death, Minamoto no Tamekane wrote a biographical account of him in eulogy form entitled *Kōya rui,* and his biography is also included in the *Nihon ōjō gokuraku-ki* of Yoshishige no Yasutane.

Kyōshin 教信 (d. 866)

Lay Buddhist of the early Heian period who devoted his life to the practice of *nembutsu,* the ritual invocation of the name of the Buddha Amida. He lived in a hut alongside the post station at Kako in the province of Harima, had a wife and family, and worked for a living. At the same time, he spent his lifetime invoking Amida's name, and as a result came to be called Amidamaru. It is said that when he was on the point of death, he made his way by means of spiritual powers to the temple of Kachio-dera in Settsu, where he appeared before the priest Shōnyo (781–867) and announced that he would be reborn in the Western Paradise of Amida. He is clearly a semilegendary figure at best. In later centuries, however, when Pure Land Buddhism, which advocates the practice of *nembutsu,* gained prominence, and when the temples and clergy of organized Buddhism became marred by corruption, Kyōshin came to be revered as the ideal of the lay Buddhist believer who remains in the everyday world but devotes his life to religious practice. As such, he was regarded with particular respect by such later Japanese Buddhist leaders as Eikan, Shinran, and Ippen.

Min (Bin) 旻 (d. 653)

Buddhist priest of the Asuka period. In 608 a Chinese envoy named P'ei Shih-ch'ing from the court of the Sui dynasty arrived in Japan and, on his return to China in the same year, he was accompanied by a party headed by Ono no Imoko and including the Buddhist priest Min. Min remained in China for over twenty years, finally returning in 632. His object in going to China had been to study, but while there he had observed the fall of the Sui dynasty in 618 and the founding of a new dynasty, the T'ang. Because of the experience and knowledge that he had acquired in China, he was appointed in 645 as a *kuni-hakase*, Scholar of the State, along with Takamuku no Kuromaro and joined the group headed by Prince Naka no Ōe in drawing up the measures known as the Taika Reforms. The purpose of these was to establish a new system of government of the *ritsuryō* type modeled on that of the T'ang dynasty of China and characterized by a strong centralized bureaucracy headed by the emperor.

Minamoto no Yoshiie 源義家 (1039–1106)

Military leader of the late Heian period. He was the eldest son of the warrior Minamoto no Yoriyoshi, and because the ceremony inducting him into manhood in 1045 was held at the Iwashimizu Hachiman Shrine south of Kyoto, he is also referred to as Hachiman Tarō. He joined his father in helping to put down the revolt in the province of Mutsu led by Abe no Yoritoki and Abe's sons, Sadatō and Munetō, the so-called Earlier Nine Years' War, which lasted from 1051 to 1062, and in reward for his services was named Dewa-no-kami, political head of the province of Dewa. In 1075, with the death of his father, he became the leader of the Minamoto (Genji) family. During the years from 1083 to 1087, when a struggle raged between two powerful families of northern Japan, those of Kiyohara no Iehira and Fujiwara no Kiyohira—the so-called Later Three Years' War—Minamoto no Yoshiie sided with Fujiwara no Kiyohira and succeeded in bringing the fighting to an end. As a result, the Minamoto were able to establish a base of power in the provinces of Mutsu and Dewa, the present-day Tōhoku region. He was one of the most admired heroes of the time and was the first member of the warrior class to be admitted at court.

MINAMOTO NO YOSHITOMO 源義朝 (1123–1160)

Military leader of the late Heian period. He was the eldest son of Minamoto no Tameyoshi. His younger brother Tametomo, having been sent to Kyushu, began to acquire power of dangerous proportions and was accordingly ordered by the court to return to the capital; when he failed to obey the order, his father, Tameyoshi, accepting responsibility for the disobedience, went into retirement, and Yoshitomo in 1154 became head of the Minamoto family. In 1156, when the quarrel among the court nobility known as the Hōgen uprising broke out, Yoshitomo sided with the opposite faction from that supported by his father and younger brother, and though his side emerged victorious, he soon found himself engaged in a struggle for power with its leader, Taira no Kiyomori. Kiyomori conspired with Retired Emperor Goshirakawa, the real wielder of power in the court, to block Yoshitomo's advancement, whereupon in anger Yoshitomo siezed Retired Emperor Goshirakawa as his hostage in 1159 and declared himself in revolt. He was defeated and killed in battle by Taira no Kiyomori, however, and this disturbance—the Heiji uprising—quickly came to an end. A famous scroll painting depicting the events of the uprising, entitled *Heiji monogatari emaki*, is preserved in the Boston Museum of Fine Arts.

MONONOBE NO OKOSHI 物部尾輿 (dates uncertain)

Official of the Yamato court period. The Mononobe family was prominent from early times, serving the Yamato court in the handling of military and policing duties. Mononobe no Okoshi strongly criticized his rival at court, Ōtomo no Kanamura, also a member of a prominent family, for his handling of Korean affairs and managed to bring about the downfall of the entire Ōtomo family. In 538 (the date is also given as 552), King Syŏngmyŏng of the Korean state of Paekche presented a Buddhist image and scriptures to the Japanese ruler, introducing Buddhism to Japan for the first time. Mononobe no Okoshi, declaring that the gods of Japan would be angered, strongly opposed the acceptance of the foreign religion, but another important minister of the court, Soga no Iname, accepted the image and other articles and, converting his home into a temple, paid them homage. Later, however, an epidemic broke out, and Okoshi, declaring to Emperor Kimmei that it was brought on by the anger of the gods, proceeded to burn the temple down. His son Moriya continued the opposition to Buddhism and its patrons of the Soga family, but he and his family were finally wiped out by Soga no Umako.

Nimmyō Tennō 仁明天皇 (810–850)

Emperor of the early Heian period. He was the son of Emperor Saga, but in 823 was adopted by his uncle, Emperor Junna, and in 833 was given the throne by the latter, becoming the fifty-fourth ruler. He then set up Emperor Junna's son Prince Tsunesada as heir apparent. In 842 Tomo no Kowamine, Tachibana no Hayanari, and others close to the heir apparent plotted a revolt, but they were discovered and condemned to punishment and a new heir apparent, Prince Michiyasu, was appointed. This was the so-called Jōwa disturbance, which came about because the heir apparent was not related to the Fujiwara family. The new heir apparent, Prince Michiyasu, was a son of Emperor Nimmyō and the daughter of Fujiwara no Fuyutsugu. In time he became Emperor Montoku, and the Fujiwaras were able to gather all power into their hands.

Emperor Nimmyō was fond of learning and was a skilled musician. A detailed account of his reign was compiled, the *Shoku Nihon kōki*, and is still extant; it is one of the *Rikkokushi*, the six officially sponsored histories of the early period.

Ninkai 仁海 (951 or 955–1046)

Shingon monk in the middle Heian period, founder of the Ono branch of Shingon; he was also known as Senshin. He was born in the province of Izumi and at the age of six entered the Shingon monastery on Mt. Kōya, where he studied under Gashin. He remained on Mt. Kōya until around the age of forty, devoting himself to scholarly learning. In 990 he received *kanjō*, a ceremony in Esoteric Buddhism indicating the attainment of Buddhahood, from Gengō of Daigo-emmei-in. Thereafter he took up residence in Mandara-ji in Ono east of Kyoto, working to spread the teachings of Esoteric Buddhism and gathering a group of some one thousand disciples around him.

Distressed at the declining condition of the Mt. Kōya monastery, in 1007 he submitted a petition (*Chishiki gammon*) to Emperor Ichijō asking for assistance in rebuilding the monastery. In 1023 he preached to the eminent statesman Fujiwara no Michinaga concerning the Esoteric Buddhist belief that Mt. Kōya is none other than the Pure Land, or Buddhist Paradise, and converted Michinaga to his views. He frequently carried out rain-making ceremonies, which proved effective, and hence came to be known as Ame no Shōjō, the "Rain Abbot." He served as second head of Tō-ji, head of Tōdai-ji, and finally head of Tō-ji, and rose to the ecclesiastical rank of *shōjō*. The teaching line that he headed came to be known as the Ono branch of Shingon, constituting, along with the Hirosawa branch headed by Kanchō, one of the two groups into which the Shingon sect in time came to be divided. His works include *Ono rokujō* and *Denju-shū*.

Nintoku Tennō 仁徳天皇 (early fifth century)

The sixteenth Emperor of Japan; reigned around the fifth century. According to traditions recorded in the *Nihon Shoki*, his reign is credited with many achievements in foreign relations and agriculture. It saw the influx into Japan of large numbers of Korean settlers, and with them the culture and techniques of China; large areas of land were opened to cultivation in the Kinai district (the Kobe-Kyoto-Nara region); a capital was established at Naniwa (present Osaka); and envoys were sent to China. The references to the kingdom of "Tsan" (Chinese reading) or "Ya" in the official Chinese histories of the Sung and Liang dynasties are believed to refer to his reign.

That this period saw the power of the Yamato court grow rapidly and reach its peak is graphically witnessed by the huge burial mound in Sakai City, Osaka Prefecture, which is generally known as the Tumulus of the Emperor Nintoku. The largest royal tumulus in the world, it has an overall length of 477 meters. The width of the square front section is 305 meters and its height 27 meters, while the round rear section is 245 meters in diameter and 30 meters in height, with three moats encircling the whole. It is an eloquent symbol of the new power of the state and authority of the monarch in the fifth century.

Nomi no Sukune 野見宿禰 (first century B.C.–first century A.D.)

Warrior of the ancient period. According to legend, in the time of Emperor Sujin (first century A.D.) there was a strong man called Taima no Kehaya who boasted that he could overpower anyone pitted against him. The emperor, hearing of another man of great strength named Nomi no Sukune in the province of Izumo, had him brought to court and arranged for the two to engage in a sumo wrestling contest, from which Nomi no Sukune emerged the victor. This is said to be the origin of Japanese style wrestling. Nomi no Sukune did not return home but remained in the service of the emperor. According to the custom of the time, when a person of importance died, a number of his or her attendants were buried alive with the body so that they might accompany their lord in death. Emperor Sujin was distressed at this practice, and when the empress died, he asked his courtiers if there were some way that it could be avoided. Nomi no Sukune then sent for a hundred potters from the province of Izumo and had them make clay images of men and horses that could be ranged around the grave mound to take the place of the human beings. This, the legend states, was the beginning of the practice of burying *haniwa* with the dead.

ŌJIN TENNŌ 應神天皇 (third–fourth centuries)

Emperor of the ancient period. According to legend, his father, Emperor Chūai, died suddenly while on his way to attack the state of Silla in Korea. His mother, Empress Jingū, though already pregnant with the future Emperor Ōjin, successfully carried out the expedition against Silla and returned to Japan, giving birth to her son at the province of Tsukushi in Kyushu. On his mother's death, he became the fifteenth ruler of Japan. Though there is some doubt about the earlier rulers, it is believed that Emperor Ōjin was an actual historical figure. He is said to have reigned for forty years, during which Achi no Omi introduced the art of weaving, Wani presented books, and other foreigners who had settled in Japan introduced wine making and other elements of mainland culture. It was thus a period when the Yamato court increased in power both internally and externally. His grave mound, situated in Habikino in Osaka Prefecture, measures 418 meters in length and, along with that of his son, Emperor Nintoku, which is the largest grave mound in the world, gives evidence of the remarkable degree of power and prospertity that the Yamato state had attained at this time.

ŌMI NO MIFUNE 淡海三船 (722–785)

Scholar of the late Nara period. In his youth he became a Buddhist monk, assuming the name Genkai, but he later returned to lay life and took up a position at court. In 756, however, he was penalized for speaking out in criticism of the court. In 764, when Emi no Oshikatsu rose up in revolt, Ōmi no Mifune condemned his actions and was rewarded by promotion in rank, Along with Isonokami no Yakatsugu, he was famous as one of the outstanding scholars of the time, and in 772 he was appointed head of the *daigaku*, a school of higher learning set up by the state, which was somewhat comparable to a modern university but restricted in enrollment to sons of the aristocracy. In conjunction with Ishikawa no Natari and others he engaged in the compilation and editing of historical materials, and in 779 he wrote a biography of Ganjin, a Chinese priest who came to Japan, entitled *Tōdaiwajō tōseiden*. In addition he is said to have been the one who selected and assigned the Chinese style posthumous names such as Jimmu, Suizei, etc. by which the early Japanese rulers are now known.

Ono no Imoko 小野妹子 (early seventh century)

Court official of the Asuka period. He was a member of a powerful family said to have come from Ono in the district of Shiga in Ōmi Province; the element *ko* in his name, though nowadays usually used only in women's names, was a title of respect. On behalf of Prince Shōtoku, regent for Empress Suiko, he went in 607 as envoy to the court of Emperor Yang of the Sui dynasty in China. Previously Japan in her relations with China had been treated as a vassal state, but Ono no Imoko was dispatched with the request that this situation be changed and the two countries deal as equals. The request was denied, but as a result of the mission, formal trade relations were established with China, and the continental influences that are reflected in the art works of the Hōryū-ji and other temples and that make the Asuka so important a period in the development of Japanese culture began to enter the country. In Chinese historical works Ono no Imoko's name is written with the characters 蘇因高, in modern Mandarin pronounced Su Yin-kao.

Osakabe Shinnō 刑部(忍壁)親王 (d. 705)

Imperial prince of the Asuka period; son of Emperor Temmu. At the time of the Jinshin uprising in 672, when Emperor Tenji's son, Prince Ōtomo, was engaged in a struggle for succession to the throne with Emperor Tenji's younger brother, Prince Ōami (the future Emperor Temmu), he accompanied his father and was active in the fighting in the east, which ended in victory for his father.

At the command of Emperor Mommu, he undertook an enlargement and revision of the previously devised system of laws, known as the *ritsuryō*, or penal and civil code, presiding over the compilation of the so-called *Taihō ritsuryō*, Penal and Civil Code of the Taihō era, which was completed in 701 and put into effect the following year. The purpose of the code was to make Japan, both in name and fact, a bureaucratic state after the Chinese model. From the time of its promulgation, therefore, Japan was, institutionally speaking, under the rule of a single central government headed by the emperor and guided by the laws of the *ritsuryō*, and though changes in the way in which power was actually exercised came about later with the founding of the Kamakura, Muromachi, and Edo shogunates, in name at least, the shoguns were regarded as merely acting on the delegated authority of the emperor, who remained the ruler and actual head of the state.

Ōtomo no Kanamura 大伴金村 (fifth–sixth centuries)

Military leader of the Yamato court period. Ōtomo no Kanamura, who wielded military power at the early Yamato court, was ordered by Emperor Buretsu when the latter was still heir apparent to attack and wipe out Heguri no Matori and his sons. Having carried out the task and won the emperor's favor, he gained even greater prestige at court. When Emperor Buretsu died, Kanamura set up Emperor Keitai as successor and gathered all power into his own hands. In 512 the Korean kingdom of Paekche requested that four districts of its neighbor, the Japanese tributary state of Mimana (Imna) be ceded to it. When the matter was discussed at the Japanese court, Kanamura favored granting the request and saw to it that the matter was so decided. After the death of Emperor Keitai, the successors backed by Kanamura, emperors Ankan and Senka, both died after ruling for only brief periods, and a candidate supported by Mononobe no Okoshi, Emperor Kimmei, came to the throne. Subsequently Kanamura was accused by Mononobe no Okoshi of having accepted bribes from Paekche in the settlement of the Mimana affair. He thereupon retired to his home and did not take any further part in affairs of state; as a result the power of the Ōtomo family declined.

Rōben 良辨 (689–773)

Buddhist priest of the middle Nara period. Some accounts give his birthplace as the province of Ōmi, other as the province of Sagami. Legend states that when he was a child he was carried off by a large eagle and transported to the Kasuga Shrine in the province of Yamato, where he was found by the eminent priest Gien and raised to manhood. Thirty years later he was finally reunited with his mother.

Whatever the truth of the legend, it is certain that Rōben studied Buddhism under Gien. He was treated with great favor by Emperor Shōmu, and it has even been said that he was the one who persuaded the emperor to undertake the building of the Tōdai-ji. In 733 he built the Kensaku-in, the forerunner of the present Sangatsu-dō of the Tōdai-ji. Later, when Emperor Shōmu decided to build the Tōdai-ji, Rōben was put in charge of the construction and worked with Gyōki and others to bring it to completion in 752. He was made the first head of the new temple.

RYŌGEN 良源 (912–982)

Buddhist priest of the middle Heian period. He was born in the province of Ōmi (present-day Shiga Prefecture) and became a monk in 928, entering the monastery on Mt. Hiei as a follower of the Tendai sect. He won reknown for engaging in doctrinal debates with exponents of other sects. At the same time he became friendly with Fujiwara no Morosuke, a high court official, accepting Morosuke's son Jinzen as his disciple, and with Morosuke's help set about rebuilding the temples of Mt. Hiei, which had earlier been destroyed by fire. In 966 he became the eighteenth *zasu*, or head of the Tendai sect, and in 960 he drew up a set of regulations in twenty-six sections that were designed to put an end to the drinking, brawling, and other forms of immoral conduct that had begun to appear among the members of the religious community. Ryōgen thus worked to restore the Tendai sect to its original purity and prestige, but at the same time, because of his connections with the aristocracy, he made it more difficult for persons of humble birth who entered the clergy to rise to high ecclesiastical position.

RYŌNIN 良忍 (ca. 1072–1132)

Monk of the Tendai sect in the late Heian period, famous as the institutor of the *yūzū nembutsu.* In his youth he was a regular priest of the Enryaku-ji temple on Mt. Hiei, but he later withdrew to a retreat at Ōhara in the northern foothills of the mountain, where he devoted himself to *nembutsu* practice. The type of *nembutsu* he practiced is known as *yūzū nembutsu*, or "circulating *nembutsu.*" The exact nature of the practice is not clear, but it appears to be based upon the concept that the *nembutsu* or ritual invocation of the name of the Buddha Amida performed by one man can be "circulated" to other men, and their *nembutsu* circulated to him, so that all persons together can be reborn in the Pure Land, the paradise of the Buddha Amida. The concept of *yūzū nembutsu* was later taken over and developed by Yūkan (1649–1716), who founded the Yūzū Nembutsu sect that remains in existence today. Ryōnin was also renowned for his knowledge of *shōmyō*, the type of singing used in Buddhist ceremonies. He is listed in the Tendai teaching line as a disciple of Ryōga.

Saga Tennō 嵯峨天皇 (786–842)

Emperor of the early Heian period. He was the second son of Emperor Kammu. In 809 his elder brother, Emperor Heizei, abdicated because of illness and turned the throne over to him, making him the fifty-second ruler of Japan. The following year the so-called Fujiwara no Kusuko revolt broke out, an abortive attempt by Fujiwara no Kusuko and her brother to restore Emperor Heizei to the throne, but order was restored by Sakanoue no Tamuramaro and his associates. This same year the emperor set up the Kurōdodokoro, an office directly under the supervision of the ruler designed to handle confidential documents and other matters of state, and assigned Fujiwara no Fuyutsugu and Kose no Notari to head it. In 823 he abdicated, making way for Emperor Junna.

The emperor took an active part in cultural as well as political matters, working enthusiastically to introduce elements of Chinese culture to Japan. On his order the *Ryōunshū* was compiled, the first collection of *kanshi*, or poems written in Chinese by Japanese, to be compiled on imperial command, and he also directed the compilation of legal codes and works of history. He was an outstanding calligrapher, along with Kūkai and Tachibana no Hayanari comprising the so-called Sampitsu, or Three Masters of Calligraphy, of the time.

Saichō (Dengyō Daishi) 最澄(傳教大師) (766 or 767–822)

Buddhist monk of the early Heian period; founder of the Tendai sect in Japan; his posthumous title is Dengyō Daishi. He was born in Ōmi Province, the son of a family named Mitsu-no-obito. He entered the clergy in 780 under a monk named Gyōhyō. In 785 he received formal ordination as a priest at Tōdai-ji in Nara, but thereafter immediately withdrew to a hermitage on Mt. Hiei northeast of Kyoto, where he devoted himself to strict religious observances. At this time he became interested in the teachings of the T'ien-t'ai, or Tendai, sect of Buddhism, which had previously been largely ignored in Japan. The T'ien-t'ai sect was founded by the Chinese monk Chih-i (538–597), who in his various writings set forth a world view and system of religious practice based upon the Lotus Sutra.

Around 797, Saichō began to emerge from seclusion and to become active in society, gradually gaining fame as a religious leader. In 804 he journeyed to China along with his disciple Gishin and others. At Mt. T'ien-t'ai in Chekiang, he studied T'ien-t'ai doctrines and *vinaya,* monastic discipline, under Tao-sui and Hsing-man. He also received instruction in meditation from Hsiao-jan and in Esoteric Buddhism from Shun-hsiao of Yüeh-chou. Thus Saichō's Buddhism came to include four elements, Tendai doctrine, *vinaya* (*ritsu*), meditation (*zen*), and Esoteric Buddhism (Mikkyō), and this combination remained characteristic of Tendai Buddhism as it was transmitted in Japan.

Saichō returned to Japan in 805. In 809 he became acquainted with Kūkai, another important Buddhist leader of the time, but in 815 the two broke off relations. In 817 Saichō set out on a tour to spread his teachings in eastern Japan. He became involved in a religious dispute with Tokuichi, a learned monk of the Hossō sect residing in Aizu. To support his position, Saichō wrote such works as *Shōgon jikkyō, Shugo kokkai-shō,* and *Hokke shūku.* In 818 he petitioned the emperor for permission to establish a Mahayana ordination platform on Mt. Hiei, the following year writing a work called *Kenkairon* to support his request, but he met with strong opposition from the older sects of Buddhism in Nara. It was only after his death in 822 that permission was finally granted.

Saichō's thinking centers about these two issues of the doctrinal debate with Tokuichi and the question of the ordination platform. In the former, Tokuichi had upheld the Hossō sect's teaching that the potentiality to attain Buddhahood differs according to the individual. In response to this, Saichō argued that human beings are all equally endowed with the potentiality for enlightenment. On the latter issue, he asserted that Mahayana Buddhism should have a set of *vinaya,* or rules of discipline, that was distinctively its own. The older schools of Buddhism in Japan, though teaching Mahayana doctrines, had followed the rules of discipline laid down in Hinayana Buddhism. As may be seen, Saichō was idealistic in his thinking and did not hesitate to expound views that put him in direct opposition with the older factions in Japanese Buddhism. In this respect he stands in contrast to Kūkai, his eminent contemporary who was likewise working to bring about revolutionary changes in Buddhism, but who was more tolerant and flexible in his attitude. In the centuries following Saichō's death, Tendai Buddhism flourished, with Enryaku-ji on Mt. Hiei as its chief center of activity. It produced such distinguished monks as Ennin and Enchin and served as the training ground for all the important religious reformers of the Kamakura period.

Sakanoue no Tamuramaro 坂上田村麻呂 (758–811)

Military leader of the early Heian period. The members of the Sakanoue family were hereditary military leaders in the service of the court. Tamuramaro's father, Karitamaro, demonstrated his bravery at the time of the Emi no Oshikatsu uprising in 764, and Tamuramaro in turn came to enjoy the favor of Emperor Kammu and to be entrusted with the military affairs of the court. In 794 he was sent on an expedition against the Ezo people, who lived in the Tōhoku region of northern Japan, and in 797 was given the newly created title of *seii-taishōgun* (roughly, "commander-in-chief against the barbarians"), the first time the military title of *shōgun* was used. In 801 he was dispatched on a second expedition against the Ezo, this time at the head of a force of over forty thousand soldiers. In 802 he built the Izawa Fort at a site in the present-day city of Mizusawa in Iwate Prefecture, which served as a base in exercising control over the Ezo.

After his death, his grave in Kyoto, called the Shōgunzuka, became an object of veneration among military men, and it was said that they would customarily visit it to pay their respects before setting off to battle. He is also said to have been the founder of the Kiyomizu-dera in Kyoto.

Seiwa Tennō 清和天皇 (850–880)

Emperor of the early Heian period. He was the fourth son of Emperor Montoku, but in spite of the fact that he had three elder brothers, he was declared heir apparent in the year of his birth because his mother was the daughter of the powerful minister Fujiwara no Yoshifusa. In 858 he became the fifty-sixth ruler and the first child under ten years of age to ascend the throne. Because of his youth, all affairs of government were handled by his grandfather, Fujiwara no Yoshifusa, who in 866 was officially appointed *sesshō*, regent, the first person not a member of the imperial family or the Buddhist clergy to hold the title. Yoshifusa also arranged for Emperor Seiwa to marry Takaiko, the younger sister of his adopted son Mototsune, and saw to it that the son born from this union was declared emperor. Thus Emperor

Seiwa was unable to exercise any political power, but was completely under the control of the members of the Fujiwara family. The descendants of his son Prince Sadasumi became the founders of the Genji (Minamoto family), the military leaders of the late twelfth century.

Shinjō (Shim-sang) 審祥 (d. 742)

Buddhist monk of the Nara period and the founder of the Kegon sect of Buddhism in Japan. He was a native of the Korean state of Silla. He went to China and studied under Fa-tsang (643–712), who gave final shape to the doctrines of Hua-yen (Kegon) Buddhism. Shinjō later transmitted these teachings to Japan. Writings of the Kegon sect had been introduced to Japan in 736 by the Chinese monk Tao-hsüan (Dōsen; 702–760), but had not yet become well known. In 740, the monk Rōben requested Shinjō, then residing in Daian-ji in Nara, to lecture on Kegon teachings at Rōben's temple, Konshō-ji (later called Tōdai-ji). Shinjō in time came to enjoy the patronage of Emperor Shōmu and gained great distinction. Consequently, he is regarded as the first patriarch of the Kegon sect in Japan, and Rōben as the second patriarch. Among his disciples were Jikin, Enshō, and Gonchi; he left a work entitled *Kegon kishin kangyō hōmon*. It should be noted, however, that the above biographical data is based entirely upon the account compiled by the Kamakura period monk and historian of Buddhism Gyōnen (1240–1321) and needs to be subjected to further research.

Shōbō 聖寶 (832–909)

Shingon sect monk of the early Heian period; his posthumous title is Rigen Taishi. He was born in the province of Yamato and, his abilities having been recognized by Kūkai's disciple Shinga (801–879), he went to Nara around the age of twenty to study the doctrines of the Sanron, Hossō, and Kegon sects of Buddhism. He founded a subtemple in Tōdai-ji known as Tōnan-in, which served as a training center in Sanron Buddhism and in later times became the main instrument for the transmission of Sanron teachings. He studied Shingon, or Esoteric Buddhism, under Shinga and Shinnen and received *kanjō*, the ceremony in Esoteric Buddhism indicating the attainment of Buddhahood, from Shinga's disciple Gennin at Tō-ji in Kyoto. In 874 he founded a temple called Daigo-ji at Daigo Kasatoriyama southeast of Kyoto. In his later years he served as head of Tōdai-ji and of Tō-ji. His teaching line was carried on and developed by his disciple Kanken and later became the basis for the Ono branch of Shingon Buddhism. He also took a great interest in Shugendō, a system of Buddhist practices and ceremonies carried out in the mountains, and erected an image of Nyoirin Kannon on Mt. Kimbu at Yoshino. In later times he was revered as the restorer of Shugendō Buddhism, which had been founded two centuries earlier by En no Ozunu. He is thus an unusual figure in Japanese Buddhism, combining a knowledge of the Nara sects of Buddhism with Shingon teachings and the practices associated with Shugendō.

Shōmu Tennō 聖武天皇 (701–756)

The forty-fifth sovereign and third sovereign of the Nara period, he reigned from 724 to 749; his personal name was Obito, and his religious name Shōman. He was the eldest son of Emperor Mommu; his mother, Miyako, was a daughter of Fujiwara no Fuhito.

Since he was still a child in 707 when Emperor Mommu died, his grandmother, Empress Gemmei, took the throne and was followed by his aunt, Empress Genshō. In 714 he was designated heir apparent and in 724 ascended the throne. His consort was Kōmyōshi, a daughter of Fujiwara no Fuhito; she became his wife while he was still heir apparent and was declared empress in 729.

During the early part of Emperor Shōmu's reign, the government was dominated by Prince Nagaya, a grandson of Emperor Temmu, but he was suspected of plotting treason and committed suicide in 729. Thereafter power passed into the hands of Fujiwara no Muchimaro and his three brothers, sons of Fujiwara no Fuhito. But all four brothers died in an epidemic in 737 and were succeeded in power by Tachibana no Moroe, a half-brother of Empress Kōmyō, along with the Buddhist prelate Gembō and Kibi no Makibi, who had formerly been sent to China as a student.

In 741, Emperor Shōmu, acting on proposals submitted by these advisors, ordered that an officially sponsored temple (*kokubun-ji*) and nunnery (*kokubun-niji*) be set up in each province to pray for good fortune and the safety of the state.

During his reign, Emperor Shōmu twice dispatched embassies to T'ang China and became an enthusiastic importer of Chinese culture. Art, architecture, and the daily lives of the aristocracy came under strong Chinese influence, and the period, know by the era name Tempyō, proved to be one of the most brilliant and creative in the history of Japanese culture.

Meanwhile, struggles for power continued at court. In 740, Fujiwara no Hirotsugu, hoping to restore the Fujiwara family to eminence, raised a revolt in northern Kyushu. After the revolt was put down, the capital was moved several times to Kuni, Shigaraki, and Naniwa. In 743, Emperor Shōmu ordered the construction of a giant image of the Buddha Vairocana to insure peace and prosperity to the state. The expense and labor of this undertaking, however, proved a heavy burden upon the common people and caused much grumbling against the government, which served to intensify the struggle for power at court. In 749, when the casting of the image, known as the Great Buddha of Tōdai-ji, was completed, Emperor Shōmu abdicated in favor of his daughter, Princess Abe, who became known as Empress Kōken. He was initiated into the clergy by the famous monk Gyōki, taking the religious name Shōman and thereafter devoting himself to religious affairs. In 752 he attended the "eye-opening" ceremony that marked the completion of the Great Buddha of Tōdai-ji. After his death in 756, his personal belongings were turned over to Tōdai-ji for safekeeping, where they were housed in a storehouse known as the Shōsō-in and have survived in almost perfect condition to the present, constituting a priceless record of the art and material culture of Nara period Japan as well as objects from T'ang dynasty China.

Shōtoku Taishi 聖徳太子 (574–622)

Political and cultural leader of the Asuka period and one of the most highly revered figures in all of Japanese history. His father was the thirty-first sovereign, Emperor Yōmei; his mother was Empress Anahobe-no-hashibito. The prince was named Umayado, or Horse Stable Door, reportedly because his mother, in the course of a walk about the palace grounds, gave birth to him when she reached the royal stables. The posthumous title Shōtoku Taishi means Crown Prince of Holy Virtue.

In his youth the prince studied Buddhism under Hyeja (Ehi), a monk from the Korean state of Koguryŏ, and Confucianism under a Korean scholar named Hakka (Kakuka). He proved to be a highly diligent and intelligent student and was said to have been widely read in both religious and secular works.

In 592 the powerful government leader Soga no Umako ordered the assassination of the thirty-second sovereign Emperor Sushun. The latter was succeeded as ruler by Empress Suiko, the niece of Soga no Umako and aunt of Prince Shōtoku, who thereupon became crown prince. He handled affairs of state in her place, guiding the imperial house through a period of particular difficulty.

In 589 the Sui dynasty had succeeded in uniting all of China under its rule, while on the Korean peninsula the state of Silla, which had earlier overthrown Japan's ally Imna, continued to grow in power. The prince considered sending an army to attack Silla and attempt to restore the state of Imna, but nothing came of these plans; instead he concentrated his attention upon internal affairs.

He announced that the Buddhist religion should be the foundation of the state, and to this end founded various temples such as Shitennō-ji in present-day Osaka, Kōryū-ji in present-day Kyoto, and Hōryū-ji and Chūgū-ji in the Nara area. Hōryū-ji, which was founded in 607, continues in existence today in close to its original form and constitutes an invaluable example of Asuka period Buddhist architecture. The prince also engaged in the study of Buddhist texts and produced *gisho* (commentaries), which are still extant, on three major Mahayana sutras, the Lotus Sutra, Vimalakīrti Sutra, and the Sutra of Queen Śrīmālā. By encouraging Buddhism, he no doubt hoped to promote social harmony and morality. At the same time he helped to advance the level of learning and art in Japan and to make the Asuka period one of the most brilliant eras in Japanese culture.

On the political scene, the prince in 603 established a system of twelve cap-ranks for court officials. The purpose of this was to encourage the recognition of individual talent in the government and counteract the emphasis that had hitherto been placed upon family and clique connections. The following year, he promulgated the Seventeen Article Constitution, a document in Chinese that lays down the principles of government. Drawing upon Buddhism and Chinese Confucian and Legalist thought, it sets forth the ideal of a centralized state headed by the emperor and administered by a government-appointed bureaucracy. The document did much to inspire the Taika Reforms of 646 and exerted a strong influence on later legal and governmental codes. The prince also undertook the compilation of the first Japanese historical works, *Tennō-ki* and *Koku-ki*—texts dealing with the history of the imperial house and the country as a whole. It was around this time that the Japanese ruler, previously referred to by the term *ōkimi*, began to be designated by the Chinese term *tennō*.

On the diplomatic scene, he dispatched a letter to Emperor Yang of the Sui dynasty in China in which he conveyed greetings from "The Son of Heaven of the Land of the Rising Sun to the Son of Heaven of the Land of the Setting Sun," an indication that Japan considered itself to be on an equal footing with China. He also sent Japanese students to China along with the official envoy so that they could learn more about Buddhism and Chinese culture. He died in 622 and was entombed at Shinaga in the province of Kawachi.

Soga no Iname 蘇我稲目 (d. 570)

Court official of the Yamato court period. The members of the Soga family are said to have come to prominence through their handling of fiscal matters for the Yamato court. Soga no Iname engaged in a struggle for power with Mononobe no Okoshi, leader of the conservative faction at court, and when King Syŏngmyŏng of the Korean state of Paekche presented Buddhist images and scriptures to Emperor Kimmei in 538 (the date is also given as 552), Soga no Iname took the image into his own home and worshiped it, although Mononobe no Okoshi fiercely denounced the foreign religion. Later, however, an epidemic broke out and Mononobe no Okoshi, declaring that it was caused by Soga no Iname's acceptance of Buddhism, set fire to the latter's house and burned it down. This represents the first mention of the introduction of Buddhism to Japan. Soga no Iname's son, Soga no Umako, was also a follower of Buddhism and, along with Prince Shōtoku, helped to create the distinctive culture of the Asuka period, which is noted for its temples and Buddhist works of art. Iname's daughters became consorts of Emperor Kimmei and gave birth to Emperor Yōmei and other distinguished persons, thus increasing the power and influence of the Soga family.

Soga no Iruka 蘇我入鹿 (d. 645)

Court official of the Asuka period. He was the son of Soga no Emishi and grandson of Soga no Umako. When Empress Suiko died in 628, a struggle for the succession arose between Prince Tamura, who enjoyed the support of Soga no Emishi, and Prince Yamashiro no Ōe, the son of Prince Shōtoku. The former emerged victorious, however, and ascended the throne to become Emperor Jomei. In 643 Soga no Iruka forced Prince Yamashiro no Ōe to commit suicide and thereafter was able to manage affairs of state as he pleased, even going so far as to build mansions for himself and his family that he entitled "palaces." In 645, however, he was assassinated by Prince Naka no Ōe, the future Emperor Tenji, and Nakatomi no Kamatari (Fujiwara no Kamatari), whereupon his father, Emishi, set fire to his own house and burned to death.

Soga no Umako 蘇我馬子 (sixth century)

Court official of the Asuka period. He was the son of Soga no Iname, who had engaged in a struggle for power with Mononobe no Okoshi, and the same struggle was carried on by Umako. In 587, when Emperor Yōmei died, a quarrel over the succession broke out between the prince backed by Mononobe no Okoshi's son Moriya and that backed by Umako, but Umako attacked and killed Moriya and proceeded to set up the prince he supported, who became Emperor Sushun. Being told later that Emperor Sushun hated him, however, he had the emperor assassinated and in his place set up his own niece, the consort of the deceased Emperor Bidatsu, who became Empress Suiko, appointing Prince Shōtoku as heir apparent to handle affairs of government. He, like Prince Shōtoku, was a follower of Buddhism, and founded the first temple in Japan, known as Asuka-dera. He also joined with Prince Shōtoku in compiling works on the history of Japan.

Sugawara no Michizane 菅原道眞 (845–903)

Political leader, scholar, and literary figure of the middle Heian period; after his death he was worshiped as the deity Tenjin at the Temmangū shrine. He was born in Kyoto, the third son of Sugawara no Koreyoshi, a scholar of Chinese studies. He displayed literary talent at an early age, and in 872, when he was chosen to entertain the envoy from the state of Pohai, won praise for his poetry in Chinese. After attending the state university and holding various posts, he was appointed a professor of the university in 877; he was the fourth member of his family in succession to hold that position, his great-grandfather, grandfather, and father having also been professors and the presidents of the state university as well.

In 886 he was appointed governor of the province of Sanuki in Shikoku. Upon his return to the capital, he gained favor with Emperor Uda and in 891 was selected for the important post of head of the Kurōdodokoro, an office in charge of palace affairs. This appointment took place shortly after the death of the powerful minister Fujiwara no Mototsune and suggests that Emperor Uda hoped to make use of Michizane to help curb the power of the Fujiwara family. Michizane continued to rise in office along with Fujiwara no Mototsune's son Tokihira, until in 897 Tokihira was appointed *dainagon* (great counselor) and Michizane was appointed *gon-no-dainagon* (acting great counselor). Tokihira and Michizane became in effect the most powerful ministers at court.

In 894 Michizane was chosen to head a mission to the T'ang court in China, but he submitted a memorial pointing out the risks that the journey involved and the internal disorder and decay into which the T'ang rule had fallen and recommended that the mission be abandoned. His advice was accepted, and thus ended the practice of sending regular diplomatic missions to China that had begun some 260 years earlier.

Emperor Daigo came to the throne in 893, and in 899 he appointed Tokihira minister of the left and Michizane minister of the right. This was the first time since the appointment of Kibi no Makibi in 766 that a scholar had been appointed to this high post, and it represented an extreme honor for Michizane. But it also placed him in a dangerous position, and in 901, as a result of the slanders of Tokihira, he was appointed *Dazai-no-gon-no-sochi*, or head of the administrative office (the Dazaifu) in Kyushu. The appointment was nominal, for in fact he was being condemned to banishment. He died two years later at his place of exile in Kyushu.

After his death, a number of untoward events occurred that were believed to have been caused by Michizane's angry spirit. In 923 he was declared guiltless of the charges against him and was restored to his former rank and office and in 993 he was posthumously promoted to the court rank of senior first rank and the office of *dajōdaijin* (prime minister). Earlier, a shrine had been set up in Kitano in Kyoto, where he was worshiped under the name Temma Tenjin. In time he came to be looked upon as the patron deity of learning and literature, and his cult spread throughout the country. One of the most important shrines dedicated to him is the Temmangū shrine at Dazaifu in Kyushu, at the spot where he lived and died in exile.

Michizane was known for his unusual skill in writing prose and poetry in Chinese. In 892 on imperial order he undertook the compilation of a work on Japanese history entitled *Ruijū kokushi* and he also took part in the compilation of the *Sandai jitsuroku*, an officially sponsored history in Chinese covering the period from 858 to 887. His poetry in Chinese is preserved in two works, the *Kanke bunsō* and *Kanke kōshū*, which contain over five hundred poems.

Suiko Tennō 推古天皇 (554–626)

Empress of the Asuka period; the first woman sovereign of Japan. Her father was Emperor Kimmei, her mother the daughter of Soga no Iname. When she grew up, she became the empress of her elder half-brother by a different mother, Emperor Bidatsu. Emperor Bidatsu died in 585 and his successor, Emperor Yōmei, died shortly after. The throne passed to Emperor Sushun, but in 592 he was assassinated by his uncle, Soga no Umako. Thereupon, at the urging of the court officials, Empress Suiko consented to take the throne, becoming the first woman in Japanese history to hold the title of *tennō*. Prince Shōtoku was appointed as heir apparent and, along with the high official Soga no Umako, took up the position of *sesshō* (regent) and carried out the actual business of government.

During the reign of Empress Suiko, Buddhism flourished under the encouragement of Prince Shōtoku, and the arts and learning associated with it came to constitute what is known as Asuka culture. The machinery for handling state business was put into good order, the system of twelve cap-ranks for the members of the bureaucracy was promulgated, and in 604 the so-called Seventeen Article Constitution was proclaimed, which set up a national state with the emperor at its head. Thus at this time there was an increasing consciousness of Japan as a nation, which was reflected in relations with China. In 607 Ono no Imoko was sent as official envoy to the Sui state in China with the request that Japan and China deal with one another as equals. The increasing consciousness of national identity is also reflected in the compilation of works dealing with the history of Japan, in attacks on the state of Silla in Korea, and in the firm suppression of insubordination among government officials.

Empress Suiko was said to have been a woman of great grace and beauty, correct in conduct and of impeccable character.

SUJIN TENNŌ 崇神天皇 (dates uncertain)

Emperor of the ancient period. According to the *Kojiki*, which deals with the history of Japan from the earliest times until the reign of Empress Suiko, he was the tenth ruler. Shortly after coming to the throne he is said to have taken the sacred mirror and sword that were preserved in the palace and transferred them to a place called Kasanui-no-mura, where worship was paid to the ancestress of the imperial family, the goddess Amaterasu Ōmikami. This is the origin of the great Shinto shrine at Ise. He decreed that the common people should pay taxes out of the game caught by the men and the woven products of the women, thus assuring financial support for the government, and he dispatched four generals in each of the four directions to conquer the outlying regions that had not yet been brought under control. He is thus said to be the first emperor to establish central rule over the entire country.

Whether such a person as Emperor Sujin existed or not is unclear, but the account of his reign would seem to reflect the fact that during the second and third centuries the Yamato court was gradually extending its control over an increasingly larger area of Japan.

Tachibana no Moroe 橘諸兄 (684–757)

Court official of the middle Nara period. His father was Prince Minu, a descendant of Emperor Bidatsu; his mother was Tachibana no Michiyo, also mother of Empress Kōmyō. At first he was given the title Prince Katsuragi and, as a member of the imperial family, was assigned to a post at court in 710. In 731 he was appointed to the office of *sangi*, councilor, which allowed him to take part in important deliberations of the court and other state business. In 736 he petitioned the court for permission to take his mother's name, and he was accordingly removed from the imperial family and made a commoner with the name Tachibana no Moroe. In 737 an epidemic carried off many members of the Fujiwara family who had held high office in the government, and Moroe, though he had no particular talent for politics, suddenly found himself in a position of power. With Kibi no Makibi and the priest Gembō as his advisors, he proceeded to take over the management of the state. In 740, Fujiwara no Hirotsugu called out troops in an attempt to restore power to the Fujiwara family, but his efforts ended in failure. In 749 Moroe was given the highest court rank possible for a commoner, that of *shōichii*, or senior first rank, but by this time his power had begun to wane as a new rival, Fujiwara no Nakamaro (Emi no Oshikatsu) rose to prominence. He took part in the ceremonies marking the completion of the Great Buddha of the Tōdai-ji in 752, though completely overshadowed by Fujiwara no Nakamaro. Against such a background, reports began to circulate that at a certain banquet Moroe had composed a poem that hinted at plans for a coup d'état. He was about to be condemned to punishment when special pleading from his half-sister, Empress Kōmyō, secured him a pardon. He retired from office in 756 and died the following year. After his death, his eldest son, Tachibana no Naramaro, plotted to overthrow Fujiwara no Nakamaro, but the plot was discovered and he was killed in the seventh month of the same year as his father's death.

Taira no Masakado 平將門 (d. 940)

Warrior of the middle Heian period. He was the son of Taira no Yoshikado, who had been sent by the court to bring under control the Ezo tribes of the Tōhoku region. He made his way to the capital, where he found service with the aristocracy, but failing to gain any official appointment, he returned east to his home in Kantō. In 935 he killed his uncle, Taira no Kunika, with whom he had been engaged in a dispute over his father's estate, and as a result aroused the animosity of the entire Taira family. In addition, he attempted to mediate in a quarrel among the officials of the province of Musashi (present-day Saitama and Tokyo prefectures) and instead was condemned by the court as a rebel. Later, when Fujiwara no Gemmyō of the province of Hitachi (present-day Ibaragi Prefecture) was arrested by the officials for failure to pay taxes, he called upon Taira no Masakado for assistance, and the latter responded by burning down the government offices of Hitachi. Thus Masakado, finding himself deeper and deeper in trouble of one kind or another, finally in a gesture of ultimate defiance declared himself emperor. The court sent an expeditionary force against him, and he was killed in 940.

Takaoka Shinnō 高岳親王 (799–865)

Buddhist priest of the early Heian period. The third son of Emperor Heizei, he was designated heir apparent to Emperor Saga in 809 but was removed from that position as a result of the uprising led by Fujiwara no Kusuko the following year. He later entered the clergy, assuming the religious name Shinnyo, and became a disciple of Kūkai. Troubled with doubts as to whether the Buddhism transmitted to Japan represented the true teaching of Śākyamuni, he journeyed to China in 862 and questioned various eminent members of the Chinese clergy, but they could tell him no more than he had learned from Kūkai. He thereupon resolved to go to India, the birthplace of the Buddhist faith, setting out from China in 865 at the age of sixty-six, but he died along the way at a place designated in Chinese as the state of Lo-yüeh, which scholars surmise corresponds to the area of Singapore.

TENJI TENNŌ 天智天皇 (d. 671)

The thirty-eighth sovereign of Japan, he reigned from 668 to 671. His father was Emperor Jomei; his mother was Emperor Jomei's consort, who reigned twice under the titles Kōgyoku and Saimei respectively. He was known as Katsuragi-no-miko and Naka no Ōe.

Earlier, Prince Shōtoku (574–622) had attempted to carry out governmental reforms and set up a strong centralized state with the emperor at its head, but he had been prevented from realizing his objectives by the privileged position of the powerful Soga family. After his death, the Sogas continued to increase in power until they overshadowed the imperial family. Meanwhile, China had come under the rule of the T'ang dynasty, which had dispatched armies in an attempt to conquer the states of the Korean peninsula.

The future Emperor Tenji studied Chinese thought and political doctrine under Minabuchi no Shōan, a Buddhist monk who had been sent to China some years earlier to study and who had returned to Japan in 640. The prince then joined the court official Nakatomi no Kamatari in plotting the overthrow of the Sogas, a goal that was accomplished in 645 with the murder of Soga no Iruka and the suicide of his father, Emishi. Emperor Kōtoku then came to the throne, and the prince became heir apparent, wielding the actual power of government. Under his direction, the capital was moved from Asuka to Naniwa, on the site of the present-day city of Osaka.

The Chinese system of using *nengō*, or era names, was initiated, the period beginning in 645 being designated the Taika era. In 646 various edicts were promulgated that laid down the foundations for a new political system. In summary, the new system called for (1) the nationalization of all private lands and persons held in the past by the imperial family or the other great families; (2) the establishment of an administrative system consisting of *kuni* (provinces), *gun* (districts), etc.; (3) the compilation of a register of all the persons in the nation and the institution of a system of equal distribution of land; and (4) the establishment of a new tax system that would ensure the state a sound financial basis. A centralized bureaucracy modeled after that of T'ang China was set up to carry out the administrative functions of the new government.

During the reign of Emperor Kōtoku, attention was concentrated upon the carrying out of these government measures, which came to be known as the Taika Reforms. After the death of Emperor Kōtoku in 655, the prince's mother came to the throne under the title of Empress Saimei, and the prince continued as before to play a key role in government affairs. In 660, the state of Paekche, Japan's ally on the Korean peninsula, was defeated by the forces of Silla and T'ang China. Japan dispatched an army in an attempt to assist its ally, but the army was defeated in a naval engagement at Hakusuki-no-e in Korea in 663 by the combined forces of Silla and China. Somewhat earlier, Empress Saimei had died at the army headquarters set up at Asakura-no-miya in Kyushu.

Following her death in 661, the prince acted as ruler without formally ascending the throne, but in 667 he moved the capital to Ōtsu in the province of Ōmi and in 668 ascended the throne to become Emperor Tenji. He took steps to prepare for a possible invasion of Japan by the forces of Silla and China, establishing defenses along the shore in western Japan. He also dispatched envoys to China to reestablish diplomatic relations between the two countries. He ordered Nakatomi no Kamatari, now renamed Fujiwara no Kamatari, and others to compile a code of laws that was in time promulgated under the name *Ōmi ryō*, or Ōmi Civil Code. In 670 he had a nationwide register of families compiled, known as the Kōgo'nenjaku, which served as a model for similar registers in later periods. He died in 671 and was buried in Yamashina in the area east of the present-day city of Kyoto. Following his death, a struggle over the succession broke out between his son Prince Ōtomo and his younger brother Prince Ōama; from the cyclical designation for the year, it came to be known as the Jinshin uprising. Prince Ōama emerged victorious and ascended the throne to become Emperor Temmu. Emperor Temmu's descendants died out during the Nara period, and the late eighth century rulers Kōnin and Kammu and their successors were descended from the line of Emperor Tenji.

Toba Tennō 鳥羽天皇 (1103–1156)

Emperor of the late Heian period. The son of Emperor Horikawa, he ascended the throne on his father's death in 1107 to become the seventy-fourth ruler of Japan. Earlier, in 1086, Emperor Shirakawa had turned over the throne to his son, Emperor Horikawa, so that, as a retired sovereign and father of the ruler, he might exercise power more freely, and this system of government, known as *insei* or government by an ex-sovereign, continued to be practiced by Emperor Shirakawa's successors. Accordingly, Emperor Toba in 1123 turned over the throne to his son, Emperor Sutoku, and with the death of his father in 1129, became the actual wielder of power through the *insei* system. Emperor Toba was a devout follower of Buddhist teachings, building temples and leaving instructions for his burial at the Anrakuju-in, a temple that he himself had founded.

Ten days after his death in the seventh month of 1156, a struggle broke out between his son, Retired Emperor Sutoku, and Emperor Goshirakawa. Known as the Hōgen uprising, it split not only the imperial family but many of the great aristocrat families such as the Fujiwara as well, some members of a single family supporting one side, some the other; it ended in victory for the supporters of Emperor Goshirakawa. Active in the strife were military leaders such as Taira no Kiyomori and Minamoto no Yoshitomo. As a result, these men of the warrior class were able to acquire power within the court, and in the end, one of them, Taira no Kiyomori, succeeded in establishing control over the court and setting himself up as a virtual dictator.

Toneri Shinnō 舎人親王 (*676–735*)

Court official of the early Nara period. The son of Emperor Temmu, he was ordered by his father to compile the *Nihon Shoki;* the work was completed in 720 and presented to Empress Gemmei. A history of Japan in thirty chapters compiled under the auspices of the state and covering the period from the mythical beginnings of the nation to the end of the reign of Empress Jitō (697), it is one of the most valuable sources for the study of ancient Japanese history. With the death of Fujiwara no Fuhito in 720, Prince Toneri assumed the highest official post and took charge of the management of the state. In 729, when it was learned that Prince Nagaya was plotting a revolt, Prince Toneri, along with Prince Niitabe, confronted him and forced him to commit suicide. Through the efforts of Fujiwara no Nakamaro, Prince Toneri's son Prince Ōi was eventually able to ascend the throne, becoming the forty-seventh sovereign, Emperor Junnin.

Wake no Kiyomaro 和氣清麻呂 (*733–799*)

Court official of the late Nara period. He was born in the province of Bizen, present-day Okayama Prefecture. His elder sister Hiromushi became lady-in-waiting to Empress Shōtoku (formerly Empress Kōken), and through her introduction he entered court service around 765. Sometime after, Empress Shōtoku was informed that the god of the Usa Hachiman Shrine in the province of Bungo had conveyed word through one of his attendants that it would be all right for the empress to turn over the throne to her favorite, the priest Dōkyō. In the eighth month of 769 the empress dispatched Wake no Kiyomaro to the Usa Hachiman Shrine to consult the god for confirmation, but he returned with word that the god would not give premission for any such action. For this answer Kiyomaro was subjected to punishment and exiled to the province of Ōsumi. After the death of Empress Shōtoku in 770, however, Dōkyō was stripped of power and Kiyomaro was pardoned and recalled to service at the court. In 781 Emperor Kōnin died and Emperor Kammu came to the throne, and in 784 he moved the capital from Heijō-kyō in Nara to Nagaoka-kyō in the province of Yamashiro and set about creating a new political regime. Kiyomaro was active in the creation of the new capital, but when the man who had planned the move, Fujiwara no Tanetsugu, was assassinated, and other difficulties and obstacles developed, Kiyomaro suggested that the capital be moved once more, this time to a site in Yamashiro to be called Heian-kyō, the present city of Kyoto. The emperor adopted his suggestion, and the capital was accordingly moved in 794. As a result of the services rendered on this occasion Kiyomaro was awarded land and won the confidence of the emperor. In 798 he asked to be relieved of court duties, but the request was denied and he died the following year.

WANI 王仁 (dates uncertain)

Foreigner of the ancient period who settled in Japan. He is said to have come to Japan from the Korean state of Paekche in the time of Emperor Ōjin, bringing with him copies of the *Lun-yü* (Confucian *Analects*) and the *Ch'ien-tzu-wen* (*Thousand Character Classic*), a rhymed work one thousand characters in length compiled by Chou Hsing-ssu, thus becoming the first person to introduce books to Japan. He became tutor to the heir apparent and, along with Achi no Omi, was put in charge of the handling and drafting of documents for the court.

It is not clear whether he was Korean or Chinese, and indeed it is not even certain that he actually lived. However, as the Yamato court in the period around the fourth century began to grow in size and complexity, it employed foreigners to draw up documents and handle written records, and Wani may be conveniently regarded as representative of the earliest of these.

YAMATO TAKERU-NO-MIKOTO 日本武尊

Legendary hero of ancient times whose story appears in the *Kojiki* and *Nihon Shoki*. He was the son of Emperor Keikō, the twelfth sovereign according to traditional reckoning; his name was originally Ousu-no-mikoto.

From childhood he was noted for his bravery, and at the age of fourteen was ordered by the emperor to go to southern Kyushu to put down an uprising of the Kumaso people. Disguised as a woman, he made his way into a banquet held by the chief of the Kumaso, where he attacked and killed the chief. Before he died, the chief declared, "I have never met anyone as brave as you. From now on, you should be known as Yamato Takeru,"—the Brave Man of Yamato. The prince, after subjugating the region of southern Kyushu, proceeded to attack enemies in the region of western Honshu and then returned to Yamato in triumph.

When the prince was twenty-six, the Azuma Ebisu people of eastern Honshu rose up in rebellion, and the emperor accordingly dispatched him to attack them. On his way, he stopped to pray at the shrine at Ise dedicated to Amaterasu Ōmikami, the ancestress of the imperial family. There his aunt Yamato-hime-no-mikoto, who was priestess of the shrine, gave him a sacred sword called Ame-no-murakumo-no-tsurugi, which belonged to the shrine. When he reached the region of Suruga in present-day Shizuoka, he was attacked by enemies who attempted to kill him by setting fire to the grass of the plain. But he was able to escape by mowing down the grass with the sword, which accordingly became known as Kusanagi-no-tsurugi or the "Grass-mower Sword."

Thereafter he proceeded to Sagami, Kazusa, and the region of northeastern Honshu known as Hidakami-no-kuni, subjugated the inhabitants and then, after visiting various other regions, returned to Owari in present-day Aichi. There he deposited the sword Kusanagi, where it is still worshipped at the Atsuta Shrine in Nagoya. He set off to attack enemies at Mt. Ibuki, but was taken ill. He returned to Owari, and then set out once more, but died at a place called Nobono in the northern part of Ise Province. He was thirty at the time. He was buried there, but it is said that a white bird flew up from the grave mound and went off to the west. It alighted at two places, Kawaragi in Yamato and Furuichi in Kawachi, at both of which grave mounds were erected to the white bird.

It would appear that Yamato Takeru-no-mikoto was not a historical person, but rather a legendary figure symbolizing the brave exploits of the numerous military leaders who worked to extend the power of the Yamato court and bring the rest of the country under its rule. The tales associated with the figure of Yamato Takeru embody the ideals of vigor and bravery associated with the aristocratic warriors of ancient times and also contain a moving element of tragedy and pathos.

YOSHISHIGE NO YASUTANE 慶滋保胤 (d. 1002)

Scholar of the middle Heian period; he was the son of Kamo no Tadayuki but later adopted the surname Yoshishige. He studied under Sugawara no Fumitoki and was skilled in writing poetry and prose in Chinese. He also took a deep interest in Buddhism and in 964 joined with other scholars and monks in forming the Kangakue, an association of clergy and laymen devoted to the study of the Lotus Sutra. Though he held a post in the government, he became increasingly weary of the secular society of the time, with its numerous evils and injustices. In 982 he wrote a prose piece in Chinese entitled *Chiteiki*, or "Record of the Pond Pavilion," in which he described the social ills of the time and lamented his failure to gain recognition in the world. In 984 he compiled a work called *Nihon ōjō gokuraku-ki*, containing biographies of persons who were believed to have been reborn in the Western Paradise of the Buddha Amida. In 986 he became a member of the clergy, adopting the religious name Jakushin, and thereafter traveled about the country performing religious exercises. Along with the priest Genshin, he played an important role in the formation of the Nijūgo Zammaie, a society devoted to the propagation of *nembutsu*, the ritual invocation of the name of the Buddha Amida. He had a disciple, Ōe no Sadamoto, who also took the religious name Jakushin.

MEDIEVAL PERIOD

Asai Nagamasa

Ashikaga Yoshimasa

Ashikaga Takauji

Ashikaga Yoshimitsu

Ashikaga Yoshiaki

Ashikaga Yoshimochi

Ashikaga Yoshiteru

Eison

Chōgen

Enni Bennen

Dōgen

Godaigo Tennō

Gokomatsu Tennō

Gomurakami Tennō

Hōjō Masako

Hōjō Sanetoki

Hōjō Sōun

Hōjō Takatoki

Hōjō Tokimune

Hōnen

Hosokawa Katsumoto

Ippen

Kusunoki Masashige

Lan-hsi Tao-lung

Mansai Jugō

Minamoto no Yoriie

Minamoto no Yoritomo

Myōan Eisai

Nichiren

Nisshin

Nitta Yoshisada

Ōtomo Sōrin

Sanjōnishi Sanetaka

Shinran

Shūhō Myōchō

Shunjō

Shun'oku Myōha

Taira no Kiyomori

Takeda Shingen

Uesugi Kenshin

Wu-hsüeh Tsu-yüan

Medieval Period

Akamatsu Norimura 赤松則村 (1277–1350)

Military leader of the period of the Northern and Southern Courts. The Akamatsu were a warrior family with their base in the manor of Sayo in Harima Province. In 1332 Akamatsu Norimura was ordered by Imperial Prince Morinaga to raise troops and attack the Hōjō army, and later he joined Chigusa Tadaaki in marching on Kyoto and ovethrowing the Hōjō family. In 1333, when the so-called Kemmu Restoration took place and Emperor Godaigo returned to Kyoto to rule in person, Norimura was made *shugo*, constable, of Harima, a post that gave him full control of the province, but this was later taken away from him and, angered, he joined forces with Ashikaga Takauji in opposing the Kemmu government. Their first attempt at revolt failed, but Norimura continued to assist Takauji, fighting in various areas, and in 1336 joined Takauji's younger brother Naoyoshi in defeating Kusunoki Masashige at the battle of Minatogawa in Harima and overthrowing the Kemmu government. In reward for his services, he was once more appointed constable of Harima. He was an ardent follower of Zen Buddhism, inviting the monk Sesson Yūbai to come to the province to found the Hōun-ji, and in his late years he himself became a monk with the religious name Enshin.

Asai Nagamasa 淺井長政 (1545–1573)

Warrior of the late Muromachi period; son of Asai Hisamasa and father of Yodogimi, concubine of Toyotomi Hideyoshi. Known in childhood as Saruyasha, later as Shinkurō, he married Oda Nobunaga's younger sister and in 1564 joined Nobunaga in capturing the Kannon-ji castle in the province of Ōmi (Shiga Prefecture), defeating the warrior Rokkaku Yoshikata and his son and gaining control of half the province of Ōmi. The following year Oda Nobunaga installed himself in Kyoto in the service of Shogun Ashikaga Yoshiaki, thereby expanding his own power, whereupon Nagamasa joined with Asakura Yoshikage and the Hongan-ji temple in doing battle with Nobunaga. He made a truce with Nobunaga at one stage, but fought again and was defeated at the battle of Anegawa in Ōmi in 1570. From then on his fortunes tended to wane; he joined with the Asakura family and the monks of the Enryaku-ji temple on Mt. Hiei in resisting Nobunaga. However, in 1571 Nobunaga burned down the temples on Mt. Hiei, then in 1573 defeated Asakura Yoshikage. Finally, he attacked Nagamasa in Odani Castle, and Nagamasa, unable to hold his forces back, committed suicide in the castle at the age of twenty-eight.

Ashikaga Takauji 足利尊氏 (1305–1358)

Shogun of the period of the Northern and Southern Courts. The Ashikagas were a branch of the Genji family, and because there was an old saying that the Genji and the Heike would take turns wielding political power, it is said that Takauji's forefathers had for a long time plotted how they might overthrow the Hōjō family, who exercised control of the Kamakura shogunate and were descended from the Heike. In 1331 Emperor Godaigo carried out a coup d'état to free himself from shogunate control. Ashikaga Takauji and others were dispatched by the shogunate to go to Kyoto and restore control, but in the fourth month of 1333 Takauji declared himself an ally of the emperor and attacked and defeated the shogunate troops in Kyoto. Meanwhile Nitta Yoshisada and others attacked Kamakura and overthrew the shogunate, thus clearing the way for the so-called Kemmu Restoration, which centered around Emperor Godaigo. The emperor, to show how deeply he appreciated the assistance that Takauji had rendered, bestowed on him a new character for his name, the element *taka* to be written with the character meaning "honored," which was part of the emperor's own name, Takaharu. But the new government that Emperor Godaigo formed was made up largely of court aristocrats, and men of the warrior class such as Takauji, who had done the actual fighting in the struggle to overthrow the Kamakura shogunate, could hardly help but feel disgruntled. Amidst this atmosphere of discontent, Takauji in 1335 at Kamakura declared himself in open defiance of the court. For a while he was forced by the imperial armies to retreat to Kyushu, but in 1336, after defeating the forces of Kusunoki and Nitta, he entered Kyoto once more, set up the Muromachi shogunate, and became the first shogun. Emperor Godaigo retired to the mountains in the Yoshino area, south of Kyoto, whereupon Takauji set up a new ruler, Emperor Kōmyō, as his rival. From this time until 1392 there were two emperors, one in Kyoto and one in the Yoshino area to the south, and the period is accordingly referred to as that of the Northern and Southern Courts.

In 1336 Takauji promulgated a set of laws called the *Kemmu shikimoku*, which made it clear that he intended to carry on the traditions of the Kamakura shogunate and conduct a military style of government. Takauji placed himself at the head of administrative affairs and appointed his younger brother Tadayoshi to head those pertaining to the judiciary, but later dissension developed between the two, and in 1352 Takauji killed his brother. He made frequent attempts to heal the breach between the factions of the Northern and Southern Courts, but all ended in failure. He died in 1358 of a tumor.

According to a text written at the time, the *Baishōron*, Takauji was generous by nature and freely gave away weapons and other valuable goods. Though he defied Emperor Godaigo and engaged in a struggle with him, when the emperor died in 1339, Takauji founded a temple, the Tenryū-ji, expressly for the purpose of bringing ease to the departed emperor's soul. He also drew up plans for the founding of a new temple in each province of the country. These steps were taken on the suggestion of Musō Soseki, an eminent Zen monk whom Takauji respected greatly. Takauji himself was a devout believer in Buddhism, and there are extant religious paintings that he executed with his own hand.

The Muromachi shogunate that Takauji founded continued in existence until 1572. It reached its peak of power under the third shogun, Yoshimitsu, but later it began to wane, and from the time of the Ōnin War, which arose because of dissension within the shogunate itself and lasted from 1467 to 1477, the entire country was plunged into strife, and the Muromachi shogunate lost all vestiges of its former authority.

Ashikaga Yoshiaki 足利義昭 (1537–1597)

Last shogun of the Muromachi period. The son of the twelfth shogun of the Muromachi shogunate, Ashikaga Yoshiharu, he became a monk with the religious name Kakkei and headed the Ichijō-in of the Kōfuku-ji in Nara. In 1565 Matsunaga Hisahide killed Yoshiaki's elder brother, the thirteenth shogun Ashikaga Yoshiteru, and tried to set up the brothers' cousin Ashikaga Yoshihide as shogun. Kakkei, fearing for his own safety, fled from the temple and returned to lay life, taking the name Yoshiaki and working to revive the fortunes of the Muromachi shogunate. In 1568, having been told that the character *aki* ("autumn") in his name was inauspicious, he replaced it with another character read *aki* meaning "bright." In the second month of the same year Ashikaga Yoshihide became the fourteenth shogun, but Yoshiaki, with the help of Oda Nobunaga, entered Kyoto in the ninth month, removed Yoshihide from the position of shogun, and in the tenth month himself became the fifteenth shogun. He did not get along well with Oda Nobunaga, however, and after unsuccessfully attempting to oppose Oda, he was driven out of Kyoto in 1573. With this, the Muromachi shogunate came to an end both in name and fact. He continued in his efforts to overthrow Oda Nobunaga but without success, and in 1587 he placed himself under the protection of Toyotomi Hideyoshi.

ASHIKAGA YOSHIMASA 足利義政 (1436–1490)

Shogun of the middle Muromachi period. He was the son of the sixth Ashikaga shogun, Yoshinori. On his father's death in 1441, his elder brother Yoshikatsu became shogun, but Yoshikatsu died of dysentery two years later and Yoshimasa succeeded him to become the eighth shogun. At first he governed with the assistance of Hatakeyama Mochikuni and other leaders of the great vassal families, but later these were replaced in power by Yoshimasa's wife, Hino Tomiko, and a number of underlings who had managed to maneuver themselves into positions of authority. The sad state into which the Muromachi shogunate had fallen in Yoshimasa's time may be seen in the fact that the government was thirteen times obliged to issue orders for a *tokusei*, a general cancellation of debts.

Because Yoshimasa had no son, he persuaded his younger brother, who had become a Buddhist monk, to reenter secular life and, with the name Yoshimi, appointed him heir to the shogunate with Hosokawa Katsumoto to act as his advisor. In 1464, however, Yoshimasa's wife, Tomiko, gave birth to a son, named Yoshihisa, and set about working to have him made heir, enlisting the assistance of the powerful feudal leader Yamana Sōzen. As a result, a struggle ensued between the two rival factions headed by Hosokawa and Yamana respectively, the other great families taking sides with one or the other. For over ten years, from 1467 to 1477, the opposing armies fought in Kyoto and its environs. The struggle, known as the Ōnin War, resulted in Yoshihisa becoming shogun, but in the process Kyoto was reduced to ashes and the power of the Muromachi shogunate fell to a new low. In addition, the great warrior families who had engaged in the struggle were so debilitated that they could not defend themselves against ambitious retainers who aspired to replace them in power. The social upheaval spread throughout the country, ushering in the period known as the Sengoku Jidai, or Era of Civil Strife, which lasted for one hundred years and saw many of the old warrior families overthrown by men of more humble birth who fought and schemed their way to power.

In 1483 Yoshimasa built the Ginkaku, the famous Silver Pavilion, in the hilly area known as Higashiyama on the east side of Kyoto and retired there, patronizing the arts of the Nō drama and the tea ceremony and helping to create the ideals known in the vocabulary of Japanese aesthetics as *sabi* and *yūgen*. He built what is probably the first real tea ceremony room, the Dōjinsai, and in other ways left a profound imprint on the development of Japanese culture. From the location of his villa, the distinctive culture associated with the time of Yoshimasa has come to be called Higashiyama culture. Though occurring in a time of unrest and conflict, the Higashiyama culture is looked upon as being one of the high points of the Ashikaga shogunate.

Ashikaga Yoshimitsu 足利義満 (1358–1408)

Shogun of the early Muromachi period. Yoshimitsu was a grandson of Ashikaga Takauji, the founder of the Muromachi shogunate, and after the death of his father, Yoshiakira, he succeeded him in 1368 to become the third shogun. But though the leaders of the Muromachi shogunate might hold the title of shogun, which proclaimed them the supreme military commanders of the nation, their control over the powerful warrior families in the provinces was still tenuous. Yoshimitsu set about devising various ways to strengthen and consolidate the control of the shogunate. In 1391 he defeated in battle the leader of the Yamana family, which was said to control territories amounting to one-sixth of the entire country, and the following year he succeeded in healing the breach between the Northern and Southern Courts that had so long divided the state, arranging for the ruler of the Southern Court to abdicate in favor of the ruler of the Northern Court, whom Yoshimitsu supported, Emperor Gokomatsu. Through these measures, he greatly strengthened the stability of the shogunate. In 1394 he was given the title of *dajōdaijin*, or prime minister, the highest post in the court bureaucracy, becoming the first member of the warrior class to hold it since Taira no Kiyomori. Thus he found himself the holder not only of the highest military position, that of shogun, but of the highest civil position as well, first in the courtiers' world as in the warriors'. He thereupon turned the shogunate over to his son, Yoshimochi, and in 1395 shaved his head and became a member of the Buddhist clergy. This last act, however, was a mere formality by which he hoped to control the affairs of state more effectively by freeing himself from worldly ties. In 1399 his forces defeated and killed in battle Ōuchi Yoshihiro, a powerful warrior who controlled six provinces in the southwest part of Honshu. In 1401 he sent an envoy to the Ming court in China, requesting the opening of trade between the two countries. In his request Yoshimitsu, representing himself as the king of Japan, asked to be allowed to send articles of tribute to the Ming ruler in exchange for Chinese currency. The Ming recognized his title as king and complied with the request, and Yoshimitsu was thus able to exercise complete control over the flow of Chinese currency into the country. Yoshimitsu constructed a large villa for himself on a hill north of Kyoto called Kitayama, part of which remains in existence today as the temple of Kinkaku-ji, the Golden Pavilion. He worked to introduce new elements of culture from Ming China, and under his patronage ink painting and the writing of poetry and prose in Chinese, which was particularly associated with the monks of the Gozan, the Five Great Zen Temples of Kyoto, flourished. It was also at this time that Zeami completed the creation of the Nō drama. The culture of this period, which is one of the most outstanding in the cultural history of the nation, is often referred to as Kitayama culture from the location of Yoshimitsu's villa north of Kyoto.

Ashikaga Yoshimochi 足利義持 (1386–1428)

Shogun of the middle Muromachi period. His father, Yoshimitsu, turned over the shogunate to him in 1394, making him the fourth shogun, but until his father's death in 1408 he was not allowed to exercise actual power. Thereafter, with the assistance of Mansai Jugō and others, he took control of the government, but he adopted policies quite different from those of his father. His father had expressed the wish that after his death he might be given a posthumous title by the court, but when the court complied by confering such a title, Yoshimochi modestly declined to allow his father to be so honored. He also discontinued the trade with Ming China that his father had begun, on the grounds that it was undignified.

In 1416 Uesugi Zenshū led a revolt in the Kantō region, and Yoshimochi's younger brother, Yoshitsugu, began plotting to join the revolt, whereupon

Yoshimochi killed his brother and defeated and killed Uesugi Zenshū in battle. In 1423 he turned over the shogunate to his son, Yoshikazu, but Yoshikazu died of dissipation in 1425, and Yoshimochi resumed control of the government until his own death in 1428.

Ashikaga Yoshinori 足利義教 (1394–1441)

Shogun of the middle Muromachi period. The son of Ashikaga Yoshimitsu, he entered the Buddhist clergy at an early age, took the religious name Gien, and in time advanced to the highest position in the Tendai sect, that of *zasu*, or head of the sect. In 1428 his elder brother, Shogun Yoshimochi, died and, Yoshimochi's son having died earlier without leaving an heir, there was no one in the direct line to succeed to the shogunate. Thereupon the four brothers of Yoshimochi drew lots to see which would become shogun, and Gien emerged as the winner. At first he took the name Yoshinobu but later changed it to Yoshinori. In 1432, in an effort to improve the financial state of the government, he reopened the trade with Ming China that his brother Yoshimochi had earlier suspended. He also launched an attack on his kinsman Ashikaga Mochiuji, who controlled the Kantō region, and in 1439 forced him to commit suicide. In this way Yoshinori worked to strengthen the power and prestige of the shogunate, filling everyone about him with fear and apprehension. One of those who had borne the brunt of his oppression, the military leader Akamatsu Mitsusuke, finally assassinated him in 1441, and in turn was attacked and forced to commit suicide by Yamana Sōzen.

Ashikaga Yoshiteru 足利義輝 (1536–1565)

Shogun of the late Muromachi period. He was the eldest son of the twelfth shogun of the Muromachi shogunate, Ashikaga Yoshiharu, but though his father held the title of shogun, it carried with it little actual power, since the period was one of almost incessant strife and civil war, and both father and son were obliged to flee from Kyoto and take refuge in the province of Ōmi. In 1546 Yoshiteru became the thirteenth shogun and returned to the capital, attempting to exercise power with Hosokawa Harumoto to assist him in the position of *kanrei* (chief administrator), but a struggle broke out between Hosokawa Harumoto and his vassal Miyoshi Nagaharu, and the shogun was once more obliged to flee to Ōmi. Miyoshi Nagaharu having emerged the victor in his struggle with Hosokawa Harumoto, he invited Shogun Yoshiteru to return to the capital. As Miyoshi Nagaharu grew older, however, his power passed into the hands of his vassal Matsunaga Hisahide. When Nagaharu died in 1564, Yoshiteru attempted to sieze power from Matsunaga Hisahide, but in the fifth month of the following year he was attacked by Hisahide's forces and obliged to commit suicide. This process, in which a vassal overthrows his lord only to be overthrown in turn by his own vassal, is known in Japanese as *gekokujō* and is characteristic of this period, an age of warfare and social upheaval when actual ability counted far more than birth or position.

Benkei 辨慶 (d. 1185)

Buddhist priest of the early Kamakura period. In literary works describing the struggle between the Taira and Minamoto families such as the *Heike monogatari* and the *Gikeiki*, Benkei, also called Musashi-bō Benkei, appears as a faithful retainer of Minamoto no Yoshitsune, but there is some doubt as to whether he is an actual historical personage. He was said to have been born in Kumano on the Kii Peninsula, and since there is a record of a monk by the same name residing in the monastery on Mt. Kōya, which is not far from Kumano, it is thought to be he. In the temples of the time there were two types of monks, those who devoted themselves to learning and those who bore arms for the protection of the temple; it is reasonable to suppose that Benkei, who in legend is noted for his military prowess, belonged to the latter group. He is said to have been active in assisting Minamoto no Yoshitsune to overthrow the Taira family, but later, when dissension developed between Yoshitsune and his elder brother Yoritomo, Benkei accompanied his lord in fleeing to Hiraizumi in Mutsu and died with him in the battle of Koromogawa. A number of dramatic works centering on the figures of Yoshitsune and Benkei have been written and remain popular today.

Chōgen 重源 (1121–1206)

Priest of the early Kamakura period; he first studied the doctrines of Shingon Buddhism at the Daigo-ji near Kyoto, and went by the name Chōgen of the Shunjōbō. Later he studied Pure Land Buddhism under its famous propagator Hōnen. During the years from 1167 to 1176 he made three trips to China, where he continued his Buddhist training and, it is said, also studied architecture and building techniques. At this time the struggle for power between the Taira and Minamoto families was raging, and in 1180 the great Tōdai-ji temple of Nara, which had sided with the latter, was burned to the ground by Taira no Shigehira. Its reconstruction was undertaken by the government, and Chōgen was ordered to direct the work. The buildings that he erected employ a type of architecture known as *tenjiku-yō*, which makes use of the unit construction system. For the casting of the great bronze Buddha image, an artisan named Ch'en Ho-ch'ing (Chin Nakei in Japanese reading) was summoned from China, while the noted sculptors Unkei and Kaikei were assigned the task of carving wooden images. The work was completed in 1203, and the main hall, though later reconstructed, remains today the largest wooden building in existence. Chōgen was an ardent believer in Pure Land teachings and adopted the name Namu-Amidabutsu. He left a record of the reconstruction of the Tōdai-ji entitled *Namu-Amidabutsu sazenshū.*

Dōgen 道元 (1200–1253)

Zen monk of the early Kamakura period, founder of the Sōtō branch of Zen; his literary name was Kigen. He was born in Kyoto in an aristocrat family; his father was Kuga no Michichika, his mother the daughter of Fujiwara no Motofusa. He lost both parents at an early age and in 1212 entered the monastery on Mt. Hiei, becoming a disciple of Kōen, the head of the Tendai sect. But he entertained doubts about the validity of Tendai teachings, and, after studying for a time in 1214 under Kōin of Onjō-ji, he became a disciple of Eisai, a master of the Rinzai branch of Zen who resided at Kennin-ji in Kyoto. In 1217, after Eisai's death, he placed himself under Eisai's disciple Myōzen. In 1223 he accompanied Myōzen on a journey to China. After traveling about from one temple to another, he achieved final enlightenment under the master Ju-ching (1163–1228) of Mt. T'ien-t'ung. From Ju-ching he received the pure teachings of the Ts'ao-tung (Sōtō) branch of Zen, compiling a work called the *Hōkyōki*, which records the questions and answers exchanged between himself and Ju-ching.

He returned to Japan in 1227 and resided for a time at Kennin-ji. The same year he wrote a work entitled *Fukan zazengi* in which he propounded Zen teachings in their pure form. Around 1230 he moved to An'yo-in in Fukakusa in Kyoto and in 1233 founded a temple called Kōshō Hōrin-ji on the site of the old Gokuraku-ji in Fukakusa. His fame soon spread abroad and he acquired a number of disciples, among them Ejō. But he was faced with increasing opposition from the monks of Mt. Hiei, and in 1243 accepted an invitation from Hatano Yoshishige to move to the province of Echizen. In 1244 he took up residence in Daibutsu-ji in Echizen and in 1246 changed the name of the temple to Eihei-ji. In time it became the headquarters of the Sōtō branch of Zen and remains so today.

In 1247 Dōgen journeyed to Kamakura at the invitation of Hōjō Tokiyori, regent of the Kamakura shogunate, but soon returned to Eihei-ji, where he devoted himself to Zen meditation and the training of his disciples. He fell ill in 1252, and the following year, having turned over the care of Eihei-ji to his disciple Ejō, he journeyed to Kyoto, where he died.

In his way of life, Dōgen rejected all striving for worldly fame or profit. He also rejected the use of various types of religious practices in combination, declaring that one should devote oneself solely to *zazen*, Zen meditation, which represents the proper practice for Buddhists from the time of Śākyamuni on; the doctrine is known in Japanese as *shikan taza*. A second doctrine that he stressed, called *shūshō ittō*, insists that enlightenment does not exist apart from religious practice, but that religious practice is synonymous with enlightenment. In addition to the works mentioned above, he wrote the *Gakudō yōjinshū* and *Eihei kōroku*. His most important work, however, is the *Shōbō genzō*, which he began in 1231 and continued to work on up to the time of his death. It covers a wide variety of topics, from highly philosophical questions to the rules for the daily life of a Zen monk. The chapters that deal with the basic nature of the world of enlightenment (*Genjō kōan*) and the relationship between existence and time (*Uji*) have been particularly admired by present-day philosophers. The work is also important as the first philosophical work to be written in Japanese, Chinese having previously been the medium for writings of such a nature. The record of Dōgen's words and actions compiled by Ejō under the title *Shōbō genzō zuimonki* provides an excellent introduction to Dōgen's thought.

Eison 叡尊 (1201–1290)

Kamakura period monk of the Ritsu, or Vinaya, sect; his personal name was Shien and his posthumous title Kōshō Bosatsu. He was born in the province of Yamato and at first studied Esoteric Buddhism, but later determined to revive the teachings and observances of the Vinaya sect, which emphasizes the rules of monastic discipline. In 1236 he carried out a ceremony in which he administered to himself the vows of ordination. He took up residence in

Saidai-ji, one of the seven great temples of Nara, which had fallen into a state of disrepair. There he worked to revive the fortunes of the temple and to spread the Vinaya teachings. At the same time he was very active in social movements, preaching and administering to convicts and members of the outcast class and promoting observance of the Buddhist prohibition against taking life. In 1262 he was invited by the military leader Hōjō Sanetoki to come to Kamakura. There he lived in the Shaka Hall of Shinshōryō-ji and won many converts to his teachings. After a stay of only a few months, he returned to the capital area, living first in Kyoto and then in Saidai-ji, where he resumed his various activities. When the Mongol forces attacked Kyushu in 1274, he held a great ceremony to pray for divine protection and he was also active in undertakings to benefit society such as the repairing of the Uji Bridge. Retired Emperor Kameyama was among his converts. The school of Vinaya teaching that he founded is known as the Saidai-jiryū and is strongly influenced by Esoteric Buddhism. Among Eison's writings are his autobiography entitled *Kanjin gakushō-ki*, an account of his visit to eastern Japan entitled *Kantō ōkan-ki*, and others. Among his disciples, Ninshō was of particular eminence.

ENGETSU (CHŪGAN) 圓月 (1300–1375)

Zen monk of the period of the Northern and Southern Courts. Born in Kamakura, he entered a temple at the age of eight and began religious training. In 1318, hoping to be able to go to China, he journeyed as far as Kyushu, but the Kamakura shogunate refused him permission to leave the country; it was not until 1325 that he was finally allowed to depart. After studying in China for a number of years, he returned to Japan in 1332, residing first at the Kenchō-ji and later at the Engaku-ji. In 1333 the Kamakura shogunate was abolished, and Emperor Godaigo assumed the direction of the government. These changes occasioned considerable unrest among the people. Engetsu thereupon submitted a memorial to the throne pointing out the abuses and ill effects attendant upon the reforms that were being carried out in the political system.

Engetsu was an accomplished writer of Chinese verse, and his collected works, the *Tōkai ichiōshū*, ranks as one of the earliest and finest products of the *Gozan bungaku*, the body of prose and poetic works written in Chinese by Zen monks of the late Kamakura and Muromachi periods.

ENNI BENNEN 圓爾辨圓 (1202–1280)

Rinzai Zen monk of the middle Kamakura period; his posthumous title is Shōichi Kokushi. He was born in the province of Suruga. He first studied the doctrines of Tendai and other older sects of Buddhism but later undertook Zen training under Eichō and Gyōyō. He went to China in 1235 and traveled about from region to region visiting various Zen masters. He spent a lengthy period studying under Wu-chu Shih-fan of Ching-shan, in time becoming his Dharma heir. He returned to Japan in 1241 and settled for a time in northern Kyushu, residing at Sufuku-ji and Shōten-ji and working to spread Zen teachings. He became known to Regent Kujō Michiie, who invited him to Kyoto in 1243. There he founded a temple called Tōfuku-ji at the place on Higashiyama where Michiie's country villa was situated. He was on intimate terms with members of the court and administered Buddhist vows to the retired emperors Gosaga, Gofukakusa, and Kameyama. He also visited Kamakura and counted the statesman Hōjō Tokiyori among his converts. He had many close relations with the older sects of Buddhism and at one time held the office of *daikanjin* in Tōdai-ji in Nara. His thinking represents an amalgamation of Zen and the doctrines of the older sects, and it is clear that he did not, like some Zen leaders, feel any antagonism toward such sects. His teaching line, known as the Shōichi-ha, for a time flourished greatly. His most important disciples were Tōzan Tanshō, Mukan Fumon, Hakuun Egyō, and Mujū Dōgyō. His works include *Sangyō yōryaku* and *Kana hōgo.*

GIDŌ SHŪSHIN 義堂周信 (1325–1388)

Zen monk of the period of the Northern and Southern Courts. He was a follower of the Rinzai branch of the Zen sect and was also known as Kūge Dōjin. In his youth he entered the Tendai monastery on Mt. Hiei, but at the age of seventeen began study under the Zen monk Musō Soseki. In 1359 he was invited by the Kantō *kanrei* (governor of the eastern regions) Ashikaga Motouji to come to Kamakura, where he resided in the Engaku-ji, and in 1380, at the invitation of Shogun Ashikaga Yoshimitsu, he went to Kyoto and took up residence at the Nanzen-ji, where he enjoyed great favor with Yoshimitsu. He is one of the outstanding figures of the so-called *Gozan bungaku*, the body of literature written in Chinese by Zen monks of the Kamakura and Muromachi periods, and his poems and prose works were said to have won admiration even in China. A collection of his poems in

Chinese, the *Kūgeshū*, is extant, along with other works including the *Kūge nikkushū*, a diary that contains valuable data on the society and politics of the time.

Godaigo Tennō 後醍醐天皇 (1288–1339)

The ninety-sixth sovereign, he reigned from 1318 to 1339. He was the second son of Emperor Gouda; his personal name was Takaharu. At this time it was the custom to choose the rulers alternately from two rival branches of the imperial family known respectively as the Daikaku-ji line and the Jimyō-in line. Godaigo belonged to the former. When he first came to the throne, power was still in the hands of the *insei* (cloistered government) of his father, Retired Emperor Gouda, but from 1321 on Godaigo was able to rule in person. He selected such talented officials as Yoshida Sadafusa, Kitabatake Chikafusa, Hino Suketomo, and Hino Toshimoto to assist him, encouraged learning and the military arts, and instituted various reforms in government affairs.

Perceiving that the military clans were beginning to lose faith in the power of the Kamakura shogunate, he laid plans to overthrow the shogunate and restore power to the throne, but twice, in the Shōchū disturbance of 1324 and the Genkō disturbance of 1331, his plans were discovered. In 1331 his headquarters at Mt. Kasagi was attacked by the shogunate forces and he was taken captive. The following year he was exiled to the island of Oki.

Meanwhile, various military leaders began uprisings, and in 1333 the Kamakura shogunate was overthrown. Godaigo escaped from Oki and made his way back to the capital, where he formed a new government made up of both courtiers and military leaders and began to rule in person. He instituted a number of measures designed to restore the powers and ceremonies that had marked the imperial rule in its period of greatest flourishing in the past; from the era name, these measures are known collectively as the Kemmu Restoration. But he tended to favor the courtiers over the military leaders, which led to discontent among the latter. In 1335 one of the most powerful of these, Ashikaga Takauji, raised the standard of revolt in eastern Japan, and after only two years of existence the Kemmu Restoration government was overthrown. In 1336 Kusunoki Masashige and other important military supporters of Godaigo's cause were killed in battle, and Godaigo fled south to Mt. Yoshino in Yamato. Ashikaga Takauji thereupon set up a new ruler, Emperor Kōmyō of the Jimyō-in line of succession.

Godaigo retained possession of the imperial regalia and continued to proclaim himself the legitimate sovereign, establishing what was known as the Southern Court at his headquarters at Mt. Yoshino. But with the death in battle of his supporters Kitabatake Akiie and Nitta Yoshisada in 1338, his military power waned and he faced growing disappointment and loneliness. After abdicating in favor of his son, Emperor Gomurakami, he died in 1339 in his palace on Mt. Yoshino. He was buried on the mountain and, at his own request, was given the posthumous name Godaigo; this last symbolizes the respect that he held for the great Heian period ruler Emperor Daigo (898–930) and his own fervant hopes of imitating Daigo's example.

Gokameyama Tennō 後亀山天皇 (d. 1424)

Emperor of the period of the Northern and Southern Courts. When Ashikaga Takauji turned against Emperor Godaigo and challenged his right to rule, he set up a rival, Emperor Kōmyō, in Kyoto and forced Emperor Godaigo to retire to the mountains of Yoshino to the south, thus initiating the period of the Northern and Southern Courts. In time Emperor Godaigo was succeeded in the line of the Southern Court by Emperor Gomurakami, whose son was Emperor Gokameyama. Emperor Gokameyama in 1383 received the throne from his elder brother, Emperor Chōkei, becoming the ninety-ninth sovereign, but in 1393 the supporters of the Northern Court proposed that peace be arranged between the rival factions, and Gokameyama was persuaded to abdicate in favor of the claimant of the Northern Court, Emperor Gokomatsu. When the conditions upon which the peace had been arranged were not observed, he removed once more to Yoshino in 1410 and for a while worked to revive the fortunes of the Southern Court, but in 1416 he was prevailed upon by the Muromachi shogunate to return to Kyoto.

Gokomatsu Tennō 後小松天皇 (1377–1433)

Emperor of the early Muromachi period. He was the son of Emperor Goen'yū, a ruler of the Northern Court, the line of succession backed by the Muromachi shogunate at the time of the split between the Northern and Southern Courts. In 1382 he succeeded his father as ruler of the Northern Court, and in 1392, through the mediation of Shogun Ashikaga Yoshimitsu, it was arranged that he should receive from the ruler of the Southern Court, Emperor Gokameyama, the sword, mirror, and jewel, sacred regalia symbolic of the position of emperor. He was thus able to hold a proper coronation ceremony, becoming the one hundredth sovereign. Thus the split between the Northern and Southern Courts, which began when Emperor Godaigo retired to the Yoshino region in the south and a rival ruler, Emperor Kōmyō, was set up in Kyoto in 1336, was finally brought to an end.

Gomurakami Tennō 後村上天皇 (1328–1368)

The ninety-seventh sovereign of Japan and second emperor of the Southern Court, he reigned from 1339 to 1368. He was the son of Emperor Godaigo; his personal name was Yoshinaga. Growing up in the troubled times of the Northern and Southern Courts, he lived from childhood in an atmosphere of martial readiness and spent his adult years attempting to regain control of the capital and the government. In 1334, when his father was ruling in Kyoto, he was appointed protector of the region of far northern Honshu, though he was only six at the time; Kitabatake Akiie, the eldest son of Kitabatake Chikafusa, was assigned to serve him. When Ashikaga Takauji rebelled against the authority of the court, the prince went to Kyoto in 1335 and again in 1337 with the aim of attacking Takauji. He was eventually defeated, however, and forced to retreat to Yoshino, where his father resided as sovereign of the Southern Court.

In 1339 he set out for eastern Japan accompanied by Kitabatake Chikafusa. While at sea, he encountered a violent storm and was forced to return to Ise. He returned to Yoshino and the same year was declared heir apparent. With the death of Emperor Godaigo shortly after, he ascended the throne, continuing, like his father, to reside at Yoshino. He made several attempts to regain control of Kyoto, but by this time the military power of the Southern Court had waned, and all his efforts were unsuccessful. When the forces of the Northern Court launched an attack on his residence at Yoshino, he was forced to move about to Anō, to Sumiyoshi, and to the Kanshin-ji temple in Kawachi. He died in temporary quarters at Sumiyoshi in 1368 at the age of forty. He was a distinguished poet, one hundred of his poems being included in the imperial anthology entitled *Shin'yō wakashū*.

Gouda Tennō 後宇多天皇 (1267–1324)

Emperor of the late Kamakura period. He became heir apparent in 1268, and in 1274 received the throne from his father, Emperor Kameyama, to become the ninety-first sovereign. In 1287 he abdicated in favor of his cousin, who became Emperor Fushimi. Ordinarily the throne passed to a direct descendant, but because Emperor Gosaga had died in 1272 without leaving any clear instructions as to who his successor should be, a struggle broke out between Emperor Gofukakusa and Emperor Kameyama, each trying to insure that his own heirs should succeed to the throne. The contention lasted for over one hundred years (leading eventually to the so-called period of the Northern and Southern Courts [1336–92], when the descendants of Emperor Gofukakusa claimed the throne in Kyoto, while the descendants of Emperor Kameyama made the same claim from their retreat in Yoshino to the south). In an attempt to put a stop to the quarrel, Emperor Gouda, who in spite of his abdication some years earlier had retained considerable power, arranged for the throne to pass to his son, Emperor Godaigo, in 1321, but this did not heal the strife.

Gyōnen 凝念 (1240–1321)

Scholar-monk of the Kegon sect in the late Kamakura period. He was born in the province of Iyo in Shikoku. He entered the priesthood at Tōdai-ji in Nara at the age of seventeen and studied under Enshō. He also received instruction in Kegon Buddhism from Shūshō, in Pure Land teachings from Chōsai, and in Shingon from Shinkū. On the basis of his wide familiarity with the teachings of many different sects, he wrote over one hundred works on various aspects of Buddhism. Particularly famous are his first work, entitled *Hasshū kōyō* (1268), an introduction to Buddhist doctrine that won him wide acclaim and remains today one of the best books on the subject; a systematic exposition of Kegon doctrine entitled *Kegon hokkai gikyō* (1295); the *Sangoku bukkyō dentsū engi* (1311), the first work to attempt to deal systematically with the history of Indian, Chinese, and Japanese Buddhism; and the *Jōdō hōmon genryū-shō* (1311), which deals with Pure Land teachings.

Harada Kiemon 原田喜右衛門 (ca. 1555–ca. 1599)

Overseas trader of Sakai city in the Momoyama period; he was baptized and took the Christian name Paulo. Early in his life he and his assistant Harada Magoshichirō, whose Christian name was Gaspar, engaged in trade with the Philippines. On the basis of the experience so acquired, he urged Toyotomi Hideyoshi, through the latter's close advisor Hasegawa Sōjin, to undertake the conquest of the Philippines. In 1592, when the envoy from the Philippine government, a Franciscan named Father Juan Cobos, was leaving Japan to return to Luzon, Harada went along in a separate ship, heading the second Japanese mission to the Philippines urging the government there to acknowledge Japanese sovereignty and submit tribute, a similar mission having been dispatched the previous year. Because Cobos' ship was wrecked on the way, however, Harada returned to Japan without carrying out his mission. The following year, he was ordered by Hideyoshi to undertake a visit to Taiwan, though the aim of this mission was apparently to establish friendly relations with that region. Presumably because of the merit acquired through these activities, Hideyoshi granted him a domain in the province of Satsuma in Kyushu.

Hino Tomiko 日野富子 (1440–1496)

Wife of the middle Muromachi period Shogun Ashikaga Yoshimasa. The Hino, an aristocratic family dating back to Heian times, had produced several members active at the time of the Northern and Southern Courts. The family also provided wives for the Ashikaga shoguns Yoshimitsu, Yoshimochi, and Yoshinori. Tomiko became the fourth member of the group, marrying Shogun Ashikaga Yoshimasa. Because Yoshimasa was a person of weak character, the real power was wielded by Tomiko's elder brother, Hino Katsumitsu. Yoshimasa, having no son of his own, had adopted his younger brother, Yoshimi, and indicated that he should become the next shogun. In the following year, however, Tomiko gave birth to a son named Yoshihisa and, being a woman of very strong disposition, she determined to fight for her son's right to become shogun, enlisting the help of Yamana Sōzen, one of the powerful military leaders of the time. In 1467 fighting broke out between Yamana Sōzen and Hosokawa Katsumoto, the guardian of Yoshimi and leader of the opposing faction, the beginning of the prolonged period of civil strife known as the Ōnin War, and in 1473 Tomiko finally persuaded her husband to turn over the position of shogun to her son, Yoshihisa. In addition to being strong willed, she was noted for her love of money, which led her to set up toll barriers and take other measures that aroused criticism among the populace.

Hōjō (Taira) Masako 北條(平)政子 (1157–1225)

The wife of Minamoto no Yoritomo, founder of the Kamakura shogunate and a prominent military leader. She was the eldest daughter of Hōjō Tokimasa, a member of a branch of the Taira family having its base of power at Hōjō in the province of Izu. In 1159, Minamoto no Yoshitomo was defeated in battle by Taira no Kiyomori. Yoshitomo's son Yoritomo was exiled to Izu, where he was befriended by Hōjō Tokimasa and formed an alliance with Tokimasa's daughter Masako. In 1180 Yoritomo, responding to an order by Prince Mochihito, raised troops and set out to attack the Taira forces, but he was defeated and for a time went into hiding at Izusan. He entered Kamakura in the tenth month of the same year, where he was joined by other members of the Minamoto clan and their military forces. At this time, Masako was given recognition as his lawful wife and was thereafter treated with utmost respect. In time she bore two sons, Yoriie and Sanetomo.

Upon the death of her husband in 1199, she became a Buddhist nun, but played a very active role in politics as guardian of her son Yoriie, the second shogun. She set up a council composed of her father and twelve other important ministers that was entrusted with the conduct of government affairs. When Yoriie fell ill in 1203, Masako and her father laid plans to give the control of the western provinces to Yoriie's younger brother Sanetomo and control of the eastern provinces to Yoriie's son Ichiman. Yoriie's father-in-law, Hiki Yoshikazu, and the other members of the Hiki family, angered at what they considered the injustice of such an arrangement, laid plans to overthrow the Hōjō family. When word of this leaked out, Hōjō Tokimasa and Masako wiped out the Hiki family, had Ichiman assassinated, and removed Yoriie from the position of shogun, replacing him with Sanetomo. But Tokimasa began plotting to do away with Sanetomo as well, whereupon Masako joined with her brother Hōjō Yoshitoki in protecting Sanetomo and driving Tokimasa out of power.

In 1218, Masako journeyed to the capital and made secret arrangements to set up a member of the imperial family as heir to Sanetomo. The following year, however, when Sanetomo was assassinated by Yoriie's son Kugyō, Masako instead set up as shogun Fujiwara no Yoritsune, an infant great-grandson of Yoritomo's younger sister. In 1221, a struggle known as the Jōkyū disturbance broke out between the court and the shogunate. Masako sent military forces to attack the capital and put down the resistance and thereafter established the Rokuhara *tandai* (headquarters) in Kyoto to insure shogunate control of the court and the region of western Japan. She also appointed her brother Yoshitoki to act as *shikken* (regent) to the shogun. When Yoshitoki died, the office of regent passed to his son Yasutoki and thus the custom of members of the Hōjō family acting as regents for the Kamakura shoguns and handling affairs of state in their name was firmly established. Because of the key role that Masako played in the wielding and consolidation of power, she came to be referred to as Ama Shogun, the Nun Shogun.

Hōjō Sanetoki 北條實時 (1225–1276)

Military leader of the middle Kamakura period. The son of Hōjō Saneyasu and grandson of Yoshitoki, he held a number of important positions in the Kamakura shogunate. Because he had a country estate at Kanazawa in the province of Musashi, he was also called Kanazawa-shi.

Sanetoki was very fond of learning and built up a large collection of books gathered from all over Japan or imported from China and had copies made of the rarer items. He moved the entire collection to a temple called Shōmyō-ji in Kanazawa, where the books were maintained and arrangements were made whereby interested persons could consult or borrow them. Known as the *Kanazawa bunko,* it was the only library facility in existence in the Kamakura period. At present in the Kanazawa Ward of the city of Yokohama in Kanagawa Prefecture, the site of the *Kanazawa bunko,* there is a prefectural library that houses some twenty thousand rare books originally in Sanetoki's collection.

Hōjō Soun 北條早雲 (1432–1519)

Military leader of the late Muromachi period. He was said to have been born in Ise and at first went by the name Ise Shinkurō Nagauji. He became a Buddhist monk and assumed the religious name Sōun. Later, his son changed the family name to Hōjō. He began his career as a retainer to the lord of Suruga, Imagawa Yoshitada, and when a revolt broke out in the region in 1476 and Yoshitada was killed, Sōun assisted the lord's son, Imagawa Ujichika, to restore order. In reward for his services, he was made lord of the castle of Kōkoku-ji. In 1491 he siezed the province of Izu from Ashikaga Masatomo, and in 1495 he killed Ōmori Fujiyori, the lord of Odawara Castle, and took possession of the castle, making it his base of operations. In 1518 he completed the take-over of the province of Sagami and then proceeded to take advantage of a quarrel within the Uesugi family to extend his power into the province of Musashi as well. From then on until the overthrow of his descendants by Toyotomi Hideyoshi in 1590, he and his line held dominion over the entire Kantō region. To distinguish his family from the other family of the same name that served as regents for the Kamakura shogunate, it is often called the Go-Hōjōshi, or Later Hōjō family.

Hōjō Takatoki 北條高時 (1303–1333)

Military leader of the late Kamakura period. In 1316, while still in his teens, he was raised to the highest position of power in the Kamakura shogunate, that of *shikken* (regent), the shogun at this time being a mere figurehead. This unusual situation came about because the members of the Hōjō family who had previously held the position of *shikken* had one after another died of sickness. Because of his youth, the actual power of government was wielded by Nagasaki Takatsuna and his associates, and it is said that Takatoki devoted himself entirely to a life of pleasure and took no cognizance of political affairs. As a result, the authority of the shogunate waned until 1325, when Emperor Godaigo felt confident enough to plan its overthrow. Takatoki was able to frustrate his plans, but in 1331 Emperor Godaigo made a second attempt, which proved successful. In 1333 the forces of Nitta Yoshisada and the other leaders who were loyal to the emperor attacked Kamakura, and Takatoki and his family were obliged to commit suicide. At one point, in 1326, Takatoki, because of illness, became a monk, but up until the time of his death he retained his authority in the government.

Hōjō Tokimasa 北條時政 (1138–1215)

Military leader of the early Kamakura period. The Hōjō family was descended from the Taira and controlled the province of Izu. In 1159, when Tokimasa was still a young man, a struggle broke out between the Taira and the Minamoto families. Known as the Heiji uprising, it ended in the defeat and death of the Minamoto leader Yoshitomo and the exile of his son Yoritomo to the province of Izu. Though Yoritomo was technically a criminal, Hōjō Tokimasa treated him generously, giving him his daughter Masako for a wife and supporting him in his efforts to overthrow the Taira. When these efforts proved successful and Yoritomo founded the Kamakura shogunate, Tokimasa continued to assist him, negotiating on his behalf with the court and persuading the emperor to recognize the newly established *shugo* (constables) and *jitō* (stewards) system. In 1199 Yoritomo died, and his son Yoriie became shogun, but in 1203 Tokimasa replaced him with another son of Yoritomo, Sanetomo, and created the position of *shikken* (regent) for himself, which allowed him to act as assistant to the shogun and exercise the actual power of government. The office of *shikken* passed down to Tokimasa's descendants, fifteen of them holding it in succession; in this way the Hōjō family continued to control the Kamakura shogunate.

Hōjō Tokimune 北條時宗 (1251–1284)

Military leader of the middle Kamakura period. The eldest son of Hōjō Tokiyori, in 1268 he became the eighth *shikken*, or regent, of the Kamakura shogunate. Around this time envoys began to come to Japan from the Mongol, or Yüan, dynasty of China demanding that Japan acknowledge itself a tributary state of Yüan. Yüan at this time was under the rulership of Kublai Khan, the fifth of the Mongol emperors and grandson of Genghis Khan, the founder of the dynasty. Later, in 1271, he adopted Yüan as the official name of his dynasty, and in 1279 conquered the Southern Sung and united all of China under his rule. In 1259 Kublai, as part of his campaign to subjugate all of Asia, had forced the Korean state of Koryŏ to become a tributary, and now he prepared to use it as a base for an attack on Japan should the Japanese refuse to acknowledge his authority. When the Mongol envoys came with their demands, Tokimune refused to heed them, instead beginning preparations to defend the country against attack. In 1274 a force of over thirty thousand Mongol and Korean soldiers crossed over from the mainland in a fleet of some nine hundred ships and invaded Hakata in northern Kyushu. The Japanese defenders were easily thrown back, but a violent storm arose in the Japan Sea, inflicting heavy damage on the invaders' ships and obliging them to withdraw. From the era name of the time, this is called the Bun'ei campaign. In 1275 Kublai sent another envoy demanding the submission of the Japanese. This time Tokimune executed the envoy and began construction of a stone battlement along the coast of northern Kyushu to fend off any future Mongol attack. In 1281 the Mongol forces appeared again to attack Kyushu, but once more they met with a violent storm that forced them to withdraw. This second attack is known as the Kōan campaign, again from the era name of the time. Collectively, the two Mongol assaults are referred to as the "campaign of the Yüan pirates." Hōjō Tokimune laid plans to launch a counteroffensive against the Mongols and spent large sums of money on military preparations, moves that put a heavy strain on the finances of the shogunate and were one of the causes of its eventual downfall.

Hōjō Yasutoki 北條泰時 (1183–1242)

Military leader of the early Kamakura period. The eldest son of Hōjō Yoshitoki, he led the attack on Kyoto in the Jōkyū disturbance of 1221 and defeated the forces of the emperor. With the death of his father in 1224, he replaced him in office to become the third *shikken*, or regent, of the Kamakura shogunate and the actual wielder of authority in the government. In 1232 he promulgated the *Jōei-shikimoku*, also known as the *Kantō-goseibai-shikimoku*, a code of laws for the warrior class that fixed in writing what had heretofore been merely custom. The first attempt to draw up a constitution for the military government, its spirit continued to be influential long after the disappearance of the Kamakura shogunate and was reflected even much later in the practices of the Edo shogunate.

Yasutoki was a devout Buddhist, expressing particular admiration for the religious leader Myōe of the Kōzan-ji in Kyoto and founding a number of temples. Under his leadership the Kamakura shogunate enjoyed its period of greatest political stability.

Hōjō Yoshitoki 北條義時 (1163–1224)

Military leader of the early Kamakura period. The eldest son of Hōjō Tokimasa, he joined the forces of Minamoto no Yoritomo in the struggle to overthrow the Taira family and establish the Kamakura shogunate. His father aspired to depose the third shogun, Minamoto no Sanetomo, and make himself the head of the military government, but Yoshitoki joined with his elder sister Masako in thwarting his father's plans, principally because he feared that his father's insatiable thirst for political power was arousing antagonism among the other warrior groups in the government. In 1205 he succeeded his father to become the second *shikken*, or regent, nominally acting as assistant to the shogun but in practice wielding the actual power of government. In 1213 he engaged in a struggle with his most potent rival among the military leaders, Wada Yoshimori, and succeeded in wiping out him and his family, thus making the Hōjō virtual dictators of the shogunate. In 1221, when the forces centering around the imperial court attempted to overthrow him in a move known as the Jōkyū disturbance, he quickly restored order, crushing the power of the court nobility, which until this time had constituted an independent political body controlling the western part of Japan. This completed the process by which the shogunate extended its rule over the entire country.

Hōnen 法然 (1133–1212)

Priest of the early Kamakura period, founder of the Jōdo sect of Buddhism; his posthumous name is Genkū. He was born in Mimasaka, the son of Uruma no Tokikuni, the *ōryōshi* (military governor) of the region. His father was killed in a quarrel in 1141, whereupon he entered the priesthood, becoming a disciple of Kangaku of a local temple called Bodai-ji. In 1145 (or possibly 1147) he entered the monastery on Mt. Hiei and studied Tendai doctrine under Genkō and Kōen. Discouraged by the corrupt state into which Buddhism had fallen, he went into retirement at Kurodani on Mt. Hiei in 1150, where he studied the rules for monastic discipline and the Pure Land teachings of the Tendai sect under Eikū. In 1175 he read the commentary on the *Kuan-wu-liang-shou-ching* (*Kammuryōju-kyō*; one of the three Pure Land sutras, containing an account of the Buddha Amida and the glories of his Paradise) by Shan-tao (631–81), a celebrated monk of T'ang China, and became convinced that it was possible to attain rebirth in Paradise merely by the repetition of the invocation of Amida (*Namu Amida Butsu*). He left Mt. Hiei the same year and lived for a time at Hirotani west of Kyoto, later moving to Ōtani on Higashiyama, the site presently occupied by Chion-in. In 1186 he expounded his doctrines to a group of eminent monks of various sects of Buddhism at Ōhara, and from 1189 on was very active in spreading his teachings, often calling on the courtier Kujō Kanezane. In 1198 he wrote his most important work, the *Senchaku hongan nembutsu-shū*. As the number of his disciples and lay followers increased, the older sects of Buddhism, fearful of his growing power, exerted their influence to oppose him. In 1207 the practice of the *nembutsu*, the invocation of Amida, was banned, and Hōnen was banished to Shikoku. He was pardoned the same year and stayed at Kachio-dera in Settsu. He returned to Kyoto in 1211, where a disciple set down on paper his famous *Ichimai kishōmon*, containing the essence of the Pure Land teachings. He died the following year.

His thought is based upon the traditional Pure Land teachings of Tendai, which stress that all living beings are in fact Buddhas and that the present world is none other than the Pure Land of enlightenment. In Tendai, the *nembutsu* was only one of a number of religious practices to be observed, and consisted of a difficult form of meditation in which one visualized the Buddha in one's mind. Hōnen, however, interpreted the Pure Land as a separate realm in which one is reborn after death. He taught that the invocation of the name of Amida alone was all that was needed to insure such rebirth, thus greatly simplifying the religious practices required of the believer. His thinking was colored by the belief that the world had entered the period of *mappō* or "the latter days of the Buddhist Law," when individuals could no longer hope to achieve enlightenment by their own efforts. At the same time, he worked vigorously to take Buddhism out of the hands of the clergy and aristocrats and to establish it as a means of salvation for the people as a whole. That is why the new sect that he established grew with such speed and why it was so vigorously opposed by the older sects of Buddhism and the court. His writings and sayings are collected and preserved in *Saihō shinan-shō* and *Kurodani shōnin gotō-roku.* His disciples included such eminent figures as Shōkū, Shōkō, and Shinran. The present-day Jōdo sect derives from the teaching line of Shōkō.

Hosokawa Katsumoto 細川勝元 (1430–1473)

Military leader of the middle Muromachi period. The Hosokawa, followers of Ashikaga Takauji, were given posts in the Muromachi shogunate, and from the time Hosokawa Yoriyuki was appointed to the position of *kanrei* (chief administrator) so that he might act as assistant to Shogun Ashikaga Yoshimitsu, generation after generation of this family occupied important offices in the shogunate. Katsumoto likewise held the position of *kanrei* for four years beginning in 1445, and again from 1452 to 1464.

In the eleventh month of 1464, Shogun Ashikaga Yoshimasa, having no son of his own, adopted his younger brother Yoshimi as his son and heir and appointed Katsumoto to act as his guardian. The following year, however, the shogun's wife, Hino Tomiko, gave birth to a son and called on Yamana Sōzen, one of the powerful military leaders of the time, to help her have the child declared heir to the shogun. As a result, in 1467 the two opposing factions drew up their forces in Kyoto, those of Hosokawa Katsumoto on the east side of the city, those of Yamana Sōzen on the west, and the period of civil strife known as the Ōnin War began. But in the third month of 1473, long before the strife was brought to an end, Yamana Sōzen, the commander of the western camp, died, and two months later Hosokawa Katsumoto fell victim to an outbreak of plague.

IMAGAWA YOSHIMOTO 今川義元 (1519–1560)

Military leader of the late Muromachi period. The Imagawa family were said to have gotten their start as owners of the Imagawa manor in the province of Mikawa. Yoshimoto's father, Ujichika, became *kokushu* of the Tōkai region, controling the provinces of Suruga and Tōtōmi. Yoshimoto at first became a monk, but when his eldest brother died without an heir, he engaged his next eldest brother in a struggle for power and, emerging victorious, became heir to the Imagawa family. He later extended his power into the neighboring provinces, defeating the lord of Mikawa, Oda Nobuhide, and adding that province to the two already under his control. Tokugawa Ieyasu, the founder of the Edo shogunate, spent his childhood as a hostage in the house of Imagawa Yoshimoto. Yoshimoto arranged marriage alliances between his family and those ruling the provinces around him, gaining political allies in this way, and in 1560, hoping to unite the country under his rule, he set out with his forces to march on the capital, but he was opposed by Oda Nobunaga at Okehazama and died in battle.

IPPEN 一遍 (1239–1289)

Buddhist monk of the middle Kamakura period and founder of what in time became the Ji sect; his posthumous name is Chishin. He was the son of Kōno Michihiro, a member of a wealthy family of the province of Iyo in Shikoku. On the death of his mother in 1248, he entered the priesthood, taking the religious name Zuien. In 1251 he went to Tsukushi province in Kyushu and became a disciple of Shōtatsu, himself a disciple of Shōkū of the Seizan line of Jōdo (Pure Land) Buddhism. At Shōtatsu's direction he also studied under Kedai, and took the name Chishin. He returned to his home on his father's death in 1263 and left the priesthood, taking up ordinary lay life. Around 1271, however, family quarrels led him to enter the priesthood once more. He visited the religious centers at Zenkō-ji, Mt. Kōya, and Kumano, and also carried out religious practices in the mountain forests of his native region.

In 1274, while on a pilgrimage to the temples and shrines of Kumano, he underwent a mystical experience and thereafter changed his name to Ippen. He traveled about the country carrying out a practice known as *fusan*, the distributing of tallies to believers assuring them that they would be reborn in the Western Paradise of the Buddha Amida. In 1279, while in the province of Shinano, he began the practice known as *odori-nembutsu*, an ecstatic song and dance performed in honor of Amida. Because Ippen in his later years had no fixed dwelling, but abandoned all possessions and constantly traveled about from place to place, he came to be called Sute-hijiri, the "Abandoning Saint," or Yugyō-shōnin, the "Wandering Saint."

The *nembutsu* practice that he taught was in some ways closely allied with the type of *nembutsu,* or incantatory invocation, of Amida's name already made popular among the people by the Jōdo sect. At the same time, however, Ippen's *nembutsu,* though based on Jōdo teachings, in some ways resembled Zen practice, since it called upon the believer to free himself from all relative concepts and become completely identified with the *nembutsu* formula *Namu Amida Butsu.* When Ippen was about to die, he declared, "All my teachings have come to an end. I have become the *Namu Amida Butsu.*" He then proceeded to burn all his books and writings, so that nothing from his own hand remains in existence. In time, however, his disciples compiled a record of his teachings preserved in two works, *Ippen shōnin goroku* and *Banshū hogo-shū.* Accounts of his life are found in two famous illustrated works, *Ippen hijirie,* also known as *Rokujō engi,* compiled by Shōkai; and *Ippen shōnin ekotoba-den.*

Two teaching lines were established by his disciples Shōkai and Shinkyō (Tea) respectively, and though they quarreled, that established by Shinkyō, which became the Ji sect, flourished in later times. During the middle ages, the sect exercised an important influence on the fine arts and performing arts. It continues in existence today, with its headquarters at Shōjōkō-ji in Fujisawa, Kanagawa Prefecture.

I-SHAN I-NING (ISSAN ICHINEI) 一山一寧 (1247–1317)

Chinese Zen monk of the Rinzai branch who took up residence in Japan; he was born in T'ai-chou. He traveled about to various Zen centers in China to study under eminent teachers, among them Wu-teng Hui-yung, and also studied the Vinaya and T'ien-T'ai (Tendai) schools of Buddhism. He gained enlightenment under Wan-chi Hsing-mi of Yü-wang-shan and became his Dharma heir. At this time, the Sung dynasty had been overthrown by the invading Mongols (1279), who founded a new dynasty called the Yüan. Kublai Khan, the emperor of the Yüan, had failed in his two attempts to invade and conquer Japan and therefore decided to send an eminent monk to Japan to establish peaceful relations between the two countries. I-shan was chosen for the mission and given the honorary title Miao-tz'u Hung-chi ta-shih. Accompanied by Hsi-chien Tzu-t'an, Shih-liang Jen-kung, and others, he arrived in Japan in 1299, bearing official messages from China. Regent Hōjō Sadatoki suspected I-shan and his group of acting as spies and for a time had them held in confinement at Shuzen-ji, a temple in Izu. But because I-shan had won so many followers among the Japanese monks and laity, he was eventually allowed to return to Kamakura, where he lived at Kenchō-ji and Engaku-ji and accepted Hōjō Sadatoki as one of his followers. In time his fame reached the imperial court in Kyoto, and retired emperors Kameyama and Gouda also became followers. In 1313 he was invited to replace the newly deceased Kian Soen as head of Nanzen-ji in Kyoto. Retired Emperor Gouda often used to visit him at Nanzen-ji to receive instruction and bestowed the honorary title of *kokushi*, national teacher, upon him posthumously.

I-shan never mastered the Japanese language, but communicated with his students and gave them instruction principally by writing in Chinese. He played an important role in establishing pure Chinese style Zen in Japan. He was a highly educated man who was widely read in Confucianism and popular literature and exercised considerable influence upon the development of *Gozan bungaku*, the prose and poetry written in Chinese by Japanese Zen monks of the period. Many of the most outstanding Zen monks of the time such as Kōhō Kennichi, Musō Soseki, and Kokan Shiren received instruction from him. Among his direct disciples, the most distinguished was Sesson Yūbai, and through him the so-called I-shan line of Zen teaching flourished. A work known as *Issan Kokushi goroku*, preserving a record of I-shan's teachings, has been handed down.

JŌKEI 貞慶 (1155–1213)

Buddhist monk of the Hossō sect in the early Kamakura period; he was a son of Fujiwara no Sadanori. He was ordained as a priest in 1165 and studied the teachings of the Hossō sect at Kōfuku-ji in Nara, but later determined to live the life of a recluse. In 1193 he withdrew to Mt. Kasagi north of Nara. In his closing years he lived in Kaijūsen-ji, a temple near Mt. Kasagi. He observed strict rules of monastic discipline and devoted his entire life to study and religious practice. According to the work known as *Yuishikiron dōgakushō*, he labored to put the traditional Hossō doctrines of Kōfuku-ji into finished form; at the same time he was influenced by Esoteric Buddhism Zen, and *nembutsu* practices. In addition to his more technical works, he also wrote introductory works dealing with actual religious practices, such as his *Hossō shinyōshō* and *Kan'yū dōhōki*. He opposed the Jōdo, or Pure Land, sect founded by his contemporary Hōnen, which centered about devotion to the Buddha Amida, and wrote a work entitled *Kōfuku-ji sōjō* advocating faith in the Bodhisattva Miroku (Maitreya).

Kakunyo 覺如 (1270–1351)

Buddhist priest of the late Kamakura period. He was a great-grandson of Shinran, the founder of the Jōdo Shinshū sect of Buddhism. He began as a student of the Tendai sect and in 1286 became a monk of the Kōfuku-ji in Nara. The following year he received instruction in the doctrines of the Jōdo Shinshū sect from the priest Nyoshin. In 1290 he journeyed around the Kantō region visiting sites associated with Shinran, and in 1300, when Nyoshin died in the province of Mutsu in the far north of Japan, Kakunyo replaced him as propagator of the Jōdo Shinshū faith in the Mutsu region. In 1308 he returned to Kyoto and the same year was presented by Emperor Gofushimi with the area called Ōtani in Kyoto, the site of Shinran's grave. He proceeded to repair the grave and build a temple on the site called the Hongan-ji. He did his best to preserve the unity of the group centering around the Hongan-ji, stressing the view that Shinran in the first generation, Nyoshin in the second, and himself in the third were the true leaders of the Jōdo Shinshū religious community. Among his writings are the *Hōonkō-shiki* and the *Kudenshō*.

Keian Genju 桂庵玄樹 (1427–1508)

Zen monk of the late Muromachi period. Born in the province of Nagato, he entered the Nanzen-ji in Kyoto at the age of nine and became a monk of the Rinzai branch of Zen. In 1467 he accompanied the Japanese embassy to Ming China, where he lived in Hangchow and Suchow and studied the *Shang shu* (or *Shu ching*) and other texts, returning to Japan in 1473. At this time Kyoto had been all but destroyed in the Ōnin War, which lasted from 1467 to 1477, and to avoid the strife Genju retired to the province of Iwami and later went to Kyushu. In 1478 he was invited by Shimazu Tadamasa, the lord of Satsuma, to come to his domain and lecture on Confucianism, and in 1481 in cooperation with the *karō* (chief retainer) of the Shimazu family, Ijichi Shigesada, he brought out an edition of the *Ta-hsüeh chang-chü* (Japanese: *Daigaku shōku*) by the Sung Neo-Confucian philosopher Chu Hsi, thus becoming one of the first to introduce the doctrines of Neo-

Confucianism to Japan. Genju continued to reside in Satsuma and lecture on Confucianism until his death, and the line of scholars that he founded, known as the *Satsunan gakuha*, flourished in the succeeding centuries.

Keizan Jōkin 瑩山紹瑾 (1268–1325)

Zen monk of the late Kamakura period who revived the fortunes of the Sōtō branch of Zen; his posthumous title was Butsuji Zenji. Born in the province of Echizen, he entered the priesthood at an early age and studied under Koun Ejō and Tettsū Gikai of Eihei-ji, both of whom were disciples of Dōgen, the founder of Eihei-ji and early proponent of Sōtō Zen teachings in Japan. He also studied under monks of the Rinzai branch of Zen such as Tōzan Tanshō, Hakuun Egyō, and Muhon Kakushin. He gained full enlightenment in 1294 under Tettsū Gikai and became his Dharma heir. After Gikai's death in 1303, he succeeded him as head of Daijō-ji in the province of Kaga. He also founded the temples Sōji-ji and Eikō-ji in the nearby province of Noto, spreading Sōtō teachings through the Hokuriku region of northwestern Honshu. The Sōtō branch had in the past confined itself to the pure Zen teachings introduced to Japan by Dōgen, but Keizan combined these with elements drawn from Esoteric Buddhism and Shinto and worked to put the prayers and ceremonies of the sect into order, actively seeking to spread its doctrines among the common people. He thus laid the foundations for the striking spread of Sōtō Zen in rural regions that was later to take place. His writings include *Denkōroku*, *Zazen yōjin-ki*, and *Keizan shingi*. Among his disciples, Meihō Sotetsu and Gazan Shōseki were particularly outstanding. The latter is the founder of the so-called Gazan teaching line that became the central teaching line of the Sōtō branch of Zen.

Kitabatake Akiie 北畠顯家 (1318–1338)

Military leader of the period of the Northern and Southern Courts. He was the eldest son of Kitabatake Chikafusa, and in 1333, when the Kamakura shogunate was overthrown and Empero Godaigo took over the direction of the government, both he and his father were appointed to high positions. In the eighth month of that year he was put in charge of the province of Mutsu and, in the service of Imperial Prince Yoshinaga, he helped to restore order to the troubled area of Dewa in northern Japan. In 1335, when Ashikaga Takauji rebelled, Akiie attacked him and drove him out of his position in Kamakura; the following year he joined with Nitta Yoshisada and Kusunoki Masashige in pressing the attack on Takauji and forcing him to flee to Kyushu. Akiie then returned to his territory in the north, but Takauji once more rallied his forces and took possession of Kyoto. The emperor ordered Akiie to the attack again, and he fought with the Ashikaga forces at Aonobara in the province of Mino while marching towards Kyoto, but he failed to gain the upper hand and, obliged to fall back from one position to another, he was finally defeated and killed at Ishizu in Izumi Province.

KITABATAKE CHIKAFUSA 北畠親房 (1293–1354)

Statesman and military leader of the period of the Northern and Southern Courts and author of the *Jinnō shōtōki*; he was the son of Acting Dainagon Kitabatake Moroshige. His great-grandfather, grandfather, and father had all been court officials in the service of the Daikaku-ji line of emperors, and as a result Chikafusa himself entered the service of Emperor Godaigo. In time he came to be numbered, along with Madenokōji Nobufusa and Yoshida Sadafusa, as one of the emperor's three most trusted ministers. The emperor entrusted him with the upbringing of his second son, Prince Yonaga, but when the prince died prematurely in 1330, Chikafusa in grief retired from active life and took Buddhist vows. With the Kemmu Restoration a few years later, when Emperor Godaigo began to rule in person, Chikafusa returned to political life and eventually advanced to the court rank of junior first rank and the post of *daijin* (minister).

In 1333, when Chikafusa's eldest son, Akiie, was appointed governor of Mutsu and ordered to serve the emperor's son Prince Munenaga, Chikafusa accompanied him to Mutsu, taking up residence in the government office at Taga. In 1335, when Ashikaga Takauji began his revolt in Kamakura and assumed the title of *seii-taishōgun*, Akiie was given a military title and ordered to launch an attack on Takauji, who had taken up a position in Kyoto. Chikafusa joined his son and Prince Yoshinaga in the attack, which eventually forced Takauji to flee to Kyushu. But Takauji quickly recovered from the blow, returned east, and occupied Kyoto once more. Emperor Godaigo was placed in confinement, and Emperor Kōmyō of the Jimyō-in line ascended the throne. Chikafusa at this time was in Ise, where he and his second son, Akinobu, were attending Prince Munenaga and working to maintain control of the area. He made arrangements for Emperor Godaigo to retire to the nearby region of Yoshino, where the emperor established the so-called Southern Court and challenged the legitimacy of the Northern

Court in Kyoto. Thereafter, Chikafusa remained a key figure in the activities of the Southern Court.

Chikafusa's eldest son, Akiie, in 1335 returned to Mutsu in the service of Prince Yoshinaga, but in 1337 he was ordered by Emperor Godaigo to march west and attack the forces loyal to Takauji. He died in battle in 1338 at an engagement at Ishizu in Izumi. The same year, Chikafusa set out from Ise with his second son, Akinobu, who had been appointed to replace Akiie as assistant governor of Mutsu, and Prince Norinaga. At sea the ships encountered a severe storm, and Prince Norinaga and Akinobu were driven back to Ise. Chikafusa managed to reach the coast of Hitachi, where he established bases of power in the castles of Oda and Seki. With the fall of the castle of Seki in 1343, however, he returned to Yoshino. Thereafter he joined forces with Kusunoki Masatsura in an attempt to seize control of Kyoto. They were successful for a time, but Masatsura was killed in battle in 1348, and thereafter the military power of the Southern Court declined rapidly. Chikafusa died in 1454 at Anō, where the Southern Court had moved some years before.

The historical work entitled *Jinnō shōtōki* was written during Chikafusa's years in Seki Castle, when he received word that Emperor Godaigo had died and Prince Yoshinaga, whom Chikafusa had served so long, had succeeded him to become Emperor Gomurakami. Beginning with the famous declaration, "Great Japan is the land of the gods," the work stresses the divine descent of the imperial line and the legitimacy of the Southern Court and was intended for the education of the youthful emperor. A second work, the *Shikigenshō*, traces the history of official ranks and titles and was likewise written for presentation to Emperor Gomurakami. Both works give ample evidence of Chikafusa's wide learning in the fields of history and the teachings of Neo-Confucianism, Buddhism, and Shinto.

Kokan Shiren 虎關師錬 (1278–1346)

Rinzai Zen monk of the late Kamakura period, he was a native of Kyoto; he also went by the names Kaizō Oshō and Fūgetsu Shujin. In 1285 he began Zen training under Tōzan Tanshō of Sanshō-ji, a disciple of Enni Bennen and follower of the Shōichi teaching line. In 1287 he formally entered the clergy. In 1292, after the death of Tōzan Tanshō, he became a disciple of Kian Soen of Nanzen-ji, a Dharma heir of the Chinese monk Wu-hsüeh Tsu-yüan (Mugaku Sogen). From 1293 on, he traveled about to various temples in Kyoto and Kamakura, studying under numerous Zen masters, among them the Chinese monk I-shan I-ning (Issan Ichinei). He also studied Esoteric Buddhism at Ninna-ji and Daigo-ji, and received instruction in Confucianism, the *Book of Changes*, and works of Chinese literature such as the *Wen hsüan* from Sugawara no Arisuke and Minamoto no Arifusa.

In 1314 he built a residence in Kyoto called Saihoku-an, but two years later moved to Hongaku-ji, a temple in the province of Ise. He returned to Kyoto in 1322, living in Kaizō-in, and the same year completed his major work, the *Genkō shakusho* in thirty chapters. The work, written in Chinese, is a history of Japanese Buddhism centering about the biographies of eminent monks from the time of the introduction of Buddhism to Japan down to the period of the writer. It is said that Kokan Shiren undertook the writing of the book out of shame when he found himself unable to answer questions on the history of Japanese Buddhism put to him by the Chinese monk I-shan I-ning. He drew upon a wide range of source materials and revised the work three times; as a result, it continues today to be one of the most valuable basic sources on the subject. It also reflects the strong sense of national identity that was a characteristic of the age in which the author lived.

In 1326, Kokan moved to Sanshō-ji, and later resided in Tōfuku-ji and Nanzen-ji, ending his life at the former. His other writings include *Butsugo shinron*, a commentary on the *Lankāvatāra Sutra*, an anthology of parallel prose entitled *Zengi gemonshū*, a collection of his sayings entitled *Jūzen shiroku*, and his collected poems and prose pieces in Chinese, *Saihokushū*. He was one of the forerunners of the *Gozan bungaku*, the literature in Chinese written by Japanese Zen monks, and had many eminent disciples such as Mugan Soō, Shōkai Reiken, and Taidō Ichii, who were also distinguished writers of Chinese. He was on close terms with members of the imperial family such as emperors Kameyama, Godaigo, and Gokōmyō. Emperor Gomurakami posthumously bestowed upon him the title of *kokushi*, and he is thus known as Kokan Kokushi.

Kujō Kanezane 九條兼實 (1149–1207)

Statesman of the early Kamakura period. The son of Fujiwara no Tadamichi, he took the surname Kujō from the Kujō area of Kyoto where his mansion was situated. In similar fashion, his elder brother Motozane took the surname Konoe; Motozane's descendants continued to serve as close personal associates of the emperor down to the time of the Second World War.

In 1166 Kanezane was promoted to the position of minister of the right and became a man of importance in the political world of the time, but he did not get along well with Taira no Kiyomori, and when the latter moved the capital to Fukuhara at the site of the present-day city of Kobe in 1180, Kanezane chose to remain behind in Kyoto. When the great struggle between the Taira and the Minamoto families broke out, he sided with the latter, joining the forces that supported its leader, Minamoto no Yoritomo. In return, when the Minamoto family emerged victorious and founded the Kamakura shogunate, Kanezane was able with their backing to climb to the highest position at court. However, because of interference from Retired Emperor Goshirakawa, he was not always able to have his way, and it was not until the death of Goshirakawa in 1192 that he could exercise control freely. In the same year Minamoto no Yoritomo was appointed *seii-taishōgun*, the highest military title that could be conferred by the court, indicating that the emperor both in name and in fact recognized the existence of the Kamakura government. The move came about through the efforts of Kanezane, who saw it as a symbol of harmony between the court and the military power. Kanezane married his daughter to Emperor Gotoba, hoping to have the son that was born from the union made ruler so that he might further consolidate his power, but the machinations of Minamoto no Michichika drove him from office in 1196. He made an attempt to regain his position in the government, but because of the death of Yoritomo in 1199, his efforts ended in failure. In his late years he became a Buddhist monk with the religious name Enshō, rendering assistance to Hōnen, the founder of the Jōdo sect. He was fond of learning, and his diary, known as the *Gyokuyō*, is one of the most important sources for the history of the period.

Kusunoki Masashige 楠木正成 (d. 1336)

Military leader of the period of the Northern and Southern Courts. Nothing is known for certain of his background or date of birth, though it would appear that he conducted some kind of business in the province of Kawachi. In 1331 he participated in the coup d'état carried out by Emperor Godaigo against the Kamakura shogunate, engaging in battle with the shogunal armies. In 1333, when the shogunate was overthrown and Emperor Godaigo assumed personal direction of the government, Masashige was appointed *shugo* (constable) and put in charge of the province of Kawachi and other areas. When Ashikaga Takauji revolted in 1335, Masashige and others attacked him and forced him to flee to Kyushu. Masashige then attempted to persuade Emperor Godaigo to make peace with Takauji, but the emperor would not heed this advice. The following year Takauji returned from

Kyushu at the head of a large force. Masashige engaged him in battle at Minatogawa in the province of Settsu but was defeated and committed suicide.

Lan-hsi Tao-lung (Rankei Dōryū) 蘭溪道隆 (1213–1278)

Chinese Rinzai Zen monk of the middle Kamakura period; his posthumous title is Daikaku Zenji. Born in Shu in the area of present-day Szechwan, he studied Zen under Wu-ming Hui-hsing (Mumyō Eshō) and became his Dharma heir. In 1246, at the invitation of the statesman Hōjō Tokiyori, he came to Japan with his disciples I-weng Shao-jen (Giō Shōnin) and Lung-chiang Ying-hsüan (Ryūkō Ōsen). The following year, he journeyed from Hakata to Kyoto and then on to Kamakura. In 1253, when Tokiyori founded the temple named Kenchō-ji in Kamakura, Tao-lung became head of it. In 1265 he relinquished the position to Wu-an P'u-ning, another Chinese monk who had just come to Japan, and went to Kyoto, where he took up residence in Kennin-ji. While in Kyoto, he preached before Emperor Gosaga. Three years later, he returned to Kamakura at the bidding of Hōjō Tokimune. As a result of slanders, he was for a time sentenced to banishment. In his later years, however, he was pardoned and returned to Kamakura, residing at Jufuku-ji. Before his arrival in Japan, Japanese Zen had consisted of a mixture of Zen and the teachings of Esoteric Buddhism and the Tendai sect. Tao-lung, however, introduced the pure form of Zen current at the time in Sung China and subjected his followers to a rigorous course of religious training, thus helping to initiate a new era in the history of Japanese Zen. He was particularly respected among the samurai of Kamakura, many of whom were his followers. His teaching line is known as the Daikaku-ha. His principal disciples were Ikō Dōnen, Tōkei Tokugo, Mukyū Tokusen, and Yakuō Tokuken. His teachings are preserved in a work entitled *Daikaku zenji goroku.*

Mansai Jugō 満済准后 (1378–1435)

Buddhist priest of the middle Muromachi period. He was the son of Imakōji Morofuyu, a member of the aristocracy. He became a monk at the Daigo-ji near Kyoto and in 1395 advanced to the highest position among the monks.

Mansai enjoyed the profound trust and respect of Shogun Ashikaga Yoshimitsu, who made him his *yūshi,* or adopted son without inheritance rights. In return Mansai assisted both Yoshimitsu and his successors, the shoguns Yoshimochi and Yoshinori, in the management of government affairs. Mansai was a conscientious diary keeper, and the sections dealing with the years from around 1411 to 1435 have been preserved. Describing such events as the peasant uprising in the province of Ōmi in 1428 and the struggle for power that preceded the selection of Yoshinori as shogun, it is one of the primary sources for the history of the period. In 1428 Mansai was given the honorary title *jugō*, indicating that he was entitled to the same respect due to a consort of the imperial family, and is hence known as Mansai Jugō.

Minamoto no Yoriie 源頼家 (1182–1204)

Shogun of the early Kamakura period. His father, Minamoto no Yoritomo, having died in 1199, Yoriie succeeded him in 1202 to become the second shogun of the Kamakura shogunate. Hōjō Tokimasa, the father of Yoriie's mother, Masako, greedy for power, conspired to have Yoriie done away with, enlisting the help of Anō Zensei, but in the fifth month of 1203 Yoriie killed Zensei. In the seventh month of the same year Yoriie, having fallen gravely ill, turned over the authority of government to his eldest son, Ichiman and his younger brother Semman, later known as Sanetomo. Hiki Yoshikazu, the grandfather of Ichiman, who shared power in the government with Hōjō Tokimasa, concluded that this was a scheme on the part of Tokimasa and consulted with Yoriie on ways to overthrow Tokimasa, but instead Yoshikazu and his grandson Ichiman were both killed by Tokimasa in the ninth month of 1203. Learning of the murder of his son, Yoriie commanded Wada Yoshimori and his associates to attack Tokimasa, but Yoshimori instead went over to Tokimasa's side. Yoriie was thereupon forced to turn over the position of shogun to his younger brother, Minamoto no Sanetomo, and was confined in the Shuzen-ji temple in the province of Izu, where in the seventh month of 1204 he was put to death by Tokimasa.

Minamoto no Yoritomo 源頼朝 (1147–1199)

Shogun of the early Kamakura period; first shogun of the shogunate system of government. He was the third son of Minamoto no Yoshitomo. In 1159, at the time of the struggle between the Minamoto and Taira families known as the Heiji disturbance, he had his first taste of battle, but the Minamoto forces having been defeated, he attempted to flee to the eastern provinces. He was caught, however, and brought back to Kyoto, where he would under oridinary circumstances have been executed, but the pleas of the nun Ike no Zenni, stepmother of the leader of the Taira forces, Taira no Kiyomori, saved his life. The following year he was exiled to Hirugakojima in the province of Izu and remained in that region for the next twenty years, living the life of a banished criminal. In the interval, he married Masako, the daughter of a powerful military leader of the area, Hōjō Tokimasa, and watched for an opportunity to revive the fortunes of the Minamoto family.

In 1180 Prince Mochihito, a son of Emperor Goshirakawa, began laying plans to overthrow the Taira family, sending out an order to the provinces for supporters and engaging the Taira forces in battle, but he was defeated and killed. Meanwhile Yoritomo, responding to the order, gathered together a body of troops and engaged an ally of the Taira at Ishibashiyama, but he, too, was defeated and fled by sea to the province of Awa. There he gathered to himself the support of the Chiba and other powerful families of the Kantō region, and with their aid succeeded in entering Kamakura in the province of Sagami and establishing a base of operations, gradually extending his power from there. In the tenth month of 1180 he already felt confident enough to engage the Taira forces at Fujigawa, inflicting a defeat. Then, after wiping out the Satake family in the province of Hitachi, he set up the Samuraidokoro, a military office whose function was to regulate the lives and affairs of Yoritomo's retainers, and thereafter joined with Minamoto no Yoshinaka, also known as Kiso Yoshinaka, and others in extending the control of the Minamoto throughout the Kantō and Tōkai regions. In 1183 Yoshinaka was able to enter Kyoto, the Taira forces having fled to the west, but the violent and dictatorial manner in which he conducted himself in Kyoto highly displeased Yoritomo, who sent out an order for Yoshinaka's overthrow. Yoritomo's younger brother Yoshitsune thereupon attacked and killed Yoshinaka in 1184. This same year Yoritomo set up the Kumonjo, later renamed the Mandokoro, the administrative organ for the shogunate or military government, and the Monchūjo, the office for handling legal affairs, thus laying the foundations for a new system of government that in time would replace the court bureaucracy.

In 1185 Minamoto no Yoshitsune completed the destruction of the Taira family at the battle of Dan-no-ura in the province of Nagato, but Yoritomo, declaring that Yoshitsune was conspiring with the court, proclaimed him a traitor and called for his arrest. Yoshitsune fled into hiding, whereupon Yoritomo used the search for him as a convenient excuse to set up *shugo*, or constables, officials whose duty was to regulate the military affairs of the various provinces, and *jitō*, or stewards, who were to do the same for the private manors, persuading the court to give its approval to the system. In this way he managed for the first time to establish military rule over the entire country. Meanwhile it was discovered that Yoshitsune had taken refuge with the Fujiwara family in the province of Mutsu, and on orders from Yoritomo he was attacked in 1189 and forced to commit suicide. In 1192 Yoritomo received from the court the title *seii-taishōgun*, making him the highest military officer of the state, and with this the process of establishing a military government was brought to completion. This is the beginning of feudalism in Japan.

Minamoto no Yoshitsune 源義經 (1159–1189)

Military leader of the early Kamakura period. He was the son of Minamoto no Yoshitomo and Tokiwa Gozen and in his youth was called Ushiwakamaru. In the twelfth month of 1159 his father, Yoshitomo, turned against the leader of the Taira family, Taira no Kiyomori, in the action known as the Heiji uprising, but in the first month of the following year Yoshitomo was killed in battle. Tokiwa Gozen tried to flee with her children but was siezed by the Taira forces. Later she married Fujiwara no Naganari and for a while Yoshitsune lived in the home of the latter, but around 1169 he entered the temple north of Kyoto called Kuramadera to become a monk. The religious life seems not to have been to his liking, for around 1174 he left Kyoto and, eluding the Taira soldiers that had been sent to pursue him, made his way to the home of Fujiwara no Hidehira, a powerful lord of the province of Mutsu.

In 1180, hearing that Minamoto no Yoritomo, his elder brother by a different mother, had raised troops and was attempting to overthrow the Taira, he joined in the campaign. In 1183 another relative who had entered the struggle, Yoshitsune's cousin Minamoto no Yoshinaka, succeeded in driving the Taira forces from the city of Kyoto, but he behaved defiantly toward Retired Emperor Goshirakawa, who controlled the imperial court, and as a consequence Yoshitsune was sent at the head of an army to restore order, attacking and killing Yoshinaka in 1184. Yoshitsune then continued the pursuit of the Taira forces, which had fled to the west, and at the battle of Dan-no-ura in the third month of 1185 finally destroyed them. Shortly after, however, dissension developed between Yoshitsune and his elder brother Yoritomo, who had remained in Kamakura, over the disposition of Taira hostages. Retired Emperor Goshirakawa, determined to exploit the rift between the brothers, commanded Yoshitsune to attack Yoritomo. Yoritomo then dispatched his retainer Tosabō Shōshun to assassinate Yoshitsune, but Yoshitsune succeeded in siezing and killing him instead. In order to evade the pursuers that Yoritomo sent after him, Yoshitsune fled from province to province, finally taking refuge with Fujiwara no Hidehira in Mutsu, where he had lived as a youth. When Hidehira died in the tenth month of 1187, however, Yoritomo ordered Hidehira's son, Fujiwara no Yasuhira, to attack Yoshitsune, an order that he carried out in 1189, forcing Yoshitsune to commit suicide. He performed the deed in hopes of thereby retaining control of the province of Mutsu, but he, in turn, was killed by the forces of Yoritomo, who took over control of the area. Yoshitsune, along with his famous retainer Benkei, is the subject of a number of dramatic works that are still frequently performed today such as the Kabuki plays *Ataka-no-seki no kanjinchō* and *Yoshitsune sembonzakura.*

Mōri Motonari 毛利元就 (1497–1571)

A powerful daimyo in western Japan in the age of civil wars during the late Muromachi period. He was the second son of Mōri Hiromoto; his childhood name was Shōjumaru. In 1516 his elder brother Okimoto died and he assisted his elder brother's son Yukimatsumaru in managing the affairs of the family. But in 1523 Yukimatsumaru died, and Motonari became head of the family. The Mōri family, which resided in Yoshida in Aki, was relatively weak and situated between the two much more powerful Ōuchi and Amako families. At first it allied itself with the Amako, but as a result of a dispute in the Mōri family it later went over to the side of the Ōuchi. Motonari gradually overwhelmed the other powerful families of the provinces of Aki and Bingo and in 1540 inflicted a defeat on the Amako family. In 1546 he turned over the nominal leadership of the family to his son Takamoto but continued to exercise power.

In 1551 Ōuchi Yoshitaka, head of the Ōuchi family, was killed by his retainer Sue Harukata. In 1555 Motonari attacked and defeated Sue Harukata at Itsukushima and in one stroke added all of the Ōuchi lands to his own, thus laying the foundation for his spectacular rise to power. Thereafter he challenged the power of the Ōtomo family, wiped out the Amako, and in time made himself master of a territory embracing the ten provinces of Aki, Suō, Nagato, Bitchū, Bingo, Inaba, Hōki, Izumo, Oki and Iwami, as well as parts of Buzen in Kyushu and Sanuki in Shikoku. He died in the sixth month of 1571.

Musō Soseki 夢窓疎石 (1275–1351)

Zen monk of the late Kamakura and early Muromachi period, founder of the Tenryū-ji teaching line of Rinzai Zen. He was born in Ise and raised in the province of Kai. He entered the priesthood at the age of eight and at first studied the doctrines of the Tendai and Shingon sects. At nineteen he entered the Zen sect, studying under the Chinese master I-shan I-ning (Japanese: Issan Ichinei) and Kōhō Kennichi and became the Dharma heir of the latter. Not wishing to associate himself with the men in power at the time, he lived in seclusion in the mountains of Kai and Mino provinces. In time, however, his name became known, and in 1325 he was summoned to the capital by Emperor Godaigo to become head of Nanzen-ji. Later, at the invitation of the members of the powerful Hōjō family, he went to Kamakura to head Engaku-ji. He also founded Erin-ji in Kai, Zuisen-ji in Kamakura, and Rinsen-ji and Saihō-ji (Kokedera) in Kyoto.

After the death of Emperor Godaigo, he was treated with great respect by the shogun Ashikaga Takauji and his brother Tadayoshi. He persuaded Takauji and his brother to establish a temple and pagoda in each of the provinces of the country to pray for the souls of those who had been killed in the recent civil disturbances and also prevailed upon Takauji to found Tenryū-ji in the western suburbs of Kyoto, a temple dedicated to the repose of the soul of Emperor Godaigo. Musō Soseki became the first head of the temple, which was completed in 1345. Takauji dispatched trading ships to China to obtain funds for the erection of the temple, and these came to be known as *Tenryū-ji bune*. In 1346 Musō Soseki turned over the direction of the temple to his disciple Mukyoku Shigen and in 1351 died at Rinsen-ji nearby.

Soseki wrote various works, including *Kokushi goroku*, *Muchū mondō*, *Hōwa-shū*, and *Kokukyō-shū*. He was skilled in the composition of poetry in Chinese and Japanese and also designed and constructed beautiful gardens at Saihō-ji and other temples. In addition, he played an important role in political affairs, working to negotiate a settlement in the disagreement between the Northern and Southern Courts. He is said to have had some ten thousand disciples, among whom the above-mentioned Mukyoku, Shun'oku Myōha, Gidō Shūshin, and Zekkai Chūshin are particularly famous. All were men of learning and skilled writers of Chinese verse and prose and occupy a prominent place in the literary movement known as *Gozan bungaku*.

Musō Soseki was three times honored during his lifetime as a *kokushi* (national master), receiving the titles Musō, Shōkaku, and Shinsō from emperors Godaigo, Kōgen, and Kōmyo respectively. After his death, he was four more times honored with the title *kokushi*, so that he became known as the National Master of Seven Reigns. Thus, although he himself preferred a life of retirement, he was respected and honored by the leaders of the nation and exercised his talents in a wide variety of religious, artistic, and political activities. In his religious teachings, he showed a tendency to fuse Zen with the doctrines of other sects, particularly those of Esoteric Buddhism. In this respect he stands in marked contrast to his famous contemporary Shūhō Myōchō, better known as Daitō Kokushi, who taught a meticulously pure form of Zen.

Myōan Eisai 明庵榮西 (1141–1215)

Zen monk of the early Kamakura period who introduced the Rinzai branch of Zen to Japan; his literary name was Yōjōbō. The name Eisai may also be read Yōsai. He was born in Kibitsu in the province of Bitchū. He entered the clergy at a young age and studied at various places such as Mt. Hiei, An'yō-ji in Kibitsu, and Daisen in Hōki, receiving instruction in Tendai Esoteric Buddhism from Jōshin, Kikō, Ken'i, and others. In 1168 he journeyed to China, at this time under the Sung dynasty, spending about half a year there and returning to Japan with the latest writings of the Tendai sect. But this failed to satisfy him and he took up residence at Seigan-ji, a temple in Kyushu, where he waited for another opportunity to visit China. In 1187 he set out once more, hoping eventually to reach India, but was unable to realize this goal. At Mt. T'ien-t'ai in China, he met the Zen master Hsü-an Huai-ch'ang and later accompanied him to Mt. T'ien-t'ung. There he received sanction as a successor to the Zen and Vinaya teachings of the Huang-lung line of the Lin-chi (Rinzai) branch of Zen. He returned to Japan in 1191 and stayed for a time in Kyushu, founding Shōfuku-ji in Hakata and other temples, where he propagated Zen and Vinaya.

At this time there was a monk named Dainichi Nōnin who proclaimed himself a Zen master and was active in the area of the capital, propagating what came to be called the Daruma school of Zen. Eisai's activities were regarded as in a class with those of Nōnin and were attacked by the established sects of Buddhism. As a result of their agitation, Eisai was ordered by the court in Kyoto to cease his Zen activities. He went to Kyoto and in 1198 wrote a work entitled *Kōzen gokoku-ron* in which he made clear that his Zen was different from that taught by Nōnin and argued that it was conducive to the general welfare and national security. Later he went to Kamakura, where he won over to his teachings Hōjō Masako, the wife of the founder of the Kamakura shogunate, and the second shogun, Minamoto no Yoriie. In 1200 he founded Jufuku-ji in Kamakura and two years later founded Kennin-ji in Kyoto. Eisai's attitude was marked by tolerance and adaptability, and he made many compromises with the older forms of Buddhism. In this respect he stands in marked contrast to Dōgen, another monk who worked to introduce Zen to Japan and who rigorously guarded the purity of the teaching from contamination with other sects. Eisai was active in the propagation of Tendai Esoteric teachings as well as Zen, writing many works on the subject and founding a school known as Yōjō-ryū. In order to further the spread of his teachings, he cultivated the friendship of persons in the court and shogunate. He is famous also for the steps he took to popularize the cultivation and drinking of tea, writing a work entitled *Kissa yōjō-ki* (first draft 1211, revised version 1214) in which he praised the medicinal values of the beverage. His disciples include Eichō and Myōzen. Myōzen, in turn, was the teacher of Dōgen, who is regarded as the founder of the Sōtō branch of Zen in Japan.

Nichiren 日蓮 (1222–1282)

Buddhist monk of the middle Kamakura period, founder of the Nichiren sect. He was born at Kominato in Awa Province, the son of a fisherman. In 1233 he entered the nearby temple of Kiyomizu-dera, studying under Dōzembō. He became a member of the clergy in 1237 and the following year went to Kamakura to study Buddhism. After returning home in 1242, he entered the monastery of Mt. Hiei in Kyoto and studied the doctrines of the Tendai sect. He became convinced that the *Hokekyō* (Lotus Sutra), which formed the basis of Tendai teaching, represented the highest expression of truth. He returned home in 1253, and on the twenty-eighth day of the fourth month, took the first step toward the formation of a new sect of Buddhism by devising the mantra *Namu Myōhō Rengekyō*, "Homage to the Lotus of the Wonderful Law." The mantra, called a *daimoku*, was believed to encompass all the truth and merit of the Lotus Sutra, and its recitation came to constitute the chief religious practice of the Nichiren sect.

Nichiren shortly after set out for Kamakura, where he began to gather a group of disciples and lay believers around him. He declared that the nation was suffering from endless natural disasters and social upheavals because it failed to observe the teachings of the Lotus Sutra and predicted that Japan would suffer the even greater disaster of foreign invasion if it did not abandon its erroneous ways. In 1259 he wrote a work entitled *Shugo kokka-ron*, in which he expressed these ideas, and in 1260 wrote a similar work, *Risshō ankoku-ron*, which he presented to the former regent Hōjō Tokiyori. His prophecies of foreign attack in time came true when the Mongols launched two attempts to invade Kyushu.

Nichiren's sharp attacks on other sects of Buddhism involved him in increasing difficulty and in 1261 he was exiled to Izu Peninsula. He was pardoned in 1263 and returned to Kamakura, but he continued to preach his doctrines with even greater vigor than before. He was once more arrested by the authorities and banished to the island of Sado in 1271. The hardships of exile only deepened his sense of mission, and at this time he produced his most important works such as the *Kaimokushō* (1272) and *Kanjin honzonshō* (1273). He was pardoned in 1274 and returned for a time to Kamakura. Realizing that his views would never be heeded, however, he retired to Mt. Minobu in the province of Kai. In 1282, illness obliged him to leave the mountain in search of a place to convalesce, but while en route to a hot spring, he died at Ikegami in Musashi.

Nichiren's thinking may conveniently be divided into two parts, that representative of the period before his exile to Sado, and that of the period following exile. In the earlier period, though he stressed the supreme authority of the Lotus Sutra, his teachings remained within the confines of Tendai doctrine. In the period following his exile, however, his thinking underwent fundamental changes. He began to lay emphasis upon the figure of the eternal Śākyamuni and saw himself as the true disciple of this eternal Buddha. He also asserted that, while Tendai teachings confined themselves to the realm of theory (*ri*), his own teachings represented the true practice or actualization (*ji*) of Buddhism. He wrote many works in addition to those mentioned above. The numerous letters that he wrote to followers and believers have long been prized for the moving way in which they reveal the richly human side of his personality.

Ninshō 忍性 (1217–1303)

Buddhist monk of the Ritsu (Vinaya) sect in the middle Kamakura period who devoted much effort to social welfare; he is also known as Ryōkan or Ninshō Bosatsu. In 1240 he entered the priesthood under Eison of Saidai-ji in Nara and devoted his efforts to caring for lepers and persons of the outcast class. He is said to have founded the Kitayama Jūhachikendo, a hall for the shelter and care of lepers in Nara, which remains in existence today.

In 1252 he journeyed to eastern Japan and took up residence in Mimura-ji in the province of Hitachi, where he worked to spread his teachings. In 1261 he went to Kamakura, where he lived in the Shaka Hall of Shōryō-ji. The statesman Hōjō Shigetoki and his son Naritoki were both followers of Ninshō, and when Shigetoki built a temple called Gokuraku-ji in Kamakura, Ninshō took up residence as the first head of it. He thereafter set up facilities in Gokuraku-ji for the care of lepers and other sick persons, and was also active in other types of social welfare such as road repairing and well digging in various regions of the country. In addition, he was famous for carrying out Shingon style prayers and incantations. He opposed the famous Buddhist leader Nichiren, who was preaching in Kamakura at this time, and lent his support to the shogunate in its measures to curb Nichiren's activities. At the time of the second Mongol attack on Japan in 1281, he won fame for the ceremonies that he carried out to pray for divine protection. He demonstrated great ability as an administrator, serving as *bettō* (supervisor) of Eifuku-ji in Kamakura and manager of other temples in various regions. In addition to these varied activities, he set up facilities for printing books at Gokuraku-ji.

NISSHIN 日親 (1407–1488)

Middle Muromachi period Buddhist monk of the Nichiren sect; he was born at Haniya in the province of Shimōsa. In his youth he entered a temple of the Nichiren sect called Hokekyō-ji in Nakayama in his home province, studying under Nichiei, Nissen, and Nissatsu. In 1433 he was appointed *dōshi*, or teacher, for the Kyushu area and took up residence in Kōshō-ji in the province of Hizen. He strongly attacked the members of the Nichiren sect of his time for failing to guard the doctrinal purity of the sect. As a result of such criticisms, he was officially expelled from Nakayama Hokekyō-ji in 1437.

In 1439 he appealed to the shogun Ashikaga Yoshinori, calling upon him to reject all other sects and to support the pure teachings of the Nichiren sect. The following year he wrote a doctrinal work entitled *Risshō chikokuron*, which he intended to present to the shogun in order to reiterate his appeal, but the matter came to light before he had presented the work and he was arrested and put in prison. There he was subjected to various tortures, among them the placing of a heated metal pot on his head. As a result, he came to be known as "Pot-crowned Nisshin." In 1441 he was pardoned and thereafter traveled about the country preaching. His vehement attitude aroused opposition in many quarters and often brought him suffering, but gradually his followers and supporters grew in number. In his late years he founded a temple in Kyoto called Hompō-ji, where he devoted himself to the guidance of his followers.

NITTA YOSHISADA 新田義貞 (d. 1338)

Military leader of the period of the Northern and Southern Courts. It is not certain whether he was born in 1301 or 1302. The Nitta, a warrior family descended from the Genji (Minamoto), had their base at the district of Nitta in the province of Kōzuke. In 1331, when Emperor Godaigo attempted to sieze power from the Kamakura shogunate, Yoshisada was one of a group of military leaders who were dispatched by the shogunate to restore control, but midway in the mission he returned to his home in Kōzuke, raised a force of men, and joined Ashikaga Yoshiaki in attacking Kamakura instead, bringing about the overthrow of the Kamakura shogunate in 1333. In the sixth month of the same year, he joined the group centering about Emperor Godaigo in carrying out the so-called Kemmu Restoration, whereby the emperor was once more made the actual ruler of the country. In 1335, when Ashikaga Takauji began a revolt at Kamakura, Yoshisada engaged him in battle at Take-no-shita in Hakone but was defeated. He continued the struggle against Ashikaga Takauji's forces, encountering them in battle at various locations, but in 1338 he was defeated by the Ashikaga ally Shiba Takatsune in an engagement in Echizen and died in the combat.

ŌE NO HIROMOTO 大江廣元 (1148–1225)

Statesman of the early Kamakura period. The Ōe family was famous for having produced many court officials and scholars during the Heian period. Hiromoto likewise began his career as an official in the service of the court, but in 1184 he was invited by Minamoto no Yoritomo to come to Kamakura and take up an important position in the new military government. In 1185 Hiromoto presented a plan for the appointment of shogunate officials, to be known as *shugo* (constables), and *jitō* (stewards), to supervise the various provinces and manors throughout the country. Minamoto no Yoritomo adopted the plan and saw to it that the court gave its approval. In this way the court, which heretofore had exercised at least nominal control over the entire country, was obliged to recognize the rulership of the newly arisen warrior class. In 1221, when the struggle known as the Jōkyū disturbance broke out between the court and the shogunate, Hiromoto once again worked for the welfare of the shogunate, helping it to strengthen its position and consolidate its control over the capital and further demonstrating his power and political acumen.

Ōsen Keisan 横川景三 (1429–1493)

Zen monk of the late Muromachi period. He entered the priesthood at an early age and underwent religious training at the Sōkoku-ji in Kyoto. To avoid the troubles of the Ōnin War, he took refuge in the province of Ōmi, but returned to Kyoto in 1472 and resided at the Sōkoku-ji and later the Nanzen-ji. At this time Zen monks generally won fame either by becoming outstanding scholars or by acting as political advisers. Ōsen Keisan followed the former course, and was allowed to accompany the Japanese embassies to Korea in 1472 and 1474 and the embassy to China in 1475. So great was the respect accorded his ability in Chinese studies that he was selected to compose the official letters that were sent to the courts of China and Korea. A collection of his verse and prose in Chinese, the *Keikashū*, has been handed down and holds a place of importance in the *Gozan bungaku*, the body of poetry and prose works written in Chinese by the Zen monks of the late Kamakura and Muromachi periods.

Ōtomo Sōrin 大友宗麟 (1520–1587)

Military leader of the late Muromachi period. He was born into the Ōtomo family, which from Kamakura times on held control of the province of Bungo. His father, Yoshiaki, enlarged the domain until it embraced the provinces of Buzen, Bungo, Chikugo, and Higo—that is, almost half of the island of Kyushu—and traded with the Europeans who came to Japan. (In 1545 a disabled Portuguese ship drifted ashore at Tanegashima off southern Kyushu, and for the first time the exact location of Japan became known abroad.) In 1550 Yoshiaki became involved in a family dispute and was killed, and his son Sōrin, at that time called Yoshishige, succeeded him as head of the family. He, like his father, engaged in constant battles with the rulers of neighboring provinces to enlarge the territory under his command. He also carried on a flourishing trade with the Portuguese ships and in that connection was persuaded to give permission to the Jesuits to preach in his domain. In 1551 he wrote a letter to the king of Portugal and sent it, along with a delegation, to Dom Alfonso de Noronha, the governor of Goa in India.

In 1578 he was baptized and took the Christian name Francisco, and in 1582 he joined with the other Christian daimyo Ōmura Sumitada and Arima Harunobu in sending a delegation to the Pope in Rome. His embracing of the Christian faith, however, was probably at least in part a strategy to insure that he could buy arms and other goods from the Europeans. After being baptized, he engaged Shimazu Yoshihisa, lord of the Satsuma, Ōkuma, and Hyūga domains, in battle and was defeated at Mimikawa in Hyūga. His power began to decline, and when in 1586 the Shimazu family reopened attacks on him, he appealed to Toyotomi Hideyoshi for assistance. This provided Hideyoshi with a convenient opportunity to attack the Shimazus and, after forcing their surrender, to bring all of Kyushu under his control. Sōrin died in 1587.

Ōuchi Yoshitaka 大内義隆 (1507–1551)

Military leader of the late Muromachi period. He was the son of Ōuchi Yoshioki, who had his base at Yamaguchi in the province of Suō (the present-day city of Yamaguchi in Yamaguchi Prefecture) and extended his control over the neighboring provinces of Nagato, Aki, Iwami, and others. With the death of his father in 1528, Yoshitaka became head of the family and worked to widen the area under its control, in 1535 siezing the region of northern Kyushu. Hoping to engage in foreign trade, he fought with the Hosokawa family over the rights to such trade and, emerging victorious, began to conduct trading missions with Ming China and Korea. He met twice with the Jesuit missionary Francis Xavier, in 1550 and 1551, and gave Xavier permission to preach Christianity in his domain. During this period, many of the courtier families, in order to escape the troubled conditions in Kyoto, sought protection under Yoshitaka, and Yamaguchi soon became a flourishing center of cultural life, but in 1551 one of Yoshitaka's vassals, Sue Harukata, attacked his master and Yoshitaka was forced to commit suicide.

Rennyo 蓮如 (1415–1499)

Buddhist priest of the late Muromachi period. He was the son of Sonnyo, the seventh head of the Hongan-ji branch of the sect of Buddhism called Jōdo Shinshū. His mother died when he was six, and he was brought up by his father at the Hongan-ji in Kyoto, which at that time had been reduced to a state of extreme poverty. Determined to revive the fortunes of the sect, he became a priest at the age of seventeen, and when his father died in 1457, he succeeded him to become the eighth head of the Hongan-ji branch. He began to work vigorously to propagate the teachings of the sect, but in 1465 the monks of the Enryaku-ji, alarmed at Rennyo's success, attacked and burned his temple and he was obliged to flee to the province of Ōmi. From there he made his way to Yoshizaki in the province of Echizen, where he established a temple known as the Yoshizaki Dōjō and began spreading the doctrine in the Hokuriku area.

Rennyo, taking full advantage of the written word to propagate his teachings, wrote a number of *ofumi*, or pastoral letters, explaining in simple language the principles of Jōdo Shinshū and, utilizing the social and political organization of the farming villages, set up *kō*, religious clubs, to act as links between the temples and the congregation. As a result of his lively missionary activities, the influence of the sect spread all the way to the Ōshū region of far northern Japan. In 1475 he left Yoshizaki and returned to Kyoto, rebuilding the Hongan-ji at Yamashina. There he began working to gather together the different branches of the sect and unite them under Hongan-ji leadership, in time making Jōdo Shinshū the largest sect of Buddhism in Japan. Even after turning over the management of temple affairs to his son Jitsunyo in 1489, he continued to be active in religious concerns, and in 1496 at the age of eighty-one he supervised the founding of the Ishiyama Hongan-ji in Osaka.

Sanjōnishi Sanetaka 三條西實隆 (1455–1537)

Courtier, scholar, and poet of the Muromachi period; he was the second son of the *naidaijin* (minister of the interior) Sanjōnishi Kimiyasu. He lost both parents at an early age but entered government service and held various offices at court, eventually in 1506 advancing to the post of minister of the interior and the rank of senior second rank. He thereafter retired from public service and in 1516 entered the Buddhist clergy, taking the religious name Gyōkū.

He lived at the time of the Ōnin War and the beginning of the period of the warring states, when the country was torn by repeated outbreaks of civil strife. He served under four emperors, Gohanazono, Gotsuchimikado, Gokashiwabara, and Gonara, at a time when the imperial household wielded very little power and was in dire financial straits. As a result, he spent much effort persuading the shogunate and other important parties to contribute funds for the carrying out of court ceremonies.

He was a distinguished poet and was initiated into the *Kokin-denju*, a series of secret interpretations of words and phrases in the *Kokinshū*, by the poet Iio Sōgi. He also received instruction in *renga* (linked verse) from Iio Sōgi and assisted him in compiling the *Shinsen Tsukubashū*, a *renga* anthology. He received instruction in *The Tale of Genji* from Sōgi and Botanka Shōhaku and lectured on the text and compiled a commentary of his own on it. From Ichijō Kanera he received instruction in ancient court rituals and practices. After the death of Ichijō Kanera in 1481, he served as a leading authority in matters pertaining to Japanese poetry, calligraphy, court ritual and practice, and matters pertaining to incense. He associated widely not only with members of the imperial family and the court, but with members of the shogunate and other military leaders as well, helping to preserve and hand on traditional Japanese culture at a time when social disorder threatened its survival. In addition to his scholarly and poetic works, he kept a journal, the *Sanetaka-kō ki*, which provides invaluable information on the history of the period, and made many transcriptions of early works of Japanese literature.

Sesson Yūbai 雪村友梅 (1290–1346)

Zen monk of the period of the Northern and Southern Courts. He was born in the province of Echigo and at an early age began Zen study under I-shan I-ning (Japanese: Issan Ichinei), a Chinese monk who had come to Japan and was residing at the Kenchō-ji in Kamakura. In 1307, at the age of eighteen, he went to China, which was then under the rule of the Yüan, or Mongol, dynasty. Earlier, in 1274 and 1281, the Mongols had dispatched large numbers of troops in two attempts to invade and conquer Japan, but both had ended in failure and, unable to forget their resentment against the Japanese, in 1312 they arrested Sesson and held him in confinement. In 1326 he was at last released and resided in Ch'ang-an for three years. Because of his great learning, he won the respect of the Yüan ruler, Emperor Wen-tsung, who bestowed on him the title Pao-chüeh Chen-k'ung on the occasion of his departure. He returned to Japan in 1329 after a stay of twenty-two years abroad and took up residence in a succession of temples. He was particularly skilled in the writing of Chinese verse and prose and is regarded as one of the founders of the Gozan literary movement. His works are preserved in a collection entitled *Bingashū.*

Shinran 親鸞 (1173–1262)

Buddhist monk and founder of the Jōdo Shin sect in the middle Kamakura period; he also went by the names Han'en, Shakkū, Zenshin, and Gutoku Shinran. He was born in Kyoto, the son of Hino Arinori. He entered the religious life at the age of eight, becoming a disciple of Jien. He spent a number of years at the Jōgyō-zammai-dō on Mt. Hiei devoting himself to religious practices, but left the mountain in 1201 in order to search for the true way to salvation. He became a follower of Hōnen, who taught that practice of the *nembutsu*—ritual invocation of the name of the Buddha Amida—alone was sufficient to assure one of rebirth in the Pure Land (Jōdo) presided over by Amida. In 1204 he was permitted to make a copy of Hōnen's principal work, the *Senchaku hongan nembutsu-shū.*

In 1207 the older sects of Buddhism launched a vigorous movement against Hōnen and his disciples, which resulted in the punishment of a number of them. Hōnen was exiled to the island of Sado and Shinran to the province of Echigo. Shinran was pardoned in 1211, but did not return to Kyoto; instead he went to Hitachi and Kasama in eastern Japan, where he worked to spread his teachings among the farmers. His most important work, the *Kyōgyō shinshō* in six chapters, appears to have been written during his stay in the east. In his late years he returned to Kyoto, but continued to send letters of guidance to his followers in the eastern regions.

His thought is characterized by a deepening and extension of the doctrines of Hōnen and emphasizes absolute reliance upon the saving powers of Amida. He also taught the doctrine of *akunin shōki,* according to which Amida's salvation is intended above all for evil human beings who cannot avoid living lives of sin. He himself violated the traditional prohibition against marriage for the clergy, openly taking a wife, and called himself Gutoku Shinran, the "Stupid Shavepate," who is "neither priest nor layman." In his late years he advocated a life of spontaneous action in which complete reliance is placed upon Amida. He and his wife, Eshin-ni, had several children, among them a son named Zenran and a daughter named Kakushin-ni. Zenran turned away from Shinran's teachings and caused his father great grief in Shinran's old age. Kakushin-ni's grandson Kakunyo founded a temple called Hongan-ji at the site of Shinran's grave in the Ōtani section of Kyoto, which in the following centuries was headed by Shinran's descendants and served as the headquarters of the Jōdo Shin sect.

In addition to the works mentioned, Shinran also wrote *Jōdo monrui jushō*, *Gutoku-shō*, and others. The *Mattō-shō* is a collection of his letters, while the *Jōdo wasan* contains poems giving expression to his teachings. The *Tannishō*, a record of his sayings and actions compiled by his disciple Yuien, conveys a realistic picture of his faith and the spiritual anguish that he suffered at times, while the *Eshin-ni monjo*, a collection of his wife's letters, provides valuable historical material on his life and makes clear the deep love that existed between the two.

Shūhō Myōchō 宗峰妙超 (1282–1337)

Rinzai Zen monk of the late Kamakura period, he is best known by his posthumous title Daitō Kokushi. He was born in the province of Harima. At the age of ten he entered a temple on Mt. Shosha, studying under a monk named Kaishin and receiving instruction in the rules of monastic discipline and the teachings of the Tendai sect. Convinced that the truth could not be attained through such academic study, he determined to take up Zen practice and to that end traveled about visiting various Zen masters in Kyoto and Kamakura.

At the age of twenty-two, he began study under Kōhō Kennichi (1241–1316) at Manju-ji in Kamakura. Kōhō Kennichi was a Dharma heir of the Chinese Zen monk Wu-hsüeh Tsu-yüan and the teacher of Musō Soseki. Kōhō shortly after conferred *inka* upon Shūhō Myōchō, the mark of approval indicating that he was qualified to become a Zen master. But Shūhō felt the need for more rigorous training, and journeyed to Kyoto, where he became a disciple of Nampo Shōmin (1235–1308), better known as Daiō Kokushi.

Nampo had studied in China and become a Dharma heir of the Chinese Zen master Hsü-t'ang Chih-yü (Kidō Chigu), and on his return to Japan had spent a number of years teaching Zen in Kyushu. In 1307, Shūhō accompanied Nampo to Kenchō-ji in Kamakura, where he attained final enlightenment. He received *inka* from Nampo, but was ordered to spend twenty more years in religious practice before attempting to become a teacher. After Nampo's death, he went to Kyoto, where he lived in retirement in a retreat on Higashiyama known as Ungo-an. During this period, he copied out the text of the *Ching-te ch'uan-teng lu*, a work containing biographies of

Chinese Zen monks compiled by Tao-yüan at the beginning of the eleventh century, and engaged in discussions with a monk of Shōun-an, a retreat attached to Ryūshō-ji. He is also said to have mingled with the crowd of beggars living under the Gojō Bridge.

Around 1315, Shūhō gained the support of Akamatsu Enshin, a Zen monk from a distinguished family who later became a statesman and military leader. He moved to a small residence in the Murasakino area of Kyoto, founding what in time became the renowned Zen temple Daitoku-ji. He later won as converts to his teaching Retired Emperor Hanazono and Emperor Godaigo. In 1325 he engaged in a doctrinal debate with representatives of the Tendai sect in the presence of the court and emerged the victor; the affair is known as the Shōchū no Shūron, "Sectarian Debate of the Shōchū Era." In 1326 construction was completed on the main hall of Daitoku-ji, and he became more active than ever in the teaching of Zen. In 1335 he wrote his famous "Testamentary Admonitions," a brief statement designed to guide his disciples after his death, which is today regularly recited in Rinzai Zen temples, and drew up a set of rules, the *Jiki jūjō*, to insure that temple discipline would not become lax. In 1337 he entrusted all his affairs to his disciple Tettō Gikō, and died the same year of illness.

Shūhō's style of Zen teaching placed great emphasis upon the need for the student to delve deep within himself. He was much influenced by the teaching line deriving from the tenth century Chinese Zen master Yün-men (Ummon) and composed a number of excellent *jakugo*, or brief critical comments appended to the koans handed down from the past. (Koans are problems or themes for meditation assigned by the Zen master to his students to help them achieve understanding and a proper attitude.) His writings are collected in the *Daitō kokushi goroku* and *Kana hōgo*. The *Kaian kokugo* consists of passages taken from the *Daitō kokushi goroku* with critical comments added by Hakuin Ekaku. In addition to Tettō Gikō already mentioned, his disciples include Kanzan Egen (1277–1360), famous as the founder of Myōshin-ji, another important Zen temple in Kyoto. The posthumous title Kokushi was bestowed upon him by Retired Emperor Hanazono.

Shunjō 俊芿 (1166–1227)

Buddhist monk of the Ritsu sect in the early Kamakura period; his personal name was Gazen, his literary name Fukaki, and his posthumous title Daikō Shōbō Kokushi. He was born in the province of Higo in Kyushu. In 1180 he began religious study under Shinshun of a temple called Jōraku-ji in Higo, and in 1184 he formally entered the clergy. In 1185 he received the 250 commandments for a monk at Kanzeon-ji in Dazaifu, and thereafter traveled about the country studying the doctrines of the Tendai, Shingon, and Ritsu sects. In 1194 he founded a temple called Shōhō-ji at Tsutsugatake in his native province.

In 1199 he journeyed to China, at this time under the rule of the Sung dynasty. There he studied the doctrines of the Ch'an (Zen), T'ien-t'ai (Tendai), and Vinaya (Ritsu) sects and of Esoteric Buddhism. At the same time he associated widely with Chinese of many different types and acquired a knowledge of contemporary Confucianism, calligraphy, and other subjects. He returned to Japan in 1211, bringing with him a large number of Chinese books. He won over to his religious teachings a member of the powerful Utsunomiya family, Utsunomiya Nobufusa, and through his assistance undertook to restore an ancient temple on Higashiyama in Kyoto known as Sen'yū-ji. The name of the temple had previously been written with characters meaning "Immortal's Outing," but he substituted characters meaning "Spring Bubbling," also read Sen'yū or Sennyū. He made it a center for religious training in a combination of Buddhist teachings drawn from the Zen, Ritsu, Tendai, and Shingon sects, and the sects advocating practice of the *nembutsu*, or invocation of the Buddha Amida. Thereafter the Ritsu sect represented by Sen'yū-ji came to be known as Hokkyō (Northern Capital) Ritsu, to distinguish it from the Nankyō (Southern Capital) Ritsu of Nara, and in time developed a distinctive tradition of its own.

In 1224 he traveled to eastern Japan to spread his teachings. He had a wide knowledge of Buddhism as it was transmitted both in Japan and in China and played a role of particular importance in introducing Sung dynasty thought and learning to Japan. He is said to have been the first person to introduce to Japan the teachings of the Neo-Confucian philosopher Chu Hsi (1130–1200). He wrote the *Sanzen biken* and several other works, and a biography of him by the monk Shinzui exists, entitled *Sen'yū-ji Fukaki hōshi-den*.

Shun'oku Myōha 春屋妙葩 (1311–1388)

Rinzai Zen monk of the early Muromachi period; his posthumous title was Chikaku Fumyō Kokushi, and he employed the literary names Kaishitsu and Fugyōshi. He was born in the province of Kai and was a nephew and leading disciple of Musō Soseki. He possessed great political and administrative ability and, while residing at such Kyoto temples as Tenryū-ji and

Daikōmyō-ji, attracted many followers, including Emperor Gokōgon. But he clashed with the Buddhists of the Tendai sect, who were jealous of the eminence that Zen enjoyed, and in 1371 he and his disciples retired to a temple in Tango Province called Ummon-ji. He had occasion during this period to meet Wu-i K'o-ch'in, Chung-yu Tsu-ch'an, and other Chinese monks who had come to Japan as envoys of the Ming dynasty. The poems and letters that he exchanged with them have been collected in a work entitled *Ummon ikkyoku.*

In 1379 he returned to Kyoto and took up residence in Ungo-an in Tenryū-ji and later moved to Nanzen-ji. He was the first person to hold the post of *sōroku*, or registrar of monks, an office that acted as supervisor of Zen temples of the Rinzai branch. He won the shogun Ashikaga Yoshimitsu over to his teachings and founded Sōkoku-ji, a Zen temple in Kyoto that in time rose to great prominence. He also played an important role in the production of the "Gozan editions," books that were edited and printed by the Zen monks of the time, and helped lay the foundations for the so-called *Gozan bungaku*, the literature in Chinese written by the Zen monks. His disciples included Enkan Bonsō.

TAIRA NO KIYOMORI 平清盛 (1118–1181)

Military leader of the late Heian period. He was the son of Taira no Tadamori, and because of his father's influence at court, became well known at a very early age. In 1156 a struggle broke out between Emperor Goshirakawa and his elder brother, Retired Emperor Sutoku, and the nobles proceeded to take sides with one or the other faction, members of the same family often finding themselves on opposite sides. Taira no Kiyomori joined Minamoto no Yoshitomo in supporting Emperor Goshirakawa, who emerged victorious. This conflict, known as the Hōgen uprising, though it originated with the imperial family and the court nobles, was settled by families of the newly arisen military class such as the Taira and Minamoto and showed just how powerful the men of this class had become. It also served to increase the influence of such men over the court, which by this time had become all but powerless.

In 1159 Minamoto no Yoshitomo tried to wrest power from his rival Kiyomori, holding Emperor Goshirakawa as hostage, but Kiyomori quickly defeated and killed Yoshitomo, putting an end to what is known as the Heiji uprising. From this time on, Kiyomori was unchallenged, and in 1167 he assumed the highest position in the government, that of *dajōdaijin*. He married his daughter Tokuko to Emperor Takakura, and when a son was born from the union, he quickly had him declared ruler in an effort to consolidate the power of the Taira family (Heike). The child ruler, known as Emperor Antoku, died in tragic circumstances a few years later.

From his base in Fukuhara, in the present-day city of Kobe, Kiyomori worked to establish trade with China. In addition, the members of his family controlled over half the territory of the country, so that it was said that if one were not a Taira, he was not fit to be regarded as a human being. When Kiyomori died of fever in 1181, however, the son of Minamoto no Yoshitomo, Yoritomo, determined to avenge his father's death, defied the Taira by declaring himself in revolt, and after four years of fighting he had succeeded in destroying them and founding a military government, the Kamakura shogunate.

Shortly after the downfall of the Taira family, the story of their dramatic rise and fall was made into a romance, the *Heike monogatari* (*The Tale of the Heike*), which is regarded as one of the masterpieces of Japanese literature.

Taira no Tadamori 平忠盛 (1095–1153)

Military leader of the late Heian period. His father was Taira no Masamori, a warrior who held territory in the provinces of Ise and Iga, which he donated to Retired Emperor Shirakawa, the actual wielder of power at the time, becoming one of the retired emperor's attendants. Tadamori likewise served the retired emperor, and after successfully putting down the pirates who infested the Inland Sea, he was admitted to the court nobility.

He was interested in trade with China, and in 1133 appropriated the goods from a Chinese merchant vessel that had landed at the manor of Kanzaki in the province of Hizen in Kyushu. Thus he built up a position of military and economic strength at court, providing a base for his son Kiyomori, who in time made the Taira the most powerful family in the land.

Takeda Shingen 武田信玄 (1521–1573)

Military leader of the late Muromachi period. His given name was Harunobu, Shingen being a religious name. He was the eldest son of Takeda Nobutora, lord of the province of Kai in present-day Yamanashi Prefecture; the Takeda family was descended from the famous Minamoto family of Heian and Kamakura times. In 1536, after undergoing the ceremony marking his admission into manhood and assuming the name Harunobu, he set out on a military campaign against the neighboring province of Shinano. In 1541 he drove his father, who had lost the support of the people of Kai, out of the domain and himself became the nineteenth lord of the Takeda family. In 1555, having seized control of the province of Shinano, he found himself in fierce confrontation with Uesugi Kenshin, the lord of the province of Echigo, which corresponds to present-day Niigata Prefecture, and the series of battles that they fought at a place near the Shinano border called Kawanakajima and that ended in 1561 are famous in history.

In 1568 Shingen occupied the province of Suruga, present-day Shizuoka, extending his power in all directions. In 1572, hoping to make himself master of all Japan, he raised a powerful army and began moving towards Kyoto. He engaged the combined forces of Oda Nobunaga and Tokugawa Ieyasu at Mikatagahara in Tōtōmi, present-day Shizuoka, and defeated them, but the following year he fell ill and died in the field, his aspirations to supreme power unrealized. Shingen was not only the finest military strategist of the so-called Warring States era at the end of the Muromachi period, but also distinguished himself as an administrator, carrying out various engineering projects on the mountains and rivers and working to improve agricultural conditions in the lands under his control. He was also fond of learning and the arts, composing poetry in Chinese and Japanese, and was a devout Buddhist.

Tokiwa Gozen 常盤御前 (d. 1137)

Woman of the early Kamakura period. Her name was Tokiwa; Gozen is a title of respect. She came from a humble background and served as a maid-in-waiting, but was said to have been very beautiful. For this reason Minamoto no Yoshitomo took her as a concubine, and she bore him three children, Imawaka, Otowaka, and Ushiwaka. In 1159 Yoshitomo was killed in the Heiji uprising, and Tokiwa was seized by the Taira forces, but Taira no Kiyomori, struck by her beauty, freed her and is even said to have made her his concubine. Later she became the wife of Fujiwara no Naganari and bore him a son named Yoshinari. Of her three children by Minamoto no Yoshitomo, Ushiwaka grew up to be the famous warrior Minamoto no Yoshitsune.

Uesugi Kenshin 上杉謙信 (1530–1578)

Military leader of the late Muromachi period. He was the son of Nagao Tamekage, who controlled the province of Echigo. In 1547 he succeeded his father as heir of the Nagao family and ruler of Echigo. In 1552 the ruler of the Kantō region, Uesugi Norimasa, hard pressed by the forces of the Hōjō family, came to him for assistance, and the following year the ruler of the province of Shinano, Murakami Yoshiharu, also came to him seeking aid. He then joined Uesugi Norimasa in attacking the Hōjō, and in conjunction with Murakami Yoshiharu engaged in a series of battles with Takeda Shingen in the region of Kawanakajima in Shinano, though these latter engagements did not end in a clear victory for either side. In 1561 he received from Uesugi Norimasa the name of that distinguished family, changing his name from Nagao Kagetora to Uesugi Masatora, and the following year, when Shogun Ashikaga Yoshiteru granted him the use of the element *teru* from his own name, he became Uesugi Terutora. In 1570 he made peace with the Hōjō family, and later became a Buddhist monk with the religious name Kenshin. Hoping to unite the country under a single rule, he set off for the capital with a large body of troops, but he fell ill along the way and died without realizing his ambitions.

Uesugi Norizane 上杉憲實 (1411–1466)

Military leader of the middle Muromachi period. He was appointed *shitsuji*, or steward, to Ashikaga Mochiuji, who controlled the Kantō region, and it was hoped that he would bring about harmony between his lord and the Muromachi shogunate, but in 1429, when Ashikaga Yoshinori became the sixth shogun of the Muromachi shogunate, Mochiuji grew openly defiant. Norizane cautioned him against such behavior, but succeeded only in incurring suspicion, and in 1438 he left Kamakura. Mochiuji sent forces to pursue him, whereupon Shogun Yoshinori took advantage of the opportunity to attack Mochiuji, the whole incident being known as the Eikyō uprising.

The following year Uesugi Norizane founded the Ashikaga Gakkō, the only school of higher learning in the Muromachi period, at the site of the present-day city of Ashikaga in Tochigi Prefecture. He appointed the monk Kaigen to head it, drawing up rules for its operation, building up a library, and instituting courses of instruction. Later he was temporarily put in charge of the Kantō region, but in 1449 he entered the Buddhist priesthood and, in company with his younger brother Dōetsu, also a priest, he traveled about from province to province. He died in Suō, the domain of the Ōuchi family.

WADA YOSHIMORI 和田義盛 (1147–1213)

Military leader of the early Kamakura period. The grandson of the warrior Miura Yoshiaki, he adopted the surname Wada from the village of Wada on the Miura Peninsula, in present-day Kanagawa Prefecture, where he lived. In 1180 Yoshimori joined Minamoto no Yoritomo in launching an attack on the Taira family, and the following year he was appointed head of the Samuraidokoro, the office set up to handle affairs pertaining to the military class. Later he fought by the side of Minamoto no Yoshitsune in the engagements that brought about the final overthrow of the Taira. Yoshimori, a man of simple and straightforward disposition, was very popular among his fellow samurai and held a position of considerable authority in the Kamakura shogunate. In 1203, the second shogun, Minamoto no Yoriie, ordered Yoshimori and his associates to attack Hōjō Tokimasa, but Yoshimori instead went over to the side of Tokimasa and foiled the shogun's scheme. Hōjō Tokimasa in turn, jealous of Yoshimori's power, joined with one of Yoshimori's own kinsmen, Miura Yoshimura, in plotting his ruin. He subjected Yoshimori to insult until in anger the latter called out his troops to attack the Hōjō family, whereupon Miura Yoshimura betrayed him to his enemies and he was killed in battle.

WATARAI IEYUKI 度會家行 (1256–1362)

Shinto priest of the period of the Northern and Southern Courts. The great Shinto shrine of Ise, where the ancestors of the Japanese imperial family are worshiped, is divided into two parts, the Gegū, or Outer Shrine, dedicated to the deity Toyouke no Ōkami, and the Naigū, or Inner Shrine, dedicated to the deity Amaterasu Ōmikami. The Outer Shrine is presided over by priests of the Watarai family, the Inner Shrine by priests of the Arakida family.

Traditionally the Outer Shrine was regarded as inferior in status to the Inner Shrine, but in Kamakura times the members of the Watarai produced a group of works known as the *Shintō gobusho*, or "Five-Part Writings of Shinto," in which they argued that the Outer Shrine was superior to the Inner Shrine. Their views came to be known as Ise or Watarai Shinto.

Watarai Ieyuki, a member of the family and follower of the doctrines of Ise Shinto, worked to provide a theoretical basis for the *Shintō gobusho*, adopting elements from Confucian and Buddhist teachings that he felt to be compatible with Shinto and, in writings of his own such as the *Ruijū jingi hongen*, putting into final form the doctrines of Ise Shinto.

In 1336, when Emperor Godaigo was attacked by Ashikaga Takauji and forced to take refuge in the wilds of Mt. Yoshino, Watarai Ieyuki sided with the emperor and gathered together troops to support his cause. He was a close friend of the scholar Kitabatake Chikafusa and guided the latter to the place where Emperor Godaigo was in hiding. In later years, when Kitabatake Chikafusa came to write his historical work, the *Jinnō shōtōki*, which begins with the famous declaration that "Japan is a divine nation," he drew heavily on the ideas of Watarai Ieyuki to support his interpretations of history.

Wu-an P'u-ning (Gottan Fu'nei) 兀菴普寧 (1197–1276)

Chinese Zen monk of the Southern Sung period, he belonged to the Rinzai branch of Zen; he was known as Tsung-chüeh Ch'an-shih (Shūgaku Zenji). Born in Shu in the area of present-day Szechwan, he at first studied Confucianism, but later turned to Buddhism. He devoted himself to Zen practice and in time became a Dharma heir of Wu-chun Shih-fan. He resided at a temple called Wu-hsi-ssu in Ch'ang-chou. The political situation in China at this time was highly unstable as the Mongols grew in power and threatened the continuance of Sung rule. To avoid the confusion, P'u-ning accepted an invitation from the statesman Hōjō Tokiyori and in 1260 came to Japan. He lived at first at Shōfuku-ji in Hakata in Kyushu, but later, at the urging of Enni Bennen, a Japanese Zen monk whom he had known in China, he moved to Tōfuku-ji in Kyoto. Still later, he moved to Kenchō-ji in Kamakura at the invitation of Hōjō Tokiyori. Tokiyori treated him with great reverence, went to him in person to receive instruction in Zen, and in time gained enlightenment. But after Tokiyori's death in 1263, P'u-ning was left without a patron and soon found himself the victim of rumor. He left Kamakura and, after spending time with Tōgan Ean in Kyoto and Gokū Keinen in Kyushu, he returned to China. In his closing years he lived in Lung-hsiang-ssu in Wen-chou. A *goroku*, or record, of his teachings is extant.

Wu-hsüeh Tsu-yüan (Mugaku Sogen) 無學祖元 (1226–1286)

Chinese Rinzai Zen monk of the middle Kamakura period; his personal name was Tzu-yüan (Shigen) and his posthumous titles were Bukkō Zenji and Emman Jōshō Kokushi. He was born in Ming-chou and in time became a Dharma heir of the Zen master Wu-chun Shin-fan. China at this time was in a state of turmoil as the Mongol forces grew in strength and in 1279 finally overthrew the Southern Sung dynasty, making themselves rulers of China. During this period, Tsu-yüan was studying under Huan-hsi Wei-i (Kankei Iitsu) at Mt. T'ien-t'ung. It is said that he showed no sign of alarm when faced by the invading Mongol soldiers, but on the contrary won their admiration by his fearless attitude. In 1279 at the invitation of the statesman Hōjō Tokimune he went to Japan along with Chung-t'ang Chüeh-yüan (Kyōdō Kakuen) and others, taking up residence in Kenchō-ji in Kamakura. In 1281, when the Mongols launched their second attack on Japan, he strongly influenced Tokimune in the latter's decision to meet them with all possible resistance. In 1282 he founded a temple called Engaku-ji in Kamakura, where he devoted himself to the religious training of the Kamakura samurai. Because of the painstaking manner with which he guided his followers, his style of teaching came to be referred to as *rōba* Zen, "old-woman's Zen." His teaching line came to be known as the Bukkō-ha. His principal disciples were Kōhō Kennichi and Kian Soen. Through the efforts of Kōhō Kennichi's disciple Musō Soseki, the line attained a position of great eminence.

Yamana Sōzen 山名宗全 (1403–1473)

Military leader of the middle Muromachi period. His name was originally Yamana Mochitoyo; later he turned over the leadership of his family to his son and became a monk, taking the religious name Sōzen, though this move was a pure formality and he continued to exercise authority in family affairs. He was a vigorous man with a ruddy complexion and was accordingly nicknamed Aka-nyūdō, Red-faced Monk; he was also known for his savage behavior. In the time of Shogun Ashikaga Takauji (1305–56), the head of the Yamana family held control over eleven provinces in the San'in area of western Honshu along the Japan Sea and was therefore called Rokubun-no-ichi Dono, or Lord of One-sixth of the Country, there being sixty-six provinces in Japan at that time. By Sōzen's time, however, the number of provinces under Yamana control had dwindled to three. When the *shugo* (constable) Akamatsu Mitsusuke revolted and assassinated Shogun Ashikaga Yoshinori in 1441, Sōzen attacked and wiped out the assassin, and as a reward was given control of five more provinces, bringing the number in his domain to eight. At the time of the Ōnin War, which began in 1467, he heeded the wishes of Hino Tomiko, the wife of Shogun Ashikaga Yoshimasa, by becoming commander of the forces drawn up on the west side of the capital, engaging in a protracted struggle with Hosokawa Katsumoto, the commander of the forces occupying the east side, but he died in the third month of 1473, long before the war was brought to a conclusion.

Yoshida Kanetomo 吉田兼俱 (1435–1511)

Shinto leader of the Muromachi period. The Yoshida family originally bore the name Urabe and served the court as diviners and advisors on the *on'yō*, or yin-yang, system of thought. Their position at court was rather low, but after they became priests of the Yoshida Shrine in Kyoto, which was dedicated to the patron deity of the Fujiwara family, their status improved, and by Kanetomo's time they occupied a place of considerable importance at court.

With the decline in the power of the court nobility that had taken place at this period, however, it was no easy matter to provide for the operation and upkeep of a religious establishment such as the Yoshida Shrine, and Kanetomo accordingly took steps to improve the shrine's position. Shinto beliefs at this time were closely interwoven with those of Buddhism, while the Shinto pantheon, with its *yaoyorozu no kami*, "myriads of gods," lacked any form or hierarchical organization. Kanetomo set out to create a new type of Shinto, known as Yuitsu (Unitarian) Shinto, in which the earlier Shinto and Buddhist beliefs were combined with elements borrowed from the Yin-yang and Five Elements cosmological systems of ancient Chinese philosophy, and stress was placed upon the unity rather than the diversity of the pantheon. Kanetomo's ambition was to gather all of the gods of Japan into a single shrine on the top of Mt. Yoshida, but when he announced in 1489 that the deity of the Ise Shrine, one of the most sacred in all Japan, had transferred its presence to the Yoshida Shrine, he was vigorously attacked by the priests of the Ise Shrine, and his efforts ended in failure. He did succeed, however, in winning recognition of the right of the Yoshida Shrine to assign ranks to the deities of the various local shrines.

Kanetomo was a thinker as well as a religious leader and wrote several works on Shinto beliefs and practices, attempting to organize the religion on a nationwide scale. The school of Shinto that he founded is also called Yoshida Shinto in recognition of Kanetomo's role in its creation.

Zekkai Chūshin 絕海中津 (1336–1405)

Rinzai Zen monk of the early Muromachi period, he was a distinguished writer of poetry and prose in Chinese and a leading figure in *Gozan bungaku.* His posthumous title was Butchi Kōshō Kokushi, his literary name Shōken Dōjin, and he was also referred to as Kai Oshō and Kai-ō Daizenji. He was born in Tosa in Shikoku, a son of the prominent Tsuno family of that province. In 1348 he went to Kyoto and entered Tenryū-ji, a Zen temple headed at that time by Musō Soseki. In 1350 he shaved his head and entered the priesthood; he was given the name Chūshin and studied Zen under Shun'oku Myōha, a leading disciple of Musō Soseki. After the death of Musō Soseki in 1351, he joined Gidō Shūshin and other monks who had been studying at Tenryū-ji in moving to another Zen temple in Kyoto, Kennin-ji, where he studied under Ryūzan Tokken. In 1364 he went to Kamakura and studied under Seizan Jiei and Daiki Hōkin of Kenchō-ji.

In 1368 he voyaged to Ming China in company with Nyoshin Ryōsa and Nyoshin Chūjo, where he became a disciple of Chi-t'an Tsung-le, also known as Ch'üan-shih Ch'an-shih, of the temple called Chung-chu-ssu in Hangchow. While pursuing his Zen training, he also studied the writing of poetry in Chinese and took lessons in calligraphy from Chu-an Ch'an-shih. He also traveled about to other Zen training centers such as Ling-yin-ssu and Tao-ch'ang-shan to meet eminent Zen masters. In 1376, he was summoned to an audience by Emperor T'ai-tsu, the founder of the Ming dynasty. In response to the imperial command, he composed a four-line poem in Chinese dealing with the shrine in Kumano dedicated to Hsü Fu, a Chinese who according to legend journeyed to Japan in ancient times. The emperor was so impressed that he composed a poem in response.

Zekkai returned to Japan the same year and took up residence in Ungo-an in Kyoto, but was invited by Shōkai Reiken to take the position of *shuso,* chief of trainees, in Tenryū-ji. In 1380 he moved to Erin-ji in the province of Kai. In 1383 he returned to Tenryū-ji, but incurred the anger of the shogun Ashikaga Yoshimitsu and in 1384 retired to a place called Zenihara in Settsu. At the invitation of the statesman Hosokawa Yoriyuki, he founded a temple called Hōkan-ji in the province of Awa in Shikoku. Later, when the misunderstanding between him and the shogun was dispelled, he returned to Kyoto, residing at Tōji-ji and Sōkoku-ji.

Like Gidō Shūshin, who was born in the same province as Zekkai and belonged to the same Zen teaching line, he was an outstanding figure in *Gozan bungaku*, the "Literature of the Five Mountains," the works of poetry and prose written in Chinese by monks of the prominent Zen temples of Kyoto and Kamakura, living at a time when that literature was at the peak of its development. But while Gidō was of a scholarly nature, Zekkai possessed the emotional and otherwordly temperament of a poet. Japanese Zen literature in the past had been under the influence of the Chinese Zen literature of the Sung and Yüan dynasties, but Zekkai introduced elements adopted from the Zen literature of the newly founded Ming, particularly that of the Taie school. He was especially skilled in composing parallel prose and long poems using a five-character line. He had a command of Chinese that far surpassed that of most of his countrymen, and his works were highly admired in China as well as in Japan. His poems and prose writings in Chinese have been collected in a work entitled *Shōkenkō.*

EARLY MODERN PERIOD

Abe Masahiro

Akechi Mitsuhide

Aoki Kon'yō

Asano Naganori

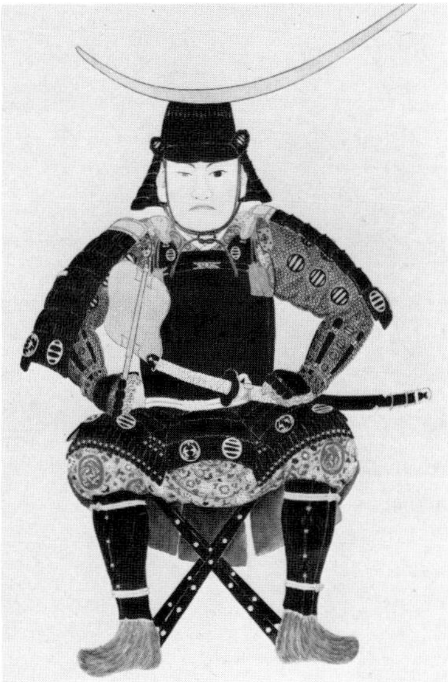
Date Masamune

Egawa Tarozaemon

Hakuin Ekaku

Fujita Tōko

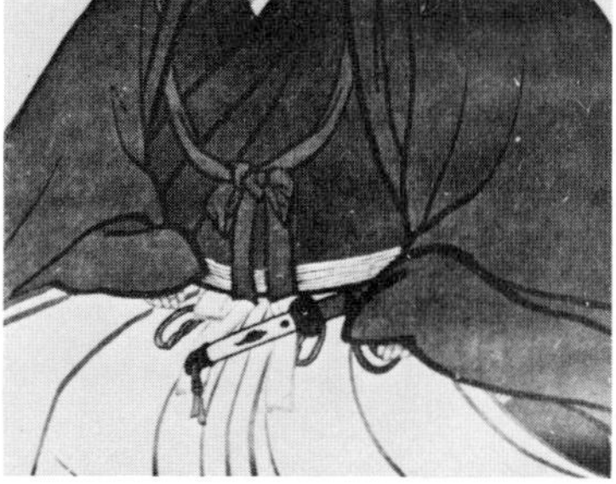
Hanaoka Seishū

Gomizuno-o Tennō

Hanawa Hokiichi

Hayashi Shihei

Hasekura Tsunenaga

Hiraga Gennai

Hirata Atsutane

Honda Masanobu

Ii Naosuke

Ishida Baigan

Ishida Mitsunari

Jiun Onkō

Kaibara Ekiken

Katō Kiyomasa

Kumazawa Banzan

Maeno Ryōtaku

Matsudaira Sadanobu

Matsuura Shigenobu

Mōri Terumoto

Mizuno Tadakuni

Nakae Tōju

Mogami Tokunai

Ninomiya Sontoku

Oda Nobunaga

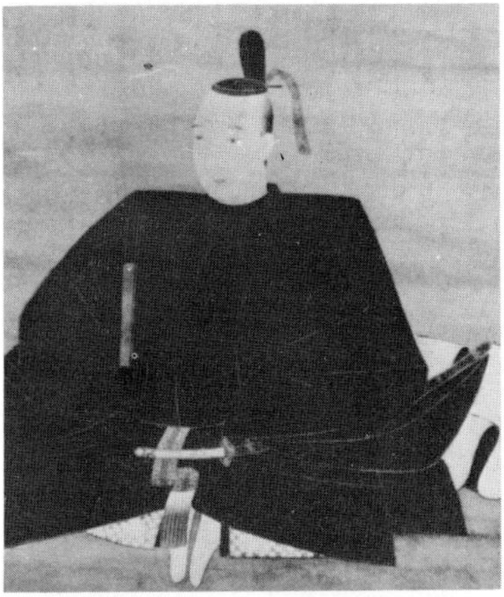

Oda Nobutada

Ogata Kōan

Ōgo (Mokujiki Shōnin)

Ōishi Yoshio

Ōshio Heihachirō

Sakamoto Ryōma

Sakuma Shōzan

Satō Nobuhiro

Sūden

Sugita Gempaku

Suminokura Ryōi

Takadaya Kahei

Takano Chōei

Takashima Shūhan

Takuan

Tenkai

Tokugawa Iemitsu

Tanuma Okitsugu

Tokugawa Ieyasu

Tokugawa Yoshinobu

Toyotomi Hideyori

Toyotomi Hideyoshi

Watanabe Kazan

Yamada Nagamasa

Yamaga Sokō

Yamazaki Ansai

Yanagisawa Yoshiyasu

Yin-yüan

Yoshida Shōin

Early Modern Period

ABE MASAHIRO 阿部正弘 (1819–1857)

Rōjū (councilor of state) of the Tokugawa shogunate in the late Edo period. He was the son of Abe Masakiyo, lord of the domain of Fukuyama in the province of Bingo. His childhood name was Gōzō, but he was later known as Kazue; his literary name was Yūken. In 1836 he succeeded his elder brother Masayasu as lord of the domain, which received a revenue of 100,000 *koku* of rice a year, and was given the honorary title of Ise-no-kami. In 1840 he became *jisha-bugyō*, official in charge of temples and shrines for the shogunate. During his term in office, he succeeded in disciplining Nikkei, a priest of the Chisen-in, a subtemple of Hokekyō-ji at Nakayama in Shimōsa. Nikkei as a man of religion had enjoyed special confidence with the women of the shogun's private quarters and had taken advantage of this fact to secure improper advantages. Masahiro won widespread renown by having him banished to a distant island, a daring move, since Nikkei's close connections with the women of the shogun's household had previously protected him from disciplinary measures.

In 1843, at the age of twenty-four, Masahiro became a *rōjū*, or councilor of state. When Perry arrived in Japan in 1853 and demanded the opening of the country to trade relations, he consulted with the various daimyo and decided to open the country. The following year, he concluded a friendship treaty with the United States and opened the two ports of Shimoda and Hakodate; this was followed by similar treaties with Russia, England, and Holland. At Masahiro's insistence, however, trade was not at this time permitted at the ports that had been opened. He worked to stabilize the position of the shogunate by emphasizing a policy of cooperation with the daimyo and the imperial court. In 1855 he recommended Hotta Masayoshi to the position of *rōjū* and stepped down himself. In addition to the foregoing, his achievements include the removal of the ban on the construction of large ships; the establishment of a shogunate naval force; the setting up, under the stimulus afforded by a knowledge of Western armed forces, of the Kōbujō, a forerunner of the military academy known as the Kōbusho; and the spread of a knowledge of Western culture through the creation of the Yōgakusho, the forerunner of the Bansho Shirabesho, a shogunate center for Western studies. Such able and progressive officers of the shogunate as Kawaji Toshiakira, Tsutsui Masanori, Iwase Tadanari, Nagai Naomune, and Egawa Hidetatsu were all promoted to office by him. He died in the seventh month of 1857 at the age of thirty-eight.

Adams, William (Miura Anjin) 三浦按針 (1564–1620)

The captain of a Dutch ship named the *Liefde*, which was stranded on the shore of Bungo in Kyushu in 1600; he is the first Englishman known to have visited Japan. He was born in Gillingham in Kent. In 1598, when a group of Dutch merchants in Rotterdam dispatched a fleet of trading ships to the Far East, he joined the expedition as a pilot. The ships passed through the Straits of Magellan and had reached the Moluccan Islands when they were blown off their course by a typhoon and arrived in Japan in the third month of 1600. The party consisted of Adams and twenty-one other seamen.

Adams, along with one of the seamen named Jan Joosten, were given an audience by Tokugawa Ieyasu. Adams gained the confidence of Ieyasu and was presented with a small piece of territory at the village of Hemi in the district of Miura in Sagami, with an annual stipend of 250 *koku* of rice. For this reason, he took the surname Miura, to which the people of the time added the name Anjin, the Japanese word for "pilot." He was also given a house in the Nihonbashi section of Edo, and the area where it was situated as a consequence came to be called Anjin-chō. He acted as advisor to Ieyasu, handling matters pertaining to foreign trade, and on Ieyasu's orders also undertook to build several Western style sailing ships. He did his best to promote relations between England and Japan, and when John Saris arrived at the head of a fleet of English ships in the fifth month of 1613, he helped arrange for the opening of an English trading office at Hirado in the tenth month of 1613.

But Ieyasu died in 1616, and the second shogun Hidetada pursued quite different policies from those of his predecessor. As a result, the trading rights of the English were gradually reduced, and Adams found his services less in demand than previously. He lived out his last years in rather straitened circumstances and died at Hirado on the sixteenth day of the fifth month

(April 24) of 1620. He was around the age of fifty-six. Three years after his death, the English trading office at Hirado was shut down, and the English withdrew from Japan.

Akechi Mitsuhide 明智光秀 (1528–1582)

Military leader who was active in the struggles for power during the sixteenth century; his common name was Jūbei. The facts concerning his early career are uncertain, but he is known to have entered the service of the military leader Oda Nobunaga and to have been entrusted with important duties. In 1568, when Nobunaga and his forces entered Kyoto, he and Murai Sadakatsu were charged with maintaining order among the populace. In 1575 Nobunaga bestowed on him the surname Koretō, and he came to be known as Koretō Hyūga-no-kami. The following year, he joined Araki Murashige in attacking Ishiyama Castle in Settsu, a stronghold of the followers of the Pure Land sect of Buddhism in what is now the city of Osaka. In 1577, he and Takikawa Kazumasu attacked another defiant group of Pure Land believers at Saiga in the province of Kii. Later, he was ordered by Nobunaga to besiege Hatano Hideharu at his castle in Yakami in Tamba. In order to bring about a peaceful settlement, he handed over his own mother as a hostage to Hideharu, meanwhile persuading Hideharu to submit and allow himself to be taken to Nobunaga's castle in Azuchi. Nobunaga thereupon had Hideharu put to death, and Hideharu's vassals retaliated by putting Mitsuhide's mother to death, a move that was said to have caused Mitsuhide to hate Nobunaga. In 1582, Tokugawa Ieyasu, another powerful military leader, was visiting Nobunaga at his castle in Azuchi, and Mitsuhide was ordered to take charge of his entertainment. Meanwhile, another of Nobunaga's subordinates, Toyotomi Hideyoshi, who was besieging the castle of Takamatsu in Bitchū, asked Nobunaga for reinforcements. Nobunaga ordered Mitsuhide to dispense with the entertaining of Tokugawa Ieyasu and to go to the assistance of Hideyoshi. Instead of doing so, however, Mitsuhide turned against Nobunaga and, in the summer of the same year, attacked him at his headquarters in the Honnō-ji temple in Kyoto, forcing him to commit suicide. He in turn was attacked and defeated by Hideyoshi at Ōyama Castle in Yamazaki southwest of Kyoto. He fled in the direction of his stronghold in Sakamoto in Ōmi, but was mobbed and killed by villagers at Okurisu on the way.

Amakusa Tokisada 天草時貞 (d. 1638)

Leader of the Shimabara Revolt. His father, Masuda Jimbei Yoshitsugu, had been a retainer of the Christian daimyo Konishi Yukinaga, and after the defeat of Yukinaga at the battle of Sekigahara, had taken up residence in Amakusa in the province of Higo, present-day Kumamoto Prefecture. As a child Tokisada was so talented and beautiful that he was nicknamed Tendō, "Angel." The lord of the region of Amakusa at this time, Terazawa Katataka, was relentless in his enforcement of the official ban on Christianity, at the same time exacting extremely heavy taxes from the peasants under him, and as a result there was widespread discontent among his subjects. The former retainers of Konishi Yukinaga, who were Christians, proclaiming that Tokisada was capable of performing a miracle, in 1637 chose him as their leader and started a revolt of the peasants and Christians in the area of Amakusa and Shimabara, taking up a position in the castle of Hara, which had formerly belonged to the Arima family. At first they successfully held off the attacks of the government forces, but in the second month of 1638, their food supplies having been exhausted, they were finally forced to surrender. Tokisada, already wounded, was beheaded by a retainer of the Hosokawa family and his head taken to Dejima in Nagasaki for exposure. He was said to have been only sixteen at the time of his death.

Andō Nobumasa 安藤信正 (1819–1871)

Lord of the castle of Taira in the province of Iwaki and a *rōjū* (councilor of state) in the closing years of the Edo period. He was the eldest son of Andō Nobuyoshi; in childhood he went by the names Kinnoshin and Kinnosuke, but after his coming-of-age assumed the name Nobuyuki and later Nobumasa. In 1847 he succeeded his father as lord of the castle of Taira. He was given the honorary title of Tsushima-no-kami, by which he was commonly known. In 1853 he was appointed to the post of *jisha-bugyō* (official in charge of religious affairs for the shogunate). He advanced in office until in 1860 he became a *rōjū* (councilor of state) to the shogun, being assigned to handle foreign affairs. When the *tairō* (senior councilor of state) Ii Naosuke was assassinated in the fourth month of the same year, he became the leading councilor of state. He was faced with various problems regarding foreign affairs, among them the conclusion of a commercial treaty with Prussia, the assassination of Henry C.J. Heusken, the interpreter of the American legation, and the appearance of a Russian warship at Tsushima Island.

He was a supporter of the *kōbu-gattai* policy, which sought to strengthen relations between the imperial court and the shogunate. To further this aim, he arranged for Kazunomiya, the younger sister of Emperor Kōmei, to become the wife of the shogun Tokugawa Iemochi. But this last action aroused the enmity of the forces who were working for restoration of power to the emperor. In 1862 he was attacked and wounded by members of this group outside the Sakashita Gate. As a result, he resigned from the position of councilor of state. But he was accused of irregular conduct in arranging for an heir to succeed Ii Naosuke and was deprived of lands amounting to a revenue of 20,000 *koku* of rice. In 1868, when fighting broke out between the forces of the emperor and those loyal to the shogunate, he joined other domains of northern Honshu in resisting the imperial forces. When the hostilities had ended, the imperial government ordered him to be placed under house confinement for the rest of his life. He was pardoned the following year, but died in 1871 at the age of fifty-two.

Andō Shōeki 安藤昌益 (eighteenth century)

A physician and critic of feudalism and the conventional systems of morality, he was active during the middle of the Edo period, though the exact dates of his lifetime are impossible to determine. His name was Yoshinaka, and he also went by the literary name Kakuryūdō. Very little is known about his life, and it was not until 1899, when his works were discovered and introduced to the world by Dr. Kanō Kōkichi, that he first began to attract attention for the originality of his thought. It would appear that he was the second son of a samurai named Nakamura, a retainer of the fief of Okudono in the province of Mikawa. He was adopted into the Toda family, who were physicians in the fief of Hachinohe in Mutsu, present-day Aomori Prefecture. It is possible that the adoption was later cancelled, though the evidence is unclear; it is certain, however, that around 1744–45 he made his living as a townsman doctor in Hachinohe.

From his writings, it would appear that during the Hōreki era (1751–63) he lived in "the city of Akita Castle," as Akita was called at that time, in the province of Dewa, present-day Akita Prefecture. His disciples included Kamiyama Sen'an, a physician of Hachinohe, and other samurai of the same fief, as well as Akashi Ryūei of Kyoto and Shizu Teichū of Osaka. He wrote a work in 101 chapters entitled the *Jizen shin'eidō*, of which 15 chapters in manuscript form are extant; and two other works, *Jizen shin'eidō* in three chapters and *Tōdō shinden* in four chapters, exist in printed form.

In his thought, *shizen* (nature) is treated as an interrelated process in which all creatures participate as they pursue their various activities. He describes this process by the term *gosei kasshin*, the "living truth of reciprocal individuality," and because this process itself constitutes the working of nature, he labels it *shizen shin'eidō*, or the "way of natural truth." Nature, in his view, transcends all conceptual and moral categories. For this reason, he called for the rejection of the moral teachings of both Confucianism and Buddhism, with their emphasis upon goodness alone and their recognition and support of social differences. He likewise attacked the Tokugawa feudal system, which sought justification for its existence in the ideals of Confucianism and Buddhism, rejecting it with a finality that is unmatched among the various thinkers of the Edo period. He asserted that the ideal of human life should be "productivity," by which he meant agriculture, denying the right of any group in society to exist without producing its own food. He advocated a complete egalitarianism that refused to recognize any social, economic, or political distinctions, and called for strict monogamy and equal rights for women. In spite of his thoroughly egalitarian approach, however, he failed to envision any kind of cooperative spirit that might serve to integrate society, which has been cited as the principal flaw in his system as a social thinker.

Aoki Kon'yō 青木昆陽 (1698–1769)

Scholar of Confucianism and Dutch learning in the middle Edo period. His father, Tsukudaya Han'uemon, was according to some accounts a merchant of the province of Ōmi, according to others a fish seller of Nihonbashi in Edo. Kon'yō studied under the Confucian scholar Itō Tōgai in Kyoto and became an expert in economic affairs. He was treated with favor by the magistrate Ōoka Tadasuke, and through the latter's introduction gained employment in the Tokugawa shogunate. He was assigned to a series of posts connected with the supervision of official archives, and in 1767 was promoted to the post of director of the Momijiyama Bunko, the shogunate library. At the same time he traveled about the country collecting rare old documents that he found in the possession of temples and shrines. At the order of the eighth shogun, Tokugawa Yoshimune, he joined Noro Genjō in applying himself to Dutch learning, at first studying under the head of the Dutch trading office, who resided in Edo, and later gaining permission to travel to Nagasaki to continue his studies there. He is regarded as the founder of the orthodox school of Dutch learning in the Edo period. Among his works are *Oranda moji ryakkō* ("Notes on Dutch Letters"), *Oranda kaheikō* ("Notes on Dutch Currency"), etc. In addition, he became interested in the cultivation of the sweet potato as a means of relieving famine. He wrote a work called *Banshokō* on the subject, which he presented to Shogun Yoshimune in 1735, and as a result the sweet potato came to be widely cultivated, winning for Kon'yō the name Kansho-sensei, "Sweet Potato Scholar."

ARAI HAKUSEKI 新井白石 (1657–1725)

Scholar and statesman of the middle Edo period who played a leading role in the shogunate as adviser to the sixth shogun Tokugawa Ienobu. His personal name was Kimiyoshi, his common name Kageyu, and his literary name Hakuseki. His father, Arai Masanari, was a samurai in the service of Tsuchiya Toshisada, lord of the domain of Kururi in Kazusa, and Hakuseki was born in the domain residence in Edo. When Hakuseki was twenty, his father was dismissed from the service of the Tsuchiya family, and Hakuseki as a result was obliged to live in very straitened circumstances. He devoted himself to intensive study, however, determined to gain some kind of official employment. To this end, he turned down a proposal of a marriage alliance with the family of Kawamura Zuiken, a wealthy merchant of Osaka.

In 1683, at the age of twenty-five, Hakuseki entered the service of Hotta Masatoshi, the *tairō* (chief state councilor) of the shogunate. With the downfall of the Hotta family in 1685, he was once more reduced to hardship. He was offered a stipend in 1691, but felt obliged by circumstances to reject it. During this period, when he was around the age of thirty, he became a disciple of Kinoshita Jun'an, a teacher of the Chu Hsi school of Neo-Confucianism, and was counted among the latter's most outstanding students. In 1693, on the recommendation of his teacher, he became a lecturer on Confucianism to Tokugawa Ienobu, lord of Kōfu, and soon came to be highly trusted. In 1709, Ienobu was chosen to succeed Tokugawa Tsunayoshi as the sixth shogun, and Hakuseki accordingly became an official in the shogunate. He ranked in importance with the chamberlain of the shogun Manabe Akifusa and was in a position to advise the shogun in person on questions of state, making Hakuseki a figure of great influence in the shogunate. In 1711 he was given the honorary position of governor of the province of Chikugo and the following year was assigned a stipend of 1,000 *koku*, honors that were all but unprecedented for a man of scholarly background in the Edo period.

Tokugawa Ienobu died in 1712, but his successor to the shogunate,

Ietsugu, was still a child, and Hakuseki therefore continued to play a key role as adviser on matters of state. Upon Ietsugu's death in 1716, however, when Tokugawa Yoshimune, lord of the domain of Kii, became shogun, Hakuseki found his advice no longer wanted and he retired from government service, devoting his remaining years to writing and research. He died in 1725.

As a statesman, Hakuseki sought to realize the Confucian ideal of benevolent government, carrying out reforms in matters of ritual and administration and emphasizing the arts of peace. As adviser to the shogun Ienobu, he brought about the abolishment of the excessively severe laws against cruelty to dogs and other living creatures that had been promulgated by Ienobu's predecessor, Tokugawa Tsunayoshi, and pardoned some eight thousand persons who had been condemned to punishment under them. He also took steps to insure justice in legal affairs, had the *Buke shohatto*, the basic legal code for members of the samurai class, rewritten in more easily comprehensible language, and changed rituals and ceremonies to make them conform to those in use at the imperial court in Kyoto. He carried out currency reforms, substituting sound currency for the badly debased currency that had been issued in Tokugawa Tsunayoshi's time. He also imposed restrictions on the foreign trade carried out at Nagasaki in order to stop the drain of gold, silver, and copper. In 1711, when supervising the reception of envoys from Korea, he decided that the shogun should be referred to in Chinese by the title *ō*, or "king," a step that aroused considerable controversy among scholars, since it seemed to infringe upon the nominal authority of the emperor. Underlying all his measures was the Confucian ideal of government as an instrument of moral instruction and leadership, and it is appropriate that his period in power should have been known as *shōtoku no chi*, or "the rule of upright virtue."

As a scholar, Hakuseki placed particular emphasis upon rationalism and careful documentation, attempting to find ways to translate the ideals of Chu Hsi Confucianism into actual practice. His works include *Koshitsū*, a study of the so-called Divine Age of Japanese history in terms of rationalistic humanism; *Seiyō kibun* and *Sairan igen*, works on Western geography, which are based on information gathered in his interviews with the Italian missionary Sidotti, who was arrested in 1708 for illegally entering the country; *Hankampu*, a historical gazetteer of the feudal domains; and *Dokushi yoron*, a collection of historical essays. He is also well known for his diary, the *Arai Hakuseki nikki*, and his excellent autobiography, *Oritaku shibanoki*.

Arima Harunobu 有馬晴信 (1567–1612)

Momoyama and early Edo period Christian daimyo; he was born in the castle of Arima in Hizen in Kyushu, the second son of the lord of the domain, Arima Yoshinao. He became the adopted son of his elder brother Yoshizumi, and in 1572, at the age of four, succeeded to the domain. At the time of Toyotomi Hideyoshi's campaign against Kyushu, he was guaranteed the safety of his domains by Hideyoshi and took up residence in the castle of Hinoe. He also took part in Hideyoshi's two campaigns against Korea and distinguished himself in battle. At the time of the crucial battle of Sekigahara in 1600, he at first sided with the forces loyal to Hideyoshi's heir but immediately went over to the opposite side, that headed by Tokugawa Ieyasu, attacking the domain of Konishi Yukinaga. In 1608, an officially licensed trading ship that he had dispatched to the kingdom of Champa in Vietnam was attacked by the Portuguese while stopping en route in Macao. The following year, when the Portuguese vessel *Madre de Deus* came to Nagasaki from Macao, Arima attacked it by way of retaliation. In 1612, he was unjustly accused of trying to enlarge his domain. He was deprived of his lands and exiled to the province of Kai. In the sixth month of the same year, he committed suicide there. This incident led to the order issued in 1612 outlawing Christianity in territory under direct control of the shogunate.

Arima was a Christian, having been baptized in 1579 by the Jesuit Visitor Alessandro Valignano. At first he took the name João, but later changed it to Protasio. He presided over the founding of a seminary and a training center for novices in the domain of Arima and in 1582 joined the Kyushu Christian daimyos Ōmura Sumitada and Ōtomo Yoshishige in dispatching a mission to the Pope in Rome. When Toyotomi Hideyoshi in 1587 ordered all Catholic Fathers to leave Japan and outlawed the teaching of Christianity, many missionaries and believers took refuge in the domain of Arima, where they were given protection. The Christian seminaries, in addition to giving ordinary instruction, also taught Western style music, painting and sculpture, and the manufacture of organs and other musical instruments as well as watches, thus playing an important part in the introduction of Western style art and technology to Japan.

Asada Gōryū 麻田剛立 (1734–1799)

An astronomer of the mid-Edo period. His true surname was Ayabe, and by profession he was a Confucian physician. His common name was Yasuaki, and his literary names Seian and Shōan. The second son of Ayabe Kensai, he studied astronomy and the calendar from early childhood, at the same time acquiring a knowledge of medicine. Around 1770 tried to resign his post as domain physician but was refused, so he left the domain and went to Osaka. Changing his name to Asada Gōryū, he set up as a practicing physician and at the same time continued his studies of astronomy and the calendar, making telescopes and reflectors with which he carried out observations. He also read Dutch works and made studies of the Western calendar and acquired so many pupils that in time they came to form an "Asada school." In 1795, the Tokugawa shogunate commanded him to study the reform of the calendar, but he declined, recommending instead three outstanding pupils—Takahashi Yoshitoki, Hazama Shigetomi, and Adachi Nobuaki. He similarly rejected invitations from the heads of other domains, out of deference to the head of the Kitsuki domain, which he had left.

Asano Naganori 浅野長矩 (1667–1701)

Lord of the domain of Akō in the province of Harima, he was the son of Asano Nagatomo; his childhood name was Mataichirō. In 1675 he became lord of the domain with a revenue of 53,500 *koku.* In the fourth month of 1701, he and Date Muneharu were ordered by the shogunate to supervise the reception of an imperial messenger. He requested Kira Yoshinaka, who was in charge of protocol involving the shogunate and court, to instruct him in the necessary etiquette. Insulted by the manner in which Kira treated him, however, Naganori drew his sword and severely wounded Kira. Kira, who was proud of his family and station, was said to have tended toward arrogance and to have been particularly unpopular among the lesser daimyo. Since the incident took place within Edo Castle and violated the strict shogunate ban on the drawing of swords within the castle, Naganori was ordered to commit *seppuku* the same day and his lands were confiscated. Ōishi Yoshio, chief retainer of the Asano family, and others of the domain asked the shogun to allow Naganori's younger brother Nagahiro to inherit the Asano estate, but permission was refused. At the end of the following year, Ōishi and his followers avenged the death of their lord by attacking and killing Kira in his residence in Edo. This is the famous revenge of the so-called Forty-Seven Rōnin, celebrated in kabuki, puppet drama, and popular literature of the Edo period and still one of the best-known incidents in Japanese history.

Bankei Eitaku 盤珪永琢 (1622–1693)

Rinzai Zen monk of the Edo period; his posthumous names are Butchi Kōsai Zenji and Tahiō Shōgen Kokushi. He was born in the province of Harima. Around the age of eleven he began the study of the Confucian text known as the *Great Learning* but was troubled by doubts concerning the meaning of the key term *ming-te*, "illustrious virtue." The quest for understanding eventually led him to the religious life. In 1638 he entered the priesthood under the guidance of Umpo Zenshō of a local temple called Zuiō-ji. He thereafter traveled about the country in pursuit of religious training. He returned to his home in 1645, where he indulged in such severe religious practices that he became ill. In 1647 he finally attained enlightenment and at the same time recovered his health. He once more traveled about devoting himself to religious training and in 1657 became the Dharma heir of Bokuō Sogyū, a disciple of Umpo Zenshō in the Shōtaku teaching line of Rinzai Zen. He thereafter devoted himself to activities in various areas, founding a temple called Ryūmon-ji in his native province, one called Nyohō-ji in Iyo in Shikoku, and one called Kōrin-ji in Edo, as well as restoring Jizō-dō in Yamashiro Province. In 1672 he for a time became head of Myōshin-ji in Kyoto, the main temple of the Rinzai line to which he belonged.

Bankei's teaching is referred to as *Fushō-zen*, or "Uncreated Zen," because it rejects all human artifice and seeks to attain a state of absolute freedom by returning to the Buddha nature inherent within all persons. He was particularly critical of the type of Zen teaching that employs difficult koans in Chinese. He himself used simple, everyday language in his teaching and attempted to spread an understanding of Zen among the common people. This aspect of his teachings influenced Tejima Toan, a disciple of Ishida Baigan and proponent of the religious doctrines known as Shingaku. Bankei left no writings, but a *goroku*, or record, of his teachings was compiled by his disciples.

Chaya Shirōjirō 茶屋四郎次郎

Wealthy merchants of the Momoyama and early Edo periods. The founder of the Chaya family, Kiyonobu (1545–96), was the son of a Kyoto clothing merchant and commonly went by the name Shirōjirō, which became hereditary in the family. At an early date he entered the service of the Tokugawa family, at that time lords of the domain of Mikawa, and in 1582, when Oda Nobunaga was murdered at the Honnō-ji in Kyoto, he managed by a clever strategy to save his master, Tokugawa Ieyasu, at the time in Sakai, from danger in the ensuing political confusion. Thereafter, while operating a clothing store in Kyoto, he continued his close association with the Tokugawas, laying the foundation for the future prosperity and eminence of the Chaya family.

The second head of the family, Kiyotada (d. 1603), the son of Kiyonobu, took over the management of the family business on his father's death, acting as official supplier of clothing and personal effects for Tokugawa Ieyasu. In 1612 he received from the government the *shuin* (vermilion seal) allowing him to engage in foreign trade, dispatching ships to Cochin China and conducting a lively and lucrative commerce in Japanese and foreign goods.

Munekiyo (d. 1622), a younger son of Kiyonobu and third head of the family, at first became the adopted son of the chief administrator of the city of Nagasaki, Hasegawa Fujihiro, but because of the early death of his elder brother Kiyotada in 1603, he took over the leadership of the Chaya family. Enjoying the favor and confidence of Ieyasu, he joined with Hasegawa Fujihiro in carrying on foreign trade and implementing the government's prohibitions against Christianity. In 1604 he received from the Tokugawa shogunate official permission to import and distribute raw silk from China. Thus, until the closing of the country in 1635, the Chaya family was able to reap vast profits as officially licensed traders and importers of raw silk. After the closing of the ports, they made a living as clothiers, with their main office in Kyoto and a branch office in Nagoya to serve the lord of Owari, and another branch in Wakayama to serve the lord of Kishū, both domains being in the possession of members of the Tokugawa family.

CHENG CH'ENG-KUNG 鄭成功 (1624–1662)

Chinese military leader and Ming loyalist. His name in Japanese pronunciation is Tei Seikō, and he is popularly known by the appellation Kokusenya, which has passed into European languages as Coxinga. He was born at Hirado in the province of Hizen, his mother a Japanese of the Tagawa family, his father a Chinese named Cheng Chih-lung, who came to Japan at the age of seventeen and eventually took over leadership of the Chinese residents there. In 1644 Chih-lung became a pirate chief, his forces dominating the South China Sea. The imperial house of the Ming dynasty, which at this time was rapidly succumbing to the invading Manchu (Ch'ing) forces, appointed him an admiral and ordered him to launch an attack on its enemies. In 1646 Chih-lung requested military assistance from the Tokugawa shogunate but, his request denied, he surrendered to the Ch'ing and was later put to death.

Ch'eng-kung first went to China in 1630 at the age of six. Inheriting his father's warships and other property on the death of the latter, he carried on trade with Nagasaki and the regions of Southeast Asia. Using the rich profits acquired through these enterprises to purchase arms, he carried on the resistence against the Ch'ing forces in Fukien and Kwangtung provinces of southern China. In 1648, hoping to restore the Ming dynasty to power, he requested aid from the shogunate, and in 1658 he sent a second embassy to Japan with a similar plea, but his efforts met with no success. In 1661, having failed in an attempt to take Nanking, he drove the Dutch out of Formosa, which they had previously occupied, and took possession of the island. In the same year the Ch'ing dynasty ordered its subjects to move inland from the seacoast and forbade them to launch merchant ships or engage in foreign trade, a move which struck a severe blow to Ch'eng-kung's ambitions for wealth and power, and the following year fever brought an end to his colorful career. His son Cheng Ching and others of the family for a time were active in transporting goods between Nagasaki and Southeast Asia, but in 1683 they acknowledged loyalty to the Ch'ing dynasty, bringing to an end the Cheng family's role in Nagasaki trade. Cheng Ch'eng-kung's exploits, much fictionalized, are the subject of Chikamatsu Monzaemon's dramatic masterpiece, *Kokusenya kassen*, or *The Battles of Coxinga.*

DAIKOKUYA KŌDAYŪ 大黒屋幸太夫 (1751–1828)

Seaman and castway of the late Edo period. He was born in a village called Minami Wakamatsu in the province of Ise and when grown moved to Shiroko, a seaport on the Ise coast, and became a seaman. In 1782 he set sail for Edo with sixteen other men in a ship called the *Shinshō Maru* loaded with rice from the domain of Kishū, but midway they were blown off their course by violent winds, drifting for eight months until they were finally cast up on the island of Amchitka in the Aleutians. After remaining on the island for four years, they were rescued in 1787 by a Russian and taken to the port of Kamchatka on the Siberian mainland. In 1788 they set out from there, making their way to Okhotsk and Yakutsk and in 1789 finally reaching Irkutsk in the Lake Baikal region. There they became acquainted with a teacher named Laxman, who assisted them to submit a petition for repatriation to the governor-general of Siberia, but their request, though several times submitted, was each time denied. Leaving the rest of the party behind, Laxman then took Kōdayū to the Russian capital at St. Petersburg, and in 1791 he was granted audience with Catherine II and given permission to return to Japan. He was presented by the empress with a gold medal and was treated with great kindness by the members of the imperial family and the high officials, residing in the capital for half a year. In 1792 he made his way back to Irkutsk, and there he and the two other seamen remaining from the original party accompanied Adam Laxman, a Russian envoy to Japan, landing at Nemuro in Hokkaido. He was forty-one at the time of his return to Japan. The following year he was subjected to thorough cross-examination by the shogun and high shogunate officials, and for the remainder of his life was kept in mild confinement within the grounds of a garden for medicinal plants at Banchō in Edo.

Date Masamune 伊達政宗 (1567–1636)

Military leader of the Momoyama and early Edo periods. In childhood named Bontenmaru, he was the eldest son of Date Terumune, lord of Yonezawa in the province of Dewa, present-day Yamagata Prefecture. In 1584, when his father was killed, he succeeded him as lord of the domain, and the following year carried out revenge on his father's killer, Hatakeyama Yoshitsugu, at Nihonmatsu. In 1589 he defeated another long-time enemy of the family, Ashina Yoshihiro, and took over control of the region of Aizu, in present-day Fukushima Prefecture, moving his residence to Kurokawa Castle in Aizu. The following year, however, he was berated by Toyotomi Hideyoshi for his tardiness in joining the campaign against Odawara Castle, which Hideyoshi was then conducting, and was obliged to give up possession of the three districts of Aizu that he had recently acquired and return to his former residence in Yonezawa. In 1591 he journeyed to Kyoto, had an interview with Hideyoshi, and succeeded in clearing himself of any suspicion of disloyalty. After returning to his domain, he put down a revolt raised by the Ōsaki and Kasai families and moved his residence to Iwatezawa in the Tamatsukuri district of Mutsu, present-day Miyagi Prefecture.

In 1592–93, at the time of the so-called Bunroku era campaign against Korea, he fought in various encounters in the Korean peninsula and won merit. After the death of Hideyoshi, he allied himself with Tokugawa Ieyasu, fighting on Ieyasu's side at the battle of Sekigahara in 1600 and leading the attack on the forces of Uesugi Kagekatsu of Aizu, in reward for which he was given possession of the district of Karita in Mutsu. In 1603 he constructed

Aoba Castle in Sendai and moved his residence there, becoming the first lord of Sendai. In 1613, at the urging of the Franciscan missionary Luis Sotelo, he dispatched his retainer Hasekura Tsunenaga to head a mission to Spain and Rome, but though the members of the mission were received by the king of Spain and the Pope and returned to Japan in 1620, they failed to realize the objectives set them, which were to open up trade relations with the Spanish domains in the New World and arrange for the establishment of a bishopric in the province of Mutsu. During the campaigns against Osaka Castle in 1614 and 1615, Masamune once more fought for the Tokugawa cause, distinguishing himself in attacks on the Toyotomi generals. By 1634, two years before his death, Masamune had succeeded in becoming one of the most powerful lords of the Tokugawa regime, commanding a large domain centered around the province of Mutsu, receiving a stipend of 620,000 *koku* of rice, and laying a firm foundation for the later prosperity of the fief of Sendai.

Dazai Shundai 太宰春臺 (1680–1747)

Confucian scholar of the middle Edo period. He at first served as a retainer to Matsudaira Tadanori, lord of Izushi in the province of Tajima, present-day Hyōgo Prefecture, but later retired from service and went to Kyoto to study the Chu Hsi school of Neo-Confucianism, the officially approved version of Confucian teaching at this time, under Nakano Kiken. Following this, he studied under Andō Tōno, a disciple of Ogyū Sorai, and when he felt he had made sufficient progress, went to Edo to study under Sorai himself. Sorai, at this time one of the most eminent scholars of Confucianism and Chinese culture, rejected the interpretations of Chu Hsi and the other Neo-Confucian philosophers and attempted through philological research to discover the original meaning of the ancient texts of Confucianism. Shundai proved to be one of Sorai's most distinguished students and in time opened a school of his own, called the Shien, and devoted himself to a life of teaching and writing. Sorai had taught a Confucianism that embraced both the study of poetry and literature and attention to practical concerns of economic and political life, but Shundai in the main carried on and developed the latter strain, in 1729 completing his best-known work, the *Keizairoku*, or "Discussion of Economics," in which he rejected mercantilism and emphasized the prime importance of agriculture, stating the classic theory of feudal economics. In addition to this and a supplementary work on economics, *Keizairoku shūi*, he wrote *Seigaku mondō*, an attempt to define the true teachings of Confucius, and a work on composition and rhetoric entitled *Bunron*.

Egawa Tarōzaemon Hidetatsu 江川太郎左衛門英龍 (1801–1855)

Military expert of the late Edo period. He was the second son of Egawa Hidetake, a *daikan*, or local administrative official of the shogunate, in Nirayama in the province of Izu; in addition to the names Tarōzaemon and Hidetatsu he is also known by the literary appellation Tan'an. At the age of thirty-four he succeeded his father as administrative official of Nirayama, applying himself to his duties with great seriousness. In 1836 he restored order after a peasant uprising had broken out in the district under his supervision, and he also made frequent tours of inspection through the district, apprising himself of conditions among the people, promoting men of talent, encouraging the practice of vaccination and the building up of grain reserves, and gaining for himself a reputation as an outstanding administrator. He was especially interested in matters of coastal defense and the manufacture of guns and acquired a considerable knowledge of military science and conditions in the West through his association with Watanabe Kazan and other experts in such matters. In 1841 he studied gunnery under Takashima Shūhan and the following year was designated by the shogunate as an instructor in gunnery; he gave instruction to men from over 130 domains, his students including Sakuma Shōzan, Kawaji Toshiakira, and Hashimoto Sanai.

In 1843 he constructed a reverberatory furnace at Nirayama and succeeded in casting cannon; later he constructed a large furnace at Nakamura in Izu for the casting of guns. The previous year he submitted to the shogunate a work entitled *Nōhei no gi*, or "Proposal for a Peasant Army," which contained the first tentative suggestions toward a system of universal military conscription. With the arrival of Perry's ships in 1853, he was promoted to a post in the shogunate having to do with finance and he began construction of a battery emplacement at Shinagawa on the outskirts of Edo, a work that was completed the following year. He died shortly after at his residence at Honjo in Edo. He was a man who was not only interested in all fields of learning, but possessed a surprisingly high level of competence in a number of them. He left a work on gunnery entitled *Teppō chiryōsho*, as well as a number of excellent paintings from his hand.

Fujita Tōko 藤田東湖 (1806–1854)

Confucian scholar of the Mito domain in the late Edo period; he was a leading exponent of the movement to restore power to the emperor and expel the foreigners. His personal name was Takeki, his common name was Hinkei, and his childhood name Takejirō, which was later changed to Toranosuke. He was the son of Fujita Yūkoku, a distinguished scholar of the fief of Mito. In 1824, when a British ship landed in Hitachi, where the Mito domain was situated, Tōko, acting on orders from his father, planned to attack and cut down the foreigners as an expression of antiforeign sentiment, but the plan failed.

On his father's death he became head of the family and was appointed a member of the Shōkōkan, an institution sponsored by the domain and devoted to the writing of history and other scholarly matters. In 1829 he was appointed acting director of the Shōkōkan. This same year a dispute arose over who should succeed to the position of lord of Mito. Tōko supported Tokugawa Nariaki, and when Nariaki was chosen as daimyo, Tōko enjoyed his confidence and set about introducing various administrative reforms. In 1837, on Nariaki's orders, he produced an annotated edition of the laws governing the clan school, entitled *Kōdōkan-ki jutsugi*, which contained a characteristic expression of the Mito domain's views on the need to honor the emperor and resist foreign encroachment. Tōko also wrote such works as the *Seiji keizai-ron* and *Jōge fuyū no gi*. In 1844, when Nariaki aroused the displeasure of the shogun and was forced to relinquish his position as daimyo, Tōko was at the same time placed under house confinement. Nariaki was pardoned and restored to his post in 1848, at which time Tōko once more became his close adviser. During this period he wrote the *Kaiten shishi*, *Hitachi-obi*, and other works. In the great Ansei earthquake that struck Edo on the second day of the tenth month of 1854, he was crushed to death in the ruins of the Mito clan residence at Koishikawa.

Fukan Zai Fabian 不干齋ファビアン (1565?–1621)

A Japanese *irmao*, or brother of the Jesuit order, he was a talented writer and produced various works supporting the work of the order and, after his apostasy, attacking Christianity. He was born in the province of Wakasa, the son of a Buddhist priest, and in youth was trained for the Buddhist priesthood. Later he embraced the Christian faith and received instruction at the Takatsuki seminary, in 1586 entering the Society of Jesus. He resided for a time in Bungo in Kyushu, but because of fighting in the area later moved about to Yamaguchi, Shimabara, and Amakusa. In 1586 he produced a condensation of the *Heike monogatari* in colloquial language and also was connected with the printing of the *Esopu monogatari* (a Japanese translation from Latin of *Aesop's Fables*) and *Kinkushū*, a collection of proverbs. He taught Japanese literature at the Collegio in Nagasaki and at other Christian schools. In 1605 he wrote a devotional work entitled *Myōtei mondō*, which was cast in the form of a dialogue between two Japanese women, and the following year engaged in a debate with Hayashi Razan, the leading Confucian advisor to the Tokugawa shogunate, concerning the earth and the nature of the universe. In 1608 feelings of dissatisfaction and involvements with a woman led him to renounce Christianity and in 1620 he wrote a work entitled *Ha Daiusu*, attacking the Christian religion.

Gomizuno-o Tennō 後水尾天皇 (1596–1680)

Emperor of the early Edo period. Named Kotohito, he was the third son of Emperor Goyōzei. In 1611 he ascended the throne to become the 108th sovereign. In 1620 he took the daughter of the second Tokugawa shogun, Hidetada, whose name was Kazuko, to be his empress. Earlier, in 1615, Hidetada had issued the *Kuge-shohatto* (Ordinances for Courtly Families), a code of laws designed to restrict the freedom and movement of the emperor and the members of the court, and in 1629 Emperor Gomizuno-o, increasingly angered by shogunate interference, abdicated, turning over the throne to his daughter, who became Empress Meishō, the 109th sovereign, though he continued until his death some fifty years later to take an active part in matters of state. He was fond of learning and art, eagerly listening to lectures on the Confucian *Four Books* and such classics of Japanese literature and poetry as the *Tales of Ise* and *Kokin wakashū*. He was an accomplished poet, his works being collected in a volume entitled the *Ōsōshū*. A devout Buddhist, he received instruction from the eminent monk Takuan. He built the Shugaku-in Detached Palace in the northeastern suburbs of Kyoto and was also an expert in flower arrangement. After a long life devoted to cultural activities, he was buried in the Sennyū-ji, where so many of the members of the imperial family are interred.

Gotō Mitsutsugu 後藤光次 (1571–1625)

Metalworker of the early Edo period. His personal name was Shōzaburō, and he was said to have borne the surname Yamazaki, though his origins are uncertain; he was a native of Kyoto. The founder of the Gotō family, Yūjō, was an expert in metal-carving who served Shogun Ashikaga Yoshimasa and later retired to devote his time to fashioning metal decorations and fixtures for swords. His descendents carried on his work and prospered. Mitsutsugu became a disciple of Tokujō, the fifth head of the house, specializing in metal-carving and the minting of coins, and in 1593 became the adopted son of the fourth head of the house, Kōjō. Around 1595, when Gotō Tokujō was ordered by Toyotomi Hideyoshi to leave Kyoto and go to the Kantō region, Mitsutsugu went in his place, proceeding to Edo, where Tokugawa Ieyasu had his castle. He was given a house at Hommachi Itchōme, a site now occupied by the Bank of Japan, and put in charge of the Kinza, an office that handled the minting of gold coins. In addition to supervising the minting and appraisal of gold coins, he also assisted in the setting up of the Ginza, an office that did the same thing for silver coins. He thus played an important role in establishing the monetary system of the Tokugawa shogunate. His heirs, who continued to use the name Shōzaburō, served generation after generation as supervisors of the Kinza until 1810, when the eleventh Shōzaburō was convicted of a crime. The first Shōzaburō, Mitsutsugu, also served Tokugawa Ieyasu as an advisor on questions of foreign trade.

Hakuin Ekaku 白隠慧鶴 (1685–1768)

Zen monk of the middle Edo period who revived the Rinzai branch of Zen in Japan; his posthumous title is Shinki Dokumyō Zenji, and he went by such literary names as Kōrin, Sendai-ō, and Sara Juka Rōnō. He was born in the province of Suruga and entered the priesthood in 1699 under Tanrei of Shōin-ji. He thereafter traveled about, studying with such masters as Baō of Mino and Shōtetsu of Takada in Echigo, and in 1708 attained enlightenment under Shōtetsu. Dissatisfied with this, he set out to visit Dōkyō Etan (Shōju Rōjin), a monk of Shinano noted for the rigor of his religious training. Hakuin spent eight months under Dōkyō, devoting himself to strenuous practice, and at the end of the period became his Dharma heir. He then continued his travels about the country, pursuing meditation and other religious practices until he all but injured his health. He returned to his home in 1717 and took up residence in Shōin-ji, the temple of his first teacher, Tanrei, who by this time was dead.

He devoted himself to restoring vitality to the Rinzai branch of Zen, rescuing it from dry formalism and gaining a reputation for his religious fervor. Soon a number of disciples from different parts of the country had gathered around him. Though he was for a time *shuso* (chief monk) of Myōshin-ji in Kyoto, he had no interest in positions of eminence but devoted all his energies to spreading Buddhist teachings among the common people. In his later years he founded a temple on the Izu Peninsula called Ryūtaku-ji, but spent his last days at Shōin-ji.

His writings are extremely numerous and varied and include *Kaian kokugo*, *Orategama*, and *Yasen kanwa*, as well as simple pieces designed for the instruction of the common people such as *Otafuku jorō konahiki-uta*. He is also famous for his paintings and calligraphy, which are frequently tinged with satirical humor. He had many disciples, among whom Tōrei Enji and Gazan Jitō were of particular distinction. Nearly all the teaching lines of Rinzai Zen in Japan today trace themselves back to Gazan Jitō.

HAMADA YAHYŌE 濱田彌兵衞 (seventeenth century)

Ship captain in the employ of the early Edo period overseas trader Suetsugu Heizō of Nagasaki; he played a major role in the clash between the Japanese and the Dutch in Formosa. At this time the Ming dynasty in China maintained an official ban upon all overseas trade, but the Japanese were able to carry out a lively trade in secret with the Chinese ships at Formosa. In 1624 the Dutch set up a base in the southern part of Formosa and thereafter began attempting to interfere with the Japanese trade. The Japanese, for their part, vigorously defended their prior claim to trading rights and did what they could to oppose the Dutch. In 1626 Hamada Yahyōe sailed to Formosa in one of Suetsugu's ships, but because of Dutch interference, he was forced to abandon his cargo there and return to Japan.

Subsequently, Pieter Nuyts, the governor of the Dutch base in Formosa, came to Japan in an attempt to explain the affair to the shogunate officials, but his mission was frustrated by interference from Hamada and Suetsugu. In the fourth month of 1628, Hamada went to Formosa once more with two armed ships and a force of 480 crewmen. He and his men stormed the governor's residence in Zeelandia and compelled Governor Nuyts to exchange hostages with the Japanese and to conclude a peace agreement before they withdrew and returned to Japan. As a result of this incident, Japanese-Dutch relations were disrupted, and the shogunate for a time forbade the Dutch to carry on trade with Japan. Later, however, Nuyts was handed over to the Japanese, and with the death of Suetsugu in 1630, the affair came to an end. Nuyts was confined in the Ōmura prison but was pardoned in 1636 and left Japan for Batavia.

HANAOKA SEISHŪ 華岡青洲 (1760–1835)

Dutch, or Western style, surgeon of the middle Edo period; his personal name was Furuu, his common name Zuiken; Seishū was his professional name. He was born in Nishiyama, a village in the Kaminaka district of the province of Kii, the son of a Dutch style surgeon. In 1782 he went to Kyoto to study Koihō, a branch of traditional Chinese medicine, under Yoshimasu Nangai, and also studied Dutch style surgery under Yamato Kenryū. Returning to his home in 1785, he devoted his efforts to the care of his patients, at the same time pursuing his studies in an effort to develop methods that would combine the best of both Chinese and Western medicine. After many years of strenuous effort, he succeeded in developing a drug that would serve as a general anesthetic, which he called *mafutsusan*. In 1805, through the use of this anesthetic, he performed a successful operation for breast cancer, some years before a comparable use of a general anesthetic was developed in the West, thus gaining lasting fame in the annals of medical history. From 1802 on he served as an official physician of the fief of Kii and in 1833 became personal physician to the lord of the fief. He trained numerous disciples and contributed greatly to the development of surgical arts in Japan. Included among his various writings and records of his medical teachings are such works as the *Shōka sagen*, *Sanka sagen*, *Shōkan kōgi*, *Nyūgan-ben*, and *Seishū zatsuwa*.

HANAWA HOKIICHI 塙保己一 (1746–1821)

Scholar of Japanese studies of the late-middle Edo period; his childhood name was Toranosuke and his literary name was Suiboshi. He was born in the province of Musashi, the son of a farmer named Ogino Uhei. In 1752 at the age of six he lost his sight. In 1760 he went to Edo and studied acupuncture under a *kengyō*, or highest-ranking blind official, named Amatomi Sugaichi. In his enthusiasm for learning, he also studied Japanese fiction and poetry, Shinto, the legal and administrative system of early times, and other subjects under such men as Hagiwara Sōko, Kawashima Kirin, and Yamaoka Matsuakira. In 1769 he became a disciple of the eminent scholar Kamo no Mabuchi, specializing in the *Rikkokushi*, the six official histories of early Japan written in Chinese, but he had been at such studies little over half a year when Kamo no Mabuchi died.

In 1775 he was assigned the rank of *kōtō*, the second highest official rank for blind persons, and took the surname Hanawa, and in 1783 he was raised to the rank of *kengyō*. In 1785 he was invited to the domain of Mito, where he worked to produce collated editions of the *Gempei seisuiki* and other texts. In 1786 he printed sample volumes of what was to be his most important work, the compendium of early texts entitled the *Gunshō ruijū*. In 1793 he received permission from the shogunate to found a school of Japanese studies called the Wagaku Kōdansho. His students included such men as Yashiro Hirokata, Matsuoka Tokikata, Inayama Yukinori, and Ishihara Masaaki.

Over a period of more than forty years he supervised his students in the task of collecting and collating the texts that went into the *Seihen Gunsho ruijū*, which contains a total of 1,779 works and has been of incalculable importance in the study of Japanese history and culture and the preservation of source materials. After the publication of this great work, he was ordered by the shogunate to undertake the compilation of a lengthy encyclopedia on military affairs entitled the *Buke myōmokushō*. While he was in the midst of this task, and of gathering together texts for a continuation of the *Gunsho ruijū*, he died. The continuation eventually appeared under the title *Zoku Gunsho ruijū*. The *Gunsho ruijū* and its continuation contain a total of 2,103 works and have been of enormous value in preserving historical and literary texts that might otherwise have become lost. These two works constitute Hanawa Hokiichi's most important contribution to scholarship, one that continues to be appreciated down to the present day.

Hasegawa Sahyōe Fujihiro 長谷川左兵衛藤廣 (1567–1617)

Official who played an important role in trade and foreign relations in Nagasaki in the early Edo period. He was said to have been the son of a carpenter of the province of Hitachi. His younger sister was a favored concubine of Tokugawa Ieyasu and had received permission to engage in *shuin* ("vermilion-seal") trade, foreign trade carried out in officially licensed ships. Hasegawa entered the service of Tokugawa Ieyasu in 1602 and in 1606 succeeded his deceased elder brother Shigeyoshi as *bugyō* (governor) of Nagasaki. In this post he had occasion to deal with the foreign traders who came to the port and proved himself highly capable in managing the port, supervising the foreign trade carried out by the Japanese "vermilion-seal" vessels and vessels from abroad and enforcing the prohibitions against Christianity.

In 1608, a trading vessel belonging to Arima Harunobu, the lord of Hizen, put in at the port of Macao. A dispute arose between the crew and the citizens of Macao, which resulted in the death or injury of many of the Japanese. The following year, the commander of the trading fleet, Andre Pessoa, came to Nagasaki in the vessel *Madre de Deus* to request the shogunate to prohibit Japanese ships from calling at Macao. Hasegawa, however, acting in conjunction with Arima Harunobu, attacked the vessel. Pessoa and his crewmen, realizing that the situation was hopeless, set fire to their powder casks and blew themselves up along with their ship.

In 1614, when Tokugawa Ieyasu attacked the Toyotomi family at the Winter Siege of Osaka Castle, Hasegawa was ordered by the shogunate to request the daimyo of the Kyushu region to dispatch their forces. The following year, he was transferred to the post of magistrate of the city of Sakai. His nephew Gonroku Fujimasa succeeded him as governor of Nagasaki and proved equally diligent in enforcing the prohibitions against Christianity. Hasegawa was said to have played an important role in promoting the general use of the abacus. He is buried in the Seikyō-ji in Sakamoto in Shiga Prefecture.

Hasekura Tsunenaga 支倉常長 (1571–1622)

Retainer of Date Masamune who headed an embassy to the Pope. In youth he was called Yoichi, and later Rokuemon. In 1613 Date Masamune decided to dispatch an embassy to Spain and Rome in order to establish trading relations with the West, and chose Hasekura Tsunenaga to head it. The party embarked from Tsuki-no-Ura in Mutsu, where the Date domain was situated, in the ninth month, with a Spanish Franciscan named Luis Sotelo to act as guide. The ship, having crossed the Pacific, arrived in Acapulco in Mexico the following year. The party then proceeded across the Atlantic, landed at Sanlucar in Spain, and journeyed by way of Sevilla to Madrid. In 1615 Hasekura presented a letter from Date Masamune to King Philip III and received baptism, taking the Christian name Don Filippo Francesco Faxecura. The party then continued from Barcelona to Rome, where Pope Paul V received them in audience. Hasekura presented letters and gifts from Date Masamune, and the Pope in turn honored him with the rights of a Roman citizen.

Hasekura, however, was unable to obtain permission to carry on trade, which was the main object of his journey, and consequently delayed his departure for home. Finally despairing of success, he embarked on the homeward journey, once more accompanied by Sotelo. He parted from Sotelo in Manila, from which he embarked in 1618, and in 1620 finally returned to

Tsuki-no-ura. By this time Christianity had been placed under interdict by the Tokugawa shogunate, and as a result it was impossible to make use of the unusual experience and understanding that Hasekura had acquired in the course of his travels. He died on the first day of the seventh month of 1622.

Hashimoto Sanai 橋本左内 (1834–1859)

Political activist of the late Edo period. His father, Hashimoto Chōkō, was a physician in the fief of Fukui in Echizen; Sanai is also known by the name Keigaku. At the age of six he began the study of Chinese characters and calligraphy and later studied medicine and learned to conduct clinical examinations. In 1848 he studied under Yoshida Tōkō and the following year went to Osaka and became a student in the Tekitekisaijuku, a school for the study of Dutch or Western learning headed by Ogata Kōan, where he became acquainted with Umeda Umpin and Yokoi Shōnan. In 1852 his father died and he returned to Fukui to take over his father's medical practice. In 1854 he went to Edo and studied Western medicine and science under Sugita Seikei and Chinese under Shionoya Tōin, at the same time becoming acquainted with Fujita Tōko. In 1857 he was appointed head of the Meidōkan, a school operated by the domain of Fukui, and devoted himself to carrying out reforms in the domain administration.

Having learned something of the world situation from the various teachers and acquaintances mentioned above, many of whom were thinkers and political activists themselves, he developed his own theories as to what course Japan should follow in meeting the demands of the foreign powers for the opening of trade and argued that Japan should ally itself with Russia. Later, in 1858, when the shogunate signed trade agreements with five of the foreign powers and a dispute over the succession to the shogunate arose, he went to Kyoto as a representative of the lord of Fukui, Matsudaira Yoshinaga, arguing in favor of the opening of the ports and supporting Hitotsubashi Yoshinobu as the successor to the shogunate. The powerful shogunate official Ii Naosuke, however, succeeded in arranging for the shogunate to pass to a candidate of his own selection and, in order to stifle opposition, took vigorous measures against his critics. Sanai was ordered to be placed under surveillance, and in the tenth month of the following year he was put to death.

Hayashi Shihei 林子平 (1738–1793)

Expert on administrative and military affairs of the middle Edo period; his common name was Tomonao and his literary name was Rokumusai. His father, Okamura Gengohyōe Yoshimichi, was in the service of the shogunate in Edo, but because his elder brother Tomomasa was a retainer to the Date family in Sendai, Shihei and his family moved to Sendai in 1756. He was friendly with Kudō Heisuke and Fujitsuka Shikibu, a Shinto priest of the Shiogama Shrine, men who, like himself, were concerned about Japan's position in the world. He took a particular interest in matters pertaining to economics and national defense, traveling throughout the domain to observe conditions first hand. He also acquired what knowledge he could of conditions in the West. Three times he submitted proposals to the lord of the domain calling for reforms in the educational and defense system and steps to restrain the merchants, encourage production, provide lands for the samurai so that they could engage in farming, and improve the financial situation of the domain. He also made three trips to Nagasaki, taking particular note of reports of Russian expansion toward the south. In 1785 he wrote a work entitled *Sangoku tsūran zusetsu*, and the following year another entitled *Kaikoku heidan*, both stressing the importance of coastal defense. But because his views on military matters often contradicted those of the shogunate, in 1792 the wood blocks from which the works were printed were confiscated by the authorities and Shihei was ordered confined to his elder brother's house in Sendai. He died there the following year on the twenty-first day of the six month.

Hiraga Gennai 平賀源内 (1728–1779)

Scientist, technician, and man of letters of the middle Edo period. His personal name was Kunitomo, his common name Gennai, and he went by such literary names as Fūraisanjin, Kyūkei, and Fukuuchi Kigai, the last used in his role as a writer of *jōruri* (puppet) drama. He was the son of a minor official of the domain of Takamatsu in Shikoku. In 1752 he went to Nagasaki, where he first became acquainted with Dutch learning, the science and technology of the West as it filtered into Japan through the Dutch merchants there. In 1756 he went to Edo, where he took up the study of herbal medicine under Tamura Ransui, and the following year began Confucian studies under the members of the Hayashi family. In addition, in cooperation with Tamura Ransui he arranged an exhibition of useful animals, plants, and minerals at

Yushima in Edo, repeating the exhibition three times. The study of the specimens for the exhibition provided him with the material that later went into an encyclopedia he completed in 1763 entitled *Butsurui hinshitsu.*

His abilities were recognized by the lord of his native fief of Takamatsu, who assigned him a stipend, but in 1761 he became a *rōnin,* a masterless samurai, and continued to pursue his various interests. He was forbidden by the lord of the domain from taking service with any other family, but in 1770 he for a time served the shogunate, which employed him to translate works from Dutch. It was the period when Tanuma Okitsugu held power in the shogunate, actively encouraging industry, foreign trade, and the opening of new lands for cultivation. In this atmosphere of experimentation, Hiraga Gennai turned his attention to the development of a variety of products. In 1764 he produced a heat-resistant asbestos cloth called *kakampu,* and from 1766 on carried out mining activities for gold and iron in Chichibu. In 1770 he went to Nagasaki once more, where he learned Dutch methods of pottery manufacture and taught them to the people of Sanuki in Shikoku, the products being known as Gennai ware. He began sheep-raising in Sanuki and produced woolen goods known as Kunitomo cloth. In 1776 he produced a replica of a friction electric motor, which he received from a Dutch interpreter in Nagasaki; known as an *erekiteru,* it attracted considerable attention at the time. For some years in the past, he had also interested himself in Western styles of realistic painting. He thus displayed an interest and talent for many different kinds of activities. But all of his ventures were a commercial failure, and his efforts to interest the shogunate in them proved to be of no avail.

He sought an outlet for his frustrations in the writing of fiction, producing works in the genre known as *sharebon* such as *Nenashigusa* (1763) and *Hōhiron* (1774). These works satirized the follies of the times, particularly the scramble for profit, at the same time lamenting the fact that the nation as a whole took so little interest in the development of industry. He also wrote plays for the *jōruri,* or puppet drama, beginning with a work performed in 1770 called *Shinrei yaguchi no watashi,* and in time became one of the outstanding *jōruri* dramatists of Edo. In 1779 he was sent to prison for an offense and died there.

Gennai showed no talent for scientific theory but was highly apt in matters of practical technology. He holds a place of importance as one of the pioneers of modern Japanese science and at the same time played a significant role in the literary development of the *sharebon* and *jōruri* genres, representing one of the most unusual and widely talented figures of the middle Edo period.

Hirata Atsutane 平田篤胤 (1776–1843)

Scholar of Japanese studies and Shinto thinker of the late Edo period. He was born in Akita, the son of a samurai named Ōwada, and in his youth studied Confucianism. In 1795 he ran away from his native domain and went to Edo. In 1800 he became the adopted son of a samurai of the domain of Matsuyama named Hirata. He proclaimed himself a disciple of the eminent scholar of Japanese studies Motoori Norinaga, stating that he began instruction under Motoori in 1801. But since Motoori died in that year, it would appear that Hirata was never actually a disciple. In 1803 Hirata wrote his first work, entitled *Kamōsho*, an attack on the *Bendōsho*, a work by the Confucian thinker Dazai Shundai. The following year he adopted the literary name Masuganoya and set himself up as a teacher.

In 1806 he wrote *Honkyō gaihen*, a work of great importance in the development of his thought, though it remained in manuscript during his lifetime and was not widely known until the latter part of the Meiji period. The work was clearly written under the influence of Christianity as it was known in China in late Ming times and emphasizes the concepts of a supreme deity and a life after death. Many works followed, among the more important being *Tama-no-hashira* (1812), a work on cosmology that was written under the influence of the *Sandaikyō* by Motoori Norinaga's disciple Hattori Chūyō (1756–1824); the *Koshiden* (1825), a commentary on Hirata's own considerably rewritten version of the *Kojiki*; and others such as *Kodō taii* (1811), *Koshichō* (1818), and *Tamadasuki* (1831). All the above works deal with Hirata's interpretation of Shinto beliefs. In these, he establishes Ame-no-minakanushi-no-kami as the supreme deity of the Shinto pantheon and, rejecting the vague underworld called Yominokuni posited by traditional Shinto, substitutes a world of the dead presided over by the deity Ōkuninushi-no-kami, who judges the souls of the deceased. To support his contentions, he turned to the study of legends concerning the afterlife preserved in India and China, asserting that all such legends derived originally from Japan. Such ethnocentricity and the supreme position accorded to Japan in his thought fitted well with the concept of reverence for the emperor, and as a result Hirata's thought exerted considerable influence over the movement to drive out the foreigners and restore power to the emperor that came to prominence at the end of the Edo period, as well as over the measures to make Shinto the state religion that were carried out in the early Meiji period.

He is said to have had 550 disciples while he was alive, and after his death the number of persons calling themselves his followers swelled to over 1,300.

His unusual views were attacked as unorthodox by the followers of Motoori Norinaga, and the shogunate likewise looked upon them as dangerous and placed a ban upon his writings in 1841. Hirata was ordered to return to his domain and died in Akita two years later.

HONDA MASANOBU 本多正信 (1538–1616)

Daimyo who contributed to the founding of the Tokugawa shogunate. His childhood name was Yahachirō, and his other given names were Masayasu and Masayuki; he held the honorary title of Sado-no-kami. As a young man he served under Tokugawa Ieyasu, but in 1563 joined the Sakai family and others in a popular revolt in Mikawa that defied the authority of Ieyasu and the following year was forced to retire to the province of Kaga in the north. Later he was pardoned and allowed to resume service under Ieyasu. When Ieyasu assisted Oda Nobunaga in defeating the Asakura forces at Anegawa in Ōmi, he took part in the battle and achieved distinction. Subsequently he played an active role in the campaign to defeat Uesugi Kenshin and in the battle of Sekigahara in 1600. When Ieyasu took up residence in the Kantō area, Honda was assigned to the domain of Amanawa in Sagami with an annual stipend of 10,000 *koku* of rice. He assisted Ieyasu in the building of Edo Castle. In the time of the second shogun Hidetada he served as a *rōjū* (councilor of state), and he and his son Masazumi both exercised considerable power.

Though Honda Masanobu's domain at its largest provided a stipend of only 30,000 *koku*, he was the most eminent of Ieyasu's ministers, and it is said that Ieyasu's actions followed the policies laid down for him by Honda. The *Honsaroku*, a work on the shogunal government that is attributed to him, contains the statement: "The way to govern is to make certain that the peasants have neither an excess of goods nor an insufficiency." This in fact was the basic policy adopted by the Tokugawa shogunate. Honda died in the sixth month of 1616.

HONDA TOSHIAKI 本多利明 (1744–1821)

Thinker and writer on economic and governmental affairs in the late Edo period. His common name was Saburōuemon, and his literary names were Hokui and Rodonsai. He was born in Murakami in the province of Echigo. At the age of seventeen he went to Edo in search of teachers, and there studied mathematics, astronomy, and swordsmanship. At the age of twenty-three he opened a private school in the Otowa area of Edo and hence came to be called Otowa-sensei. Later he turned over the direction of the school to his disciple Sakabe Hironao and embarked upon an extensive tour of the country to observe the geography and special products of its various regions. He also acquired a knowledge of the geography and customs of foreign countries, as well as of the techniques involved in astronomical observation, navigation, metal refining, and the production of explosives, by reading translations of Western works on the subject. He took a particular interest in the development of Ezochi, as the island of Hokkaido was then known, and sent his disciple Mogami Tokunai along as a member of an official scouting party to observe the region. In 1801 he himself acted as captain of a ship called the *Ryōfū Maru* on a voyage to Hokkaido and thereafter advocated the opening of the island to colonization.

Around 1809 he for a time entered the service of the Maeda family, lords of the domain of Kaga, but soon resigned. In views communicated to Matsudaira Sadanobu and other important statesmen of the time, he urged the government to encourage trade through officially supervised shipping activities, to take steps to ensure a more equitable distribution of goods and prices and to relieve the grain shortages that caused unrest in the cities, and to seize economic power from the wealthy merchants and instead exploit it to strengthen and enrich the nation as a whole. The progressive nature of his views at times shows an affinity with the mercantilist ideas of Western thinkers. He wrote a great many works, among them the *Keisei hisaku, Saiiki monogatari, Chōkiron, Tokai shimpō,* and *Ezo dōchihen.* Since none of them were printed during his lifetime, however, he avoided incurring government censure for the boldness of his proposals. He died in Edo in the eleventh month of 1821.

HOSOKAWA GRACIA 細川ガラシア (1562–1600)

The third daughter of Akechi Mitsuhide and wife of Hosokawa Tadaoki. Her marriage to Hosokawa Tadaoki was arranged by Oda Nobunaga and took place in 1579. She bore him three sons, Tadataka, Okiaki, and Tadatoshi. In the sixth month of 1682 her father, Akechi Mitsuhide, assassinated Oda Nobunaga at the Honnō-ji in Kyoto. As the daughter of a traitor, she was viewed with suspicion, and her marriage was dissolved. Later, at the suggestion of Tokugawa Ieyasu, Toyotomi Hideyoshi gave permission for the marriage ties to be resumed. Through her husband, she became acquainted with the famous Christian daimyo Takayama Ukon and adopted his faith, receiving baptism in 1687 and taking the Christian name Gracia. Tadaoki was not pleased at his wife's deepening religious devotion, but he was frequently away on military campaigns or other business, at which time she would attend church. At the time of the great battle of Sekigahara in 1600, Ishida Mitsunari, hoping to sway the loyalty of the followers of the Toyotomi family who had gone over to the side of Tokugawa Ieyasu, attempted to have their wives and children seized and taken as hostages to Osaka Castle. Gracia, knowing that her husband had joined the Tokugawa forces and fearful that he would be swayed by concern for her safety, refused to be taken as a hostage but instead had herself beheaded by the chief retainer of the fief, Ogasawara Shōsai. Such a step was necessary because suicide would have violated the precepts of her faith.

Hosokawa Tadaoki 細川忠興 (1563–1645)

A military leader of the early Edo period and an expert in the tea ceremony. He was the son of Nagaoka Fujitaka but was adopted by Hosokawa Terutsune. His childhood name was Kumachiyo, later changed to Yoichirō, and late in life he assumed the Buddhist name Sōritsu and the literary name Sansai. Under the Muromachi shogunate he held the title of *ōtozamashū*, and later became page to Oda Nobunaga, being assigned to the fief of Tango north of Kyoto with an annual stipend of 120,000 *koku* of rice. When Akechi Mitsuhide assassinated Oda Nobunaga at the Honnō-ji in Kyoto, Mitsuhide attempted to persuade Tadaoki, who was his son-in-law, to side with him, but Tadaoki refused and joined his father, Nagaoka Fujitaka, in supporting Toyotomi Hideyoshi. He distinguished himself in Hideyoshi's service at the battles of Shizugatake, Komaki, and Odawara and in the two campaigns against Korea.

In the battle of Sekigahara in 1600 he sided with Tokugawa Ieyasu and was rewarded with the domains of Buzen and Bungo in Kyushu, from which he received a revenue of 400,000 *koku* of rice a year; he resided in Kokura Castle. In 1619 he went into retirement because of illness, shaved his head, and assumed the name Sansai Sōritsu. He was a man of highly refined tastes and accomplishments and was particularly honored as an outstanding disciple of the great tea master Sen no Rikyū. He also excelled as a judge of teabowls and other utensils used in the tea ceremony. In addition, he was noted for his ability as a swimmer. His wife, the third daughter of Akechi Mitsuhide, who was baptized into the Christian faith and took the name

Gracia, is likewise renowned for her role in the turbulent events of this period.

Hotta Masayoshi 堀田正睦 (1810–1864)

A high official in the shogunate in the late Edo period and an advocate of the policy of opening the country to foreign trade. His given name was originally Masaatsu, his literary name was Kenzan, and he held the honorary official titles of Sagami-no-kami and later Bitchū-no-kami. He was adopted as heir by his elder brother Hotta Masachika and in 1825 became lord of the domain of Sakura in Shimōsa with an annual stipend of 110,000 *koku* of rice. He had great enthusiasm for Dutch studies, encouraging his retainers to study Dutch and Western medicine and military affairs with such persistence that he came to be referred to as the Rampeki, or "Dutch maniac."

In 1835 he was assigned to the post of *jisha-bugyō* (official in charge of temples and shrines), in 1837 became Osaka *jōdai* (governor of Osaka Castle), and in 1841 advanced to the position of *rōjū* (councilor of state). He resigned in 1843, but in 1855 was made *rōjū shuseki*, or head councilor of state. He placed particular trust in the *kanjō-bugyō* (superintendent of the treasury) Kawaji Toshiakira and the *metsuke* (overseer) Iwase Tadanari, and did his best to promote the opening of the country.

In 1858, when a trade and navigation treaty was signed between Japan and the United States, he journeyed in person to Kyoto in an attempt to receive imperial ratification of it, but the highly complex nature of relations between the court and the shogunate at this time caused his mission to fail. Meanwhile a dispute over the succession to the shogunate developed. Hotta supported Hitotsubashi Yoshinobu for the post, but Yoshinobu's rival of the Kii branch of the Tokugawa family, Tokugawa Iemochi, won the position and appointed Ii Naosuke as *tairō* (senior councilor). As a result, Hotta was dismissed from the office of councilor of state and went into retirement. In 1862 he was accused of committing errors of foreign policy while serving as a councilor of state and was placed under house arrest for an indefinite period and his fief reduced. He died in Sakura Castle in the third month of 1864. The collection of Dutch books and translations of foreign works that he gathered together remains today in the possession of Sakura High School.

Ii Naosuke 井伊直弼 (1815–1860)

Statesman of the late Edo period. He was the fourteenth son of Ii Naonaka, lord of the domain of Hikone in the province of Ōmi, present-day Shiga Prefecture. In 1846 he became the adopted son of his elder brother, Naoaki; in 1850 succeeded to the position of lord of Hikone and the title of Kamon-no-kami that traditionally accompanied it and devoted his energies to the improvement of affairs within the domain. He was also assigned to supervise the defenses of the province of Sagami, present-day Kanagawa Prefecture, and of Haneda and Ōmori in Edo Bay.

Japan at the time faced many problems, both internal and external, particularly that of how to answer the demands of America and other countries for trading treaties, and to these was added a dispute over the succession to the shogunate, which arose when the thirteenth shogun, Tokugawa Iesada, died in 1858 without an heir. Ii Naosuke, who in the fourth month of 1858 had been appointed to the post of *tairō* (senior councilor of state) in the shogunate, set about working toward a settlement of these problems, arranging for Tokugawa Iemochi to succeed as shogun and, without waiting for approval from the imperial court, concluding trade treaties with America and four other foreign powers. These moves aroused fierce opposition from the Mito and Hitotsubashi branches of the Tokugawa family, but Ii Naosuke, in the action known as the Great Persecution of the Ansei period, suppressed the opposition by jailing its leaders. This stimulated further opposition from the samurai of Mito and Satsuma, who advocated the policy of *sonnō-jōi*, or reverence for the emperor and expulsion of the foreigners, and in the third month of 1860 a group of them intercepted him outside the Sakurada Gate as he was on his way to Edo Castle and assassinated him. He was forty-five at the time of his death.

Imamura Eisei 今村英生 (1671–1736)

Scholar of Dutch learning in the middle Edo period. He was born in Nagasaki in a family that, since the time of his grandfather Imamura Ichizaemon, had served as official interpreters of Dutch. At the age of twenty-four Eisei passed the Dutch language examination and began a career as interpreter that lasted for forty-two years until his death; in 1707 he was promoted to the rank of senior interpreter. In 1708, when the Italian missionary Giovanni Battista Sidotti came to Japan, Eisei acted as interpreter for him, and the following year, when Sidotti was taken to Edo and the scholar and statesman Arai Hakuseki was ordered to cross-examine him, Eisei once again served as interpreter. Hakuseki's record of the examination, the *Seiyō kibun*, circulated widely in manuscript, and was the first work to provide Japanese of the time with a knowledge of conditions in the Western world. In 1727 Eisei also interpreted for a Dutch horse-trainer named H. J. Keijser, who was invited to serve in Edo by Shogun Yoshimune. In addition to his duties as an interpreter, he was ordered by the shogunate to translate Dutch works on botany, horsemanship, the treatment of ailments in horses, and animal raising.

Inatomi Ichimu 稲富一夢 (1552–1611)

Active in the Momoyama and early Edo periods, he was the most important early exponent of the Inatomi school of gunnery. He was born in Tanabe in the province of Tango, present-day Kyoto Prefecture. He went by the given names Sukenao and Naoie and later was assigned the title of Iga-no-kami; in his late years he entered the Buddhist priesthood, taking the name Ichimusai. He studied gunnery under his grandfather Naotoki, the founder of the Inatomi school, and was said to have displayed amazing talent in his grasp of the subject. His ability was recognized by Toyotomi Hideyoshi, who ordered him to act as instructor in gunnery to Hosokawa Tadaoki, the lord of Tango. In 1600, at the time of the great battle of Sekigahara, he was commanded to guard the life of Hosokawa Gracia, the Christian wife of his lord Tadaoki, but she, fearful of becoming a hostage in the hands of her husband's enemies, committed suicide and Inatomi, having failed his responsibility, fled into hiding. For a time he was in great danger from the wrath of Tadaoki, but Tokugawa Ieyasu intervened on his behalf and he escaped punishment. He served Ieyasu and his successor to the shogunate, Hidetada, and later entered the service of Ieyasu's son Yoshinao, the lord of the fief of Owari. A description of his gunnery techniques is preserved in the *Ichiryū ippen no sho* in eleven chapters and the *Gokui* in nine chapters.

Inō Tadataka 伊能忠敬 (1745–1818)

Geographer of the middle Edo period. He was the third son of Jimpo Toshizaemon Sadatsune of Kozutsumi village in the province of Kazusa, but in 1762 he became the adopted son of a saké brewer named Inō Nagayoshi. While working to revive the fortunes of the Inō family, he applied himself to the study of mathematics, astronomy, and surveying. In 1793 he turned over the management of family affairs to his eldest son, Kagetaka, and took up a life of retirement at Fukagawa in Edo. A few years later, at the age of fifty, he became a student of Takahashi Yoshitoki, an official astronomer in the service of the shogunate, studying various methods of astronomical observation and matters pertaining to the calendar; he was the first person in Japan to observe the culmination of the planet Venus.

In 1800, on the recommendation of Yoshitoki, he was ordered by the shogunate to undertake a land survey of Ezochi, as the island of Hokkaido was known at that time, and produced one map at a scale of 1/43,600 and a second at one-tenth of that scale. In 1801 he was further ordered to survey the Tōkaidō coastline from the Izu Peninsula north to the province of Mutsu, and the following year to do the same for the Japan Sea coast of northern Honshu. This was followed by surveys of the areas east of Owari and Echizen, and in 1804 of surveys of western Honshu, Shikoku, Kyushu, and the smaller islands of Oki, Tsushima, and the Gotō group. In 1815 he surveyed the islands off the Izu Peninsula, the Kantō region, and the area around Edo, intending to produce a complete map of Japan, but he died in the fourth month of 1818 before he could bring the task to completion. His disciples, however, kept his death a secret while they hurriedly worked to finish the undertaking, only revealing it when they presented the completed map to the shogunate in 1821. Tadataka left a number of works, among them journals of his surveying activities.

Ishida Baigan 石田梅巖 (1685–1744)

Founder of *shingaku.* He was born in the province of Tamba north of the city of Kyoto, the second son of a farming family. In 1695 at the age of seventeen he became an apprentice in Kyoto and, after returning once to his home, in 1707 went to Kyoto a second time and took service with a merchant family named Kuroyanagi. In his spare time he applied himself to scholarship, studying for a time under Oguri Ryōun. Later he gave up business activities and in 1729 opened a lecture hall in Kyoto in order to expound his own teachings. All instruction was free of charge, and although at first attendance was poor, in time he began to draw increasingly large crowds until he was obliged to set up lecture halls in a number of places throughout the city. His teaching, which combines elements drawn from Confucianism, Buddhism, Taoism, and Shinto, stresses the key role of *shin* or *kokoro*, the heart or mind, and hence is known as *shingaku.* Designed to improve the nature of society and emphasizing such virtues as harmony, frugality, patience, and honesty, his doctrines were expounded with such clarity and enthusiasm that they won many followers among the common people and came to be referred to as *chōnin-gaku*, or the creed of the townsmen. At the same time he also defined the ideals appropriate to the warrior class as well and attracted a number of samurai and monks to his school.

He is said to have been an extremely kind and thoughtful teacher, sending to inquire about the health of any of his regular listeners who happened to be absent, and in 1740, when crop failures brought on widespread famine among the common people of Kyoto, he and his followers collected contributions for the relief of the poor. Among those who carried on his teachings were Sugiura Shisai, Chishima Toan, Tomioka Michinao, and Saitō Zemmon. Baigan himself published only two works, the *Tohi mondō* and *Saikaron*, but his disciples compiled a collection of his sayings, the *Ishida sensei goroku*, and another of his unpublished writings, the *Ishida sensei ikō*. He remained unmarried all his life, devoting his energies entirely to the education of the common people.

Ishida Mitsunari 石田三成 (1560–1600)

Military leader of the Momoyama period. As a boy he won recognition of his talents and was taken into service by Toyotomi Hideyoshi, acting as an usher and arranger of interviews between his master and the local leaders at the time of Hideyoshi's campaign in the western part of Japan. In 1585, when Hideyoshi was made *kampaku*, he was given court rank and assigned to an office that allowed him to take part in the most secret and vital business of the state. He participated in Hideyoshi's campaigns against Korea in the Bunroku and Keichō eras, and at the time of the peace negotiations he escorted the Ming envoy to the port of Nagoya in Kyushu and there worked out the seven conditions upon which Japan was willing to end the war. In addition he played an important role in the great land survey that Hideyoshi ordered to be carried out by the various daimyo in their domains; in recognition of his services he was in 1595 made lord of the fief of Sawayama in the province of Ōmi, where he demonstrated his ability as a civil administrator. In 1598 he was chosen by Hideyoshi to be one of the five *bugyō* (magistrates) in charge of government affairs. After Hideyoshi's death he opposed the ambitions of Tokugawa Ieyasu and, joining with Uesugi Kagekatsu of Aizu and a number of other daimyo who were indebted to Hideyoshi and loyal to his memory, he called out his troops in 1600, but in the ninth month of the same year he and the others of his group were defeated by Ieyasu and his allies at the battle of Sekigahara. He was captured on Mt. Ibuki and taken to Kyoto, where, along with Konishi Yukinaga and Ankokuji Ekei, he was beheaded at the Rokujōgawara execution ground.

ITAKURA KATSUSHIGE 板倉勝重 (1545–1624)

Shogunate official of the early Edo period. Born in the province of Mikawa, he entered the priesthood at an early age, taking the religious name Kōyo Sōtetsu. In 1561 his father, Yoshishige, was killed fighting in the service of Tokugawa Ieyasu, and after his elder and younger brothers had also been killed in battle, Ieyasu ordered him to return to lay life and take over the leadership of the family. In 1586 he was appointed *machi-bugyō*, or chief administrative official, of the city of Sumpu, enjoying the confidence of Ieyasu, and when Ieyasu took up residence in Edo, he appointed Katsushige as *machi-bugyō* of Edo and at the same time made him *Kantō-gundai*, or overseer of Ieyasu's lands in the Kantō region. In 1601 he was transferred to the post of *shoshidai* in Kyoto, his duties being to keep watch on the imperial court and the region around the capital. He continued in the post for twenty years, distinguishing himself by his capability and strict adherence to the law. He received a stipend of over 16,000 *koku* and was given the title of Iga-no-kami. In 1620 he turned over his position to his son Shigemune and retired from official life.

ITAKURA SHIGEMASA 板倉重昌 (1588–1638)

Military leader of the early Edo period. The second son of Itakura Katsushige, he entered the service of Tokugawa Ieyasu in 1603, and in 1609 was assigned to the domain of Fukamizo in Mikawa with a stipend of 1,000 *koku*. At the time of the winter seige on Osaka Castle in 1614, Shigemasa was sent as envoy from Ieyasu to negotiate a peaceful settlement with Toyotomi Hideyori, a mission that he carried out successfully, returning with Hideyori's promise of cooperation. In 1633 his income was raised to 15,000 *koku*. In 1637, when the Shimabara Rebellion broke out in western Kyushu, he was sent as envoy of the shogun to Arima, where he led an army made up of contingents from the neighboring domains of the Matsukura, Hosokawa, and Nabeshima families, but the attack did not proceed as successfully as had been hoped. The Edo shogunate thereupon dispatched Matsudaira Nobutsuna to the scene of action. Learning that Matsudaira was on the way and fearing it would mean his disgrace, Shigemasa mounted a concerted attack on Hara Castle, where the rebels were ensconced, leading the attack in person; he was killed in the fighting.

Itō Gemboku 伊東玄朴 (1800–1871)

Physician of the late Edo period. Born in Kanzaki in the province of Hizen in Kyushu, he became the adopted son of Itō Yūshō, a samurai of the domain of Saga. Determined to become a physician, he went to the city of Saga and studied Western learning under Shimamoto Ryōjun, also known as Ryōshō. From there he proceeded to Nagasaki, studying the Dutch language under Inomata Denjiemon and medicine under von Siebold, a German doctor attached to the Dutch trading office. In 1826 he made a brief trip to Edo, returning almost immediately, but went again to Edo and in 1833 began practice as a physician, calling his residence the Shōsendō and offering training in medical matters to younger men. Earlier, in 1828, when von Siebold was found to have in his possession a map and other forbidden articles and was arrested by the authorities, many of his former students were implicated in the affair, but Itō managed to avoid entanglement and in the following year adopted the name Gemboku, by which he is commonly known.

In 1841 he became a physician of the domain of Saga, and in 1845, when the lord of the domain, Nabeshima Kansō, had some smallpox vaccine imported from Holland, Gemboku successfully vaccinated Kansō's daughter and thereafter performed vaccinations on the populace in general. In 1857 he set up a vaccination center in the Kanda district of Edo, which later became the Center for Western Medicine and eventually the medical department of Tokyo University. The following year he was appointed physician to the shogunate. Many of his disciples were active in medical, educational, and government circles in late Edo and early Meiji times, among the more notable being Aoki Kenzō, Terajima Munenori, Ogata Kōan, Sano Tsunetami, and Kanda Takahira. His work on medical practice is entitled *Iryō seishi.*

Itō Mansho (Mancio) 伊東満所 (1570–1612)

Japanese Christian of the Momoyama period. He was the son of Itō Shurinosuke, a close relative of the Christian daimyo of the domain of Bungo,

Ōtomo Sōrin. In 1582, when three of the Christian daimyo of Kyushu Ōmura, Ōtomo, and Arima, dispatched a group of four youths on a mission to the Pope and the king of Spain, he was chosen by Ōtomo Sōrin to be one of them, and though he was only eleven at the time, he acted as spokesman for the group. In Rome he was made an honorary citizen and raised to the ranks of the nobility with the title Cavaliere di Speron d'oro. The group returned to Nagasaki in 1590, and the following year Itō was summoned to an audience with Toyotomi Hideyoshi and gave an account of what he had seen and heard in Europe. The same year he entered the novitiate at Amakusa in Kyushu, becoming a member of the Jesuit order. During the period around 1606–07 he assisted in giving instruction at a seminary sponsored by the Arima family, and later became a regular member of the priesthood. In the year of his death, the Edo shogunate issued the first of its orders outlawing Christianity.

Itō Tōgai 伊藤東涯 (1670–1736)

Confucian scholar of the middle Edo period. His personal name was Nagatane and he was the eldest son of Itō Jinsai, a celebrated Confucian scholar of Kyoto. His father, rejecting the interpretations of the Chu Hsi and Wang Yang-ming schools of Neo-Confucianism, had attempted to discover the original teachings embodied in the Confucian *Analects* and in Mencius, founding a new school known as the Kogakuha, or School of Ancient Learning, and expounding his teachings at a private academy called the Kogidō at Horikawa in Kyoto. Tōgai faithfully carried on his father's teachings, though he added nothing of his own. His scholarship was praised by the leading authority on Chinese studies in Edo at the time, Ogyū Sorai, but he seems to have taken little notice of this fact. He was invited to the domain of Kii by the lord of the fief but declined to accept the invitation, preferring to devote his time to teaching and writing. His interests cover a broader range of subjects than those of his father and include Chinese and Japanese institutional history and the history and literature of Korea. He produced a great many works, among them the *Seidotsū*, *Bengiroku*, and *Kogaku shiyō*. Itō Tōgai and his father gave instruction to townsmen and samurai alike and both had large numbers of disciples; among Tōgai's more notable disciples were Okuda Sankaku, Sawamura Kinsho, Matsuzaki Jikei, and Aoki Kon'yō. The books and papers of Tōgai and his father are now in the collection of the Tenri Library in Nara Prefecture.

JOOSTEN VAN LODENSTEIJN, JAN (ca. 1560–1623)

He was the son of a prominent family of Delft in the Netherlands. In Japan he is known as Yayōsu. He was one of the senior officers of the Dutch far eastern trading ship *Liefde*, which in 1600 was stranded on the shore of Bungo Province, present-day Ōita Prefecture in Kyushu. In company with William Adams, another officer of the ship, he journeyed to Edo and was received in audience by Tokugawa Ieyasu. He won the confidence of the future shogun and was given a residence in Edo. The place name Yaesugashi, which continues in use in present-day Tokyo, is derived from his name. In 1609, when a Dutch trading office was set up in Hirado, he played a very active part in negotiations between the shogunate and the Dutch traders.

He also sent trading ships bearing the *shuin* (vermilion-seal patent) of the shogunate to various countries of Southeast Asia. Later, hoping to return to the Netherlands, he took ship to Batavia, but was unable to make satisfactory arrangements there and decided to go back to Japan. In the summer of 1623, however, his ship foundered on a reef of the Paracel Islands in the South China Sea and he was drowned. While in Japan he married a Japanese woman and had a son who also sent trading ships to Southeast Asia.

JIUN ONKŌ 慈雲飲光 (1718–1804)

Middle Edo period priest of the Shingon sect, he was a native of Osaka; he used such literary names as Hyakufuchi Dōji and Katsuragi Sannin, and was commonly referred to as Jiun Sonja. In 1730 he became a disciple of Ninko Teiki and entered the priesthood. For three years beginning in 1733 he studied Confucianism in Kyoto under Itō Tōgai, and for another three years beginning in 1741, he studied Zen under Daimai Zenji in Shinano Province. In 1744 he took up residence in Chōei-ji, a temple in Takaida in Kawachi near Osaka. In 1749 he compiled the *Kompon sōsei*, a system of religious life and practice based upon the rules for monastic discipline laid down in the time of Śākyamuni, the founder of Buddhism. The expounding of this system was a passion that dominated his activities for the remainder of his life. In 1758 he built a retreat on Mt. Ikoma called Sōryū-an and took up the study of Sanskrit in order to gain a better knowledge of early Buddhism. The results of his studies are contained in a work in one thousand chapters entitled *Bongaku shinryō*. Earlier Japanese Buddhist thinkers and scholars had in most cases relied upon Chinese translations of works in Sanskrit, and Jiun thus holds a place of special importance as the first Buddhist scholar in recent centuries to turn his attention directly to original Sanskrit sources. In 1771 he moved to Amida-ji in Kyoto and devoted himself to religious teaching. He expounded what he called *Jūzenkai*, or Ten Rules of Discipline, that he believed should be observed by Buddhists, and wrote a work entitled *Jūzen hōgo* explaining them. In his late years, he moved to Kōki-ji, a temple on Mt. Katsuragi in Kawachi, where he developed and advocated his own type of Shinto known as Jiun Shinto. In addition to the works already mentioned, he wrote *Hito to naru michi* and others. He is also famous for his calligraphy.

Kaibara Ekiken 貝原益軒 (1630–1714)

Confucian scholar of the early Edo period. He was born into a samurai family that for generations had served the domain of Kuroda in Chikuzen Province, Kyushu; his father was a medical official of the domain. Ekiken, who was a follower of the Chu Hsi school of Neo-Confucianism, spent much of his life traveling about to Nagasaki, Edo, and Kyoto and studying under various scholars, but he had no single person whom he acknowledged as his teacher. Living at the time of the Genroku era, when a commercial and money economy was beginning to flourish, his thinking is marked by a strongly empirical and positivist tone. In the field of natural science he wrote a work entitled *Yōjōkun* ("Rules for Nourishing Life") in which, based upon his own experience, he gave advice on diet and other matters concerning health, and he also wrote on the subject of medicinal and food plants. These and his other works, unlike the usual scholarly treatises of the time, are written in a style that is very simple and easy to read and they enjoyed widespread popularity during the Edo period.

He compiled a genealogy of the Kuroda family and a gazetteer of the province of Chikuzen as well as keeping many journals of his travels. In his works entitled *Shinshiroku* and *Ekiken jukkun* he expounded his views on the essential dignity and equality of man, an equality that transcends the class divisions of feudal society. Ekiken had only two disciples, Takeda Shun'an and Kōzuki Gyūzan, but because of the great number of his works and their practical nature, he had an incalculable influence upon his time.

Kamiya Sōtan 神屋宗湛(紙屋宗旦) (1553–1635)

Wealthy merchant and tea master of the early Edo period; His family for generations had been residents of Hakata in Kyushu. His grandfather

Kamiya Jutei studied processes of metal refining in Ming China and opened up the Ōmori silver mines in Iwami Province, acquiring great wealth as a result. In 1569 the city of Hakata was reduced to ashes by the contending armies of the Ōtomo and Mōri families, but Sōtan managed to escape harm by fleeing to Karatsu in Hizen. Thereafter he traveled to various ports of Korea and China, conducting trade, accumulating wealth, and gaining a through knowledge of the situation abroad.

In 1586 he entered the priesthood at the Zen temple of Daitoku-ji in Kyoto. He became an expert in the tea ceremony, associating with such other tea masters as Sen no Rikyū and Tsuda Sōkyū and from time to time being invited by Toyotomi Hideyoshi to the latter's famous tea parties, where he mingled with the great lords of the nation. At the time of Hideyoshi's campaigns against Korea (1592 and 1597), he helped in the construction of the military installations at the port of departure for the troops at Nagoya in Kyushu and thereafter busied himself with the supplying of arms and other necessities to the Japanese armies. After the death of Toyotomi Hideyoshi, he was well treated by Tokugawa Ieyasu.

He was called upon by the Kuroda family, lords of the domain of Fukuoka, where his native city of Hakata was situated, to take charge of the supplying of funds and laborers for the construction of Fukuoka Castle. At the same time he worked to develop local industries in the domain. Mining, silver-working, the extracting of wax from the berries of the *haze* (wax sumac) tree, the manufacture of weights and measures, the weaving of a special kind of cloth called *Hakata-ori*, and other industries were opened up and developed by him. His diary, the *Sōtan nikki*, covers the period from 1586 to 1613 and deals with matters pertaining to the tea ceremony, giving invaluable information on the lavish tea parties held by Toyotomi Hideyoshi and other great lords of the period.

Katō Kiyomasa 加藤清正 (1562–1611)

Military leader of the Momoyama period. He was born in Nakamura in the province of Owari and as a child was called Toranosuke. Because his mother was a cousin of the mother of Toyotomi Hideyoshi, he became a retainer of Hideyoshi, distinguishing himself in the attack on Tottori Castle in Inaba, in the battle against Akechi Mitsuhide at Yamazaki, and in particular at the battle of Shizugatake, where he won the distinction of being named among the *shichihonyari*, the seven most outstanding warriors of the battle. In 1586 he was made lord of Kumamoto Castle in Higo, and in the campaigns against

Korea (1592 and 1597) he again won distinction, leading the vanguard in company with Konishi Yukinaga.

After the death of Hideyoshi, when a struggle for power developed between Ishida Mitsunari and Tokugawa Ieyasu, Kiyomasa and others of the militarist party proved useful to Ieyasu because of their opposition to Mitsunari and the civilian party, and although Kiyomasa did not take part in the battle of Sekigahara in 1600, he aided Ieyasu's cause by putting down Mitsunari's supporters in Kyushu; as a reward, he was confirmed by Ieyasu in his possession of the lands he held in Higo. Later he was ordered by Ieyasu to construct the keep of Nagoya Castle in Owari and served Ieyasu in other ways, but at the same time he continued to show concern for the safety of Hideyoshi's heir, Hideyori.

Though his talents were principally military, he was also an able administrator and won the admiration of the people of his domain by opening up the Kikuchi River for navigation and carrying out other projects that benefited them. For a time he also dispatched ships to carry on trade with Southeast Asia. His death in 1611 was a windfall for Ieyasu, clearing the way for the final overthrow of the Toyotomi family.

Katsuragawa Hoshū 桂川甫周 (1751–1809)

A physician and student of Dutch learning in the middle Edo period; his personal name was Kokuzui, his formal name Kōkan, and his literary name Getchi. His family for generations served as physicians to the Tokugawa shogunate, Hoshū representing the fourth generation to hold such a position. He was eighteen when he assumed the post of *okui* (physician) to the shogun. In 1771 he helped prepare a translation of a Dutch work on dissection, being the youngest member of the group of translators. The work, entitled *Kaitai shinsho*, represents the earliest translation of a European medical text into Japanese. In 1772 he was ordered by the shogunate to confer with the head of the Dutch trading office in Nagasaki on the occasion of the latter's visit to Edo. In 1776 he had occasion to meet the Swedish physician Karl Peter Thunberg, who was attached to the Dutch trading office, received medical instruction from him, and was given a certificate to that effect. In 1783 he was awarded the highest rank of physician, *hōgen*, and in 1794 was appointed professor of surgery in the Igakkan, the medical school maintained in Edo under the auspices of the shogunate.

In addition to his medical interests, he was active as a writer and translator. Gathering information from Daikokuya Kōdayū, a Japanese seaman who was shipwrecked and detained in Russia for a time, as well as from others like him, he wrote the *Hokusa bunryaku* and *Hyōryūmin goranki.* He also produced the *Roshia-shi* and *Rokoku jijitsu-shō,* works giving information on Russia that were in part translated from Dutch sources. In addition, his writings include works on geography and medicine such as the *Chikyū zenzu, Bankoku zusetsu, Oranda yakusen, Kaijō biyōhō,* and *Geka taisei.* Because no works on Western internal medicine had been translated, he persuaded Utagawa Genzui to translate such a work (Japanese title: *Naika senyō*) by the Dutch scholar Johannes de Gorter. He died in 1809 at the age of fifty-eight. The seventh generation physician of the same family, Katsuragawa Kunioki, also used the name Hoshū and was active in Dutch studies at the end of the Edo and the beginning of the Meiji period.

Kawaji Toshiakira 川路聖謨 (1801–1868)

Shogunate official in charge of finance and foreign affairs in the late Edo period. His father was a samurai named Naitō, but he became the adopted son of Kawaji Sanzaemon; his younger brother was Inoue Naokiyo, who held the title of Shinano-no-kami. He was first appointed to office in the shogunate in 1818 and thereafter held a series of posts having to do at various times with the treasury, the local administrations of the island of Sado and the cities of Nara and Osaka, coastal defense, and foreign relations. As official in charge of coastal defense, he was obliged to deal with the arrival of Commodore Perry and his squadron of American ships at the harbor of Uraga in 1853. When the Russian envoy Putiatin arrived at Nagasaki the same year, Toshiakira was put in charge of receiving him, exchanging memoranda with him concerning preferential rights and most favored nation treatment at such a time as trade relations should be established, and persuading him that in order to establish Russo-Japanese boundaries in the Kurile Islands and Kamchatka it was preferable that both countries send inspection parties to the area. The following year, when Putiatin returned to Japan, this time arriving at Shimoda, Toshiakira concluded a treaty of Russo-Japanese friendship with him.

In the dispute over the succession to the shogunate, he opposed the opinion of the high official Ii Naosuke and in 1859 was deprived of his post as minister of foreign affairs; it was restored to him in 1863, but at that time he declined it because of ill health. He published a work entitled *Kaikoku zushi* ("Illustrated Gazetteer of the Maritime Nations"), set up an office for the handling of books from abroad, and made other contributions to the culture of the time. On April 12, 1868, the day after the shogun handed over Edo Castle to the imperial forces, he committed suicide in his sickbed.

Kawamura Zuiken 河村瑞軒(隨見) (1618–1700)

Wealthy merchant of the middle Edo period. He was born in the village of Ukura in the province of Ise; Zuiken is a religious name taken when he entered the Buddhist clergy; later he returned to lay life under the name Hiradayū. He went to Edo at the age of twelve, at first working as a wagon puller, later as a pickle merchant, and finally, after becoming a head of day laborers employed in engineering projects for the shogunate, he opened a lumber business in Edo. In 1657, when the so-called Great Fire of the Meireki era destroyed much of the city, he hurried off to Fukushima in the Kiso region, bought up large quantities of lumber, and transported it to Edo, amassing a huge profit in the enterprise. Following this, he acquired further wealth by undertaking various engineering projects for the shogunate.

Not content merely to carry out projects for others, he displayed his own skill and ingenuity by opening up a new route for shipment of rice from the Tōhoku region of northern Japan to Edo, a process that had previously required a year to complete. By his new route, known as the *higashi-mawari*, or eastern circuit, rice was transported down the Abukuma River to Arahama on the Pacific coast, where it was carried by ship around the Bōsō Peninsula to Edo. In 1672 he devised a second route, the *nishi-mawari*, or western circuit, by which rice from northern Japan was brought around through the Shimonoseki straits, through the Inland Sea, and thus to Edo, a process that could be completed in three months. In 1683 he undertook a project to clear the outlets of the Yodo River in the Osaka region, conducting extensive work on the Aji, Nagara, and Nakatsu rivers. He wrote a work entitled *Nōkakun* ("Instructions for Farm Families"), and was on close terms with such eminent scholars as Arai Hakuseki and others, often assisting them in their financial needs. In recognition of his services, the shogunate in 1698 made him a *hatamoto*, or direct vassal of the shogun.

Kinokuniya Bunzaemon 紀國屋文左衞門 (1665–1734)

Wealthy merchant of the middle Edo period. He was born in the province of Kii, though the exact location of his birthplace is a matter of dispute. The region of Kii was famous for its tangerines, which commanded a very high price in Edo because of the difficulty of transporting them there by sea. In spite of the risks, however, Bunzaemon took a load of them to Edo by ship and succeeded in turning a very large profit. On the return voyage he loaded his ship with salted salmon, an item in short supply in western Japan, and further added to his wealth. Later he set up a lumber business in the Hatchōbori district of Edo and in time became a supplier of lumber for the shogunate, providing the material used in the building of the Komponchū-dō of the Kan'ei-ji temple in Ueno.

He ranked with Naraya Mozaemon as one of the wealthiest merchants of the time and, under the name Kibun Daijin, was frequently made the subject of kabuki plays and other forms of Edo popular literature. There is even a popular song of the period that mentions "white sails seen in the darkness offshore, the tangerine boats from the province of Kii." He took up the writing of haiku, studying under the poet Takarai (Enomoto) Kikaku and adopting the literary name Senzan, but with the fall from power of the statesman Yanagisawa Yoshiyasu, his fortunes rapidly declined and he lived out his last years in retirement in the Fukagawa section of Edo.

The facts of his life have become so entangled with legend that they are often difficult to make out, and it has been suggested that, while the original Kinokuniya made his money by shipping tangerines, it was a successor by the same name who became a wealthy lumber merchant. It is also possible that the story of Kinokuniya has become confused with that of another wealthy lumber dealer and shipping agent of approximately the same period, Kawamura Zuiken.

Kinoshita Jun'an 木下順庵 (1621–1698)

Confucian scholar of the early Edo period. His personal name was Sadatomo, and after his death his disciples referred to him as Kyōsei-sensei. Born in Kyoto, he manifested a talent for literature and learning at a very early age, and when he was only twelve composed a piece called *Taiheishō*, or "Hymn to Perfect Peace." He studied under the Confucian scholar Matsunaga Shakugo and later accompanied the lord of Tajima to Edo, but returned to Kyoto and opened a school in the Higashiyama section of Kyoto. He was invited by Maeda Tsunanori, the lord of Kaga, to come to his domain, but he recommended that the orphaned son of his teacher, Matsunaga Shakugo, be invited instead, whereupon Maeda Tsunanori generously provided a stipend for both men.

In 1682 Jun'an was invited by the shogunate to come to Edo and lecture to

Shogun Tsunayoshi and, along with the Confucian scholar Hayashi Nobuatsu and others, was put in charge of compiling the *Butoku taiseiki*, a biography of Tokugawa Ieyasu. Though he himself was a staunch follower of the Chi Hsi school of Neo-Confucianism, he took a liberal stand in matters of philosophical belief. His poems and prose in Chinese are collected in a work called the *Kinri bunshū*. He was particularly outstanding as a teacher, and numbered among his disciples such famous scholars and statesmen as Arai Hakuseki, Muro Kyūsō, Amenomori Hōshū, Gion Nankai, Sakakibara Kōshū, Nambu Nanzan, Miyake Kanran, and others.

Kondō Morishige 近藤守重 (1771–1829)

Hatamoto of the late Edo period and explorer of the Kurile and Sakhalin area. Also known as Kondō Jūzō, he was a *hatamoto*, or direct vassal of the shogun, and in 1798 was ordered by the shogunate to undertake a mission to Matsumae Ezochi, the present-day island of Hokkaido, remaining in the area until 1802 and exploring the Chishima (Kurile) Islands. He set up markers indicating that the territory belonged to Japan and did his utmost to facilitate the defense and colonization of the region. In 1807 he was ordered to conduct a second survey of the area and this time explored Rishiri Island. In 1808 he was made an official of the Momijiyama Bunko, the shogunate library in Edo Castle, and for the following eleven years he devoted himself to the writing of works on currency and foreign countries. In 1819 he was assigned to an administrative post in Osaka and in 1824 to a similar post in Nagasaki, but in 1827 he was punished because of a crime committed by his son and remained out of favor until his death two years later. Among his numerous writings are works dealing with economics, legal systems, geography, exploration and the history of Japanese contacts with foreign lands.

Konishi Yukinaga 小西行長 (d. 1600)

Christian daimyo of the Momoyama period. He was the son of Konishi Ryūsa a wealthy merchant of the port city of Sakai in the province of Izumi. He first served Ukita Naoie, a military leader under the powerful Mōri family of western Japan, but later became a vassal of Hideyoshi, distinguishing himself at the battle of Yamazaki, which took place after the assassination of Oda Nobunaga in 1582, at the battle of Shizugatake the following year, and in other encounters. He thus played an important part in assisting Hideyoshi to gain control of the entire country and became one of his most trusted retainers. Meanwhile, in 1584 he was baptized a Christian and took the name Augustine, being referred to by the European missionaries of the time as Don Augustin. In 1587 he won distinction in the campaign against Kyushu, and the following year helped to put down the peasant rebellion in the province of Higo, present-day Kumamoto Prefecture; in recognition for these accomplishments he was given a fief of 240,000 *koku* in the same province, where he devoted himself to protecting the Christians within his domain and carrying out acts of charity.

In 1592, when the so-called campaign of the Bunroku era against Korea took place, he was ordered by Hideyoshi to lead the vanguard and was the first to land at Pusan, after which he captured Seoul and went on to occupy Pyongyang. The following year he returned to Japan and labored to bring the peace negotiations that were then going on to a successful conclusion. When efforts to arrange a peaceful settlement failed, he took part in the second Korean invasion in 1597 but withdrew with the other leaders on the death of Hideyoshi the following year. In 1600 he joined Ishida Mitsunari and the others who opposed Tokugawa Ieyasu at the battle of Sekigahara but was defeated and, on orders from Ieyasu, was taken to Kyoto and put to death at the Rokujōgawara execution ground.

Kozeki San'ei 小關三英 (1787–1839)

Physician and scholar of Dutch learning in the late Edo period. Born in the domain of Shōnai in Dewa, he studied Dutch medicine under Yoshida Kukoku and became close friends with one of his fellow students, Takano Chōei. At the age of twenty-three he produced a translation of a world atlas entitled *Sekai chishi*. In 1822 he became a lecturer in the medical school of the domain of Sendai; the following year he went to Nagasaki to study under the German doctor von Siebold and thereafter became physician to the lord of Kishiwada. In 1834 he went to Edo and took a position in the office for the translation of foreign books, which was operated by the shogunate, and around this time joined with Takano Chōei, Watanabe Kazan, Suzuki Shunzan, and others, seventeen men in all, to form an association called the Shōshikai for the study of Dutch learning and the discussion of current problems.

In 1839 the shogunate, stung by the criticisms expressed by some of the members of the association, took stern measures to suppress it, arresting

Takano Chōei and Watanabe Kazan in the action known as the Bansha imprisonment; San'ei, knowing that he would never be able to stand prison life because of the poor condition of his health, committed suicide. His principal translations are the *Taisei naika shūsei*, later published under the title *Seii gembyōryaku*; the *Yochishi*; and the *Ponaparuto senki*.

Kudō Heisuke 工藤平助 (1732–1800)

Physician and administrator of the middle Edo period. He was the third son of Nagai Taiun, a physician of the domain of Kii, and at the age of twelve became the adopted son of Kudō Jōan, also a doctor, of the domain of Sendai. On reaching maturity he practiced medicine in Sendai, and in 1754 was made physician of the fief of Sendai and took up residence in Edo. He studied Confucianism under Hattori Nankaku and Aoki Kon'yō and, becoming friendly with such students of Dutch learning as Nakagawa Jun'an, Noro Genjō, and others, took up the study of Western subjects. Later he journeyed to Nagasaki and studied Dutch language and culture under one of the Dutch merchants there. In 1786 at his recommendation, Ōtsuki Gentaku was summoned to be a physician of the domain of Sendai, and together they conducted a survey of the herbs and other medicines to be found in the domain. In time he was also called upon to take part in administrative affairs of the fief.

He was much concerned over the possibility of Russian expansion into the region of Ezochi, as Hokkaido was known at that time, and in 1783 addressed a memorial on the subject to Tanuma Okitsugu, the highest ranking shogunate official of the period. In a work entitled *Aka Ezo fūsetsukō*, or "Reports of the Red Ezo" (i.e., Russians), he urged that steps be taken to protect the coastline and harbors of Japan, particularly in the northern region, and suggested that trade relations be established with Russia. His work had a great influence on the thinking of Hayashi Shihei, another scholar of Sendai who concerned himself with problems of coastal defense and national security.

Kumazawa Banzan 熊澤蕃山 (1619–1691)

Confucian scholar of the early Edo period. He was born into a Kyoto family named Nojiri but was adopted by his mother's father, Kumazawa Morihisa. In 1634 he took service under Ikeda Mitsumasa, the lord of Bizen (present-day Okayama Prefecture), but in 1639 left his position because of poor health and went to live with his grandfather at Kirihara in the province of Ōmi (Shiga Prefecture). There he devoted himself to study and in 1642 became a disciple of Nakae Tōju, an exponent of Yōmeigaku, the doctrines of the Ming Confucian scholar Wang Yang-ming, who emphasized the importance of practice over theory. In 1645 he returned to the service of Ikeda Mitsumasa, this time at a very substantial stipend, and applied himself to problems of land and water utilization and the prevention of famine in the fief of Bizen. But the success that he achieved in these undertakings aroused the criticism of rivals within the domain, and in 1658 he asked permission to retire and moved to Kyoto, where he devoted his time to writing and teaching.

As his fame increased, a number of persons associated with the court came to study with him, and this aroused the suspicions of the *shoshidai*, the official appointed by the Edo shogunate to superintend the court. As a consequence he left Kyoto in 1667 and lived on Mt. Yoshino and in other mountainous regions in the capital area, but because of criticisms of the shogunate that he expressed in his writings, he was arrested in 1669. He was first turned over to the fief of Akashi in present-day Hyōgo Prefecture for surveillance but was later moved to Kōriyama in Yamato and then to Furukawa in Shimōsa (Ibaraki Prefecture), where he died in confinement. His most important writings are the *Daigaku wakumon*, *Shūgi washo*, and *Shūgi gaisho*.

Maeno Ryōtaku 前野良澤 (1723–1803)

Physician and highly successful student of Dutch learning in the middle Edo period. His personal name was Yomisu, his formal name was Shietsu, and he used the literary names Rakuzan and Ranka; Ryōtaku was probably a common name. His father was Taniguchi Shinsuke, a samurai of Chikuzen in Kyushu, but he died when Ryōtaku was still very young. Ryōtaku was brought up by an uncle, Miyata Sentaku, a physician of the fief of Yodo near Osaka, and was later adopted by Maeno Tōgen, a physician of the fief of Nakatsu in Kyushu. At first he studied the traditional style Chinese and Japanese medicine as taught by Yoshimasa Tōdō, but in 1769 he was introduced to Dutch medical works by Saka Kōō of the domain of Yodo. Around this time he became a disciple of Aoki Kon'yō and began study of the Dutch language. In 1770 he accompanied Okudaira, the lord of the domain of Nakatsu, on a trip home from Kyushu and, obtaining a hundred-day leave of absence, went to Nagasaki to continue his Dutch studies.

In 1771, at the invitation of the physician Sugita Gempaku, he joined in observing dissections carried out on the bodies of executed criminals in Kozukahara in Edo. (According to the custom of the time, the actual dissection was carried out by menials while the doctors looked on.) Ryōtaku compared what he saw with the information found in a Dutch book he had acquired at Nagasaki entitled *Ontleedkundige Tafelen* (1734), a translation of a German work entitled *Anatomische Tabellen* by J. A. Kulmus. Impressed with the accuracy of the work, he set about, with the assistance of Sugita Gempaku, Nakagawa Jun'an, Katsuragawa Hoshū, and Mine Shuntai, to translate it into Japanese. The translation was completed in 1774 and published under the title *Kaitai shinsho*. This was the first translation of a work of European science to be produced in Japan.

From this time on, he devoted his energies almost entirely to translation, introducing works not only on medicine but on such other fields as language, astronomy, geography, and military science. The titles include *Kanrei higen*, *Jingen shisetsu*, *Jigaku shōsei*, *Oranda yakusen*, *Oranda chikujō-sho*, *Kamsatsu kashi*, and *Roshia hongi*. He carried out his studies and translation work under the patronage of the lord of the Nakatsu domain, who was moved by his boundless energy and enthusiasm to refer to him as "our Dutch freak." Ryōtaku did not have a large number of disciples, though the group included men such as Ōtsuki Gentaku and Ema Ransai, and he numbered among his friends Kudō Heisuke and Takayama Hikokurō. He died in the tenth month of 1803.

Mamiya Rinzō 間宮林藏 (1780–1845)

Explorer of the region north of Japan in the late Edo period and discoverer of the Mamiya Straits. His personal name was Rinsō. He was the son of a farm family of the district of Tsukuba in Hitachi; his birth date is sometimes given as 1776. His talents were recognized by a shogunate official named Shimojō Yoshinosuke, and arrangements were made for him to be educated in Edo. In 1796 he became a *fushin-yaku-yatoi*, or construction worker in the service of the shogunate, advancing to a slightly higher post in 1799. In 1800 he was sent as a *goyō-yatoi*, or employee of the shogunate in the Ezochi or Hokkaido region, to explore the Chishima (Kurile) Islands. While on this assignment, he met the surveyor Inō Tadataka and learned surveying techniques from him. In 1803 he carried out a land survey in western Ezo. In 1808, after having been promoted to the level of *fushin-yaku-kaku*, he was dispatched along with Matsuda Denjūrō to explore Karafuto (Sakhalin).

Matsuda explored the western shore of Sakhalin while Mamiya explored the eastern shore. Mamiya was forced by bad weather to suspend his explorations for a time, but in 1809 set out once more and this time discovered that Sakhalin is an island, a fact hitherto unknown. The body of water that separates it from the mainland was named the Mamiya Straits, and its existence was made known to the West by the German physician Siebold. Later he was sent to explore the seven islands off the shore of the Izu Peninsula. In 1828, when Siebold was found to have in his possession a map of Japan, and he and his Japanese associates were imprisoned, Mamiya was suspected of having informed on one of them, Takahashi Kageyasu. As a result, he spent a rather friendless old age. His writings include the *Tōtatsu kikō*, *Kita Ezo zusetsu*, and *Hokui kōshō*, all based on his own explorations of the regions north of Japan. He died in the second month of 1845.

Matsudaira Nobutsuna 松平信綱 (1596–1662)

A statesman of the early Edo period. He was the eldest son of Ōkōchi Hisatsuna; his childhood name was Kamechiyo, which was later changed to Chōshirō. He was adopted by his uncle Matsudaira Masatsuna. In 1604 he became a page in the service of Tokugawa Iemitsu, and in 1622, when Iemitsu was selected to be the third shogun, Nobutsuna came to play an important role in government affairs. In 1633 he became an assistant councilor of state (*rokuninshū*, later called *wakadoshiyori*), and in 1635 he was advanced to *rōjū*, or councilor of state. He was made daimyo of the fief of Kawagoe in Musashi with an annual stipend of 75,000 *koku* of rice. During the years 1637–38 he replaced Itakura Shigemasa, who had been killed in battle, in putting down the Shimabara Revolt in Kyushu. He also played a part in frustrating the planned rebellions of Yui Shōsetsu and Bekki Shōsaemon, in rebuilding Edo after the disastrous fire of 1657, and in helping to work out the machinery of government for the Tokugawa shogunate and to establish it on a firm footing. He died in the second month of 1662.

Matsudaira Sadanobu 松平定信 (1758–1829)

A statesman and reformer of the shogunate in the middle Edo period. His childhood name was Katamaru, and his literary names Rakuō and Kagetsuō. He was the third son of Tayasu Munetake and a grandson of the eighth shogun, Tokugawa Yoshimune. In his youth he studied Confucianism and calligraphy under Ōtsuka Takayasu and was skilled in the composition of Japanese and Chinese poetry, painting, and the military arts. In 1774 he became the adopted son of Matsudaira Sadakuni, lord of the domain of Shirakawa, and in 1783 succeeded his foster father as daimyo. He worked to encourage devotion to learning and the military arts within the domain and promoted forestation and the improvement of agriculture. As a result of these enlightened measures, and of his attention to frugality and the efficient transportation of foodstuffs, not a single person within the domain died of starvation during the terrible Temmei famine (1782–87), which elsewhere in the country claimed millions of lives.

In 1787, when the *rōjū* (councilor of state) Tanuma Okitsugu fell from power, Sadanobu replaced him and the following year began carrying out the governmental changes, which, because of the era name, are commonly referred to as the Kansei Reforms. His first measures were to promote men of ability in his administration and to encourage simplicity and thrift. Concerned about the possibility of Russian encroachment to the south, he also submitted plans for coastal defenses to protect Edo Bay. He meted out punishment to officials and merchants doing business with the government who were guilty of corruption, reduced the *sukegō*, or conscript labor tax, imposed upon the farmers living along the main highways, and otherwise lightened the burdens imposed upon the peasant class. In order to provide honest employment for the numbers of persons who had drifted into Edo from the farming communities, he established centers for that purpose. Finally, he initiated a policy of not assigning government office to any person who did not adhere to the officially sanctioned Chu Hsi School of Neo-Confucianism; the measure has come to be known as the Kansei prohibition of unorthdox learning.

In 1793 he retired from his duties in the shogunate and devoted all his attention to his own domain of Shirakawa, where he established an official school of Confucian studies called the Rikkyōkan. In 1810, acting on orders from the shogunate, he cooperated with the domain of Aizu in establishing cannon emplacements along the shore of the Bōsō Peninsula at the entrance to Edo Bay. He distinguished himself not only as a statesman but as a poet, critic, and man of letters as well, and also took an interest in archeological matters. His works include the *Seigo*, *Bukkaron*, *Kagetsu sōshi*, *Taikan zakki*, *Sansōshū*, *Uge no hitokoto*, *Shūshinroku*, and *Shūko jusshu*. He died in the fifth month of 1829.

Matsuura Shigenobu 松浦鎮信 (1549–1614)

Daimyo of the domain of Hirado in Kyushu in the early Edo period. He held the honorary title of Hizen-no-kami, and later that of Shikibu-kyō Hōin, and hence was referred to by the European merchants visiting Hirado as Hōin-sama. He was the son of Matsuura Takanobu and in 1587 succeeded his father as lord of Hirado. He was among the most famous and well informed of the lords of Kyushu, and in 1587 assisted Toyotomi Hideyoshi in bringing the island under control. Later, at the time of Hideyoshi's campaigns against Korea, he presented Hideyoshi with a map of Korea and, joining the fighting forces, distinguished himself in battle.

In 1600 he sided with Tokugawa Ieyasu at the battle of Sekigahara and was subsequently confirmed in the possession of his domain. He took an interest in foreign trade and gave permission to the Dutch to open a trading office at Hirado. In 1613 similar permission was given to the English, and for a time Hirado flourished side by side with Nagasaki as a center of foreign trade. Through Matsuura's intervention, John Saris, the head of the British East India Company at Hirado, was able to obtain an interview with Tokugawa Ieyasu. Matsuura was also noted as an expert in the tea ceremony. When he returned from the Korean campaigns, he brought back with him as prisoners a number of Korean potters who contributed greatly to the advancement of the pottery industry in the area. He died in 1614.

Mitsui Takatoshi 三井高利 (1622–1694)

A highly successful merchant of the early Edo period and the founder of the Mitsui family fortunes. His common name was Hachirōbei. From the middle ages, the Mitsui family had been retainers to the Sasaki family, lords of a domain in the province of Ōmi. At the beginning of the Edo period, a Mitsui Takatoshi (written 高俊) set up in business as a saké merchant and pawnbroker in Matsuzaka in Ise. The Mitsui Takatoshi who is the subject of this article was the first Takatoshi's fourth son. By lending money to the daimyo and to needy farmers and buying and selling rice, he managed to acquire a considerable fortune and in 1673 opened clothing goods stores in Kyoto and Edo under the shop name Echigoya. By demanding cash at the time of purchase rather than in the customary semiannual or annual payments and by selling goods at a low margin of profit and concentrating upon a large volume of sales he was able to succeed in business. In 1683 he opened a money exchange in Edo, and in 1691 set up businesses in Osaka.

He had many sons and divided them up into six families, the Kita-no-Mitsui, to which the eldest son succeeded and which acted as the head family, and five branch families such as the Rokke-no-Mitsui, etc. In late Edo times the Mitsui were commissioned by the shogunate to handle the transfer of funds between Edo and Osaka, and in this way laid the foundation for their later prosperity in industry and commercial enterprises.

MIURA BAIEN 三浦梅園 (1723–1789)

Independent and creative thinker of the middle Edo period; his personal name was Susumu, his formal name, Yasusada; Baien was his professional name. He was born in the village of Tominaga, the district of Kunisaki, in the province of Bungo in Kyushu, the son of a physician named Giichi. In 1739, at the age of sixteen, he studied the writing of poetry and prose in Chinese under Ayabe Keisai, a resident of the castle town of Kitsuki, and later became a student of Fujita Keisho, a teacher of the *kogaku*, or "ancient learning," school of Confucianism. Around 1743 he compiled a collection of his verse in Chinese entitled *Dokushōshū*. He embarked upon a walking tour in 1745 that took him to Nagasaki, Dazaifu, Kumamoto, and other important cities and historical sites of Kyushu. In 1747 he was invited by the Kurushima family, lords of the fief of Kusu in his native province, to enter official service, but he steadfastly declined the invitation, preferring to devote all his time to his studies.

Around 1751 he began developing his highly original concept of *jōri*, a term that has been translated as the "logic of things," which denotes a system of natural order underlying man and the universe and is comparable to present-day principles of logic, mathematics, physics, and ethical science. In the years that followed, he labored to formulate a logical system of thought based upon this concept, and in 1775, at the age of fifty-two, set forth his ideas in a work entitled *Gengo*. In another work, *Zeigo*, he presents a critique of other systems of thought based upon his own concept of *jōri*, and in his *Kango* discusses the application of his thinking to the fields of government and morality. In addition, he wrote a work on human physiology, *Shinsei yodan*; a treatise on such economic questions as currency and prices, *Kagen*; and various other works. He died in his native village of Tominaga at the age of sixty-six.

Miyazaki Yasusada 宮崎安貞 (1623–1697)

Agronomist of the early Edo period; his common name was Buntayū. He was the second son of Miyazaki Giuemon, a samurai of the domain of Hiroshima in Aki. In 1647 he entered the service of the domain of Fukuoka in Kyushu with a yearly stipend of two hundred *koku* of rice. When he had passed the age of thirty, he resigned his post and took up the life of a farmer in the village of Meubara in the Shima district of the Fukuoka domain. He studied Chinese works on agriculture and botany, and at the same time traveled extensively along the Inland Sea and through the Kyoto, Osaka, Ise and Shima Peninsula regions, talking with elderly farmers and questioning them on their experience. The result of these labors was a work in ten chapters entitled *Nōgyō zensho* ("Agricultural Encyclopedia"). A Confucian scholar of the domain of Fukuoka named Kaibara Rakuken made various changes in the text and added a chapter of his own, and another Confucian scholar, his elder brother, Kaibara Ekiken, contributed a preface. The work was printed in 1697, and Miyazaki died in the tenth month of the same year at the age of seventy-four.

The work deals with the subject of agriculture in general and also includes chapters on grains, vegetables, wild vegetables, fruit trees and other types of useful trees, herbs, and methods of cultivation. Miyazaki was influenced by Chinese Confucian ideas regarding the nature and importance of agriculture, but he combined these with a practical knowledge of the subject gained from personal experience, creating in the *Nōgyō zensho* a uniquely Japanese exposition of the subject.

Mizuno Tadakuni 水野忠邦 (1794–1851)

A high official of the Tokugawa shogunate who, during the Tempō era (1830–44), attempted to carry out various fiscal and governmental reforms in order to strengthen the power of the shogunate. He was born in Edo, the second son of Mizuno Tadamitsu, lord of the fief of Karatsu in Hizen; in childhood he went by the name Otogorō. In 1805 he was made heir to his father, and in 1812, at the age of eighteen, became lord of Karatsu and set about reforming the finances of the domain. In 1817 he was made a *jisha-bugyō* of the Tokugawa shogunate, a high official who had supervision over the temples, shrines, and religious affairs of the country. In the same year he was removed from his former fief in Hizen in Kyushu and made lord of Hamamatsu in Tōtōmi. He continued to rise in office in the shogunate until in 1834, at the age of forty, he became *rōjū-shuseki*, or chief councilor of state, taking over effective control of all affairs of government.

In 1841, with the death of shogun Tokugawa Ienari, he set about instituting a series of reforms that, because of the era name, came to be known as the Tempō Reforms. In terms of foreign policy, he adopted Western gunnery techniques and took steps to strengthen the coastal defenses and in 1842 rescinded previous orders to attack and repulse all foreign vessels, allowing vessels that were in difficulty to receive supplies of food, water, and fuel. In internal affairs he issued orders designed to enforce greater frugality and to reduce prices. In 1843 he announced his famous Jōchirei, a plan to place all lands in the immediate vicinity of Edo and Osaka under control of the shogunate, the owners to be given lands elsewhere by way of compensation, which aroused a storm of protest. The severity of his measures, particularly those designed to curb luxury and manipulate prices, provoked resentment among the samurai, the ladies of the shogun's household, and the merchants, and in 1843, while still in the midst of promulgating his reforms, he was forced to step down from the position of councilor of state. He was recalled to the post for a brief time, but was once more dismissed and even deprived of his domain. He remained in disgrace for the rest of his life, dying of illness in 1851.

Mogami Tokunai 最上徳内 (1755–1836)

Explorer of Hokkaido, the Kurile Islands, and Sakhalin in the late Edo period. He was the son of a farm family of the village of Tateoka in the province of Dewa. He became a servant in the household of Yamada Tonan, a physician in the shogunate. Later he entered the private school in Edo operated by the geographer and economist Honda Toshiaki, studying astronomy, geography, surveying, and navigation under him. In 1785, when Honda Toshiaki was incapacitated by illness, he took Honda's place in participating, along with Aoshima Toshizō, in a party sent out by the shogunate to explore Ezochi, as Hokkaido was called at that time, and the Chishima (Kurile) Islands. The party succeeded in carrying out a survey of the southern Kuriles.

In 1789, when the Ainu of Kunashiri rose up in revolt, Mogami acted as guide to the investigation party sent out by the shogunate. In recognition of his services, he was advanced from the post of *fushin-yaku shitayaku*, a rather lowly position in the shogunate, to that of *fushin-yaku*. In 1791 he conducted another exploration of the southern Kuriles, and the following year of Karafuto (Sakhalin). In 1798 he and Kondō Jūzō (Morishige) sailed to the island of Etorofu. In 1807 he became a *shirabeyaku-nami*, or supernumerary invesitgation official in the *Hakodate-bugyō*, the shogunate administrative office in Ezochi. When the Russian envoy Laxman escorted to Matsumae the Japanese seaman Daikokuya Kōdayū, who had been shipwrecked in Siberia, Mogami was assigned to receive him. In 1826, when the German doctor von Siebold, who was attached to the Dutch trading office in Nagasaki, visited Edo, Mogami lent him a copy of the survey map of Ezochi, helped him to compile a glossary of Ainu words, and presented him with botanical specimens from Ezochi. Siebold, in his work on Japan entitled *Nippon*, duly records the debt that he owes to Mogami. Mogami's own writings include the *Ezo sōshi*, *Sekijin mondō*, *Matsumae shiryaku*, and *Doryōkō settō*. He died in the ninth month of 1836.

Mōri Terumoto 毛利輝元 (1553–1625)

Powerful daimyo and military leader of western Honshu in the late sixteenth and early seventeenth century; he was the eldest son of Mōri Takamoto and the grandson of Mōri Motonari. In childhood he went by the names Yukitsurumaru and Shōtarō; the eleventh Ashikaga shogun Yoshiteru gave him permission to use the element *teru* from his own name to make up the name Terumoto.

With his father's death in 1663, Terumoto became head of his father's domain, but since he was only nine at the time, his grandfather Mōri Motonari attended to administrative matters. Thereafter Terumoto and his grandfather launched a campaign against the Amako family of Izumo and eventually made themselves masters of a domain comprising ten provinces in the San'in and San'yō regions of western Honshu. Motonari died in 1571, but thereafter Terumoto was aided by his uncles Kikkawa Motoharu and Kobayakawa Takakage and was able to retain control over his vast holdings.

In 1573 the military leader Oda Nobunaga drove the fifteenth Ashikaga shogun Yoshiaki out of Kyoto and put an end to the Ashikaga shogunate. Yoshiaki sought refuge with opponents of Oda Nobunaga in various parts of the country and attempted to carry on resistance to him. In 1576, with the aid of Mōri Terumoto, he took up residence in Tomo in the province of Bingo, which was a part of Terumoto's domain. At this time, the powerful Hongan-ji temple, situated at Ishiyama in present-day Osaka, was allied with Yoshiaki in resisting Oda Nobunaga. Nobunaga launched an attack on the temple, which was heavily fortified, but Mōri Terumoto came to its aid by supplying it with arms and provisions by sea. Nobunaga thereupon decided to launch an attack on the Chūgoku region of western Honshu where Terumoto's domains were situated, dispatching his subordinate Hashiba (later Toyotomi) Hideyoshi to lead the attack. Terumoto put up a stout resistance, but was several times defeated in combat.

In 1582, Hideyoshi laid siege to the castle of Takamatsu in Bitchū, the stronghold of one of Terumoto's vassals. Terumoto and his uncles hastened to relieve the siege, preparing for a decisive battle with Hideyoshi, when news came that Hideyoshi's commander, Oda Nobunaga, had been assassinated at Honnō-ji in Kyoto. Hideyoshi thereupon arranged a peaceful settlement with Terumoto and hastened back to Kyoto. Thereafter Terumoto became a follower of Hideyoshi, joining him in his campaign against Kyushu in 1587. In 1590, when Hideyoshi carried out his campaign against Odawara, Terumoto remained in Kyoto to guard the city. This was the year that Hideyoshi finally brought all of Japan under his control.

In 1591 Terumoto filled in the delta area at the mouth of the Ōta River and built Hiroshima Castle, abandoning his former residence at Kōriyama and moving to the new castle. The same year he received from Hideyoshi patents recognizing his right to a domain comprising nine provinces and a revenue of 1,120,000 *koku* of rice. In 1595 he was given the court post of acting *chūnagon* and in 1598 was chosen to be one of the five *tairō* (senior councilors) who were to form the regency during the minority of Hideyoshi's son Hideyori. He thus became one of the most powerful and eminent daimyo in the nation.

After Hideyoshi's death in 1598, Terumoto continued to aid and support his son and successor Toyotomi Hideyori. At the time of the great battle of Sekigahara in 1600, Terumoto remained at Osaka Castle to guard Hideyori and did not take any direct part in the hostilities. But since he had been allied with the losing side, he was severely reprimanded by Tokugawa Ieyasu, the victor and new ruler of the country. Terumoto was stripped of almost two-thirds of his domains and was left merely with the possession of the provinces of Suō and Nagato in far western Honshu and a revenue of 370,000 *koku*. Terumoto thereupon shaved his head and entered the Buddhist clergy, taking the religious name Sōzui. He turned over the supervision of his domain to his son Mōri Hidenari, but continued to keep an eye on the management of affairs. In 1604 he built a castle at Hagi on the Japan Sea, making that the administrative center for the domain.

These measures taken against the Mōri family naturally occasioned a sharp reduction in the stipends of the numerous retainers of the family, who were obliged to move from Hiroshima to the new domain headquarters in

Hagi, and left them with deep feelings of resentment against the Tokugawa shogunate. This is one of the reasons why the domain, commonly referred to as Chōshū, took a leading part in the movement to overthrow the shogunate in the nineteenth century.

Motoki Einoshin 本木榮之進 (1735–1794)

An interpreter of Dutch at Nagasaki in the middle Edo period. He was the grandson of Motoki Shōdayū, who held the post of *daitsūji*, or chief interpreter. His personal name was Yoshinaga and he also went by the common names Jindayū and Einoshin; his *gō* (literary name) was Rankō. In 1748 he became a *keiko tsūji*, or apprentice interpreter, and in 1788 was made a chief interpreter. Earlier, in 1744, he and his fellow officials Yoshio Kōzaemon, Nishi Zenzaburō, and others requested permission to study some of the Dutch books in their possession. When permission was granted by the government authorities, Motoki devoted full time to the work of translation. In addition to Dutch, he also had a knowledge of Latin and French and was well informed in matters pertaining to astronomy, geography, medicine, botany, the calendar, and production methods. He was highly respected both by the shogunate and the lords of the various domains for his ability as a translator.

His translations include a two-volume work entitled *Seijutsu taiyō kyūri ryōkai-setsu*, the first work to introduce the Copernican theory to Japan. A forerunner of the astronomical studies and translations of his disciple Shizuki Tadao, it exercised a profound influence upon the thinkers of the time. In 1794 he requested permission to retire from his duties, and was officially rewarded as a recognition for his diligent service. His other works include the *Oranda honzō* in two volumes; a work on the Western calendar entitled *Oranda eizoku koyomi wage*; a work on sundials and moondials entitled *Nichigetsukei wage*; and a work in four volumes entitled *Tenchi nikyū yōhō*, which explains the use of celestial and terrestrial globes.

Motoki Shōzō 本木昌造 (1824–1875)

The first man to use lead movable type in Japan and to employ Western style printing methods. His formal name was Nagahisa and his literary name Kosō. He was the fourth son of Kitajima San'yata of Nagasaki; he was later adopted by an official interpreter of Dutch named Motoki Shōzaemon and succeeded his foster father in the post of interpreter. He took a great interest in Western technological methods, particularly those involved in printing, and in 1848 purchased a Dutch-made printing press and a font of type for printing European languages. In 1855, when a government-operated movable type printing office was set up in Nagasaki, he was assigned to it. At the same time, he acted as interpreter for the Dutch instructor on steamships attached to a government school of naval warfare called the Nagasaki Kaigun Denshūjo, and had occasion to study chemistry, physics, and methods of iron manufacture under a Dutch physician.

In 1860 he was assigned to the government iron manufacturing office in Nagasaki and, after the Meiji Restoration in 1868, became head of the office. In 1869 he opened a private school and, in order to raise funds for its support, began to consider how to employ movable type printing for commercial ends. The following year, under the guidance of an American named William Gamble, he set up a printing school and succeeded in casting his own type. He established branch printing offices in Osaka and Tokyo, but never developed them into commercial ventures. He also set up a printing office in Yokohama, from which he published a newspaper called the *Yokohama Mainichi Shimbun*. He died in September, 1875.

Mukai Genshō 向井元升 (1609–1677)

Physician of the early Edo period; he was born in Hizen in Kyushu. His father's name was Kaneyoshi, and his own name, Kuromatsu, which he later changed to Genshō.

At the age of seven he moved with his father to Nagasaki, where he studied astronomy, geography, and the lore of medicinal herbs. In 1630 he determined to become a physician and, after much hardship and study by himself, he mastered Chinese style medicine and began to gain a reputation for his skill. He was also an enthusiastic exponent of Confucianism and in 1647 received permission from the Nagasaki city authorities to set up a temple in honor of Confucius there. He also set up a school where he taught Confucianism and worked to improve the morals of the citizens of Nagasaki. His heirs continued in later years to preside over the temple as Confucian scholars. From 1688 on, at the request of the shogunate they also undertook the task of examining books imported from China to make certain that none pertaining to Christianity were allowed into the country.

In 1658 Mukai moved with his wife and family to Kyoto. He was called upon to treat many members of the imperial family and court and was widely known for his skill. He wrote over ten works on medicine and medicinal herbs, including the earliest work on herbs to be compiled in the Edo period, the *Hōchū biyō wamyō honzō*. His second son was Mukai Kyorai (1651–1704), one of the leading disciples of the haiku poet Matsuo Bashō, and his third son, Mukai Rochō (1656–1727), was a noted Confucian scholar and haiku poet.

Christovão Ferreira (1580–1650; Japanese name Sawano Chūan), a Portuguese Jesuit who was arrested for missionary activities in 1633 and who renounced his faith, was ordered by the shogunate to make a Japanese translation of a European work on astronomy. When the work appeared, Mukai Genshō wrote a refutation of it entitled *Kenkon bensetsu*. Mukai's work had a great influence upon Japanese intellectual circles in later times and played a decisive role in convincing people that the earth is round.

NAKAE TŌJU 中江藤樹 (1608–1648)

Confucian scholar of the early Edo period. Born in the village of Ogawa in the province of Ōmi, his personal name was Hajime. His father having died, he was adopted at the age of eight by his grandfather Nakae Yoshinaga, a samurai of the domain of Yonago, and when Katō, the lord of Yonago, was transferred to the domain of Ōsu in Iyo Province in Shikoku, Tōju and his grandfather accompanied him there. Upon his grandfather's death in 1622, Tōju became head of the family and an official in the local administration. Fond of learning, at the age of sixteen he studied on his own Chu Hsi's commentaries on the *Four Books* and acquainted himself with the teachings of the Chu Hsi school of Neo-Confucianism. At the age of twenty-six he left the service of the Katō family and returned to his home in Ōmi, his reason being that he wished to take care of his aged mother, though it is probable that political and academic rivalries within the domain contributed to his decision. At his home in Ōmi on the west shore of Lake Biwa, he gathered about him a group of friends and young people from the neighboring villages and opened a school; because an old wisteria grew in the garden near the room where he taught, he came to be called Tōju-sensei, Wisteria Tree Master.

Around the age of thirty-two he developed a great fondness for the works of the Chinese Taoist school of philosophy, and his teachings took on a strongly religious bent. The *Okina mondō*, a work compiled by his disciples, gives a detailed account of his thought at this time and records his conviction that man should live as nobly as the gods. At the age of thirty-six he began a study of the complete works of the Ming Neo-Confucian philosopher

Wang Yang-ming, who opposed the teachings of Chu Hsi and emphasized the importance of translating one's beliefs into positive action. Converted to Wang Yang-ming's views, he became the first exponent of the Yang-ming, or Yōmei, school of Neo-Confucianism in Japan. He wrote a number of commentaries on Confucian texts in which he expounded his mature philosophy, stressing the prime importance of self-examination and spiritual purity and emphasizing the inner equality of all men, an equality that transcends social differences of class and occupation. As a result, his teachings appealed not only to the samurai, but spread among members of the peasant class as well, and in time he came to be referred to as The Saint of Ōmi. Ikeda Mitsumasa, lord of the domain of Okayama, expressed great admiration for his doctrines, inviting Tōju to lecture to him, providing for the upbringing of Tōju's son, and taking into his service one of Tōju's principal disciples, Kumazawa Banzan.

Nakagawa Jun'an 中川淳庵 (1739–1786)

Physician and scholar of Dutch learning of the middle Edo period. His family were for generations physicians in the domain of Obama in Wakasa Province. He was interested in the study of plants, particularly herbs, and the development of natural products. Making many new discoveries in these fields, he even produced, joining with Hiraga Gennai, a kind of asbestos cloth called *kakampu.* In 1770 he succeeded his father as physician and head of the family. At the same time, becoming interested in Western science and medicine, he began the study of Dutch under the physician Yasutomi Kiseki and, when the opportunity presented itself, called on the Dutch merchants who periodically came to Edo to pay their respects to the shogun.

In 1771 he joined with Maeno Ryōtaku, Sugita Gempaku, and others in undertaking a Japanese translation of a Dutch work entitled *Ontleedkundige Tofelen* (1624), which in turn was a translation of a German work on anatomy by a physician named Johann Adam Kulmus, and after much labor published the completed translation in 1774 under the title *Kaitai shinsho.* This was the first translation of a Western medical work to appear in Japan and laid the foundation for the introduction and development of Western medical practices. In 1775 Jun'an, along with Katsuragawa Hoshū, studied medicine and natural science under Carl Peter Thunberg, a Swedish physician who was attached to the Dutch trading office at Nagasaki, and in return helped Thunberg to carry on his studies in botany. He was also friendly with the head of the Dutch trading office, Isaac Titsingh; after Titsingh returned to Holland, Jun'an continued to exchange documents and articles related to research with him. In 1778 he became private physician to the lord of Obama and in time received a stipend amounting to 140 *koku.* He left a number of writings and translations dealing with Western medicine and other subjects.

Nichiō 日奥 (1565–1630)

Buddhist monk of the early Edo period, founder of the Fuju-fuse branch of the Nichiren sect. He was born in Kyoto, the son of a wealthy merchant, and entered the priesthood at the age of eleven under Nitten of Myōkaku-ji in Kyoto. In 1592 he replaced Nitten as head of Myōkaku-ji. In 1595, the military dictator Toyotomi Hideyoshi, as part of his policy to bring religious organizations under tighter control, announced plans to hold a memorial service for his deceased parents in the Hall of the Great Buddha of Hōkō-ji in Kyoto, summoning a number of monks from all the various Buddhist sects to participate. The Nichiren sect, however, forbids its priests and laypersons to recite sutras for or receive alms from persons belonging to other sects, the prohibition being known as *fuju-fuse.* Hideyoshi's invitation thus posed a serious problem. Nichiō and three other monks adamantly refused to take part in the ceremony and withdrew from Myōkaku-ji.

In 1599 Hideyoshi's successor to power, Tokugawa Ieyasu, arranged a debate between Nichiō and another monk of the Nichiren sect who in the past had proven more conciliatory in attitude. Nichiō refused to modify his position and as a result was banished to the island of Tsushima. He was pardoned in 1612 and returned to Kyoto, where his followers began to increase in number. The branch of the Nichiren sect headed by Kuon-ji of Mt. Minobu, fearful of his growing power, took steps to oppose him. In 1630 Tokugawa Ieyasu once more ordered him to take part in a religious debate. Nichiō, too ill to participate in person, sent his disciple Nichiju to represent him. The result was that Nichiō and his followers were once more subjected to severe restraint. Throughout the remainder of the Edo period, the Fuju-fuse branch of the Nichiren sect, as Nichiō's group came to be known, was strictly outlawed, though it continued to exist in secret, guarding the purity of its beliefs until the ban on it was finally lifted in 1874.

NINOMIYA SONTOKU 二宮尊徳 (1787–1856)

Administrator and specialist in agricultural affairs who worked vigorously to restore prosperity to the farming villages in the late Edo period; his common name was Kinjirō. He was the son of a middle-class farm family of the village of Kayama, Ashigara District, in the province of Sagami. His family's livelihood was wiped out by the floods of the Sakawa River, and both his parents died when he was still a child. But from his youth he was noted for his devotion to learning and diligence, and by around the age of twenty-four he had succeeded in reestablishing the Ninomiya family. Later he was requested by the Hattori family, chief retainers of the fief of Odawara, to help the family out of the financial difficulties into which it had fallen. He succeeded in reorganizing the family's finance, displaying unusual talent in the process. He also exerted great effort in restoring many abandoned farm villages in the fiefs of Odawara, Karasuyama, and Shimodate. He was particularly noted for the leadership that he demonstrated in carrying out engineering projects in the villages and opening up new lands for cultivation.

Many farmers of the time, because of the financial pressures upon them, had abandoned their farms and villages. In restoring health to the farming communities, Ninomiya insisted that the yearly levies and taxes imposed upon the farmers by the lord of the fief be kept at a fixed level and employed any surplus funds that became available to improve agricultural facilities or to invest in activities profitable to the farm community. At the same time, he worked to impress upon the farmers the importance of simple, frugal ways of living and of diligence.

As his fame spread, he attracted the attention of the Tokugawa shogunate, which in 1842 appointed him to take charge of public works projects. In 1853 he undertook to restore prosperity to the farming villages in the domain of the Tōshō-gū in Nikkō, the shrine dedicated to the founder of the Tokugawa shogunate, but he fell ill and died before completing the task. His ideas and methods were carried on by his principal disciples such as Tomita Takayoshi and Agoin Shōshichi, and the Hōtokusha, a society that he founded for the purpose of spreading his teachings, continued to be active throughout Japan in the Meiji period and thereafter. However, his ideas, with their emphasis upon filial piety, frugality, and diligence, were designed originally to meet the needs of an agricultural class existing within a strictly regulated feudal system. In the years since the Second World War, when the emphasis in Japan has shifted to individualism, democracy, and technological advancement, his ways of thought have ceased to appeal to the working classes and no longer enjoy their former popularity. His writings include the *Hōtokuki* and the *Sansai hōtoku kimmō roku.*

NISHI GEMPO 西玄甫 (d. 1684)

Physician and interpreter of the early Edo period. He was born in Nagasaki; his given name was Kichibei. He first acted as an interpreter of Portuguese, but in 1641, when the Dutch trading office at Hirado was moved to Dejima in Nagasaki, he became an interpreter of Dutch. In 1656 he was appointed *daitsūji*, or chief interpreter, and in 1673 was summoned to Edo to act as an official surgeon and interpreter for the shogunate. He was awarded the honorary title of *hōgen* and changed his name to Gempo.

He began the study of surgery under the Portuguese missionary Christovão Ferreira (Sawano Chūan), who had apostatized and was employed by the Japanese as an interpreter. He continued his studies of Western medicine under various Dutch physicians of Dejima. In 1668 he received a diploma in Western medicine from the Dutch doctor Arnold Dirckz and later studied with another Dutch doctor named Willem ten Ryne. Adding his own ideas to what he had learned, he established himself as a Western style physician. He also joined with Mukai Genshō in writing the *Kenkon bensetsu*, a refutation of a Portuguese work on astronomy, which Sawano Chūan had earlier translated into romanized Japanese, and wrote other works such as the *Shokoku miyagesho.* He died in Edo in 1684.

NISHIKAWA JOKEN 西川如見 (1648–1724)

Astronomer of the middle Edo period. His family were local officials in Nagasaki, one of their duties being to oversee the importation of raw silk from China. Sometime after the age of twenty he turned his attention to scholarship, studying Confucianism under Nambu Sōju, a Kyoto scholar; he also acquired a knowledge of astronomy, though from whom or by what process it is not known. In 1697 he retired from his official post, but continued to pursue his astronomical studies with even greater energy than before. In 1719 he was invited to come to Edo and discuss matters pertaining to astronomy with Shogun Yoshimune. He was a man of wide interests, and in addition to works on astronomy he also wrote on the subjects of land utilization popular education, and trade; two works on the last subject, the *Kai tsūshōkō,* ("Study of the China Trade") and the *Nagasaki yawagusa*

("Nagasaki Notes") are of particular importance in the study of overseas trade in the Edo period. In 1899 his descendants published his collected writings in seventeen volumes entitled *Nishikawa Joken isho.*

ODA NOBUNAGA 織田信長 (1534–1582)

Powerful military leader of the late Muromachi-Momoyama periods; he played a large role in helping to unify Japan after the decades of civil strife that had troubled it and in opening the way for the modern era. He was born in 1534, the second son of Oda Nobuhide, a member of the Oda family, who were lords of Nagoya Castle in the province of Owari, present-day Aichi Prefecture; in childhood he went by the name Kichihōshi. In 1546 he underwent his coming-of-age ceremony, and the following year took part in his first military engagement. His father died in 1551, and at the age of seventeen he succeeded him, but in 1555 seized the castle of Kiyosu in the same province and transferred his residence there. In 1559 he attacked Iwakura, another castle in Owari Province, and thus succeeded in gaining control of the western part of the province.

In 1560, when Imagawa Yoshimoto, a military leader with his base in Suruga Province to the east, led a large army in an invasion of Owari, Nobunaga defeated him in a surprise attack at Okehazama, gaining wide renown for his daring and skill in battle. He then launched an attack on Saitō Tatsuoki, one of the lords of the province of Mino to the west, seizing the castle of Inokuchi and, after renaming it Gifu, made it his new residence. In 1568 he gained control of the province of Ōmi and escorted Ashikaga Yoshiaki into Kyoto, where Yoshiaki became the fifteenth and last of the Ashikaga shoguns. In 1570 he attacked the combined armies of Asai Nagamasa of Ōmi and Asakura Toshikage of Echizen, inflicting a decisive defeat on them at Anegawa in Ōmi through the use of firearms, which had recently been introduced to Japan from the West. The following year he made a fierce attack on the Buddhist monks of the Tendai sect, who had their headquarters on Mt. Hiei and had allied themselves with his enemies of the Asai and Asakura clans, burning down all the temples on the mountain and breaking the power of the sect. In 1575 he engaged the forces of Takeda Katsuyori, a powerful military leader of the province of Kai, in the battle of Nagashino in Mikawa Province, allying himself with Tokugawa Ieyasu, a leader of Mikawa. The battle, which ended in defeat for Takeda's forces, is noteworthy as the earliest encounter in which firearms were used on a large scale in open warfare.

In 1576 he constructed a magnificent castle at Azuchi on the east shore of Lake Biwa, from which he planned to exercise domination over the entire country. In 1580 he conducted a successful campaign in Osaka against the Ishiyama Hongan-ji, the headquarters of the Shin sect of Buddhism, which was responsible for leading numerous *ikkō ikki* (peasant uprisings) in the Kinki and Hokuriku regions. In 1582 he joined with his ally Tokugawa Ieyasu in invading the province of Kai and wiping out the forces of Takeda Katsuyori. He then set off in the same year for western Japan, intending to assist his subordinate Hashiba Hideyoshi, who was besieging the castle of Takamatsu in Bitchū, one of the castles belonging to the powerful leader Mōri Terumoto. While staying at the Honnō-ji in Kyoto, however, he was surrounded and attacked by a large force led by one of his own generals, Akechi Mitsuhide, and was driven to commit suicide at the age of forty-eight.

Several reasons may be cited to explain Nobunaga's remarkable success in his campaign to unify the nation. First, he made his base in the provinces of Owari and Mino, which were near Kyoto and were large rice producing regions, and he was thus assured of plentiful supplies of food and money for his armies. Second, he built up professional fighting forces that were independent of the peasantry and showed great skill and inventiveness in utilizing firearms, armored ships, and other new devices of warfare. Finally, he instituted land surveys to gain more efficient control of the peasantry, did away with toll barriers, and took other steps to encourage free trade, and in this way undermined the power of the old aristocratic clans and Buddhist establishments and laid the foundations for a new system of government. It remained for his subordinate Hideyoshi to carry to completion the task that he had begun and to unify all of Japan under a single rule.

ODA NOBUO 織田信雄 (1558–1630)

Prominent military leader of the Momoyama period, he was the second son of Oda Nobunaga; in his youth he went by the name Chasen. In 1569 Nobunaga, for reasons of political expediency, arranged for Nobuo to become the adopted son of Kitabatake Tomonori, the governor of the province of Ise. In 1574 he successfully put down the *ikkō ikki*, a peasant uprising led by Buddhist priests of the Shin sect, which broke out at Nagashima in Ise, and in 1575 he succeeded his adopted father to become governor of the province. When Oda Nobunaga was attacked and driven to suicide by Akechi Mitsuhide in 1582, he did not actively join with Hashiba Hideyoshi and the others in punishing the assassin, and for that reason he was not among those who were considered to succeed Nobunaga. He was allowed to resume the surname Oda, however, and was made lord of the castle of Kiyosu in the province of Owari.

In 1583, having fallen out with his younger brother Oda Nobutaka, he attacked and killed the latter at Gifu. In 1584 he sided with Tokugawa Ieyasu against Hashiba Hideyoshi at the battles of Komaki and Nagakute, but when peace was restored, he once more allied himself with Hideyoshi. He participated in Hideyoshi's campaign to gain control of Kyushu in 1587 and again in the attack on the castle of Odawara in 1590, but quarreled with Hideyoshi over the disposition of the spoils and, incurring Hideyoshi's wrath, was banished to Karasuyama in the province of Shimotsuke in present-day Tochigi Prefecture. Through the intervention of Tokugawa Ieyasu, however, he was later pardoned and once more became a close associate of Hideyoshi.

He did not participate actively in the battle of Sekigahara in 1600, when Tokugawa Ieyasu and his followers clashed with the supporters of Hideyoshi's heir, but he communicated in secret with Ieyasu and sent him information concerning the situation in the Kyoto-Osaka region. He sided with the Tokugawa forces once more when, in 1614 and 1615, they attacked Osaka Castle and wiped out Hideyoshi's heir and his supporters, and after the battle was presented with fiefs in the provinces of Yamato and Kōzuke. He died in Kyoto in 1630.

Oda Nobutada 織田信忠 (1557–1587)

Military leader of the Momoyama period, he was the eldest son of Oda Nobunaga. Born in the castle of Kiyosu in Owari, present-day Aichi Prefecture, he was known in childhood as Sampōshi, but with his coming-of-age ceremony in 1572 he assumed the name Kankurō. The same year he took part in the attack on Asai Nagamasa in the castle of Odani in Ōmi, distinguishing himself for his military prowess. In 1574 he joined his father in helping to put down the *ikkō ikki*, a peasant revolt led by priests of the Shin sect of Buddhism, that had broken out at Nagashima in Ise. When his father moved to the newly built castle of Azuchi in Ōmi in 1576, he became the lord of Gifu Castle. In 1577 he helped to put down another *ikki* revolt in Saiga in the province of Kii and the same year went on to attack and wipe out Matsunaga Hisahide and his son Hisamichi, who were ensconced in a castle on Mt. Shigi in Yamato and were opposing Nobunaga.

In 1578 he assisted Hashiba Hideyoshi in the campaign to wipe out resistance in the province of Harima. He led the vanguard in an attack on Takeda Katsuyori in the province of Kai in 1582, attacked Takeda again at the castle of Takatō in Shinano, and finally wiped out the Takeda forces in another battle in Kai. The same year, when he and his father were in residence in Kyoto, Akechi Mitsuhide attacked Nobunaga at the Honnō-ji, driving him to suicide. Nobutada, determined to resist Akechi Mitsuhide's attacks and avenge his father's death, took up a position in Nijō Castle, but though he struggled valiantly, he found himself overpowered and committed suicide.

Ogata Kōan 緒方洪庵 (1810–1863)

Physician and scholar of Dutch learning of the late Edo period. He was the son of Ogata Iin, a samurai of the domain of Ashimori in Bitchū. He went to Osaka and studied Western medicine under the physician Naka Ten'yū and later, at the age of twenty, studied Dutch learning under Tsuboi Shindō in Edo. He also studied under Udagawa Genshin and then went to Nagasaki in 1836 to receive instruction from a Dutch physician named Johannes Erdewin Niemann. Eventually at the age of twenty-eight he returned to Osaka, where he began practice as a physician and opened a school called the Tekitekisai-juku or Tekijuku to give instruction in Dutch learning.

Among his students were Murata Zōroku (Ōmura Masujirō), Hashimoto Sanai, Ōtori Keisuke, Nagayo Sensai, Fukuzawa Yukichi, and Sano Tsunetami, all men who played prominent roles in the political and cultural life of late Edo and Meiji times. He had as many as a thousand students at his school, and in addition to teaching, kept up a medical practice and wrote and translated works on medicine. His *Byōgaku tsūron*, published in 1849, was the first work on pathology in Japanese, and he also produced a systematic translation of works on internal medicine, and in 1858 published a work on the treatment of cholera entitled *Korori chijun*. When cowpox vaccine was first imported to Japan, he played an important role in encouraging the practice of vaccination. In 1862 he was summoned to Edo to become physician to the shogun and head of the shogunal school of Western medicine, being given the honorary title *hōgen*.

Ōgimachi Tennō 正親町天皇 (1517–1593)

Emperor of the late Muromachi and Momoyama periods. He was the eldest son of Emperor Gonara, and when the latter died in 1557, he succeeded him to become the 106th sovereign. This was a time of great social unrest; the finances of the imperial household were at their lowest ebb, and it was therefore impossible to hold a proper coronation ceremony. In was not until three years later, when one of the great daimyo of the Chūgoku region, Mōri Motonari, donated a sum of money for that purpose, that the ceremony could finally be carried out. In the years following, the move toward the unification of the country under a single military leader gained momentum, and at the same time the responsibility of supporting the imperial household was taken over by the military leaders who were working for unification. Oda Nobunaga and Toyotomi Hideyoshi worked to restore the fortunes of the imperial household, and through their efforts the palace was rebuilt and the court ceremonies were once again carried out in proper fashion. Emperor Ōgimachi reigned for thirty years and in 1586 ceded the throne to his grandson, who became Emperor Goyōzei.

Ogiwara Shigehide 荻原重秀 (1658–1713)

Shogunate finance minister of the middle Edo period. He began his career as a lower official in the *kanjōsho* (finance office) of the shogunate and gradually worked his way up until in 1696 he became one of the highest officials in the office with a stipend of 3,500 *koku*. At that time the shogunate was in very dire financial straits, and in an attempt to relieve the situation Shigehide persuaded Shogun Tsunayoshi to allow him to debase the currency and increase the amount in circulation. Lowering the value of the currency brought about a degree of confusion in prices, but the increase in the amount had the effect of hastening the growth of a pure money economy, which previously had been hindered by the lack of sufficient currency. However, it was discovered that there was a certain amount of connivance between him and the officials in charge of minting currency and the lumber merchants, and this and other aspects of the policy aroused widespread criticism. The scholar Arai Hakuseki exposed the improprieties in Shigehide's fiscal policy, three times submitting memorials to Shogun Ienobu, Tsunayoshi's successor, and in 1712 Shigehide was dismissed from his post. He died the following year, it is said from self-inflicted starvation.

Ōgo (Mokujiki Shōnin) 應其(木食上人) (1537–1608)

Buddhist monk and *renga* poet of the Momoyama period. He was a samurai who was born in the province of Ōmi and served the Sasaki family, but when the latter's fortunes declined, he went to Mt. Kōya and became a monk. In 1585, when Toyotomi Hideyoshi was preparing to attack Mt. Kōya, he visited Hideyoshi and succeeded in persuading him to call off the attack and agree to a peaceful settlement, thus saving the temples from destruction. At the same time, he gained the trust of Hideyoshi, and on the occasion of Hideyoshi's death he was appointed to take charge of the funeral. In 1600, when the armies of the various daimyo were gathering for the battle of Sekigahara, he did his best to negotiate peace, but learning that the armies of the western camp had been defeated and that Tokugawa Ieyasu had emerged the victor, he retired to the Handō-ji in Ōmi.

Ōgo was a distinguished writer of *renga*, or linked verse, and after studying under Satomura Jōha, he published the *Mugonshō* in three chapters in 1603, a kind of handbook on how to compose *renga* and one of the most important works in the history of *renga*.

Ōgo was popularly called Mokujiki Shōnin, or Tree-eating Saint, because when he was practicing religious austerities he would retire to the mountains and, refusing to eat any cultivated grain or vegetables, would live entirely on the nuts and fruits of trees. He is not to be confused with another monk named Myōman (1718–1810), who was also nicknamed Mokujiki Shōnin and who is famous as a sculptor of Buddhist deities.

Ōishi Yoshio 大石良雄 (1659–1702)

Samurai of the domain of Akō in Harima; his common name was Kinai, which he later changed to Kuranosuke. His great-grandfather Ōishi Yoshikatsu, who was in the service of Asano Nagashige, was made *karō* (chief retainer) as a result of his achievements in the siege of Osaka Castle and assigned a stipend of 1,500 *koku* of rice. His father died young, and it was Yoshio who succeeded his grandfather as chief retainer of the Akō domain. In 1701, just twenty-five years after he assumed that post, the lord of the domain of Akō, Asano Naganori, was ordered to take charge of the reception of an imperial envoy at the castle of the shogun in Edo. The shogunate official Kira Yoshinaka failed to give him proper instruction in the rules of ceremony to be observed, and as a result he was publicly humiliated. In anger he drew his sword and wounded Kira, though such conduct was strictly forbidden within the confines of Edo Castle. Asano was punished by being deprived of his domain and ordered to commit suicide.

Ōishi Yoshio went into retirement in Yamashina near Kyoto, where he plotted with other *rōnin* (masterless samurai) of the domain of Akō to restore the Asano family to its former position. When it became clear that this was hopeless, they determined to take revenge on their lord's enemy. Though beset by many difficulties, a band of forty-seven *rōnin* headed by Ōishi succeeded one snowy night at the end of 1702 in breaking into Kira's residence in Edo and putting him to death. On orders from the shogunate, Ōishi was held in custody in the Edo residence of Hosokawa Tsunatoshi, the lord of the domain of Kumamoto. In the third month of the following year, he and the others of his group were ordered to commit suicide. Ōishi and his band were made the heroes of the kabuki drama entitled *Kanadehon Chūshingura* and have remained extremely popular figures in Japanese history down to the present day.

Ōkura Nagatsune 大藏永常 (b. 1768)

Agronomist of the late Edo period. Born in Kuma-machi, Hida-gun, Bungo Province (Ōita Prefecture). His common names were Kamedayū, Tokubei, Kinai, and Kidayū, his formal name was Takezumi, and he was also known as Kiō, Juwaen, and Kōyōen. At first he hoped to become a Confucian scholar, but was persuaded by his father to take up the study of agriculture, and for some ten years wandered about Kyushu, acquiring the techniques of sugar growing employed in Satsuma and spreading them to other districts. In 1796 he went to Osaka and took up the sale of saplings and agricultural implements, and during the same period visited various districts in the Kinki and Chūgoku areas to continue his study of agriculture. In 1810 he went to Edo and toured the Kantō area, then in 1816 returned to Osaka. After a few years he went to Edo again and published a large number of works on agriculture, recommending the clans of the Kantō area to take up industry and at the same time planning, with his friends, to open up various uninhabited islands. He also worked to develop industry in the lands of the shogunate and the Tanaka clan in Suruga (Shizuoka Prefecture). In 1834 he was introduced to the Tahara clan by Watanabe Kazan and worked for the clan for a while. At one stage he received the patronage of the celebrated *rōjū* Mizuno Tadakuni and became *kōsan-kata*, official in charge of promoting industry, but following the latter's fall from power went to Edo, where he devoted himself to writing. He wrote more than thirty books, including

Nōkaeki, Rōnō chawa, Nōgu benri ron, Seikatsu roku, Aburana roku, Kōeki kokusan kō.

Ōmura Masujirō 大村益次郎 (1824–1869)

Military expert of the late Edo and Meiji periods. He was the son of a physician of the province of Suō; his name was originally Murata Zōroku but was changed to Ōmura Masujirō in 1865. He pursued Chinese and Dutch studies and the study of medicine under Umeda Yūsai, Hirose Tansō, Ogata Kōan, Okuyama Seishuku, and the German doctor von Siebold. In 1853 he entered the service of the domain of Uwajima, Shikoku, supervising military preparations, the translation of works on military subjects, and the construction of warships. In 1856 he went to Edo and opened a school called the Kyukyodō, but shortly after he was invited to become an instructor in the shogunal office for the handling of foreign books, and the following year was transferred to the Kōbusho, a military academy that had recently been established by the shogunate. In 1860 he entered the service of the domain of Chōshū, training students in Western studies, and in 1866, when the shogunate dispatched forces to conduct a punitive expedition against Chōshū, Masujirō led the soldiers of the domain and successfully repulsed them.

Under the new government formed at the time of the Meiji Restoration he served with distinction as an official in the office of military defense, and in 1869 was appointed *hyōbu-tayū* (vice-minister of war) and put in charge of the reform of the military system. In the ninth month of the same year he visited Kyoto to conduct a study on the manufacture of machines and the establishment of a naval academy, and while there was attacked by a group of Chōshū samurai headed by Kumashiro Naoto. He died shortly after of his wounds.

Ōmura Sumitada 大村純忠 (1533–1587)

Christian daimyo of the late Muromachi and Momoyama periods. As lord of the Ōmura domain in the province of Hizen in Kyushu, he had long been interested in the prospects of foreign trade, and in 1562 he opened the harbor of Yokoseura in Hizen for the use of Portuguese trading ships and built a church there. The following year he was baptized and took the Christian name Bartolomeo, thus becoming the first of the Christian daimyo. In 1570 on the advice of Father Cosmo de Torres he opened the port of Nagasaki, and in 1580 donated the area around Nagasaki and Mogi to the Jesuits, so that the region became a center of both trade and missionary activities. In 1582, on the advice of the religious inspector Valignani, Sumitada joined with Ōtomo Sōrin, Arima Harunobu, and others in sending a mission to the Pope in Rome to express reverence and report on the progress of the Church in Japan. The mission consisted of a fifteen-year-old boy named Itō Mancio, a fourteen-year-old named Chijiwa Miguel, and two other youths. In the fifth month of 1587, however, both Ōmura Sumitada and Ōtomo Sōrin died, and the same year Toyotomi Hideyoshi issued an order banning Christianity, initiating an era of persecution and martyrdom for the Christians in Japan.

Ono Ranzan 小野蘭山 (1729–1810)

Naturalist of the late Edo period. Born in Kyoto, he began at the age of twelve to study under Matsuoka Joan an expert in botany. After the death of his teacher six years later, he continued his studies on his own and at the age of twenty-four opened a school on Maruta-machi in Kyoto. His lectures were collected and put into order by his grandson and one of his students named Okamura Shun'eki and were published in fourty-eight chapters during the years 1803–05 under the title *Honzō kōmoku keimō*, constituting the largest work on the subject of Japanese botany produced in the premodern period. When he was seventy he was invited by the shogunate to come to Edo and talk on botany at the Saijukan, and from this time until his death he lectured at the shogunal medical school. During the years from 1800 to 1806, when he was already over seventy, he made walking trips through many of the provinces for the purpose of collecting botanical specimens. His principal works are *Honzō kōmoku keimō kōsansetsu*, *Honzō kōmoku bemmoku bengo*, and *Inzentekiyō*.

Ōoka Tadasuke 大岡忠助 (1677–1751)

Machi-bugyō (city magistrate) of Edo in the middle Edo period. In early life he used the given names Tadayoshi and Kumema, later changing to Ichijūrō and Tadaemon. He was adopted by Tadazane, a member of his father's family. In 1700 he inherited the family estate, and some years later became *kachi-gashira* ("head of the foot-soldiers," a shogunate post). In 1712 he was appointed *bugyō* (magistrate) of Yamada, in which capacity he judged a boundary dispute between the clans of Yamada in Ise and Matsuzaka in Kii, deciding against Matsuzaka but thereby gaining the favor of Yoshimune, the lord of Kii. In 1716 he became *fushin bugyō* (supervisor of construction and civil engineering works for the shogunate), then the following year was promoted to *bugyō* of Edo and given the title Echizen-no-kami. In his new post he set about the task of putting the criminal code down in writing, and worked towards the establishment of the Edo guilds of firefighters.

In later years he was again promoted to *bugyō* of shrines and temples, and his annual stipend was increased to a total of 10,000 *koku*, which placed him on a level with the daimyo. His official headquarters was at Nishi Tahei in the province of Mikawa. He was renowned as a judge and is the subject of many, probably apocryphal, anecdotes, though his fairness at least is witnessed by his verdict in the Ise-Kii case. In recent years his journal of his official duties has been discovered and published.

Ōshio Heihachirō 大鹽平八郎 (1793–1837)

Confucian scholar of the late Edo period. He was the son of a police officer named Ōshio Yukitaka of the Temma section of Osaka and in time succeeded to his father's post. He studied the Chu Hsi school of Neo-Confucianism under the Confucian scholar Hayashi (Matsudaira) Jussai in Edo, but later became an advocate of the doctrines of the Ming Neo-Confucian scholar Wang Yang-ming, who emphasized the importance of translating one's moral convictions into positive action. At the age of twenty-six he was promoted to the post of police examiner and gained considerable reputation for the diligence with which he pursued his duties, but ten years later he turned over his post to his son Kakunosuke and devoted all his time to teaching the doctrines of Wang Yang-ming, or as he is known in Japanese pronunciation, Ō Yōmei.

In 1836 the Osaka area was afflicted by severe famine, and the following year Heihachirō, unable to bear the sight of the suffering it caused, submitted a letter to the local authorites requesting that they take steps to relieve the distress of the people. When his pleas went unheeded, he sold the books from his own library and used the proceeds to bring what relief he could to the victims of the famine. He also circulated an appeal throughout the Osaka and Kyoto region calling upon men of like mind to join him in action. On the nineteenth day of the second month he led an armed insurrection, going about the city setting fires and attacking the establishments of the rich merchants, but the rioters were quickly suppressed and Heihachirō and his son Kakunosuke fled into hiding. Near the end of the third month they were discovered and surrounded by the government forces, whereupon they committed suicide. Heihachirō's uprising was the first armed action led by members of the upper class to challenge shogunate authority since the time of the Shimabara Rebellion in the early seventeenth century and served as an omen of the increasing unrest and opposition that the shogunate was to face in the near future.

ŌTSUKI GENTAKU 大槻玄澤 (1757–1827)

Physician and scholar of Dutch learning of the middle Edo period. Also known as Shigetaka or Bansui, he was the son of a physician of the domain of Ichinoseki in the province of Mutsu. He began his studies under Tatebe Seian, a physician of the same domain, and at the age of twenty-one went to Edo to study medicine and Dutch learning under Sugita Gempaku and Maeno Ryōtaku. Later he went to Nagasaki to continue his studies, and in 1782 wrote a guide to Dutch learning entitled *Rangaku kaitei*, which proved to be very helpful to persons interested in familiarizing themselves with the subject. In 1786 he became a physician in the service of the Sendai clan, taking up residence at Kyōbashi in Edo and opening a private school called the Shirandō, where he gave instruction in Dutch learning. It was here that, in 1794, he held a gathering to celebrate *Oranda shōgatsu*, Dutch New Year, the first time that the solar calendar New Year's Day was observed among the Japanese.

Among his students at this time were Hashimoto Sōkichi, Inamura Sampaku, and Udagawa Genshin. In 1806 he and his son Genkan were appointed to the office of the shogunate that had charge of the translation of foreign books; he also undertook to produce a revised and enlarged version of the *Kaitai shinsho*, a work on anatomy and dissection by his teacher Sugita Gempaku, completing the task after some twenty years of labor and publishing a new edition in fourteen chapters entitled *Jūtei kaitai shinsho*. In addition he compiled an atlas of the world entitled *Kankai ibun* in fifteen chapters, which he presented to the shogunate. He produced more than three hundred chapters of translations and original works, and his miscellaneous writings have been collected in a two volume work entitled *Bansui sonkyō*.

Sakai Tadakiyo 酒井忠清 (1623–1681)

Fudai daimyo of the early Edo period. The *fudai* daimyo were the feudal families that had already sworn allegiance to Tokugawa Ieyasu before the battle of Sekigahara in 1600; the Sakai family were lords of the domain of Maebashi in present-day Gumma Prefecture, Tadakiyo becoming lord of the domain in 1637 on the death of his father. In 1651, when Tokugawa Ietsuna became the fourth shogun, Tadakiyo was sent as the shogun's envoy to the imperial court in Kyoto to thank the emperor for his congratulations, and in the same year he was raised in rank and given the title Uta-no-kami. In 1653 he was advanced to the important administrative post of *rōjū*, and in 1666 to the highest post of all, that of *tairō*.

Because Shogun Ietsuna was ailing and because so many of the great lords who had dominated the scene at the time of the founding of the Edo shogunate had by this time died, Tadakiyo was able to exercise power as he pleased. He also played a part in settling a dispute that arose within the Date family of the domain of Sendai.

Tadakiyo's mansion was situated outside the Ōte Gate of Edo Castle, near the signboard ordering persons who were entering the castle to dismount from their horses, and he was accordingly given the nickname *geba shogun*, "Dismount Shogun." In 1680 his fief was increased in size, but with the death of Shogun Ietsuna shortly after, he fell from power, and in 1681 was removed from the post of *tairō* by the fifth shogun, Tsunayoshi.

Sakamoto Ryōma 坂本龍馬 (1835–1867)

Tosa samurai of the late Edo period. He was born in the domain of Tosa, present-day Kōchi Prefecture, the son of a local landlord and saké maker, but he turned over the family business to his younger brother and at the age of seventeen went to Edo and studied swordsmanship under the swordmaster Chiba Shūsaku. In 1854, when Perry and his squadron of American ships arrived at Uraga and demanded the opening of the country, Ryōma, concerned for the future of Japan, joined the group of samurai of the domain of Mito who were calling for expulsion of the foreigners. The following year, when he returned to Tosa, he met the painter Kawada Shōryū and learned from him something of the international situation, Kawada having earlier talked with a Japanese castaway named Nakahama Manjirō, who had been repatriated from America. Impressed by what he had learned, Ryōma returned to Edo and remained there until 1858. In 1861 he joined the Tosa group headed by Takechi Zuizan, which favored return of power to the emperor, and was active in the Kyoto and Osaka area.

In 1862, dissatisfied with the conservative policies of the Tosa domain, he left Tosa without permission and became a student of Katsu Kaishū, an adviser on naval affairs to the Edo shogunate, receiving a European style education and assisting Katsu in the setting up of a naval training station for the shogunate in Kobe. The training station was closed down in 1863, but through the introduction of Katsu, Ryōma went to the fief of Satsuma in Kyushu and later, with the backing of Satsuma leaders, gathered a group of friends and opened a shipping and trading company called the Shachū. In 1864 he began trying to bring about cooperation between the two great fiefs of western Japan, Satsuma and Chōshū, and in 1866 at Kyoto succeeded in forming an alliance between the two designed to work for the overthrow of the shogunate. In 1867, through the intervention of a high official of Tosa named Gotō Shōjirō, he was pardoned for having earlier left the fief without permission, and, with the backing of Tosa, formed an organization called the Kaientai to engage in enterprises similar to those of the Shachū but on a larger scale. Finally, in hopes of solving the grave internal and external problems that faced the nation, he persuaded the lord of Tosa, Yamanouchi Yōdō, to talk the shogun into returning the power of government to the emperor, thus bringing to an end the three-hundred-year rule of the Tokugawa family. In the same year, however, when he was in Kyoto at a meeting with Nakaoka Shintarō, he was attacked and killed by agents of the shogunate. The type of government that he envisioned for Japan was a federation of feudal lords centering around the emperor.

Sakuma Shōzan 佐久間象山 (1811–1864)

Late Edo period scholar of Western learning. He was the son of Sakuma Kuniyoshi, a samurai of the domain of Matsushiro in Shinshū, present-day Nagano Prefecture; his given name was Kunitada, Shōzan being a literary appellation. From an early age he showed great fondness for learning and in 1833 went to Edo to study Neo-Confucianism of the Chu Hsi school under Satō Issai, head of the officially sponsored Hayashi family school. In 1836 he was ordered by the lord of Matsushiro to return to his home and teach the sons of the samurai of the fief. In 1839 he went to Edo a second time and took charge of the school, which was maintained in the official residence of the Matsushiro domain, at the same time opening a school in Kanda called the Shōzan Shoin and giving instruction there.

In 1841 at the direction of the lord of Matsushiro, Sanada Yukitsura, who held the position of *rōjū* (councilor of state) in the shogunate, he went to Nirayama on the Izu Peninsula to receive instruction in Western style gunnery from Egawa Tarōzaemon, a shogunate official who, among other things, was proficient in military science, and presented to the government a proposal for measures to be taken for coastal defense. From around 1844 he began to pursue Western studies more intensively and in 1848, following the information contained in a Dutch work, he succeeded in casting several cannon. With this his fame at last began to spread, and promising students from all over the country flocked to him asking for instruction.

In 1853, when Perry's ships first arrived at Uraga, he sent a letter expressing his opinions to the shogunate and, in company with Yoshida Shōin, attempted to board the ships and obtain passage aboard, but the plan ended in failure. As a result of the incident he was imprisoned in Edo and later sent back to Matsushiro for confinement there, but this did not sway his determination to continue to pursue Western studies and improve his scientific knowledge.

In 1864 he was ordered by the shogunate to go to Kyoto and confer with the shogun's advisor, Tokugawa Yoshinobu, and other important government officials who were there, attempting to convince them of the need to open the country as soon as proper steps had been taken to introduce Western scientific knowledge and strengthen the defenses of the state, but he was attacked and killed by a member of the group that advocated expulsion of foreigners. Among his disciples were many such as Katsu Kaishū, Sakamoto Ryōma, Yoshida Shōin, and Hashimoto Sanai, who played important roles in the late Edo and Meiji Restoration periods.

Sakura Sōgorō 佐倉宗五郎 (dates uncertain)

Farmer of the early Edo period. His real name was Kiuchi Sōgorō and he was the son of the *nanushi*, or village head, of Kimitsu in the domain of Sakura, the province of Shimōsa, in present-day Chiba Prefecture. At that time the lord of the domain of Sakura, Hotta Masanobu, occupied the position of *rōjū*, a high administrative post in the shogunate, and had imposed extremely heavy taxes upon the farmers in his domain. Sōgorō joined with the other peasants of the domain in appealing to the authorities for a lessening of the tax burden, but when these appeals had no effect, he made his way alone to Edo and, in spite of strict prohibitions against such action, accosted the shogun as he was passing in procession and begged him to look into the matter. It is said that his request was granted, but that he and his wife and children, four persons in all, were condemned to suffer death nevertheless. The story of his deed circulated widely among the common people of the Edo period, who, like him, suffered under the burden of excessive taxation, and was even made the theme of a play performed on the kabuki stage. Though the story may have acquired fictional elements in the process of its popularization, there is historical evidence to prove that such a person as Sakura Sōgorō actually existed.

Satō Issai 佐藤一齋 (1722–1859)

Confucian scholar of the late Edo period. His common name was Sutezō, Issai being his literary name. Born into the family of the chief retainer of the Iwamura clan in the province of Mino (Gifu Prefecture), he entered the personal service of the lord of the clan in 1790, at the age of eighteen, and studied Confucianism together with Hayashi (Matsudaira) Jussai, the lord's son. In 1791 he went to Osaka, where he became a pupil of the Confucian scholar Nakai Chikuzan, then later went to study with the Confucian scholar Minakawa Kien in Kyoto. In 1793 he became a pupil of Hayashi Nobuatsu, who was in charge of educational affairs for the shogunate. When in time his old friend Matsudaira Jussai became head of the Hayashi family and Confucian scholar to the shogunate, Issai became his assistant, and in 1805 became head of the Confucian academy run by the Hayashi family. In 1841, when Issai was sixty-nine, Jussai died and Issai was selected to succeed him as official Confucian scholar to the shogunate. In the capacity he worked to spread the teachings of the Chu Hsi school of Neo-Confucianism (Shushigaku), which the Tokugawa shogunate encouraged as the orthodox form of Confucianism in Japan.

His Confucianism did not concentrate solely on theory, but also took in elements of the doctrines of Wang Yang-ming (Yōmeigaku), with its emphasis on action. This, together with his dignified and sincere personality and his wide learning, brought him many pupils, among them such outstanding later figures as Watanabe Kazan, Sakuma Shōzan, and Yokoi Shōnan. He wrote many works, *Kinshiroku* and *Genshiroku* being among the best known.

Satō Nobuhiro 佐藤信淵 (1769–1850)

Agronomist and thinker of the late Edo period. A native of Okachi in the province of Ugo (Akita Prefecture). For four generations his family had been studying agriculture and mining, and at the age of twelve Nobuhiro was taken by his father on a tour of the Ezo territories (Hokkaidō) and the Ōu district as a means of giving him instruction in agricultural matters. Unfortunately, his father died just as they reached the Ashio copper mine in the province of Kōzuke (Gumma Prefecture). In accordance with his father's dying wish, he went alone to Edo, where he became a pupil of the *rangakusha* (student of Dutch or Western learning) Udagawa Genzui, and also studied astronomy, geography, and surveying, among other things, with the scholar Kiuchi Taizō. In 1785 he left Edo with his teacher Genzui and went to the Tsuyama domain in the province of Mimasaka (northern Okayama Prefecture), where he gave advice on reforming the clan government.

From 1786 onward he toured Kyushu, Shikoku, and other areas, deepening his knowledge. Returning eventually to Edo, he studied with Yoshikawa Genjūrō, official Shinto scholar to the shogunate, then became a pupil of Hirata Atsutane, with whom he studied *kokugaku* (the school of learning, first appearing in the mid-Tokugawa period, that sought to return to the true Japanese national spirit via the study of the Japanese classics; with time, it acquired an increasingly nationalistic flavor). In 1814 he was admonished by the shogunate on a matter connected with Shinto but persisted and was placed in a state of semiconfinement in Adachi district in the province of Musashi (Saitama Prefecture). He continued nevertheless to devote himself to his studies and to writing books, so that his fame eventually spread among the daimyo and the public in general. He also became friendly with the contemporary *rangakusha* Watanabe Kazan and Takano Chōei; as a result, he was caught in the shogunate's move to suppress progressive students of European science made in 1839 and barely escaped punishment. Following this, at the request of the *rōjū* (councilor of state) Mizuno Tadakuni, he prepared a work entitled *Fukkohō gaigen* in which he discussed state control of industry. He also gave advice to various daimyo on agricultural affairs, the economy, and maritime defense, and published a large number of works, among them *Nōsei honron*, *Keizai yōroku*, *Bōkaisaku*, and *Suiriku sempōroku*.

SEKI TAKAKAZU 關孝和 (1642–1708)

Japanese style mathematician of the middle Edo period. He was the second son of Uchiyama Shichibei, a retainer of the shogunate, and is said to have been born at Fujioka in Kōzuke, present-day Gumma Prefecture; his father was later adopted into the Seki family. His father served Tokugawa Tsunatoyo, lord of the castle of Kōfu, and later, when Tsunatoyo was adopted as heir to the fifth shogun, Tsunayoshi, Takakazu became a samurai under the direct jurisdiction of the shogunate, being assigned to the post of *onando kumigashira*, the office in charge of clothing and furnishings for the shogun. It is said that he studied mathematics under Takahara Yoshitsugu, though this is uncertain.

In 1674 he wrote a work on mathematics entitled *Hatsubisampō*. Judging from this, he took as his point of departure the traditional Chinese type of calculation done with an abacus and called *tengen-jutsu*, but proceeded to develop a system of his own that anticipated the later inductive method of calculation known as *tenso-jutsu*. In terms of modern mathematics, his system corresponds to the algebraic method. In addition, he labored to work out a theory of the equilateral polygon and to discover the *enri* (principle of the circle) that would enable one to determine the area of a circle of globe. An examination of the *Katsuyō sampō*, a work published after Takakazu's death by his principal disciple, Tatebe Takahiro, reveals that Takakazu's mathematics had advanced to the point where they could compare favorably with European mathematics of the seventeenth century. Though he was of course deprived by the seclusion policy of the Tokugawa government of any opportunity to learn about European natural science, he made a brilliant contribution to the development of Japanese mathematics, and his methods, carried on by his numerous disciples and known as the Seki school, dominated the world of mathematics in Japan from the middle Edo period on.

SHIBATA KYŪŌ 柴田鳩翁 (1783–1839)

Teacher of *shingaku* in the late Edo period. He was born in Kyoto; his parents died when he was very young, and he experienced great hardship as a child. Seven years after losing his father, he went to Edo to work but, failing to gain success, he returned to Kyoto and became a lacquerer. In 1810 he turned to the profession of storyteller and at last began to advance in the world. His fondness for learning, however, led him in 1821 to become a student of Satta Tokken, a teacher of *shingaku*, the system of popular ethics expounded some one hundred years earlier by Ishida Baigan, which combined elements drawn from Buddhism, Confucianism, Taoism, and Shinto. In 1825 he made up his mind to devote his full time to the propagation of *shingaku* teachings among the common people, and in 1826 received certification as a teacher from the Meirinsha, the *shingaku* school.

Though he lost his eyesight the following year, he did not allow this to deter him, but pursued an active career, carrying on his teaching activities not only in Kyoto but in twelve provinces of the surrounding area. Expounding the *shingaku* doctrines in an interesting and easily comprehensible manner, he succeeded in winning many adherents among the peasants and townsmen and even attracted men of the noble and samurai class as well. He left an autobiography, the *Yoshinashikoto*, and his son compiled a collection of his sayings, the *Kyūō dōwa*, which was printed in 1834.

Shibukawa Shunkai 澁川春海 (1639–1715)

Student of astronomy and the calendar in the early Edo period. His common name was Sukezaemon, Shunkai being his literary name. Born the elder son of Santetsu, first head of the Yasui family, one of four families that provided opponents for the shogun when he wished to play *go*. Showing a taste for learning at an early age, Shunkai became a pupil of Yamazaki Ansai and studied the Chu Hsi school of Neo-Confucianism (*Shushigaku*), as well as Shinto. He also studied astronomy and the calendar with scholars such as Ikeda Shōi and Okanoi Gentei, and for many years thereafter carried out observations of the heavenly bodies, which led to the discovery that the "Semmyō calendar" drawn up by Hsü Ang of T'ang China, which had been in use in Japan for 823 years, was full of errors. Accordingly, he devised what was known as the "Jōkyō calendar," based on the "Juji calendar," China's most highly developed calendar, with revisions to suit conditions in Japan. This calendar was officially adopted by the shogunate in 1684, and Shunkai was taken on as official shogunate astronomer, successive generations of his descendants continuing to hold the post following his death. In 1699, he also published *Temmon Seizō-zu*, which consisted of Chinese maps of the stars with the addition of new constellations. He also wrote books such as *Nihon chōreki* and *Temmon keitō*, which contributed greatly to the development of astronomy in Japan.

Shizuki Tadao 志筑忠雄 (1760–1806)

Scientist of the middle Edo period. Also called Tadajirō or Ryūho, he was born into the Nakano family of Nagasaki in the province of Hizen but was at an early age adopted into the Shizuki family. The members of the Shizuki family had for generations acted as interpreters for the foreigners trading at Nagasaki, the only family in the domain permitted to do so, and Shizuki Tadao likewise at the age of seventeen began service as an interpreter of Dutch, but left his position the following year because of illness. Later he devoted himself to intensive study of astronomy under Motoki Enoshin, and in 1802 he completed a translation of a Dutch work entitled *Inleiding tot de waare Natuuren sterrekunde of de Natuuren Sterrekundige Lessen*, which in turn had been translated from a work in English on physics and astronomy by the Oxford don John Keil, for the first time making available in Japanese information on the Copernican system, air pressure, the refraction of light, and similar scientific subjects. In addition he wrote varied and original works on astronomy, physics, the Dutch language, and other subjects, contributing greatly to the introduction and spread of scientific knowledge in Japan.

Sūden 崇傳 (1569–1633)

Rinzai Zen monk of the early Edo period; his personal name was Ishin, and his posthumous title Enshō Honkō Kokushi. He was born in Kyoto, the son of Isshiki Hidekatsu, a retainer of the Ashikaga family. His father died in the overthrow of the Ashikaga shogunate in 1573, whereupon he entered Nanzen-ji, becoming a disciple of Gempo Reisan. He went to Kamakura in 1605 to become head monk of Kenchō-ji, but returned to Kyoto the following year and devoted all his efforts to restoring Nanzen-ji. In 1608 he was summoned into the service of Tokugawa Ieyasu, the founder of the Tokugawa shogunate. In 1610 he built a temple called Konchi-in in Sumpu, where Ieyasu was living in retirement, and took up residence there. Under Ieyasu's direction, he handled documents pertaining to foreign relations. He encouraged the government in its anti-Christian policy and took part in drafting the various proclamations outlawing Christianity and ordering the foreign missionaries out of the country. He was also active in affairs pertaining to the regulation of Buddhist institutions and in other domestic affairs, participating in the formulation of the ordinances known as *Jiin hatto*, *Kuge shohatto*, and *Buke shohatto*.

It is said the Sūden drew to Ieyasu's attention the inscription on the bell of Hōkō-ji. The bell had been contributed by Toyotomi Hideyori, the son of Ieyasu's former rival for power, Toyotomi Hideyoshi, and the inscription contained the characters used for Ieyasu's name. Ieyasu, claiming that the intent was to put a curse on him, used the inscription as a pretext to make war on the Toyotomi family, eventually wiping them out. Sūden was also active in the so-called purple robe affair of 1627–29, in which the shogunate countermanded orders given by the emperor to grant purple robes and other marks of honor to members of the Buddhist clergy, opposing the imperial court and the temples and working to strengthen the power of the shogunate. Thus, although a member of the clergy himself, he played an important role in extending and stabilizing the authority of the shogunal government in the early Edo period. As a result, he came to be referred to as Kokui no Saishō, the Premier in Monk's Robes. In 1619 he moved the Konchi-in to Edo and was commonly called Konchi-in Sūden. His writings include two diaries entitled *Ikoku nikki* and *Honkō kokushi nikki*, which convey a clear picture of his political activities.

SUGITA GEMPAKU 杉田玄白 (1733–1817)

Physician and student of Western science in the latter half of the Edo period. His original given name was Tasuku and his literary name Isai, Gempaku being his common name. He was the son of Sugita Teishin, physician to the Obama domain (Obama City, Fukui Prefecture) and was born at the residence of the clan lord at Ushigome in Edo. He conceived the desire to become a physician when he was sixteen or seventeen and at his father's recommendation began to study Confucianism with Miyase Ryūmon and Dutch-style surgery with Nishi Gentetsu, physician to the Tokugawa shogunate. In 1753 he was made clan physician at the age of twenty and in 1757 set up a practice in Nihonbashi-dōri in Edo. Around this time he joined with other men such as Hiraga Gennai and Nakagawa Jun'an, also a physician to the Obama clan, in a society devoted to the study of herbs. In 1769, when he was thirty-six, his father died and he was promoted to the rank of personal physician to the lord of the clan.

In 1771, at the age of thirty-eight, he observed the internal organs of an executed criminal at Kozukahara, Senju (in present Adachi Ward, Tokyo) and, comparing his findings with the Dutch anatomical work *Ontleedkundige Tofelen*, which he had obtained via the lord of the clan, was so astonished at the book's accuracy that he set about making a Japanese translation in collaboration with Maeno Ryōtaku, Nakagawa Jun'an, and others. After much laborious work the task was finally completed and published under the title *Kaitai shinsho* in 1774, when Gempaku was forty-one. The first genuine translation of a Western work into Japanese, it marked the beginning of a new epoch in the study of Western sciences in Japan and in the development of Western style medicine in particular. The following year, he published *Kyōi no gen* as a reply to violent criticisms of him made by exponents of traditional Chinese herbal medicine. He continued thereafter to devote himself to the practice of medicine, research, and writing; at the same time, he found time to teach at the Tenshinro Academy, turning out many outstanding pupils, men such as Ōtsuki Gentaku, and made lasting achievements in the development of Western studies.

He wrote many works on medicine, including *Kaitai yakuzu* (1773), which gives an account of the structure of the human body; *Oranda iji mondō* (1795), a collection of letters giving questions and answers concerning the study of Western sciences and the new medicine; *Keiei yawa* (1802), an account of his studies of medicine during his earlier years; and, at the very end of his life, *Rangaku kotohajime* (1815), in which he reminisces on his labors in translating *Kaitai shinsho*; as well as various didactic works dealing with national policy and contemporary society.

SUMINOKURA RYŌI 角倉了以 (1554–1614)

Rich merchant of the Momoyama and early Edo periods. A native of Kyoto, his family name was actually Yoshida, but because the family had for generations been in the money-lending business they came to be called Suminokura ("corner storehouse"). Ryōi's father, Sōkei, was a doctor, but Ryōi, dreaming of a more ambitious and exciting career, allowed his younger brother to take over his father's medical practice, while he devoted himself to overseas trade and engineering projects. In 1592 he received from Toyotomi Hideyoshi one of the *shuinjō* (vermilion-seal patents), granting him permission to engage in overseas trade, and for the next forty-four years, until the final closing of the country in 1636, he and his son Soan conducted a large number of trading missions to the Annam and Tonkin regions, from which they reaped large profits.

In addition, in 1606 he undertook a project to clear the Ōi River west of Kyoto and open it up for navigation, and the following year he was ordered by the Edo shogunate to do the same for the Fuji River. Some years later he conducted operations to dredge and improve the flow of the Kamo and

Takase rivers in Kyoto, opening up an avenue for water transport between Kyoto and Fushimi, where connection was made with other waterways leading to Osaka. Ryōi also drew up plans for an extensive project involving Lake Biwa, but unfortunately he died before he could put them into effect. He is buried at the Nison-in at Saga in Kyoto.

Suzuki Shōsan 鈴木正三 (1579–1655)

Sōtō Zen monk of the early Edo period, he was born in the province of Mikawa. He was a member of the warrior class and fought with the Tokugawa against the Toyotomi forces in the battle of Sekigahara and the winter and summer campaigns against Osaka Castle, distinguishing himself on the field. But from an early age he had been troubled by questions relating to the nature of life and death and had associated with such Zen monks as Taigu and Gudō. In 1620 he finally abandoned lay life and entered the priesthood, traveling about to various temples and going into retirement to conduct religious practices on his own. In 1624 he built a small hermitage for himself at a place called Ishi-no-taira in Mikawa. In 1632 he turned his hermitage into a temple called Onshin-ji; thereafter he became known as Sekihei Dōjin, or Priest of Sekihei, Sekihei being the Sino-Japanese reading of the place name Ishi-no-taira. He attained full enlightenment in 1639.

His younger brother Suzuki Shigenari distinguished himself in the action to put down the peasant rebellion in Shimabara in Kyushu and was accordingly appointed to act as local governor of Amakusa, one of the regions involved in the revolt. For this reason, Shōsan went to Amakusa in 1641 where he worked to spread Buddhist teachings. His aim was to adapt his teachings to the particular class to which his listeners belonged, whether samurai, peasant, artisan, or merchant, and to instill a kind of faith that would have meaning in terms of the daily life of the believers. To accomplish this, he wrote various works such as *Bammin tokuyō*, *Fumoto no kusawake*, *Mōanjō*, *Nembutsu zōshi*, and *Futari bikuni*, which employ a simple, colloquial style suitable for readers of the lower classes. The last two works, which contain didactic tales, are important in literary history as early examples of the type of works of popular fiction known as *kanazōshi*. An account of his late years is preserved in a work entitled *Roankyō* by his disciple Echū.

TAKADAYA KAHEI 高田屋嘉兵衛 (1769–1827)

Shipping agent of the late Edo period. He was born in the island of Awaji in present- day Hyōgo Prefecture and in 1792 built a large boat of 1,700 *koku* capacity and, loading it with goods, began trading with western and northern Honshu and with Ezochi, as Hokkaido was known at that time. In 1798 he expanded the scale of his enterprise, establishing a branch office in Hakodate. The following year when the shogunate, hoping to strengthen the defenses of Ezochi and speed its colonization, asked for volunteers to undertake exploration of the island of Etorofu, the largest of the Chishima (Kurile) Islands, Kahei responded and set up a shipping route to Etorofu, opening new fishing grounds in the process. In 1801, in reward for the role he played in the development of Ezochi, he was allowed to bear a surname and carry a sword, though he was a member of the merchant class and these privileges were ordinarily reserved to the samurai. He was also made a regularly employed boatman of the shogunate and put in charge of the operation of shogunate boats and the exploitation of the fishing grounds.

In 1806 he was ordered to take over the selling of Ezochi products, and he accordingly fixed his main office at Hakodate, maintaining branch offices in Hyōgo and Osaka, and with some ten or more large boats began trading Ezochi products for those of the home islands, acquiring huge profits in the process. In 1812, in retaliation for the arrest of a Russian sea captain named Vasili Mikhailovi Golovnin by shogunate officials on Kunashiri Island, Kahei was seized by the crew of a Russian ship and taken to Kamchatka. The following year, when he was allowed to return to Japan, he worked for the release of Golovnin and played a role in bringing about a reconciliation between Russia and Japan. In 1824 he turned over his business to his younger brother and retired to his native village to live out his remaining years.

TAKAHASHI YOSHITOKI 高橋至時 (1764–1804)

Astronomer of the middle Edo period. Commonly known by the name Sakuzaemon, he was born in Osaka, the son of a lower-grade samurai named Tokujirō in the service of the shogunate. In 1778 Yoshitoki succeeded his father as head of the family and, though poor, devoted himself to learning, taking instruction in mathematics and matters pertaining to the calendar from Matsuoka Yoshikazu. Around 1788 he began studying under Asada Gōryū, the leading astronomer of the time, making improvements in the various instruments used for astronomical observation at the same time that he devoted his energies to studies of the calendar. In time his fame as an astronomer began to spread, and in 1795, on the recommendation of his teacher, Asada Gōryū, he was selected to fill the post of *temmonkata*, official astronomer to the shogunate, and, along with his fellow student and friend Hazama Shigetomi, was ordered to devote himself to calendrical reform.

In 1796 he conducted observations of the position of the sun each day at noon from the observatory in Kyoto, and on the basis of these calculations produced a new calendar, known from the era in which it was promulgated as the Kansei-reki, or Kansei Calendar. In 1803 he succeeded after great labor in completing a work entitled *Rarande rekisho kanken* in eleven chapters, a translation of a European work on astronomy by the Frenchman Lalande, and, along with his son Kageyasu, did much to advance the study of astronomy and the calendar in Japan. One of his principal disciples, Inō Tadataka, was ordered by the shogunate to carry out a land survey of all of Japan, and the fact that he was able to complete the task was due in large part to the efforts of his teacher. Unfortunately Yoshitoki died of illness at the relatively young age of forty.

Takano Chōei 高野長英 (1804–1850)

Late Edo period physician and scholar of Dutch learning. Born into the Gotō family in the city of Mizusawa in the province of Mutsu, present-day Iwate Prefecture, he was adopted into the Takano family at an early age. In 1820, at the age of sixteen, he went to Edo and became a student of the physician and scholor Sugita Hakugen, the following year studying Dutch internal medicine under Yoshida Chōshuku. In 1825 he journeyed to Nagasaki and entered the Narutakijuku, the medical school opened by Philipp Franz von Siebold, a German doctor attached to the Dutch trading office there. In 1828, when Siebold came under suspicion of spying, many of his students were condemned to punishment, but Chōei managed to escape difficulty and make his way back to Edo, where he set up practice as a town doctor in Kōjimachi and in his spare time devoted himself to writing and translating.

Around 1832 he joined with other scholars of Dutch learning such as Watanabe Kazan and Kozeki San'ei to form the Shōshikai, a society for the study of Western European culture and discussion of current problems. In 1838 he wrote a work called the *Yume-monogatari* ("Dream Stories") in which he criticized the shogunate for its order to attack and repel any foreign ships approaching Japanese shores, and the following year, in the action known as the Bansha imprisonment, he and others of the Shōshikai were arrested and sentenced to life imprisonment. Chōei, however, was not humbled, and while in prison wrote another work, the *Tori no nakune*, pointing out the error of the shogunate's way of governing.

In 1844 fire broke out in the prison where he was confined, and he succeded in escaping, fleeing Edo and making his way in secret about the country. In 1848 he settled for a time in the domain of Uwajima, in present-day Ehime Prefecture in Shikoku, where he lectured on Dutch learning and continued his translation labors, and the following year he went to Kagoshima in Kyushu at the invitation of the lord of the domain, Shimazu Nariakira, and translated a work on military science. In 1850, having disfigured his face with chemicals, he secretly made his way to Edo and set up business as a doctor once more under the assumed name Sawa Sampaku, at the same time continuing to translate works on military science. In the same year, however, the shogunate officials discovered his whereabouts and surrounded the house, upon which he committed suicide. He left a number of original works and translations on medicine and military science and played a role of great importance in the introduction of Western scientific learning to Japan, helping to prepare the way for the modernization of the country.

TAKASHIMA SHŪHAN 高島秋帆 (1798–1866)

Gunnery expert of the late Edo period. His given name was Mochiatsu, and he is also called Shirōdayū and Kihei; his family had for some generations been *machidoshiyori*, or city officials, in Nagasaki. His father, Shirōbei, was a student of the Ogino school of gunnery. In 1814, at the age of sixteen, Shūhan succeeded to his father's post, and in the 1830s he began intensive study of Western style gunnery under a Dutch resident of Nagasaki. In 1840, having gathered together some three hundred disciples, he organized them into a large-scale musket battalion, and the same year he petitioned the Nagasaki city government for the adoption of Western style firearms.

Through the assistance of Egawa Hidetatsu, a shogunate official who was interested in Western military science, he arranged to hold gunnery maneuvers at Tokumarugahara (in the present-day Itabashi ward of Tokyo), greatly impressing the high shogunate officials who had gathered to watch. He was chosen to be a samurai under the jurisdiction of the shogunate and ordered to give lessons in gunnery to Egawa Hidetatsu. Having attracted widespread attention through these activities, he aroused the opposition of the more conservative elements in the government bureaucracy and as a result of their machinations was for a time imprisoned, but with the arrival of American ships in 1853 he was pardoned and released. The same year he petitioned the shogunate, urging the immediate adoption of Western firearms and the establishment of proper defense measures, arguing that if these steps were taken, there would be no danger in opening the ports to foreign trade. At the same time he joined Egawa Hidetatsu in the work of casting cannon, building emplacements for them, and taking other steps for military preparedness. In 1856 he was promoted to the position of official gunnery instructor for the shogunate. His methods were known as the Takashima or Western Style school of gunnery and were carried on after his death by his numerous disciples.

Takasugi Shinsaku 高杉晉作 (1839–1867)

Late Edo period Chōshū samurai active in the anti-shogunate movement. He was born in the city of Hagi in present-day Yamaguchi Prefecture and as a youth studied in the Meirinkan, the school for sons of the samurai run by the fief of Hagi. From 1857 on, he studied at the Shōka Sonjuku, a school in Hagi headed by Yoshida Shōin, proving himself to be a student of exceptional talent. In 1860 he was appointed head of the Meirinkan and the following year he became a close associate of the heir to the fief.

In 1862 he accompanied shogunate officials on a journey to Shanghai and witnessed in person the havoc wrought in China by the Taiping Rebellion. After returning to Japan he became active in the *sonnō-jōi* movement, which advocated restoration of power to the emperor and the expulsion of the foreigners, and he took part in the attack on and burning of the British legation at Shinagawa in Edo. In 1863, after a period of withdrawal in Kyoto and Hagi, he directed a bombardment of foreign vessels in the straits of Shimonoseki and formed the Kiheitai, a special battalion of fighting men drawn from the farmers, artisans, and merchants of the domain to strengthen the Chōshū military forces. In 1864, when the joint forces of America, Britain, France, and Holland bombarded and occupied Shimonoseki, Takasugi Shinsaku was sent to discuss terms for a settlement and succeeded in arranging a peaceful conclusion to the affair. In 1864, after Chōshū forces had attempted an abortive coup d'état in Kyoto and had been subdued by the shogunate army, Shinsaku found himself in disagreement with the leader of the conservative faction within the domain and withdrew, but the following year he called out the military forces of the domain, massed them at Shimonoseki, and persuaded the leaders of the domain to declare themselves in favor of the overthrow of the shogunate. In 1866 when the shogunate once more sent its armies against Chōshū, Shinsaku led his Kiheitai and inflicted a decisive defeat, but he collapsed of illness and died in the fourth month of the following year before he could witness the final overthrow of the shogunate, which represented the culmination of his labors.

TAKAYAMA UKON 高山右近 (1552–1614)

Christian daimyo of the Momoyama period. The son of Takayama Tomoteru, lord of the province of Hida, he was named Nagamasa or Tomonaga and was baptized under the name Justo; Ukon is a popular appellation. He was baptized a Christian, along with his father, at an early age. In 1578, when his superior Araki Murashige turned against Oda Nobunaga, Ukon, who was at that time lord of the castle of Takatsuki in Settsu, present-day Osaka Prefecture, found himself surrounded by Nobunaga's forces, but at the urging of the Portuguese missionary Organtin Gnecchi, he was persuaded to go over to the side of Nobunaga. In 1582, when Nobunaga was killed at the Honnō-ji by his vassal Akechi Mitsuhide, Ukon joined the forces of Hideyoshi in attacking Mitsuhide at Yamazaki, helping to defeat the latter and winning merit. As a reward, he was made lord of the domain of Akashi in the province of Harima in 1585.

In 1587 Hideyoshi, at that time on a campaign in Kyushu, suddenly issued a command ordering the suppression of Christianity and the expulsion of the missionaries from Japan, but Ukon, refusing to abandon his faith, gave up his domain and went into retirement in the island of Shōdo in the domain of another Christian daimyo, Konishi Yukinaga. In 1588 Hideyoshi ordered Yukinaga to move to the province of Higo in present-day Kumamoto Prefecture in Kyushu and at the same time placed Ukon under the surveillance of Maeda Toshiie, lord of the province of Kaga (Ishikawa Prefecture). When Ukon arrived in Kanazawa, the castle town of Kaga, he was made a retainer of Toshiie and treated with great respect, being called upon to give instruction in the tea ceremony to his lord. In 1590 he accompanied Toshiie in participating in Hideyoshi's campaign against Odawara Castle, but though he distinguished himself in battle, he was unable to dispel the resentment that Hideyoshi still bore against him.

In 1614, when Tokugawa Ieyasu, then military leader of the nation, issued another command forbidding Christianity, Ukon and the other Christian believers were ordered to be expelled from Japan. In the eleventh month of the same year, Ukon, accompanied by the members of his family and a group of missionaries and Christian believers, departed from Nagasaki and on the twenty-first day of the twelfth month arrived in Manila, where they were enthusiastically greeted by the governor-general, the archbishop, and a crowd of citizens. In the second month of 1614, some forty days after his arrival, however, Ukon fell sick and died, ending his life of hardship at the age of sixty-two.

TAKUAN 澤庵 (1573–1645)

Buddhist priest of the early Edo period. He was the son of a samurai of the domain of Izushi in the province of Tajima, present-day Hyōgo Prefecture, and entered the priesthood at an early age. In 1592 he went to Kyoto and entered the Sangen-in, a subtemple of the Daitoku-ji, one of the head temples of the Rinzai branch of the Zen sect. In 1609 he became the 154th *jūji*, or chief priest, of Daitoku-ji. In 1620 he returned to his home in Izushi and lived for the following seven years in retirement in a small hut on a hill behind the Sōkyō-ji, but in 1627 he went to Kyoto once more, this time to protest the action of the Edo shogunate in the so-called purple robe affair. Emperor Gomizuno-o had ordered that purple robes, a mark of special honor, be presented to Shōon Sōchi, the chief priest of Daitoku-ji, and other eminent members of the Buddhist clergy, but the shogunate countermanded the order. As a result of his protests against the action of the government, in 1629 Takuan was exiled to Kami-no-yama in Uzen in present-day Yamagata Prefecture, but he was pardoned three years later and allowed to return to Kyoto.

In 1634 he became special spiritual advisor to Emperor Gomizuno-o and the third Tokugawa shogun, Iemitsu, and in 1636 he was invited by Iemitsu to come to Edo and was treated with great favor and trust. In 1639 he became the first abbot of the Tōkai-ji, a temple in Shinagawa founded by Iemitsu. Emperor Gomizuno-o requested that Takuan give him instruction in Buddhist doctrine and presented him with a writing from his own hand. Takuan died in 1645 at the Tōkai-ji. He left a number of works pertaining to Buddhism, the tea ceremony, calligraphy, and swordsmanship, as well as poems in the *waka* and *haiku* forms, the texts of which have been collected in the *Takuan oshō zenshū*.

Tanaka Kyūgu 田中邱愚 (1662–1729)

Shogunate civil official of the middle Edo period. He was born in the village of Hirasawa in the district of Tama in Musashi Province. He was the second son of a farmer named Hachirōuemon, who in his spare time traded in silk goods. When Kyūgu grew up he carried on his father's enterprises, but in 1704 he was asked to become the adopted son of Tanaka Hyōgo, the village head and official of the Kawasaki stop on the Tōkaidō highway. In 1707 he succeeded his foster father as *nanushi*, or village head, bit by bit proving his ability as an administrator.

During the interval from 1711 to 1715 he studied Confucianism under Ogyū Sorai in Edo and the classics and history under Narushima Dōchiku. In 1721 he wrote a work in seventy-seven sections entitled the *Minkan seiyō* in which, speaking from his own experience as a farmer and local official, he discussed such problems as taxation and water control, and through his teacher Dōchiku had it presented to the shogunate. In 1723 he was consulted by Shogun Yoshimune on questions of agriculture administration and water utilization and, his talents at last being duly recognized, was selected for service in the shogunate. He first turned his attention to projects designed to further the control and utilization of the Arakawa and Tamagawa rivers, after which, in 1726, he was ordered to undertake repairs on the embankments of the Sakawa River in the province of Sagami, present-day Kanagawa Prefecture; these he carried out with great success, using a special method of his own devising. In 1729, in recognition of his accomplishments, he was made a *daikan* (administrator for lands directly under the control of the Tokugawa shogunate) of the province of Musashi, the region around present-day Tokyo. Unfortunately, he died shortly after having received this unusual honor, leaving behind him several works on water control.

Tanuma Okitsugu 田沼意次 (1719–1788)

An important shogunate official of the middle Edo period, he rose from the position of an ordinary samurai to that of *rōjū*, or councilor of state. His childhood name was Ryūsuke, but he later came to be called Tonomo-no-kami Okitsugu. His father, Senzaemon Okiyuki, was a samurai of the fief of Kii in present-day Wakayama Prefecture, but when Tokugawa Yoshimune, the lord of Kii, was summoned to Edo to become the eighth shogun, Okiyuki and Okitsugu accompanied him, Okitsugu serving as page to Yoshimune's eldest son, Ieshige. In 1734 Okiyuki died, leaving Okitsugu as his heir. In

1745 Tokugawa Ieshige succeeded his father to become the ninth shogun, and Okitsugu continued as before to act as his personal attendant, exercising his innate cleverness and enjoying great favor with his lord. He advanced repeatedly in station and in 1758 was presented with the fief of Sagara in the province of Tōtōmi, thus rising to the rank of a provincial landholder.

In 1760 Ieshige died and was succeeded by his son Ieharu, the tenth Tokugawa shogun. Okitsugu continued to enjoy favor as before; in 1767 he was appointed *sobayōnin*, or intermediary between the shogun and the councilors of state, and in 1772 he himself became a councilor of state. At the time of his appointment to this office the peasantry were sorely troubled by natural disasters, famine, and the burden of heavy taxes, and agricultural revenues had fallen off. In order to create new sources of revenue for the shogunal government, Okitsugu encouraged the export of copper and dried fish and shellfish from the port of Nagasaki, bringing into the country quantities of foreign gold and silver in exchange. He also created monopolies on certain commodities such as copper, iron, and ginseng, and collected fees from merchants and manufacturers in exchange for recognition of various monopolistic rights. Borrowing capital from the merchants, he undertook a large-scale project to drain Lake Imba in the province of Shimōsa and convert it to farm land, and laid plans for the opening up of Ezochi, as the island of Hokkaido was known at the time. But, positive and forward-looking as many of his plans were, his alliances with the great merchants led to widespread bribery and corruption in the government and frequent violations of the law. Moreover, in the latter years of his period in power, particularly during the years of the great famine that broke out in 1783 and spread throughout the country, life became increasingly difficult for the peasants and townspeople. It is not surprising, therefore, that with the death of Tokugawa Ieharu in 1786, Okitsugu, along with his son Okitomo, who had also held a high position in the shogunate, fell abruptly from power. He died shortly after.

Tenkai 天海 (1536–1643)

An eminent priest of the Tendai sect and political advisor to the Tokugawa government in the early Edo period, he is also known as the founder of the Kan'ei-ji at Ueno in Edo. His childhood name was Heitarō, and he later went by such names as Zuifū and Nankōbō; after his death he was given the title Jigen Daishi. He is said to have been born in the province of Aizu, present-day Fukushima Prefecture. At an early age he entered a local temple called the Ryūkō-ji and began the study and practice of Buddhism. In time he made his way to the Enryaku-ji and Onjō-ji (Miidera), the two principal temples on Mt. Hiei, the headquarters of the Tendai sect, and later went to the Kōfuku-ji in Nara for further study. In 1560 he entered the Ashikaga School in Kōzuke Province, where he devoted himself to the study of Confucianism. In 1589 he had his first interview with Tokugawa Ieyasu at Edo Castle and won the confidence of the future founder of the Tokugawa shogunate.

In 1590 he went to study under a priest named Gōkai of the Muryōju-ji in Kawagoe Semba in Musashi Province, and in honor of his teacher changed his name to Tenkai. In 1599 he was assigned a temple of his own, the Kita-in in Kawagoe Semba. In 1613 Ieyasu made him head of the Nikkō-san, an important Tendai temple at Nikkō in Shimotsuke. After the death of Ieyasu in 1616, he journeyed to Kyoto to ask the emperor to bestow a posthumous title upon Ieyasu. At the same time he himself was raised to the position of *daisōjō*, the highest ecclesiastical rank. In 1617 he removed the body of Ieyasu from its temporary burial place at Mt. Kunō in Suruga and escorted it for reburial to Nikkō. In 1624 at the command of the second shogun, Tokugawa Hidetada, he founded the Tendai temple known as the Tōei-zan Kan'ei-ji on a hill called Shinobugaoka in the Ueno section of Edo. During his lifetime he enjoyed the confidence of three shoguns, from Ieyasu to Iemitsu, and played an important role as an advisor to the government on both foreign and domestic affairs. In 1637 he began the printing of a new edition of the *Daizōkyō* (Tripitaka), which came to be known as the Tenkai Edition, but died at the age of 107 before the undertaking was completed.

TOKUGAWA HIDETADA 徳川秀忠 (1578–1631)

The second Tokugawa shogun, he was born at Hamamatsu Castle in the province of Tōtōmi, the third son of Tokugawa Ieyasu. In childhood he went by the name Nagamaro and later Takechiyo, the name his father had held as a child; after his coming-of-age ceremony in 1587, he assumed the name Hidetada. In 1590 he journeyed to Kyoto and had his first audience with Toyotomi Hideyoshi. In 1595 he married the third daughter of Asai Nagamasa, a military leader of the province of Ōmi. In 1600 he lead a campaign against Uesugi Kagekatsu, a powerful lord of the domain of Aizu, but had advanced no farther than Utsunomiya in Shimotsuke when he learned that Ishida Mitsunari and other powerful opponents of his father had raised an army in the Kansai region and were preparing to defy Ieyasu. At the command of his father, he set off for Kansai to meet the attack, proceeding by way of the Tōsandō region, but along the way became engaged in hostilities with Sanada Masayuki, lord of the castle of Ueda in Shinano Province. As a result, he did not arrive in time to participate in the decisive battle that took place between his father and his father's opponents at Sekigahara in Mino, a fact for which he was severely scolded by Ieyasu.

In 1605 the imperial court bestowed on him the rank of shogun in the Nijō Castle in Kyoto, and he thus succeeded his father as the second shogun of the Tokugawa line. In the years that followed, he devoted himself to strengthening the power and authority of the Tokugawa family. He joined his father in the attacks on Osaka Castle in 1614–15 that led to the overthrow of Hideyoshi's heir Hideyori and the destruction of the Toyotomi family and its supporters. In 1623 he journeyed to Kyoto and received sanction to turn over the position of shogun to his second son, Iemitsu. The following year he retired to the Nishinomaru section of Edo Castle, where he lived until his death in 1631.

Tokugawa Iemitsu 徳川家光 (1604–1651)

The third Tokugawa shogun, he was the second son of Tokugawa Hidetada; his mother was the daughter of Asai Nagamasa, a military leader of the province of Ōmi, and his wet nurse was Kasuga-no-tsubone. In childhood he went by the name Takechiyo. In 1614–15, when his father and grandfather marched west to attack and overthrow the forces of the Toyotomi family at Osaka Castle, he remained in Edo to guard Edo Castle, though still only a child. With his coming-of-age ceremony in 1620, he assumed the name Iemitsu. In 1623 he journeyed with his father to Kyoto and received commission from the imperial court to succeed his father in the position of shogun.

During the 1630s, he took various steps to consolidate the power of the Tokugawa family and insure the effective functioning of the feudal system of government. In 1633 he drew up regulations making clear the number of troops and armament the *hatamoto* (samurai directly under the command of the shogunate) were expected to have ready in the event of warfare in return for the particular lands and stipends bestowed upon them. In 1635 he revised the *Buke shohatto*, a code of laws promulgated by Ieyasu that regulated the duties and functions of the daimyo and samurai, and established the system of *sankin-kōtai*, which obliged the daimyo to reside part of the time in Edo and to leave their wives and children in Edo as hostages during the periods when they returned to their domains, thus insuring that they would not contemplate revolt. He prohibited the building of large ships and took other steps to tighten the control of the government over the feudal lords, decreeing that any infringement of the regulations should be subject to the severest penalties. In the same year, in order to prevent the spread of Christianity, he forbade Japanese to engage in foreign trade or to leave the country.

In 1637–38, when a revolt broke out among the Christians of the Shimabara Peninsula of Kyushu in opposition to the oppressive rule of the Matsukura clan, he dispatched a large army to the area and in time succeeded in stamping out all resistance. From this time on he took increasingly stern measures against Christianity, in 1639 prohibited Portuguese ships from coming to Japan, and in time succeeded in closing off the country entirely from the outside world, the only exception being the highly restricted and government supervised trade that took place through the port of Nagasaki. This system of national seclusion remained in effect until the arrival of American warships in 1853 forced the opening of the country. Thus Iemitsu brought to final form the system of feudal rule initiated by his grandfather Ieyasu.

Tokugawa Iemochi 徳川家茂 (1846–1866)

The fourteenth of the Tokugawa shoguns, he was the eldest son of Tokugawa Saijun, a former lord of the domain of Kishū, and in 1849 he himself became lord of Kishū. In 1858, when the thirteenth shogun, Iesada, fell dangerously ill, a struggle over who should be his successor developed, the progressive daimyo Matsudaira Yoshinaga and his group supporting the candidacy of Hitotsubashi Yoshinobu (who later became fifteenth shogun), the conservative statesman Ii Naosuke, who held the position of *tairō* (senior councilor of state), supporting Iemochi. Such was the power of Ii Naosuke that his judgement prevailed and Iemochi became the fourteenth shogun in 1858.

In an attempt to allay some of the criticisms that had been raised against the shogunate because of its signing of trade treaties with the United States and other foreign powers, Iemochi in 1861 followed the advice of shogunate officials in taking as his bride Princess Kazunomiya, the younger sister of Emperor Kōmei, thus endeavoring to establish harmonious relations between the imperial court and the shogunate. In 1862 he further attempted to promote harmony and bring about reform in the shogunate by appointing his former rival Hitotsubashi Yoshinobu and the latter's backer Matsudaira Yoshinaga to important posts in the government. In 1863 he journeyed to Kyoto to discuss problems related to the opening of the ports to foreign trade directly with the imperial court, but his trip did not accomplish the results he had hoped for. In 1864, when he journeyed to Kyoto once more, he persuaded the court to sanction him in launching a punitive attack on the forces of the fief of Chōshū, who were enthusiastic supporters of imperial rule and advocates of the expulsion of the foreigners, but who in their zeal had become all but uncontrollable. Peace between the parties was restored for a time, but in 1866 Iemochi launched a second expedition against Chōshū, leading his forces in person. Before he could accomplish his objective, however, he died of illness at Osaka Castle at the age of twenty.

Tokugawa Ienari 徳川家斎 (1773–1841)

The eleventh of the Tokugawa shoguns, he was the eldest son of Hitotsubashi Haruzumi, being born in the latter's Edo residence. His mother was the daughter of Iwamoto Masatoshi. In his childhood he was known by the name Toyochiyo. In 1781 he became the adopted son of the tenth shogun, Tokugawa Ieharu, residing in the Nishinomaru section of Edo Castle, and when Ieharu died in 1787, he succeeded him as shogun. He thereupon dismissed the *rōjū* (councilors of state) who had held power under his predecessor and summoned Matsudaira Sadanobu, lord of the fief of Shirakawa in present-day Fukushima Prefecture, to be head councilor. Sadanobu instituted a number of reforms designed to encourage frugality, restore prosperity to the farmers, and improve the fiscal state of the shogunate. Sadanobu was obliged to step down from power in 1793, but he was succeeded as head of the *rōjū* by Matsudaira Nobuaki, who continued to work to restore health to the government. After Nobuaki retired from office, however, the shogun Ienari took personal charge of affairs of state. The result was a relaxation of discipline in government and a return to sumptuous living among the shogun's family and retinue in Edo Castle. The level of popular morality declined and the shogunate found itself more pressed than ever for funds.

In 1837 Ienari turned over the position of shogun to his son Ieyoshi and again took up residence in the Nishinomaru section of the castle, but he continued to exercise power from behind the scenes. His rule as shogun lasted for a total of fifty years and appeared on the surface to be a peaceful and orderly one, though in fact the farmers were growing poorer and more hard-pressed than ever, city life was marked by corruption and decadence, and the Tokugawa shogunate was showing an increasing inability to cope with the problems of government.

Tokugawa Ieyasu 徳川家康 (1542–1616)

An outstanding military leader, he was the founder of the Tokugawa shogunate, which, with its headquarters in Edo, ruled Japan for two and one-half centuries. He was born in the province of Mikawa in present-day Aichi Prefecture, the eldest son of Matsudaira Hirotada, lord of the castle of Okazaki. His mother was the daughter of Mizuno Tadamasa, lord of the castle of Kariya in the same province. In childhood he went by the name Takechiyo, and later used the names Motonobu, Motoyasu, and Ieyasu. In youth he was sent as a hostage to Imagawa Yoshimoto, a powerful military leader in the province of Suruga just east of Mikawa, but in 1560, when Oda Nobunaga made a surprise attack on Yoshimoto and killed him in battle, Ieyasu was freed from the role of hostage and allowed to return to his home in Okazaki.

The following year Ieyasu formed an alliance with Oda Nobunaga, who controlled the province of Owari to the west, and spent the years from that time until 1568 putting down the *ikkō ikki*, the Buddhist-led peasant uprisings, in Mikawa and restoring order to the province. In 1570 he moved his residence to Hamamatsu in the province of Tōtōmi and the same year joined with Oda Nobunaga in attacking and wiping out the forces of Asakura Yoshikage, the lord of the province of Echizen, at the battle of Anegawa in Ōmi Province. In 1572, Takeda Shingen, a powerful military leader of the province of Kai, led a large army and laid siege to the castle of Hamamatsu. Ieyasu engaged his enemy at Mikatagahara in the vicinity of the castle but, although he struggled valiantly, he was finally defeated. Shingen fell ill and died shortly after, however, and Ieyasu was able to retain possession of his domain. In 1575 he joined his ally Oda Nobunaga in attacking and defeating a highly trained army headed by Shingen's son Takeda Katsuyori at Nagashino in Mikawa, and in 1582 he and Nobunaga once again attacked Katsuyori in his home province of Kai and wiped him out. As a result of the victory, Ieyasu gained dominion over the province of Suruga.

In 1582 Nobunaga, who had clearly entertained ambitions of uniting the entire country under his control, was attacked and killed at the Honnō-ji in Kyoto by his subordinate Akechi Mitsuhide. Ieyasu was at the time in residence in the city of Sakai just south of Osaka and, having only a small force with him, was in fear for his own safety, but he managed to make his way back home without incident. He then immediately embarked upon a campaign against Kai and Shinano, joining them to the three provinces of Mikawa, Tōtōmi, and Suruga already under his control to make himself the master of a total of five provinces. In 1584 he engaged in battle with Oda

Nobunaga's successor Toyotomi Hideyoshi at Komaki and Nagakute in Owari, but before any decisive victory had been won by either party, peace was arranged between them and Ieyasu acknowledged Hideyoshi as his superior. In 1590, at the command of Hideyoshi, Ieyasu led the vanguard in an attack on Odawara Castle, the stronghold of the Hōjō clan, which held dominion over the Kantō region, and after gaining victory, was given possession of the provinces of Izu, Sagami, Musashi, Kōzuke, Kazusa, and Shimōsa, which had formerly belonged to the Hōjō. The same year he took up residence in Edo Castle and began making a careful survey of the area and productivity of the lands under his control, at the same time handing out fiefs to the men who had assisted him to power and working out the details of an efficient system of feudal government.

When Hideyoshi died of illness in 1598, Ieyasu was left as the most powerful of his military supporters, and in accordance with Hideyoshi's dying wishes took up residence in Fushimi Castle in Kyoto and began directing the affairs of the nation in the name of Hideyoshi's heir, Hideyori. His conduct, however, aroused displeasure among a great many of Hideyoshi's former supporters. In 1600 Ieyasu set out to attack one of those who most openly defied him, Uesugi Kagekatsu of the domain of Aizu. He had proceeded as far as Oyama in Shimotsuke when Ishida Mitsunari and other disgruntled leaders of the Kansai region, taking advantage of his absence, organized an army to set out against him. The two forces met in battle at Sekigahara in Mino, and Ieyasu and his supporters won complete victory.

In 1603 Ieyasu was appointed by the emperor to the post of shogun and officially established the shogunate in Edo. In 1605 he turned over the office of shogun to his son Hidetada and retired to the castle of Sumpu in Suruga, but continued to wield power behind the scenes. In 1614–15 he led two campaigns against Hideyoshi's heir, Hideyori, at Osaka Castle, which ended in the death of Hideyori and the total defeat of Ieyasu's opponents, thus bringing the entire nation under Tokugawa rule. Ieyasu died in 1616 at Sumpu Castle, and the following year was given a sumptuous burial at the Tōshō-gū at Nikkō.

Tokugawa Tsunayoshi 德川綱吉 (1646–1709)

The fifth shogun of the Tokugawa line, he was born in Edo Castle, the son of the third shogun, Iemitsu. In 1651 he was made lord of the castle of Tatebayashi in the province of Kōzuke. In 1680 the fourth shogun, Ietsuna, who was Tsunayoshi's elder brother, fell gravely ill, and because he had no heir, Tsunayoshi was made his adopted son. When Ietsuna died the same year, Tsunayoshi succeeded to the position of shogun. He thereupon dismissed Sakai Tadakiyo from the post of *tairō* (senior councilor of state), the highest ministerial position in the shogunate, and in 1681 appointed Hotta Masatoshi to the position. In 1684, however, Hotta Masatoshi was assassinated in Edo Castle, and thereafter, in 1688, Tsunayoshi raised Yanagisawa Yoshiyasu to the post of *sobayōnin*, or intermediary between the shogun and the *rōjū* (councilors of state), and relied heavily upon him.

In the early part of his term as shogun, Tsunayoshi ruled with considerable sternness, punishing daimyo who had violated the law and in 1683 issuing orders regulating the type of clothing the populace could wear. He was a patron of learning and took steps to encourage the study and spread of Confucianism. Thus in 1690 he founded the Seidō in the Yushima section of Edo, a temple dedicated to the worship of Confucius, and decreed that the Chu Hsi school of Neo-Confucianism should be the official doctrine of the state, appointing the scholar Hayashi Nobuatsu to the post of *daigaku-no-kami*, or head of the state university sponsored by the shogunate. In 1687, however, he issued an edict enjoining kindness to birds, fish, insects, and other living creatures and, because he himself had been born in the Year of the Dog, calling for special respect in the treatment of dogs. The unusually heavy penalties decreed for violators of the edict and the severity with which it was enforced aroused widespread popular resentment and were damaging to his reputation as a ruler.

The latter part of his rule coincided with the Genroku era (1688–1703), when the cities of Edo and Osaka flourished and the townsmen began to develop a lively literature and culture that was distinctively their own. At the same time, the life of both the townsmen and the samurai became marked by increasing luxury, and the shogunate found itself sinking deeper into debt each year. In 1696 Ogiwara Shigehide, who held the post of *kanjō-bugyō*, superintendent of the treasury for the shogunate, attempted to remedy the situation by debasing the value of the gold and silver currency, but this precipitated a sudden rise in prices and created great confusion in the economic world. The revenge of the fourty-seven *rōnin* of Akō, an event that attracted wide attention and was to become famous in Japanese literature and drama, took place shortly before the end of his rule.

TOKUGAWA YOSHIMUNE 徳川吉宗 (1684–1751)

The eighth Tokugawa shogun, he is noted for the efforts he made to restore efficiency and financial health to the shogunate and improve the state of the nation. He was born in Wakayama Castle, the fourth son of Tokugawa Mitsusada, the lord of the fief of Kishū (Kii Province). His mother was Oyuri-no-kata, the daughter of Kose Rokuzaemon. In childhood he went by the names Genroku and Shinnosuke, and later was called Yorikata. In 1697 he had an audience with the fifth shogun, Tsunayoshi, at the official residence of the fief of Kishū in Edo. In 1705, as a result of the sudden deaths of his father and elder brothers, he was unexpectedly raised to the position of lord of the fief of Kishū. In 1716 the seventh shogun, Ietsugu, died without leaving an heir, and Yoshimune, because of his reputation for keen intelligence, was chosen by the high shogunate officials to succeed to the position of shogun. He set about taking measures to correct the numerous abuses in government that had grown up and to suppress the luxury and lawlessness prevailing in society at the time. He turned his attention first to the selection of able men for official positions, at the same time strengthening the enforcement of the laws and encouraging frugality and the practice of the military arts.

In order to relieve the fiscal distress of the shogunate, he set up in 1722 a system whereby the daimyo were called upon to make contributions to the shogunal government, thereby alleviating the financial crisis. In 1723 he took measures to punish those *daikan* (local tax officials) of the shogunate who had abused their positions and instituted reforms in the organization of the Kanjōdokoro, the fiscal office of the shogunate. Beginning around 1722, he initiated steps to open up new lands for cultivation and increase productivity, at the same time reforming the tax laws and devising ways to enlarge the tax revenues. In order to facilitate the introduction of advanced scientific techniques and industrial developments from Europe, he relaxed the restrictions against the import of Dutch books in 1720. Around 1727 he also began to encourage the cultivation of sugarcane, sweet potatoes, ginseng, and other plants. As a result of such policies, the financial position of the shogunate was considerably improved. In 1742 he promulgated a new penal code in 103 articles entitled the *Kujikata osadamegaki* and took other steps to insure legal reform. However, although he exerted every effort during his thirty-some years in power to stabilize the price of rice, he met with only limited success. Dearth continued to force drastic rises in the price, leading to riots and disturbances in many local areas, and as a result he did not enjoy a very favorable reputation with the populace as a whole.

Tokugawa Yoshinobu (Keiki) 徳川慶喜 (1827–1913)

The fifteenth and last of the Tokugawa shoguns, he was the seventh son of Tokugawa Nariaki, lord of the fief of Mito, and was born in the Mito residence at Koishikawa in Edo. As a child he went by the name Shichirōmaro. In 1838 he went to Mito, where he studied in the official school of the clan, the Kōdōkan. In 1847 at the order of the shogun he went to Edo and became the adopted heir of the Hitotsubashi family. In 1848 he underwent his coming-of-age ceremony and changed his name to Yoshinobu, which is also sometimes read Keiki. In 1857 he was considered as a possible successor to the thirteenth shogun, Iesada, along with Tokugawa Yoshitomi (Iemochi) of the fief of Kishū, but because of the backing of the powerful minister Ii Naosuke the choice fell upon the latter. In the sixth lunar month of 1858, when Ii Naosuke, acting in his capacity as *tairō* (senior councilor of state) signed a trade agreement between Japan and the U.S.A., Yoshinobu expressed his opposition, and as a result he was forbidden to enter Edo Castle.

In 1860 Ii Naosuke was struck down by assassins outside the Sakurada Gate of Edo Castle, and after this conditions in the shogunate began to move in a direction favorable for Yoshinobu. In 1862 he was appointed guardian to the youthful shogun Iemochi, and in conjunction with his supporter Matsudaira Yoshinaga, who had also been appointed to a key post in the government, he gained effective control of the shogunate. He initiated the so-called *kōbu-gattai* movement, which sought to promote harmony and cooperation between the imperial court (*kō*) and the shogunate (*bu*). To further this end, he journeyed to Kyoto in 1863 and on the shogun Iemochi's behalf attempted to explain the complex question of the opening of the ports to the court and gain its approval. In 1864 he made a second trip to Kyoto in an effort to stabilize the political situation.

In the eighth month of the same year, the forces of the clan of Chōshū, who were clamoring for the expulsion of the foreigners, surrounded the imperial palace and clashed with the palace guards at the Hamaguri Gate. At this time Yoshinobu acted as commander of the palace guards and succeeded in repulsing the attackers and putting down the attempted coup. In 1866, Shogun Iemochi set off at the head of a force of government troops to attack the Chōshū forces, who were still in revolt, but died of illness at Osaka Castle. In the following year Yoshinobu succeeded him to become the fifteenth Tokugawa shogun.

Because of the trend of events at the time, Yoshinobu was persuaded on November 9 of the same year, 1867, to resign the position of shogun and proclaim the return of the power of government to the throne. In the first month of 1868 the new government of the Meiji Restoration was formed, but hostilities soon broke out between the troops loyal to the shogunate and the forces of the new government, which were made up mainly of fighting men from the domains of Satsuma and Chōshū. Yoshinobu left Osaka Castle, where he had been staying, and proceeded by warship to Edo, where he made it clear that he had no intention of opposing the will of the new Emperor Meiji and was placed under surveillance. In the fifth month of the same year Yoshinobu officially turned over Edo Castle to the government forces and retired to Mito. Later the main branch of the Tokugawa family was given jurisdiction over the province of Suruga in present-day Shizuoka Prefecture, and Yoshinobu moved to Sumpu, now called Shizuoka City. He lived the remainder of his life until 1913 in quiet retirement.

Tominaga Nakamoto 富永仲基 (1715–1746)

Thinker of the middle Edo period. Known also as Kichibei, he was the son of a soy sauce maker of Amagasaki-chō in Osaka. His father, Kichizaemon, was a scholar of sorts and helped to found the Kaitokudō, a school for the education of Osaka townsmen. Brought up in a home where learning was honored, Nakamoto from childhood showed a fondness for scholarship and around the age of ten entered the Kaitokudō, studying under Miyake Sekian and taking instruction in the Wang Yang-ming school of Confucianism, which emphasized the importance of action as well as knowledge. Around the age of fifteen he wrote a work entitled *Setsuhei,* in which he pointed out what he believed to be errors in the Confucian classics; it is said that his teacher Miyake Sekian disowned him as a result, though the facts are uncertain. Later he studied the writing of Chinese poetry and prose under Tanaka Tōkō, a friend of the eminent scholar of Chinese language and literature Ogyū Sorai. He also assisted in the task of reprinting and collating an eight-thousand-volume collection of Buddhist scriptures in the possession of the Mampuku-ji, a Zen temple near Kyoto founded by the Ming loyalist monk Yin-yüan. Eventually he opened a school of his own in Bingo-chō in Osaka, teaching at the same time that he carried on his research.

In 1746 he produced a work entitled *Okina no fumi,* in which he sharply criticized the Shinto, Confucianism, and Buddhism of his time and called for greater sincerity and moral fervor in the lives of his fellow countrymen. In 1745 he completed a work, the *Shutsujō gogo,* in which, drawing upon his profound knowledge of Buddhism, he expressed severe criticism of the Buddhist scriptures. The book aroused bitter opposition among the Buddhist clergy but had the salutary effect of encouraging a more historical approach to the study of the religious texts. Nakamoto was of weak constitution and often suffered from poor health, but he overcame this handicap to become one of the most learned and creative scholars of the time, producing in his short lifetime a number of works remarkable for their insight and originality.

Toyotomi Hideyori 豊臣秀頼 (1593–1615)

The second son of Toyotomi Hideyoshi, the great military leader who unified Japan at the end of the sixteenth century, he was born in Osaka Castle. As a child he was known by the name Hiroimaru. His mother was Yodogimi, the eldest daughter of Oda Nobunaga's younger sister Odani-no-kata. Hideyoshi, because his first son had died in infancy, doted on the boy and had him brought up at Fushimi Castle in Kyoto. Lacking a son of his own, Hideyoshi had earlier adopted an heir named Hidetsugu, but in 1595 Hidetsugu incurred his foster father's displeasure and was forced to commit suicide. This left Hideyori as sole heir.

In 1598 Hideyoshi, aware that death was near, called upon Tokugawa Ieyasu and the other powerful military leaders of the time to support his son, repeatedly demanding that they swear oaths of fealty, and succumbed to illness shortly after. In 1599 Hideyori, in accordance with his father's dying wishes, took up residence in Osaka Castle. Meanwhile Tokugawa Ieyasu continued to grow in power, and relations between him and such rivals as Ishida Mitsunari became increasingly strained. The result was the great battle of Sekigahara in 1600 between Ieyasu and his followers and Ishida Mitsunari and the other military leaders who supported Hideyori, which ended in the defeat of the latter. Hideyori, however, was allowed to remain in Osaka Castle and to retain dominion over the three nearby provinces of Settsu, Kawachi, and Izumi.

In 1603, Hideyori's military supporters, in an effort to ensure his safety, arranged a marriage between him and Sen-hime, the daughter of Tokugawa Hidetada, Ieyasu's third son. In the winter of 1614, however, Ieyasu found an excuse to launch an attack on Osaka Castle, and though hostilities were suspended for a time, a second attack in the summer of 1615 ended in the total defeat of Hideyori's supporters. Hideyori and his mother, Yodogimi, committed suicide while the castle went up in flames about them.

Toyotomi Hideyoshi 豊臣秀吉 (1536–1598)

The military and political leader who succeeded in uniting the country and bringing an end to the turbulence of the so-called Warring States era. At first he went by the name of Kinoshita Tōkichirō and later Hashiba Hideyoshi, but in time the emperor bestowed upon him the surname Toyotomi, by which he was thereafter known. He was born in the village of Nakamura in the province of Owari, present-day Aichi Prefecture, the son of a farmer named Kinoshita Yaemon. In 1543 his father died, and in 1551 he left home and entered the service of Matsushita Kahei, lord of the castle of Kunō in the province of Tōtōmi. In 1558 he entered the service of the powerful military leader Oda Nobunaga of Owari, and in 1566, at the command of his lord, he built the castle of Sunomata on the border between Owari and Mino, thus facilitating attacks upon his lord's powerful opponent, the Saitō family of Mino. In 1570 he distinguished himself in the attacks on the military leader Asai Nagamasa of Ōmi, and as a reward he was in 1573 put in charge of the former domains of the Asai family. In 1574 he built a castle for himself at Nagahama in Ōmi on the shore of Lake Biwa.

In 1576 he engaged in a campaign against the powerful Mōri family, which had gained control of a number of provinces in the area west of Kyoto. The campaign dragged on for some years, but in 1582, when he was besieging the castle of Takamatsu in the province of Bitchū, he received word that his lord, Oda Nobunaga, had been assassinated at the Honnō-ji in Kyoto by one of his subordinates, Akechi Mitsuhide. Hideyoshi immediately ceased hostilities against the Mōri family, withdrew his troops, and hastened back to Kyoto, where he engaged and defeated Mitsuhide at the battle of Yamazaki, thus laying the groundwork that in time permitted him to become the successor to Nobunaga.

In 1583 he led his forces in an attack upon his rival Shibata Katsuie, defeating him at the battle of Shizugatake in Ōmi and eventually pursuing him to his castle in Echizen, where Katsuie committed suicide. In the same year, Hideyoshi began work on the great castle of Osaka, which was to be his residence in future years. In 1584 he launched an attack upon his most formidable rival, Tokugawa Ieyasu, whose base of power was in the province of Mikawa, engaging him in battle at Komaki and Nagakute in Owari, but instead of pressing for a decisive engagement he concluded peace with Ieyasu and was eventually able by political stratagems to persuade the latter to acknowledge fealty to him.

In 1585 he attacked the powerful military leader Chōsokabe Motochika and gained control of the island of Shikoku, and in 1587 he brought to submission the Shimazu family, which had heretofore controlled the island of Kyushu. In the same year, while encamped at Hakata in northern Kyushu, he suddenly issued an order calling for the expulsion from the country of all Christian missionaries. The following year he took control of the port of Nagasaki and the surrounding area, which had previously been controlled by the Jesuits, and placed it under his direct jurisdiction, at the same time taking charge of the foreign trade conducted by Portuguese vessels at the port. In 1590 he attacked the Hōjō family, who were powerful military leaders in the Kantō region, approaching their castle at Odawara from the land and sea and forcing it to surrender. In the same year he went on to march against the remoter regions of northeastern Honshu, until at last he had brought the entire country under his command.

Hideyoshi's principal political measures may be summed up as follows. He continued the policy begun by Oda Nobunaga of conducting careful land surveys to determine the exact area of land under cultivation and its yield and set up a system to collect taxes in rice directly from the farmers. He handed out lands as rewards to his followers and required that they perform military service in return. He conducted a *katanagari*, or "sword hunt," confiscating all swords and other weapons from the peasants and establishing clear distinctions between the samurai or warrior class and the peasantry. He placed all major cities and areas containing gold or silver mines under the direct supervision of the government in Kyoto and took steps to mint coins and establish a uniform currency throughout the country. Finally, he encouraged overseas trade, issuing official patents to powerful merchants, giving them permission to engage in such trade. When he had completed the task of uniting the country and bringing order to the feudal system, he turned his attention to foreign conquest, in 1592 and again in 1597 dispatching troops to invade Korea in an attempt to force the ruler of Korea to recognize his sovereignty, but in 1598 he died of illness at his castle in Fushimi just south of Kyoto, and his plans to conquer Korea and eventually China ended in complete failure.

Udagawa Genzui 宇田川玄随 (1755–1797)

Scholar of Dutch learning in the middle Edo period. From the time of his father, Udagawa Michinori, his family served as physicians in the fief of Tsuyama in Mimasaka; he was born in the Tsuyama official residence in Edo. Apprised of the importance of Dutch learning by Katsuragawa Hoshū, the physician to the shogun, he made up his mind at twenty-four to learn

Dutch. Hoshū had a high regard for his ability and urged him to translate a work on internal medicine by a Dutch medical expert named Johannes de Gorter. While continuing to pursue his studies of the Dutch language under Ishii Tsuneuemon, he began work on the translation, completing it ten years later. In eighteen chapters, it was entitled *Seisetsu naika senyō* and was published in 1793, the first work to introduce Dutch internal medicine to Japan. Genzui intended to revise and improve the translation, but he died before he could carry out the task; the work was taken over by his adopted son, Genshin (or Shinsai), who in 1822 brought out a revised and enlarged edition entitled *Zōho jūtei naika senyō*. Genzui produced many other works on Western medicine, botany, and other subjects, among them the *Ensai meibutsukō*, *Tōzai byōkō*, and *Ensai sōmokuryaku*. In his late years he moved to the Kayaba section of Edo, where he died.

UDAGAWA YŌAN 宇田川榕庵 (1798–1846)

Scholar of Dutch learning of the late Edo period. The son of Ezawa Yōju, a physician of the fief of Ōgaki in Mino, he was later adopted by Udagawa Genshin (or Shinsai) and became a physician to the lord of the domain of Tsuyama. From his youth he was fond of natural history and collected medicinal herbs and other specimens. Later he studied Dutch learning under Baba Kokuri and proved himself to be especially talented in languages. In 1816, at the age of eighteen, he wrote a work entitled *Seisetsu botanikakyō* on the subject of Western botany.

In 1826 he succeeded his foster father Shinsai as a shogunate official in charge of translation and participated in the largest officially sponsored translation project of the pre-Meiji period, the rendering of a French encyclopedia by N. Noel Chomel into Japanese under the title *Kōsei shimpen*. He also wrote a work entitled *Shokubutsu keigen*, in which he presented the first systematic description of botany in Japanese. Also, in a translation of William Henry's *Elements of Experimental Chemistry*, done from a Dutch translation of the work and entitled *Seimi kaisō*, he succeeded in freeing chemistry from its earlier position in Japan as an adjunct to medicine and herbal lore by establishing it as a separate science in its own right. Through these and other works, he thus made a major contribution toward establishing modern Western style methods of study of the natural sciences in Japan.

He was a close friend of the German doctor von Siebold and numbered among his disciples Itō Keisuke, Totsuka Seikai, and Udagawa Kōsai.

WATANABE KAZAN 渡邊崋山 (1793–1841)

Scholar and painter of the late Edo period. He was the son of Watanabe Sadamichi, a samurai and important official of the domain of Tahara in Mikawa Province, and was born in the Tahara official residence in Edo. His personal name was Sadayasu; his common name, Nobori; Kazan was his literary name. He studied Confucianism under Satō Issai and Matsuzaki Kōdō, but because the fief of Tahara was small and his stipend meager, he decided to take up painting in order to supplement his income, studying under Shirakawa Shizan and later Kaneko Kinryō and Tani Bunchō. He also took an active part in the administration of the fief, advancing in office until in 1832 he was appointed *karō* (chief retainer) and was made responsible for coastal defense in the area.

It was around this time that he first became interested in Dutch learning—that is, the study of European science and civilization as it was conveyed to Japan through Dutch teachers and textbooks—joining with Takano Chōei, Kozeki San'ei, and others to form a society called the Shōshikai devoted to the investigation of European culture and the discussion of the current situation in Japan and abroad. In 1838 he wrote a work entitled *Shinkiron* in which he criticized the shogunate for the order that it issued in 1825 calling on all coastal domains to attack and repel any foreign ships that might approach Japan. In 1839 occurred the so-called Bansha imprisonment, a move by the shogunate to suppress the members of the Shōshikai and other liberal-minded students of Dutch learning, and Kazan was put in prison along with Takano Chōei, but through the efforts of his teacher Matsuzaki Kōdō he was released and allowed to return home to Tahara, where he was kept under surveillance. Later, fearing that he might cause embarrassment to his lord, he committed suicide. In addition to the *Shinkiron* already mentioned, he wrote several other works such as *Seiyō jijō onkotaegaki* and *Gekizetsu wakumon* in which he expressed his sincere concern for the future of the nation.

As a *bunjin-gaka* (scholar-painter), Kazan holds a place of importance in the art history of the period. He studied the techniques of Shen Nan-p'in, a Chinese painter who came to Nagasaki in 1731 and was noted for his realistic depictions of flowers and birds, and of the *ukiyo-e* painters, and was skilled in the execution of both landscapes and human figures. He is particularly noted for his unusual portraits in which he employed a chiaroscuro technique borrowed from Western painting to create a three-dimensional effect. Among the best-known representatives of this style are the portrait of Takami Senseki in Tokyo National Museum, the portrait of Satō Issai in the possession of the Kawada family, and the portrait of Ichikawa Beian belonging to the Shimomura family. He had many disciples, most notable among them being Fukuda Hankō, Tsubaki Chinzan, and Okamoto Shūki.

WATARAI NOBUYOSHI 渡會延佳 (1615–1690)

Shinto leader of the early Edo period and reviver of the Ise or Watarai school of Shinto. His family name was Deguchi, his common name Yosaburō or Shinano, and his literary name Jikian. He was the son of a priest of the Outer Shrine of Ise. At the time of his birth, Ise Shinto had fallen into decline because of the strength of a rival school known as Yoshida Shinto. Watarai did not study under any distinguished teacher, but seems rather to have been self-educated. In time he became a *gon-negi*, an acting priest in the Outer Shrine. Outside of a few trips to Edo, he seems scarcely ever to have left the Ise region, but spent his entire life in research and lecturing. He also collected and published earlier works, establishing a library known as the Toyomiyasaki Bunko, in these and other ways laboring to revive the fortunes of Ise Shinto.

In his thinking, he followed the traditional doctrines of the Ise school, expounding the trinity of deities made up of Ame-no-minaka-nushi-no-kami, Kunitokotachi-no-kami, and Toyouke Daijingū, and placing great emphasis on the so-called Five Classics of Shinto. But he also gave evidence of considerable Confucian influence, particularly from the thought of the *Book of Changes*. In addition, he stressed everyday morality, in particular extolling the virtue of honesty, thus introducing into Ise Shinto elements that reflect the intellectual and spiritual climate of early Edo times. His principal work is *Yōfukuki*, in addition to which he wrote *Nakatomi no harai mizuho-shō*, *Shindai no maki kōjutsushō*, *Jingu hiden mondō*, and many others. He had numerous disciples, among them his son Watarai Nobutsune.

YAMADA NAGAMASA 山田長政 (d. 1630)

Adventurer of the early Edo period, he was born in the province of Suruga; his ordinary given name was Nizaemon. For a time in his youth he served as palanquin bearer to Ōkubo Tadasuke, lord of the fief of Numazu, but around 1611 he journeyed in a *shuinsen*, or vessel officially authorized to carry on foreign trade, to Siam, where he was active in the Japanese community that had grown up in the suburbs of Ayuthia, the capital of the kingdom, and in time became head of the community. When Siamese envoys came to Japan, he frequently sent letters and gifts by way of them to important officials in the Tokugawa shogunate, and he also dispatched his own merchant vessels to Japan, Malacca, and Batavia and exchanged letters and gifts with Jan Pieterszoon Coen, the governor general of the Netherland East Indies, thus playing an active part in both commerce and diplomacy. He also headed an army of Japanese that took part in the civil and foreign wars of Siam and distinguished himself by his military prowess.

In 1628 he was awarded the highest official title in Siam, that of Okya Senaphimuk. With the death of the king of Siam in the same year, he helped to end the struggle that ensued over the succession and to place the king's son on the throne, but because of the apprehension that he aroused in other members of the royal family, he was appointed governor of the region of Ligor and was dispatched from the capital the following year to take up his new post. While there, he engaged in battle with an invading army from Patani. He was wounded in the encounter and died of poison applied to his wounds by the Siamese. His son Okon Senaphimuk succeeded him as governor of Ligor but, meeting with opposition from the Siamese, he burned the city of Ligor to the ground, set off for Cambodia, and died in an encounter with the Siamese army. The Japanese settlement at Ayuthia was attacked and burned and thereafter ceased to be of importance. The Sengen Shinto Shrine in Shizuoka Prefecture formerly had in its possession a wooden plaque of a warship, which had been presented to the shrine by Yamada Nagamasa, but it was destroyed by fire in 1778 and only a copy of it remains today.

YAMAGA SOKŌ 山鹿素行 (1622–1685)

Early Edo period Confucian, exponent of the *kogakuha*, or "school of ancient learning," and founder of the Yamaga school of military science. His personal name was Takaoki or Takasuke, his common name Jingoemon, and his literary name Sokō. His father had originally been a samurai in the domain of Kameyama in Ise, but later became a dependent of Machino Yukiyori, a samurai of the domain of Aizu in Mutsu. Sokō was born in Aizu and in 1627 accompanied his father to Edo. In 1630 he became a student of Hayashi Razan, a celebrated Confucian scholar in the service of the Tokugawa shogunate, studying the Chu Hsi school of Neo-Confucianism under him. He also studied the Kōshū school of military science under Obata

Kagenori and received a certificate indicating his mastery of its teachings. From these two teachers he also received instruction in Imbe and Ryōbu Shinto. By around 1641, he had succeeded in acquiring a wide knowledge of both Japanese and Chinese religious and philosophical teachings.

In 1652 he was invited by Asano Naganao, lord of the domain of Akō in Harima, to enter the service of the domain. He received a stipend of 1,000 *koku* of rice, an unusually large amount for a Confucian scholar, and lectured the samurai of the domain on military matters. In 1656 he wrote three works, *Bukyō yōroku, Shūkyō yōroku,* and *Chikyō yōroku,* in which he argued that the teachings of Confucianism should play a practical role in the daily life of members of the warrior class.

He left the service of the lord of Akō in 1660, and in 1665 wrote *Bukyō shōgaku.* Shortly after, he also compiled a collection of his writings and conversations in forty-five chapters entitled *Yamaga gorui.* One section of this, a three-chapter work called *Seikyō yōroku,* was published separately and soon attracted attention. In it, Sokō criticized the officially supported teachings of the Chu Hsi school of Neo-Confucianism as being too theoretical in nature and called for a return to the ways of Confucius and the other sages of antiquity, expounding views that came to be known as the *kogakuha,* or "school of ancient learning." As a result of his criticisms of Neo-Confucianism, he was ordered into banishment in Akō the following year.

At Akō, he wrote *Buke jiki, Chūchō jijitsu,* and other works in which he argued that, in its history and natural features, Japan was in no way inferior to China, and criticized the ordinary run of Japanese Confucian scholars for their excessive adulation of Chinese culture. In 1675 he was given permission to return to Edo, where he opened a school in his own home called the Sekitokudō. He gave instruction in Confucianism and military science and is said to have had a total of over four thousand students.

During his period of exile in Akō, he was very well treated by the lord of the domain and numbered among his students Ōishi Yoshio and other samurai who, as the so-called Forty-seven Rōnin, later became famous for the manner in which they avenged their lord's death. The late Edo period Confucian and patriot Yoshida Shōin, it may be noted, was a teacher of the Yamaga school of military science and educated a number of the young men who were to play a crucial role in the Meiji Restoration. Sokō's grave is situated in the temple called Sōsan-ji in Ushigome in Shinjuku Ward, Tokyo.

YAMAGATA BANTŌ 山片蟠桃 (1748–1821)

Osaka merchant and scholar of the late Edo period; his common name was Masuya Kouemon. He was born in the village of Kazume, the district of Inami, in the province of Harima, the second son of a farmer named Hasegawa Kohei. In 1760, at the age of twelve, he became heir to his uncle Masuya Kyūbei, who operated a branch store for the wealthy Osaka merchant Masuya Heiemon. On reaching the age of adulthood in 1764, he abandoned his childhood name Sōgorō and took the name Kyūbei the Fourth. From 1772 on, he acted as guardian to the head of the Masuya establishment, who was still a young boy, overcoming various financial difficulties and improving the fortunes of the business. In time, by carrying on astute dealings with the Date family, lords of the fief of Sendai, and other prominent daimyo, he was able to reap large profits and to establish the Masuya as one of the largest and most powerful merchant houses of Osaka.

While tending to business matters, he also devoted himself to scholarship, enrolling in the Kaitokudō, the well-known private school established in Osaka for the education of townsmen, studying Confucianism under its directors, Nakai Chikuzan and his brother Nakai Riken. Later he took up the study of Western astronomy and calendrical matters under Asada Gōryū, taking a deep interest in matters pertaining to the technology and culture of the West, known at this time as Dutch learning. With the wealth at his disposal, he built up a large collection of books pertaining to astronomy, geography, and history, as well as books and articles imported from the West.

Around 1804 his sight began to fail, and in time he went blind, but he continued at his scholarly endeavors. In 1820, at the age of seventy-two, he completed a major work in twelve chapters entitled *Yume no shiro*, which deals with a wide range of subjects such as astronomy, geography, history, and economics and is noted for its critical spirit and highly rational and scientific approach. He also produced other works such as the *Taichiben*, which treats questions relating to prices, particularly the price of rice, leaving behind him a reputation as one of the most outstanding townsman scholars in Osaka history.

YAMAMURA SAISUKE 山村才助 (1770–1807)

Geographer and student of Dutch learning in the late Edo period; his personal name was Masanaga, his common name Saisuke, and he used the professional name Muyū Dōjin. He was born in the Fukagawa area of Edo, in the official residence of the fief of Tsuchiura; his father's name was Tsukasa, his mother's name Maki. At an early age he began studies under his uncle on his mother's side, the renowned Confucian scholar Ichikawa Kansai. After reading the *Sairan igen*, a work on the countries of the West written in 1713 by Arai Hakuseki, he determined to devote himself to the study of world geography. In 1789 he entered the Shirandō, a private school established by Ōtsuki Gentaku for the teaching of Dutch learning. In 1796, after examining all the Eastern and Western materials pertaining to world geography that he could lay his hands on, he wrote his first work, the *Gaiki seigokō*.

In 1802 he completed what has come to be recognized as the finest work on world geography to be produced in the Edo period, the *Teisei zōyaku Sairan igen*. This was followed in 1805 by a work on the ancient history of the West entitled *Seiyō zakki*. In addition, at the command of the Tokugawa shogunate, he produced a translation in eight chapters of a work on Russia entitled in Japanese *Roshia kokushi* (published in 1848), as well as such other works as the *Kai ichiran zusetsu* (1806), *Indoshi*, and *Ajia shotōshi*, all of them contributions of prime importance to the study of world geography. Unfortunately, he died of illness at the age of thirty-seven.

YAMAWAKI TŌYŌ 山脇東洋 (1705–1762)

Physician of the middle Edo period; his personal name was Hisanori; Tōyō was his professional name. He was the eldest son of Shimizu Ritsuan, a native of Kameyama in Tamba who was residing in Kyoto. In his youth he studied medicine under Yamawaki Genshū, who had also been his father's teacher, and in 1726 became the adopted son of Genshū and carried on his adopted father's medical practice, Later, under Gotō Konzan, he studied *koihō*, or traditional Chinese medicine, particularly that associated with the Chin and T'ang dynasties (roughly, the period from the fourth to the tenth centuries). Through his researches, he contributed greatly to the development and spread of *koihō* type medicine and in time came to be numbered among the four leading experts in that field.

In 1754 he joined Kosugi Genteki and other physicians in carrying out dissections on the bodies of executed criminals in the suburbs of Kyoto, and through these studies discovered that the traditional theories pertaining to the internal organs were in error at various points. In 1759 he produced a work entitled *Zōshi* in which he described the true structure of the internal organs of the human body, the first of its kind in Japanese medical history and a contribution of immeasurable importance. He conducted further dissections on the bodies of executed criminals and gained increasing fame, but died in 1762 at the age of fifty-seven. In addition to the *Zōshi*, his writings include the *Yōjuin isoku* and the *Saisei yogen*.

Yamazaki Ansai 山崎闇齊 (1618–1682)

Early Edo period Confucian and Shintoist of highly individual character; he was born in Kyoto. His personal name was Yomishi, his common name Kaemon, and his literary name Ansai, and as a Shinto leader he went by the literary name Suika. His father, Yamazaki Jōin, was a masterless samurai of Himeji, who made his living as an acupuncturist.

In his youth Ansai was sent to the Buddhist monastery on Mt. Hiei, but he left the monastery and in 1632 entered Myōshin-ji, one of the major Zen temples of Kyoto. In 1636 he moved to Kyūkō-ji, a temple in the domain of Tosa in Shikoku, becoming a full-fledged Zen monk. There he became acquainted with Nonaka Kenzan, an official of the Tosa domain who was attempting to introduce administrative reforms based upon the ideals of Confucian doctrine. Through him, he met Kenzan's teacher, Tani Jichū, the founder of Neo-Confucian studies in Tosa, and under him studied the Chu Hsi school of Neo-Confucianism. In 1642 he renounced the Buddhist religion and became a Confucian.

Shortly thereafter, he returned to Kyoto and in 1655 opened a school there. He was a forceful educator, extolling Chu Hsi's teachings as the highest expression of Confucian thought and laboring to instill their essential principles in his students. In 1657 he made a visit to the Grand Shrines of Ise, where he found himself greatly attracted to Shintoism. He studied Shinto under Yoshikawa (Kikkawa) Koretari in Edo, and by combining Shinto teachings with the metaphysics of Chu Hsi Neo-Confucianism, in time developed a new school of Shinto known as Suika Shinto, which emphasized the essential unity of Shintoism and Confucianism.

After going to Edo in 1658, he became the teacher of such distinguished personages as Inoue Masatoshi, lord of the domain of Kasama in Hitachi, and Katō Yasuyoshi, lord of the domain of Ōzu in Iyo, and also came under the patronage of Hoshina Masayuki, lord of the domain of Aizu and younger brother of the third shogun Tokugawa Iemitsu. Thereafter he divided his time between Edo and Kyoto, teaching half a year in each, but after the death of Hoshina Masayuki in 1671, he settled down in Kyoto and devoted himself to writing.

He had some six thousand disciples, of whom the eminent Confucian scholars Satō Naokata, Miyake Shōsai, and Asami Keisai were the most outstanding. Satō and Asami were both somewhat critical of Ansai's views on Shinto, and as a consequence were expelled from his school, though in later times they came to be recognized as the legitimate transmitters of Ansai's teachings. Asami Keisai's disciple Miyake Kanran is particularly noteworthy for the role he played in transmitting the teachings of Ansai to the domain of Mito. He was in the service of Tokugawa Mitsukuni, lord of the domain of Mito, and participated in the compilation of the *Dai-Nihon shi*, the great history of Japan sponsored by Mitsukuni. Ansai's views on the essential unity of Shinto and Confucian teachings formed the basis for the idealization of the imperial family and institution that characterized the Mito scholars. Other well-known figures who, though they lived considerably later, were much influenced by Ansai's views on the reverence due to the imperial house and who attempted to translate them into reality include the eighteenth century scholars Takenouchi Shikibu and Yamagata Daini and the nineteenth century scholar Umeda Umpin, all of whom were arrested because of their antishogunate sentiments and died as a result. Ansai left a large number of works, which have been collected in the *Yamazaki Ansai zenshū*. He is buried in the grounds of Kōmyō-ji (Kurodani) in Kyoto.

YANAGISAWA YOSHIYASU 柳澤吉保 (1658–1714)

Rōjū (councilor of state) in the Tokugawa shogunate and lord of the fief of Kōfu. He went by the common names Chikara and Yatarō and in youth by the names Fusayasu and Yasuaki. He was the fifth son of Yanagisawa Yasutada, a retainer of Tokugawa Tsunayoshi, the lord of Tatebayashi in Kōzuke. After his father retired from active service, he was appointed head of the *koshōgumi*, or castle guard. In 1680, when Tokugawa Tsunayoshi became the fifth shogun, Yoshiyasu was taken into the service of the shogunate, being appointed a *ko'nando* (personal attendant) to the shogun. In 1685 he was given the title of Dewa-no-kami and was thereafter gradually promoted until by 1688 he had reached the status of daimyo with a yearly stipend of 12,030 *koku* of rice and held the post of *sobayōnin*, chamberlain to the shogun. It was in Yoshiyasu's time that the post of *sobayōnin* first became one of great power and authority. In 1694 he became lord of the castle of Kawagoe in the province of Musashi with a stipend of 70,000 *koku*. The same year he was made a *rōjū-kaku*, assistant councilor of state, and in 1698 became a *rōjū-jōseki*, or chief *rōjū*.

In 1701 he was given the surname Matsudaira, the former surname of the Tokugawa family, and was allowed to borrow the element *yoshi* from the personal name of the shogun, being renamed Yoshiyasu; his eldest son Yasusada was at the same time renamed Yoshisato. In 1704 he was relieved of the domain of Kawagoe and enfeoffed instead as lord of Kōfu, a domain customarily entrusted to a member of the Tokugawa family, with a stipend of 150,000 *koku*. The shogun Tsunayoshi from time to time visited the residence of Yoshiyasu, a fact that, along with his brilliant and rapid rise to power, occasioned wide resentment among Yoshiyasu's contemporaries. He won favor with the shogun through his talent and sagacity, but he was also fond of learning and took into his service such noted Confucian scholars as Ogyū Sorai and Hosoi Heishū, arranging for them to lecture and debate in the presence of the shogun when the latter was visiting in his home. He also took an interest in the compilation of historical works and sponsored the printing of Chinese historical texts.

From the distinguished haiku poet and scholar of Japanese literature Kitamura Kigin he received initiation into the *Kokin denju*, a body of interpretations concerning the *Kokinshū* that were handed down in secret and imparted only to persons of special qualification in the art of poetry. He also took a deep interest in Zen doctrine and practice and was himself an ardent practitioner of Zen training. In 1709, with the death of the shogun Tsunayoshi, he went into retirement, entering the Buddhist clergy and taking the religious name Hozan. He died in 1714 at his country estate, the Rikugien, in the Komagome section of Edo. The garden of the latter is still in existence, constituting one of the most outstanding examples of Edo period landscape gardening.

Yin-yüan (Ingen) 隱元 (1592–1673)

Zen monk of Ming China who came to Japan in the early Edo period. Also known as Yin-yüan Lung-ch'i, in Japanese pronunciation Ingen Ryūki, his family name was Lin and he was born in Fu-ch'ing in the province of Fukien. He entered the priesthood at the age of twenty and began training at Mt. Pu-t'o-lo. At twenty-eight he went to Mt. Huang-po to study under the Zen Master Chien-yüan, later succeeding his master as head of the temple there and founding what is known as the Huang-po (Japanese: Ōbaku) school of Rinzai Zen. In 1654, ten years after the Ming dynasty was overthrown and the rulership of China had passed into the hands of the Ch'ing or Manchu dynasty, Yin-yüan was invited by the monk Itsuzen of the Kōfuku-ji in Nagasaki to come to Japan, an invitation that, probably because of the triumph of the Manchus over his homeland, he readily accepted.

He resided first at the Kōfuku-ji and later at the Sōfuku-ji and Fukusai-ji in Nagasaki and the Fumon-ji in the province of Settsu, where he gained considerable fame. In 1658 he took up residence in the Rinshō-ji in the Yushima section of Edo and was received in audience by Shogun Ietsuna, being granted permission to found a temple of his own at Uji, southeast of the city of Kyoto. This temple, called Mampuku-ji of Mt. Ōbaku, became the first temple of the Ōbaku school of Rinzai Zen in Japan.

Yin-yüan enjoyed favor among the members of the imperial family and the court nobles, and when he fell ill in 1673 he was presented by Retired Emperor Gomizuno-o with the title Daikō Fumyō Kokushi. He died the same year at the age of eighty-one and was given the posthumous title Shinkū Daishi. His writings and teachings are preserved in a number of works, among them the *Fushō kokushi kōroku*, *Ōbaku goroku*, and others.

YODOGIMI 淀君 (d. 1615)

Concubine of the military dictator Toyotomi Hideyoshi and mother of his heir, Hideyori; she lived a life characterized by dramatic reversals of fortune. Known by the personal name Chacha, she was the eldest daughter of Asai Nagamasa, a daimyo who held a domain in the northern part of Ōmi Province and resided in Odani Castle. Her mother, known as Oichi-no-kata or Odani-no-kata, was a younger sister of the military leader Oda Nobunaga.

In 1573 Asai Nagamasa defied Nobunaga and was attacked and wiped out by the latter. At this time Chacha, her mother, and her two younger sisters were taken into custody by Nobunaga. (One of her younger sisters later became the wife of Kyōgoku Takatsugu, the other the wife of Tokugawa Hidetada, the second of the Tokugawa shoguns.)

In 1582, after the assassination of Oda Nobunaga, Chacha's mother married Shibata Katsuie, one of Nobunaga's generals. Chacha and her sisters accompanied their mother to her new home in the castle of Kita-no-shō in Echizen. But the following year Shibata Katsuie was defeated in battle by Toyotomi Hideyoshi, and the castle of Kita-no-shō fell into the hands of the latter. Chacha's mother committed suicide, and Chacha and her sisters were led off to Hideyoshi's headquarters.

After having been intimately involved in the tragic downfall of two domains, Chacha's fortunes took a turn for the better. She became a concubine of her captor Hideyoshi and soon enjoyed great favor. In 1589 she took up residence in Yodo Castle south of Kyoto and the same year bore Hideyoshi his first son, Tsurumatsu, who died in infancy. Chacha by this time was the most highly favored of Hideyoshi's concubines and was referred to by him as Yodo-no-nyōbō or Yodo-no-mono. She was commonly known as Yodo-dono and later by the nickname Yodogimi.

In 1590 she accompanied Hideyoshi on his campaign against Odawara and in 1592 resided at his headquarters in Nagoya when he launched his first campaign against Korea. In 1593 she returned to Hideyoshi's principal residence, Osaka Castle, where she bore his second son, Hideyori. Neither Hideyoshi's wife, a daughter of the Sugihara family, nor any of his other concubines had borne him any sons, and as a result Yodogimi's position outshone even that of Hideyoshi's wife.

After Hideyoshi's death in 1598, Yodogimi remained in Osaka Castle and plotted with Ishida Mitsunari and other prominent leaders concerning possible ways to stem the rising power of Tokugawa Ieyasu and restore the Toyotomi family to eminence. But Hideyoshi's followers were split into two factions, those siding with Yodogimi and the more militant group siding with Hideyoshi's wife of the Sugihara family. After Ishida Mitsunari was defeated by Tokugawa Ieyasu at the battle of Sekigahara in 1600, the power of Yodogimi's group waned, and it became apparent that Ieyasu was not to be overthrown. Yodogimi's continued efforts at resistance all met with failure, and in the two attacks on Osaka Castle in the winter of 1614 and the summer of 1615, the last vestiges of resistance to Tokugawa rule were wiped out. In the latter attack, the castle was destroyed by fire, and Yodogimi and her son Hideyori committed suicide. Yodogimi was something over forty at the time of her death. Hideyori's wife, Sen-hime, the daughter of the second shogun Tokugawa Hidetada, was rescued from the flames and sent to Edo, where the following year she married Honda Tadatoki.

YODOYA TATSUGORŌ 淀屋辰五郎 (dates uncertain)

Wealthy Osaka merchant family of the early and middle Edo period. Originally named Okamoto, the first head of the family, Tsuneyasu Yosaburō, moved from the manor of Okamoto in Yamashiro to Osaka in the time of Toyotomi Hideyoshi and took up residence in Jūsannin-chō, where he began a lumber business under the shop-name Yodoya. After the completion of Osaka Castle, he opened up the area of Naka-no-shima and moved there, a fact reflected in the names Tsuneyasu Bridge and Tsuneyasu-chō, which are still in existence today.

Gentō, the second head of the family, opened up the Utsubo area, contributing greatly to the growth of the city, and acquired enormous wealth by receiving permission to engage in the government-controlled trade in raw silk imported from China and by activities in the rice market. It was at this time that the famous Dōjima rice exchange was first established at the south end of Yodoya Bridge. Gendō was fond of the tea ceremony and *renga* (linked verse) and was a close associate of Kobori Enshū, Takimoto Shōjōbō, and other men of prominence in the artistic and cultural life of the time.

The family continued to prosper under subsequent leaders, but in 1705, in the time of the fourth head of the family, Saburōuemon, the family was accused by the government of indulging in excessive luxury and was ordered to cease all its business activities. The vast economic power that had been in the possession of the Yodoya family passed into the hands of the money-changers of the Semba district, but the incident left the Osaka merchants with a profound feeling of distrust toward the Edo shogunate. It is commonly asserted that Yodoya Tatsugorō was the name of the fourth head of the family, but further study is needed before the history of the family can be ascertained for certain.

Yoshida Shōin 吉田松陰 (1830–1859)

Thinker, educator, and patriot of the late Edo period; he was born in Hagi, the second son of Sugi Yurinosuke Tsunemichi, a samurai of the domain of Chōshū. His personal name was Norikata, his common name Torajirō, and he went by such literary names as Shōin and Nijūikkai Mōshi. He was adopted by his uncle Yoshida Taisuke, a teacher of the Yamaga school of military science, at the age of four and became the heir of the family the following year. He also received instruction from another uncle, Tamaki Bunnoshin. He was a very apt pupil and at the age of nine lectured on military science in the presence of the lord of the domain. By the age of seventeen, he was acknowledged as an expert in the teachings of the Yamaga school and the following year became an instructor in his own right.

In 1850 he made a tour of Kyushu and in 1851 accompanied the lord of his domain to Edo, where he made many friends and came under the influence of various teachers. Among the latter, his contacts with Sakuma Shōzan, an advocate of Western learning and military science, were particularly important. He became Sakuma's disciple and remained deeply under his influence for the rest of his life.

While in Edo, he slipped away from the domain residence and embarked on a tour of northeastern Honshu, visiting the domain of Mito and coming under the influence of the Mito scholars and patriots. But on his return to Edo, he was accused of traveling without proper permission and was ordered to return to Hagi, where he was deprived of his stipend and samurai status. He was soon forgiven by the lord of the domain, however, and was given permission to spend the following ten years traveling about to other areas to study. In 1853 he embarked once more on a series of travels that took him back to Edo. The same year, Perry appeared with his squadron of ships at Uraga and began pressing for the opening of the country. Shōin went to Uraga to observe the foreigners and, becoming more convinced than ever of the superiority of Western style armaments, determined to travel abroad. He hastened to Nagasaki at the news that a Russian official party had put into port there, only to find on his arrival that the Russians had already departed. He returned to Edo, and in 1854, when Perry appeared once more, he and a disciple named Kaneko Jūsuke went to Shimoda and attempted to stow away on one of the American warships, but they were apprehended and placed under arrest.

Shōin was sent back to Hagi, where he was placed in confinement. For the following five years until his death, he devoted his time to writing and teaching. He was released from prison in 1855, transferred to house confinement, and in time opened a small private school called the Shōka Sonjuku on the grounds of the house where he was confined. There he gave instruction to a large number of disciples, at the same time vigorously supporting the *sonnō-jōi* movement, which called for the expulsion of the foreigners and the restoration of power to the emperor. His students included such promising young men as Takasugi Shinsaku, Kusaka Genzui, Itō Hirobumi, and Yamagata Aritomo, who later played important roles in overthrowing the Tokugawa shogunate and carrying out the Meiji Restoration.

Fired by hatred for the shogunate and patriotic zeal, Shōin conceived the idea of assassinating the high shogunate official Manabe Akikatsu. Word of the plot leaked out, and the domain authorities, fearful of being implicated, placed him under arrest once more. Meanwhile, the shogunate learned of the affair, and Shōin was sent to Edo and imprisoned there. It was the time of the Great Persecution of the Ansei era, when the shogunate was taking the harshest measures against its adversaries. Shōin was executed in 1859 at the age of twenty-nine. In time two shrines were established to pay honor to his spirit, one in Hagi and the other in Setagaya Ward in Tokyo.

Yoshikawa Koretari 吉川惟足 (1616–1694)

Shinto leader of the early Edo period, he was born in Edo; he went by the literary names Sōzan Inshi and Shigodō. His father, a samurai, died when Koretari was very young; the boy was adopted by a merchant family of the Nihonbashi section of Edo. He showed no interest in business activities, however, and in 1651 moved to Kamakura, where he lived in retirement and devoted himself to reading and composing Japanese poetry. In 1653 he went to Kyoto and became a disciple of Hagiwara Kaneyori, an exponent of the branch of Shinto known as Yoshida Shinto. In 1656 he received the so-called *Himorogi iwasaka no den* from Hagiwara Kaneyori, thus being initiated into the inner secrets of the doctrine, and was recognized as the successor to the line of Yoshida Shinto. He later returned to Edo, where he set about working to rescue Shinto from the state of decline into which it had fallen.

He propounded the doctrines of Shinto principally among the higher officials of the shogunate and the daimyo. Among the latter, Tokugawa Yorinobu, lord of the domain of Kii, Hoshina Masayuki, lord of the domain of Aizu, and Tsugaru Nobumasa, lord of the domain of Hirosaki, were particularly ardent followers, and the latter two were initiated into the secrets of the sect. As a result of Koretari's efforts, Shinto came to be recognized as a way of life and thought worthy to be ranked beside Confucianism and Buddhism. In 1682 he was appointed *Shintōkata*, or official Shinto representative in the shogunate, a post that passed down to his descendants in succeeding generations.

In matters of doctrine he followed the traditional principles of Yoshida Shinto as laid down by Yoshida Kanetomo, which emphasized the primacy of Shinto over other teachings, and sought to systematize the traditions it handed down in secret. Though his intention was to reject the teachings of Buddhism and Confucianism, it is clear that he was strongly influenced by the latter, and his doctrines are noteworthy for the way in which they accord with the thinking of the feudal society of the time. Thus, while emphasizing the importance of the primal deity Kunitokotachi-no-mikoto, Koretari explains the creation of the world in terms of the Chinese theories of the yin and yang and the five elements and stresses the unity of gods and human beings. He also dwells upon the ethical relations of daily life, in particular the importance of the relationship between ruler and subject. His works include *Shindai no maki kaden kikigaki*, *Shindai no maki Koretari shō*, *Shintō daiichū*, *Shintō kōdan*, and others. Sources for his life include his autobiography, entitled *Yoshikawa Shigodō kotogaki*, and a biography compiled by his disciples entitled *Yoshikawa Shigodō gyōjōki*.

Yoshio Kōsaku 吉雄幸作 (1724–1800)

Surgeon and interpreter of Dutch of the middle Edo period; his personal name was Nagaaki, he also for a time went by the name Kōsakuemon, and in his old age by the professional name Kōgyū. His family had for generations been interpreters of Dutch in Nagasaki, and from the time of his grandfather Juzan they took an interest in medicine as well. In 1737 he became a *keiko tsūshi*, apprentice interpreter, and advanced in rank until in 1748 he was promoted to the position of *daitsūshi*, or senior interpreter. Thereafter he served nine times as *nemban daitsūshi*, or senior interpreter for the year, and until 1790 held the post of *tsūshi metsuke* (superintendent of interpreters).

While fulfilling his duties as an interpreter, he applied himself to the study of astronomy, geography, botany, and particularly medicine. He read a work on medicine by the German doctor Joseph Jacob Plenck in Dutch translation, which greatly advanced his knowledge and allowed him to become something of an expert in surgery. He also studied under the Swedish doctor Carl Peter Thunberg, who visited Japan during the Temmei era (1781–89), and assisted Thunberg in his studies of Japan. Among his students in what came to be known as the Yoshio school of surgery were his younger brother Yūjirō, Maeno Ryōtaku, and Sugita Gempaku, as well as a large number of others, his students being said to have numbered over six hundred. When Maeno, Sugita, and others produced and published the *Kaitai shinsho*, a translation of a Dutch work on dissection, he was invited to write the introduction. In his later years he was accused of making an error in the translation of a letter sent from the head of the Dutch trading office in Nagasaki to the shogunate, and was condemned to punishment, but was pardoned shortly after. He shaved his head and entered the Buddhist priesthood, taking the name Kōgyū, and was ordered to act as *Bangaku shinan*, instructor in Western learning. He died in the eighth month of 1800.

Yui Shōsetsu 由井正雪 (1605–1651)

Specialist in military science who headed an attempted revolt in the early Edo period. He was said to have been the son of a dyer who went by the shop name of Konya in Yui in the district of Ihara in the province of Suruga, though the facts are uncertain. In 1616, at the age of eleven, he studied under Takamatsu Hambei and first became acquainted with the life stories of such famous military leaders of the past as Minamoto no Yoshitsune, Kusunoki

Masashige, and Takeda Shingen. At the age of sixteen he went to Edo and for a time was employed in a shop called the Tsuruya there, but later took up the study of military science under Kusunoki Fuden. In 1630 he set off on a journey to the province of Kii and other areas of the country.

In 1633, at the age of twenty-eight, he succeeded his teacher Kusunoki Fuden as a lecturer on military science. His fame gradually spread, and he was invited to lecture on his speciality to Tokugawa Yorinobu, the lord of the fief of Kishū in Kii, and Ikeda Mitsumasa, the lord of the fief of Bizen. Meanwhile he gathered around him a large number of men of military bent and *rōnin* (masterless samurai). Shortly after the death of the third shogun, Tokugawa Iemitsu, in 1651, he and one of his followers named Marubashi Chūya began laying plans to seize control of the country. According to the plot, Marubashi was to attack and occupy Edo Castle, while Yui himself assaulted Kunōzan, a hill near Sumpu Castle in Suruga, gaining possession of the military funds of the Tokugawa family, and then was to proceed to an attack on Sumpu Castle itself. Before any action had been taken, the plot was discovered and the inn where he was staying in Suruga was surrounded. He and his fellow conspirator committed suicide.

In the early years of the Edo period, the shogunate, after establishing control over the country, had deprived a number of daimyo of their domains, thus creating a large class of *rōnin*, or masterless samurai. The attempted revolt by Yui Shōsetsu and his associates may be taken as a typical manifestation of the discontent that prevailed among this group in Japanese society at the time. The incident is often referred to as the Keian disturbance from the name of the era when it occurred.

Zeniya Gohei 錢屋五兵衛 (1773–1852)

Merchant and shipping agent of northern Japan in the late Edo period. He was born in the castle town of Kaga, the present-day city of Kanazawa in Ishikawa Prefecture, to a family that for some generations had made a living as money changers. His father attempted to expand into the shipping business but failed because of unfavorable conditions in the financial world. Gohei, however, who was a man of boldness and imagination, succeeded in taking advantage of the expanding opportunities for trade along the Japan Sea coast at the beginning of the nineteenth century, reviving his father's shipping enterprise and reaping large profits from the transport of goods to and from the Ezochi (Hokkaido) and Aizu (Fukushima) regions. In addition, around 1830 he made arrangements through an important official of the fief of Kaga named Okumura Hidezane for permission to act as a specially appointed trader for the fief and thereafter developed a very lively export trade in rice and other products of the Kaga domain. Something of the scale of this enterprise can be surmised by the fact that he opened branch offices in Edo, Osaka, and many other cities and maintained a fleet of twenty ships, each large enough to carry over a thousand *koku* of rice. In this way he enriched the domain of Kaga and built up a huge fortune for himself, becoming one of the most powerful merchants in the country. In his late years he formulated a plan to fill in Lake Kahokugata and convert it into farmland but was frustrated by the violent opposition of the fishermen in the area and, his patron Okumura having fallen victim to the schemes of a rival official, he died in prison at the age of seventy-nine.

ZUSHO HIROSATO 調所廣郷 (1776–1848)

Samurai of Satsuma in the late Edo period. He was born into the Kawasaki family of Satsuma in Kyushu but in 1778 became the adopted son of one Zusho Kiyonobu; he is often called Shōzaemon. In 1790 he was appointed *chabōzu* for the fief, a post that involved taking charge of the tea ceremony and other duties, and in 1798 he became *sadō*, director of the tea ceremony, for the lord of the fief, Shimazu Shigehide. He held a succession of posts after this until, in 1825, he became *sobayōnin* to Shimazu Narioki, his duties being to act as intermediary between the lord of the fief and the *karō* (chief retainer). In 1827 he was given an extraordinary promotion by Shigehide and Narioki and put in charge of the finances of the domain, which were in very bad condition, and he held other high offices, in 1833 reaching the rank of *karō*.

In 1835 he asked the wealthy merchants of Kyoto, Edo, Osaka, and the fief of Satsuma for a very sizeable loan, to be repaid without interest over a period of 250 years, and succeeded in getting it. In addition he raised large sums of money by setting up monopolies operated by the fief on sugar and other Satsuma products and by conducting clandestine trade with the Ryūkyū Islands, so that by 1840 he had solved the financial difficulties of the domain. He also made improvements in the military system of the fief, and in general laid the foundation for the important role that Satsuma was to play at the end of the Edo period in overthrowing the shogunate and instituting the Meiji Restoration.

MODERN PERIOD

Asanuma Inejirō

Ashida Hitoshi

Dan Takuma

Enomoto Takeaki

Fukuzawa Yukichi

Godai Tomoatsu

Gotō Shimpei

Gotō Shōjirō

Hamada Hikozō

Hara Takashi

Hamaguchi Osachi

Hatoyama Ichirō

Hiranuma Kiichirō

Honda Kōtarō

Hirota Kōki

Hoshi Tōru

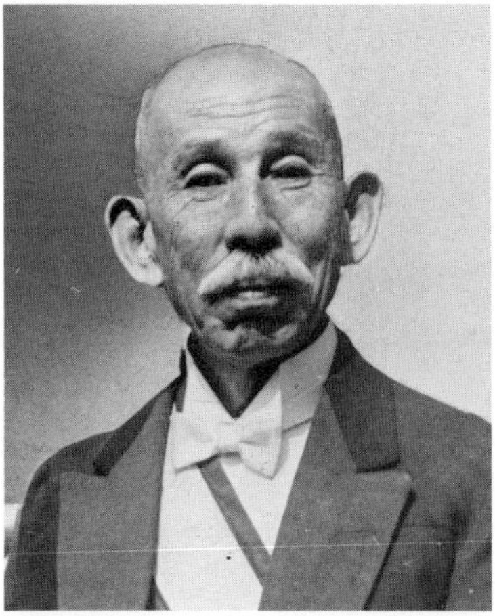
Hozumi Nobushige

Hozumi Yatsuka

Ikeda Shigeaki

Inoue Junnosuke

Inoue Kaoru

Inoue Kowashi

Inukai Tsuyoki

Ishibashi Tanzan

Ishii Kikujirō

Itō Hirobumi

Itagaki Taisuke

Iwakura Tomomi

Iwasaki Yatarō

Kanō Jigorō

Kagawa Toyohiko

Katayama Sen

Katayama Tetsu

Katō Hiroyuki

Katō Takaaki

Katō Tomosaburō

Katsu Kaishū

Kawakami Hajime

Katsura Tarō

Kido Takayoshi

Kishi Nobusuke

Kiyoura Keigo

Kita Ikki

Kojima Korekata

Kitazato Shibasaburō

Komura Jutarō

Konoe Fumimaro

Kōtoku Shūsui

Kurozumi Munetada

Maejima Hisoka

Makino Tomitarō

Makino Nobuaki

Matsukata Masayoshi

Meiji Tennō

Mori Arinori

Miyake Setsurei

Mutsu Munemitsu

Nakae Chōmin

Niijima Jō

Nakamura Masanao

Nishi Amane

Nishida Kitarō

Nogi Maresuke

Noguchi Hideyo

Nomura Kichisaburō

Okada Keisuke

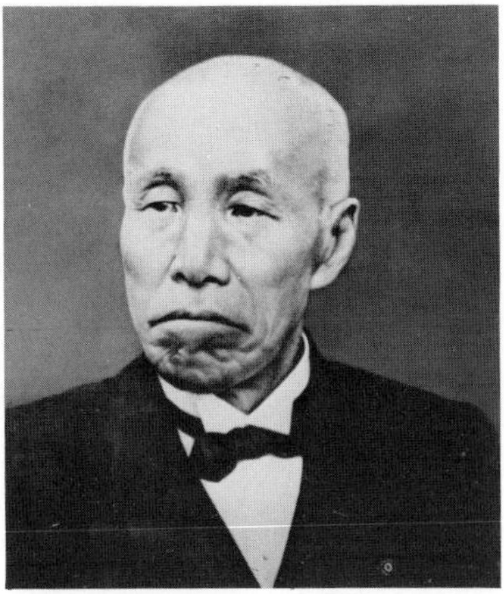

Ōkuma Shigenobu

Ozaki Yukio

Ōkubo Toshimichi

Saigō Takamori

Saionji Kimmochi

Sanjō Sanetomi

Saitō Makoto

Shibusawa Eiichi

Shidehara Kijūrō

Sugiura Shigetake

Soejima Taneomi

Suzuki Kantarō

Suzuki Mosaburō

Takamine Jōkichi

Suzuki Umetarō

Tanaka Giichi

Takahashi Korekiyo

Terajima Munenori

Tōjō Hideki

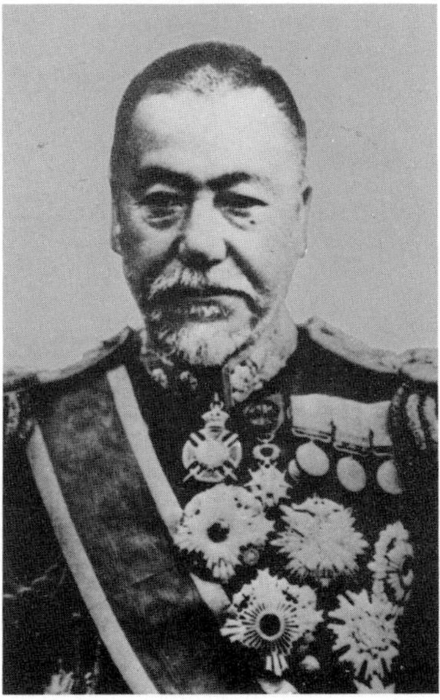

Tōgō Heihachirō

Tomonaga Shin'ichirō

Tsuda Umeko

Uemura Masahisa

Uchimura Kanzō

Ugaki Kazushige

Wakatsuki Reijirō

Yamagata Aritomo

Yamamoto Gombei

Yamamoto Isoroku

Yanagida Kunio

Yoshino Sakuzō

Yoshida Shigeru

Yukawa Hideki

Modern Period

Abe Isoo 安部磯雄 (1865–1949)

Christian socialist and leader of the socialist movement of the Meiji, Taishō, and Shōwa periods; he was born in Fukuoka Prefecture. He studied at Dōshisha, a Christian college in Kyoto, and was baptized by its founder and head, Niijima Jō. After graduation, he preached Christianity in Okayama. He went to America in 1891 to study theology and socialism, and on his return to Japan became a professor of Dōshisha and later of Waseda University in Tokyo. In 1898 he formed the Socialist Study Society. In 1900 he renamed it the Socialist Society and assumed the post of director. In 1901 he joined with Katayama Sen, Kōtoku Shūsui, and others to form the Shakai Minshutō, or Social Democratic Party. The group drafted statements calling for total disarmament for the sake of universal peace and the brotherhood of mankind, but were immediately outlawed and forced to disband. During the Russo-Japanese War, Abe voiced his opposition, declaring that the war was not in the economic interest of the Japanese people as a whole and calling upon Japan to become the "Switzerland of Asia." In 1905 he joined with Ishikawa Sanshirō in publishing a magazine called *Shinkigen*.

In 1910, after Kōtoku Shūsui and other socialists were arrested on suspicion of plotting to assassinate the emperor, he in effect separated himself from the movement advocating the practice of socialism. During the more liberal years of the Taishō period, however, he returned to the movement, and was looked upon as the leader of right-wing socialism in Japan. In 1924 he became head of the Fabian Society and in 1926 chairman of the Shakai Taishūtō, or Social Populace Party. In 1928, in the first election to be held under the universal manhood suffrage law, he was elected a member of the Diet. He was chosen chairman of the Social Mass Party. After the Pacific War, he acted as an advisor to the Japan Socialist Party. He is also famous as the founder of the baseball club of Waseda University, being referred to as "the father of Japanese student baseball." In addition, he was an ardent advocate of birth control.

ADACHI MINEICHIRŌ 安達峰一郎 (1869–1934)

Late Meiji, Taishō, and Shōwa era diplomat and doctor of laws; he was born in Yamagata Prefecture. In 1892 he graduated from the law course of Tokyo Imperial University and entered the Ministry of Foreign Affairs. In 1905 he accompanied the Japanese ambassador plenipotentiary Komura to the conference at Portsmouth, where the treaty concluding the Russo-Japanese War was drawn up and signed. He served as minister to Mexico from 1913 to 1916, as minister to Belgium in 1917, as ambassador to the same from 1921 to 1927, and as ambassador to France from 1927 to 1930. He also participated in the drawing up of the Kellogg-Briand Peace Pact of 1928. In addition, he served as Japan's representative to the League of Nations from the time of its founding in 1919, attending the first ten general meetings and in his eloquent French explaining Japan's position before the other delegates. In 1930 he was elected a judge to the Permanent Court of International Justice with the highest number of votes and was selected for the position of presiding judge. When he died of illness in Amsterdam in 1934, he was given a state funeral by the Dutch government in recognition of his lifelong efforts for the attainment of international peace. In addition to his activities on the diplomatic scene, he was renowned as an authority on international law. In 1921 he became an associate of the Institut de Droit International, and in 1925 a member of the Imperial Academy of Japan. He was also a member of the Belgian Academy and an honorary professor of the University of Louvain.

ANEZAKI MASAHARU 姉崎正治 (1873–1949)

Critic and scholar of religion; he was born in Kyoto. After attending the Third High School there, he entered the philosophy course of Tokyo Imperial University in 1893, where he studied under Inoue Tetsujirō and Raphael Koeber. He was a fellow student and close friend of Takayama Chogyū, who later became an important thinker and critic. He graduated in 1896. While in school, he took up the study of religion and contributed articles to such magazines as *Tetsugaku zasshi* and *Taiyō*. In 1897 he joined Ōnishi Hajime, Kishimoto Nobuta, and others in establishing a society called the Teiyūkai for the purpose of carrying out critical and nonsectarian studies of religion.

During the years from 1900 to 1903 he studied in Germany and England, pursuing religious studies under such scholars as P. Deussen, H. Oldenberg, and T. W. Rhys-Davids and concentrating on the subject of Indian philosophy. In 1904 he received his Ph.D.; his thesis on Buddhism is entitled *Genshinbutsu to hosshinbutsu.* In 1905, when a course in religion was set up at Tokyo Imperial University, he was appointed professor to teach it. Thereafter he gave his time to teaching and research, occasionally responding to invitations to lecture on the history of Japanese religion in European and American universities. In 1923 he became a member of the Japan Academy. The same year he was appointed to head the Tokyo Imperial University library, where he worked to repair the severe damage inflicted upon the library by the Kantō earthquake. He retired from teaching in 1934 and in 1939 became a member of the Upper House of the Diet.

Though his activities were varied, he is most important for having introduced Western methods of objective and critical study of religion to Japan. In addition to the work mentioned above, his writings include *Shūkyōgaku gairon* (1900) and others. His writings on Indian religion, particularly Buddhism, are of special importance. *Kompon bukkyō,* a study of the Buddhism of the time of Śākyamuni published in 1910, throws great light upon the thought of Buddhism in its earliest stage and established the term *kompon bukkyō* or "fundamental Buddhism" as a designation for early Buddhism as distinguished from Buddhism in its later stages of development. Under the influence of his friend Takayama Chogyū, he became a follower of Nichiren Buddhism and in 1916 published a work on Nichiren entitled *Hokekyō no gyōja Nichiren,* which continues to attract readers today. In his late years he took up the study of Christianity in Japan, in 1925 publishing a collection of articles on the subject entitled *Kirishitan shūmon no hakugai to sempuku.* In 1910–11 he published a translation of Schopenhauer's *Die Welt als Wille und Vorstellung* under the title *Ishi to genshiki to shite no sekai,* which initiated a vogue for Schopenhauer's thought.

Aoki Shūzō 青木周藏 (1844–1914)

Meiji period diplomat; he held the title of viscount. He was born in the fief of Chōshū and became the adopted son of a physician named Aoki Kenzō. In 1873, while studying in Germany, he became a first-class secretary in the Ministry of Foreign Affairs, serving in the Japanese legation in Germany.

During the period from 1874 to 1879 he served as minister to Germany, Austria, and Holland. After his return to Japan in 1879 he assisted Minister of Foreign Affairs Inoue Kaoru in the latter's attempts to bring about revision of Japan's treaties with foreign powers, but these efforts ended in failure. The period from 1880 to 1885 was spent in the posts of minister to Germany, Holland, and Norway. In 1889 he became acting minister of foreign affairs and an advisor to the Privy Council. He served as minister of foreign affairs in the Yamagata Aritomo cabinet and conducted negotiations with the British in efforts to carry out treaty revision. Because of the so-called Ōtsu Incident in 1891, in which a Japanese police officer attacked and wounded the Russian Crown Prince Nikolai, he was obliged to accept responsibility and resign his position, thus bringing to an end his negotiations on treaty revision. In 1892 he was appointed minister to Belgium and Germany. In 1894, while serving as minister to England, he succeeded in accomplishing the first step toward treaty revision with the signing of a commerce and navigation treaty between England and Japan. In 1900, while serving as minister of foreign affairs in the second Yamagata cabinet, he played a role in dispatching Japanese troops to China to assist in putting down the Boxer Rebellion. In 1906 he was appointed ambassador to the United States, but he was obliged to resign this post in 1908 because of difficulties over the question of Japanese immigration to America. Upon his return to Japan, he once more became an advisor to the Privy Council.

Arahata Kanson 荒畑寒村 (1887–)

Socialist leader of the Meiji, Taishō, and Shōwa periods; he was born in Yokohama; his personal name is Katsuzō, Kanson being a literary name. After completing higher elementary school, he entered the naval shipbuilding yard at Yokosuka as an apprentice worker. After reading an editorial in a newspaper called *Yorozu Chōhō*, he determined at the age of fifteen to join the socialist movement. He became a member of the Heiminsha, an organization formed by Sakai Toshihiko and others, traveling about and spreading the word of socialism while he made his living as a peddler. Along with the other members of the organization, he continued to speak out in opposition to the Russo-Japanese War. Around this time he became acquainted with Tanaka Shōzō, a leader in the fight against industrial pollution, and at the age of nineteen published a work entitled *Yanaka mura metsubō-shi*, which ranks as a classic in the literature on environmental pollution. In 1908 he was arrested along with Ōsugi Sakae and others for displaying an anarchist slogan at a gathering in the Kanda district of Tokyo and was imprisoned for a year and a half. As a result, he escaped being implicated in the lèse-majesté affair in 1910, when a number of socialists were arrested on suspicion of plotting to assassinate the emperor. In 1912 he joined Ōsugi in publishing a magazine called *Kindai shisō* to spread the ideas of *anarcho-syndicalisme.*

In 1922 he became secretary of the newly formed Communist Party of Japan, and the following year visited the Soviet Union. When the Communist Party was reconstituted in 1927, he did not become a member, however, but separated himself from the prevailing ideology of the party. He joined Sakai Toshihiko and Yamakawa Hitoshi in publishing a magazine called *Rōnō,* becoming a leading member of the so-called Rōnō, or Labor-Farmer, group, which regarded the socialist revolution as the most important objective at hand. He was imprisoned and released a total of seven times, but remained faithful to his convictions. After the conclusion of the war, he became a Socialist Party member of the Diet in 1946, but in 1948 he voiced solitary opposition to the budget of the Ashida cabinet and as a result withdrew from the Socialist Party. After his retirement from political affairs, he devoted all his attention to writing. In 1974 he received an Asahi Cultural Award. His most recent publication is *Heiminsha jidai.*

Araki Sadao 荒木貞夫 (1877–1966)

General of the army in the Taishō and Shōwa eras; he held the title of baron. He was born in Tokyo and graduated from the Military Academy and the Military Staff College. He served as a captain in the Russo-Japanese War in 1904. In 1907 he was attached to the Russia section of the General Staff and in 1909 was assigned to duty in Russia. In 1914 he became an instructor in the Military Staff College. During the First World War he was attached to the Russian Army and soon came to be known in military circles as an expert on Russian affairs. He served as a staff officer for the Japanese forces dispatched to Siberia in 1918, in 1923 advanced to the rank of major general, in 1924 became commander of the gendarmerie, and in 1927 became a lieutenant general.

After serving as head of the Military Staff College, divisional commander in Kumamoto, and head of the Department of Military Education, he was appointed War Minister in the Inukai Tsuyoki cabinet in 1931. During this time he began emphasizing the period of crisis that Japan faced, calling for spiritual rearmament and gathering about him a group of young officers dedicated to radical reform. The plans for a coup d'état, which came to light in October, 1931, before they could be put into effect, called for Araki to be made prime minister. Araki, along with General Masaki Jinzaburō, was a key figure in the Kōdō, or Imperial Way, faction in the Army, and even after the May 15 incident in 1932, when Prime Minister Inukai was assassinated, Araki remained on as war minister, working to support the members of his faction. When the young officers of the Imperial Way attacked and killed a number of government officials on February 26, 1936, Araki took a sympathetic view of their action and as a result was obliged to retire from active duty and enter the reserve. In 1938, he became minister of education in the first Konoe cabinet, working to promote militaristic education throughout the country. After the Pacific War he was tried by the International Military Tribunal for the Far East as a first-class war criminal and was sentenced to life imprisonment, but was released from prison in 1955 because of illness and later pardoned.

Arisugawa-no-miya Taruhito 有栖川宮熾仁 (1835–1895)

Member of the imperial family who played an active role in public affairs in the late Edo and Meiji periods, he was the eldest son of imperial prince Arisugawa-no-miya Takahito and was born in Kyoto. His mother was of the Saeki family. In his youth he went by the name Yoshi-no-miya. Though the tendency of the court at the time was to act in concord with the shogunate, the prince supported the *sonnō-jōi* movement, which sought to overthrow the shogunate and restore power to the emperor. After the Hamaguri Gate incident of 1864, when the Chōshū forces attempted to seize control of Kyoto, he was relieved of his office as *kokuji-goyōgakari* and placed under house confinement. In 1868, when the shogunate was abolished and power restored to the emperor, he was appointed president of the new government.

In the Boshin War, which broke out between the imperial forces and the forces remaining loyal to the shogunate, he was appointed governor-general of the eastern expedition. He led the imperial forces to Edo, where he took control of Edo Castle, and then proceeded to put down resistance in the Tōhoku region. In 1870 he was made minister of military affairs. Shortly after, when it came to light that the domain of Fukuoka was counterfeiting currency, the central government executed the officials of the domain who were responsible. When the domains were abolished in 1871, the lord of the domain became governor of Fukuoka. He was removed from this post by the central government, which fearing opposition from the people, appointed Prince Arisugawa to fill the position. In 1875 he became a member of the

Genrōin (Senate), and the following year became president of the Genrōin. When the internal uprising known as the Seinan War broke out in 1877, he was appointed commander of the expeditionary forces dispatched to put down the resistance, and in recognition of his accomplishments in doing so, was made a general of the army. In 1880 he became minister of the left. In 1882 he journeyed to Russia to represent Japan at the coronation of the czar, and thereafter toured Europe and America. In 1885 he became head of the General Staff Office, and in 1894, with the outbreak of the Sino-Japanese War, acted in his capacity as head of the General Staff Office to set up the imperial headquarters in Hiroshima, but died of illness before the formal conclusion of the war.

Arita Hachirō 有田八郎 (1884–1965)

Diplomat and political leader of the Shōwa period; he was born on the island of Sado in Niigata Prefecture. His elder brother was the financier and political leader Yamamoto Teijirō (1870–1937). After graduating from the law course of Tokyo Imperial University in 1909, he entered the Ministry of Foreign Affairs. He was assigned to various overseas posts and in 1927 became head of the Asian Bureau, ranking along with Shigemitsu Mamoru as one of the ministry's most influential experts in Asian affairs. He served as minister to Australia in 1931 and in 1932 became vice-minister of foreign affairs. In 1934 he was appointed ambassador to Belgium. In 1936 he became minister of foreign affairs in the Hirota cabinet, which was organized after the February 26 incident. The same year, he concluded the Japan-German Anti-Comintern Pact. Thereafter he served as minister of foreign affairs in the Konoe (first), Hiranuma, and Yonai cabinets, handling the country's diplomatic affairs at the time of the outbreak of hostilities between Japan and China. He opposed the strengthening of military ties with Germany and attempted to prevent the worsening of relations between Japan and America, but he was replaced as minister of foreign affairs in 1940 by Matsuoka Yōsuke, and thereafter the pro-Axis faction came to dominate the Ministry of Foreign Affairs. He became a member of the Upper House of the Diet in 1938. In 1953, after the Pacific War, he was elected to the Diet. He was a reform candidate for mayor of Tokyo in the elections of 1955 and 1959, but was defeated both times. In his late years, he sued the novelist Mishima Yukio for invasion of privacy because of resemblances between his own political career and that of a character in one of Mishima's novels, but the matter was settled out of court.

Asanuma Inejirō 淺沼稲次郎 (1898–1960)

Statesman and leader of the socialist movement in the Shōwa period. He was born in Miyakejima in Tokyo and in 1923 graduated from the political science department of Waseda University. While in college, he came under the influence of democratic thought and later of the theories of socialism and joined the socialist movement. After graduating, he joined the Japan Miners' Union, taking part in the strike against the Ashio Mines in Tochigi Prefecture. He also joined the Japan Farmers' Union and worked to support its labor disputes in various parts of the country. In 1925 he became chief secretary of the Nōmin Rōdōtō (Farmer Labor Party). After the party was disbanded, he became a member of the standing committee of the Zenkoku Rōnō Taishūtō (National Labor Farmer Popular Party). In 1926 he headed the organizing section of the Rōdō Nōmintō (Labor Farmer Party). In these and other ways, he participated in the struggle to establish proletarian political parties, though the difficulties faced by the movement at this time were very great.

In 1933 and thereafter he was twice elected to the Tokyo City Council, and he also served as city vice-chairman. In 1936 he was elected to the Lower House of the Diet, serving a total of nine terms as a member of that body. In 1945 he took part in the forming of the Japan Socialist Party, and from 1948 served as chief secretary for eleven years. When the Socialist Party split into two factions, he allied himself with the right-wing faction but did all he could to act as mediator between the two groups. In 1960, as a member of the central executive committee of the party, he played a key role in the movement to oppose the revision of the Security Treaty between Japan and the United States. The same year, when he was attending a public meeting of the heads of the three major political parties at Hibiya Hall, he was stabbed to death on the speaker's platform by a right-wing youth. In spite of his prominence, he continued in later life to live in a very simple apartment and was widely admired for his unassuming manner.

Ashida Hitoshi 蘆田均 (1887–1959)

Statesman of the Shōwa period, he held the degree of Doctor of Laws. Born in Kyoto, he graduated from the law course of Tokyo Imperial University in 1912 and entered the Foreign Ministry. He served in Russia, France, Turkey, and other countries, holding such posts as embassy secretary, foreign secretary, and embassy councilor. With the beginning of the

Manchurian Incident in 1931, however, he found himself in disagreement with the government policy in Manchuria and he accordingly resigned and left the service of the Foreign Ministry. In 1932 he was elected to the Lower House of the Diet, and thereafter continued to be reelected, holding office for a total of ten terms. During this period, he spoke out against the incursions of the military and Japan's expanding military front, allying himself with the Seiyūkai political party. He also held the position of president of *The Japan Times*, an English language newspaper.

In the postwar era, he served as minister of welfare in the Shidehara Kijūrō cabinet in 1945. He joined with Hatoyama Ichirō in helping to form the Minshutō (Democratic Party), and in 1947 became president of the party. He adopted a policy of alliance with the Socialist Party, and was appointed foreign minister in the Katayama Tetsu cabinet formed the same year. After the resignation of the Katayama cabinet in 1948, Ashida formed a cabinet of his own with himself as prime minister and foreign minister. Like the Katayama cabinet, it represented a coalition of three political groups, the Democratic Party, the Socialist Party, and the Kokumin Kyōdō (National Alliance). But it was subjected to frequent interference from the General Headquarters of the Occupation forces and was unable to function effectively. Meanwhile, a scandal involving the Shōwa Electric Company led to the arrest of Nishio Suehiro and other important cabinet ministers, and the cabinet resigned en masse. Ashida was also active in the formation of the Jiyū Minshutō (Liberal Democratic Party), but later became alienated from the mainstream of the party. He wrote several works on foreign affairs such as *Saikin sekai gaikōshi* and *Kakumei zenya no Roshia*, and in 1929 was awarded the degree of Doctor of Law for his *Kokusaihō oyobi kokusai seiji yori mitaru Kokkai narabi ni Kumpu kaikyō no chii*, a study of the Black Sea and the Bosporus and Dardanelles straits from the point of view of international law and politics.

BABA TATSUI 馬場辰猪 (1850–1888)

Statesman of the early Meiji period, he was born in Tosa in Shikoku, the son of a samurai of the domain. Shortly after the Meiji Restoration, he went to Tokyo and studied in the Keiō Gijuku, the forerunner of present-day Keiō University. During the years from 1870 to 1878 he studied abroad, principally in England, specializing in British and Roman law and also studying political science and sociology. While abroad, he formed an association of Japanese students studying in foreign countries. After his return to Japan, he continued his contacts with the group, joining with Ono Azusa and others to form a cultural organization called the Kyōson Dōshū, which devoted its time to research and the advancement of learning. In 1881 he participated in the founding of a political party known as the Jiyūtō (Liberal Party), and thereafter was active as a party member and a reporter for the party newspaper *Jiyū Shimbun*. Because of conflicts of opinion with Itagaki Taisuke, the head of the party, however, he later gave up his membership. He founded a school called the Meiji Gijuku and set up an office for legal consultation, but in 1885 was arrested on suspicion of violating the laws governing the possession of explosives. In time he was released and in 1886 went to the United States, where he traveled about giving lectures on Japanese culture. He died in Philadelphia in 1888.

Dan Takuma 團琢磨 (1858–1932)

Business leader of the Meiji, Taishō, and Shōwa periods; he held the degree of Doctor of Engineering and the title of baron. He was the son of a samurai of the domain of Chikuzen in northern Kyushu; his name was originally Kamiya Komakichi, but he was later adopted into the Dan family of the same domain. In 1871 he and Kaneko Kentarō, another native of Chikuzen whose younger sister later became Dan's wife, joined the Iwakura mission to Europe and America. He enrolled in the Massachusetts Institute of Technology, where he specialized in mining. After graduating, he returned to Japan in 1878 and taught English at a school in Osaka, and in 1881 became an assistant professor of Tokyo University. In order to make use of his knowledge of mining, he transferred to the mining division of the Ministry of Public Works in 1884 and was assigned as an engineer to the Miike Mines in Kyushu.

In 1887–88 he was sent to England to conduct a survey of mining technology, and during his absence the government sold the Miike Mines to the Mitsui family. Upon his return to Japan, he therefore entered the employ of the Mitsui family. It is said that Dan's reputation as an engineer was one of the reasons the Mitsui were willing to offer an unusually large price for the purchase of the mines. As manager of the Miike Mines, Dan faced the problem of underground flooding, but he solved it by using English-made Davy pumps, which removed the water and allowed for a large increase in productivity. In 1894 he became chairman of the board of directors of the Mitsui Mining Company. In 1914 he was appointed chief director of the Mitsui Partnership Company. He abandoned the commercialistic policies of Masuda Takashi, the previous director of the Mitsui interests, and ventured into the field of heavy industry, becoming the most important leader in the Mitsui *zaibatsu* and a key figure in the financial world.

In 1921–22 he headed a group of Japanese business leaders on an inspection tour of Europe and America. He also served as the first director of the Nihon Kōgyō Kurabu, the Industry Club of Japan, an employers' organization formed in 1917 to offset the unionizing efforts of the left-wing organizers. In 1922 he became president of the newly established Japan Economic League, assuming a role of leadership in financial affairs. In 1929, when the Hamaguchi cabinet drafted a proposal for a law permitting the formation of labor unions, Dan became leader of the various capitalist groups organized to combat the measure. Although the proposal passed the Lower House of the Diet, he succeeded in having it killed in the Upper House. In 1932 he was shot to death at the entrance to the Mitsui main office by Hishinuma Gorō, a member of the right-wing organization Ketsumeidan. His death was a great blow to the Mitsui *zaibatsu* and brought about a change in its management policies under the leadership of Ikeda Shigeaki. The composer and member of the Japan Art Academy Dan Ikuma is his grandson.

Deguchi Onisaburō 出口王仁三郎 (1871–1948)

Religious leader of the Taishō and Shōwa periods and co-founder, along with Deguchi Nao (1836–1918), of the religion called Ōmoto-kyō. He was the son of a poor farm family of Sogabe in Kyoto Prefecture; his name was originally Ueda Kisaburō. He ceased formal education in the midst of primary school and thereafter worked at various occupations. In 1898 he had his first mystical experience and the same year met Deguchi Nao. A carpenter's widow who lived in great poverty, she experienced divine possession in 1892 and thereafter attracted a group of believers about her, centered in the Ayabe area of Kyoto Prefecture. In 1900, Onisaburō married her fifth daughter, Sumi, and took the family name Deguchi; in 1904 he adopted the personal name Onisaburō. He thereafter worked with his mother-in-law Nao to spread their religious teachings, which became known as Ōmoto-kyō. They soon won a wide following.

In 1921 Onisaburō was accused of lèse-majesté and subjected to government suppression. He later joined forces with right-wing leaders and went to Manchuria, where he set up an organization called Kurenai Manjikai, founded the Sekai Shūkyō Rengōkai (Federation of World Religions) in 1925, and participated in the Esperanto movement. In 1935 he was once more arrested on charges of lèse-majesté, and the buildings that housed the headquarters of his religious organization were completely destroyed. After being released on bail in 1942, he lived quietly in retirement, hoping for an opportunity to revive his religious organization. He was crippled by a stroke before he could realize his hopes, though the Ōmoto-kyō has undergone a marked revival in the postwar period. Onisaburō's voluminous writing, the *Reikai monogatari* runs to a total of eighty-one volumes. In addition, he displayed unusual talent as a poet, calligrapher, painter, and potter. Taniguchi Masaharu, the founder of the religion known as Seichō no Ie, and Okada Mokichi, founder of Sekai Meshiya-kyō, were both originally followers of Ōmoto-kyō.

Ebina Danjō 海老名彈正 (1856–1937)

Pastor of the Congregational Church in Japan and a Christian leader of Meiji, Taishō, and Shōwa times; he was born in the province of Chikugo, present-day Fukuoka Prefecture in Kyushu, the son of a samurai of the domain of Yanagawa. He attended the official school of the domain, studying Chinese, but in 1872 entered the Kumamoto Western School. There he came under the influence of a foreign instructor named L. L. Janes and was converted to Christianity, joining with Kozaki Hiromichi, Yokoi Tokio, Kanamori Tsūrin, and others in the group of thirty-five converts known as the Kumamoto Band. In 1876, upon completing the course of the Kumamoto Western School, he enrolled in Dōshisha, a Christian school recently founded in Kyoto by Niijima Jō. In 1879 he graduated from Dōshisha and became pastor of the Annaka Church in Gumma Prefecture, also traveling about to different areas of Japan to spread the message of Christianity.

In 1887 he founded the Kumamoto English School and Kumamoto Girls School, and in 1890 set up the Japan Missionary Society in Kyoto. In 1897 he became pastor of the Hongō Church in Tokyo, a position that he held for the following twenty-four years. For eight years beginning in 1920, he served as president of Dōshisha College. His Christianity included within it elements suggestive of the code of the Japanese warrior and of nationalistic thinking, which led him to be attacked by representatives of orthodoxy such as Uemura Masahisa. In 1900 he founded a magazine called *Shinjin*, which dealt with philosophical, cultural, and political issues from a Christian point of view and exercised an important influence upon the cultural and social movements of the time.

Enomoto Takeaki 榎本武揚 (1836–1908)

Naval leader in the service of the shogunate and statesman of the Meiji period; he held the title of viscount. His common name was Kamajirō, and his literary name Ryōsen. He was born in Edo, the second son of an official in the service of the shogunate. In 1856 he became a naval trainee under the sponsorship of the shogunate in Edo and in Nagasaki received instruction from Dutch naval officials. He specialized in mechanics and also studied chemistry under a medical official named Pompe van Meerdervoort. In 1858 he returned to Edo and was appointed a teacher in the naval training school there. When the shogunate placed an order for the construction of a warship with the Dutch, Enomoto was sent to Holland to supervise the construction and continue his studies. He left for Holland in 1862, reaching there the following year. He witnessed the hostilities then taking place between Denmark and Prussia and in Holland studied ship construction and operation, gunnery, and international maritime law. When the ship, named the *Kaiyō Maru*, was completed, he sailed it to Japan, reaching home in 1867.

In 1868 he was appointed vice-chief of the Navy, but although the shogunate collapsed and Edo Castle was opened to the imperial forces, Enomoto refused to hand over the warships. Instead, in the *Kaiyō Maru* and with six other shogunate warships following, he slipped away from the moorings off Shinagawa in Edo Bay and made his way north, passing through Sendai Bay, until he reached Ezochi, as Hokkaido was known at the time. There he went ashore and took up a position in the Goryōkaku, a fortress in the city of Hakodate, where he proclaimed the formation of his own government and resisted the government forces. He was eventually persuaded to surrender the following year by Kuroda Kiyotaka, a staff officer of the government forces. Through Kuroda's efforts, he was spared the death penalty and instead was imprisoned in Tokyo and pardoned in 1872.

Following his release, he was employed by the Agency for the Colonization of Hokkaido, headed by Kuroda, and was put in charge of mining surveys in the area. He, however, disagreed with the American advisor named Capron over the proper way to develop Hokkaido. In 1874 he was given the rank of vice admiral in the navy and was sent to Russia as envoy extraordinary and minister plenipotentiary. In 1875 he signed the agreement that gave Russia the island of Karafuto (Sakhalin) in exchange for the Kurile (Chishima) Islands. In 1879 he became chief assistant to the foreign minister, and in 1880–81 served as navy minister. In 1882 he was made envoy extraordinary and minister plenipotentiary stationed in China and assisted the ambassador plenipotentiary Itō Hirobumi in concluding the Tientsin Treaty of 1885 between China and Japan.

The same year, when the first cabinet was formed under Itō Hirobumi, Enomoto was made minister of communications, being the only former shogunate official to be represented in the cabinet. He remained in the same position in the Kuroda cabinet that followed, but in 1889, when Minister of Education Mori Arinori was assassinated, Enomoto was shifted to that position. In 1890 he became an advisor to the Privy Council. In 1891, when Foreign Minister Aoki Shūzō resigned because of the attack on the Russian Crown Prince Nikolai (Ōtsu Incident), Enomoto replaced him as foreign minister in the Matsukata cabinet. In 1894 he became minister of agriculture and commerce in the second Itō Hirobumi cabinet, but he later resigned when he accepted responsibility for the poisonings caused by pollution from the Ashio Copper Mine. In addition to his official duties, he also acted as head of various organizations. Thus he was vice-president and later president of the Tokyo Geographical Society, which he proposed and founded in 1874. In 1892 he organized a Resettlement Society, which had plans for helping Japanese to emigrate to Mexico, devoting his own time to its direction, but the society's plans ended in failure in 1898.

Etō Shimpei 江藤新平 (1834–1874)

Statesman of the early Meiji period and leader of the Saga Rebellion. He was born in the village of Yae in the province of Hizen, the son of a lesser samurai of the domain of Saga. His personal name was Taneo, and his *gō* Nampaku. He studied under Edayoshi Shin'yō, a scholar of the Saga domain and elder brother of the statesman Soejima Taneomi, and in 1859 became an official in the service of the domain. In 1862 he left Saga without receiving official permission and went to Kyoto, where he associated himself with the courtiers and joined the movement to restore power to the emperor and expel the foreigners. Later he was sentenced by the Saga authorities to be held in room confinement for an indefinite period. With the restoration of power of the emperor in 1868, he was pardoned and became a military official in the headquarters of the imperial army assigned to march on Edo. After the army reached Edo and took over control of Edo Castle, Etō played an important part in civil administration and also recommended that the capital be moved from Kyoto to Edo. In 1869 he returned to Saga and devoted himself to carrying out reforms in the administration of the domain, but the same year he was ordered to return to the service of the central government, being assigned to an office in charge of institutional affairs. In company with Mori Arinori and Kanda Takahira, he helped to plan and set up deliberative organs and a legal system for the new government.

In 1871, after the old feudal domains were abolished and prefectures set up in their place, Etō served as vice-minister of education and vice president of the Sain, a legislative body. In 1872 he became minister of justice and, in connection with the establishment of a police system, was ordered to make a tour of Europe, but the plan never materialized, Kawaji Toshiyoshi being dispatched instead to inspect the police systems of various countries. While serving as minister of justice, Etō worked to reform the judicial system, endeavoring to separate the courts from the administrative offices of the government and to establish the independence of the judicature. He enacted a new criminal code known as the *Kaitei ritsurei,* edited a translation of the French legal code entitled *Mimpō sōan,* and in other ways labored to bring about constitutional government in Japan.

In 1873 he became a councilor of state and expressed sympathy with Saigō Takamori's call for an expedition against Korea, but the plans for such an expedition were thwarted by opposition from Iwakura Tomomi and Ōkubo Toshimichi, who had just returned from their inspection tour of Europe, and Etō resigned his position as councilor. In 1874 he joined Itagaki Taisuke and others in petitioning the government for creation of an elected legislature. Around the same time, responding to invitations from those who favored an attack on Korea, he returned to Saga, where he became the leader of the disaffected samurai groups who opposed the policies of the government. In the same year, he joined with Shima Yoshitake and others in raising an armed rebellion in Saga, but it was quickly suppressed by government troops. Etō went into hiding, but was arrested in Kōchi Prefecture. He was sent back to Saga, tried on the spot, and executed. In the general amnesty that accompanied the promulgation of the Meiji Constitution in 1889, he was posthumously cleared of the charges against him.

Fujii Nittatsu 藤井日達 (1885–)

Shōwa period Buddhist priest, leader of the postwar peace movement, and founder of the type of Buddhism known as Nihonzan Myōhō-ji. He was born in Kumamoto Prefecture and entered the priesthood in 1903. The following year he graduated from Nichiren Daigaku (present-day Risshō University). In 1917 he carried out a fast and prayer service in front of the Imperial Palace, calling for a realization of Nichiren's ideal of *Risshō ankoku,* national government based upon the true teachings of the Lotus Sutra. The following year he went to Manchuria, where he traveled from place to place beating on the kind of hand drum called *uchiwadaiko*, preaching Buddhism, and establishing temples known as Nihonzan Myōhō-ji. He later carried on similar activities in Japan, China, India, and Burma. In India he became friendly with Gandhi. In marked departure from the spirit of Gandhi's teachings, however, he cooperated willingly with the militaristic elements in Japan and the advocates of Japanese expansion abroad. With the defeat of Japan in 1945, he decided that his past actions had been in error, and became an exponent of nonresistance and unarmed pacifism. He was active in the movement to ban the atomic and hydrogen bombs and in demonstrations against the United States military base at Sunagawa. Though he does not have a numerous following in Japan, his group represents the largest Buddhist sect in India.

FUKUDA (KAGEYAMA) HIDEKO 福田(景山)英子 (1865–1927)

Meiji period pioneer in the women's liberation movement, she was the daughter of a lower ranking samurai of the domain of Bizen in present-day Okayama Prefecture; her family name was Kageyama. In 1882 in Okayama she attended a speech by the feminist leader Kishida Toshiko (Nakajima Shōen) and thereupon determined to take part in the women's movement. In 1883 she and her mother opened a school for women, but it was closed the following year on the grounds that it violated the regulations concerning public meetings. She went to Tokyo, where she devoted herself to the popular rights movement, but she became implicated in the Osaka Incident, a scheme by left-wing elements in the Liberal Party to aid the cause of political reform in Korea, and was arrested in Nagasaki. After her release from prison in 1889, she joined Ōi Kentarō, another participant in the Osaka Incident, in a lecture tour through the Kansai region, and for a time became his common-law wife. She later separated from him and in 1892 married Fukuda Tomosaku, who died in 1900.

As a step toward the economic independence of women, she established a technical school for women. She was a close friend of Ishikawa Sanshirō and frequently participated in the Heiminsha, the socialist organization to which he belonged, gradually becoming a supporter of socialism herself. In 1904 she published her autobiography entitled *Warawa no hanshōgai*. In 1907 she established a women's magazine called *Sekai Fujin*, in which she reported on the progress of the feminist movement in foreign countries and worked to further the movement in Japan. She also published articles by Abe Isoo and other socialist leaders. To help support herself and her activities, she traveled about selling material for Japanese style clothing, but in 1909 the magazine she had established was banned. She worked vigorously to promote and protect the political freedom of women and at the same time played an important role in the movement to better the position of the workers and farmers.

Fukuoka Takachika 福岡孝弟 (1835–1919)

Meiji period statesman; he held the title of viscount; his common name was Tōji. Born in the domain of Tosa in Shikoku, he served as a *kōri-bugyō* (district magistrate), and in 1867 became a member of the central administration of the domain. In 1867 he was ordered by the lord of Tosa to go to Kyoto in company with Gotō Shōjirō, another samurai of Tosa, where they persuaded Shogun Tokugawa Yoshinobu to return the power of government to the imperial court. In contrast to the men of the domains of Satsuma and Chōshū, who were working to overthrow the shogunate by force, Fukuoka and the others of his group from Tosa supported the *kōbu-gattai* policy of harmonious relations between the shogunate and the court and aimed at a government made up of a coalition of the powerful clans.

Fukuoka served as a councilor in the newly formed Meiji government and took part in the drafting of the five-article Charter Oath, which laid down its principles. To the original draft prepared by Mitsuoka Hachirō (better known as Yuri Kimimasa), he added the sentence: "A council of the feudal lords shall be set up, and all matters settled by open discussion." In addition, he did his best to bring about the publication of a written definition of the polity, served as a member of a group set up to study forms of parliamentary government, and in other ways helped to lay the foundation for parliamentary government. In 1870 he became junior councilor in Kōchi (Tosa), and thereafter, as acting senior councilor, he joined with the senior councilor Itagaki Taisuke in carrying out the reforms in the domain of Kōchi. In 1872 he became chief assistant to the minister of education and to the minister of justice; in 1875 he became a member of the Genrōin, and in 1881 a councilor of state and minister of education. In 1882, at the instigation of Itō Hirobumi, he persuaded Itagaki, the head of the Jiyūtō (Liberal Party), to withdraw from the popular rights movement and arranged for him to make a trip abroad. In 1883 Fukuoka became head of the Sanjiin, a legal organ of the government, and in 1891 an advisor to the Privy Council.

Fukuzawa Yukichi 福澤諭吉 (1835–1901)

Thinker, educator, and popularizer of Western culture in the late Edo and Meiji eras. He was born in Osaka, the son of a samurai of the domain of Nakatsu in Kyushu. His father was a man of talent and learning, but because of his relatively low social position, was unable to employ his talents to the full or to escape from poverty and hardship. This fact deeply influenced the young Yukichi and inspired in him a strong distaste for the emphasis upon birth and family background that characterized traditional Japanese society. In 1854, at the urging of his elder brother, he went to Nagasaki to pursue the study of Dutch and Dutch learning. He left Nagasaki the following year and went to Osaka where he entered a school for Dutch studies headed by Ogata Kōan, a Western style physician. In 1857 he became head student of the school, and the following year, on orders from his domain, he opened a school for Dutch studies in Teppōzu in the Tsukiji section of Edo, which in time grew to be Keiō University. Though devoting all his attention to Dutch studies, he discovered through actual contacts with Westerners that the Dutch language was not widely known or understood. In 1858 he accordingly turned his attention to English, which he studied on his own.

In 1860 he went to America in the ship *Kanrin Maru* as an attendant to Kimura Settsu-no-kami, official in charge of warships and head of the embassy sent by the shogunate to ratify the trade treaty between Japan and the United States. After his return to Japan, he was made an official in charge of translations pertaining to foreign affairs. In 1861 he was once again sent abroad as a member of an official mission of the shogunate, visiting France, England, Germany, Russia, and other countries. The journey gave him a first-hand knowledge of the civilization of the more advanced countries of the West and allowed him to observe their cultural and political systems. On the basis of the knowledge he acquired, he published in 1866 a work entitled *Seiyō jijō* ("Conditions in Western Lands"). The work appeared just at a time when many people in Japan were beginning to turn away from the violent antiforeign sentiment of earlier years and to become more receptive to Western ways and ideas, and it did much to encourage this trend. In 1864 he advanced to a higher post in the service of the shogunate and in 1867 was once more sent to America. At this time he purchased a number of Western books, and after his return to Japan devoted himself to the study of a variety of fields of learning. In 1868 he moved his school to Shinsenza in the Shiba area and renamed it the Keiō Gijuku.

After the termination of the shogunate and the founding of the Meiji government, he voluntarily took the status of a commoner and devoted his energies to the spread of Western ideas and civilization through education and the mass media. In 1869 he began a publishing venture under his own direction. In 1870 he prepared a survey of the police systems of Western countries at the request of the Tokyo prefectural government and in this connection the following year moved his school to the Mita area of Tokyo, where it remains today. In 1873 he joined with Katō Hiroyuki, Tsuda Mamichi, Nakamura Masanao, Nishi Amane, and other intellectuals in forming a society for the encouragement of Western studies known as the Meirokusha, which published a journal called *Meiroku Zasshi.* He also published various works of his own such as *Gakumon no susume* or *Bummeiron no gairyaku* in which, under the influence of British style utilitarianism, he emphasized the importance of independence, pride in self, and the promotion of measures that are of practical benefit to society. At this time the craze for Western learning and culture may be said to have reached its peak in Japan.

From 1875 on, however, when the popular rights movement came to the fore, Fukuzawa Yukichi emphasized the importance of a compromise between popular rights and the rights of the government, a position that in effect made him a critic of the popular rights movement. After the government shakeup of 1881, he advocated the enhancement of national prestige and harmonious cooperation between government officials and citizens and supported the government's policy of expansion on the Asian mainland. In the last position he is said to have been influenced by his support of Kim Ok-kyun, a reformer and one of the founders of the Korean Independence Party, who was a member of the pro-Japanese faction in Korea. Yukichi's thinking at this time is well illustrated in the *Jiji Shimpō,* a newspaper that he founded in 1882.

Godai Tomoatsu 五代友厚 (1835–1885)

Patriot and business leader of late Edo and Meiji times; he was born in the domain of Satsuma in Kyushu. It is said that at the age of thirteen he made a globe of the world that was entirely of his own design. In 1854 he became an official in the domain administration and in 1857 went to Nagasaki, where he studied navigation, gunnery, mathematics, and surveying under a Dutch officer. In 1859, on orders from his domain, he stowed away on a vessel used by the shogunate for foreign missions called the *Chitose Maru,* in this way making his way to Shanghai. There he purchased a German steamship and, naming it the *Ten'yū Maru,* acted as its captain. From around this period, having gained a knowledge of the world situation, he advocated the opening of Japan to foreign trade and communication. He also began to take a deep interest in trade himself.

In 1863, when a British naval squadron attacked Kagoshima in Satsuma, Godai's ship was seized, and he and Terajima Munenori were taken prisoner by the British. He later managed to escape at Yokohama, but for a time the men of his domain believed that he had deserted to the enemy and he was forced to make his way in secret to Edo and Nagasaki. In 1865, on orders from his domain, he joined a group of fourteen students who were being sent to Europe, studying in England and later traveling about France, Holland, and Germany to observe the state of industrial development in these countries. What he saw at this time influenced him profoundly. After returning to his domain in 1866, he urged the establishment of basic industries in the domain and also set up a spinning mill, the first in Japan, in fulfillment of a contract he had made while in Europe with a Frenchman named Montblanc. In these and other ways, he helped to promote the industrialization of Satsuma.

In 1868 he became a *san'yo* (junior councilor) and an official in charge of foreign affairs in the newly formed Meiji government. He later held various other posts in connection with foreign affairs and the regulation of trade, particularly in Osaka Prefecture, and also played an important part in matters pertaining to the Osaka Mint and Customshouse. In 1869 he was transferred to a post as an accounting official in Yokohama, but he resigned two months later and entered the world of business. He soon demonstrated great talent in business affairs, in the same year setting up the Gold and Silver Assay Office in Osaka. In 1876 he established a salt manufacturing plant and also went into mining activities. In 1878 he established the Osaka Stock Exchange and Commercial Meeting Hall and later the Osaka Commercial Training School, in these and other ways contributing to the expansion and modernization of business activities in Osaka. But, as the scandal concerning the sale of government property in 1881 revealed, he maintained close contacts with the men of his own domain who were in power in the government and used these connections to his advantage in his business dealings.

Gotō Shimpei 後藤新平 (1857–1929)

Statesman of the Meiji, Taishō, and early Shōwa periods; he held the title of count. He was born in what later became Iwate Prefecture and, determining in his youth to become a doctor, attended the official school of his domain. Later he attended the Sukagawa Medical School in Fukushima Prefecture. In 1881, after graduating, he became director of the Aichi Hospital and head of the Aichi Medical School. In 1882, when Itagaki Taisuke, the president of the Liberal Party, was attacked and wounded during a speaking appearance in Gifu, Gotō took charge of the treatment of his injuries. The same year, Gotō entered government service in the Health Bureau attached to the Home Ministry. After a period of study in Germany, he became director of the Health Bureau in 1892. Because of his involvement in the dispute over inheritance in the family of Viscount Sōma, however, he was sentenced to half a year in prison.

When the Sino-Japanese War broke out in 1894, he strongly urged the establishment of a quarantine system patterned on that of Europe and America in order to protect the health of the Japanese forces. His advice was heeded, and as head of the first army military office to be established in Japan, he worked for the duration of the war to spread an understanding of quarantine methods throughout the country. In 1898 he went to Taiwan, which had become a Japanese possession as a result of the war, where he assisted Governor-General Kodama Gentarō as civil administrator. The unusual skill and success that he displayed in the post revealed that he had a natural talent for the administration of colonial affairs. He was particularly successful in dealing with opposition from the local population and handling matters pertaining to monopoly enterprise and railroad development.

He later became a member of the Upper House of the Diet. In 1906, in recognition of his activities in Taiwan, he was made president of the South Manchuria Railway Company. During the period from 1908 to 1911, he served as minister of communications in the second and third Katsura Tarō cabinets and at the same time served as president of the Railway Bureau and vice-president of the Colonization Bureau, playing a very active part in Japanese affairs in Manchuria. In 1916 he became home minister in the Terauchi Masakata cabinet and a member of the interim foreign policy investigation commission. In 1918 he became foreign minister, advocating Japanese economic expansion in China, dispatch of troops to Siberia, and other measures indicative of a vigorous foreign policy. In 1920 he became mayor of Tokyo, and in 1923 home minister in the second Yamamoto Gombei cabinet. He also headed the agency that was established to plan and oversee the rebuilding of Tokyo after the disastrous Kantō Earthquake, at this time gaining something of a reputation as a tall talker. In the same year, 1923, he held private talks with the USSR representative Ioffe with a view to bringing about a restoration of Japanese-Russian relations. These talks laid the foundation for the Japan-Soviet treaty, which was in time concluded. After retiring from his official positions, Gotō devoted himself to broadcasting enterprises, the leadership of youth groups, and the movement to improve the ethical conduct of government.

Gotō Shōjirō 後藤象二郎 (1838–1897)

Late Edo and Meiji period statesman; he held the title of count. He was born in the domain of Tosa in Shikoku and was a close friend of Itagaki Taisuke, another important Meiji period statesman from Tosa. He studied the civil and military arts under his relative Yoshida Tōyō and also Ōishi Susumu, a samurai of the fief of Yanagawa. In 1863 he went to Edo and studied navigation in the Kaiseijo, a school for Western studies set up by the shogunate, and also received instruction in English from Ōtori Keisuke. He returned to his domain in 1864 and became an inspector general, founding the business establishment known as the Kaiseikan and in other ways playing an important role in strengthening the economic and military situation of the domain. In 1865 he traveled to Satsuma, Nagasaki, and Shanghai, looking for ways to develop overseas trade, and he also questioned Sir Ernest Mason Satow, a British official interpreter stationed in Japan, in order to find out all he could about the British parliamentary system. He was strongly influenced by Sakamoto Ryōma, another native of Tosa, who at this time was engaged in trade and shipping and who favored restoration of power to the emperor.

In 1867, Gotō persuaded Yamanouchi Yōdō, the lord of the domain of Tosa, to request that the shogunate restore power to the emperor. Accordingly, Gotō, Teramura Sazen, Fukuoka Tōji (Takachika), acting as spokesmen for Yamanouchi, called on the shogun Tokugawa Yoshinobu in Kyoto and requested that he resign so that imperial rule could be reestablished. At the same time, in reply to those domains that called for violent overthrow of the shogunate, he supported his lord Yamanouchi in urging the establishment of a council of the more important daimyo. In 1868 he became a *san'yo* (junior councilor) in the newly formed Meiji government and was also put in charge of foreign affairs, helping to make plans for the emperor to receive the foreign envoys in audience as a symbol of the new regime. At this time he succeeded in rescuing the British minister Sir Harry Smith-Parkes from an assassination attempt, an act for which he was awarded an honorary sword by Queen Victoria. The same year he was made an official in the Foreign Affairs Bureau, and also played an important role in government affairs as a military overseer and advisor to the General Affairs Bureau.

After the reorganization of the governmental system, he held the posts of junior councilor and governor of Osaka Prefecture. In 1871 he became chief assistant in the Ministry of Works and participated in the abolition of the feudal domains and the establishment of the prefectural system. In 1873 he became a councilor of state and director general of the legislative body known as the Sain, but found himself in opposition to Ōkubo Toshimichi on the Korean question and, like others who favored an expedition against Korea, withdrew from the political scene. From this time on, he took an interest in the movement toward party government and in 1874 he joined with Itagaki and others in forming the Aikoku Kōtō and petitioning the government for the creation of an elected legislature. He continued to oppose the policies of the Ōkubo government, but returned to official service as a result of the conciliatory meeting held in Osaka in 1875. He held the position of head of the Genrōin, but retired from political life once more. For a time he managed the Takashima coal mines in Kyushu but failed in the enterprise. In 1881 he joined Itagaki and others in forming the Jiyūtō (Liberal Party). Once more, however, he gave in to the conciliatory policies of the government and persuaded Itagaki to accompany him on a trip to Europe. In Austria they attended lectures by Lorenz von Stein, one of the leading theoreticians of the people's rights movement. Gotō, after his return to Japan, attempted to lend assistance to Kim Ok-kyun, the leader of the Korean Independence Party, but his efforts ended in failure.

In 1887, when opposition to the government increased because of its failure to carry out treaty revision, Gotō played a central role in the movement to bring about a fusion of the opposition parties. But he allowed himself to be bought off by the government, assumed a cabinet post, and thereafter worked to frustrate the movement he had formerly led. Thus, during the years from 1889 to 1893 he served as minister of communications, and after 1893 as minister of agriculture and commerce. While continuing to proclaim himself a member of the people's rights movement, he in fact worked in collusion with the government leaders and on more than one occasion actually betrayed the real members of the people's rights movement.

Hamada Hikozō 濱田彥藏 (1837–1897)

Late Edo and Meiji period import-export merchant and the founder of the first Japanese newspaper; he was the son of a farmer of the province of Harima; his youthful name was Hikotarō, and he also went by the name

Joseph Heco. In 1850 he set out by ship for Edo but was shipwrecked in a typhoon. He was rescued by an American trading ship and taken to San Francisco, where he was educated and baptized a Catholic. In 1858 he acquired US citizenship, becoming the first Japanese American; he went by the name Joseph Heco. In 1860 he accompanied Dorr, the newly appointed US consul in Kanagawa, to Japan, serving as his interpreter, and was also active in affairs pertaining to the United States, England, Russia, and other foreign countries. But antiforeign feeling ran high in Japan at this time, and since he was regarded as a foreigner, he began to fear for his safety and resigned his job as an interpreter. For a while he returned to the United States and at that time had an opportunity to meet with President Lincoln.

He went to Japan once more in 1862, and in 1863, when the domain of Chōshū opened fire on the vessels of England, America, France, and Holland in the Shimonoseki Straits, he was aboard the American ship. The same year, he resigned the position in the American consulate that he had previously held and opened an import-export business in Yokohama. He also published an account of his shipwreck in Japanese. In 1864, he began publication of a Japanese language newspaper called the *Kaigai Shimbun* in Yokohama, printing it from woodblocks. Later he engaged in import-export business in Nagasaki, where he became friendly with Itō Hirobumi and Kido Takayoshi, both leaders in the Meiji government. In 1872 he took a position in the Finance Ministry of the newly founded Meiji government, where, under the direction of Shibusawa Eiichi, he worked in cooperation with an Englishman named Alexander Allen Shand to draw up regulations for banks in Japan. He resigned his position in 1874. In 1895 he published a work entitled *The Narrative of a Japanese*, the first autobiography of a Japanese to appear in English.

Hamaguchi Osachi 濱口雄幸 (1870–1931)

Bureaucrat and statesman of the Meiji, Taishō, and Shōwa eras; he was born in Kōchi Prefecture. He graduated from the political science department of Tokyo Imperial University in 1895 and entered the Ministry of Finance. After serving as chief revenue officer of Yamagata Prefecture, he held various posts as a bureau chief and head of the Monopoly Bureau, and in 1912 became vice-minister of communications under Minister of Communications Gotō Shimpei. Later, at the urging of Gotō, he joined the political party known as the Rikken Dōshikai and became active in party politics. In 1914, after the Siemens bribery scandal had forced the resignation of the Yamamoto cabinet, he became vice-minister of finance in the second Ōkuma Shigenobu cabinet, serving under Minister of Finance Wakatsuki Reijirō.

In 1915, while holding this post, he was also elected a member of the Lower House of the Diet from Kōchi Prefecture. For a period of some ten years from 1916 on, he represented the Kenseikai (an outgrowth of the Rikken Dōshikai) and others, which later became the Rikken Minseitō, in its opposition to the Seiyūkai of Hara Takashi, and is particularly famous for his controversy with Minister of Finance Takahashi Korekiyo in which he advocated budget reduction. In 1924, when the Kiyoura Keigo cabinet was overthrown and Katō Takaaki formed a new cabinet made up of the three political parties advocating protection of the constitution, Hamaguchi became minister of finance and in 1926 became minister of home affairs in the Wakatsuki Reijirō cabinet. In 1927, when the political party known as the Rikken Minseitō was formed, he became its president.

In 1929 he became prime minister and formed his own cabinet. Reversing the policies of his predecessor Tanaka Giichi, he announced a ten-point platform for his cabinet and later carried out budget reductions and lifted the embargo on gold. In addition, through his Foreign Minister Shidehara Kijūrō, he adopted a policy of international conciliation, overriding the opposition of naval and military leaders in making Japan a signatory of the agreement drawn up at the London Disarmament Conference. As a result, he was strongly attacked by elements in the Privy Council and in military and right-wing circles. It was a period of severe financial distress due to the world depression, and living conditions for most Japanese were increasingly difficult. Amid this atmosphere of tension, Hamaguchi was attacked and severely wounded at Tokyo Station by a right-wing youth. In order to quell the confusion in the Diet and insure the ratification of the London agreement, he forced himself to appear in the Diet in spite of his critical condition. As a result, his condition worsened, and in April he turned over the post of prime minister and the presidency of the Rikken Minseitō to Wakatsuki Reijirō. He died in August of the same year. He was a man of sincere character and grave bearing; known popularly as the "Lion Prime Minister," he lived a life of strict integrity.

HARA TAKASHI 原敬 (1856–1921)

Statesman of the Meiji and Taishō periods; he was born in the city of Morioka, the grandson of the *karō* (chief retainer) of the domain of Nambu in the Tōhoku region. In his youth he went by the name Kenjirō; his literary name was Issan. His name Takashi can also be read Kei. In 1870 he entered the official school of the domain and the following year transferred to the Kyōkan Gijuku, a school for English studies maintained by the lord of the domain of Nambu in Tokyo. Lack of funds, however, forced him to withdraw from school. In 1873 he was baptized a Christian, taking the name David Hara. In 1874 he became a servant and student under a French missionary, accompanying him to the Niigata area and studying French with him. In 1875 he separated himself from his family and set himself up as the head of an independent branch of the family, at the same time changing his social status from *shizoku* (former samurai) to commoner. In 1876 he entered the law school operated by the Ministry of Justice, but in 1879, when complaints arose over the dormitory meals, he busied himself in the affair as a student representative and was expelled from school for his pains.

The same year, he became a reporter for the *Yūbin Hōchi Shimbun* and in 1882 was invited to take the post of editor-in-chief of the *Daitō Nippō* in Osaka. During this period, he gained favorable notice from the statesman Inoue Kaoru and the same year resigned his newspaper position and went to Tokyo, where he took a post in the Foreign Ministry. In 1883 he was appointed consul in Tientsin in China. While in this post, he met frequently with the Chinese statesman Li Hung-chang in negotiations occasioned by the uprising in Korea known as the Second Seoul Incident. In 1885 he participated in the drawing up of the Tientsin Treaty, which restored peaceful relations between Korea and Japan, gaining recognition from Itō Hirobumi for his ability. During the period from 1885 to 1889, he served as foreign secretary in the Japanese legation in Paris. On his return to Japan, he was transferred to the Ministry of Agriculture and Commerce, where he served under three successive ministers of agriculture and commerce, among them Inoue Kaoru and Mutsu Munemitsu.

In 1892, when Mutsu Munemitsu retired from political life, Hara resigned his post in the Ministry of Agriculture and Commerce. The same year, Mutsu returned to active life to become foreign minister in the second Itō Hirobumi cabinet, and Hara returned to the Foreign Ministry, where he headed the Trade Bureau. In 1895 he advanced to the post of vice-minister of foreign affairs. In 1896, after the conclusion of the Sino-Japanese War, he was sent to Korea as envoy extraordinary and minister plenipotentiary, but he resigned that post with the death of Mutsu Munemitsu in 1897. The same year he became editorial director of the *Osaka Mainichi Shimbun* and the following year became president. During these years in public and private office he published a number of books and translations relating to the problem of the revision of Japan's treaties with the Western powers.

In 1900, at the request of Itō Hirobumi, he assisted the latter in forming a political party called the Seiyūkai, drawing up plans for its organization and serving as its first chief secretary. The same year, he succeeded Hoshi Tōru, minister of communications in the fourth Itō Hirobumi cabinet, becoming the first native of the Tōhoku region to hold a cabinet post. Following this, he established a foothold in the financial world, serving as president of the Kitahama Bank in Osaka from 1901 to 1903 and as vice-president of Furukawa Mining from 1905 to 1906. In 1902 he was elected to the Lower House of the Diet and three times served as minister of home affairs, in the first and second Saionji Kimmochi cabinets (1906–08, 1911–12) and the first Yamamoto Gombei cabinet (1913–14). During these terms in office, he abolished the *gun* (district) land division system and worked to limit the power of Yamagata Aritomo and the other leaders of the clan faction in the government and to promote the influence of the political parties. In 1914, on the retirement of Saionji Kimmochi, he was elected to serve as the third president of the Seiyūkai. In 1918, when rice riots brought about the downfall of the Terauchi Masakata cabinet, Hara became the first party politician to be called upon to form a cabinet. He gained wide popular support as the "commoner prime minister," since he had adamantly refused to be promoted to the nobility. He and his cabinet took measures to suppress the socialist movement and dissolved the Diet because of their opposition to the proposed law on universal suffrage. In the subsequent election, the Seiyūkai emerged with an absolute majority, but signs of party corruption repeatedly appeared. In 1921, after serving over three years as prime minister, Hara was assassinated in Tokyo Station by an eighteen-year-old youth in the employ of the National Railway. He was known as a master politican and showed great skill in political affairs and ability as a leader.

HATOYAMA ICHIRŌ 鳩山一郎 (1883–1959)

Statesman of the Taishō and Shōwa periods; he was born in Tokyo. His father, Hatoyama Kazuo, was a Meiji period statesman and lawyer who at one time headed the Lower House of the Diet. His mother, Haruko, was active in women's education in the Meiji, Taishō, and Shōwa periods and founded Kyōritsu Women's University in Tokyo. After graduating from the English law course of Tokyo Imperial University in 1907, he began a career as a lawyer. In 1912 he became a member of the Tokyo City Council and in 1915 was elected to the Lower House of the Diet. He thereafter served fifteen terms as a member of the Lower House and at the same time held such posts as chief secretary of the Seiyūkai, head of the Tokyo City Council, and chief secretary of the Tanaka Giichi cabinet. He served as minister of education in the cabinets of Inukai Tsuyoki and Saitō Makoto. In 1933, however, when as minister of education he forced Kyoto Imperial University to dismiss one of its professors, Takigawa Yukitoki, because of leftist views, he drew strong criticism from the League of University Professors for interfering with academic freedom and autonomy. During the Pacific War, he took a stand against those who called for unconditional support of the war effort.

After the conclusion of the war in 1945, he formed the Nihon Jiyūtō (Liberal Party of Japan) with himself as president. The party emerged victorious in the 1946 elections, and he was on the verge of forming a cabinet when the General Headquarters of the Occupation forces ordered him purged from public office. He was depurged in 1951 and began a struggle against the main faction of the Liberal Party headed by his rival, Yoshida Shigeru. In 1954 he formed the Nihon Minshutō (Democratic Party of Japan) with himself as president and continued his opposition to Yoshida. By gaining the support of the Socialist Party he was at last able to realize his dream of becoming prime minister and set about forming the first Hatoyama cabinet. In 1955 he formed his second cabinet and then, merging the conservative forces to create the Jiyū Minshutō (Liberal Democratic Party), he proceeded to form his third cabinet. A dispute developed over who should be president of the new party, but in 1956 Hatoyama was elected to be the first president. The same year he went to Moscow on his own initiative, where he signed a joint agreement restoring diplomatic relations between Japan and the Soviet Union. He thereafter withdrew from public life.

HIGASHIKUNI (HIGASHIKUNI-NO-MIYA) NARUHIKO
東久邇(東久邇宮)稔彥 (1887–)

Shōwa period army general and military leader. A member of the imperial family, he was born in Kyoto, the ninth son of Imperial Prince Kuninomiya Asahiko. His wife was the ninth daughter of Emperor Meiji. In 1906 he became the founder of a new family called Higashikuni-no-miya. After graduating from the Military Academy and the Military Staff College, he spent the period from 1920 to 1927 in France. During this period, he studied at the French military academy and experienced a kind of freedom of life and movement such as he could never know in Japan. After returning to Japan he served as a division commander and chief of the Army Aviation Headquarters. In 1938 he was sent to North China as commander of the Second Army. In 1941, after the Konoe cabinet had resigned en masse and relations between Japan and the United States had reached a critical stage, there was a movement to establish a cabinet headed by a member of the imperial family, and he was regarded as a likely candidate for the post of prime minister. These plans came to nothing, however, and he spent the war years as General Commander of Defense. When the war situation worsened, he aligned himself with the forces opposing Prime Minister Tōjō and took part in moves to bring about peace.

In August of 1945, in an effort to guide the country through the confusion following upon the surrender, he replaced Suzuki Kantarō as prime minister, becoming the first, and so far the only member of the imperial family to hold that position. He formed a cabinet with Konoe Fumimaro as minister of state without portfolio and Ogata Taketora as chief secretary of the cabinet. He and his cabinet signed the instruments of surrender and carried out various measures demanded by the termination of the war such as the disbanding of the army and navy. But in October they received a blow to their effectiveness when the General Headquarters of the Occupation Forces ordered them to do away with the special police force and the laws pertaining to the maintenance of public order, and they resigned en masse. Higashikuni was purged from public life, but was later depurged in 1952. In 1947 he removed himself from status in the imperial family, his surname thereby changing from Higashikuni-no-miya to Higashikuni.

Hiranuma Kiichirō 平沼騏一郎 (1867–1952)

Statesman and judicial official of the Taishō and Shōwa eras; he held the title of baron; his literary name was Kigai. He was born in the domain of Tsuyama in present-day Okayama Prefecture. In 1888 he graduated from the English law course of Tokyo Imperial University and immediately took a position as a judge in the Ministry of Justice. After serving as head of the Civil Penalties Bureau of the Ministry of Justice, in 1911 he became vice-minister of justice. The following year he became public prosecutor general and president of the Supreme Court. He pursued investigations with utmost severity and was said to have wielded greater actual power than any other person in the judicial field at the time. In recognition of his abilities, he was selected to be minister of justice in the Yamamoto Gombei cabinet in 1923. The same year, when an attempt was made on the life of the crown prince at Toranomon in Tokyo, he accepted responsibility for the incident and resigned his post. At the same time, he was appointed a member of the Upper House of the Diet. Around this period he began to display a strong spirit of nationalism, heading the Kokuhonsha, a right-wing organization, and engaging in other activities of a similar nature. He also became president of Nihon University.

In 1924 he was made an advisor to the Privy Council, and the following year became vice-president of the Privy Council. During this period, he expressed strong opinions concerning efforts to save the Bank of Taiwan and the ratification of the agreement reached at the London Disarmament Conference, attacking the government for its conciliatory policies. In 1936 he became president of the Privy Council. In 1939, with the outbreak of the Second World War, he became prime minister and formed his own cabinet, but he lacked an understanding of foreign affairs and was unable to keep up with new developments on the international scene such as the signing of the Russo-German Non-aggression Pact, and as a consequence his cabinet resigned en masse. In the Konoe Fumimaro cabinet of 1940 he served as both home minister and minister of state. In 1945 he once more became president of the Privy Council and, in spite of clear indications that Japan was heading for defeat, vehemently opposed all efforts to bring the Pacific War to a conclusion. After the war, he was designated an A-class war criminal by the Occupation authorities. He was tried by the International Tribunal for the Far East on conspiracy and other charges, was found guilty, and condemned to life imprisonment. He died of illness in prison.

Hiratsuka Raichō 平塚らいてう (1886–1971)

Leader of the women's movement in the Taishō and Shōwa periods; her personal name was Haru, Raichō being her literary name. She was born in Tokyo; her father was vice-president of the Board of Audit. She attended Ochanomizu Girls' High School and in 1906 graduated from the home economics course of Japan Women's University. In 1911 she founded a women's literary magazine called *Seitō* ("Bluestocking"). The magazine's motto, "In the beginning woman was the sun," represented the first proclamation on behalf of women's rights in Japan and was thereafter adopted as the slogan for groups engaged in the struggle to improve the position of women. In 1914 she left home and went to live with Okumura Hiroshi. In her role as an authority on women's affairs, in 1918 she engaged in a dispute with the woman poet Yosano Akiko and others concerning the protection of motherhood, and the same year married Okumura Hiroshi.

In 1920 she joined with Ichikawa Fusae and others in forming the New Women's Society and became active in the women's suffrage movement. She and her associates called for revision of section five of the Peace Preservation Laws, which limited women's political activities. As a result of their efforts, a revision of the law was passed by the Diet in 1922. In 1929, Hiratsuka formed an all-women consumers' union called Warera no Ie, with herself as director, and in 1930 she joined the Proletarian Women's Art Alliance formed by Takamura Itsue and others. In the postwar period, she spoke out for the preservation of the new Japanese constitution. In 1953 she became president of the Federation of Japanese Women's Organizations. In 1954 her "Japanese Women's Appeal," a call to all the women of the world to help ban the H-bomb, led to the holding of the World Mothers' Convention.

Hirota Kōki 廣田弘毅 (1878–1948)

Taishō and Shōwa period diplomat and political leader; he was born in present-day Fukuoka City, the son of a stonecutter; his childhood name was Jōtarō. In his youth, he was influenced by the nationalistic thinking of the Gen'yōsha, a patriotic society formed by ex-samurai in Fukuoka in 1881, though he never formally became a member of the society. At the conclusion of the Sino-Japanese War, when Russia, Germany, and France forced Japan to return the Liaotung Peninsula to China, he realized the importance of the role of diplomacy in international affairs and gave up earlier ambitions for a military career in favor of the diplomatic profession. While still a student in the law course of Tokyo Imperial University, he was requested by Yamaza Enjirō, a native of Fukuoka and head of the Bureau of State Affairs in the Foreign Ministry, to conduct a secret tour of inspection of the Manchuria-Korea region because of the dangerous state of Russo-Japanese relations in the area, a task that he carried out successfully.

After his graduation in 1905, he served for a time as an official in the office of the Resident-General of Korea. The following year, having passed the examination for diplomatic service, he entered the Ministry of Foreign Affairs. After holding posts in China and England, he became a section chief in the Commerce Bureau of the Ministry of Foreign Affairs. In 1923, he was made head of the Bureau of European and American Affairs. He became minister to Holland in 1926, and ambassador to the Soviet Union in 1930. After holding talks with the Russian representative, Lev Mikailvich Karakhan, during 1931-32, he succeeded in concluding an accord between Japan and the Soviet Union concerning commercial fishing grounds. In 1933 he became foreign minister in the Saitō cabinet, replacing Uchida Kōsai, who had retired because of illness. He continued in this post in the succeeding Okada cabinet, working to counteract the tendency toward isolation that resulted from Japan's withdrawal from the League of Nations. In 1935 he negotiated with the Soviet Union for the purchase by Manchuria of the North Manchuria Railway (formerly known as the Chinese Eastern Railway) and improved relations between Japan and the Soviet Union. He also worked to do the same with China, arranging for the two countries to exchange ambassadors rather than ministers, though the Kwantung Army continued to follow its own policy with regard to North China.

After the February 26 incident in 1936, when young army officers attacked and killed a number of high government officials, Hirota became prime minister and formed his own cabinet, at first serving as foreign minister also, but later appointing Arita Hachirō to that post. He had to contend with interference from the militarists, which forced him to restore the system of appointing only men on active duty to the posts of war and navy ministers. He signed the Japan-German Anti-Comintern Pact and worked to provide more funds for national defense. But when the Seiyūkai representative Hamada Kunimatsu made a speech in the Diet criticizing the militarists for meddling in government matters, it aroused the ire of War Minister Terauchi Hisaichi, and the resulting opposition between the army and the political parties brought about cabinet dissension that forced Hirota and his cabinet to resign. In 1937 he became foreign minister in the Konoe cabinet, but hostilities between Japan and China broke out shortly after, and he was unable to restore peace. The following year, he turned over the post to Ugaki Kazushige.

In 1940 he became a councilor to the Yonai cabinet and was counted among the high officials who took part in deliberations on who should succeed to the post of prime minister. During the war, he was dispatched to Thailand in 1942 as congratulatory ambassador on the conclusion of an economic agreement between the two countries. In 1945, when it became increasingly apparent that Japan was heading for defeat, he was requested by Foreign Minister Tōgō Shigenori to meet with the Soviet ambassador Y.A. Malik and ask Russia to act as a mediator in negotiating peace, but the plan came to nothing. After the war, he was tried by the International Tribunal for the Far East as an A-class war criminal and, without ever taking the witness stand to defend himself, was condemned to death, the only civilian official among those so sentenced. His wife Shizu had already committed suicide in 1946.

HONDA KŌTARŌ 本多光太郎 (1870–1954)

Meiji, Taishō, and Shōwa period physicist and metallurgist; he was born in Aichi Prefecture. In 1897 he graduated from Tokyo Imperial University, where he studied magnetism and geophysics under Nagaoka Hantarō. From 1907 to 1911 he continued his researches in Europe, studying metallography at Göttingen University. Upon his return to Japan he became a professor of Tōhoku Imperial University. Until his retirement from the post of president of the university in 1940, he conducted numerous researches in the field of metallurgy, trained young men in the sciences, and founded the Steel Research Center, which later became the Research Institute for Iron, Steel, and Other Metals of Tōhoku University. He is particularly noted for his efforts to apply measuring methods employed in physics to the field of practical metallurgy.

In 1917 he perfected high-quality steel known as KS steel, which was superior to the magnet steel used at the time in Europe and America, and in 1933 produced an improved version, NKS, or New KS steel. This last surpassed in quality the MK steel that had been perfected two years earlier by Mishima Tokushichi. He also served as a member of the Aviation Research Center, the Institute of Physical and Chemical Research, and the Imperial Academy. In his late years he served as president of the Tokyo College of Science and held other posts in education. In 1937 he was among those to receive the first Cultural Award.

HOSHI TŌRU 星亨 (1850–1901)

Statesman of the Meiji period. He was born in Edo, the son of a poor craftsman. When his mother remarried, he became the stepson of a physician named Hoshi Taijun. For a time he was adopted into another family and studied English at the school for Western studies operated by the shogunate in Edo. Later, however, he returned to the Hoshi family. After the Meiji Restoration, he went to Osaka, where he taught in an English language school. One of those receiving instruction in English from him happened to be the future statesman Mutsu Munemitsu, and the two became close friends. In 1870 he taught at the school for Western studies in the domain of Obama, and in 1872 became a translation official in the government of Kanagawa Prefecture, of which Mutsu Munemitsu was governor. On this and many subsequent occasions, Hoshi benefited from the assistance of his friend Mutsu. In 1874 he became customs director of Yokohama. While retaining his status as a government official, he went to England for further education, studying law for three years in the Middle Temple and receiving the degree of barrister. After his return to Japan he became a lawyer in the Ministry of Justice.

Around this time he joined the popular rights movement and began to make a name for himself as a skilled debater. Having joined the Jiyūtō (Liberal Party), he was soon playing a leading role in its attacks upon its opponent, the Rikken Kaishintō (Progressive Party). He also took part in the management of the *Jiyū Shimbun*, the newspaper that disseminated the party's views, and was active in the movement to oppose the government. While on a speaking tour in the Niigata region in 1884, however, he was accused of insulting an official of Niigata Prefecture and charges were brought against him. He joined with Kataoka Kenkichi and other leaders of the popular rights movement in laying plans to petition the government for freedom of speech, reduction of land taxes, and changes in foreign policy, a plan that was carried out in 1887. In 1889 he was accused of violating the Peace Preservation Regulations and was forced to leave the capital area and the following year was imprisoned for violating the regulations against secret publications. He was released as a result of the general amnesty proclaimed at the time of the promulgation of the Meiji Constitution and journeyed abroad.

After his return to Japan he was elected to the Lower House of the Diet in 1892 and later became speaker of the house, but was forced out of office by the schemes of his political enemies. He stood for election once more, however, and was reelected. After the Sino-Japanese War, he went to Korea for a time, acting as a legal advisor in connection with reforms in the internal administration of the country, but he did not achieve any outstanding success in this role. In 1896 he became an envoy extraordinary and minister plenipotentiary to America, playing a distinctive part in dealing with problems concerning Japanese immigration to America that arose with the American annexation of Hawaii. In 1898, when the Jiyū and Shimpo combined to form the Kenseitō and the first party cabinet was formed, he hastened back to Japan. He later cooperated with Itō Hirobumi in the founding of the Rikken Seiyūkai, and in 1900 became minister of communications in the fourth Itō cabinet. He proceeded to extend his influence by becoming a member of the Tokyo city council, but his stubborn attitude made him many enemies, and he was also implicated in charges of bribe-taking that were brought against members of the council. In 1901 he was assassinated by Iba Sōtarō, a sword instructor who was active in Tokyo educational affairs and was outraged at Hoshi's conduct.

Hozumi Nobushige 穂積陳重 (1855–1926)

Legal scholar of the Meiji and Taishō periods; he was the son of a samurai of the domain of Uwajima in Shikoku and the elder brother of Hozumi Yatsuka; he held the title of baron. He was among the first Japanese to hold the degree of doctor of law; for a time he bore the surname Irie. He studied at the Meirinkan, the official school of his native domain. In 1870 he was selected by the domain to go to Tokyo for further study, where he entered the Daigaku Nankō, the forerunner of Tokyo Imperial University. In 1876 he was sent to England by the Ministry of Education, where he studied at the Middle Temple. Upon his graduation in 1879 he received the title of barrister at law. The same year he went to Germany, where he studied at Berlin University, and returned to Japan in 1881. He was immediately appointed an instructor in the Law School of Tokyo Imperial University, and the following year advanced to the rank of professor, a position that he held until 1912.

In 1890 he was appointed a member of the Upper House of the Diet, and in 1893, as a member of the Code Investigation Commission, he joined with Ume Kenjirō and others in drafting the Meiji Civil Code. At a time when the legal world in Japan was dominated by French concepts of law, he helped to introduce the empirical approach of English law. At Tokyo University he established the first lectures on the principle of law, propounding his view of law as evolutionary in nature. In 1912 he became an advisor to the Privy Council and a member of the Imperial Academy (later head of the Academy); in 1925 he became president of the Privy Council. His works include *Hōritsu shinkaron*, which expounds his theory of the evolutionary nature of law, as well as *Go'ningumi seidoron* and *Inkyoron*. His wife was the eldest daughter of the financier Shibusawa Eiichi. His eldest son, Hozumi Shigetō (1883–1951), was also a professor of Tokyo University, specializing in civil law, and in addition served as a Supreme Court judge.

Hozumi Yatsuka 穂積八束 (1860–1912)

Legal scholar of the Meiji and Taishō periods; he was the son of a samurai of the domain of Uwajima in Shikoku and the younger brother of Hozumi Nobushige. He studied at the official school of the domain and later Tokyo Imperial University. After his graduation in 1884, he went to Germany to study public law. He attended the universities of Berlin, Strassburg, and Heidelberg, and was particularly influenced by Professor P. Laband, becoming a supporter of the principle of absolute monarchy. Upon his return to Japan, he became a professor of Tokyo Imperial University, lecturing on constitutional law.

In 1891 a controversy arose over the promulgation of the civil code that had been drafted some time earlier by the French lawyer Boissonade. Hozumi published an article warning that the promulgation of the civil code would destroy the traditional Japanese concepts of loyalty and filial piety and led the movement to postpone the date of its enforcement. As a result, the civil code was subjected to revisions that emphasized the authority of the father as head of the family and preserved many traditional customs and attitudes concerning the superiority of the family over the individual. He later joined in a controversy with Minobe Tatsukichi and Uesugi Shinkichi, both scholars of constitutional law and professors of Tokyo University, concerning the nature of the imperial institution. Hozumi supported Uesugi in the latter's view of the divine right of the emperor, attacking Minobe's view of the emperor as an "organ of the state." In addition to his teaching position, Hozumi held the position of court councilor and member of the bureau for the investigation of the imperial household system. His works include *Kempō taii* and others.

Ikeda Shigeaki 池田成彬 (1867–1950)

Business and political leader of the Taishō and Shōwa periods; he was born in Yonezawa, the son of a samurai of the domain of Yonezawa; the name Shigeaki is commonly read Seihin. In 1888 he graduated from Keiō Gijuku, the forerunner of Keiō University, and took a position as an editorial writer for the *Jiji Shimpō*, a newspaper founded by Fukuzawa Yukichi, but resigned after three weeks and joined the Mitsui Bank. At this time, the Mitsui Bank was under the direction of Nakamigawa Hikojirō (1854–1901), who employed a number of graduates of Keiō Gijuku in his efforts to modernize banking procedures. Ikeda was one of this group, which included Fujiyama Raita, Mutō Sanji, Fujiwara Ginjirō, and Kobayashi Ichizō, all in later years prominent leaders of Japanese capitalism. Ikeda's talents were recognized by Nakamigawa, who in 1901 made him his son-in-law. After serving as head of the Ashikaga branch of the bank, he went to Europe and America in 1898, visiting various countries in order to study their banking methods. He returned to Japan the following year and in 1904 became head of the business department. In 1909 he advanced to the position of a managing director, and in 1919 to that of chief managing director.

During the twenties and early thirties he successfully steered the Mitsui Bank through any number of financial crises and raised it to a position of unrivaled leadership in the financial world, at the same time establishing the Mitsui *zaibatsu* as one of the largest business combinations in Japan. In 1931, just before Japan went off the gold standard, he made huge profits by buying up quantities of US dollars, a move that aroused worldwide criticism. It is said that he was listed for assassination by the right-wing organization Ketsumeidan along with Dan Takuma, the top leader of the Mitsui *zaibatsu*. Dan was, in fact, assassinated by the Ketsumeidan in 1932, and in 1934 Ikeda moved into a position of power as managing director of the Mitsui Partnership Company. He effected a number of measures to modernize the operation of the *zaibatsu* such as seeing that the members of the Mitsui family retired from positions of prominence, making public the identity of the stockholders, and putting into effect a system of compulsory retirement. In accordance with the last, he himself retired from his position in 1936. In 1937 he became president of the Bank of Japan. He resigned after less than half a year because of illness, but during his period in office led the bank in the initial steps to broaden its activities by investing in industrial as well as commercial ventures.

In 1938 he became minister of finance and minister of commerce and industry after the reorganization of the first Konoe cabinet. He retired from political activity in 1939, though his name was mentioned from time to time as a candidate for the offices of minister of finance or prime minister. He became an advisor to the Privy Council in 1941 and held a position of prime importance in the wartime financial world. In 1945, after the conclusion of the war, he was listed as an A-class war criminal suspect, but was removed from the list in 1946. He remained barred from public office for the remainder of his life, but played an important role as a covert advisor to the Yoshida cabinet. His writings include *Zaikai kaiko* and others.

Inoue Enryō 井上圓了 (1858–1919)

Thinker and educator of the Meiji period; he was the son of the head of a local temple of the Shin sect in the Santō District of Niigata. His childhood name was Kishimaru and his literary name, Hosui. He attended the official school of the domain of Nagaoka, his home town, and later the school of the head temple of the sect in Kyoto. He entered Tokyo Imperial University, graduating from the philosophy course in 1885. He specialized in Indian thought and in 1896 received his doctorate. He utilized Western philosophical theory to present a systematic analysis of Buddhist thought and on the basis of this theoretical framework offered criticisms of Christianity. He also labored to combat superstition by examining various tales of ghosts and spirits and attempting to offer rational explanations of them. His aim was to exercise a positive influence upon the thinking of the society of his time and to that purpose he invited Katō Hiroyuki and others to join him in forming the Tetsugakkai (Philosophy Society) in 1884. He also helped Miyake Yūjirō and others to found the magazine *Nihonjin* in 1887 and established a school called the Tetsugakkan (present-day Tōyō University) in the Hongō section of Tokyo. He traveled about on lecture tours throughout Japan and to Manchuria and Korea as well, and died in Dairen in 1919. His works include *Shinri kinshin*, *Bukkyō katsuron*, *Yōkai kōgiroku*, and others.

INOUE JUNNOSUKE 井上準之助 (1869–1932)

Financial and political leader of the Taishō and Shōwa periods, he was born in the region of present-day Ōita Prefecture in Kyushu. After graduating from Tokyo Imperial, University in 1896, he took a position with the Bank of Japan. During the period 1897–99, he resided in England, studying banking practices under Alexander Allen Shand, an Englishman who had helped to set up the Japanese banking system at the beginning of the Meiji period. After returning to Japan, he served as head of the Osaka branch of the Bank of Japan, and in 1906 was promoted to the position of head of the Business Division, an unusually rapid advance for a person of his age. In 1908 he was assigned to duty in America. He returned to Japan in 1911, in 1913 became president of the Yokohama Specie Bank (the forerunner of the Bank of Tokyo), and in 1919 became president of the Bank of Japan. In both of the latter positions, he succeeded Mishima Yatarō, a native of the domain of Satsuma and member of the Upper House of the Diet.

In 1923 he left the post of president of the Bank of Japan to become finance minister in the Yamamoto cabinet, the first one-hundred-percent Bank of Japan man to hold that position. In the confusion following the Great Kantō Earthquake, he pulled the country through its financial difficulties by declaring a moratorium. With the fall of the Yamamoto cabinet in 1924, he was selected to be a member of the Upper House of the Diet and continued to act as a mediator in affairs of the financial world. At the time of the financial panic of 1927, he once more became president of the Bank of Japan, but resigned after thirteen months.

In 1929 he became finance minister in the Hamaguchi cabinet and joined Hamaguchi's political party, the Minseitō. He shouldered the responsibility for economic planning during the period of financial panic, pursuing a deflationary policy and in 1930 lifting the embargo on gold. But when England went off the gold standard, it struck a blow to Japan's policy of free gold export, and the situation was made more serious by the sudden outbreak of fighting by Japanese forces in Manchuria. When the Hamaguchi cabinet was replaced by that of Inukai of the Seiyūkai late in 1931, the new finance minister, Takahashi Korekiyo, restored the embargo on gold. Inoue, after his retirement from political office, was chosen to be senior manager of the Minseitō. As head of the election committee, he was on his way to lend his support to a candidate in February of 1932 when he was assassinated by Onuma Shō, a member of a right-wing organization known as the Ketsumeidan, as part of its movement to create social confusion.

Inoue Kaoru 井上馨 (1835–1915)

Leader in the movement in late Edo times to restore power to the emperor and a statesman of the Meiji and Taishō eras; his literary name was Seigai and he held the title of marquis. He was born in the fief of Chōshū and in his youth went by the name Monta. He studied Dutch learning, English, and Western style gunnery and became an enthusiastic supporter of the *sonnō-jōi* movement, which advocated restoration of power to the emperor and the expulsion of the foreign traders, and in 1862 participated in the attack and burning of the British legation at Shinagawa in Edo. In 1863, on orders from his fief, he joined Itō Hirobumi in escaping from the country in secret and journeying to England. During his period of study in London, he became acutely aware of the impracticability of attempts to expel the foreigners from Japan and in 1864, upon receiving news that the ships of four foreign nations had been fired upon in the Shimonoseki Straits by the Chōshū forces, he hastened back to Japan and did his best to arrange a peaceful settlement to the affair. Later, he was attacked and wounded by members of the opposing faction in his fief, but he recovered and joined Takasugi Shinsaku in the movement to overthrow the shogunate.

With the establishment of the Meiji government in 1868, he became a councilor and officer in charge of foreign affairs. In 1871 he was made chief assistant of finance and later minister of finance, playing an active role in the organization of the new government and the handling of its foreign and fiscal affairs. But because of factional struggles within the government, he retired from public life in 1873 and devoted his energies to various business enterprises. As a result of the movement to quiet criticisms against the government (the outcome of a meeting of influential statesmen known as the Osaka Conference), he returned to political life in 1875, becoming a member of the Genrōin (Senate). In 1876 he was made a vice-envoy extraordinary and minister plenipotentiary and sent to Korea with the chief envoy Kuroda Kiyotaka to settle difficulties that had arisen between the two countries as a result of the Kanghwa Incident the previous year; the outcome was the trade agreement known as the Kanghwa Treaty.

After returning to Japan, he set off for a visit to Europe to study fiscal and economic matters. On his return to Japan in 1878 he became a councilor of state and minister of public works and the following year was transferred to the post of minister of foreign affairs. In 1884 he went once more to Korea as an envoy extraordinary and minister plenipotentiary to settle difficulties arising out of the Second Seoul Incident, negotiating and signing the Seoul Treaty the following year. The same year he became minister of foreign affairs in the first Itō cabinet and devoted all his efforts to seeking revision of Japan's treaties with foreign powers, but because of his policies for thoroughgoing Westernization, he aroused the opposition of Minister of Agriculture and Commerce Tani Kanjō and the French legal advisor to the government Gustave Emile Boissonade and others and was forced to retire.

In 1888 he became minister of agriculture and commerce in the Kuroda cabinet and in 1892 became minister of home affairs in the second Itō cabinet. With the outbreak of the Sino-Japanese War in 1894, because of his thorough knowledge of Korean affairs, he was dispatched to Korea once more as an envoy extraordinary and minister plenipotentiary. He devoted his energies to carrying out reforms in the Korean government. In 1898 he became minister of finance in the third Itō cabinet, and later a *genrō* (personal counselor) to the throne. In 1902 he supported Itō in urging the government to draw up an *entente cordiale* with Russia, but these efforts were brought to nothing with the signing of the Anglo-Japanese alliance in the same year. He was also active in the forming of the first, second, and third Katsura cabinets and the Ōkuma cabinet. Throughout his life he remained a staunch friend and supporter of Itō Hirobumi.

Inoue Kowashi 井上毅 (1843–1895)

Meiji period statesman; he used the literary name Goin and held the title of viscount. Born in the fief of Kumamoto in Kyushu, he was well versed in Japanese and Confucian studies and noted for his literary skill. In 1870 he went to Tokyo and entered the Ministry of Justice. He accompanied Etō Shimpei, the minister of justice, on an inspection tour of France and Germany. Upon returning to Japan, his abilities gained recognition from the statesman Ōkubo Toshimichi, and he was appointed chief secretary in the Ministry of Home Affairs and later in the Executive Council. After Ōkubo's death, he became closely associated with Iwakura Tomomi and Itō Hirobumi, and in 1881 was assigned by Iwakura to the group charged with the task of making preparations for the drawing up of a constitution.

With the assistance of Karl Friedrich Hermann Roesler, a German advisor to the Ministry of Foreign Affairs, he wrote several works such as *Daikōryō*, *Sairyō*, and *Ikensho*, which outline the foundations for a constitution and regulations for the imperial household. In 1886 he joined Itō Miyoji, Kaneko Kentarō, and others working under the direction of Itō Hirobumi in drafting what was to become the Meiji Constitution, strongly German in influence, emphasizing the powers of the sovereign, and known in Japanese as the *Dai-Nihonteikoku Kempō*. He also played a central role in the drafting of the Imperial House Law. In 1888, with the completion of these two documents, he became chief of the Bureau of Legislation. With the creation of the Privy Council, an advisory body that consulted on matters pertaining to the promulgation and interpretation of the constitution, he made various proposals concerning its organization and functions and himself became a chief secretary in the Privy Council. He took part in its deliberations and helped to define the interpretation of the constitution and the Imperial House Law. In 1890 he joined Motoda Eifu in drafting what was to become the Imperial Rescript on Education, defining the educational principles for the nation, and assisted in the drafting of various other imperial edicts and laws. After serving as an advisor to the Privy Council, he became minister of education in 1893 in the second cabinet of Itō Hirobumi, drawing up regulations for the establishment of public high schools and encouraging industrial education.

INOUE TETSUJIRŌ 井上哲次郎 (1855–1944)

Philosopher and educator of the Meiji and Taishō periods; he was born in what later became Fukuoka Prefecture in Kyushu; his literary name was Senken. After graduating from Tokyo Imperial University in 1880, he was selected by the Ministry of Education to be sent abroad for further study. From 1884 to 1890 he studied philosophy in Germany under Eduard Von Hartmann, a representative of the central faction of the Hegelian school, and others. Upon his return to Japan, he devoted his time to teaching at Tokyo University, working to introduce German philosophy. As a result of his efforts, German idealism became the dominant school in Japanese philosophical circles. He also took a great interest in traditional Japanese thought, publishing works such as *Nihon Yōmei gakuha no tetsugaku, Nihon kogakuha no tetsugaku,* and *Nihon Shushi gakuha no tetsugaku,* which deal with various schools of Japanese Confucianism in the Edo period. His aim appears to have been to achieve a synthesis of Eastern and Western thought. He wrote a commentary on the Imperial Rescript on Education entitled *Chokugo engi,* which provided a philosophical foundation for the educational policy of the Meiji government. He also took an active part in criticizing Christianity, claiming that its doctrines were inconsonant with the Japanese national polity. In all, he played an important role in encouraging nationalistic trends in the moral climate of the period.

INUKAI TSUYOKI 犬養毅 (1855–1932)

Meiji, Taishō, and Shōwa period political leader; he was born in the region that later became Okayama Prefecture; his literary name was Bokudō. In 1875 he went to Tokyo and became a student in Keiō Gijuku, where he made the acquaintance of Ozaki Yukio. At the time of the Seinan War in 1877, he became a correspondant for the newspaper called *Yūbin Hōchi* and was sent to Kyushu to cover the fighting. He developed a strong admiration for the chief editor of the newspaper, a former shogunate official named Kurimoto Joun, and was much influenced by him. In 1880 he withdrew from Keiō Gijuku, and along with his classmates Toyokawa Ryōhei and Asabuki Eiji, founded a magazine published every ten days called *Tōkai Keizai Shimpō* in which he advocated protectionist trade policies.

In 1881 at the invitation of Yano Fumio he took a position as a government official in the Institute of Statistics, but with the government shakeup in the same year, he withdrew from official life along with Ōkuma Shigenobu.

In 1882 he participated in the formation of the Rikken Kaishintō (Progressive Party) headed by Ōkuma. For a while he served as chief editor of the *Akita Nippō*. At the time of the Seoul Incident in 1884, he was sent to Korea as a special correspondant for the *Yūbin Hōchi*. After his return to Japan, he transferred to the staff of the *Chōya Shimbun*. In 1885 he was elected a member of the Tokyo Prefectural Assembly. In 1888 he joined in the formation of the Daidō-danketsu, an antigovernment organization led by Gotō Shōjirō that advocated popular rights, and drafted the prospectus for the organization. In 1890 he entered the first general election as a candidate from Okayama and won election to the Lower House of the Diet. He was thereafter repeatedly reelected, serving a total of nineteen terms.

At the time of the formation of the second Matsukata cabinet in 1896, he acted as advisor to Ōkuma Shigenobu, the head of the newly formed Shimpotō, who became foreign minister in the cabinet. He also played an important part in 1898 when the Jiyūtō and Shimpotō merged to form the Kenseitō, or Constitution Party. In the first Ōkuma cabinet formed in the same year, he succeeded Ozaki Yukio as minister of education, but retired from political life shortly after when the Kenseitō split up and the cabinet fell. In 1910 he founded a political party called the Rikken Kokumintō. In 1913 he joined Ozaki Yukio to become one of the leaders of the first Movement to Protect the Constitution, opposing the Katsura cabinet and becoming known, along with Ozaki, as one of the "gods of constitutional government." In 1922 he dissolved the Kokumintō and instead formed an organization known as the Kakushin Kurabu, or Reform Club. In 1924 he headed one faction of the second Movement to Protect the Constitution, which was launched to oppose the Kiyoura cabinet. In the Katō Takaaki cabinet that was formed the same year from the three constitution protection groups, he served as minister of communications.

In 1925, when the universal male suffrage law was passed, he merged the Kakushin Kurabu with the Seiyūkai and retired from political life. He continued to take the side of the opposition parties and minority factions who opposed the domain cliques in power in the government. In 1929, after the death of Tanaka Giichi, he was chosen to be Tanaka's successor as head of the Seiyūkai and thus returned to political life. In 1931, after the fall of the Wakatsuki cabinet, he became prime minister and formed his own cabinet. He had hardly been in office half a year when, in the so-called May 15 incident, he was attacked at his official residence by a group of young naval officers and assassinated. He was known for his sympathy toward Asian liberation movements and was a supporter of such men as Kim Ok-kyun, founder of the Korean Independence Party, the Chinese revolutionary leader

Sun Yat-sen, and R. B. Bose, head of the Indian independence movement, who at one time or another had fled to Japan. He was a distinguished calligrapher, had a wide knowledge of Chinese culture, and was noted for his refinement and integrity.

Ishibashi Tanzan 石橋湛山 (1884–1973)

Journalist and statesman of the Taishō and Shōwa periods; he was born in Tokyo. His father had at one time been chief priest of the Kuon-ji at Minobu, one of the most important temples of the Nichiren sect of Buddhism. In 1907 Ishibashi graduated from the literature department of Waseda University. He took a position with a newspaper, the *Tokyo Mainichi Shimbun*, but left it in 1909. In 1911 he went to work for a magazine of social criticism, the *Tōyō Keizai Shimpō*, publishing in its pages articles embued with a thoroughgoing liberalism and dealing with such issues as universal suffrage or expressing disapproval of the dispatch of Japanese troops to Siberia. He also took a very active part in various social and political movements, joining the Association for the Realization of Universal Suffrage in 1911, the Pacific Problems Study Institute and the Friends of Armament Reduction in 1921, and the Monetary System Study Institute in 1922.

With the beginning of the Shōwa period in 1926, as Japan's economic situation worsened, he spoke out frequently in print on such problems as the lifting of the gold embargo or emergency fiscal measures, though his outlook became increasingly less liberal. In 1941 he became president of the company publishing the *Tōyō Keizai Shimpō*. At the same time, he also served as a committee member in a number of important government organizations such as the Investigation Bureau of the cabinet, the Key Industries Control and Operation Committee of the Ministry of Commerce and Industry, the Cabinet Planning Board, and the Expert Committee of the Ministry of Commerce and Industry. In 1944, when it became increasingly apparent that Japan was likely to suffer defeat in the Pacific War, he recommended Finance Minister Ishiwata Sōtarō to set up a Special Investigation Office of Wartime Economy within the Finance Ministry. The purpose of this office was to study the question of Japan's economic reconstruction in the postwar period, a problem that was thus already under investigation before the war had come to a conclusion.

After the end of the war in 1945, Ishibashi participated in the formation of the Jiyūtō, or Liberal Party. He served as finance minister in the first

Yoshida Shigeru cabinet in 1946 and adopted an inflationary policy. In the same year he resigned as president of the *Tōyō Keizai Shimpō.* In 1947 he was ordered purged from public office by the Occupation authorities. He spoke out in print in protest against this action and in 1951 was depurged. The same year he was accused of antiparty activities and, along with Kōno Ichirō, was expelled from the Liberal Party by its president, Yoshida Shigeru, but was reinstated after his election to the Lower House of the Diet. In 1954 he joined Hatoyama Ichirō in helping to form the Minshutō, or Democratic Party, and three times served as minister of international trade and industry in succeeding Hatoyama cabinets. In 1956 he succeeded Hatoyama as president of the Jiyū Minshutō (Liberal Democratic Party) and formed his own cabinet, but he was forced by illness to resign after less than three months and to turn over the office of prime minister to Kishi Nobusuke. He thereafter served as president of Risshō University and in 1957 was awarded an honorary doctoral degree by Waseda University. Though a member of the conservative camp, he worked to promote cultural exchange between Japan and China and the Soviet Union, serving as chairman of the Japan-Soviet Union Society and urging the restoration of diplomatic relations with the People's Republic of China.

Ishihara Kanji 石原莞爾 (1889–1949)

General of the army active in the Shōwa period; he was born in Tsuruoka in Yamagata Prefecture. He graduated from the Military Academy and Military Staff College and served as an instructor at the latter. From 1922 to 1924 he was stationed in Germany, but on his return to Japan, resumed his teaching duties. In 1928 he was made a lieutenant colonel and became a staff officer in the Kwantung Army, which was stationed in Manchuria. The Kwantung Army was working to extend military control over the area and in 1931 created the so-called Manchurian Incident, which led to the spread of Japanese power and the establishment of the new state of Manchukuo. In 1932 Ishihara was a member of the Japanese delegation to the League of Nations in Geneva. In 1933 he became commander of the Sendai infantry regiment, and in 1935 head of the tactical section of the General Staff Office, making certain that Japan would be prepared in the eventuality of a conflict with the Soviet Union. In 1937 he succeeded in blocking the formation of the Ugaki Kazushige cabinet, and shortly after was promoted to the rank of major general.

With the outbreak of hostilities between Japan and China in July of the same year, he advocated measures to prevent any widening of the conflict, arguing that Japan's defense against the Soviet Union would be endangered. In September he was made assistant chief of staff of the Kwantung Army, but found himself in conflict with the chief of staff Tōjō Hideki. In 1938 Ishihara was transferred to the relatively unimportant post of commander of the Maizuru garrison and ceased to have a voice in important military decisions, and after serving as a divisional commander in Kyoto, he entered the reserve in 1941. He spent the year 1941–42 as a professor of Ritsumeikan College in Kyoto, but by this time General Tōjō had become war minister and prime minister and applied severe pressure on the Tōa-remmei, a civilian ideological group headed by Ishihara. Ishihara was a man of great self-confidence and talent and developed a unique theory of warfare that combined elements of Nichiren Buddhism with the study of European military history. After the war, he was summoned to give testimony at a special court session in Sakata in Yamagata held by the International Military Tribunal for the Far East.

Ishii Kikujirō 石井菊次郎 (1866–1945)

Diplomat of the Meiji, Taishō, and Shōwa periods; he was born in the province of Awa, later a part of Chiba Prefecture; he held the title of viscount. After graduating from the law department of Tokyo Imperial University in 1890, he entered the Foreign Ministry, serving in the Japanese legations in Paris and Inchon in Korea. He was stationed in Peking in 1900 when the Boxer Rebellion broke out and the foreign legations were besieged. After the siege was lifted and he returned to Japan, he was made a secretary of the Foreign Ministry and later chief of the telephone section of the general affairs bureau. In 1908 he became vice-minister under Foreign Minister Hayashi Tadasu. In 1912 he was minister plenipotentiary to France and in 1914 he became foreign minister in the Ōkuma Shigenobu cabinet, taking over the management of foreign affairs after the resignation of Katō Takaaki. He concluded the fourth Russo-Japanese agreement and took appropriate measures on the outbreak of the First World War. In 1916 he became a member of the Upper House of the Diet.

In 1917 he went to America as minister plenipotentiary and concluded the so-called Ishii-Lansing agreement by which Japan and America attempted to reconcile their approaches to the China question. In 1927 he was a minister plenipotentiary to the Geneva Disarmament Conference and in 1929 became an advisor to the Privy Council. In 1933 he served as Japan's representative to the International Economic Conference. From this period on, he held a position of respect and importance as a veteran of the diplomatic world. In 1940, when the Privy Council was holding deliberations concerning the concluding of a tripartite pact with Germany and Italy, he warned the government to proceed with utmost caution. Shortly before the end of the Pacific War, he was killed in an American bombing raid. He is regarded by scholars of diplomatic history as a man who was extraordinarily skilled in matters of diplomacy.

ITAGAKI TAISUKE 板垣退助 (1837–1919)

Meiji period statesman, champion of popular rights, and president of the Jiyūtō (Liberal Party); he held the title of count. He was the son of a distinguished family of the domain of Tosa in Shikoku, and in the closing years of the Edo period supported the movement to restore power to the emperor. But he found himself in disagreement with Gotō Shōjirō and others in his domain who favored cooperation between the court and the shogunate, and in 1865 went to Edo, where he studied Dutch style military science. When the Boshin civil war broke out in 1868, he entered Kyoto as commander of a battalion. As a staff officer of the general command, he accompanied the imperial forces when they moved east to put down resistance, distinguishing himself in the fighting at Aizu. During the campaign in Aizu, he is said to have first conceived the ideas that later led him into the popular rights movement. In 1869 he became a *san'yo* (councilor) in the newly formed Meiji government. In 1870 he became a major councilor in Kōchi, the prefecture that had been created out of the old domain of Tosa, and set about reforming the domain administration. In 1871 he returned to service in the central government, serving as a councilor of state and working to deal with problems arising from the abolishment of the domains and establishment of the prefectural system.

In 1873 he resigned from the government as a result of the dispute over Korean policy, along with Saigō Takamori, Etō Shimpei, and others. Unlike Saigō and Etō, however, he contemplated no recourse to military resistance. Instead, he determined to try to break the hold that the leaders from the domains of Satsuma and Chōshū had upon the government through political action. He petitioned the government for creation of an elected legislature, and along with Kataoka Kenkichi and others instituted the popular rights movement, founding the political organizations known as the Aikoku Kōtō and the Risshisha in Kōchi.

In 1875 he attended a meeting in Osaka that was designed to bring about a conciliation between the government and the popular rights group. As a result, he temporarily resumed his position as councilor of state, along with Kido Takayoshi, but resigned again because of disagreements of opinion. In 1878 he revived the Aikokusha, an organization he had helped found earlier in 1875, and in 1880 renamed it the Kokkai Kisei Dōmei, playing a leading role in the popular rights movement. In 1881, after a shuffle in government leadership, the emperor promised the establishment of a national assembly at the end of ten years, and Itagaki thereupon formed the Jiyūtō (Liberal Party) with himself as president. But he found himself faced with strong opposition from the government and made his way forward with the greatest difficulty. In 1882, when he was in Gifu on a speaking tour, he was stabbed by a would-be assassin and is reported to have shouted in defiance, "Itagaki may die but freedom will never die!" Shortly after, he and Gotō Shōjirō left the country and journeyed to Europe to avoid the criticisms against them and the movement. He returned to Japan in 1883 but, when the movement was intensifying, proceeded to dissolve the Jiyūtō because he felt he could no longer exercise effective control over the more radical elements in the lower echelons of the party. Previously, the party had been moving to identify itself with the interests of the farming population. But Itagaki's decision to dissolve it effectively frustrated all such efforts and greatly retarded the systematic promotion of the popular rights movement throughout the country as a whole.

After the fusion of opposition parties had been disrupted by disagreements over treaty revision and other questions, he became president of the Rikken Jiyūtō, which was established in 1890. He served as minister of home affairs in the second Itō Hirobumi cabinet in 1896 and in 1898 held the same post in the so-called Ōkuma-Itagaki cabinet, the first party cabinet in Japanese history. In 1900, when Itō Hirobumi founded the Seiyūkai, Itagaki retired from the political scene and thereafter devoted his time to social work. As the first to take up the cause of popular rights and the foremost leader in the movement, he holds a place of prime importance in the political history of the Meiji period.

Itō Hirobumi 伊藤博文 (1841–1909)

Leading statesman of the Meiji period; he held the title of duke. He was born in the fief of Chōshū and as a boy went by the name Toshisuke. His parents were poor farmers, but he was later adopted by the Itō family. In

1856 he was a foot soldier in the defense forces at Uraga, whose duty was to guard the entrance to the Bay of Edo, and there gained recognition from the head official from the fief of Chōshū. After returning to Chōshū he was enabled, through the introduction of the official, to enter the Shōka Sonjuku, a private school headed by Yoshida Shōin, and later went to Nagasaki to learn Western methods of military drill.

In 1859 he accompanied Kido Takayoshi (Kōin) on trips to Edo and Kyoto, made the acquaintance of a number of outstanding young samurai from various other fiefs, and came under strong influence of the *sonnō-jōi* movement, which advocated restoration of power to the emperor and expulsion of the foreigners. In 1862 he joined Takasugi Shinsaku, Inoue Kaoru, and others in attacking and burning the British legation at Shinagawa in Edo. In 1863 he was promoted to the rank of samurai and, on orders from his fief, joined Inoue Kaoru and others in leaving the country and journeying to England. After half a year of study in London, he received word that the Chōshū forces had fired upon the ships of four Western powers in the Straits of Shimonoseki and hastened back to Chōshū to attempt to arrange a peaceful settlement of the affair. During his journey abroad he became aware that efforts to expel the foreigners from Japan were misguided and thereafter devoted his energies to the movement to overthrow the shogunate and restore power to the throne, assisting Takasugi Shinsaku in strengthening the alliance between the fiefs of Satsuma and Chōshū that had been formed by Sakamoto Ryōma.

With the establishment of the Meiji government in 1868, he was appointed a councilor of state, judge in the Bureau of Foreign Affairs, and Osaka judge; later he became governor of Hyōgo Prefecture. In 1869 he became a lesser assistant in the ministries of Finance and Civil Affairs, working in cooperation with Ōkuma Shigenobu, chief assistant in the Ministry of Finance, on measures to open up the country and to establish a railway system. In 1870 he went to America to study fiscal and currency affairs, and after his return to Japan became chief of taxation, chief of currency, and major assistant in the Ministry of Public Works, playing a leading role in the process of abolishing the old feudal domains and setting up a prefectural system. In 1871 he accompanied Iwakura Tomomi in an inspection mission to Europe and America, acting as vice-envoy. After the return of the mission in 1873, a dispute arose among the leaders of the government over Saigō Takamori's proposal for military action against Korea, resulting in Saigō's resignation. Itō thereupon became a councilor of state and minister of public works and joined with Ōkuma Shigenobu in supporting Ōkubo Toshimichi. After the assassination of Ōkubo in 1878, Itō, while continuing as a councilor of state, became minister of home affairs and found himself in opposition to Ōkuma. In 1881, because of disagreement over the establishment of a constitutional form of government, he ousted Ōkuma from office and assumed political leadership himself.

In 1882 Itō went to Europe to study constitutional systems, particularly that of Germany, and upon his return to Japan joined with Inoue Kowashi, Itō Miyoji, and others in drafting a constitution for Japan. At the same time, as head of the Bureau for Organizational Studies and minister of the imperial household he worked to revise the cabinet system and the rules governing matters pertaining to the imperial household. Thus he played a major role in shaping the Meiji Constitution (*Nihonteikoku kempō*) and the Imperial House Law (*Kōshitsu tempan*), securing the financial situation of the imperial household, setting up the Sūmitsuin (Privy Council), and in other ways laying the foundations for the Japanese government system of modern times. In 1885 he formed the first cabinet with himself as prime minister and minister of the imperial household, and later he also became president of the Privy Council. The same year he went to Korea as envoy extraordinary and minister plenipotentiary to negotiate with the Chinese minister plenipotentiary Li Hung-chang over difficulties arising from the Second Seoul Incident of the previous year; these negotiations ended in the signing of the Tientsin Treaty. In 1890 he became president of the House of Peers in the newly established Diet, and the following year lent his support to the Matsukata cabinet and became a *genrō* (personal counselor) to the throne. In 1892 he formed the second Itō cabinet, devoting his energies to administrative reform, restoration of legal rights, expansion of the navy, and tax increases. In 1894 he was obliged as prime minister to carry out the country's entry into the Sino-Japanese War. In 1895 as minister plenipotentiary he negotiated with Li Hung-chang the Treaty of Shimonoseki, which brought the war to a conclusion.

In 1898 he formed the third Itō cabinet, but met with strong opposition from the Kenseitō (Constitutional Party) and became aware of the need to form a political party of his own. This he did in 1900, setting up the Rikken Seiyūkai with himself as president. The same year he formed the fourth Itō cabinet but resigned after half a year and become president of the Privy Council. In matters of foreign policy he opposed the group that favored close cooperation with the British, and urged the government to draw up an *entente cordiale* with Russia, journeying to Moscow in an effort to carry out such a step, but his plans were brought to nothing by the signing of the Anglo-Japanese alliance in 1902. In 1903 he once again became president of the Privy Council. After the conclusion of the Russo-Japanese War in 1905 he became Japanese ambassador to Korea and, as a result of the Second Japanese-Korean agreement, took over control of Korea's foreign affairs, becoming the first Resident-General in Seoul in 1906. In 1907, with the Third Japanese-Korean agreement, he assumed control of Korea's internal affairs and laid the foundation for outright annexation of the country. He returned to Japan in 1909 to become president of the Privy Council for the fourth time, but soon after went to Korea once more to handle difficulties that had arisen between Japan and Russia. In October of 1909 he was assassinated in the Harbin railway station by a Korean named An Chung-gun. During his long career in political affairs he enjoyed extraordinary confidence with Emperor Meiji.

Itō Miyoji 伊東巳代治 (1857–1934)

Bureaucrat active in government affairs from the Meiji to the early Shōwa era; he held the title of baron. Born in Nagasaki, he took up Western studies and English and in 1873 was appointed an official interpreter of Hyōgo Prefecture. Through the introduction of Kanda Takahira, the governor of Hyōgo Prefecture, he became acquainted with the statesman Itō Hirobumi, who recognized his talents and appointed him to a post in the Ministry of Public Works. He accompanied Itō Hirobumi when the latter went to Europe to study constitutional systems, and after his return to Japan was in 1884 made a secretary in the Executive Council. In 1889 he moved to the post of chief secretary in the Privy Council. During this period he participated in the drawing up of the Meiji Constitution. He served as private secretary to Itō Hirobumi when the latter formed the first cabinet with himself as prime minister. He served in the second cabinet as chief secretary and in the third cabinet as minister of agriculture and commerce. In addition, for thirteen years beginning in 1891 he was president of the Tokyo *Nichinichi Shimbun*.

In 1895 he was sent to Chefoo in China in connection with the ratification of the treaty that ended the Sino-Japanese War and in 1899 became an advisor to the Privy Council. Referring to himself as a "guardian of the Constitution," he became associated with the Seiyūkai headed by Itō Hirobumi. In 1922 he urged that Japan retain its troops in Siberia, in 1927 played a part in bringing down the Wakatsuki cabinet because of the financial crisis, and as an advisor to the Japanese delegation to the London Disarmament Conference in 1930 advocated a strong stand on the part of Japan. In addition to these activities in the political arena, he served as vice-president of a group set up in 1903 to study the imperial system and played a role in revising and formulating the regulations for the imperial household.

Iwakura Tomomi 岩倉具視 (1825–1883)

Court noble and statesman of late Edo and early Meiji times; he was born in Kyoto, the son of a member of the lower nobility named Horikawa Yasuchika. He went by the childhood name of Kanemaru, but was later adopted by Iwakura Tomoyasu and took the name Tomomi; his literary name was Taigaku. In 1853 he became a student of classical Japanese poetry under the *kampaku* (chief advisor) Takatsukasa Masamichi. His abilities in time were recognized and he was made a chamberlain in the service of Emperor Kōmei. In 1858, when the senior shogunate official Hotta Masayoshi came to Kyoto to seek imperial sanction for the commercial treaty that had been drawn up between Japan and the United States, the *kampaku* Kujō Hisatada drafted a reply to be presented in the emperor's name, which left the responsibility for decisions in such matters in the hands of the shogunate. At this time Iwakura was among the group of eighty-eight nobles who protested the action and expressed strong disapproval of the treaty. In order to help restore power to the court, however, in the period 1860–61 he became a supporter of the *kōbu-gattai* faction, which favored cooperation between the court and the shogunate, arranging a marriage between the emperor's younger sister Princess Kazunomiya and the shogun Tokugawa Iemochi. As a result he incurred the anger of the antishogunate party, which was very powerful at the time, being branded one of the so-called "four villains." He was impeached, forced to resign his post, and banished from the city. He shaved his head and entered the Buddhist clergy, living in retirement in the village of Iwakura north of Kyoto under the religious name Yūzan.

During this period of retirement, he gradually came to favor the position of those who advocated the overthrow of the shogunate, and communicated in secret with patriotic samurai of various domains who were working toward that end. In 1867, when Emperor Kōmei died and Emperor Meiji came to the throne, he was pardoned and allowed to enter Kyoto once more. There he joined with Ōkubo Toshimichi of the domain of Satsuma and others in plotting to restore power to the throne. After the shogun Tokugawa Yoshinobu had agreed to resign and return the power of government to the court, Iwakura joined with the forces of the domains of Chōshū and Satsuma and in 1868 successfully carried out the coup d'état that initiated the Meiji Restoration. Iwakura acted as a key figure in the new government that was formed, holding such important positions as *san'yo*, *gijō*, *fukusōsai*, and *dainagon*. In 1871, when the feudal domains were abolished and the prefectural system established, Iwakura was appointed minister of foreign affairs. This was followed by his appointment as minister of the right and envoy extraordinary and minister plenipotentiary, when he was ordered to head a mission to Europe and the United States. Accompanied by Ōkubo, Kido Takayoshi, Itō Hirobumi as vice-envoys and a number of attendant officials and students bound for study abroad, he left Japan in the latter part of 1871. Though the negotiations with the United States concerning treaty revision did not go as had been hoped, the mission gained valuable information through its study of governmental systems in the different countries it visited and its actual observations of life in the West and returned to Japan in 1873.

During Iwakura's absence, Saigō Takamori and other members of the caretaker government had advocated the sending of a military expedition against Korea. When Iwakura returned, he vigorously opposed this idea, arguing that precedence should be given to the solving of domestic problems. A dispute arose in the Executive Council, and when the premier, Sanjō Sanetomi, was suddenly taken ill, Iwakura was called upon to act in his place. He submitted a statement of his views to the emperor and managed to gain the latter's support and in this way defeated the advocates of a Korean expedition. Early in the following year, he was attacked and wounded at Akasaka in Tokyo by former samurai who resented the stand he had taken.

He also maintained a firm opposition to the people's rights movement, which was coming to prominence at this time, insisting that the power of the emperor was supreme. In the face of demands for a constitutional system of government, he had Inoue Kowashi formulate a series of basic principles in 1881, insuring that any constitution that might be adopted would be conferred upon the nation by the emperor and would conform entirely to his wishes. Thus Iwakura established the fundamental approach that was adopted in the drafting of the Meiji Constitution and the governmental reforms that accompanied its promulgation. The same year, when opposition developed within the government between Ōkuma Shigenobu, who demanded immediate framing of a constitution and establishment of a national assembly, and Itō Hirobumi, who favored a much slower and more cautious approach, Iwakura sided with Itō and succeeded in having Ōkuma ousted from his position as councilor of state.

From late Edo times on, Iwakura had on frequent occasions submitted memorials to the emperor stating his opinion on various matters and he also contributed advice on how the imperial household should be regulated and its financial situation made secure. He worked to organize the nobility as a kind of wall of defense surrounding the imperial family, and through his positions as head of the Peers' Club and director of the office in charge of affairs pertaining to the peerage, he acted as a kind of general supervisor of the nobility. In addition, with funds invested by members of the nobility he arranged for the establishment of the Fifteenth National Bank, often referred to as the "Peers' Bank," and the Japan Railway Company. He also gave attention to the welfare of the members of the former samurai class, who constituted a kind of middle class in Japanese society, and proposed that the government take steps to ensure them a means of livelihood. In 1883, the illness that had afflicted him from the previous year worsened. He was attended by Erwin Bälz, a German doctor attached to Tokyo Imperial University, and Emperor Meiji paid a personal call to his bedside, but he died the same year, before Itō Hirobumi, who had gone to Europe to study constitutional forms of government, had returned to Japan. He was given a state funeral and posthumously promoted to the post of *dajōdaijin* (premier). As a further mark of honor, his son Iwakura Tomosada was in 1884 given the title of duke.

Iwasaki Yatarō 岩崎彌太郎 (1835–1885)

Business leader of the Meiji period and founder of the Mitsubishi *zaibatsu*; he held the title of baron. He was born in the domain of Tosa in Shikoku, the son of a *rōnin* (masterless samurai), but later acquired regular samurai status. In his youth he studied the doctrines of the Wang Yang-ming school of Neo-Confucianism and in 1854 went to Edo and became a disciple of the Confucian scholar Asaka Gonsai. He returned to Tosa the following year, however, as a result of a dispute between his father and the village officials. Because of this incident, he became acquainted with Yoshida Tōyō and Gotō Shōjirō, who were at this time instrumental in carrying out reforms in the domain administration. Later, Yoshida was assassinated, and Gotō advanced in power and influence. Iwasaki likewise came to play an increasingly active role in events, in 1865 assuming a position in the Kaiseikan, an organization established by the domain of Tosa to promote trade and productivity, journeying to Nagasaki and Osaka for that purpose. In 1867 he became official in charge of accounting in the Tosa Shōji company set up in Nagasaki, working to promote trade with Korea. In 1870, the Tosa Shōji, which had accumulated large debts with foreign merchants, was reorganized by Iwasaki under the name of the Tsukumo Company, which took over from Tosa the former company's ten or more trading ships, along with all of its credits and liabilities. In 1871, when the domains were officially abolished, the Tsukumo Company became a purely private enterprise. In 1873 it relocated in Osaka and, under the name Mitsubishi, devoted its attention to shipping.

At the time of the punitive expedition against Taiwan in 1874, the company benefited from the fact that the US declaration of neutrality prevented the ships of the American-owned Pacific Steamship Company from being used for military transport, and that the Teikoku Yūbin Jōkisen Kaisha, a Japanese shipping company that might have performed that function, had gone bankrupt. Thus, as a result of negotiations between Iwasaki and Ōkubo Toshimichi and other high officials of the government, the Mitsubishi Company undertook sole responsibility for the task of military transport. It thus succeeded in securing protection from the government in the form of subsidies and preferential treatment. But although the company became public in character, Iwasaki retained firm hold of the directorship, becoming known as a business leader with special government connections. He bought up the Shanghai line from the US-owned Pacific Steamship Company, drove the British-owned P & O Steamship Line out of business in Japanese coastal waters, and soon came to monopolize the shipping field. The company made huge profits at the time of the Kanghwa incident in Korea in 1875 and the Seinan civil war in 1877 and extended its activities into foreign exchange, marine insurance, warehousing, mining, and other enterprises. But it came under criticism at home for its monopoly on shipping, and after Ōkuma Shigenobu, one of its principal supporters, fell from power in the government, its situation worsened. In 1883 the government set up the Kyōdō Un'yu Kaisha and withdrew its sponsorship from Mitsubishi. Competition arose between the two companies, but Iwasaki died suddenly in 1885 at the height of the dispute. The two companies later merged to become the Nihon Yūsen Kaisha (NYK).

Izawa Shūji 伊澤修二 (1851–1917)

Meiji period educator; he was born in the province of Shinano, present-day Nagano Prefecture, the son of a samurai of domain of Takatō; his literary name was Rakuseki. (His younger brother Izawa Takio was governor-general of Taiwan and an advisor to the Privy Council.) After completing studies at the official school of the domain, Izawa pursued a course in Western studies in Edo and Kyoto. In 1870 he was chosen to be an officially sponsored student from his domain and attended the Daigaku Nankō in

Tokyo, the forerunner of Tokyo Imperial University. He entered the Ministry of Education in 1872 and in 1874 became head of Aichi Normal School. In 1875 he went to America in connection with a survey of methods for the training of teachers. He studied first at Bridgewater Normal School and later entered Harvard, where he studied physics and chemistry. From Alexander Graham Bell he learned how to teach lipreading and is said to have been present when Bell developed the first telephone and tried talking over the instrument.

After returning to Japan in 1878, he held various positions such as head of Tokyo Normal School and director of the Editorial Bureau of the Ministry of Education, devoting his time to the compilation of textbooks. In 1895 he was assigned to service in Taiwan, which had just come under Japanese control, acting as chief of the Educational Bureau in the office of the governor general. In 1897 he became a member of the Upper House of the Diet, and in 1899–1900 served as head of Tokyo Higher Normal School. During this period, he contributed greatly to the development of Meiji era education by introducing Western educational methods and Western music into the curriculum. In the latter endeavor, he invited L.W. Mason, who had been one of his teachers in America, to come to Japan, and with his cooperation worked to compile song books for use in the elementary schools and in other ways to lay the foundations for musical education in the Japanese school system. He also arranged for the establishment of a government school of music (the Music Department of present-day Tokyo University of the Arts), and acted as its first director, and for a time also served as head of the Tokyo School for the Blind and Dumb. In his late years he founded an organization called the Rakusekisha, in which he devoted his efforts to the correction of stammering.

Kagawa Toyohiko 賀川豊彦 (1888–1960)

Leader of the Christian social movement in the Taishō and Shōwa periods; he was born in Kobe. His father had been engaged in shipping, but he lost both parents at an early age and moved to Tokushima Prefecture in Shikoku. While still a student in Tokushima Middle School, he was baptized a Christian. In 1905 he entered the preparatory course for the theology school of Meiji Gakuin and the following year published a work entitled *Sekai heiwa-ron* ("World Peace") in the *Tokushima Mainichi Shimbun*. In 1907 he began roadside preaching of Christianity in Toyohashi in Aichi Prefecture. He transferred to Kobe Theological School and in 1909 devoted his efforts to preaching and helping the poor in the Fukiai Shinkawa section of Kobe. He graduated from Kobe Theological School in 1911, married in 1913, and in 1914 went to America, where he studied biology and theology at Princeton and Princeton Theology School. He returned to Japan in 1917 and took up life in the Kobe slums once more, arranging through the cooperation of doctors to operate a traveling clinic free of charge.

In 1919 he joined Suzuki Bunji in forming the Kansai Workers' League of the Yūaikai, the labor organization formed by Suzuki and others in 1912, serving as its chief director. In 1921 he led a strike by the workers of the Mitsui and Kawasaki shipbuilding yards, but became the object of criticism when it ended in failure. He decided to redirect his activities to the movement to organize farm cooperatives and set off to the Tōhoku region, where he preached and worked to better the lives of the farmers. In 1922 he joined Sugiyama Motojirō in the formation of the Japan Farmers' Union, the first nationwide association of farmers to be created in Japan. In 1926 he also became chairman of the central executive committee of the newly established Rōdō Nōmintō (Labor Farmer Party), but resigned at the end of the same year.

In 1927 he formed an association for the purpose of preaching Christianity in rural areas, utilizing music and visual aids to spread his message and developing other unique methods of proselytizing. Earlier, in 1920 he had published a novel entitled *Shisen o koete* ("Beyond the Line of Death"), cast in the form of the reminiscences and personal experiences of a young man of eighteen who is dying of illness. It proved to be a best seller, and the royalties aided Kagawa greatly in his social and religious undertakings. Over the years, he held various public offices such as part-time employee in the Social Bureau of the Home Ministry and in the Tokyo City Social Bureau, member of the Central Employment Agency, and advisor to the Welfare Ministry (1946).

In 1945, immediately after the conclusion of the Pacific War, he became a member of the short-lived Higashikuni-no-miya cabinet and called upon the people of Japan to participate in a general movement of repentance for the events that had passed. In 1946 he became a member of the Upper House of the Diet and participated in the formation of the Japan Socialist Party. For a time he was mentioned among the leaders of the Occupation forces as a possible candidate for prime minister, but when it was found that he had made anti-American broadcasts during the war, his name was quickly dropped. Both before and after the war, he made frequent lecture tours abroad and was particularly well known in the United States, where he was regarded as comparable in stature and importance to Gandhi. In the postwar period he became an enthusiastic supporter of the World Federation movement and in 1955 was a candidate for a Nobel Peace Prize.

Kaneko Kentarō 金子堅太郎 (1853–1942)

Statesman of the Meiji period; he held the title of count. He was born in the domain of Fukuoka in Kyushu, and on the order of Kuroda Nagatomo, lord of the domain, he went to Tokyo in 1870 for the purpose of study. In 1871 he accompanied his lord on a visit to America, where he entered Harvard University and devoted himself to law, politics, and economics. Having graduated from Harvard in 1878, he returned to Japan and became a lecturer in Tokyo University Preparatory School. In 1880 he became an acting secretary in the Genrōin and devoted himself to constitutional studies. At this time he became acquainted with Ono Azusa and others and took part in deliberations as to what type of constitution would be most suitable for Japan. After serving as a major secretary, he in 1884 became a member of the bureau for the investigation of institutional matters, in 1885 private secretary to the prime minister, in 1886 a lecturer at Tokyo Imperial University, in 1888 private secretary to the head of the Privy Council, and in 1890 a member and secretary of the Upper House of the Diet. In 1894 he became vice-minister of agriculture and commerce and in 1898 minister of justice in the second Itō Hirobumi cabinet.

Though he held an impressive variety of posts, Kaneko's most important contribution to modern Japanese history came in the years 1886–88, when he was working with Inoue Kowashi, Itō Miyoji, and others in drafting the Meiji Constitution. While Inoue in his conception of the constitution tended to stress the divine rights of the emperor and Itō to take a strongly bureaucratic approach, Kaneko, with his wide knowledge of the parliamentary systems of Western countries, did his best to invest it with a modern and liberal character, and many of the laws enacted in connection with the promulgation and functioning of the constitution show his influence.

In 1904, at the time of the Russo-Japanese War, he was active in diplomatic negotiations between Japan and the United States, and demonstrated his skill in the handling of foreign affairs. In recognition of his efforts, he was made an advisor to the Privy Council in 1906. He also headed offices that were set up for the compiling of historical materials on the imperial household and the Meiji Restoration. In addition to these activities, he traveled widely, questioning various countries concerning their opinion of the Meiji Constitution, and attended the Conference on International Law in Switzerland. In 1899 he received an honorary degree of Doctor of Law from Harvard University and was also made an honorary member of the London Alumni Association. As a statesman, he was highly trained in the principles of modern law, but his more important activities took place less often on the political stage than behind the scenes, which is where he seems to have operated most effectively.

Kanō Jigorō 嘉納治五郎 (1860–1938)

Educator, English scholar, and judo leader of the Meiji, Taishō, and early Shōwa periods; he was born in Hyōgo Prefecture. In 1875 he completed the Government Foreign Language School and in 1881 graduated from the literature course of Tokyo Imperial University. He later held positions as professor of the Peers' School, head of the Fifth and First High School, head of the Tokyo Higher Normal School (1893–97), and head of the Regular Educational Bureau of the Ministry of Education. He was also selected to be a member of the Upper House of the Diet.

In 1882 he established a center for training in the military arts called the Kōdōkan on the grounds of a temple in the Shitaya section of Tokyo. There he revived and reformed the art of jūjitsu, which had fallen into disuse after the Meiji Restoration. He incorporated into it various elements from Western style physical educational theory, physiology, and kinesiology, renamed it judo, and worked to teach and spread it in a systematic fashion. The Kōdōkan in time expanded, and Kanō made no less than thirteen trips abroad, traveling all over the world to introduce judo to foreign countries and gain international recognition for it. In 1909 he was chosen to be a member of the International Olympic Committee, and judo was represented for the first time by two Japanese athletes at the Stockholm Olympics in 1912. He was active in the movement to bring the Olympic Games to Japan and, at the general meeting of the I.O.C. (International Olympic Committee) in Cairo in 1938, he succeeded in having Tokyo chosen as the site for the Games, but he was taken sick and died while aboard the Japanese liner *Hikawa Maru* en route to Japan by way of America.

Kataoka Kenkichi 片岡健吉 (1844–1903)

Political leader of the Meiji period; he was born in the domain of Tosa in Shikoku. In 1863 he became a district official in the domain and in 1867 took part in the Boshin civil war, fighting in the cause of the emperor. After returning to his domain, he became an inspector general. When a national system of military conscription was set up, he became a member of the military and rose to the rank of naval commander. While pursuing a military career, he began around the time of the Iwakura mission of 1871 to Europe and America to take an increasing interest in politics. In 1873 he joined with Hayashi Yūzō and others to found an organization in Kōchi called the Kainan Gisha, which supported the members of the government who were calling for an expedition against Korea. When the advocates of this move were defeated, he resigned from naval service. The following year, he helped to found the political organizations known as the Aikoku Kōtō and Risshisha and became active in the people's rights movement. In 1875 he helped found the Aikokusha and in 1877 became president of the Risshisha. He petitioned the government for creation of an elected assembly, but he and Hayashi Yūzō were both arrested on suspicion of having lent aid to Saigō Takamori, the leader of the rebel forces in the Seinan War.

In 1879 he became a member of the Kōchi prefectural assembly and in 1880 helped to form the Kokkai Kisei Dōmei. He also drew up a proposal for a genuinely democratic type of constitution for Japan. In 1881 he became head of the Kōchi Shimbunsha and in 1885 he was baptized a Christian and chosen to be an elder of the Kōchi Church. In 1887 he took part in the movement to petition the government to grant freedom of speech and take other measures and was arrested for violation of the Peace Preservation Regulations. In 1890 he became a member of the Lower House of the Diet and later held the positions of president and vice president of the Lower House. In 1895 he took part in the founding of the Kenseitō (Constitution Party), and in 1900 participated in the formation of the Rikken Seiyūkai. Thus he was from the beginning one of the leaders of the people's rights movement.

Katayama Sen 片山潜 (1859–1933)

Leader of the socialist movement in the Meiji, Taishō, and Shōwa periods; he was the son of a farm family of Okayama Prefecture. He went to Tokyo and attended school while working as a printer. In 1884 he went to America where, in spite of financial difficulties, he managed to study at Yale University and elsewhere. He returned to Japan in 1896 and the following year opened a settlement house called Kingsley Hall in the Kanda area of Tokyo. He thereafter participated in the newly organized trade union movement, publishing a magazine called *Rōdō Sekai.* In 1900 he joined Kōtoku Shūsui in forming the Shakai Shugi Kyōkai (Socialist League), and in 1901 they helped to form the Shakai Minshutō (Social Democratic Party), which was outlawed the same day it was founded. He thus was one of the pioneers of the Japanese socialist movement. He opposed the Russo-Japanese War and in 1904 attended the Second International in Amsterdam as representative from Japan, where he shook hands with the Russian delegate Plekhanov in a gesture of protest against the war.

After returning to Japan, he opposed Kōtoku's calls for direct social action, advocating parliamentary reforms instead. After Kōtoku's execution on charges of plotting against the emperor, he acted as leader of the Tokyo streetcar strike in 1911–12. He went to America in 1914, where he was active among the socialist leaders of the Japanese community in America. In 1921 he went to the Soviet Union, where he was appointed a member of the permanent executive committee of the Comintern and became a leader in the international Communist movement. He took part in the drafting of the 1927 *Thèse* and the 1932 *Thèse*, and died in 1933 in Moscow. He was buried in the Kremlin. In addition to his autobiography, he wrote *Nihon no rōdō undō* and other works.

Katayama Tetsu 片山哲 (1887–)

Taishō and Shōwa period leader of the socialist movement and political leader; he was born in Wakayama Prefecture. His father was a lawyer; under his mother's influence, he became a Christian. While a student in the law course of Tokyo Imperial University, he became interested in the socialist movement led by Abe Isoo and determined to work for the realization of Christian socialism. He graduated from Tokyo University in 1912 and the following year began a career as a lawyer. In 1919 he opened an office for legal advice in the Tokyo Y.M.C.A. and the following year set up an organization called the Chūō Hōritsu Shimpōsha in Hibiya in Tokyo that published a periodical on legal affairs, in these and other ways working to democratize the legal system. He also became head of the legal division of the Japanese Federation of Labor and legal advisor to the Japan Farmers' Union. He expended great effort in working to settle legal disputes involving workers and tenant farmers and to assist the members of the proletarian class through his legal knowledge. In 1926, when the Shakai Minshūtō (Social Popular Party) was formed under the leadership of Abe Isoo, he was chosen for the post of chief secretary. He was elected a member of the Lower House of the Diet in 1930. In 1932 he became chief secretary of the Shakai Taishūtō

(Social Populace Party) that was formed when the Shakai Minshūtō merged with the Zenkoku Rōnō Taishūtō of Kawakami Jōtarō and others. In 1940 he joined Abe, Nishio Suehiro, and others in resigning from the Shakai Taishūtō in a gesture of protest against the expulsion from the Diet of Saitō Takao, a member of the Minseitō who had made an antimilitary speech in the Diet.

In 1945, after the conclusion of the Pacific War, he played a key role in the formation of the Japan Socialist Party, becoming chief secretary, and in 1946 he became chairman of the party, a post that had up until that time remained vacant. In 1947, in the first general election held under the new constitution, the Socialist Party emerged victor. Katayama became prime minister, forming a coalition cabinet along with the Minshūtō (Democratic Party) led by Ashida Hitoshi and the Kokumin Kyōdōtō (Peoples' Cooperative Party) of Miki Takeo. Katayama, however, was unable to put any of his socialist principles into action. A proposal for government supervision of the coal mines was emasculated in debate, and his cabinet, beset by all the weaknesses inherent in a coalition, was finally forced to resign en masse in 1948. Since then, the Japanese Socialist Party has never again been able to gain political control.

In 1953 he became president of the National League for the Protection of the Constitution and throughout the postwar period has been active in appealing to the Japanese people to support the new constitution. In 1956 he became the first director of the Japan-China Cultural Exchange Association, working to promote friendly relations with the People's Republic of China. In 1960, with the formation of the Minshu Shakaitō (Democratic Socialist Party), he became top advisor to the party, but was defeated in the general election in 1963 and thereafter withdrew from politics. He is an authority on works of classical Chinese literature and has written a book on the T'ang dynasty poet Li Po.

Katō Hiroyuki 加藤弘之 (1836–1916)

Scholar and social philosopher of the Meiji period. He was the son of a samurai of the domain of Izushi in Tajima Province; his common name was Toyoshi and his given name Kōzō, which, after the Meiji Restoration, he changed to Hiroyuki. He studied Chinese at the Kōdōkan, the official school of the domain and in 1852 went to Edo and studied Western gunnery and military science under Sakuma Shōzan. Thereafter he remained almost all the time in Edo, studying Dutch science and working at the Bansho Shirabesho, an institution set up by the shogunate for the study and teaching of Western learning. He also took up the study of German. In 1864 he was made a retainer of the shogunate and became a teacher in the Kaiseijo, a school that developed out of the Bansho Shirabesho and that in time became Tokyo Imperial University. He rose steadily in the shogunate administration, holding such important posts as *ōmetsuke* (head of office dealing with daimyo politics) and *kanjōgashira* (official in the accounting office).

After the Meiji Restoration, he was invited to join the newly formed government and took part in the task of working out a new governmental system and a new code of laws. In 1870 he was also appointed lecturer to the emperor and empress and for the following five years instructed them in the customs and governmental systems of Europe and America. In 1873 he joined with Mori Arinori, Nishimura Shigeki, and others to form the Meirokusha, an organization made up principally of scholars and intellectuals, and helped found a magazine called *Meiroku Zasshi* to express the opinions of the group. In 1874 he was appointed a member of the Sain, a legislative body set up at the beginning of the Meiji period, but when Itagaki Taisuke, Etō Shimpei, and others petitioned the government for the creation of an elected legislature, he expressed the opinion that such a move was premature, and a violent controversy ensued. In 1875 he became a member of the Genrōin. From 1877 he served as head of Tokyo Kaisei Gakkō, which was shortly afterward renamed Tokyo Imperial University, and later served as head of the faculties of Law and Letters and as president of the university. In 1886 he once more became a member of the Genrōin and he also served as a member of the Upper House of the Diet and as a court councilor. In 1900 he received the title of baron. After some fifty years of active life in scholarship and public affairs, he died in 1916 at the age of eighty.

In his earlier years he upheld the view that all men are born free and equal and are endowed by Heaven with certain rights, setting forth his theory in such works as *Rikken seitairyaku*, *Shinsei taii*, and *Kokutai shinron*. From around 1882, however, he began to display an increasing sympathy for the evolutionary ideas of Spencer and Hegal and, in his work entitled *Jinken shinsetsu*, he provided a theoretical foundation for the nationalistic point of view.

Katō Takaaki 加藤高明 (1860–1926)

Diplomat and statesman of the Meiji and Taishō eras; he held the title of baron. Born in the fief of Owari, he attended the Kaisei School in Tokyo and in 1881 graduated from the law department of Tokyo Imperial University. He entered the Mitsubishi Company and became acquainted with the director of the firm, Iwasaki Yatarō. In 1883 he was chosen to be sent to England, where he studied business methods under James L. Bowes. Upon his return to Japan in 1885 he became assistant manager of the firm and the following year married Iwasaki's eldest daughter. In 1888 he entered political life, serving as private secretary to Minister of Foreign Affairs Ōkuma Shigenobu and chief of the section of Political Affairs and cooperating with Ōkuma in efforts to bring about revision of Japan's treaties with foreign powers. In 1890 he moved to the Ministry of Finance, serving as a councilor. In 1894 he returned to the Ministry of Foreign Affairs and, after drawing up a defense alliance between Japan and Korea, was dispatched as envoy extraordinary and minister plenipotentiary to England, where he remained for four years. During this period he urged the Japanese government to adopt a strong policy toward Russia and to conclude an alliance with England.

In 1900 he became minister of foreign affairs in the fourth Itō cabinet and expressed adamant resistance toward the Russian occupation of Manchuria. In 1902 he was elected a member of the Diet from Kōchi Prefecture and, developing an interest in party politics, joined with Itō and Ōkuma in working to build a political party. In 1904 he became president of the Tokyo *Nichinichi Shimbun* and exerted his influence to bring about the overthrow of the militaristic Katsura Tarō cabinet. In 1906 he became minister of foreign affairs in the Saionji Kimmochi cabinet, but resigned because of his opposition to the nationalization of the railroads and the policy of the army regarding Manchuria. In 1909 he was sent to England as envoy extraordinary and minister plenipotentiary and, with Edward Grey, negotiated and signed the third revision of the Anglo-Japanese alliance. When the so-called first national Movement to Protect the Constitution brought about the downfall of the Katsura cabinet in 1913, Katō became a member of the Rikken Dōshikai, a political party formed by Katsura to combat his opponents, and after Katsura's death became president of the party. He became minister of foreign affairs in the Ōkuma cabinet in 1914, and as a result the Rikken Dōshikai was able to exert considerable influence over government policy. With the outbreak of the First World War, he persuaded the cabinet to enter the hostilities, a decision that led to Japan's seizure of the German base in Tsingtao, and following this drew up the so-called Twenty-one Demands that were presented to China. In this way he sought to expand Japan's sphere of interest on the Asia mainland, though his efforts aroused much opposition both at home and abroad.

In 1916 he formed a political party known as the Kenseikai, but remained isolated from the mainstream of political developments. In 1924 he and his followers joined with two other political parties, the Seiyūkai and the Kakushintō, in carrying out what came to be known as the second Constitution Protection Movement. As a result, Katō succeeded in overthrowing the Kiyoura cabinet and forming a cabinet made up of members from the Seiyūkai, the Kakushintō, and the Kenseikai. The Katō cabinet in 1925 enacted a law establishing universal male suffrage, but at the same time promulgated the so-called Peace Preservation Law, which allowed the government to take repressive measures against those whose political views it regarded as dangerous. Katō died in 1925 while serving as prime minister of his second cabinet.

Katō Tomosaburō 加藤友三郎 (1861–1923)

Statesman and naval leader who rose to the rank of fleet admiral; he held the title of viscount. He was born in Hiroshima, the son of a samurai of the fief of Aki. In 1873 he entered the school that later became the Naval Academy and in time graduated from the Naval Academy and the Naval Staff College. In 1883 he was commissioned as an ensign. He was sent to England in 1891 as an ordnance supervision officer and the same year became an officer aboard the warship *Yoshino*, which had been built in England at the request of the Japanese. After cruising in foreign waters, he returned aboard the ship to Japan in 1894. The same year he served in the Sino-Japanese War as gunnery lieutenant of the *Yoshino*. In 1895 he was promoted to the rank of lieutenant commander and assigned to duty in the Bureau of Naval Affairs in the Naval Ministry. The following year he was also made an instructor in the Naval Staff College, giving instruction in gunnery.

In 1898 he became commander of the warship *Tsukushi*, and from 1899 on served as the head of various sections in the Bureau of Naval Affairs. In 1904, with the outbreak of the Russo-Japanese War, he was promoted to the rank of captain and made chief of staff for the Second Fleet. In the course of the war, he advanced to the rank of rear admiral and became chief of staff of the Combined Fleet, participating in the battle of the Japan Sea aboard the flagship *Mikasa*. In 1906 he became vice-minister of the navy, in 1908 a vice admiral, in 1909 commander of the Kure Naval Yard, and in 1913 commander of the First Fleet. In 1915, after the outbreak of the First World War, he became minister of the navy in the cabinet of Ōkuma Shigenobu and continued to hold that position in the Terauchi, Hara, and Takahashi cabinets and when he himself became prime minister in 1922. He thus held a cabinet post for a total of ninety-four months, a record surpassed only by Saitō Makoto. During this period he worked to implement plans for naval expansion.

In 1921 he attended the Washington Conference as chief plenipotentiary of the Japanese delegation and in 1922 signed the naval reduction treaty on Japan's behalf. He returned to Japan the same year, and when the Seiyūkai cabinet of Takahashi Korekiyo resigned, he was appointed prime minister on the recommendation of the elder statesmen. With the support of the Seiyūkai, he formed a new cabinet centering about members of the bureaucracy and the House of Peers. Striving for democratization and peace within the country and abroad, he carried out the military reductions agreed upon at the Washington Conference, decommissioning eleven warships of the navy and reducing army personnel by over 60,000 men, and he also carried out reductions in the government administration. On the foreign field, he withdrew more than half of the Japanese forces in Siberia, which had aroused the distrust of the foreign powers, removed the Japanese garrison from Tsingtao, and resolved the Shantung question that for so long had remained unsettled between Japan and China. He was a man who was capable of taking the long view and of dealing with problems in a cool-headed and thorough manner, but he suffered from poor health and died in 1923 while holding the office of prime minister.

KATSU KAISHŪ 勝海舟 (1823–1899)

Statesman of the late Edo and Meiji periods. His given name was Yoshikuni, and he later came to be known by the name Awa; his literary name was Kaishū; he held the title of count. He was born in Edo, the son of a poor samurai in the service of the shogunate. He applied himself diligently to reading and swordsmanship and also took up Dutch studies and the study of Western military science and gunnery under Nagai Seigai. During this period he became acquainted with Sakuma Shōzan, a scholar and pioneer in the study of Western gunnery. In 1850 he opened a private school of his own where he taught Dutch studies. In 1854 he became acquainted with a shogunate official named Ōkubo Tadahiro and, at the urging of the latter, submitted a letter stating his views on coastal defense to Abe Masahiro, the senior counselor to the shogun. The letter brought him recognition from the shogunate, and in 1855 he was assigned to the task of translating Western books. Later he was transferred to the naval training institute that had been set up in Nagasaki by the shogunate.

While studying navigation and gaining what knowledge he could of the West, he also had an opportunity to sail to various parts of Japan. At this time he became acquainted with Shimazu Nariakira, the lord of Satsuma, and others like him who were endeavoring to introduce Western technology to Japan. In 1860, when an embassy from the shogunate headed by Shimmi Buzen-no-kami Masaoki was sent to America, Katsu commanded the ship *Kanrin Maru,* which carried the group across the Pacific. In 1862 he became an official in charge of warships, and in 1863 he persuaded the shogun Tokugawa Iemochi to set up a naval training center in Kobe and to place the Nagasaki ironworks under its jurisdiction, thus laying the foundation for what would later become the Japanese Imperial Navy. In 1865 he was assigned to Osaka Castle as official in charge of warships and was given the title of Awa-no-kami. But he was suspected of sheltering samurai who were connected with the naval training center and who had escaped from the jurisdiction of their domains at the time of the attempted seizure of Kyoto by the samurai of Chōshū in 1864 and he was relieved of his duties and put under house arrest.

In 1866 he was once more assigned as official in charge of warships to Osaka, where the second punitive expedition against Chōshū had been stalled by the death of the shogun Tokugawa Iemochi. In the end, however, he found himself unable to agree with the leaders of the shogunate. Meanwhile, dramatic changes were taking place on the political scene. Tokugawa Yoshinobu became shogun, Emperor Meiji ascended the throne, and the coup d'état that signaled the Meiji Restoration was carried out in Kyoto. Tokugawa Yoshinobu voluntarily resigned his position, returning the power of government to the emperor, and Katsu, convinced of the former shogun's desire to comply with the wishes of the new government, worked with Yamaoka Tesshū to insure a peaceful conclusion to the process of transfer of power. To this end, he carried out negotiations with Saigō Takamori, a leader of the imperial forces that were advancing on Edo, and as a result Edo Castle was handed over without resistance or bloodshed.

In 1869 Katsu became chief assistant to the minister of foreign affairs in the newly formed Meiji government and later became chief assistant in the Ministry of Military Affairs. For a time he held a post in Sumpu (Shizuoka), but returned to Tokyo in 1872 to become vice-minister of the navy and the following year councilor of state and minister of the navy. In 1888 he became an advisor to the Privy Council. In sum, it may be said that he was one of the ablest men in the service of the shogunate during its last days in power.

Katsura Tarō 桂太郎 (1847–1913)

Army leader and statesman of the Meiji and Taishō periods; he held the rank of full general and the title of duke. He was born in the domain of Chōshū. He served in the domain military organization called the Kiheitai organized by Takasugi Shinsaku, seeing action in the shogunate expedition against Chōshū and the Boshin civil war. In 1869 he went to Tokyo to study French military methods and later entered the foreign language school in Yokohama. In 1870 he went abroad, studying military affairs and French in Paris, and returned to Japan in 1873. In 1875 he was appointed military attaché to the Japanese legation in Germany. In 1883 he accompanied War Minister Ōyama Iwao on a tour of various European countries for the purpose of inspecting military installations. As a result of the trip, the German military expert Klemens Wilhelm Jakob Meckel was invited to Japan to teach at the Military Staff College.

In 1885 Katsura advanced to the rank of major-general, and in 1886 became vice-minister of war. During this period, under the direction of Yamagata Aritomo, he devoted himself to the tasks of establishing German military methods and adapting them to Japan's needs, reorganizing the military command, abolishing garrisons and creating new army divisions, separating the General Staff Office from the Army Command Office, and in other ways working to create a modern army. In 1890 he advanced to the rank of lieutenant general. The same year, as a member of the budget drafting committee, he succeeded in winning passage for the budget submitted to the newly created Diet by the War Ministry in spite of opposition from the popular parties, gaining recognition of his political skill in the process.

In 1894 he served in the Sino-Japanese War alongside General Yamagata, commanding the Third Division and winning renown for his exploits. In 1895 he became governor-general of Taiwan. In 1898 he became war minister in the third Itō Hirobumi cabinet and continued to hold that post until the fourth Itō cabinet of 1900. In 1900 he dispatched troops to Peking to combat the Boxers and relieve the foreign legations that were under siege. At the same time he pressed for military expansion and adopted a conciliatory attitude toward the political parties.

In 1901 he formed the first Katsura cabinet, and though he was criticized for the inferior quality of the men who made it up, he succeeded in concluding the Anglo-Japanese alliance of 1902 and handling the problems that arose in Manchuria. He acted as prime minister throughout the Russo-Japanese War, which broke out in 1904, but resigned after the Hibiya riots that broke out in Tokyo in 1905 in protest to the Portsmouth Treaty that brought the war to a close. Around this time, it became increasingly clear that Japan had designs to take over Korea. In 1908 Katsura once more became prime minister and formed his second cabinet, and in 1910 he carried out the formal annexation of Korea. He also took steps to suppress the socialist movement, as seen in the arrests carried out in connection with the so-called lèse-majesté affair of 1910. In 1912, when pressure from the military brought about the downfall of the second Saionji cabinet, Katsura, while continuing to hold the post of home minister and head of the Board of Chamberlains, formed his third cabinet. But his attempts to form a political party of his own failed, and he faced attacks both from the older cliques in the government and the other political parties, who launched a large-scale popular movement known as the First National Movement to Protect the Constitution. As a result his cabinet fell in 1913, and he died the same year in a state of despondency. He was one of the outstanding military and political leaders to emerge under the guidance of Yamagata Aritomo.

Kawai Eijirō 河合榮治郎 (1891–1944)

Economist and social thinker of the Taishō and Shōwa periods; he was born in Tokyo. After graduating from the law course of Tokyo Imperial University, he entered the Ministry of Agriculture and Commerce, where he was assigned to make a survey of factory legislation. In 1920, when Tokyo University set up a separate department of economics, he became an assistant professor in the department. In 1922 he went to England for study, and after his return was promoted to the rank of professor, lecturing on social policy. In 1932 he went to Germany for study.

He was a liberal who advocated social democracy but opposed both Marxism and nationalism. In 1936 he spoke out openly against the so-called February 26 Incident, when a group of young army officers attempted to carry out a coup d'état, condemning it as an act of fascist violence. In 1938 he likewise spoke out against the proposal by General Araki Sadao, the minister of education, that the president of Tokyo University and other imperial universities should be selected by the government. In the same year his books came under criticism in the Upper House of the Diet, and eventually four works, including *Fashizumu hihan* ("Critique of Fascism"), were banned, and he himself was indicted. In 1939 Hiraga Yuzuru, the president of Tokyo University, ordered both Kawai and another professor named Hijikata Shigeyoshi to resign their positions because of their role as leaders of rival factions within the economics department. When Kawai's case was brought before the Supreme Court in 1943, he was found guilty and condemned to pay a fine. He was thereafter deprived of any means of expressing his opinions and died of illness before the conclusion of the Pacific War.

KAWAKAMI HAJIME 河上肇 (1879–1946)

Meiji, Taishō, and Shōwa period economist, social thinker, and Doctor of Law; he was born in Yamaguchi Prefecture. He graduated from the law course of Tokyo Imperial University in 1902 and the same year became a lecturer in the agricultural course of the university. In 1905 he published a work called *Shakai shugi hyōron* ("Critique of Socialism"), which appeared serially in the *Yomiuri Shimbun* under a pen name and attracted considerable attention. With the conclusion of the work, he resigned his teaching position. For a period of two months he threw himself into the "selfless love" movement but soon withdrew when he found himself in disagreement with the leader of the movement. He also worked as a reporter for the *Yomiuri Shimbun*, but resigned in 1907 and founded a magazine called *Nihon Keizai Zasshi*, in which he attacked the free trade views of Taguchi Ukichi and argued in favor of protectionism. In 1908 he became a lecturer at Kyoto Imperial University and the following year advanced to the rank of assistant professor. He spent the period 1913–15 studying in Europe and on his return to Japan became a full professor, lecturing on economics.

In 1916, he began publishing serially in the *Osaka Asahi Shimbun* a work of fiction entitled *Bimbō monogatari*, which dealt with the problems of poverty that existed beneath the surface of Japan's post-World War One prosperity. The work attracted a wide readership and made Kawakami the most renowned scholar of economics from a journalistic point of view. But because he sought a solution to the problems of poverty in a reform of the human spirit, he came under attack from Marxist-oriented economists. This led him to take a deeper interest in Marxism, and he was very quickly converted to its teachings. In 1919 he founded a private magazine devoted to the subject, entitled *Shakai Mondai Kenkyū*, which continued publication until 1930. In 1926, when the police stepped in to suppress a Marxist student organization at Kyoto University, Kawakami's house was searched, and in 1928 he resigned his position at the university. In 1929 he joined Ōyama Ikuo and others in forming the Rōnōtō (Labor Farmer Party), but the following year called for dissolution of the party and separated himself from it. From 1932 on, he became active in underground movements, and at the request of the Japan Communist Party translated the 1932 *Thèse* into Japanese. In the same year he became a regular member of the party. In 1933 he was arrested in Tokyo at the house where he was in hiding and was put in prison. He refused, however, to compromise his integrity as a scholar. He was released in 1937 and thereafter devoted himself to the writing of his autobiography, which was completed in 1944. He died of illness in Tokyo in 1946, a year after the conclusion of the Pacific War. The poem entitled "Greetings to Comrade Nosaka," which was carried in a number of newspapers, was his last work.

Kawate Bunjirō 川手文治郎 (1814–1883)

Religious leader of the late Edo and early Meiji periods and founder of Konkō-kyō; he is also known as Akasawa Bunji and Konkō Daijin. He was the son of a farm family of the district of Asaguchi in Bitchū Province. In 1825 he became the adopted heir of the Kawate family, another farm family in the neighborhood. In 1854, when he fell critically ill, a relative speaking in a state of divine possession announced that the illness was due to a curse inflicted by Konjin, a deity originally associated with the Chinese yin-yang system of cosmology. By swearing absolute obedience to the deity, Kawate was able to recover from the illness. In 1857 his younger brother became possessed by Konjin, and around 1858 Kawate himself became capable of hearing the words of the deity. In 1859 he handed over the management of family affairs to his third son and went into retirement.

On the twenty-first day of the tenth lunar month of the same year, he received a divine command to give up farming and devote his full time to transmitting the words of the deity, an event known as Rikkyō Shinden, or the "Divine Message to Found a Religion." Thereafter, Kawate entered upon the religious life. In his teachings, the deity Konjin, who had previously been feared as a wrathful deity, is transformed into a god of love. Kawate also placed emphasis upon a life of diligence and hard work and attempted to do away with superstition. He attracted a wide following, mainly among the farm population of the Okayama area, where he was born, and by Meiji times his teachings had spread all over the country. In 1900, some years after Kawate's death, his teachings, known as Konkō-kyō, were recognized as a sect of Neo- or Sectarian Shinto. Kawate's only written work is his autobiography entitled *Konkō daijin-kaku*, which appeared in 1874.

KAZUNOMIYA 和宮 (1846–1877)

An imperial princess, who went by the name of Princess Chikako, eighth daughter of Emperor Ninkō, younger half-sister of Emperor Kōmei, and wife of the fourteenth Edo period shogun Tokugawa Iemochi; after Iemochi's death in 1866, she became a Buddhist nun with the religious name Seikan'in-no-miya. In 1860, the shogunate, as a means of strengthening ties between it and the imperial court, had proposed a marriage alliance between the emperor's younger sister and Tokugawa Iemochi, who had just become shogun. The proposal, it was said, had originally been planned by the chief shogunate official Ii Naosuke, who was assassinated the same year outside the Sakurada Gate of Edo Castle.

The princess had already become engaged to the imperial prince Arisugawa-no-miya Taruhito in 1851, and Emperor Kōmei accordingly refused the request. The shogunate, however, persisted in its petition, while at court Iwakura Tomomi, a member of the court nobility, acted as mediator in the negotiations. When the shogunate, as part of the arrangement, promised to take action to drive foreign traders out of the country, the emperor finally gave his consent, and Princess Kazunomiya was persuaded to agree as well. In 1861 she left Kyoto for Edo and the following year was married. In 1866, however, her husband, Iemochi, died of illness at Osaka Castle while undertaking an expedition to punish the domain of Chōshū for insubordination. The following year the princess's elder brother, Emperor Kōmei, also died. In 1868, when the shogunate was abolished and power was restored to the throne, the princess played an important role in pleading with the court for lenient treatment of the Tokugawa family, persuading the imperial forces to refrain from attacking Edo Castle and in other ways exerting herself on behalf of her late husband's relatives. During the years 1869–74 she resided in Kyoto, but later returned to Tokyo and died in Hakone, where she had gone for her health. She was noted for her skill in calligraphy and traditional Japanese style poetry.

KIDO KŌICHI 木戸幸一 (1889–1977)

Statesman of the Taishō and Shōwa periods; he held the title of marquis. He was born in Tokyo, the grandson of the eminent Meiji period statesman Kido Takayoshi. After attending the Peers' School, he entered the law department of Kyoto Imperial University in 1911, specializing in political science. While in college he developed an interest in economics and was influenced by the Marxist economist Kawakami Hajime, at that time a professor of Kyoto University. After his graduation in 1915, Kido entered the Ministry of Agriculture and Commerce and later became a member of the Upper House of the Diet. In 1925, when the Ministry of Agriculture and Commerce was discontinued, he entered the newly established Ministry of Commerce and Industry. At the recommendation of Konoe Fumimaro and others, he was appointed chief secretary to the home minister. Thereafter he was active in court affairs, being on close terms with the secretaries of Konoe Fumimaro, Harada Kumao, and the elder statesman Saionji Kimmochi, and was said to have had considerable influence with Saionji.

After heading the Sōchitsuryō, one of the divisions of the Department of the Imperial Household, he in 1937 became minister of education in the first Konoe Fumimaro cabinet; the following year he became welfare minister. In 1939 he became minister of education in the Hiranuma Kiichirō cabinet. With the fall of the Hiranuma cabinet in the same year, he was out of public office for a time, but in 1940, at the recommendation of Saionji, replaced Yuasa Kurahei as home minister because of the latter's resignation due to illness. In the various governmental changes and crises that followed, he headed the conference of senior statesmen and continued to serve as home minister under a succession of prime ministers until the abolition of the post of home minister in 1945. During this period he worked in close cooperation with the right-wing forces and militarists, supporting the overthrow of the pro-British and American cabinet of Yonai Mitsumasa and playing an important role in the formation of the Tōjō Hideki cabinet. After the end of the Pacific War, he was tried as an A-class war criminal by the International Military Tribunal for the Far East and was condemned to life imprisonment. In 1953 he was granted provisional release because of illness.

Kido Takayoshi 木戸孝允 (1833–1877)

Statesman of the late Edo and early Meiji periods; he was born in the domain of Chōshū. He was originally named Katsura Kogorō, but was later adopted into the Kido family; he used the given name Jun'ichirō, and the name Takayoshi is sometimes read Kōin. He studied Chinese, swordsmanship, and horsemanship, and in 1849 entered a private school in the domain run by the Confucian scholar Yoshida Shōin. In 1852 he went to Edo and perfected his study of swordsmanship under Saitō Yakurō, later becoming director of Saitō's school. He made friends among the samurai of the domain of Mito, many of whom supported the *sonnō-jōi* movement, which called for restoration of power to the emperor and expulsion of the foreigners. He studied Western style military science under Egawa Tarōzaemon and came in contact with Katsu Kaishū.

Beginning in 1858, he served in the Yūbikan, a school for the civil and military training of samurai of the domain of Chōshū who were stationed in Edo, helping to develop a group of young men who were ardent supporters of the throne. In 1862 he accompanied his lord, Mōri Takachika, daimyo of the domain of Chōshū, on a journey to Kyoto, working to drum up support for the *sonnō-jōi* movement and to make it the official policy of the Chōshū domain. In 1863, however, a coup d'état was carried out in Kyoto by his rivals of the *kōbu-gattai* faction, which favored a strengthening of relations between the court and the shogunate through a marriage alliance. As a result, the Chōshū forces were expelled from the capital. Kido remained in Kyoto in order to devote himself to the interests of the state, though his life was endangered any number of times.

In 1865 he returned to Shimonoseki in Chōshū. When the shogunate sent a punitive expedition against Chōshū, Kido worked with Ōmura Masujirō, the commander of the Chōshū forces, to employ Dutch military techniques, which contributed to the defeat of the shogunate army. Meanwhile, in 1866, Kido and others of Chōshū, through the intervention of Sakamoto Ryōma, made peace with the fief's former enemy, the domain of Satsuma, and joined the Satsuma leaders Saigō Takamori and Ōkubo Toshimichi in concluding a secret alliance to overthrow the shogunate.

In 1867 Kido persuaded the lord of Chōshū to adopt his views and in other ways did all he could to bring about a restoration of power to the emperor. He also promised Ōkubo to dispatch Chōshū troops to assist in overthrowing the shogunate, taking a leading role in events that led to the Meiji Restoration. As a result, he came in time to be referred to, along with Saigō and Ōkubo, as one of the "three heroes" of the Restoration. He also participated in the drafting of the five-article Charter Oath, promulgated in 1868, which laid down the principles for the new Meiji government.

In 1868 he became a *chōshi* (domain representative) in the Dajōkan, or Council of State, and advisor to the office of the governor (*sōsai*), taking a place beside Ōkubo as one of the key figures in the central government and working to promote the modernization of Japan through the abolition of the feudal system and the opening of the country. In 1869 he persuaded the lords of several of the most powerful domains to voluntarily return their fiefs to the emperor and in 1871 he laid the theoretical foundation for the abolishment of the feudal land system and the establishment of prefectures and worked to carry out these measures.

Earlier, in 1869, he had become a member of the Taishōin, an office for handling suggestions from the public, and had advocated an expedition against Korea as a means of unifying public sentiment in Japan. In 1870 he became a councilor of state and the following year accompanied Iwakura Tomomi on his mission to Europe and the United States as vice-minister plenipotentiary. The mission spent two years abroad, conducting preliminary negotiations for revision of Japan's treaties with the foreign powers. After returning to Japan in 1873, he urged, on the basis of his experience in Europe and America, that the government draw up detailed rules and regulations for its procedures. He also advised that priority be given to domestic problems and dismissed Saigō Takamori's proposal for an expedition against Korea as rash. In 1874 he was simultaneously appointed minister of education and minister of the interior, but resigned four months later because he opposed Ōkubo Toshimichi's action in sending troops to Taiwan. He was later appointed to a position in the Imperial Household Ministry.

For a time, Kido returned to his home in the former domain of Chōshū. In 1875, he attended the so-called Osaka Conference, a meeting between government leaders and men like Kido who had resigned from government positions in dissatisfaction. The aim was to overcome the unease and ill feeling that had arisen over the controversies concerning Korea, Taiwan, the establishment of a national assembly, and other rapid changes that had taken place on the political scene. The government leaders agreed to establish a system whereby the executive, legislative, and judiciary powers would be clearly separated, setting up a Senate (Genrōin) and Supreme Court (Daishin-in) in addition to the Council of State, and establishing an assembly of provincial officials. On these conditions, Kido, Itagaki Taisuke, and the others agreed to return to government service, Kido resuming his position as councilor of state. Later the emperor duly handed down an edict instructing that the changes in government be carried out. The same year, Kido became head of the Assembly of Provincial Officials, but he found himself in opposition to Ōkubo and Ōkuma over the question of land tax reform, and in 1876 he resigned his post as councilor of state. He later became a cabinet advisor and an official in the Imperial Household Ministry, devoting himself to the study of such questions as providing financial support for the imperial family and stipends for the aristocracy and setting up a system of noble ranks. He died of illness in 1877, in the midst of the Seinan civil war.

He was one of the most important theorists among the founders of the Meiji government, and, in contrast to the bureaucratic attitude of Ōkubo Toshimichi, was of an open and liberal mind. In spite of poor health, he was active in many fields of endeavor, and the progressive political approach he displayed in arguing for the early establishment of a national assembly has won him high esteem among scholars of political science. The year after his death, his son was made a member of the nobility and in 1884 received the title of marquis.

Kimura Hisashi 木村榮 (1870–1943)

Astronomer of the Meiji, Taishō, and Shōwa periods; he was born in Ishikawa Prefecture. In 1892 he completed the astronomical course of Tokyo Imperial University and entered graduate school to continue his studies. Studying under Tanakadate Aikitsu and others, he became aware that changes in the lattitude of the earth's axis constituted an important problem in the field of geodesy and accordingly devoted himself to the study of such changes. As a part of a worldwide effort to explore such problems, an International Latitude Observatory was founded in 1899 in Mizusawa in Iwate Prefecture, and Kimura was appointed to head it. In 1902, in addition to the two components of variation affecting changes of latitude that were previously known, he succeeded in discovering a third component of variation called the Z-term, which as a result became known as Kimura's Z-term. This was the first time that a Japanese had contributed to international scientific research and indicated that Japanese scientific investigations were ready to take their place beside those of the rest of the world. In 1911 Kimura was among the recipients in the first awarding of prizes by the Imperial Academy. In 1922, when an international conference selected the Mizusawa Observatory as the headquarters for its activities, Kimura became director of the headquarters and acted as an international leader in the study of the latitude of the earth's axis. In 1937 he became a recipient of the first Cultural Medal. In 1941 he retired from his position as head of the observatory, which he had held for forty-three years, but continued as before to devote himself to latitude studies.

Kinoshita Naoe 木下尙江 (1869–1937)

Meiji, Taishō, and Shōwa period thinker and novelist; he was born in the area of present-day Nagano Prefecture, the son of a samurai of the domain of Matsumoto. After graduating from Tokyo Semmon Gakkō, the forerunner of Waseda University, he returned to his home, where he became a convert to Christianity. He worked as a newspaper reporter and lawyer and was put in prison for his activities in the universal suffrage movement. He went to Tokyo in 1899, where he became a reporter for the *Mainichi Shimbun.* He was active in the movement to assist the victims of the Ashio Mine pollution and to do away with legalized prostitution and became a member of the Socialist League. In 1901 he participated in the founding of the Shakai Minshutō (Social Democratic Party), which was banned immediately after it was formed.

With the outbreak of the Russo-Japanese War in 1904, he joined Kōtoku Shūsui and other members of the Heiminsha in speaking out against the war. After the newspaper *Heimin Shimbun* had been forced by government pressure to suspend publication, he joined Ishikawa Sanshirō and others in publishing a magazine called *Shinkigen* that advocated Christian socialism. Meanwhile, he was active as a writer, producing *Hi no hashira* and *Ryōjin no jihaku,* antiwar novels that are regarded as among the best works of Meiji period socialist literature. In 1906, after the conclusion of the Russo-Japanese War, he became a member of the Japan Socialist Party, but withdrew almost immediately. Troubled by conflicts between the socialist movement and his religious beliefs, he separated himself from the movement and retired to the mountains in Ikaho, where he devoted himself to the writing of his autobiography, entitled *Zange,* and other works. He abandoned Christianity and moved increasingly in the direction of Buddhism, in 1910 taking up the practice of Okada-style sitting in meditation.

Kishi Nobusuke 岸信介 (1896–)

Shōwa period bureaucrat and political leader; his family name was originally Satō, the former prime minister Satō Eisaku being his younger brother. While still a student in the law course of Tokyo Imperial University, he was strongly influenced by Uesugi Shinkichi, a scholar of constitutional systems and leader of a nationalistic organization. He graduated in 1920 and entered the Ministry of Agriculture and Commerce. In 1936 he was transferred to duty in Manchuria, where he helped to further plans for industrial development. He soon attracted attention as one of the most efficient bureaucrats in Manchuria. In 1940 he was recalled to Japan and became vice-minister of commerce and industry. In 1941 he was appointed minister of commerce and industry in the Tōjō Hideki cabinet, being charged with the supervision of Japan's wartime economy. Tōjō, when he lost the support of the powerful figures in the political world, demanded the resignation of his cabinet ministers. But Kishi refused to comply, and in doing so helped to bring about the fall of the Tōjō cabinet in 1944.

After the war, he was arrested on suspicion of being an A-class war criminal, but was released in 1948. In 1952 he was elected to the Lower House of the Diet and returned to political life. He acted as chairman of the Liberal Party's Constitutional Survey Committee and, as such, advocated revision of the constitution and rearmament for Japan. After the merger of the Liberals and Democrats in 1956, Ishibashi Tanzan won out by a small margin over Kishi to become leader of the Liberal Democratic Party, and Kishi instead became minister of foreign affairs in the Ishibashi cabinet. Ishibashi resigned shortly after because of poor health, and in 1957 Kishi formed his own cabinet, followed by a second cabinet in 1958. In 1960, amidst great popular opposition concerning the revision of the Security Treaty, the newly concluded Japan-American Treaty of Mutual Security and Cooperation went into effect, and Kishi resigned immediately after. In the years since, he has remained an important figure in the Liberal Party, leading the so-called "hawk" faction and supporting the strongly anti-Communist stands of the Taiwan and South Korean governments.

Kita Ikki 北一輝 (1883–1937)

Leader of the movement for national socialism during the Taishō and Shōwa periods. He was born in Sado in Niigata Prefecture; his original given name was Terujirō. He attended Waseda University as an auditor, where he took an interest in evolutionary and socialist thought. In 1906 he published at his own expense a work entitled *Kokutai oyobi junsei shakai shugi* ("National Polity and Pure Socialism"), but the book was banned by the government. He became friendly with Kōtoku Shūsui, Sakai Toshihiko, and other socialist thinkers associated with the Heiminsha. He also became a member of the Chinese revolutionary group known as the League of Common Alliance and was friendly with Sung Chiao-jen and others of its leaders. When the Chinese Revolution broke out in 1911, he went to China and attempted to take part in it, but met with failure. Following the assassination of Sung Chiao-jen, he was ordered out of the country because of his attempts to make public the true facts of Sung's death.

After returning to Japan, he wrote an account of the revolution based upon his own experiences, which he published in 1915 under the title *Shina kakumei gaishi* ("Unofficial History of the Chinese Revolution"). In the preface to this work, he outlined the basic principles of his own concept of

Asian nationalism. In 1916 he went to China a second time, but after experiencing the May Fourth Movement of 1919 and other expressions of anti-Japanese sentiment, he returned home. Believing that Japan would in time go through a revolution of its own, he thereafter concentrated his attention upon the encouragement of national reforms within Japan. His experiences in China had taught him the importance of military power in carrying out a revolution, and therefore, after his return to Japan in 1919, he cultivated connections with the military. Meanwhile, a work that he had written in Shanghai entitled *Nihon kaizō hōan taikō* ("An Outline Plan for the Reconstruction of Japan") and that set forth the steps to be taken to put into effect his principles of Asian nationalism, began to attract attention and in time became the virtual Bible of those young army officers who advocated the carrying out of a "Shōwa Restoration."

In 1920 he joined the Yūzonsha, a right-wing society founded by Ōkawa Shūmei and others and became one of the leading theorists of the fascist movement. At the same time he maintained relations with the *zaibatsu*, receiving financial contributions from Ikeda Shigeaki, Kuhara Fusanosuke, and other leaders in the business world. He also took part in muckraking activities in connection with various political and financial scandals of the time. The ideas set forth in his *Plan for the Reconstruction of Japan* fitted well with the thinking of many persons in the early Shōwa era and in particular exercised a profound influence upon many of the younger officers of the army. Eventually they formed the ideological background for the February 26 incident of 1936, an abortive attempt at a coup d'état by a group of such officers that resulted in the assassination or injury of a number of prominent officials. Kita was arrested as a behind-the-scene backer of the affair and the following year was executed.

KITAZATO SHIBASABURŌ 北里柴三郎 (1852–1931)

Bacteriologist of the Meiji, Taishō, and early Shōwa periods; he held the title of baron. He was born in what later became Kumamoto Prefecture in Kyushu. After attending the Jishūkan, a school operated by the fief to which he belonged, he entered Kumamoto Medical School in 1871, studying under a Dutch teacher named C. J. van Mansvelt. In 1874, when Mansvert left the school, Kitazato went to Tokyo and the following year entered the Tokyo Medical School (later the medical department of Tokyo Imperial University). On completing the course in 1883, he took a position in the Health Bureau of the Ministry of Internal Affairs. In 1885 he went to Germany to continue his education, studying under Robert Koch, the founder of the science of bacteriology, devoting himself to research in that field. During his stay in Germany, he succeeded in producing a pure culture of tetanus bacilli and later discovered a method of serotherapy for the treatment of tetanus, accomplishments that won worldwide recognition in medical circles.

He returned to Japan in 1892 and urged the establishment of a research center for infectious diseases, but his pleas were unheeded. The prominent educator and intellectual leader Fukuzawa Yukichi came immediately to his aid, and through the help of the latter Kitazato was able in the same year to establish the Infectious Disease Research Center in Shiba Park in Tokyo, with himself as director, introducing the study of bacteriology and serology to Japan. In 1894, when plague broke out in Hong Kong, he was sent to the area to study the disease. Shiga Kiyoshi, one of the members of the research center working under his direction, succeeding in isolating the dysentery bacillus, and others of his group made similar important contributions.

In 1899 the research center was placed under the control of the Ministry of Internal Affairs, but Kitazato continued in the post of director. In 1914, when the research center became attached to Tokyo Imperial University, he resigned and set up his own research center, called the Kitazato Research Center. In 1917, when Keiō University established a medical department, he headed it, continuing to be active in medical education until 1928 and introducing his own particular methods of research. In addition, he worked vigorously through the Private Sanitary Association of Japan, founded in 1883, to spread a knowledge of sanitary methods among the populace as a whole. He served as chief director of the Japan Society for the Prevention of Tuberculosis; and in 1909, when the Saiseikai, an imperially sponsored organization for medical aid was established, he acted as a member of the board of trustees, in these and other ways making an important contribution to the social welfare of the nation. In cooperation with Emile von Behring he developed a serum for diphtheria and conducted research on tuberculosis. In 1906 he became a member of the Imperial Academy, in 1917 a member of the House of Peers in the Diet, and in 1923 head of the Japan Medical Association; the following year he received the title of baron.

Kiyoura Keigo 清浦奎吾 (1850–1942)

Bureaucrat and statesman of the Meiji and Taishō periods; he held the title of count. He was born in the district of Kamoto in the province of Higo, present-day Kumamoto Prefecture, the fifth son of Ōkubo Ryōshi, a Buddhist priest who headed a local temple. His childhood name was Fujaku. Later he was adopted into the Kiyoura family. As a child he studied Chinese, and in 1865 entered the Kangien, a private school in Hita in the neighboring province of Bungo (present-day Ōita Prefecture) founded by a poet and scholar of Chinese named Hirose Tansō (1782–1856). He remained there until 1870 and thereafter for a time opened a private school of his own in Kumamoto. In 1872 he went to Tokyo and, through the introduction of the governor of Saitama Prefecture, whom he had earlier known when the latter was governor of Hita, he became a member of the prefectural administration and principal of an elementary school.

In 1876 he entered the Ministry of Justice of the central government, being engaged in the formulation of a code of criminal law (promulgated in 1880) and the handling of criminal lawsuits.

In his later years he remarked that the training in law which he received at this time under Gustave Boissonade, a French lawyer who had been appointed to draft a criminal code for the Ministry of Justice, constituted, along with his years at the Kangien, one of the most formative experiences of his life. In 1881 he was transferred to the legal organ called the Sanjiin, where his talents were soon recognized by the chairman, Yamagata Aritomo. In 1884 he became head of the Bureau of Police Protection in the Ministry of Home Affairs, which at this time was headed by Yamagata; he held this post for a total of seven years. During this period, he distinguished himself in formulating the Peace Preservation Regulations and other legal measures and in modernizing the police system and he was also active in prison reform. Through these activities, he won the profound confidence of Yamagata and came to be regarded as one of the group of bureaucrat-statesmen directly allied with Yamagata. In 1891 he was selected to be a member of the Upper House of the Diet and the same year embarked on a trip abroad.

In 1898 he became minister of justice in the second Yamagata cabinet. In the first Katsura cabinet, which lasted from 1901 to 1906, he served as minister of justice, then minister of justice and minister of agriculture and commerce, and finally, in 1905, as minister of agriculture and commerce and minister of home affairs. In 1906 he became an advisor to the Privy Council. In 1914, after the fall of the Yamamoto cabinet, he attempted to form a cabinet of his own, but failed because he could get no one to fill the post of naval minister. In 1917 he became vice-chairman of the Privy Council and in 1922, chairman. In 1924, after the resignation of the second Yamamoto cabinet, he became prime minister and formed his own cabinet, but because it was made up of a special group of bureaucrats drawn mainly from the Upper

House of the Diet, and because the Seiyūhontō was recognized as the only progovernment party in the Lower House of the Diet, it aroused much opposition. The Kenseikai, Seiyūkai, and Kakushinkai banded together to carry out the so-called Constitution Protection Movement, and the Kiyoura cabinet was forced to resign after only half a year in power. Kiyoura was thereafter granted the privileges of his former posts and in 1941 was one of the high officials who participated in the council that recommended the formation of the Tōjō cabinet.

Kiyozawa Manshi 清澤滿之 (1863–1903)

Priest of the Meiji period and reformer of the Jōdo Shin sect of Buddhism; he was born in Nagoya, the son of an *ashigaru* (low-ranking samurai). In 1878 he became a priest in the Ōtani branch of the Jōdo Shin sect and entered Ikuei Kyōkō, the school attached to Higashi Hongan-ji in Kyoto. In 1882 he went to Tokyo for further study, entering the preparatory school for Tokyo University. The following year he entered the philosophy course of the university, where he studied under the American professor Ernest Fenollosa. He graduated in 1887, and in 1888 became principal of Kyoto Prefecture Middle School. At the same time he married Kiyozawa Yasuko, adopting his wife's family name, and became head of a temple called Saihō-ji in Mikawa Ōhama in Aichi Prefecture. In 1890 he resigned his position as principal of the middle school and entered upon a life of religious austerities, determined to devote himself to reforming the educational facilities of his sect.

Up to this time he had been active as a philosopher of religion, his principal ideas being summed up in a work entitled *Shūkyō tetsugaku gaikotsu*. The work, which makes a critical use of Hegelian dialectic to define the basic ideas of Buddhist philosophy, was translated into English and won favorable notice at the World Religious Conference in Chicago in 1893. In 1894 he resigned his academic position as a result of tuberculosis and moved to Suma in Hyōgo Prefecture to convalesce. At this time he devoted himself to contemplation of the inner meaning of faith, writing a work entitled *Zaishō zange-roku*. The following year he came out of retirement and, frustrated in his attempts to carry out educational reforms, determined to work for reform of the Jōdo Shin sect as a whole. To effect this, he joined with like-minded friends in 1896 in founding an organization to publish a magazine called *Kyōkai Jigen*. His aim was to introduce democratic methods in the management of the religious order, but he encountered bitter opposition and was expelled from his sect in 1897. He became convinced that institutional reform was less pressing than the need for the establishment of a sound inner spirit. In 1899, after the order expelling him from the sect had been rescinded, he went to Tokyo to supervise Shinshū University run by the Jōdo Shin sect. In 1900 he joined with his disciples Tada Kanae, Akegarasu Haya, and Sasaki Gesshō in founding a religious organization called the Kōkōdō and the following year began publication of a magazine entitled *Seishinkai*. The numerous articles that he published in it represent his efforts to promote spiritual concerns and were later collected in the volumes entitled *Seishin shugi* and *Seishin kōwa*.

In the past, followers of the Jōdo Shin sect had tended to look upon their religion as somethings concerning the family as a whole. Kiyozawa's aim was to induce believers to reexamine their faith critically in terms of modern ways of thought and personal awareness and to reaffirm it as a matter of individual conviction. His efforts led him to attach renewed importance to the Agama sutras of early Indian Buddhism and the *Tannishō* of Shinran, and he played an important role in drawing attention to these texts. Among his disciples were Soga Ryōshin and Kaneko Taiei, both leaders in the religious world of modern Japan.

Kodama Gentarō 兒玉源太郎 (1852–1906)

Meiji period military leader; he held the title of baron. Born in the fief of Tokuyama, he gained his first military experience as a soldier in a division in the imperial forces, which marched east during the Boshin War in 1868. After the Restoration, he entered the army and took part in the campaigns to put down the uprising of disaffected samurai in Saga, of the Simpūren in Kumamoto, and the rebellion led by Saigō Takamori in Kagoshima. In 1885 he became the first bureau chief in the General Staff Office, and with a German major, Klemens Wilhelm Jakob Meckel, who was employed as an advisor, worked to modernize the Japanese army system. In 1891 he became head of the Military Staff College and visited Europe to observe Western methods of military training. During the Sino-Japanese War, he became chief of staff of the imperial headquarters in Japan, and after the war advanced to the rank of lieutenant general.

In 1889 he became governor-general of Taiwan and became active in colonial affairs. Through the recommendation of Katsura Tarō he was appointed army minister in the fourth Itō Hirobumi cabinet (1900–02) and in the Katsura cabinet also held the posts of minister of home affairs and minister of education. During the Russo-Japanese War he advanced to the rank of general and, as chief of staff of the Manchurian Army, took part in the engagements at Liao-yang, Sha-ho, and Mukden and helped to lead the Japanese forces to victory. In 1906 he became chief of staff. At the same time, as head of the committee for the establishment of the South Manchurian Railway, he became involved in Japanese expansion in Manchuria, but died of illness shortly after. He was highly trusted by Emperor Meiji and was noted for his resourcefulness.

Koiso Kuniaki 小磯國昭 (1880–1950)

Army leader and statesman of the Taishō and Shōwa periods, he was the son of a samurai family of Yamagata Prefecture. He graduated from the Yamagata Middle School, Military Academy, and Military Staff College and served in the Russo-Japanese War of 1904–05 as a lieutenant. During the years from 1915 to 1917 he was a member of the General Staff Office, being assigned to handle intelligence strategy. He lent assistance to the former ruling family of the Ch'ing dynasty in China and devised plans for the Manchurian and Mongolian independence movement. In 1922 he advanced to the rank of colonel and was sent to Europe to study the methods of total warfare that had been employed in the First World War. He returned to Japan the following year and in 1926 he became an instructor in the Military Staff College. In 1930 he became head of the Bureau of Army Affairs in the War Ministry and in 1931 advanced to the rank of lieutenant general. He was one of the leaders in the plot to carry out a coup d'état in March of the same year, though the plot was not put into execution.

In 1932 he became vice-minister of war, serving under War Minister Araki Sadao, and later served as chief of staff of the Kwantung Army, commander of the Fifth Division at Hiroshima, and commander of the Chosen Army. He entered the reserve in 1938, and in 1939–40 served as minister of overseas affairs in the Hiranuma and Yonai cabinets. In 1942, after the outbreak of the Pacific War, he was appointed governor-general of Chosen (Korea). In 1944, after the resignation of the Tōjō cabinet, he became prime minister through the cooperation of Yonai Mitsumasa and was ordered to form a new cabinet. He attempted to reorganize the direction of the war effort and to improve Japan's fortunes, but with the defeat of the Japanese forces in the Philippines, the collapse of efforts to bring about a peaceful settlement with China, and the differences of opinion between himself and Foreign Minister Shigemitsu Mamoru, he and his cabinet were obliged to resign. After the conclusion of the war, he was tried by the International Military Tribunal for the Far East as a first-class war criminal and was sentenced to life imprisonment. He died of illness in prison.

Kojima Korekata (Iken) 児島惟謙 (1837–1908)

Judicial official of the Meiji period; he was the son of a samurai of the domain of Uwajima in Shikoku. His family name was originally Kaneko, which was later changed to Ogata and then to Kojima. In the troubled times at the end of the Edo period he left his domain without official permission and took part in the movement to overthrow the shogunate. After the Meiji Restoration in 1868, he was employed in the new government, serving as a local official in Niigata Prefecture and other areas. In 1871, when the Ministry of Justice was established, he became attached to it, serving as a judge in various local courts and later as a court president.

In 1891, when the Daishin'in (Supreme Court) was established, he was appointed to head it, but he had only been in this position for a few days when the so-called Ōtsu Incident occurred. At this time the Russian crown prince Nicolai Alexandrovitch (later Nicolai II) was visiting Japan, and when passing through the town of Ōtsu on the west shore of Lake Biwa, he was attacked and wounded by a police officer named Tsuda Sanzō. The government, which was headed at this time by Matsukata Masayoshi and his cabinet, as well as the *genrō* (elder statesmen), fearful of the effect the incident would have on relations with Russia, wanted to have the case handled in the same way as though Tsuda had attacked a member of the Japanese imperial family, which would have resulted in the death penalty for him. In spite of the strong pressure on him, however, Kojima took the position that the charges against Tsuda should be the same as those for attempted murder of an ordinary citizen. He succeeded in persuading the judges in charge of the case of the rightness of this view, and when Tsuda was tried in the Ōtsu district court by a special session of the Supreme Court, he was so charged and sentenced to life imprisonment. Kojima's action in guarding the independence of the judicature constituted an event of major importance in Japanese legal and political history, and he came in later times to be referred to as the "patron deity" of Japanese law.

About a year after the conclusion of the Ōtsu Incident, six Supreme Court judges, including Kojima, were accused of gambling at the card game known as *hanafuda* and were advised by the government that their resignations would be in order. Kojima denied the accusation and submitted himself to a disciplinary trial. The charges against him were dismissed because of lack of evidence, but at the urging of Minister of Justice Yamagata Aritomo and others, he agreed to accept moral responsibility for the affair and in 1892 resigned his position in the Supreme Court. In 1894 he became a member of the Upper House of the Diet and in 1898 he was elected to the Lower House. He became a member of the Upper House once more in 1905.

Komura Jutarō 小村壽太郎 (1855–1911)

Diplomat of the Meiji period; he held the title of marquis. He was born in the small fief of Obi in Kyushu and was chosen by the fief to be sent to the capital, where in 1874 he graduated from what was later to become the law department of Tokyo Imperial University. He then went to America and entered the law school at Harvard, from which he graduated in 1878. In 1880 he entered the Ministry of Justice and two years later became a Supreme Court judge. In 1884 he transferred to the Ministry of Foreign Affairs, working in the translation bureau. After a period of relative obscurity, his abilities were recognized by Minister of Foreign Affairs Mutsu Munemitsu and in 1893 he became first secretary in the Japanese legation in China. On the eve of the Sino-Japanese War, he carried on negotiations with the Chinese government as chargé d'affaires, at the same time laboring to convince the legations of the other powers in Peking that hostilities between Japan and China could not be avoided. He returned to Japan when the actual fighting began and became head of the Bureau of Political Affairs.

With the assassination of Queen Min in Korea in 1895, he was sent to Korea as a minister without portfolio and remained there as the Japanese minister. After the king of Korea transferred his residence to the Russian embassy, Komura drew up the so-called Komura-Weber Agreement, or the Russo-Japanese Agreement, on Korean affairs in 1896. After returning to Japan he became vice-minister of foreign affairs. In 1898 he became minister plenipotentiary to the United States and in 1900 minister to Sweden and Russia. During the Boxer Rebellion, he kept the Japanese government carefully informed on Russia's role in the events and after the end of the rebellion he was sent to Peking as envoy extraordinary and minister plenipotentiary to sign the final settlement.

He was an advocate of the policy of Japanese expansion on the continent and favored a warlike attitude. After becoming foreign minister in the Katsura Tarō cabinet in 1901, he strongly opposed the Russian occupation of Manchuria. At the same time he cultivated close ties with England and negotiated an agreement between Britain and Japan, known as the Anglo-Japanese Alliance, concerning their joint attitude toward Russia's policies. With the outbreak of the Russo-Japanese War, he was active on the diplomatic front and at the same time negotiated an agreement with Korea that strengthened Japan's dominance over that country. He participated in the peace conference at Portsmouth as a plenipotentiary, negotiating with the Russian representative Sergei Yulievich Vitte, and although he was unable to obtain agreement to all his demands, signed the Treaty of Portsmouth on behalf of Japan. After his return to Japan, he negotiated a treaty and agreement between Japan and China that laid the foundation for Japanese dominance in Manchuria. In addition, declaring invalid the Katsura-Harimann Memo, he took over control of the South Manchurian Railway. In 1906 he was appointed ambassador to England and in 1908 became foreign minister once more in the second Katsura cabinet. He was also active in the movement to restore tariff autonomy to Japan, the negotiation of an accord between Japan and Russia, and the Japanese annexation of Korea.

KONOE FUMIMARO 近衛文麿 (1891–1945)

Political leader of the Shōwa period; he held the title of duke (prince). He was born in Kyoto, the eldest son of one of the most distinguished families of the court nobility, which was descended from the Fujiwara family and also had close connections with the imperial family. His father, Konoe Atsumaro (1863–1904), was head of the Peers' School, president of the Upper House of the Diet, and a proponent of close cooperation between Japan and the other nations of Asia. He favored a firm policy with regard to Russia, but died just before the outbreak of the Russo-Japanese War.

Fumimaro, after completing the middle school course of the Peers' School, attended the First High School and then entered the philosophy course of Tokyo Imperial University. He later transferred to the law course of Kyoto Imperial University in order to be able to study under the economist Kawakami Hajime, whom he admired. At Kyoto University, he also came under the influence of the philosopher Nishida Kitarō. In 1916, while still a student, he was given a seat in the Upper House of the Diet because of his title of *kōshaku* (duke or prince). He graduated the following year, and for a time held a nominal post in the Ministry of Home Affairs. In 1918 he published in the magazine *Nihon oyobi Nihonjin* an article entitled *Ei-Bei hon'i no heiwa shugi o haisu* ("Criticism of British and American Style Pacifism"). In it, he attacked Britain and America for their economic imperialism and called for an end to colonialism and racial discrimination on the part of white people against the yellow race. These were principles that he continued to advocate over the years, culminating in his call in 1938 for a "New Order" in eastern Asia.

In 1919 he attended the Versailles Peace Conference as a member of the Japanese delegation headed by Saionji Kimmochi. While in Shanghai on the way to Europe, he met Sun Yat-sen, the leader of the Chinese revolution, and on the way back from the conference, he made an inspection tour of Europe and America. In 1921, after his return to Japan, he joined Mori Kaku of the Seiyūkai in organizing an association for the study of constitutions and advocated reform of the regulations pertaining to the Upper House of the Diet. In 1922, he became vice-president of the Tōa Dōbunkai, a culture organization with political overtones founded by his father (he became president in 1936). In 1926, he was appointed head of the school operated by the organization, the Tōa Dōbun Shoin. Meanwhile, in the Upper House of the Diet, he was appointed in 1922 to the most influential study committee in the Upper House and became a standing member. He left the committee in 1927, however, and instead formed an organization of the upper nobility called the Kayōkai, (Tuesday Society). In 1931 he became vice-president of the Upper House, and in 1933 president. During this period, he was in contact with various military and right-wing factions that advocated a program of reform and came to be regarded as a highly promising figure on the political scene. The elder statesman Saionji Kimmochi, in particular, was said to have held great expectations of him.

In 1936, following the attack on high government officials known as the February 26 Incident, he was recommended to the post of prime minister, but steadfastly refused appointment. In 1937, however, after the Hayashi cabinet fell as a result of defeat in the general election, he accepted the post and formed his first cabinet. A month later occurred the Marco Polo Bridge incident, which marked the beginning of prolonged hostilities between Japan and China, and though Konoe attempted to prevent the fighting from spreading, he was unsuccessful. In 1938 he announced that he would no longer deal with the Chiang Kai-shek government, a move that in effect cut off the possibility of a peaceful settlement and all but insured the continuation of the Sino-Japanese conflict. In 1939 Konoe and his cabinet resigned. He was replaced as prime minister by Hiranuma Kiichirō, while he himself became president of the Privy Council. In 1940 he played a central role in the movement to do away with political parties. He became prime minister once more, forming his second cabinet, and at the same time recommended a reform of the political system. As a result, all political parties were disbanded and replaced by the Taisei Yokusankai (Imperial Rule Assistance Association), of which Konoe was the president.

On the diplomatic front, he strengthened Japan's ties with the Axis nations, his Foreign Minister Matsuoka Yōsuke concluding the Tripartite Pact with Germany and Italy. Developments in Japanese-American relations, however, forced the Konoe cabinet to resign en masse, and Matsuoka withdrew from the scene. In 1941 Konoe set up his third cabinet and proposed a personal meeting with President Roosevelt in order to find some solution to Japanese-American differences, but his efforts were unsuccessful and, unable to restrain the prowar faction headed by War Minister Tōjō Hideki, he and his cabinet were once more obliged to resign. The Tōjō cabinet that replaced him thereupon commenced hostilities against America and Great Britain. As Japan's position in the war worsened, Konoe became worried that the imperial house would be placed in jeopardy and he accordingly sought an early end to the conflict. In 1944, he and other persons of impotance close to the emperor succeeded in forcing the resignation of the Tōjō cabinet. In February of 1945, Konoe submitted a memorial to the emperor warning of the danger of a Communist revolution. In July of the same year, he was requested by the emperor to go to the Soviet Union as a special envoy to negotiate peace, but the plan was never realized, and the following month Japan announced its surrender. In the Higashikuni-no-miya cabinet that was set up immediately afterward, Konoe was given the status of a deputy prime minister and the post of minister without portfolio. As an official in the office of the Lord Keeper of the Privy Seal, he was urged by General MacArthur to undertake the task of constitutional revision. Occupation headquarters, however, issued an order for his arrest as a possible war criminal. On the last day for his voluntary appearance before the authorities, he took poison and died.

Kōtoku Shūsui 幸徳秋水 (1871–1911)

Meiji period socialist and anarchist; he was born in Kōchi Prefecture in Shikoku. In his youth he received a Confucian education and was thoroughly dedicated to Confucian ethical ideals. Later, however, he became attracted to democratic ideas, and on completion of middle school went to Tokyo through the help of Hayashi Yūzō, a political leader from Kōchi, where he devoted himself to the popular rights movement. In 1887 he was among the large group of persons from Kōchi who were forced by the newly promulgated Peace Preservation Regulations to leave Tokyo because of their political activities. In 1888 he became a combination student and houseboy in the home of Nakae Chōmin, a proponent of Western political thought who was living in Osaka at the time, and was much influenced by his ideas and personality. When Nakae moved to Tokyo, Kōtoku accompanied him, where in 1893 he graduated from the Kokumin Eigakkai. He became a newspaper reporter, serving first on the *Jiyū Shimbun* and later the *Chūō Shimbun*, and in 1898 joined the *Yorozu Chōhō* as an editorial writer. In the same year he became a member of the Socialist Study Group, and also acted as secretary to an organization advocating universal suffrage.

During this period, he became increasingly attracted to socialism and in 1901 joined Abe Isoo, Kinoshita Naoe, and others in forming the Shakai Minshutō (Social Democratic Party), the first socialist party to be formed in Japan. The party was outlawed the same day it was formed and was forced to disband immediately. In the same year he was requested by Tanaka Shōzō, a crusader against industrial pollution, to draft a petition to present to the emperor on behalf of the victims of the Ashio Mine pollution. In 1903, on the eve of the Russo-Japanese War, when the *Yorozu Chōhō* came out in favor of a commencement of hostilities, Kōtoku, along with Sakai Toshihiko and Uchimura Kanzō, resigned from the staff. He and Sakai then formed the Heiminsha and began publication of a newspaper called *Heimin Shimbun*, which opposed military action and continued to do so even after the outbreak of the war. While the war was still in progress, the newspaper published the text of a letter sent to the Socialist Party of Russia. As a result, the paper was forced to close down in 1905, and Kōtoku was sent to jail.

After his release, he went to the United States, where he joined the American Socialist Party. In 1906 he formed the Shakai Kakumeitō (Social Revolution Party) made up of Japanese living in America. He remained in California for about half a year, during which he became increasingly influenced by anarchist thinking. After returning to Japan, he launched an appeal for direct action, proclaiming the necessity for a general strike. At the second general meeting of the Japan Socialist Party in 1907, he spoke out in opposition to Katayama Sen, Tazoe Tetsuji, and others who advocated reform by parliamentary methods. In the face of increasing harrassment from the government, he returned to Kōchi for a time to recover from an illness. With the so-called "red banner" incident in 1908, when a number of left-wing leaders were arrested for displaying anarchist and communist slogans at a gathering in Kanda in Tokyo, he went to Tokyo once more. There he joined Kanno Suga in publishing a magazine called *Jiyū Shisō*. At the time of the lèse-majesté affair in 1910, he was arrested along with other socialist leaders on suspicion of plotting to assassinate Emperor

Meiji. He was charged with being a major conspirator in the plot and was sentenced to death. In 1911 he and Kanno were among the eleven men who were executed as a result of the affair. His writings include *Nijusseiki no kaibutsu teikoku shugi* and *Shakai shugi shinzui*.

Kuroda Kiyotaka 黒田清隆 (1840–1900)

Meiji period statesman who held the title of count; he was born in Kagoshima, the son of a samurai of the fief of Satsuma. In his earlier years he went by the name Ryōsuke. In 1863 he took part in the war between Satsuma and the British. Later he entered the school of Western gunnery founded by Egawa Tarōzaemon Hidetatsu in Edo, but left the school in 1864. For the remainder of the Edo period, he devoted himself to the movement to overthrow the shogunate, working strenuously to bring about an alliance between the fiefs of Satsuma and Chōshū. He took part in the Boshin War in 1868 and in 1869 distinguished himself as leader in the attack on the Goryōkaku, the stronghold of the forces in Hakodate that remained loyal to the shogunate.

In the newly formed Meiji government he served as chief assistant to the minister of foreign affairs, and later to the minister of military affairs. In 1870 he was appointed vice-commissioner for colonization. In 1871 he went to America and returned with Horace Capron, an American agriculturalist, whom he appointed as an advisor on colonization and encouraged to draw up plans for the colonization and development of Hokkaido, at the same time putting him in charge of the establishment of the Sapporo Agricultural College. In 1872 Enomoto Takeaki, the leader of the resistance forces in Hakodate who had earlier surrendered to the government and been pardoned, was appointed commissioner of colonization. In 1874, when the system of colonial soldiers (*tondenhei*) was established in Hokkaido, Kuroda was made a lieutenant general and the same year was further appointed a councilor and head of the Commission of Colonization. He had previously made an inspection tour of Karafuto (Sakhalin) and had several times advised the government that it should abandon plans for the colonization of Sakhalin and concentrate its efforts upon the development of Hokkaido. In 1875 Enomoto, as minister to Russia, concluded a treaty whereby Japan gave Sakhalin to Russia in exchange for the Chishima (Kurile) Islands.

In the same year, the Kanghwa Incident occurred in Korea. In 1876 Kuroda was made envoy extraordinary, minister plenipotentiary, and minister without portfolio and, in company with Inoue Kaoru, journeyed to Korea, where he carried on negotiations that led to the conclusion of a friendship treaty between Japan and Korea and the opening of Korean ports to trade. In the Seinan War in 1877 he was a member of the government forces dispatched to put down the uprising, and after the death of Saigō Takamori and Ōkubo Toshimichi, acted as leader of the Satsuma faction in the government. In 1881, when the ten-year plan of the colonization commission reached its fulfillment, a scandal broke out concerning the sale of government property belonging to the commission, which aroused unfavorable comment among the public, the commission being accused of selling property at an unfair advantage to the company of Godai Tomoatsu, who was, like Kuroda, a native of Satsuma. The following year the commission was abolished and Kuroda was appointed an advisor to the Cabinet.

In 1885 he visited China and the following year made a world tour. Upon his return to Japan in 1887, he was appointed to succeed Hijikata Hisamoto as minister of agriculture and commerce in the first Itō cabinet, and with Itō's resignation, he replaced him as prime minister, forming a cabinet made up of men from Satsuma and Chōshū. In 1889, while he was in office, the Meiji Constitution was promulgated, and Kuroda immediately afterward enunciated the principle of *chōzen-shugi*, or the transcendence of party aims and loyalties. In the same year, when Foreign Minister Ōkuma Shigenobu, who was negotiating the revision of Japan's treaties with the foreign powers, was attacked and injured, Kuroda resigned the post of prime minister and was appointed an advisor to the Privy Council. In 1892 he became minister of communications in the second Itō cabinet. In 1895 he was made president of the Privy Council and continued to hold a cabinet post until 1898. In comparison with the other elder statesmen of the Meiji period, he died at a relatively early age.

Kurozumi Munetada 黒住宗忠 (1780–1850)

Religious leader of the late Edo period and founder of the Shinto sect known as Kurozumi-kyō. He was the son of a Shinto priest of the province of Bizen. As young man he was very devoted to his parents, but lost both of them in an epidemic in 1812. The shock caused him to become ill himself, and for a time his condition was critical. On the eleventh day of the eleventh lunar month of 1814, the day of the winter solstice, when he was worshiping the sun at dawn, he experienced a mystical sense of unity with the Sun Goddess Amaterasu Ōmikami, and his illness was thereafter cured. This event is referred to as *Temmei-jikiju*, the "Direct Revelation of the Heavenly

Command," and the day marks the founding of the Kurozumi religion. Kurozumi thereafter practiced the healing of sickness through prayer and gathered a group of believers about him. At the same time, he emphasized the importance of the traditional virtues taught by Confucianism and for this reason gained considerable influence among members of the samurai class, who were traditionally trained in Confucianism. In 1825 he began the observance of various religious exercises, among them a thousand-day period of withdrawal within the shrine, and laid down a set of rules for the daily life of believers entitled *Nichinichi kanai kokoroe no koto.* In 1833 he cured Ikeda Narimasa, former lord of the domain of Okayama, from an illness, and thereafter his social position was secure. In 1841 he turned over his religious duties to his eldest son, Munenobu, and went into retirement.

In his theology he stressed the importance of Amaterasu Ōmikami as the source of all creation and posited the essential unity of god and man. He taught that the human heart is an emanation of that of the deity, and by purifying it, one can be freed from all present ills. His poems and prose writings in Japanese were later compiled into a work that constitutes the sacred scripture of Kurozumi-kyō.

MAEDA EUN 前田慧雲 (1857–1930)

Buddhist scholar of the Meiji period; he was born in Kuwana in what later became Mie Prefecture, the son of the priest of a temple called Saifuku-ji of the Hongan-ji branch of the Jōdo Shin sect. As a boy he studied Chinese and Buddhist texts under a scholar in the neighborhood. In 1875 he went to Kyoto and entered the Seizan Kyōjukō, a school operated by the Hongan-ji branch of the sect. In 1878 he became a disciple of Taihō Risshi of Miidera in Ōtsu, studying the scriptures and traditional doctrines of Buddhism. With his father's death in 1880, he returned to his home for a time and became resident priest of his father's temple, but later went to Kyoto once more. He also went to Kyushu, where he studied the history of the Jōdo Shin sect under Matsushima Zenjō. He went to Tokyo in 1888, where he joined the Sonnō Hōbutsu Daidōdan, a Buddhist political organization formed by Ōuchi Seiran, and for a while was active in politics. In 1903 he received his doctorate; his dissertation was a collection of scholarly articles entitled *Daijō Bukkyō shiron.* He served as a lecturer at Tokyo Imperial University and elsewhere and later as president of Tōyō University and Ryūkoku University, the last in Kyoto. From 1905, he devoted his energies to the publication of the *Dai-Nippon Zokuzōkyō*, a continuation of the Tripitaka containing basic texts of Buddhism. In addition to the collection of articles mentioned above, his works include *Hongan-ji-ha gakuji-shi* and *Tendaishū kōyō.*

MAEJIMA HISOKA 前島密 (1835–1919)

Shogunate official and bureaucrat and business leader of the Meiji period; he held the title of baron. He was the second son of Ueno Sukeuemon, a samurai of the domain of Takada in Echigo Province; his childhood name was Fusagorō. In 1847 he went to Edo, where he studied medicine and Western style gunnery. In 1857 he entered the warship training school established by the shogunate and the following year received instruction in navigation and matters pertaining to commercial vessels from Takeda Ayasaburō in Hakodate. At the command of the Hakodate government office, he undertook a survey of the waters off the Japanese coast. In 1861 he proceeded to the island of Tsushima, but reached it only after the Russian warship that had been occupying it had withdrawn. While studying in Nagasaki, he made up his mind to travel abroad and went to Edo with that purpose in mind, but his plans did not go as he had hoped and he returned to Nagasaki. There he opened a school in company with Uryū Tora and gave instruction in English. Later he was invited by the domain of Satsuma to teach English at Kagoshima. In 1866 he was adopted as heir to a shogunate official named Maejima. He changed his given name to Raisuke and, as a retainer to the shogunate, was assigned to do translation work for the Kaiseijo, the school for Western studies established by the shogunate in Edo, and for the Hyōgo government office in Kobe.

At the time of the Meiji Restoration in 1868, he submitted a letter to Ōkubo Toshimichi, a prominent leader of the Restoration who favored moving the capital from Kyoto to Osaka, arguing that the capital should rather be moved to Edo. He held various posts in the domain of Suruga, to which the former shogun, Tokugawa Yoshinobu, had been assigned. In 1870, he took up a post in the newly formed government in Tokyo, handling tax matters in the ministries of the interior and finance; at the same time he acted as virtual director of the office in charge of transportation and communication. In 1870 he made a trip to Europe in order to study postal systems. On his return to Japan in 1871, he became chief of transportation and played a key role in setting up a modern postal system in Japan, an accomplishment that earned him the epithet "father of the post office."

In 1878 he became a member of the Genrōin and in 1880 chief assistant in the Ministry of the Interior and superintendent of transportation. With the government shake-up in 1881, however, both he and his close friend Ōkuma Shigenobu found themselves removed from office, and they set about planning the formation of a political party known as the Rikken Kaishintō (Progressive Party).

During the years 1886 to 1890, Maejima acted as president of Tokyo Semmon Gakkō, the forerunner of Waseda University. From 1888 to 1891 he also served as vice-minister of communications, presiding over the establishment of telephones as a government monopoly. In the business world, he served as president of various companies such as Kansai Tetsudō, Hokuetsu Tetsudō, and Nisshin Seimei Hoken, and he also acted as director of the Japan Seamen's Relief Association. In 1904 he was selected to become a member of the Upper House of the Diet. He is famous for advocating the abolition of the use of Chinese characters in the writing of Japanese. As early as the closing years of the Edo period, he recommended to the shogun Tokugawa Yoshinobu that Chinese characters be dropped from use in the Japanese writing system and in 1869 he repeated the recommendation to the newly formed Meiji government. In 1900 he was appointed by the Ministry of Education to serve as chairman of the committee for the investigation of the Japanese language.

Makiguchi Tsunesaburō 牧口常三郎 (1871–1944)

Religious leader and educator of the Taishō and early Shōwa periods and founder of the Sōka Kyōiku Gakkai; he was born in a fishing village in Niigata Prefecture. He moved to Hokkaido and, after graduating from Sapporo Normal School, devoted himself to the study of geography. He went to Tokyo in 1901 and in 1903 published a work entitled *Jinsei chiri-gaku.* He served as principal of an elementary school in Tokyo and at the same time devoted himself to the movement for utilitarian methods of education. In 1928, under the guidance of Mitani Sokei, he became a follower of Nichiren Shōshū, a branch of the Nichiren sect of Buddhism founded by Nikkō, a disciple of Nichiren.

In 1930, after retiring from teaching, he began publication of a four-volume work entitled *Sōka kyōikugaku taikei,* in which he criticized the values of "truth," "goodness," and "beauty" postulated by the Neo-Kantian philosophers and set forth his own theory based on the values "profit," "goodness," and "beauty." He combined this utilitarian theory of value with the religious teachings of Nichiren Shōshū, setting up an organization called the Sōka Kyōiku Gakkai, or Value-Creative Education Society. In 1941 he began publication of a magazine entitled *Kachi Sōzō* to give voice to the opinions of the organization. He gained a large number of members among primary school teachers and small businessmen. As the Pacific War grew more intense, the government took steps to bring all religious organizations under its control. Makiguchi resisted such attempts at government control, and as a result he and twenty other leaders of his group were arrested in 1943, and the Sōka Kyōiku Gakkai was destroyed. Makiguchi died the following year in prison. After the war, Makiguchi's close associate Toda Jōsei (1900–1958), who had been imprisoned with him, revived the organization under the name Sōka Gakkai. It has grown with astonishing speed and now constitutes one of the largest religious groups in Japan.

Makino Nobuaki 牧野伸顯 (1861–1949)

Statesman and diplomat of the Meiji, Taishō, and Shōwa eras; he held the title of count. He was born in the domain of Satsuma, the second son of Ōkubo Toshimichi, but was later adopted into the Makino family. In 1871 he accompanied Iwakura Tomomi on the latter's mission to Europe and America and remained in America to attend middle school in Philadelphia. When his father was assassinated in Tokyo in 1878, he withdrew from school and returned to Japan. In 1880 he entered the Foreign Ministry and was assigned to duty in London. He became acquainted with Itō Hirobumi when the latter journeyed to Europe in 1882 to study constitutional systems of government. He returned to Japan and held a succession of posts, including assistant councilor of state, councilor in the Bureau of Judicial Affairs, governor of the prefectures of Fukui and Ibaragi, vice-minister of education, and minister to Austria and Italy, and in 1906 became minister of education in the first Saionji cabinet. Thereafter he served as advisor to the Privy Council, minister of education in the second Saionji cabinet, minister of foreign affairs in the first Yamamoto cabinet, and a member of the Temporary Advisory Board on Diplomatic Affairs. In 1919 he attended the peace conference at Versailles as a plenipotentiary member of the Japanese delegation. In 1921 he became minister of the imperial household and in 1925 the Lord Keeper of the Privy Seal.

He was a strong supporter of the Satsuma faction in the government and was allied with the Saionji party. He continued until 1935 to serve as Lord Keeper of the Privy Seal, working to smooth over the differences that arose among the bureaucrats, the military leaders, and the party politicians, but he was regarded by the militarists and right-wing leaders as being too sympathetic toward Britain and the United States, and in the young army officers' uprising of February 26, 1936, he was attacked and barely managed to escape with his life. His daughter was the wife of Yoshida Shigeru, a prominent political leader of postwar Japan.

MAKINO TOMITARŌ 牧野富太郎 (1862–1957)

Botanist of the Meiji, Taishō, and Shōwa eras; he was born in what later became Kōchi Prefecture in Shikoku. He dropped out of elementary school and devoted his time to the observation of plants, studying systematic botany on his own. Later, after serving as an elementary school teacher, in 1881 he began making occasional trips to Tokyo and from around 1884 on was often to be found in the botany study room of Tokyo Imperial University, immersed in research. In 1888 he published his *Nihon shokubutsu shi zuhen* (*Illustrations of the Flora of Japan*). He later served as an assistant and lecturer at Tokyo University and after his retirement in 1939 devoted himself entirely to the classification and description of his botanical specimens. During this time he traveled all over Japan, almost single-handedly collecting specimens. His academic publications include classifications of 1,000 new species of Japanese plants, 1,500 varieties, and the astounding number of over 400,000 specimens. He thus played a major role in laying the foundations of Japanese systematic botany; in addition to his scholarly writings, he produced illustrated books and primers for the general reader, seeking to spread a knowledge of botany among the populace as a whole. In 1927 he was awarded a doctorate of science, in 1950 he became a member of the Japanese Academy, and in 1957, following his death, he was posthumously awarded a Cultural Medal.

MATSUKATA MASAYOSHI 松方正義 (1835–1924)

Meiji period statesman and financial leader; he held the title of duke. He was born in the fief of Satsuma in Kyushu and from 1850 on was very close to Shimazu Hisamitsu, brother of the lord of the fief and later lord himself. Matsukata was greatly influenced by Ōkubo Toshimichi, a samurai of Satsuma who was to become a distinguished statesman. He was involved in the Teradaya incident, a clash between two factions among the Satsuma samurai; the clash between the Chōshū forces and the imperial guards outside the

Hamaguri Gate of the imperial palace; the punitive expedition against Chōshū; and the *kōbu-gattai* movement, which sought to bring about unity between the imperial court and the shogunate; and eventually joined the movement to overthrow the shogunate. In 1866 he was put in charge of warships for the fief of Satsuma and went to Nagasaki, where he busied himself buying up foreign warships and weaponry. In 1868 he conducted successful talks with the British and French consuls concerning the extension of the earlier trade treaties between Japan and these countries, and when the Meiji government was established, helped to promote smooth relations between it and the British and French.

On the recommendation of Ōkubo Toshimichi, he was appointed governor of Hita Prefecture (in present Ōita Prefecture) in Kyūshu, in which position he worked to promote industrialization, helped to solve problems arising from the presence of the Japanese Christian community in Nagasaki, and settled the affair concerning counterfeit money that arose in Fukuoka. In 1870 he entered the central government, holding the post of chief assistant in the Ministry of the Interior. In 1874 he transferred to the Ministry of Finance, at that time headed by Ōkubo, being appointed chief of taxation, and set about to reform the system of land taxes. In 1876 he was transferred to the Ministry of Home Affairs and as head of the Agriculture Bureau worked to promote industrialization and advocated the restoration of tariff autonomy to Japan.

In 1878 he went to France as vice president of the Japanese delegation to the French Exposition and was thus out of the country at the time of Ōkubo's assassination in May of that year. Upon returning to Japan he became chief assistant in the Ministry of Home Affairs, then headed by Itō Hirobumi, and in 1880 became minister of home affairs. In 1881 he was transferred to the post of minister of finance and initiated what came to be known as the "Matsukata deflationary fiscal policy." This involved the reduction of government expenditures, imposition of new taxes, issuance of convertible notes, adoption of the gold standard, and establishment of the Bank of Japan, measures that insured a sound currency and a restoration of financial stability. He was also active in promoting other measures that helped to insure the fiscal health of the country during this period, such as the establishment of an income tax system, the imposition of additional land taxes, and revisions in the system of land evaluation. After serving as minister of finance for over ten years, he became prime minister in 1891, heading the first Matsukata cabinet. He became prime minister once again in 1896, forming the second Matsukata cabinet. In 1898 he became minister of finance, in 1903 an advisor to the Privy Council, and in 1917 minister of home affairs.

He also served as head of the Japan Red Cross. He was noted as a statesman who always remained loyal to the men of his native fief of Satsuma.

Matsuoka Yōsuke 松岡洋右 (1880–1946)

Diplomat and political leader of the Taishō and Shōwa periods; he was born in Yamaguchi Prefecture. His family, which engaged in shipping, was in economic decline, and in 1893 he went to America. After experiencing many difficulties, he succeeded in completing a bachelor of law degree at the University of Oregon. He returned to Japan in 1902 and in 1904, having passed the examination for diplomatic service, entered the Ministry of Foreign Affairs. He began his career with an assignment in Shanghai and later held posts in Russia and the United States. In 1919 he was appointed a member of the Japanese delegation to the Versailles Conference, being put in charge of relations with the press. In 1921 he retired from diplomatic service and became a director of the South Manchuria Railway Co. He left this position in 1926, and in 1927, at the request of Tanaka Giichi, the leader of the Seiyūkai, he joined Yamamoto Jōtarō and others in a tour of China designed to ascertain the political situation there. After returning to Japan, he became vice-president of the South Manchuria Railway, lending valuable assistance to its president, Yamamoto Jōtarō. He retired from this position in 1929. The same year, he attended the third meeting of the Institute of Pacific Relations held in Kyoto. There he clashed with the Chinese delegate over the Manchurian question and made an eloquent speech in English that won the admiration of Nitobe Inazō, the head of the Japanese delegation.

In 1930 he ran for election as an affiliate of the Seiyūkai and was elected to the Lower House of the Diet as a representative from Yamaguchi Prefecture. In the Diet, he spoke out against the peaceful diplomatic policy of Minister of Foreign Affairs Shidehara Kijūrō, reiterating the theme that "Manchuria and Mongolia are the lifeline of Japan!" In 1932, with the outbreak of hostilities between Chinese and Japanese forces in Shanghai known as the Shanghai Incident, he was dispatched as special envoy of the minister of foreign affairs and played an important role in assisting Shigemitsu Mamoru, the Japanese minister to China, in bringing an end to the conflict. The same year, he was appointed Japan's representative to the extraordinary meeting of the League of Nations, traveling to Switzerland accompanied by Colonel Ishihara Kanji and others. When the general meeting of the League of Nations refused recognition to the newly created "state of Manchuria," Matsuoka withdrew from the meeting in protest, a move that led him to be regarded at home as the "hero of Geneva." The same year, Japan announced its formal withdrawal from the League of Nations.

After his return to Japan, he withdrew from the Seiyūkai and formed an organization known as the Seitō Kaishō Remmei, or "League for the Dissolution of Political Parties." He also resigned his seat in the Diet and set out on a lecture tour of the country, calling for the dissolution of all political parties, cooperation on the international level with Germany and Italy, and the establishment of a new world order. In 1935 he dissolved the Seitō Kaishō Remmei and assumed the position of president of the South Manchuria Railway, but resigned in 1939. In 1940, in dissatisfaction over the foreign policy of the Yonai cabinet, he also resigned the position of cabinet councilor, which he had held from the time of the Konoe cabinet in 1937. In the same year, he became minister of foreign affairs in the second Konoe cabinet and carried out a reshuffling of personnel in the Ministry of Foreign Affairs that came to be referred to as the "Matsuoka whirlwind." He favored close cooperation with Germany and Italy and in 1940 succeeded in concluding the Tripartite Pact linking Japan with those two countries. He hoped, by gaining the cooperation of the Soviet Union as well, to form a coalition of countries that would enable Japan to settle her long-standing differences with the United States. He also formulated plans for Japanese expansion in Southeast Asia, outlining what came to be known as the Greater East Asia Coprosperity Sphere.

On his way back from negotiations with Germany and Italy over the Tripartite Pact, he stopped in Moscow and succeeded in concluding a neutrality agreement between Japan and the Soviet Union, but the German invasion of Russia in the same year destroyed his plans, and he was forced to resign from office while negotiations between Japan and the United States were still being carried out. At the end of the war, he was brought before the International Military Tribunal for the Far East as an A-class war criminal, but fell ill and died shortly after in Tokyo University Hospital. Both Satō Eisaku and Kishi Nobusuke are related to him by marriage.

Meiji Tennō 明治天皇 (1852–1912)

Emperor who reigned during the period from 1867 to 1912; his personal name was Mutsuhito; in his childhood he went by the name Sachinomiya. He was the son of Emperor Kōmei and Nakayama Yoshiko and was born in the Kyoto residence of the Nakayama family. His maternal grandfather, Nakayama Tadayasu, took charge of his upbringing. He was declared crown prince in 1860. In 1864, when forces from the domain of Chōshū attempted to seize control of Kyoto, there was bitter fighting outside the Hamaguri Gate of the imperial palace, and the future emperor underwent the experience of being under fire.

In 1867, with the death of Emperor Kōmei, he succeeded to the throne. The same year, the shogun Tokugawa Yoshinobu requested permission to return all powers of government to the throne, a request that was granted. In 1868 a decree was issued announcing to the nation the restoration of the imperial system of rule. A similar announcement was made to foreign nations, and the envoys from the various foreign powers were received in audience. In addition, the new ruler in the presence of the gods took the so-called Charter Oath, a brief statement in five parts that laid down the principles upon which the new government was to be based. The emperor at this time was only fifteen years old, having just completed the *gempuku* ceremony that symbolized his entry into adulthood. The same year, his coronation ceremony was carried out at the imperial palace in Kyoto, and Edo was renamed Tokyo (Eastern Capital). The era name was changed from Keiō to Meiji, and it was decreed that henceforth there should be only one era name to each reign. Hence the era continued to be called Meiji until the death of the emperor in 1912, and he is accordingly referred to as Emperor Meiji, though this is not his name. The emperor paid a visit to Tokyo, using Edo Castle as an imperial residence. Meanwhile, in Kyoto Ichijō Yoshiko, the daughter of Ichijō Tadaka, was proclaimed empress; she was known later as Empress Dowager Shōken. The emperor went to Tokyo once more in 1869, and though there was no formal announcement of the transfer of the capital, thereafter Tokyo in effect became the capital of the nation.

In 1871 the scholar of Chinese Motoda Eifu (Nagazane) was appointed to the emperor's entourage and charged with his education. The same year, after the feudal domains had been abolished and a system of prefectures set up, major changes were carried out in the organization of the imperial palace. Yoshii Tomozane, a friend of Saigō Takamori, was appointed to take charge of the inner palace. He thereupon dismissed the ladies-in-waiting and brought in former samurai such as Takashima Tomonosuke, Shima Yoshitake, and Yamaoka Tesshū (Tetsutarō) to be the emperor's attendants, establishing an atmosphere of sobriety and manliness. The emperor received instruction in German language and European political thought from Katō Hiroyuki and read the Japanese translation of Samuel Smiles' *Self-Help*. He also took lessons in Japanese poetry from Takasaki Masakaze, the official in charge of matters pertaining to poetry at court, and in the course of his lifetime composed some 100,000 poems in traditional style. He set an example for his people in wearing Western clothing, eating Western food, and in other ways adopting elements from Western style living. Beginning with a tour of western Japan in 1872, he made a total of six trips up to 1885, visiting the various regions of Japan, including the island of Hokkaido. He received many distinguished visitors from abroad, notably the Duke of Edinburgh in 1869 and former US president General Grant in 1879. The latter was received at the Hama Detached Palace in Tokyo, where the emperor chatted with him and was offered friendly advice on political matters. In 1891, when Crown Prince Nikolai of Russia was attacked and wounded at Ōtsu near Kyoto, the emperor went at once to Kyoto to inquire of his condition in person, and also paid a visit to the Russian warship in Kobe, thus insuring that diplomatic relations between the two countries would not be disrupted by the incident.

Some years previous in 1882, in an imperial rescript to army and navy personnel, he clarified his position as generalissimo and supreme commander of the army and navy. In 1888, when deliberations were being held in connection with the drafting of the Meiji Constitution, he personally attended all the meetings of the Privy Council and he presided over the promulgation of the constitution in 1889 and the opening of the first session of the Diet in 1890. With these moves, Japan became the first country in Asia to establish a system of constitutional monarchy. In 1890 the emperor issued the famous Imperial Rescript on Education, which defined the basic ideals for the education of the people of Japan. During the Sino-Japanese War in 1894–95, he set up imperial headquarters at Hiroshima, from which he directed the conduct of the war. He also played a very active role in the prosecution of the Russo-Japanese War of 1904–05, when Japan's fate as a nation hung in the balance. In 1906 England, Japan's ally in the war, sent Prince Arthur of Connaught to Japan to confer upon Emperor Meiji the Order of the Garter. The late years of his reign saw the annexation of Korea in 1910 and the revision of the treaties with the Western powers in 1911. He headed the country at a time when the Japanese people were engaged in the task of modernization and Westernization and were expanding Japan's power until the country was firmly established as one of the most advanced nations of Asia. For this reason, Emperor Meiji holds a place of special importance in the history of Japan. On his death in 1912, he was entombed at Momoyama in the Fushimi area of Kyoto, and a shrine, Meiji Jingū, was erected to his memory at Yoyogi in Tokyo.

Minobe Tatsukichi 美濃部達吉 (1873–1948)

Meiji, Taishō, and Shōwa period scholar of constitutions and a Doctor of Law; he was born in Hyōgo Prefecture. After completing the law course of Tokyo Imperial University, he studied in Germany. In 1902 he became a professor of Tokyo University, a position that he held until his retirement in 1934. During this period, he lectured on the comparative history of legislation and later on matters pertaining to constitutions. In contrast to scholars such as Uesugi Shinkichi, who upheld the sovereignty of the emperor, he propounded the view that the emperor should be looked upon as an organ of the state, and this disagreement led to a long-range debate on the interpretation of the constitution. In 1911 Minobe became a member of the Japan Academy. At the time of the London Disarmament Conference in 1930, debate once more broke out over the question of the constitutional rights of the various high ministers, but Prime Minister Hamaguchi and his cabinet, adopting Minobe's interpretation of the constitution, signed the Naval Treaty in spite of the objections of the naval chief of staff, a move that incurred the displeasure of the navy.

In 1932, Minobe became a member of the Upper House of the Diet. In 1935, a fellow member of the Upper House launched an attack upon him for his theory that the emperor should be regarded as an organ of the state. The incident developed into a serious political issue, Minobe was charged with lèse-majesté, and his writings were banned. He resigned his seat in the Upper House, but this did not end the affair, and in 1936 he was attacked by a hoodlum and wounded slightly. In the years following, he continued to study and write on the subject of administrative law. In 1946, after the conclusion of the Pacific War, he became an advisor to the Privy Council. He participated in the deliberations concerning the drafting of a new constitution, but it is said that he did not approve of constitutional revision so long as Japan remained under the control of the Occupation forces. His eldest son, Ryōkichi, has been elected governor of Tokyo three times since 1967.

Miyake Setsurei 三宅雪嶺 (1860–1845)

Thinker and critic of the Meiji, Taishō, and Shōwa eras; he was born in Kanazawa, the son of a doctor. His given name was Yūjirō, which he changed for a time to Yūshuku. In 1871 he entered the Kanazawa Prefectural English School and later transferred to the Aichi English School. In 1876 he went to Tokyo and entered the Kaisei School, which the following year became

Tokyo Imperial University. In 1883 he graduated from the Faculty of Letters of Tokyo Imperial University, specializing in philosophy, and took a job in the editorial office attached to the university. In 1885 he transferred to the Editorial Bureau of the Ministry of Education. Around this time he began to contribute articles and critical essays to various newspapers and magazines.

In 1888 he joined Sugiura Jūgō, Shiga Shigetaka, Inoue Enryō, and others to form a nationalistic organization known as the Seikyōsha and founded *Nihonjin*, a magazine expressing the views of the group, which sought to combat the trend toward Westernization and to emphasize the virtues of Japanese culture. His works entitled *Shinzembi Nihonjin* and *Giakushū Nihonjin*, which he wrote in 1891, are representative of the nationalistic writings appearing around the 1890s in Meiji Japan. He continued to be active in expressing his views through contributions to *Nihon oyobi Nihonjin*, *Chūō Kōron*, and other magazines, and in 1923 joined with Nakano Seigō in founding a magazine of his own called *Gakan*. In his late years he wrote a work based upon his experiences entitled *Dōjidai-kan* (later retitled *Dōjidai-shi*); in six volumes, it deals with the history of modern Japan.

Mori Arinori 森有禮 (1848–1888)

Diplomat and statesman of the Meiji period; he was born in Kagoshima, the son of a samurai of the domain of Satsuma. In his youth he went by the name Sukegorō and later Kinnojō. He studied Chinese in the Zōshikan, the official school of the domain, and also took instruction in English. In 1864 the domain set up a school called the Kaiseisho to train men in military and naval affairs, and Mori attended, specializing in naval surveying. In 1865 he was selected to be one of a group of students sent abroad by the domain for study. At this time, however, Japanese were still forbidden by law to leave the country. As a precaution, therefore, he changed his name to Sawai Tetsuma, and in this disguise managed to make his way to London. In London he studied chemistry, physics, and mathematics. He also became acquainted with an American religious leader named Harris, was converted to Christianity, and in 1867 accompanied Harris to the United States. In 1868, after the Meiji Restoration, he returned to Japan and became an official in charge of foreign affairs. He was at the same time ordered to carry out a survey of parliamentary and educational systems. In 1869, because he advocated a ban on the wearing of swords, he aroused considerable criticism and was obliged to resign his position.

He returned to his home in Kagoshima and for a time taught English, but in 1870 was recalled to service in the central government, being appointed a diplomatic official and assigned to America. While carrying out his official duties, he wrote an article in English entitled "Religious Freedom in Japan." After his return to Japan in 1873, he held various high posts in the Foreign Ministry and other branches of the government and served as minister plenipotentiary to China and England. During this period, he also joined with Nishimura Shigeki, Fukuzawa Yukichi, and other scholars and cultural leaders to form an organization called the Meirokusha to work for the enlightenment of the Japanese public. In 1884, when the cabinet system was initiated, he was appointed minister of education and in this capacity carried out various reforms and innovations to establish an educational system that would conform to the interests of the state. Because he tended to be rather extreme at times in his speech and actions, he aroused frequent opposition. In 1888, when he was about to set out for a ceremony marking the promulgation of the Meiji Constitution, he was attacked and killed at his residence by a religious fanatic.

Motoda Eifu (Nagazane) 元田永孚 (1818–1891)

Scholar of Chinese studies of the late Edo and Meiji periods. He was the son of a samurai of the domain of Kumamoto in Kyushu; his formal name was Shichū, and his literary name Tōya. He began the study of Chinese at an early age and from the age of ten attended the official school of the domain, where he gained a reputation for his brilliance. In 1858 he succeeded his father as head of the family and entered the service of the domain and in 1861 accompanied his lord to Edo. In 1867 he became administrator of Takase in Kumamoto and in 1870, after the establishment of the Meiji government, became tutor to Hosokawa Morihisa, the governor of the domain of Kumamoto. In 1871 he entered the Imperial Household Agency and in 1875 became tutor to Emperor Meiji. Thereafter he continued to rise in court service, in 1886 becoming a court advisor and in 1888 an advisor to the Privy Council. In 1891 he was given the title of baron. He enjoyed great trust and favor with Emperor Meiji. During the years from 1879 to 1882 he compiled a textbook on ethics for young people entitled *Yōgaku kōyō* and also took part in drafting the Imperial Rescript on Education, a statement on educational principles promulgated in 1890. He was a leader of the conservative faction at court and worked to establish a system of education centered about patriotism and reverence for the emperor. His writings include *Keien shinkōroku* and *Shokyō kōgi.*

Murakami Senjō 村上専精 (1851–1928)

Buddhist priest and scholar of the Meiji period; he was the son of a priest of Kyōkaku-ji, a temple of the Ōtani branch of the Jōdo Shin sect in the province of Tamba. As a boy he became an apprentice priest in another temple and later attended a private school in Himeji. After studying Yuishiki (Consciousness Only) Buddhism under Takeda Gyōchū in Echigo, he entered the Higashi Hongan-ji normal school. In 1887 he went to Tokyo, where he lectured on Buddhism at Sōtōshū University, Tetsugakkan, and Tokyo Imperial University. At the same time he set up in the Kanda area of Tokyo an institution called the Bukkyō Kōwasho, where he gave popular lectures on Buddhism. In 1890 he joined with Washio Junkyō and Sakaino Kōyō in founding a scholarly journal called *Bukkyō shirin*, playing a leading role in the study of Buddhism according to modern critical methods. In 1898 he received his Ph.D. degree. In 1901 he published a work entitled *Bukkyō tōitsu-ron* in which he argued that Mahayana Buddhism is quite different from the doctrine preached by Gautama Buddha. Though this has since become the accepted view in academic circles, it was highly offensive to the more conservative elements in the Buddhist world at the time, and Murakami was led to withdraw from the clergy as a result, though he returned to clerical status in 1912. He later served as a professor of Tokyo Imperial University, as president of Ōtani University, and became a member of the Japan Academy.

Mutsu Munemitsu 陸奥宗光 (1844–1897)

Meiji period political leader and diplomat; he held the title of count. He was born in the city of Wakayama, the son of a samurai of the domain of Kii named Date Munehiro. His childhood name was Ushimaro, and he later went by the names Kojirō, Genjirō, Yōnosuke, and the literary name Fukudō. He went to Edo in 1858 to study and later in Kyoto became a supporter of the movement to restore power to the emperor. He entered the naval school operated by Katsu Kaishū in 1863 and in 1867 left his domain without official permission and journeyed to Nagasaki, where he took an active part in the Kaientai, a marine transport and trading company organized by Sakamoto Ryōma; at this time he went by the name Mutsu Genjirō.

After the Meiji Restoration, he had occasion to meet the British minister Sir Harry Parkes and listen to his views. He thereafter met with Iwakura Tomomi, one of the leaders of the new government, in Kyoto, and urged him to open the country to trade and diplomatic relations. As a result, he was chosen for a post in the bureau in charge of foreign affairs and assigned to diplomatic service. He held such posts as governor of Hyōgo Prefecture, but later returned to Wakayama to take part in reforms in the political organization of the domain. In 1870 he went to Europe as part of an inspection tour from his domain, returning to Japan the following year. After the remaining domains were abolished and replaced by prefectures, he held the post of governor of Kanagawa Prefecture. In 1872 he was appointed head of the national tax office and set about carrying out the reforms in the land tax system that he had earlier urged the government to undertake.

In 1874, angered by the arbitrary manner in which the men of the former domains of Satsuma and Chōshū dominated government affairs, he presented an exposition of his views entitled *Nihonjin* to the statesman Kido Takayoshi and resigned his post. The following year, however, he was appointed a member of the Genrōin (Senate). At the time of the Seinan War, the revolt that broke out in Kyushu in 1877, he was accused of joining with Hayashi Yūzō, Ōe Taku, and other men of the former domain of Tosa in plotting to raise troops and move against the government. The following year he was condemned to five years in prison, being confined first to the prison in Yamagata Prefecture and later to that in Miyagi. During his period in prison, he produced a two-volume Japanese translation of Jeremy Bentham's *An Introduction to the Principle of Morals and Legislation*, which appeared in 1883 under the title *Rigaku seisō*.

He was released from prison in 1883 and the following year set off on a tour of Europe and America. In Austria he studied constitutional law and political administration under the eminent scholar Lorenz von Stein. On his return to Japan in 1886, he entered the Ministry of Foreign Affairs and in 1888 became minister to the United States. The following year he negotiated a treaty with Mexico, the first treaty that Japan concluded with a non-Asian nation in which it held equal status with the other party to the treaty. In 1890 he was appointed minister of agriculture and commerce in the first Yamagata cabinet. The same year he became a candidate from Wakayama in the first general election and was elected to the Lower House of the Diet, though he resigned the post the following year. He continued to serve as minister of agriculture and commerce in the succeeding Matsukata cabinet, but resigned in 1892 and became an advisor to the Privy Council. The same year, he became minister of foreign affairs in the second Itō cabinet. He was a highly resourceful and sharp-witted man, and soon earned the nickname "The Razor Minister."

He pressed ahead with negotiations for treaty revision, and in 1894 succeeded in signing new commercial treaties first with Great Britain and then the United States. Thus he managed to realize one of the long-standing objectives of the Meiji government. The same year saw the outbreak of the Sino-Japanese War, and in 1895 he joined Itō Hirobumi in the peace negotiations between China and Japan that led to the Shimonoseki Treaty. He resigned his post as minister of foreign affairs the same year because of illness. He went to Hawaii for a time to recuperate and, after returning to Japan, helped his friend Takegoshi Yosaburō to publish a magazine called *Sekai no Nihon*, to which he contributed articles. During his illness, he wrote his memoirs concerning the Sino-Japanese War and the diplomatic events surrounding the Triple Intervention of Russia, France, and Germany. Completed at the end of 1895, the work is entitled *Kenkenroku* and is a classic of its kind.

Nagaoka Hantarō 長岡半太郎 (1865–1950)

Physicist of the Meiji, Taishō, and Shōwa eras; he was born in what later became Nagasaki Prefecture. In 1887 he graduated from the physics course of Tokyo Imperial University. He went to Germany in 1893 for further study and on his return to Japan became a professor of Tokyo University. His early researches were concerned principally with magnetism and geophysics, particularly the study of magnetostriction, the measurement of the elasticity of rocks, and comparison of the gravitational constant of Tokyo and Potsdam, and he played an important role as a leader in Japanese steel and geophysical research. In addition, he made significant practical contributions in such varied fields as gravity measurement, optics, electromagnetics, radio wave propagation, and atomistics. He is particularly famous for his nuclear model theory, propounded in 1903, which posited the existence of the atomic nucleus, and he conducted numerous experimental researches on the atomic spectrum. He was instrumental in the founding of the Institute of Physical and Chemical Research and the science department of Tōhoku Imperial University and was active as chief researcher of the former institution. In his late years he served as the first president of Osaka Imperial University and head of the Imperial Academy. In 1937 he was among the first group to receive the Cultural Award.

Nakae Chōmin 中江兆民 (1847–1901)

Meiji period critic and advocate of popular rights; he was born in Kōchi in the province of Tosa in Shikoku; his personal name was Tokusuke, and his literary name Shūsui. He studied Chinese in the domain school and Western studies under Hosokawa Junjirō. He was chosen by his domain to go to Nagasaki, where he studied French. In 1867 he went to Edo and continued the study of French in a school headed by Murakami Hidetoshi, but was expelled because of his dissipated habits. He managed to continue studying French under a Catholic priest in Yokohama and in time was employed as an interpreter for the French minister, being sent to the Kobe-Osaka area. He returned to Edo in 1868 and enrolled in a school headed by Mitsukuri Rinshō, where he once more studied French. In 1869 he became headmaster of a private school established by Fukuchi Gen'ichirō. In 1870 he took a position as assistant professor of French in the Daigaku Nankō, which later became Tokyo University. He became acquainted with the statesman Ōkubo Toshimichi and expressed a desire to study abroad, whereupon he was allowed to accompany Ōkubo and the others in the government mission headed by Iwakura Tomomi, which left Japan in 1871. Once in America, he separated himself from the mission and went to France for study. On his return to Japan in 1874, he opened a school for French studies called Futsugaku-juku at Banchō in Tokyo. In 1875 he became head of the Gaikokugo Gakkō, or School of Foreign Languages, but soon resigned and took a position in the Genrōin (Senate). This ended the following year when a quarrel with the statesman Mutsu Munemitsu led to his resignation. He thereafter devoted full attention to the operation of his school for French studies.

In 1881 he founded a daily newspaper called *Tōyō Jiyū Shimbun* with Saionji Kimmochi, whom he had known from his days in France, as president and himself as chief editor. He used the paper to publicize French style views on popular rights and to attack the domain cliques that dominated the government, but he was obliged to suspend publication the following year. In 1882 he published a translation of Rousseau's *Contrat social* into classical Chinese and in time became known as the "Oriental Rousseau" because of his views on popular rights. In 1887 he published a work entitled *Sansuijin keirin mondō*, in which he discussed the relationship between popular rights thinking and nationalism and emphasized the need for government reforms in Japan. He supported Gotō Shōjirō in the latter's efforts to bring about a fusion of the parties opposing the government and at the end of the year was banished from the capital along with a number of other persons from Kōchi.

The following year he started publication of a daily newspaper called *Shinonome Shimbun* in Osaka. Around this time, Kōtoku Denjirō, later prominent in Socialist circles, became his disciple, and Nakae turned over the use of the literary name Shūsui to Kōtoku. In 1889, with the promulgation of the Meiji Constitution, the ban forbidding Nakae to be present in Tokyo was lifted. In 1890 he was a candidate in the first general election and was elected to the Lower House of the Diet, but he resigned the following year in disgust at the corrupt behavior of his fellow Diet members. For a year or so he served as chief editor of a daily newspaper, *Hokumon Shimpō*, published in Otaru in Hokkaido. For several years following, he tried his hand at forestry and various other activities in Hokkaido, but failed in all his ventures. In 1898, through his own efforts alone, he formed a political party called Kokumintō, but it failed to attract a following. In 1900 he participated in the Kokumin Dōmei of Konoe Atsumaro and in other ways showed himself increasingly attracted by nationalistic thinking. The same year, he was told by his doctors that, because of cancer of the throat, he had only a year or so left to live. He spent the time remaining by writing essays and critical articles, which he published in two works entitled *Ichinen yūhan* ("One Year and a Half") and *Zoku Ichinen yūhan* ("One Year and a Half, Continued).

Nakahama Manjirō 中濱萬次郎 (1827–1898)

Fisherman who was shipwrecked and taken to America in the late Edo period; he is also known as John Manjirō. He was born in Naka-no-hama, Ashizuri-misaki, in the province of Tosa in Shikoku, the son of a fisherman. He was out fishing in 1841 when he was shipwrecked in a typhoon and cast up on a deserted island. After living there for half a year, he was rescued by an American whaling vessel and taken to the United States. There, under the name John Mung, he attended school, studying English, mathematics, navigation, and surveying. He also took part in whaling activities and gold mining in California. In 1850 he left the United States aboard an American ship and, traveling by way of Honolulu and the Ryūkyū Islands, in 1851 succeeded in reaching Kagoshima in Satsuma. He was well treated by the lord of Satsuma, Shimazu Nariakira, but his native domain of Tosa, though it made use of his services, assigned him to the lowest samurai rank.

In 1853 the *rōjū* (senior councilor) Abe Masahiro arranged for him to become an official in the shogunate, and he was placed under the jurisdiction of the gunnery expert Egawa Tarōzaemon. The knowledge and ability in

English that he had acquired in America proved very useful, and he was put to work translating documents relating to foreign missions or works on navigation. He also wrote a book on English conversation and taught navigation at the naval training center set up by the shogunate. In 1860 he accompanied the official party that went to America aboard the *Kanrin Maru* to ratify the commercial treaty between the US and Japan. After his return, he directed whaling activities in the area of the Bonin Islands. He later taught English in the domains of Satsuma and Tosa. In 1869, following the Meiji Restoration, he became a professor of English in the Kaisei Gakkō, the forerunner of Tokyo University. In 1870 he accompanied the military leader Ōyama Iwao on a trip to Europe for the purpose of observing the methods of warfare employed in the Franco-Prussian War. The following year he returned to Japan because of illness.

Nakamura Masanao 中村正直 (1832–1891)

Scholar and educator of the early Meiji period; he was born in Edo, the son of a lower rank retainer of the shogunate. His common name was Keisuke, and his literary name Keiu. From his childhood he showed an aptitude for learning and in 1848 entered the Shōheikō, a school for Chinese studies established by the shogunate in Edo. In time he became an instructor in the Shōheikō and the Kitenkan, a school in Kōfu for the children of retainers of the shogunate. In 1862, at the unusually young age of thirty, he became a *jusha* (professor) in the Shōheikō. An outstanding scholar of Chinese, he at the same time took up Dutch and English studies in private and supported those who advocated the opening of the country. In 1866 he volunteered to go to England for study, but returned to Japan in 1868 because of the overthrow of the shogunate. He accompanied the last shogun to the domain in Shizuoka that had been assigned to the Tokugawa family and there worked to set up a school. With the founding of the school, he took up the position of professor of Chinese studies. At the same time he produced and published translations of Samuel Smiles' *Self-Help* and John Stuart Mills' *On Liberty* and worked to introduce modern Western thought to Japan. His translations exercised a strong influence upon the society of early Meiji times.

In 1872 he was invited to take a position in the central government, being assigned as a translator to the Ministry of Finance. In 1873 he opened a private school at Koishikawa in Tokyo called the Dōjinsha, where he taught English and Chinese. In the same year he joined Mori Arinori, Nishimura Shigeki, Fukuzawa Yukichi, and others in forming the Meirokusha, an association of scholars and intellectuals that published a magazine, *Meiroku Zasshi*, and labored to spread Western style enlightenment among the population. Nakamura also interested himself in the education of women, children, and the blind and advocated measures for its improvement.

In 1875 he became a teacher at the Tokyo Girls' Normal School and later at Tokyo Imperial University. He was also a member of the Genrōin and of the Upper House of the Diet. In 1888 he received the degree of Doctor of Literature. In addition to these activities, he played an important role in the spread of Christianity in the early Meiji period. He was among the first Japanese of the Meiji period to receive baptism and produced a Japanese translation of a Chinese work on Christian doctrine entitled *T'ien-tao su-yüan*; his translation exercised an important influence upon the missionary movement in Japan.

Nakayama Miki 中山みき (1798–1887)

Religious leader of the late Edo period and founder of the sect called Tenri-kyō. She was born in the province of Yamato, the daughter of a landowner. Around 1810 she married Nakayama Zembei, a landowner in the village of Shōyashiki (present-day Tenri City) south of Nara. She gave birth to one son and five daughters. The illness of her son and her own difficulties in childbirth caused her much suffering. In the tenth lunar month of 1839, she experienced a supernatural possession for a period of three days and three nights. After her husband's death in 1853, she was forced to endure extreme poverty, but discovered she had the power to cure illness and ease childbirth and soon attracted a following among her neighbors. In 1867 she worked out the model for her *Mikagura-uta*, songs in counting-song form that gave expression to her religious teachings. During the period from 1869 to 1882, she composed her *Ofudesaki*, writings in the form of traditional style Japanese poems.

Her teachings are salvationist and monotheistic in nature, centering upon the worship of the deity Tenriō-no-mikoto, and call upon all persons to live lives of joy based upon the principle of human equality. In spite of harsh suppression by the Meiji government, her teachings attracted a wide following, particularly among the middle and lower class farming population, and by 1880 had spread all over Japan. In 1888, the year after the founder's death, the religion was given official recognition under the name Tenri Kyōkai and attached to the Shinto office of the government. In 1908 it gained independent status as one of the sects of Neo- or Sectarian Shinto.

NANJŌ BUN'YŪ 南條文雄 (1849–1927)

Meiji period Buddhist priest and scholar of Buddhism; he was born in Gifu, the son of a priest of the Ōtani branch of the Jōdo Shin sect. He was educated at the Takakura Gakuryō, the highest educational establishment maintained by the Ōtani branch of the Jōdo Shin sect. In 1870 he became adopted heir to the priest of a temple called Okunen-ji in the province of Echizen. In 1876 the headquarters of his sect sent him to England for study. He studied Sanskrit under the eminent Indologist Max Müller and devoted himself to research in the Buddhist scriptures. He returned to Japan in 1880 and thereafter successively held the posts of lecturer at Tokyo Imperial University, professor of Shinshū University, and president of Ōtani University. In 1884 he became the first scholar in Japan to receive a Ph.D. degree. He later became a member of the Imperial Japan Academy.

While in England, he produced an English translation of the Chinese index, *Ta-ming san-tsang sheng-chiao mu-lu*, appended to the Huang-po (Ōbaku) edition of the *Daizōkyō* (Tripitaka), which appeared under the title *A Catalogue of the Chinese Translation of the Buddhist Tripitaka by Bunyu Nanjo* and served as a model for Western language studies of Buddhism. He also worked with Max Müller to edit and publish a definitive Sanskrit text of the *Sukhāvatī-vyūha* (*Muryōjū-kyō*) and with H. Kern to produce a Sanskrit text of the *Saddharmapundarīka* (*Hokekyō*), or Lotus Sutra. Such is the quality of these texts that they continue to be used today. He also produced Japanese translations and explications of Buddhist scriptures.

NIIJIMA JŌ 新島襄 (1843–1890)

Christian educator of the Meiji period; he was born in Kanda in Edo, the son of a lower ranking samurai of the domain of Annaka in Kōzuke, present-day Gumma Prefecture. In his youth he went by the name Shimeta; shortly after the Restoration, he used the name Joseph, but later settled on Jō. His father served as a secretary in the domain administration and was also a teacher of calligraphy, and as heir to his father, Niijima began the study of calligraphy at an early age. When he was thirteen, however, he was ordered by the lord of the domain to take up the study of Dutch learning, as Western science and technology were known at the time. From the age of fifteen he served as a secretary in the domain residence in Edo but at the same time attended a school called the Kaigun Denshūjo, where he studied mathematics and navigation.

Around this time he read a book by an American missionary and conceived a desire to travel abroad. Since all Japanese at this time were forbidden to leave the country, he traveled to Hakodate in Hokkaido and in 1864 managed to board an American ship bound for Shanghai. In Shanghai he boarded another American ship named *Wild Rover* and eventually reached Boston. Through the assistance of A. Hardy, the owner of the *Wild Rover*, he was able to apply himself to study and in 1870 graduated from Amherst College. He also attended Andover Theological Seminary and in 1871 was officially recognized by the Meiji government as a Japanese student abroad. When the Japanese inspection mission headed by Iwakura arrived in the United States in 1872, Niijima proved especially helpful to Tanaka Fujimaro, the member of the mission in charge of educational matters, and later accompanied the mission on its inspection of Europe, submitting a report on the educational systems he had observed.

In 1874 he graduated from Andover and, with a donation of $5,000, returned to Japan determined to found a Christian college. In 1875, through the assistance of Yamamoto Kakuma, an advisor in the Kyoto prefectural administration, and an American missionary named J. D. Davis, he was able to use the sum in setting up a school in Kyoto called Dōshisha. In the years that followed, he trained many young men who felt sympathetic toward Christianity and took them with him when he went about to various parts of Japan to spread Christian teachings. In his later years, he devoted his efforts to promoting Dōshisha to the status of a regular college, making fund-raising trips to Europe and America and persuading influential Japanese to lend their aid to his undertaking. In doing so, however, he overtaxed his health and died at the age of forty-seven.

Nishi Amane 西周 (1829–1897)

Scholar of Western studies and bureaucrat of the early Meiji period. He was born in the domain of Tsuwano in the province of Iwami, the son of a samurai physician. His common name was Michitarō; he was later called Shūsuke and, after the Meiji Restoration, Amane. He was ordered by his domain to specialize in Chinese studies, but when he was sent to Edo for that purpose, he determined to devote himself to Western studies instead, removing himself from the authority of his domain in 1854. In 1857, on completion of his studies, he was assigned a position in the Bansho Shirabesho, an institute for Western studies set up in Edo by the shogunate. In 1862 he was ordered by the shogunate to go to Holland for further study. Along with Tsuda

Masamichi, he studied political science, law, economics, and philosophy under a professor named Vissering of the University of Leyden.

Upon his return to Japan in 1865, he became a retainer of the shogunate and was made a professor of the Kaiseijo, a school for Western studies that grew out of the Bansho Shirabesho. He produced a translation of a work on international law under the title *Bankoku kōhō*. In 1867 he accompanied the shogun Tokugawa Yoshinobu to Kyoto, where the power of government was formally restored to the court. The following year, when the shogunate had been abolished and Yoshinobu assigned to a domain in Shizuoka, he accompanied him there, becoming a senior teacher of the Numazu Naval Academy and introducing Western style teaching methods.

In 1870 he was invited to take a position in the Meiji government, being assigned to the Ministry of Military Affairs, where he worked under the direction of Yamagata Aritomo to reorganize Japan's military system. In 1873 he joined Mori Arinori, Nishimura Shigeki, Tsuda Masamichi, and others in forming an association of scholars and intellectuals known as the Meirokusha; they published a magazine, *Meiroku Zasshi*, to make known their views and worked to promote the Westernization of Japan. In 1879 he became head of the Tokyo Academy, in 1882 a member of the Genrōin, and in 1890 a member of the Upper House of the Diet. In 1897 he received the title of baron. He devoted his life to introducing European and American civilization to Japan. His best known work is *Hyakugaku renkan*, which attempts to systematize a number of different fields of learning, and he also published a translation of a work by John Stuart Mill.

NISHIDA KITARŌ 西田幾太郎 (1870–1945)

Philosopher of the Meiji, Taishō, and early Shōwa periods; he was the son of a distinguished family of the Kahoku district in Ishikawa Prefecture. After completing the Ishikawa Normal School and Ishikawa Prefecture Special School (later the Fourth High School), he entered Tokyo Imperial University. He graduated from the philosophy course as a nonregular student in 1894 and returned to Ishikawa, where he became a middle and high school teacher. Troubled by discord at home and in his work, he took up the practice of Zen Buddhism. On the basis of his Zen study, he produced in 1919 a work entitled *Zen no kenkyū* in which he established the principle of "pure experience." Meanwhile, in 1909 he had become a professor of the Peers' School and later became an assistant professor and professor of Kyoto Imperial University. In 1913 he received the degree of Doctor of Philosophy.

He retired from teaching in 1928 and thereafter devoted his time to the systematizing of his philosophy, a process that around 1933–34 resulted in what has come to be known as the Nishida philosophy. It is important as the first original and independent system to emerge from Japanese philosophy, which had hitherto been completely dominated by systems of thought introduced from abroad. In addition to the work mentioned above, Nishida's other important writings include *Jikaku ni okeru chokkan to hansei*, *Hataraku mono kara miru mono e*, *Tetsugaku no kompon mondai*, and *Ippanjin no jikakuteki hansei*.

NISHIMURA KATSUZŌ 西村勝三 (1836–1907)

Meiji period pioneer in various business undertakings; his childhood name was Sampei. His father was a samurai of the domain of Sakura in Shimōsa and chief retainer of the allied domain of Sano in Shimotsuke; his elder brother Nishimura Shigeki was an exponent of Western learning and a leader in moral education. Nishimura Katsuzō, having studied Western style gunnery, began his career as a samurai in the service of the domain of Sano but later relinquished his samurai status and became a commoner, devoting himself to commercial and industrial activities. At the end of the Edo period, he made large profits through the illegal import of Western style guns, but his activities came to light, and he was for a time imprisoned on Ishikawa Island in Edo. He later separated himself from the commercial house of Ise Hei, with which he had previously been allied, and set himself up independently under the name Ise Katsu, selling firearms and ammunition and realizing huge profits.

In 1869 he received an order for military shoes from Ōmura Masujirō, who was engaged in building an army for the newly formed Meiji government, an order that he filled by importing shoes from abroad. In 1870, determined to make shoes that were better fitted for Japanese use, he set up a shoe manufacturing plant in the Tsukiji area of Tokyo and later established other leather manufacturing plants. In 1870 he set up a factory for the production of machine-knitted goods. In all these undertakings he employed the younger sons of the former samurai of his old domain, in this way helping to give employment to members of the class to which he had originally belonged.

In 1872 he opened a Western style clothing store on the Ginza in Tokyo and in 1875 began the manufacture of firebrick. In 1885 he bought up the Shinagawa glass manufacturing works, which had previously been operated by the government. The following year he went abroad, visiting factories in many different countries and taking steps to introduce the latest Western technology to Japan. About half of his early ventures ended in failure, but he played a pioneering role in the development of many different industries and helped to lay the foundation for later growth. Emphasizing the importance of technology, he encouraged industrial education and contributed to the compilation of materials on the history of industry.

NISHIMURA SHIGEKI 西村茂樹 (1828–1902)

Thinker and educator of the Meiji period; he was born in Edo, the son of a samurai of the domain of Sakura in Shimōsa, present-day Chiba Prefecture. He went by the literary name Hakuō. He studied at the Onkodō, a school at the domain residence in Edo, and at the same time took instruction in horsemanship and the handling of the sword and lance. In addition, in order to strengthen Japan's position in the face of threats from foreign powers, he also studied Western gunnery and what he could learn of Dutch and British science. He served the Hotta and Sano families, being entrusted with various important posts, and took part in the administration of the domain. After the Restoration, he held posts in the Sakura and Inba areas and participated in the local administration. In 1872 he resigned these posts and went to Tokyo, where he opened a private school and became active as an educator. In 1873 he joined with Mori Arinori and other intellectual leaders in forming a cultural organization known as the Meirokusha, publishing a magazine called *Meiroku Zasshi* and working to educate the Japanese public. In 1873 he was also ordered to serve in the Ministry of Education and in 1875 was appointed a lecturer to Emperor Meiji.

For the following twenty years or more, he held posts in the Ministry of Education and Department of the Imperial Household, helping to formulate the educational policies of the government. He was critical of the tendency of the time to imitate European and American ways and worked to set up a system of moral education for the common people based upon the teachings of Confucianism. As a member of the Ministry of Education, he helped to compile textbooks on ethics for use in the public schools and at the same time, in 1876, founded an organization to further ethical teaching known as the Tokyo Shūshin Gakusha. In 1884 this was expanded to become the Nihon Kōdōkai, a nationwide organization designed to improve the morality of the Japanese people. In 1886 he became a court adviser, in 1887 the head of the Peeresses' School, and in 1890 a member of the Upper House of the

Diet. In 1901 he was awarded a Ph.D. His most important works are *Nihon dōtokuron* and *Kokka dōtokuron,* which deal with his views on national morals, and in addition he published translations such as *Bankoku shiryaku* (a world history) and *Taisei shikan* (a European history), from books in English and German, respectively.

NITOBE INAZŌ 新渡戸稲造 (1862–1933)

Educator and scholar of agriculture and English in the Meiji, Taishō, and early Shōwa periods. He was born in Morioka, the son of a samurai of the domain of Nambu. In 1877 he entered Sapporo Agricultural College and, along with his classmate Uchimura Kanzō, became a convert to Christianity. He was said to have been at the time an avid reader of Carlyle's *Sartor Resartus.* In 1883 he entered Tokyo Imperial University, and the following year went to America and entered Johns Hopkins University in Baltimore. After graduating, he spent the years from 1887 to 1890 studying agricultural administration at various universities in Germany. While abroad, he married an American named Mary P. Elkinton. After returning to Japan, he became a professor at Sapporo Agricultural College. In 1899 he published in America a work in English entitled *Bushido, the Soul of Japan,* in which he sought to introduce to Westerners the "code of the warrior," which forms the basis of moral education in Japan. The work was widely read and translated into various languages.

Nitobe later held positions as technical expert in the office of the governor-general of Taiwan, professor of Kyoto Imperial University, head of the First High School, and professor of Tokyo Imperial University. From 1920 to 1926 he served as assistant director general of the League of Nations, playing an active part on the international scene. He held the degrees of Doctor of Agriculture and Doctor of Law and was a member of the Imperial Academy and the Upper House of the Diet. He died in Victoria in Canada while attending a conference of the Institute of Pacific Relations in 1933. He worked vigorously for international peace and in particular for better understanding between Japan and America, lecturing at many places in the United States and endeavoring to act as a bridge between the two countries. His writings include *Nōgyō honron* and other works in Japanese and English.

Nogi Maresuke 乃木希典 (1849–1912)

Military leader and general of the army in the Meiji period; he held the title of count. He was born in the Mōri family residence in Edo, the son of Nogi Maretsugu, a samurai of the domain of Chōshū. He attended the Meirinkan, the official domain school in Hagi. He lived in the home of his uncle Tamaki Bunnoshin, the teacher of the celebrated scholar and patriot Yoshida Shōin, and received training from his uncle as well. In the Boshin civil war of 1868 he served under Yamagata Aritomo, engaging in battles with the forces remaining loyal to the shogunate in the Tōhoku area. After the Meiji Restoration he went to Kyoto and enlisted at Fushimi as a member of the imperial guard. He was dispatched to help put down a disturbance in the domain of Yamaguchi. In 1871 he became a major under the newly established system of army ranks. In 1876 he took part in the action to put down an antigovernment disturbance in Hagi led by discontented samurai. In 1877 he took part in the Seinan War as commander of an infantry regiment, but on his way to the rebel encampment at Kumamoto, his regimental flag was seized by the enemy. Nogi prepared to commit suicide, and though he was finally dissuaded by those around him, the sense of disgrace caused by the incident remained with him the rest of his life.

In 1883 he became chief of staff of the Tokyo Garrison. In 1885 he was promoted to the rank of major general and the following year went to Germany along with another high army officer, Kawakami Sōroku, to study military organization and methods of warfare. After his return to Japan in 1888, he served as a brigade commander in Tokyo and Nagoya, but was obliged to retire from duty for a time because of illness, living quietly in Nasuno in Tochigi Prefecture.

He returned to duty to participate in the Sino-Japanese War in 1894 as commander of the Eleventh Brigade, capturing Port Arthur in a single day. The following year, as lieutenant general and commander of the Second Brigade, he took control of Taiwan. He returned to Japan in victory in 1896 and the same year, at the request of Kodama Gentarō, became the third governor of Taiwan. He did not prove to be suited for an administrative position, however, and in 1898 turned over the post to Kodama. He became commander of the Eleventh Brigade, but in 1901 took leave from his post and once more retired to Nasuno to convalesce. With the outbreak of the Russo-Japanese War in 1904 he was restored to duty as commander of the Imperial Guard Division. Later he became commander of the Third Army with the rank of full general. He laid siege to Port Arthur, repeatedly launching full-scale attacks, and in 1905, after much bitter fighting and with the aid of

Kodama, the commander of the Manchurian Army, he finally succeeded in taking the city. He also participated in the fighting at Mukden. He lost two of his own sons in the fighting and seems to have felt an overwhelming sense of guilt and responsibility because of the large number of men killed in the action.

After the war, he became a military councilor of state and in 1907 was advanced from the title of baron to that of count. He also served as head of the Peers' School. Emperor Meiji looked to him in particular to train the sons of the nobility, and he responded by setting an example of correct moral and spiritual education. In 1911 he went to England along with the naval leader Tōgō Heihachirō to attend the coronation of George V. In 1916, when Emperor Meiji died, General Nogi and his wife Shizuko committed suicide at their home in Akasaka on the morning of the funeral. Their action, an example of the old custom of following one's lord in death, greatly moved the people of the time. General Nogi was highly admired for his virtue, an idealist who exemplified the finest qualities of the ancient code of the warrior. He was popularly referred to as "War God Nogi" and is deified at Nogi Shrine in Akasaka, Tokyo.

NOGUCHI HIDEYO 野口英世 (1876–1928)

Meiji, Taishō, and early Shōwa period bacteriologist. He was born in Fukushima Prefecture and as a boy went by the name Yoisaku. In his youth he suffered a severe burn on his left hand, but in 1892 underwent surgery at the Watanabe Hospital in Wakamatsu City and to a large extent recovered. This experience played a part in his decision to take up the study of medicine. The following year he became a clerk in the Watanabe Hospital and began medical studies. In 1896 he went to Tokyo and, while working in the Takayama Dental College (later Tokyo Dental College), he entered a medical school called the Saisei Gakusha and continued his studies. In 1897 he passed the examination for medical practice and became a lecturer in the Takayama Dental College. The following year he entered the Research Center for Infectious Diseases and, under the guidance of Kitazato Shibasaburō, began the study of bacteriology. In 1900 he went to America and, through the assistance of a pathologist named Simon Flexner, was able to enter the University of Pennsylvania, where he received a doctorate for his researches on rattlesnake venom.

In 1903 he went to Denmark and continued his studies in the Staatens Serum Institut. The following year he returned to the United States and became a member of the Rockefeller Medical Institute, taking up permanent residence in America. The Institute attracted medical scholars from all over the world, and as a result Noguchi's achievements in bacteriology soon gained international recognition. In 1911 he succeeded in producing a pure culture of *Spirochaeta pallida* and was awarded a Japanese doctorate of medicine. He made another important contribution by proving that progressive paresis and tabes dorsalis were caused by the syphillis spirochaete. He also published researches on the causes of infantile paralysis, rabies, and trachoma.

In 1914 he became a department head in the Rockefeller Institute and was awarded a Japanese doctorate of science. In 1915 he received an Imperial Academy prize and shortly after returned to Japan, but went to America once more and began studies of yellow fever. In 1918 he journeyed to Central and South America to study the causes of yellow fever, which was rampant there. In 1923 he was recommended to become a member of the Imperial Academy. In 1928 he went to the area of the present-day state of Ghana in Africa to continue his studies of yellow fever and there contracted the fever and died. Because of his important contributions and great devotion to medical research, he is internationally renowned as one of the greatest figures of modern Japanese science.

NOMURA KICHISABURŌ 野村吉三郎 (1877–1964)

Naval leader and diplomat of the Taishō and Shōwa eras; he was the son of a former samurai of the domain of Wakayama. He graduated from the Naval Academy and Naval Staff School and in 1900 was commissioned as an ensign; by 1922 he had advanced to the rank of rear admiral. During the period from 1908 to 1911 he was stationed in Austria and Germany and from 1914 to 1918, during the First World War, was a military officer attached to the Japanese embassy in the United States, at which time he became very friendly with Franklin D. Roosevelt. In 1912 he was a member of the Japanese delegation to the Washington Conference. In 1925 he became chief of the Bureau of Naval Affairs in the Ministry of the Navy and in 1926 assistant chief of the Naval General Staff, advancing to the rank of vice admiral. Thereafter he served in succession as commander of the Kure and Yokosuka naval yards, and in 1932, as commander of the Third Fleet, was dispatched to deal with the Shanghai Incident. At the celebration of the emperor's birthday in the Shanghai New Park, he was wounded by a bomb and lost the sight in one eye.

In 1937 he entered the reserve and the same year became head of the Peers' School. In 1939 he became minister of foreign affairs in the cabinet of Abe Nobuyuki and carried on talks with US ambassador Grew. With the outbreak of the Second World War, he strove to maintain friendly relations between Japan and the United States. In 1940 he was appointed ambassador to the US. In 1941 he arranged for Kurusu Saburō to come as a special envoy to Washington to try to resolve Japanese and American differences and continued negotiations with Secretary of State Hull up until the eve of the Pearl Harbor attack in an effort to avoid conflict, but with the outbreak of the Pacific War he returned to Japan. In 1944 he became an advisor to the Privy Council. After the war, in 1953, he became president of Japan Victor Company, and in 1954 was elected to the Upper House of the Diet.

NORO EITARŌ 野呂榮太郎 (1900–1934)

Economist and Marxist theoretician of the early Shōwa period; he was born in Hokkaido. While still a student in the economics department of Keiō University, he joined Nosaka Sanzō in doing work for the Industry and Labor Research Center and was active in the Mita Social Science Studies Society and the labor school affiliated with the Japan Federation of Labor. In 1926 he was implicated in the investigation of left-wing student activities in Kyoto and charges were brought against him. In 1927 he completed his graduation thesis entitled *Nihon shihon shugi hattatsu shi* ("History of the Growth of Japanese Capitalism"), and its contents were introduced in *Shakai mondai kenkyū* (published by Shinchōsha) and other publications. In 1929 he played a leading role in the founding of the Proletarian Science Research Center. In 1930 his graduation thesis was published in book form, and the same year he became a member of the Japan Communist Party. In 1931 he participated in the planning and editing of a series of lectures on the history of the growth of Japanese capitalism prepared by a number of scholars. He thus became a leading spokesman for the theories of the so-called lecture group, which was soon engaged in a spirited controversy with the members of the "labor-farm group."

From the autumn of 1932 on, he was engaged in various illegal underground activities. As a member of the secretariat of the Central Committee of the Japan Communist Party, he worked in cooperation with Miyamoto Kenji and others to rebuild the party and, in spite of the fact that he was suffering from chest disease, continued to edit the lecture series for publication by Iwanami Shoten. In 1934 he was arrested and subjected to torture at the Shinagawa police headquarters and died thereafter in Shinagawa Hospital.

Nosaka Sanzō 野坂参三 (1892–)

Taishō and Shōwa period socialist thinker and a leader of the Japan Communist Party; he has at times gone by the name Okano Susumu. His wife Nosaka Ryō (d. 1971), was also a member of the Communist Party and active in the spread of socialism. He was born in the city of Hagi in Yamaguchi Prefecture. While a student in Keiō Gijuku in Tokyo, he joined the Yūaikai, a labor organization headed by Suzuki Bunji. After graduating, he became secretary of the organization and edited a journal that it put out. In 1919 he was sent to England as special representative of the organization, and in 1920, when the British Communist Party was founded, he became a member. After being deported from England, he visited France, Germany, and the Soviet Union and returned to Japan in 1922, where he joined the newly founded Japan Communist Party. He was arrested and imprisoned in 1923 and again in 1928 when the police took steps to suppress the Communist Party.

In 1931 he received secret instructions to go to the Soviet Union as Japanese representative to the Comintern, where he was active in maintaining contacts between the Communist movement in Japan and abroad. He also made two undercover visits to America. In 1940 he went to China, intending to return to Japan, but instead remained in Yenan, where he worked in cooperation with the Chinese Communist Party. There he organized a Japanese antiwar society made up largely of Japanese soldiers who had been taken prisoner by the Communist forces.

After the end of the war, he returned to Japan in 1946, where he received an enthusiastic welcome. In conjunction with Tokuda Kyūichi and Shiga Yoshio, he issued a joint statement calling for a flexible approach and proposing the slogan "a lovable Communist Party." At the general meeting of the party, Nosaka's doctrine of "peaceful revolution" was adopted, and the same year he was elected to the Lower House of the Diet. In 1950 he was purged from office on orders from General MacArthur, but resumed overt political activity in 1955. In 1956 he was elected to the Upper House of the Diet as representative from the Tokyo area. Since then he has served along with Miyamoto Kenji as leader of the Japan Communist Party, making certain that it maintains its independence and autonomy.

Ōi Kentarō 大井憲太郎 (1843–1922)

Political figure of the Meiji and Taishō eras; he was born in Takanami in the province of Buzen, present-day Ōita Prefecture. He first applied himself to Chinese studies, but at the age of nineteen went to Nagasaki and took up Western studies. In 1865 he went to Edo and entered the Kaiseijo, a school for Western studies that had been set up by the shogunate, where he studied French and chemistry. He worked in the Chemistry Bureau attached to the shogunate. After the Meiji Restoration, he taught Western studies for a time and entered the Daigaku Nankō, a school that later became Tokyo Imperial University. In 1871 he took a post in the Ministry of Military Affairs and in 1875 became an undersecretary in the Genrōin (Senate). At the same time, he became active in the popular rights movement. In 1876 he resigned his official position and became a lawyer.

When the Jiyūtō (Liberal Party) was formed in 1881 he became a member and went about the country making speeches. He also acted as a lawyer in cases such as the Fukushima incident of 1882, when the party members clashed with the government. In 1885 he and his associates began collecting money and arms to support the Korean independence movement. When his activities were discovered, he was arrested, but released from prison as a result of the general amnesty in 1888. He resumed his participation in the popular rights movement and helped to revive the Liberal Party, but resigned from the party because he felt it cooperated too readily with the government.

In 1892 he founded a party of his own called the Tōyō Jiyūtō and in 1894 was elected to the Lower House of the Diet. From early in his career he took an interest in social problems and the rights of labor, but after the turn of the century the advocates of socialism came forward to replace him as the leaders of such causes. In his late years he was active in the movement for universal suffrage.

Okada Keisuke 岡田啓介 (1868–1952)

Naval leader and statesman of the Taishō and Shōwa eras; he was the son of a samurai of the domain of Fukui. He graduated from the Naval Academy and Naval Staff College and, after being commissioned as an ensign in 1890, advanced rapidly until, by 1913, he held the rank of rear admiral. In 1915 he became head of the Personnel Section of the Naval Ministry. In 1917 he advanced to vice admiral and became commander of the naval dockyard at

Sasebo, head of the Bureau of Warship Construction and Maintenance, and vice-minister of the navy. In 1924 he was made a military councilor and commander of the Combined Fleet and in 1926 commander of the Yokosuka Naval Yard. After holding these important posts, he was appointed minister of the navy in the Tanaka Giichi cabinet in 1927. In 1929 he once more became a military councilor and in 1930 worked to smooth over differences of opinion within naval circles and to pave the way for Japan's signing of the agreement drawn up by the London Disarmament Conference, gaining the recognition of the elder statesman Saionji Kimmochi.

He served once more as minister of the navy in the Saitō Makoto cabinet in 1932 and the following years entered the reserve. In 1934, on the recommendation of Saionji Kimmochi, he succeeded Saitō as prime minister and formed his own cabinet, but as a result of the furor caused by Professor Minobe Tatsukichi's description of the emperor as an "organ of the state," and the necessity that it precipitated for the government to clarify the exact nature of the national polity, he was subjected to heavy pressure from right-wing military leaders and members of the Seiyūkai. In 1936, shortly after the opposition party, the Minseitō, emerged victorious in the general election, the revolt of the young army officers known as the February 26 incident occurred. One group of officers attacked the prime minister's residence, and when word was given out that Okada had been put to death, the cabinet resigned. In fact, however, he managed to escape with his life. Thereafter, as a senior statesman, he took part in the selection of men for the post of prime minister, and in 1944, toward the end of the Pacific War, played a key role in overthrowing the Tōjō Hideki cabinet.

Ōkawa Shūmei 大川周明 (1886–1957)

Nationalistic thinker of the early Shōwa period; he was born in Yamagata Prefecture. After graduating from the philosophy course of Tokyo Imperial University, he applied himself to the study of Marxism and Indian thought. While pursuing these studies, he supported himself by editorial work for the magazine *Michi* headed by Matsumura Kaiseki and by doing translation jobs for the General Staff Office of the army. In 1918 he took a position in Tokyo with the South Manchuria Railway. He served as head of the research section of the company's East Asia Economic Research Bureau and later as head of the bureau itself, and when the bureau separated from the company and became an independent organization, he became its director.

Around this time he began to advocate a type of national revolution that had strong fascist overtones, and in 1919 he joined with Kita Ikki and Mitsukawa Kametarō to form the Yūzonsha (Society for the Preservation of the National Essence). In addition to putting out *Nihonjin*, the society's official magazine, he published a number of pamphlets, devoting himself to the spread of nationalistic ideas. From 1920 on, he also held a position as professor of Takushoku University in Tokyo, lecturing on the history of colonialism. In 1926 he was awarded the degree of Doctor of Law for his study of the system of chartered colonial companies, a study that was said to have been highly praised by the eminent political scientist Yoshino Sakuzō.

Meanwhile, Ōkawa was forming close connections with a number of middle-ranking army officers. In 1931 he joined with Lieutenant Colonel Hashimoto Kingorō and other officers to form a secret society known as the Sakurakai (Cherry Society) and began planning a military coup d'état. The plans were scheduled for execution in March of 1931, and again in October, but in both cases were called off or failed to be carried out. In 1932, Ōkawa reorganized and expanded the right-wing group Kōchisha, reestablishing it as the Jimmukai with himself as its head. He called for the liberation of all nonwhite peoples and the moral unity of the world, preaching a kind of overall Asian nationalism that was strongly colored by national socialism. He thus came to rank beside Kita Ikki as one of the leading thinkers of the fascist movement in Japan in the thirties.

Ōkawa had only indirect connections with the May 15th incident of 1932, when a group of young naval officers and army cadets carried out various attacks and assassinations, but he was arrested nevertheless and condemned to five years' imprisonment. He was released in 1937 as the result of a general amnesty. He worked to drum up support for Japan's war effort in China and, after the outbreak of the Pacific War, enthusiastically advocated the establishment of what was known in the national slogans of the time as "the new order in Greater East Asia." For this purpose he wrote treatises such as that entitled *Daitōa shin chitsujo no rekishiteki seikaku* ("The Historical Character of the New Order in Greater East Asia") and also took pains to expound his ideas in academic circles.

After Japan's surrender, he was arrested as a first-class war crimes suspect, but at the public trial held before the International Military Tribunal for the Far East, he slapped one of the other defendants, the former prime minister and general of the army Tōjō Hideki, on the head. He was excused from the trial on grounds of mental disorder and was confined to a hospital. Later the charges against him were dropped and he was set at liberty. He devoted his last years to translating the Koran into Japanese. In addition to the works already mentioned, he was the author of *Kinsei Yōroppa shokuminshi* and other works.

Ōkubo Toshimichi 大久保利通 (1830–1878)

Leading statesman of the early Meiji period; he was born in the domain of Satsuma in Kyushu, the son of a lower-class samurai; his common name was Ichizō and his literary name Kōtō. He was a close friend of Saigō Takamori, another samurai of Satsuma, who was destined to play an important role in the Meiji Restoration. Ōkubo entered the service of his domain in 1846 as a keeper of records, but in 1849, because of his father's involvement in a dispute over who should succeed to the position of lord of the domain, he was condemned to exile. In 1851, when Shimazu Nariakira became lord of Satsuma, he was pardoned and permitted to return and thereafter played a key role in the reform of the domain administration. His fortunes suffered a temporary eclipse after the death of Shimazu Nariakira in 1858, but his abilities were in time recognized by the latter's younger brother Shimazu Hisamitsu, who wielded actual power in the domain.

In 1863 he became personal attendant to the lord of the domain and devoted himself to carrying out administrative reforms and promoting the *kōbu-gattai* movement, which sought to promote cooperation between the imperial court and the shogunate. But the Satsuma-British War of 1863 and the coup d'état in the eighth month of the same year, which forced seven antishogunate nobles to flee from the court, convinced him that such cooperation was impossible and he joined Saigō Takamori in going over to the side of those who advocated forceful overthrow of the shogunate.

In 1866, through the intermediary offices of Sakamoto Ryōma, a samurai of Tosa, Ōkubo and Saigō negotiated with Katsura Kogorō of the domain of Chōshū and concluded an agreement that ended the quarreling between Satsuma and Chōshū and opened the way for their concerted efforts to overthrow the shogunate. In 1867 Ōkubo concluded an agreement with Gotō Shōjirō and others to work for restoration of power to the emperor and also made contact with Iwakura Tomomi, an important court noble who supported an attack on the shogunate. This resulted in a secret pact by the domains of Satsuma, Chōshū, and Aki to call out their troops for such an attack, and later in a secret imperial order to Satsuma and Chōshū to carry out the attack. From this time on, he played an even more crucial role in the development of events on the political scene.

He helped to form a new government centering about the Emperor Meiji, offering proposals concerning changes in the court system and measures for adopting elements of foreign culture, as well as proposing that the capital be moved to Osaka. Later in the same year, when resistance to the imperial forces had largely come to an end, he took the position of *san'yo* (councilor) and worked to restore order to the city of Edo, at the same time instituting reforms in the feudal administrative system. In 1869 he became a councilor of state and was instrumental in arranging the move by which the lords of Satsuma, Chōshū, Tosa, and Hizen returned their domains to the emperor. In 1871, after deliberations with Kido Takayoshi (formerly called Katsura Kogorō) and Gotō Shōjirō, he took decisive steps to abolish the feudal domains and establish the prefectural system, making it clear that any attempt at resistance would not be tolerated. He became minister of finance in the same year and set about strengthening the financial position of the new government and working to improve the economic and military state of the country as a whole. In order to gain a first-hand knowledge of affairs in foreign countries, he joined the diplomatic embassy that left Japan at the end of 1871, participating as a vice-envoy extraordinary and minister plenipotentiary and visiting America and Europe.

Upon his return to Japan in 1873, he resumed his position as councilor of state and succeeded in driving out of power the men who had been agitating for an attack upon Korea. He established the Home Ministry, which was to become a pivotal organ in the Japanese governmental system, and with himself as home minister proceeded to display his political acumen. As head of the project to reform land taxes, he worked to improve the fiscal affairs of the government and also took measures to promote industry and assist the growth of Japanese capitalism. At the same time, he was criticized by the followers of the popular rights movement and members of the former samurai class because of the strongly despotic trend in his character.

In 1874 he dealt sternly with the samurai uprising in Saga led by Etō Shimpei and went to China in person to negotiate an indemnity after the Japanese expedition against Taiwan. At least outwardly, he attempted to placate those elements among the former samurai population who were opposed to the government. He took measures to suppress his other critics, the leaders of the popular rights movement, but at the same time he called a conference in Osaka at which he negotiated with Itagaki Taisuke, the head of the movement, persuading the latter to return to his position as councilor of state and indicating that he was willing to move toward the gradual establishment of constitutional government. He also proposed that land taxes be reduced as a means of dealing with the frequent outbreaks of rioting among the farmers. He demonstrated great skill in determining when it was wise to apply stern measures and when more conciliatory gestures were appropriate, doing his best to insure stability to the government. But discontent and outright defiance among the former samurai continued to be a problem, ending only with the Seinan War of 1877. In the period of relative peace that followed, he devoted his attention to promoting the modernization of the country. He was assassinated at Akasaka in Tokyo in 1878 by Shimada Ichirō, a disaffected samurai of the type who had so often opposed him in the past.

Ōkuma Shigenobu 大隈重信 (1838–1922)

Statesman of the Meiji and Taishō eras; he held the title of marquis. He was born in the domain of Saga in Kyushu and at the age of six entered the Kōdōkan, the official school of the domain, where he studied the Chu Hsi school of Neo-Confucianism. At the age of sixteen he joined the *sonnō-jōi* movement, which advocated restoration of power to the emperor and the expulsion of the foreign traders from Japan. As a result of such activities, however, he was forced to withdraw from school in 1855. The same year, he entered the Rangakuryō, a school for Dutch learning, devoting himself to Western and Japanese studies. After the outbreak of hostilities between the domain of Chōshū and the ships of the Western powers in 1863, he urged that Saga assist Chōshū and stressed the need for national unity in order to carry out the goals of the *sonnō-jōi* movement, but he was not able to persuade the lord of Saga to endorse his views. He then devoted himself to the founding of a school in Nagasaki known as the Chienkan for the purpose of training students in Western learning and himself studied English and mathematics under an American missionary named Guido Verbeck, who was residing in Nagasaki.

In 1866, he joined his fellow clansman Soejima Taneomi in leaving Saga without official permission and journeying to Kyoto, where they hoped to participate in plans to restore power to the emperor, but the scheme failed and Ōkuma found himself in great difficulty. With the Meiji Restoration in 1868, however, he was given the posts of *chōshi* (domain representative) and *san'yo* (junior councilor) in the new government and assigned to foreign affairs. In his capacity as the equivalent of vice-minister of foreign affairs, he was active in carrying on negotiations with the foreign powers concerning Christianity and Christian mission work in Japan. In 1869 he became lesser assistant in the Treasury Ministry and later chief assistant in the Ministry of the Interior and chief assistant in the Treasury Ministry, working to stabilize the fiscal standing of the government, establish railway and telegraph systems, and set up the Ministry of Public Works. In 1870 he became a councilor of state and in 1873 minister of the treasury. Thereafter, until he was made a full-time councilor in 1880, he pursued an inflationary fiscal policy and also spoke out against those who advocated a military expedition against Korea.

In 1874, when Japanese troops were dispatched to Taiwan, he was appointed chief of the bureau in charge of Taiwan affairs and in 1877 he similarly served as chief of the bureau that directed the government's measures to put down the revolt that broke out in Kyushu, the so-called Seinan War. While serving in these posts, he made use of the services of Iwasaki Yatarō, the founder of the Mitsubishi *zaibatsu*, in transporting military supplies and also assisted in the establishment of the Mitsubishi Steamship Company, laying the foundations for the close relations that would exist between himself and the Mitsubishi interests in later years.

In 1878, in addition to his other duties, he was made president of the bureau in charge of land tax revision. In 1881, when the popular rights movement was gaining momentum, he spoke out in favor of the immediate establishment of a national assembly, a move that placed him in opposition to the other leaders of the government and led to his dismissal from office. In 1882 he formed the Rikken Kaishintō (Progressive Party), which advocated the establishment of a British style constitutional government with regular political parties. The same year he founded Tokyo Semmon Gakkō, a school which later became Waseda University.

He served as foreign minister in the Itō Hirobumi and Kuroda Kiyotaka cabinets in 1888, negotiating with the foreign powers in an attempt to effect treaty revision, but he was criticized for being too conciliatory in approach and in 1889 was attacked and wounded by a member of a right-wing political organization called the Gen'yōsha. He was forced to undergo the amputation of his right leg and retired from office. The same year he was appointed advisor to the Privy Council. In 1896 he formed another political party known as the Shimpotō with himself as head, and through the cooperation of Matsukata Masayoshi, was appointed foreign minister once more. In 1897 he also took on the post of minister of agriculture and commerce, but he resigned his posts because of opposition to the clique of clan leaders that dominated the government.

In 1898 he merged his Shimpotō with Itagaki Taisuke's Jiyūtō, forming a new party called the Kenseitō (Constitution Party), and set about to form the first party cabinet in Japanese history with himself as prime minister and foreign minister. Internal dissension, however, led to its rapid dissolution. In 1900 he became head of the Kenseihontō. After resigning from this position in 1907, he became president of Waseda University and was active in cultural affairs as founder of the Bummei Kyōkai and the head of an organization to further efforts for the exploration of the South Pole. In 1911 he founded a magazine called *Shin Nihon* and busied himself in lecturing, writing, and entertaining foreign visitors to Japan. After 1910, for a time he withdrew entirely from political affairs, but returned to political life at the time of the first national movement to preserve the constitution in 1912, resuming his struggle against the old clique of Chōshū and Satsuma clan leaders.

In 1914, through the support of the Rikken Dōshikai group and the unanimous recommendation of the *genrō* (counselors of state), he was able to form his second cabinet, once more with himself as prime minister and foreign minister. He led Japan through the First World War, in 1914 declaring war on Germany. The following year he presented China with the so-called Twenty-one Demands, assuming a more forceful attitude toward China than in the past. In 1916 he and his cabinet resigned. Thereafter he ceased to be active in public life.

Okumura Ioko 奥村五百子 (1845–1907)

Meiji period leader in women's social work; she was born in Karatsu in the province of Hizen, the daughter of the head priest of Kōtoku-ji, a temple of the Higashi Hongan-ji branch of the Jōdo Shin sect; her father, Ryōkan, was descended from the Nijō family, a member of the court aristocracy. Her father and elder brother were supporters of the movement to restore power to the emperor and expel the foreigners from the country, and she accordingly had occasion to become friendly with distinguished supporters of the movement such as Takasugi Shinsaku, a samurai of the domain of Chōshū, and the woman poet Nomura Bōtō. She married a priest of the Jōdo Shin sect but was widowed at an early age. In 1872 she married a former samurai of the domain of Mito and helped contribute to the family funds by running a business peddling second-hand clothing. She took an interest in affairs on the Asian continent and was impressed by the arguments in favor of a campaign against Korea put forward by Etō Shimpei, a native of the same region as herself. She was divorced from her husband in 1887 and devoted all her time to public welfare work in Karatsu.

In 1897 she went to visit her elder brother in Korea, where, as a Buddhist priest, he had gone to spread the teachings of the Jōdo Shin sect. She went to Korea again in the following year and founded a business school there. In 1900 she went on an inspection tour of South China. With the outbreak of the Boxer Rebellion in the same year and the dispatch of Japanese troops to North China, she persuaded Higashi Hongan-ji to send a mission to console the troops. She herself accompanied it, and saw at first hand the need for measures to care for the wounded and assist the families of the dead that such a situation created.

In 1901, with the backing of Duke Konoe Atsumaro, the president of the Upper House of the Diet, she founded an organization called Aikoku Fujinkai (Patriotic Women's Association). The prospectus for the organization was drafted by Shimoda Utako, the director of the Peeresses' School; Lady Iwakura, the wife of Duke Iwakura, acted as president, and many other women of high social standing participated. Okumura took to the streets to publicize the organization and solicit members, touring throughout the country and lecturing, until she had built up a membership of several hundred thousand. During the Russo-Japanese War in 1904–05, although in poor health, she went to Manchuria to help minister to the officers and enlisted men in the field. In 1906 she retired to Karatsu to convalesce. The Ogasawara family, former lords of the domain of Karatsu, were longtime supporters of her activities.

Ono Azusa 小野梓 (1852–1886)

Legal scholar and government official of the early Meiji period; he was born in Sukumo in the domain of Tosa (present-day Kōchi Prefecture), the son of a low-ranking samurai. He took part in the Boshin civil war of 1868–69, fighting in northern Honshu against the forces that remained loyal to the shogunate. In 1869, after the Meiji Restoration, he went to Tokyo and entered the Shōheikō, a school formerly operated by the shogunate. When he was ordered by his domain to return home to Tosa, he gave up his samurai status and became a commoner in order to free himself from the obligation of obeying. He went to China and eventually made his way to America, where he devoted himself to study. From 1872 on, he was recognized as an official overseas student of the Finance Ministry and spent his time in London studying economic and political systems. After returning to Japan in 1874, he founded the Kyōzon Dōshū, an organization made up mainly of persons who had studied abroad, the aim of which was to encourage research and Westernization.

In 1876 he took a position in the Ministry of Justice, and later held such posts as secretary of the Genrōin and auditor of the Board of Audit. He was also active in the movement that urged the early establishment of a national assembly. In the government shake-up of 1881 he resigned his official posts, along with Ōkuma Shigenobu, and worked to establish the political party known as the Rikken Kaishintō (Progressive Party) headed by Ōkuma. In addition to his political activities, he was active in educational affairs as well. In 1882 he helped to found Tokyo Semmon Gakkō, which later became Waseda University, and in 1883 established a bookstore and publishing house called the Tōyōkan. But his health failed, and he died in 1886 at the young age of thirty-four. His principal works are *Kokken hanron* and *Mimpō no hone*.

Ōsugi Sakae 大杉榮 (1885–1923)

Anarchist and leader of the socialist movement in the Taishō period; he was born in Kagawa Prefecture. After graduating from Tokyo Foreign Language School, where he specialized in French, he decided to follow in his father's footsteps by becoming a military man. But while a student at the Nagoya Army Preparatory School he was accused of insubordination toward an officer and was expelled. From his days in Foreign Language School he had been a member of the Heiminsha, the socialist and pacifist organization formed by Kōtoku Shūsui, Sakai Toshihiko, and others. In 1906 he was arrested and imprisoned for taking part in the movement to oppose a fare rise for the Tokyo streetcars. Thereafter he was accused of various charges a total of five times and in all spent over three years in jail; it is said that each time he went to jail, he succeeded in mastering a new foreign language.

Around this time, he attended a lecture given by Kōtoku Shūsui on the occasion of his return to Japan; Ōsugi was so impressed that he determined to become a follower of anarchism and published serially in the daily newspaper *Heimin Shimbun* a translation of Kropotkin's *Appeal to Youth.* In conjunction with Arahata Kanson he published a magazine called *Kindai Shisō* in 1912 and a monthly called *Heimin Shimbun* in 1914. He also organized the Sanjikarizumu Kenkyūkai (Syndicalism Study Society), and produced numerous writings and translations dealing with anarchism, the labor movement, evolutionary theory, and the philosophy of life. He spoke out against bolshevism and exercised a considerable influence over the rising labor movement in Japan in the years following World War One.

He went to France in 1923, but was arrested in Paris and put in prison and later expelled from the country and sent back to Japan. In September of the same year occurred the Kantō earthquake that leveled Tokyo and Yokohama. In the panic and confusion that followed, a number of Koreans and left-wing leaders were arrested or massacred. Ōsugi was among those seized by the military police, and he, his wife Itō Noe, and his nephew, the last a mere boy, were all put to death by an army captain named Amakasu Masahiko.

Ōtani Kōzui 大谷光瑞 (1876–1948)

Priest of the Jōdo Shin sect, explorer, and twenty-second *hossu* (head) of the Nishi Hongan-ji branch of the sect; his religious name was Kyōnyo. He was born in Kyoto, the son of the twenty-first *hossu* Ōtani Kōson. His childhood name was Takamaro. He entered the clergy in 1885 and studied at the Peers' School and elsewhere. He went to China in 1899, and after a brief return to Japan, set out once more at the end of the year, traveling to Europe by way of India. In 1902 he left London and, after traveling through Russia, embarked upon an exploration trip of Central Asia, eventually making his way to India. In 1903, with the death of his father, Kōson, he became twenty-second *hossu.* He went to Europe for a second visit in 1909–10. In 1910 he lost his wife, Kazuko, third daughter of Duke Kujō Michitaka and elder sister of the consort of the Emperor Taishō; he remained single for the rest of his life, devoting his energies to the training of young people. He three times sent parties of explorers to Central Asia to carry out surveys of the area. Because of involvement in a financial scandal in 1914, he resigned his position as *hossu.* He turned his attention to business activities overseas and became an advocate of Japanese expansion in Asia, cooperating with the government to carry out such expansion.

Ōyama Ikuo 大山郁夫 (1880–1955)

Taishō and Shōwa period political scientist and leader of the social movement; his family name was originally Fukumoto. He graduated from Waseda University in 1905 and the following year became a lecturer there. He went to America and Germany for study in 1910 and in 1914, after his return to Japan, became a professor of Waseda. He was also active as a commentator on political affairs. He left Waseda in 1917 as a result of a disturbance at the university and became an editorial writer for the *Osaka Asahi Shimbun,* where he espoused the cause of democracy. When government censorship forced the chief editor of the newspaper to resign in 1918, he left the paper as well. The same year he joined Yoshino Sakuzō and others in forming a society for the advancement of democratic thinking known as the Reimeikai. In 1919 he began publication of a magazine called *Warera* in conjunction with Kawakami Hajime, Hasegawa Nyozekan, and others, working to spread democratic ideas. He returned to his position at Waseda University in 1920, where he was idolized by the student body.

In 1926 he helped to form the Rōdō Nōmintō (Labor Farmer Party) and became chairman of it. As a result, he was advised by the Waseda administration to retire from his teaching position, a suggestion that he complied with, though it brought on a general student strike as a gesture of protest. In 1929 he formed a new political party called the Rōnōtō (Labor Farmer Party) with himself as head and was widely referred to as "the shining chairman." In 1930 he was elected to the Lower House of the Diet, but after the Manchurian Incident in 1931, he became fearful of attacks from right-wing elements and in 1932 fled to America, where he lived as a scholar. He returned to Japan in 1947 and resumed his position at Waseda. In 1950 he was elected to the Upper House of the Diet. In his late years, he devoted much of his time to the world peace movement. In 1951 he received the International Stalin Peace Prize.

ŌYAMA IWAO 大山巖 (1842–1916)

Meiji and Taishō period military leader; he held the rank of general of the army and the title of duke. He was born in the domain of Satsuma in Kyushu and was a cousin of Saigō Takamori. He was active in the movement to restore power to the emperor. He won distinction in the Boshin civil war as commander of an artillery battalion, and on the basis of his experiences in the field, he devised a new type of artillery piece that was called a Yasuke cannon, Yasuke being his common name. In 1870 he went to Europe to observe the military methods being used in the Franco-Prussian War. In 1871 he was promoted to the rank of major general and in 1871 he went to Europe once more, studying military methods in France. In the Seinan War in 1877, he won distinction in helping to put down the rebel forces, which were led by his cousin Saigō Takamori. In 1878 he advanced to the rank of lieutenant general and became vice-chief of the General Staff Office. In 1880 he became minister of the army, in 1881 a councilor of state, and in 1882 further took on the post of chief of the General Staff Office.

In 1884 he accompanied Katsura Tarō and other distinguished army leaders in a tour of Europe and America for the purpose of observing military systems and installations. After returning to Japan, he worked in cooperation with Yamagata Aritomo, Katsura Tarō, and others to set up a modern style army in Japan. He became war minister in the first Itō Hirobumi cabinet in 1885 and remained in that post for the following ten years or more. In 1894 he took part in the Sino-Japanese War as commander of the Second Army. In 1898 he was made a general of the army and in 1899 became chief of the General Staff. In 1904 he took part in the Russo-Japanese War as commander-in-chief of the Manchurian Army. He thereafter retired from active military service. In 1914 he became home minister, a post that he held until his death two years later. He was a man of great military ability and was highly trusted by Emperor Meiji, but he had few political ambitions and was not able to restrain Yamagata Aritomo and others of the Chōshū clique from exercising their influence in army circles.

Ozaki Yukio 尾崎行雄 (1858–1954)

Party political leader of the Meiji, Taishō, and Shōwa periods; he was born in the area that later became Kanagawa Prefecture; his literary name was Gakudō. For a time he attended Keiō Gijuku in Tokyo, but transferred to a technical school, the forerunner of the engineering department of Tokyo University, in order to study dyes. In 1877 he withdrew from this school as well and, on the recommendation of Fukuzawa Yukichi, became chief editor of the *Niigata Shimbun*. Following this, he entered official life for a time at the invitation of Yano Fumio, serving as a secretary in the Institute of Statistics. With the government shakeup in 1881, he withdrew from official life along with the councilor Ōkuma Shigenobu. He assisted Ōkuma in forming the Rikken Kaishintō (Progressive Party) and became a member of the party. He also became an editorial writer for the *Yūbin Hōchi Shimbun*.

In 1884 he was elected a member of the Tokyo Prefectural Assembly. In 1887 he participated in the fusion of political parties that was formed to oppose the government and was among the group of persons who were forced to leave Tokyo under the provisions of the Peace Preservation Regulations. In 1888 he went abroad for an inspection tour of Europe and America. With the promulgation of the new constitution in 1889 he was pardoned and permitted to return to Tokyo. In the first election held in 1890, he ran as a candidate from Mie Prefecture and was elected to the Lower House of the Diet. He was thereafter elected a total of twenty-five times, continuing in the Diet until his defeat in 1953. In that year, the Diet voted to make him an honorary member in recognition of his long career in that body.

He served as minister of education in the first Ōkuma cabinet in 1898, but was obliged to resign as a result of the furor aroused by a speech he made before a group of primary school teachers. The speech was intended as an attack upon the influence of money in politics, but he unwisely opined that, should Japan for some reason become a republic, Mitsui and Mitsubishi would be the candidates for president, a type of speculation that was deemed offensive to the throne. In 1900 he parted company with Ōkuma and Inukai Tsuyoki, the political leaders he had hitherto cooperated with, and joined Itō Hirobumi in forming a political organization called the Rikken Seiyūkai. He left the organization in 1903 because he opposed its move to cooperate with the government on the latter's budget proposal. He served as mayor of Tokyo from 1903 to 1912. During this period, he sent a gift of cherry trees to the city of Washington, D.C., to be planted along the Potomac River as a symbol of Japanese-American friendship.

In 1912–13, at the time of the first Movement to Protect the Constitution, he spoke out violently against Prime Minister Katsura Tarō in the Diet, and as a result became known, along with Inukai, as one of the "gods of constitutional government." In 1914 he became minister of justice in the second Ōkuma cabinet. Following this, he joined Inukai and others in a nationwide lecture tour to drum up support for the universal suffrage movement. During the Pacific War, he was accused of lèse-majesté by the Tōjō cabinet because of a speech he made in support of the election of Tagawa Daikichirō, but he was acquitted of the charges.

He commanded great respect because of his long years of experience in the Diet. But because of his frequent withdrawals or expulsions from political organizations and his relative lack of organizing ability and cooperative spirit, he tended to become increasingly isolated in the world of politics and to wield only limited influence. In his late years, he became an advocate of world federation. His name is honored in the Ozaki Memorial Hall in the building known as the Kensei Kinenkan in Chiyoda, Tokyo.

Saigō Takamori 西郷隆盛 (1827–1877)

Statesman and military leader of the late Edo and early Meiji periods. His common name was Kichibei, later Kichinosuke, and his literary name, Nanshū. He was born in the domain of Satsuma in Kyushu, the son of an impoverished samurai of lower status; his younger brother was Saigō Tsugumichi. As a boy he attended the Zōshikan, the official school of the domain. He was influenced by Zen Buddhism and the Wang Yang-ming school of Confucianism, but the teachings of Shimazu Nisshin, which reflected both Buddhism and Confucianism and formed the basis of the Satsuma style *bushidō*, or code of ethics of the warrior, played a particularly important role in shaping his character. When he came of age, he was made a district official and put in charge of agricultural affairs.

In 1854 his talents were recognized by Shimazu Nariakira, the progressive-minded lord of the domain, and he was assigned to a post equivalent in effect to that of private secretary. He spent three years in Edo in this capacity and, after returning to Satsuma, he continued to act on secret orders from his lord, carrying out his wishes in connection with important problems of state such as the succession to the shogunate and imperial approval of the trade treaties concluded with foreign powers. With the sudden death of Shimazu Nariakira in 1858 and the political persecutions carried out by Ii Naosuke, the leaders of the important feudal domains for a time withdrew from the political scene. Saigō, who was in Kyoto at the time, determined to commit suicide and follow his lord in death, but he was dissuaded by a Buddhist monk named Gesshō. He and Gesshō left Kyoto in secret and attempted to return to Satsuma. When they were denied entrance to the domain, they resolved to take their lives and leaped from the boat in which they were riding into the sea near Kagoshima. Gesshō drowned, but Saigō was rescued. He changed his name to Kikuchi Gengo and in 1859 was banished to the island of Ōshima. In 1862, when the domain of Satsuma joined the movement to restore power to the emperor and Shimazu Hisamitsu led his troops to Kyoto, Saigō was pardoned and ordered to proceed to Kyoto. On the way, he aroused Hisamitsu's displeasure by disobeying the latter's orders when he was in Osaka, and once more he was banished, first to Tokunoshima and later to Okinoerabushima, where he was kept under house arrest.

Meanwhile, the struggle between the groups that favored court-shogunate cooperation and those that called for the overthrow of the shogunate grew in intensity, and in these tense circumstances there was strong sentiment in the Satsuma domain in favor of Saigō's recall. In 1864 Hisamitsu pardoned him, and the same year Saigō, as leader of the military forces of the group supporting cooperation between the court and the shogunate, marched on Kyoto and drove out the forces of the domain of Chōshū, which favored a violent overthrow of the shogunate. He was also active in planning the first campaign undertaken by the shogunate to punish the domain of Chōshū for its disloyalty. When the first punitive expedition failed and a second was being planned, Saigō began to become dissatisfied with attempts to effect harmony between the court and the shogunate and opposed the move. Bit by bit, he came to favor the military overthrow of the shogunate, and influenced the domain of Satsuma to support that position. Thus in 1866 he acted as respresentative of Satsuma in forming an alliance with Katsura Kogorō (Kido Takayoshi) and other leaders of Chōshū, ensuring that the domains would thereafter act in conjunction. He also devoted himself to reforming the administration of the domain of Satsuma and expanding its military and naval forces, as well as cultivating friendly relations with the British. Before long, he and Ōkubo Toshimichi were wielding most of the actual power within the domain.

In 1868 the Boshin War broke out, a struggle between the forces supporting the emperor and those remaining loyal to the shogunate, which began with skirmishes at Toba and Fushimi south of Kyoto. Saigō served as one of the leaders in the march to the east to gain control of Edo, leading the imperial forces to victory, and won particular fame for the roles that he and Katsu Kaishū played in negotiating the bloodless surrender of Edo Castle. In 1869, he returned to Kagoshima in the domain of Satsuma and devoted himself to improving the financial and military status of the domain. At the request of the central government, however, he returned to Tokyo in 1871, where he became a councilor of state and, as one of the leaders of the imperial troops, was able to play a decisive role in the abolition of the feudal domains and the establishment of a prefectural system.

In 1872 he became a marshal of the army and commander of the imperial guard and in 1873 became a full general of the army, at the same time retaining his position as councilor. While Iwakura Tomomi and other important government leaders were in Europe and America on a tour of inspection, Saigō participated in the caretaker government and was one of those supporting the decision to send troops to Korea. When Iwakura returned to Japan, he demanded that the decision be reversed; Ōkubo Toshimichi and others spoke out in his support. As a result, Saigō, along with Itagaki Taisuke and others who favored military action against Korea, resigned and withdrew from public life. Later, he became increasingly angry at the government for its treatment of former samurai of lower rank. In 1874 he set up a private school in Kagoshima, determined to remain aloof from public affairs. The samurai surrounding him, however, were growing increasingly restless in their opposition to the government, and in 1877 Saigō led them in a military uprising that became known as the Seinan War. His forces were no match for the modern conscript army of the government, however, and Saigō, finding himself surrounded, committed suicide on the battlefield in Kagoshima.

Saigō constantly proclaimed his creed to be "Reverence for Heaven and Love for Mankind," and enjoyed wide popularity because of his undoubted sincerity. In the troubled period that ushered in the Meiji Restoration, he was able to display his talent for military leadership. But he had little feeling for the methods of modern style government and could not sympathize with the views of Ōkubo Toshimichi and the other more forward-looking members of the new government. Thus, through a series of unfortunate circumstances, he ended his life as the leader of a rebel army. In 1889, when the Meiji Constitution was promulgated, he was posthumously pardoned by the government.

Saigō Tsugumichi 西郷従道 (1843–1902)

Military leader of the Meiji period; he held the rank of fleet admiral and the title of marquis. He was born in the domain of Satsuma, the younger brother of the famous statesman and military leader Saigō Takamori. He took part in the Boshin civil war and, on its conclusion in 1869, was dispatched by the government along with Yamagata Aritomo to visit Russia, Germany, and France to study military matters. On his return to Japan in 1870, he was appointed acting chief clerk of military affairs. In 1872 he became a major general in the army and in 1874 advanced to the rank of lieutenant general. In 1874, he prepared to head an expedition to Taiwan to punish the aborigines for an earlier mistreatment of a party of shipwrecked Japanese. Though the government later decided to cancel the expedition, Saigō proceeded to carry it out anyway, bearing the title of governor general of Taiwan aborigine affairs. In 1877, when his brother Takamori headed the revolt against the government known as the Seinan War, he served as commander of the Imperial Guards, proclaiming his loyalty to the emperor and refusing to join his brother's forces.

From 1878 on, he served as councilor of state and minister of education, minister of war, and minister of agriculture and commerce. After a journey to Europe, he transferred from the army to the navy, serving as the first minister of the navy in the Itō Hirobumi cabinet formed in 1885. He continued to serve in this position for the following ten years or more, until the fall of the third Itō cabinet in 1898, except for brief intervals when he served as home minister in the first Matsukata Masayoshi cabinet and temporarily as war minister in the second Itō cabinet. During this period, in 1891, occurred the so-called Ōtsu Incident, when a Japanese police officer attacked the Russian Crown Prince Nikolai, who was visiting Japan, at the town of Ōtsu. Saigō, fearing that the event would lead to international complications, assumed full responsibility for what had happened. In 1892 he joined with Shinagawa Yajirō in forming a conservative political party known as the Kokumin Kyōkai. In 1898 he became home minister in the Yamagata cabinet and was promoted to the rank of fleet admiral.

Saionji Kimmochi 西園寺公望 (1849–1940)

Meiji, Taishō, and Shōwa period political leader; he held the title of duke (prince). He was born in Kyoto, the son of Tokudaiji Kin'ito, who held the court post of minister of the right. In 1852 he was adopted into the Saionji family, also of the court nobility; for a time he went by the personal name Bōichirō: his literary name was Tōan. His elder brother Tokudaiji Sanetsune was grand chamberlain to Emperor Meiji, while his younger brother Sumitomo Kichizaemon was a business leader and held the the title of baron.

In the closing years of the Edo period, Saionji, breaking with the customs of court society, took an increasing interest in affairs of state. In 1868, when power was restored to the emperor, he became a *sanyo* (junior councilor) in the newly formed government. In the clashes between the shogunate forces and those loyal to the emperor at Toba and Fushimi, he attracted the notice of Iwakura Tomomi by his enthusiasm for battle. He participated in subsequent engagements in the San'in and Hokuriku areas, helping to bring them under imperial control. He was appointed governor of Niigata, but resigned so that he could go abroad for study. He went to France in 1871, and although Paris was in turmoil because of the establishment of the Commune, he succeeded in entering the Sorbonne, graduating in 1874. During this period he studied under the legal scholar Emile Acollas and also became friendly with Clemenceau. During his stay in France he also became acquainted with Nakae Chōmin, a scholar of French thought and intellectual leader in the Meiji period. Saionji remained in France for ten years, absorbing the liberal thinking of the time, and returned to Japan in 1880. In 1881 he founded a law school called Meiji Hōritsu Gakkō, the forerunner of Meiji University, and engaged in teaching activities. The same year he also joined Nakae Chōmin and Matsuda Masahisa in founding a newspaper called *Tōyō Jiyū Shimbun* with himself as president, pressing for the establishment of political freedom and popular rights. Iwakura Tomomi, minister of the right and the leading statesman of the time, was much startled by such behavior and urged Saionji to give up his position with the newspaper. Saionji declined to heed the advice, however, and was only persuaded to resign by a privately conveyed request from Emperor Meiji himself.

In 1882 he accompanied Itō Hirobumi when the latter journeyed to Europe to study constitutional systems, he himself concentrating upon a survey of monarchical systems. He returned to Japan in 1883 and became a member of the House of Councilors. He served as minister to Austria in 1885 and minister to Germany in 1887, and later as president of the Bureau of Decorations, vice-president of the Upper House of the Diet, and advisor to the Privy Council. He served as minister of education in the second and third Itō cabinets (1894–96, 1898), and was able to modify the educational policy of the country, tempering the strong note of nationalism that had characterized it earlier and injecting a more cosmopolitan outlook. In 1900 he became president of the Privy Council. In the same year he became one of the founding members of the Rikken Seiyūkai, the political party formed by Itō Hirobumi, supporting the movement to form political parties, and in 1903 succeeded Itō as president of the Seiyūkai. For a period following the conclusion of the Russo-Japanese War in 1905, he and Katsura Tarō took turns holding the office of prime minister, and for a time a spirit of cooperation prevailed between the Seiyūkai and the old domain cliques within the government. In his first cabinet, which lasted from 1906 to 1908, he carried out the nationalization of the railways, but his second cabinet (1911–12), by refusing to create two new army divisions, incurred the displeasure of the army and was forced to resign en masse. At the time of the resignation, Saionji was accorded treatment as a *genrō* (elder statesman) by the newly enthroned Emperor Taishō.

In 1913, when the movement to preserve the constitution was intensifying its activity, Saionji was privately requested by Emperor Taishō to place restraints on the Seiyūkai. He was unable to do so, however, and, accepting responsibility for the situation, offered to resign the position of president of the party. In 1914, Hara Takashi, who had twice served as home minister in the Saionji cabinets, was chosen to succeeded him as president, and he accordingly tendered his resignation. In 1919 he headed the Japanese delegation to the Versailles Conference, and in company with Makino Nobuaki and Chinda Sutemi represented Japan at the conclusion of the international accord. From 1924 he had the responsibility, as the last of the elder statesmen, of recommending persons for the post of prime minister to the emperor. He thus had a considerable voice in political affairs, and hoped to use it to further the cause of party government. But after the assassination of the prime minister by naval officers on May 15, 1932, no more party cabinets were formed, and the military came increasingly to dominate the government, a tendency that Saionji was unable to combat. After the appointment of Konoe Fumimaro as prime minister in 1937, he gave up his role as advisor to the emperor on the formation of cabinets. In addition to his political interests, he was a man of refined cultural tastes. While in France, he cooperated with the famous woman poet Judith Gautier in producing a volume of French translations of Japanese poetry, published in 1884, and he had a wide acquaintance among artists and intellectuals. On his death in 1940, he was given a state funeral.

Saitō Makoto 齋藤實 (1858–1936)

Statesman and naval leader of the Meiji, Taishō, and Shōwa eras; he held the title of viscount. He was born in the domain of Mizusawa in what later became Iwate Prefecture. In his early years he went by the name Tomigorō. He was a friend of the future statesman Gotō Shimpei, who was one year older and came from the same region. Saitō studied under his father, a samurai who headed a *terakoya*, or small private school, and also pursued Chinese studies in the official school of the domain. In 1870 he was selected to serve as an office boy in the prefectural office of Izawa (later a part of Iwate Prefecture) and won the admiration of the governor for the alacrity with which he acted when a fire broke out. In 1872 he went to Tokyo, and the following year entered the school that later became the Naval Academy. It was at this time that he changed his name to Makoto. He graduated from the Naval Academy in 1879 and in 1882 was commissioned as an ensign.

In 1884 he was sent to the United States for study, at the same time serving as naval attaché to the Japanese legation there. He remained in America until 1898 and, on his return to Japan, served as a member of the Naval General Staff and later as a staff officer in the command of a standing squadron. In 1897 he advanced to the rank of captain and took command of his own ship. In 1898, when Yamamoto Gombei was appointed minister of the navy, Saitō was selected to serve as vice-minister, and the two men continued to serve in these posts over a period of seven years. Meanwhile, Saitō advanced to the rank of rear admiral in 1900 and vice admiral in 1904. In 1906 Saitō succeeded Yamamoto as minister of the navy, working to reinforce Japan's naval strength in the wake of the Russo-Japanese War. He remained in that post for the following eight years, serving in five different cabinets, but in 1914 took responsibility for the Siemens affair (the disclosure of bribes passed by a German company named Siemens to affect naval contracts), and joined the other members of the Yamamoto Gombei cabinet in resigning his position. Thereafter he entered the reserve.

In 1919 he returned to active service long enough to assume the post of governor-general of Korea. Shortly after, a bomb was thrown at the carriage in which he was riding, but he escaped injury. He worked to change the character of the Japanese colonial administration in Korea from a purely military to a civil one. In 1927 he attended the Geneva Disarmament Conference as a plenipotentiary and, after his return to Japan, resigned the post of governor-general of Korea. He became an advisor to the Privy Council, but in 1929 once more assumed the post of governor-general of Korea, holding it until 1931.

On 15 May, 1932, when a group of young naval officers assassinated Prime Minister Inukai Tsuyoki, Saitō was recommended by the elder statesman Saionji Kimmochi to replace him as prime minister. He did so, announcing the formation of a "whole-nation" cabinet, that is, a coalition cabinet in which the military, the bureaucrats, and the party members were equally represented. He presided over the recognition of Manchukuo and Japan's withdrawal from the League of Nations, but in 1934, when high officials in the Finance Ministry were implicated in scandals relating to the sale of stock in the Teikoku Rayon Company, Saitō and the members of his cabinet resigned en masse. In 1935 he became Lord Keeper of the Privy Seal and served close to the emperor, but was attacked and killed by the young army officers in the February 26 incident of 1936.

Sakai Toshihiko 堺利彦 (1870–1933)

Meiji, Taishō, and Shōwa period leader of the socialist movement and early exponent of Marxism in Japan; he was born in Fukuoka Prefecture; his literary name was Kosen. He attended the First Middle School but withdrew and took up a career as a writer, supporting himself by working as a teacher and newspaper reporter while turning out works of fiction. From 1897 on, he also assisted in editing *Bōchō kaitenshi*, a history of the domain of Chōshū in the Restoration period compiled by the Mōri family, former lords of the domain of Chōshū. In 1899 he joined the newspaper called *Yorozu Chōhō*, where he wrote vigorously in support of *gembun itchi*, the movement that advocated use of the colloquial language in writing. In 1903 he founded a magazine called *Katei Zasshi*, in which he published translations and discussions of the socialist-minded novels of Emile Zola. On the eve of the Russo-Japanese War, he spoke out against the initiation of hostilities and joined Uchimura Kanzō and Kōtoku Shūsui in resigning from the *Yorozu Chōhō* because of its prowar policy. He and Kōtoku then established the Heiminsha and began publication of a newspaper called *Heimin Shimbun*, which carried a translation of the *Communist Manifesto* done by the two men.

In the dark times after Kōtoku's execution in 1911 on charges of having plotted to assassinate the emperor, Sakai founded an advertising and publishing company called Baibunsha, whereby he attempted to provide a livelihood for the members of the socialist movement and keep them from dispersing. In 1917 he ran as a candidate in the general election but lost. In 1922 he participated in the formation of the Japan Communist Party. In 1927 he and Yamakawa Hitoshi began publication of a magazine called *Rōnō* (Labor Farmer). In 1929 he was elected to the Tokyo Municipal Assembly. In 1931 he returned to his home in Fukuoka, where he opened a school for farmers and laborers. The same year, with the outbreak of hostilities between Japan and China in Manchuria, he became chairman of the Antiwar Committee of the Zenkoku Rōnō Taishūtō (National Labor Farmer Populace Party).

Sanjō Sanetomi 三條實美 (1837–1891)

Court noble and statesman of late Edo and early Meiji times; he held the title of duke. He was born in Kyoto, the son of a family that was counted among the Gosekke, or five families whose members were entitled to appointment to the post of regent. His mother was the daughter of Yamanouchi Toyokazu, lord of the domain of Tosa. He was raised on a farm in the outskirts of Kyoto and as a child went by the name Yoshimaro. He studied the Japanese classics under Tanimori Yoshiomi and in 1854 became a chamberlain. In 1858–59, when the high shogunate official Ii Naosuke carried out his purge of the courtiers, daimyo, and samurai who opposed his policies, Sanetomi's father, Sanjō Sanetsumu, resigned his position at court and entered the Buddhist clergy. He died in 1859, despairing at the course that events were taking. Sanetomi, determined to carry on his father's principles, became a supporter of the *sonnō-jōi* movement, which called for restoration of power to the emperor and expulsion of the foreigners.

In 1862 he was appointed imperial envoy and, with Anegakōji Kintomo as vice-envoy, he journeyed to Edo under the protection of the lord of Tosa and his troops to deliver to the fourteenth shogun Tokugawa Iemochi a command from the emperor urging him to carry out the expulsion of the foreigners. In 1863 he was appointed to a newly established post as commissioner of state affairs at court, where he played a leading role among the younger court nobles who were pressing for restoration of power to the emperor and expulsion of the foreigners. He maintained covert contacts with the samurai of the domain of Chōshū who were supporters of the *sonnō-jōi* movement, working to realize the aims of the movement. In 1863, however, a coup d'état at court brought into power the opposing *kōbu-gattai* movement, centering about the clans of Aizu and Satsuma, which favored cooperation between the shogunate and the imperial court. As a result, the Chōshū samurai and other supporters of the *sonnō-jōi* movement were expelled from Kyoto, and seven antishogunate court nobles, including Sanetomi, Sawa Nobuyoshi, and Higashikuze Michitomi, were obliged to flee to Chōshū (present-day Yamaguchi Prefecture). They were accompanied on this journey by a samurai of Tosa named Hijikata Hisamoto (later minister of the imperial household), who won the trust of Sanetomi and the others, and the party in time reached Mitajiri in Suō. In 1864 the shogunate launched a punitive expedition to punish Chōshū for its unruly activities, and when Chōshū meekly acknowledged its fault, Sanetomi and four other court nobles were moved from Chōshū to Dazaifu in Kyushu, where they lived in seclusion.

With the Meiji Restoration in 1868, Sanetomi returned to Kyoto, where he was restored to his former court rank and position and was assigned high posts in court administration. He was appointed inspector of the Kantō region, and after Edo Castle had been handed over to the imperial forces, he supervised the transfer of governmental power in the eastern provinces. When Edo was renamed Tokyo and a military garrison established there, he was made commander of it. After the reorganization of the governmental system in 1869, he became minister of the right and in 1871 advanced to the highest position in the government, that of *dajōdaijin* (premier). Except for a brief period in 1873 when he was replaced by Iwakura Tomomi because of illness brought on by controversy over the dispatch of an envoy to Korea, he remained in the post of premier until it was abolished in 1885 and the cabinet system set up. The same year, he became home minister in the Itō Hirobumi cabinet. After the Kuroda Kiyotaka cabinet fell in 1889, he acted for a time as both prime minister and home minister until a new cabinet was formed by Yamagata Aritomo. On his death in 1891 he was given a state funeral.

Sano Manabu 佐野學 (1892–1953)

Leader of the socialist movement in the Taishō and Shōwa periods; he was born in Ōita Prefecture. His family had for generations been physicians to the local domain. In 1917 he graduated from the political science course of Tokyo Imperial University. While still a student, he joined the socialist movement and participated in the formation of an organization called Shinjinkai made up largely of Tokyo University students and designed to further the movement. After working for the East Asia Economic Research Bureau of the Manchuria Railway, he became a lecturer at Waseda University, specializing in economics and economic history.

In 1922 he participated in the formation of the Japan Communist Party, becoming a member of the central committee. In 1923 he fled to the Soviet Union just before the first wave of arrests of left-wing leaders. He returned to Japan in 1925 and turned himself over to the government officials for sentencing. Later, he became chief editor of a newspaper called *Musansha Shimbun* and began to lay plans for reconstituting the Communist Party. In 1928 he fled to the Soviet Union once more to avoid the nationwide arrests of left-wing figures and, along with Ichikawa Shōichi, attended the Sixth Comintern, where he was chosen to be a member of the standing executive committee. In 1929 he was arrested in Shanghai while secretly directing the reestablishment of the Japan Communist Party. In 1932 he was sentenced by the Tokyo courts to penal servitude for life. While in prison, he and Nabeyama Sadachika in 1933 announced that they had given up their belief in international communism and instead advocated working for the realization of socialism in a single country, particularly in Japan. This announcement led a number of other communist followers to proclaim a similar "conversion." In 1934 Sano's sentence was reduced to fifteen years and in 1943 he was released from prison. After the war, he returned to his teaching position at Waseda University. He founded a political party called the Rōdō Zen'eitō and the Nihon Seiji Keizai Kenkyūjo (Japan Political and Economic Research Institute). His works include *Roshia keizai-shi*, *Shinchō shakai-shi*, and *Nihon kodai shiron*.

Sano Tsunetami 佐野常民 (1822–1902)

Meiji period statesman and founder of the Japan Red Cross; he was born in the domain of Saga in Kyushu; he held the title of count. From an early age he devoted himself to medicine and Western studies and he had a wide knowledge of science. In 1853 he became head of the Seirensha, an institution founded by the domain of Saga to promote Western studies and manufacture cannon, devoting himself to the study of shipbuilding. In 1855 he became an official in the naval institute founded by the shogunate. In 1867 he went to France for the opening of the Paris Exposition, touring industrial installations and studying the building of warships. He returned to Japan after the establishment of the Meiji government and undertook to reform the military system of his native domain. In 1873 he entered the Ministry of Military Affairs of the central government, devoting his energies to the establishment of a navy. He was later transferred to the Ministry of Works and held a succession of public offices, including member of the Genrōin (Senate), minister of finance, president of the Genrōin, advisor to the Privy Council, and minister of agriculture and commerce.

In addition to these activities, he became interested in European and American efforts to relieve the suffering of soldiers wounded in war. At the time of the Seinan civil war in 1877, he joined with Ogyū Yuzuru and others in forming an association called the Hakuaisha, which ministered to the sick and wounded on both sides impartially. The association later became the Japan Red Cross, and Sano, as its first director, gave great time and energy to its development. The organization played an important role at the time of the Sino-Japanese War as well. As vice-president of the National Industrial Exposition, he worked to encourage industrial growth, and he also founded the Ryūchikai, the present Japan Fine Arts Association, which encouraged the traditional arts, called for measures to protect artists, and in general contributed to the promotion of the arts and crafts in Japan.

SATŌ EISAKU 佐藤榮作 (1901–1975)

Statesman of the Shōwa period; he was born in Yamaguchi Prefecture; he was the younger brother of the statesman Kishi Nobusuke. In 1924 he graduated from the law course of Tokyo Imperial University and took a position with the Ministry of Railways. After serving as head of the Automobile Bureau in the Transport Ministry and head of the Osaka Railway Bureau, he became vice-minister of the Transport Ministry in 1947. In this last position he demonstrated great skill in dealing with the frequent strikes that disrupted the national railways at this time. He retired from office in 1948 and joined the Jiyūto (Liberal Party), becoming head of the Yamaguchi branch of the party. The same year, without taking a seat in the Diet, he became chief cabinet secretary to the Yoshida Shigeru cabinet.

In 1949 he was elected to the Lower House of the Diet and became chairman of the Political Affairs Research Committee of the Liberal Party. In 1950 he became chief secretary of the Liberal Party. In 1951 he became minister of posts and telecommunications in the third Yoshida Shigeru cabinet and in 1954, minister of construction in the fourth Yoshida cabinet. In 1954 he was involved in a shipbuilding scandal, but at the last minute was saved from arrest by Prime Minister Yoshida, who prompted Minister of Justice Inukai Ken to invoke special powers on his behalf.

When Hatoyama Ichirō formed a coalition of the conservative groups within the party, Satō joined Yoshida Shigeru in withdrawing from the party. He rejoined the party in 1957, when his elder brother Kishi Nobusuke became prime minister, taking over the post of chairman of the Executive Council of the party. In 1958 he became minister of finance in the second Kishi cabinet, in 1961, minister of international trade and industry in the Ikeda Hayato cabinet, and in 1963 assumed the additional post of state minister. In 1964, when Prime Minister Ikeda was obliged to resign from office because of illness, Satō succeeded him as president of the Liberal Party and formed his own cabinet. From then until his retirement in 1973, he was elected president of the party a total of four times. During this period he disposed of a number of important foreign and domestic problems that had been pending in the postwar period, making Japan a member of the International Labor Organization, signing a treaty with South Korea, putting through legislation to quell unrest on the university campuses, extending the Japan-United States Security Treaty, and negotiating the return of Okinawa to Japan. In 1974 he was awarded a Nobel Peace Prize.

Senoo Girō 妹尾義郎 (1891–1961)

Religious leader of the Shōwa period and advocate of Buddhist socialism. He was born in the district of Nuka (present-day Hiba) in Hiroshima Prefecture. In 1909 he was forced to withdraw from the First High School because of stomach trouble and tuberculosis of the lungs. He returned to his home to recuperate. While there he became a convert to Nichiren Buddhism through the efforts of a bean curd merchant named Matsuzaki Kyūtarō. In 1918 he went to Tokyo and became a disciple of Honda Nisshō, a priest of Tōitsukaku in Asakusa. In 1919 he organized a Nichiren sect young men's group called Dai-Nihon Nichiren Shugi Seinendan. He began publication of a magazine representing the group, called *Wakai Hito* (Young People), and a movement called *Ugoku Tera* (Movable Temple), taking an active part in social work. He leaned increasingly in the direction of socialism and in 1931 disbanded the young men's group. In its place he formed a nonsectarian Buddhist young men's group called Shinkō Bukkyō Seinen Dōmei (Shinkō Bussei) dedicated to religious reform. The group published a paper called *Shinkō Bukkyō no Hata no Motoni.* He was active in the popular front movement and in 1935 became editor and publisher of the labor magazine *Rōdō Zasshi.*

In 1936 he was arrested on suspicion of subversive activity, and in 1937 all the officers of the young men's organization were arrested and the group was disbanded. After the Pacific War, he determined to take up farm life in Minami Azumi in Nagano Prefecture, but he continued to be active in public affairs, serving as head of the Bukkyō Shakai Dōmei, the Nitchū Yūkō Kyōkai, the Tōkyō Rengō, and the Nitchō Kyōkai, all left-wing organizations. In 1959 he became a member of the Japan Communist Party. His writings include *Shinkō bukkyō no teishō* (1931), *Shakai henkaku tojō no shinkō bukkyō* (1933), and a voluminous diary, published in recent years, which constitutes an important source on the history of modern Japan.

Shaku Sōen 釋宗演 (1858–1919)

Monk of the Rinzai branch of the Zen sect in the Meiji period; his literary names were Kōgaku and Ryōgakutsu. He was born in the province of Wakasa and in 1871 entered the clergy under the direction of Okkei Shuken of Myōshin-ji in Kyoto. In 1878 he began Zen study under Kōsen Sōun (Imakita Kōsen) of Engaku-ji in Kamakura and eventually became his Dharma heir. After graduating from Keiō Gijuku, he went to Ceylon in 1886 to study Theravada Buddhism there, returning to Japan in 1889. His studies resulted in two works, *Seirontō-shi* and *Seinan no bukkyō.* In 1892 he became *kanchō* (head) of Engaku-ji and its affiliated temples and in 1903 became *kanchō* of Kenchō-ji as well. In 1893 he went to America to attend the World Religion Conference in Chicago and he made a second trip to America in 1905. He was well known as a highly active man with wide interests and experience. He acted as spiritual mentor to many Japanese intellectuals and leaders of the financial world, exercising a considerable influence over his time. Suzuki Daisetsu and Natsume Sōseki were among those who studied under him.

Shibusawa Eiichi 澁澤榮一 (1840–1931)

Business leader of the Meiji and Taishō eras and founder of the Shibusawa *zaibatsu*; he held the title of viscount. He at first went by the name Eijirō, which he later changed to Tokudayū. He was born in the district of Ōsato in present-day Saitama Prefecture. His family were wealthy farmers who also raised silkworms and indigo for dye. As a boy he studied Confucianism and swordsmanship. By the age of thirteen he was already taking part in the management of the family business and was said to have displayed a skill at it superior to that of an adult. When he was sixteen, his family was pressed for funds and subjected to insult by the lord of the domain, an experience that aroused in him a lasting resentment and feeling of distaste toward the feudal system.

In the latter years of the Edo period, when the movement to overthrow the shogunate and restore power to the emperor was gathering momentum, he responded with enthusiasm and became friendly with the groups of samurai advocating the restoration of imperial power and the expulsion of the foreigners. He joined in a plan to attack and set fire to the settlement of foreign traders in Yokohama, but the plan was thwarted before it could be put into execution and the group disbanded. While Shibusawa was living the life of a vagrant in Kyoto, he was recommended by a retainer of the family of Hitotsubashi Yoshinobu, a relative of the shogun, and entered the service of the powerful Hitotsubashi family. He proved himself highly adept at organizing agrarian troops and handling the family's financial matters. In 1866, Hitotsubashi Yoshinobu was chosen to be the fifteenth shogun, and Shibusawa became an official of the shogunate.

In 1867, when Yoshinobu's younger brother Tokugawa Akitake went to Europe to study and to be Japan's official representative to the Paris Exhibition, Shibusawa went along as a member of the group. The trip afforded him an opportunity to observe the modern production facilities and economic systems of a number of Western countries and gave him a knowledge of industrial, commercial, and financial matters that helped him greatly in his activities in later years. After the Meiji Restoration of 1868, he returned to Japan and took up residence in the domain assigned to the Tokugawa family in Shizuoka. There, with a currency loan of 500,000 *ryō* from the new Meiji government as a basis, he set up the first stock company in Japan.

In 1869 he became an official in the Ministry of Finance, devoting himself to problems associated with the abolition of the feudal domains and the establishment of prefectures, as well as with the regulation of the currencies issued by the various domains. In 1872 he became chief assistant to the finance minister, who at this time was Inoue Kaoru, but in 1873 both he and Inoue resigned because of differences of opinion between them and the other leaders of the government. Thereafter he devoted himself to business activities in the private sphere. His activities were characterized by an understanding and appreciation of the capitalist spirit, which he had acquired in Europe earlier, and by the conviction that business and morality must go hand in hand, ideals that played a major role in Japanese economic affairs. In order to provide a fiscal organ to assist the establishment of stock companies, he in 1873 headed the group that founded the First National Bank, a private organization and the first bank to be set up in Japan. In addition, he founded over five hundred companies and enterprises, including Ōji Paper, Osaka Spinning, Tokyo Artificial Fertilizer, and Tokyo Gas, as well as finance, insurance, transportation, production, chemical, and electrical corporations or industries. He was likewise determined to combat the popular attitude of reverence for officialdom and contempt for persons in private life through a program of education, working to set up a system of chambers of commerce and himself serving for a period of thirty-eight years as head of the Tokyo Chamber of Commerce and Bankers' Club.

Feudal ways of thought remained powerful in his time, commerce was looked upon as a discreditable occupation, and the merchants themselves in most cases were content to resign themselves to this state of affairs. These attitudes Shibusawa worked to overthrow, at the same time attempting to curb the excessive pursuit of profit. He insisted that business enterprises should be conducted in accordance with strict ethical principles, seeking for moral guidance in the teachings of the Confucian *Analects* and rejecting commercial methods that diverted from such principles. He looked upon trust as the only true foundation for commercial enterprises, and himself became the leading figure in the world of such enterprises. After his retirement from active business life in 1916, he devoted himself to various activities designed to promote the public welfare, among them the founding of homes for the aged. At the same time, in order to train business leaders for the future, he supported Tokyo Commercial College and other schools designed to give such training. In all, he was said to have been affiliated in one way or another with over six hundred organizations and business enterprises.

Shidehara Kijūrō 幣原喜重郎 (1872–1951)

Diplomat and statesman of the Meiji, Taishō, and Shōwa periods; he held the title of baron. His elder brother Shidehara Taira was president of Taihoku Imperial University in Taiwan. He was born in Osaka Prefecture and graduated from the law course of Tokyo Imperial University. In 1896 he passed the examination for diplomatic service and thereafter served in the Japanese consulates in Inchon in Korea, London, Antwerp, and Pusan in Korea. In 1904 he was assigned to the Foreign Ministry office in Tokyo and the following year became head of the Telegraph Section of the ministry. Around this time, he became close friends with an American advisor to the ministry named Denison and learned much from him concerning English and the language of diplomatic documents.

In 1911 he became head of the Investigation Bureau of the ministry and later served as councilor in the Japanese embassy in America and in England. In 1914 he went to Holland as envoy extraordinary and minister plenipotentiary and in 1915 he became vice-minister of foreign affairs. From then until 1919, roughly the period when the First World War was in progress, he served in that capacity under five succeeding foreign ministers. In 1919 he became ambassador to the United States, a post that he held until 1922, when he resigned and returned to Japan. In 1924 he was appointed foreign minister in the Katō Takaaki cabinet and continued in that capacity in the Wakatsuki Reijirō cabinet formed in 1926. During this time he developed the so-called Shidehara diplomacy, a policy based on international cooperation that refrained from interfering in internal affairs in China and sought to develop harmonious relations with Britain and the United States. As a result, he gained considerable trust in international circles.

In 1929, after the fall of the Tanaka Giichi cabinet, he once more became foreign minister, this time in the cabinet formed by Hamaguchi Osachi, the president of the Minseitō (Democratic Party). In 1930 Japan attended the London Disarmament Conference, and though Shidehara and Hamaguchi were accused of violating the rights of the Supreme Command, they succeeded in gaining ratification of the disarmament agreement. Shidehara was attacked by military leaders and right-wing political organizations such as the Seiyūkai for pursuing a weak-kneed policy and he likewise incurred the displeasure of the Privy Council. After Hamaguchi was wounded in an assassination attempt in November of 1930, Shidehara acted as prime minister in his place for a period of four months. He continued in the post of foreign minister in the second Wakatsuki cabinet formed in the spring of 1931, but with the development of the Manchurian Incident later in the year, the cabinet was forced to resign en masse. Shidehara largely retired from the world of politics, only continuing to hold the position of member of the Upper House of the Diet to which he had been appointed in 1926.

After the end of the Pacific War, when the Higashikuni-no-miya Naruhiko cabinet resigned in October of 1945, Shidehara became prime minister, formed a new cabinet, and immediately received orders from the general headquarters of the Occupation forces to carry out various reforms. He drafted the announcement made by the emperor at the beginning of 1946 in which the latter denied his divinity and he held discussions with General Douglas MacArthur, the commander of the Occupation forces, concerning the proposal that Japan renounce the right to make war. In March of 1946, a draft outline of proposed constitutional changes was made public, and the following month Shidehara and his cabinet resigned. He became the president of the newly formed Shimpotō (Progressive Party) and was appointed state minister in the Yoshida Shigeru cabinet that succeeded his own. In the general election of 1947 he was elected to the Diet and, after being reelected in 1949, he became Speaker of the Lower House. He died of illness in 1951 while holding this position. His wife was the daughter of the famous financier Iwasaki Yatarō and the younger sister of the wife of Katō Takaaki. After the war, he served for a time as head of the board of directors of the Tōyō Bunko, a research institute devoted to Chinese studies, and worked vigorously to revive its activities.

Shiga Kiyoshi 志賀潔 (1871–1957)

Bacteriologist and doctor of medicine of the Meiji, Taishō, and Shōwa periods; he was born in Miyagi Prefecture; his family name was originally Satō. In 1896 he graduated from the medical course of Tokyo Imperial University and immediately joined the Institute for Research in Infectious Diseases. Working under the guidance of the bacteriologist Kitazato Shibasaburō, he succeeded the following year in discovering the dysentery bacillus, an achievement that brought him worldwide fame. He went to Germany in 1901, where he studied under Paul Ehrlich at the Institut für Experimentelle Therapie in Frankfurt, specializing in biochemistry and immunology. In 1904 he cooperated with Ehrlich in publishing a work on chemotherapy and returned to Japan the following year. In 1914, when the Institute for Research in Infectious Diseases was placed under the jurisdiction of Tokyo University, he resigned along with the director, Kitazato, and in 1915 became a member of the newly established Kitazato Institute. In 1920 he became a professor of Keiō University, but resigned after half a year in order to take up duties in Seoul as head physician of the government-general of Korea.

In 1925 he became the first head of the medical department of Keijō Imperial University. In 1929 he became president of the university, a post that he held until 1931. He thus devoted more than ten years to medical education and administration in Korea. Thereafter he served as an advisor to the Kitazato Institute and continued his research in bacteriology through its facilities. In 1944 he received a Cultural Medal. From 1945 on, he resided in his birthplace, Miyagi Prefecture. In 1948 he became a member of the Japan Academy and in 1949 was made an honorary citizen of the city of Sendai. In addition to works on his field of specialization, he also wrote a biography of his teacher, Paul Ehrlich.

Shiga Shigetaka 志賀重昂 (1863–1927)

Geographer of the Meiji and Taishō periods; he was born in the city of Okazaki in present-day Aichi Prefecture; his literary name was Shinsen. After graduating from Sapporo Agricultural School (the forerunner of Hokkaido University), he became a middle school teacher in Nagano Prefecture. In 1886 he sailed on the Japanese warship *Tsukuba* on a tour of Australia and the islands of the South Pacific. He published an account of the trip in 1887 under the title *Nan'yō jiji,* which soon won him a reputation as an advocate of Japanese overseas expansion. In 1888 he joined Miyake Setsurei and others in forming a society called the Seikyōsha and publishing a magazine, *Nihonjin,* which called for the preservation of the Japanese national character. In 1894 he published a work called *Nihon fūkei-ron* extolling the beauties of the Japanese landscape, which won him many ardent readers, as well as spurring the development of alpinism in Japan.

In 1896 he entered political activity as honorary secretary of the Shimpotō (Progressive Party). In 1897 he became head of the Forestry Bureau in the Ministry of Agriculture and Forestry and in 1898 became a councilor to the Minister of Foreign Affairs. From 1902 on, he was a member of the Lower House of the Diet and an advocate of an uncompromising stance in foreign relations. In 1906, after the conclusion of the Russo-Japanese War, he participated in the group that defined the border between Russia and Karafuto, the Japanese portion of the island of Sakhalin. He made three trips around the world, in 1910, 1922–23, and 1923–24, and in 1912 published a world atlas entitled *Sekai sansui zusetsu.* He lectured on geography at Waseda University and was an honorary member of the Brazilian Geographical Society and the Royal Geographical Society of Great Britain. He is also well known for having given the scenic region in the lower reaches of the Kiso River the name "Japanese Rhine."

Shiga Yoshio 志賀義雄 (1901–)

Shōwa period political figure and leader of the socialist movement; he was born in Fukuoka Prefecture. While a student in Tokyo Imperial University, he joined a socialist organization called Shinjinkai. In 1922 he organized a nationwide Student Alliance and in 1923 joined the newly formed Japan Communist Party. The following year, after the party was disbanded, he contributed authoritative articles to a magazine called *Marukusu-shugi* (Marxism). In 1925 he graduated from the social studies course of Tokyo University. He worked with Tokuda Kyūichi to reestablish the Japan Communist Party and in 1926 became head of the political bureau of the Central Committee and chief editor of *Marukusu-shugi*. In 1927 he became a member of the Central Standing Committee and in 1928 was among those taken into custody in the March 15 mass arrest of members of the party. He spent the following eighteen years in jail, and though many of those arrested eventually renounced their political beliefs and were released from jail, he steadfastly refused to do so. He was released after the end of the Pacific War in 1945 and joined Tokuda Kyūichi in refounding the Japan Communist Party. He became a member of the Central Committee, member of the political bureau, and chief editor of the Communist newspaper *Akahata*.

In 1946 he was elected to the Lower House of the Diet, playing an active role as one of the few Communist Party members of the Diet. In 1950 he was purged from office on orders from General MacArthur and turned to underground activity. He returned to overt political life in 1955, resuming his role of leadership in the party, and was once more elected to the Diet. Earlier, in 1950, when the Cominform had criticized the Japan Communist Party, he was among the minority in the party who recognized the Soviet Union's leadership in such matters. In 1964, when controversy arose over the Partial Nuclear Test Ban Treaty, the party as a whole took an anti-Soviet stand, but he favored ratification of the treaty. As a result, he and Kamiyama Shigeo were both expelled from the party and instead founded an organization known as Nihon no Koe.

Shigemitsu Mamoru 重光葵 (1887–1957)

Taishō and Shōwa period diplomat and political leader; he was born in Ōita Prefecture in Kyushu. After graduating from the law course of Tokyo Imperial University, he entered the Ministry of Foreign Affairs. He served in various countries of Europe and America and was a member of the Japanese delegation to the Versailles Peace Conference. He later served as head of the treaty section of the Ministry of Foreign Affairs and as consul general in Shanghai. He was minister to China in 1931–32. Fighting broke out between the Chinese and Japanese in 1932 in the so-called Shanghai Incident, and he was in the midst of conducting negotiations to end the hostilities when, at a celebration in Shanghai in honor of the emperor's birthday, a Korean supporter of the Korean independence movement threw a bomb at him, causing him to lose one leg. During the period 1933–36 he served as vice-minister of foreign affairs under Hirota Kōki, the minister of foreign affairs, advising him in particular on matters relating to China. He was ambassador to the Soviet Union from 1936 to 1938, and to Great Britain from 1938 to 1941. In 1942 he became ambassador to China, and in 1943 was appointed minister of foreign affairs when the Tōjō cabinet was reorganized. He remained in this post in the succeeding Koiso cabinet in 1944, serving at the same time as minister of Greater East Asia. He resigned these posts in 1945 and became a member of the Upper House of the Diet.

With the conclusion of the Pacific War, he became minister of foreign affairs in the Higashikuni-no-miya cabinet and, along with General of the Army Umezu Yoshijirō, represented Japan at the signing of the surrender aboard the USS *Missouri* in Tokyo Bay. He was tried by the International Military Tribunal for the Far East as an A-class war criminal and was sentenced to seven years imprisonment. He was released on parole in 1950. After all restrictions on his activities had been removed, he entered the political world in 1952, serving as president of the Kaishintō (Progressive Party). In 1954 he became vice-president of the Minshutō (Democratic Party). In 1955–56 he served as minister of foreign affairs in the Hatoyama cabinet, presiding over the restoration of diplomatic relations between Japan and the Soviet Union. He was three times elected to the Lower House of the Diet. His last public appearance was as Japanese representative at the ceremonies celebrating Japan's entry into the United Nations in 1956.

Shimaji Mokurai 島地默雷 (1838–1911)

Priest of the Hongan-ji branch of the Jōdo Shin sect in the Meiji period. He was the son of a Buddhist priest of the province of Suō. After attending a nearby school, he entered the Ruiseikō, a school for the clergy in Kumamoto. In 1866 he became resident priest of a temple called Myōsei-ji in Suō. At the time of the Meiji Restoration, he determined to carry out reforms in the organization of the Jōdo Shin sect, joining with Akamatsu Renjō in 1868 in submitting proposals to that effect to the headquarters of the sect. He also cooperated with Ōsu Tetsunen in establishing a school in Hagi for the training of Buddhist followers. In 1871 he went to Tokyo, where he worked to oppose the anti-Buddhist policies of the government, recommending the establishment of a ministry of religious affairs and a bureau to handle affairs pertaining to Buddhist organizations.

In 1872–73 he and Akamatsu Renjō toured Europe to observe the condition of religion in the various countries of the continent. At this time, the Japanese government had set up an organization called Shimbutsu Gappei Daikyō-in for the purpose of bringing Buddhism under official control and establishing Shintoism as the national religion. On his return to Japan, Mokurai vehemently opposed the move and in 1875 succeeded in separating the Jōdo Shin sect from the jurisdiction of the government organization. His efforts represent a landmark in the struggle to establish religious freedom in Japan.

In 1874 he joined with Ōuchi Seiran in founding a magazine called *Hōshi Sōdan*, which attempted to advance the cause of liberalism and enlightened thinking from the Buddhist point of view. He later devoted himself to educational affairs and reforms in the headquarters of the sect. He grew increasingly nationalistic in his thinking and in 1888 joined with Miyake Setsurei and others in founding the Seikyōsha, an organization for the promotion of nationalism. The Buddhist scholar Shimaji Daitō is his adopted son.

Shimazu Hisamitsu 島津久光 (1817–1887)

The father of Shimazu Tadayoshi, lord of the domain of Satsuma, and half-brother of Shimazu Nariakira, he wielded great power in the domain and was an enthusiastic supporter of the imperial cause; he bore the title of duke. After the death of his father, Shimazu Narioki, a struggle broke out between his supporters and those of his half-brother Nariakira over who should be successor. The latter group won, and Nariakira became the lord of Satsuma. In 1858, when Nariakira died and Hisamitsu's eldest son Tadayoshi became lord of Satsuma, Hisamitsu was honored with the title of "State Father" and in fact wielded the actual power in the domain. Honoring the wishes of Nariakira, he lent his full support to the *kōbu-gattai* policy, which sought to promote cooperation between the imperial court and the shogunate.

In order to deal with the problems that faced the domain and the nation at large, he went to Kyoto in 1862. There he took steps to suppress the more fanatical of the Satsuma supporters of the movement to expel the foreigners and restore power to the emperor, ordering an attack on them at the Teradaya, an inn in Fushimi south of Kyoto. In addition, with the aim of bringing about reforms in the shogunate, he accompanied the imperial envoy Ōhara Shigetomi to Edo, where he was instrumental in preparing armaments with which to expel the foreigners, promoting Hitotsubashi Yoshinobu to the office of *hosa* (advisor to the shogun) and reorganizing the shogunate personnel.

In 1863, radical supporters of the antiforeign policy from the domain of Chōshū had become increasingly powerful in Kyoto and had succeeded in allying themselves with Iwakura Tomomi and other members of the court. To counter this situation, the Satsuma forces, centering about Hisamitsu, along with those of the domain of Aizu, on the eighteenth day of the eighth month carried out a coup d'état, which restored the supporters of the *kōbu-gattai* policy to power. Hisamitsu enjoyed the trust of Emperor Kōmei and in 1864 was given permission to take part in court affairs. He joined with Hitotsubashi Yoshinobu, Matsudaira Yoshinaga, Yamanouchi Toyoshige, Date Munenari, and others to form a council of the more important feudal lords that would have a voice in the conduct of court and shogunate affairs. Hisamitsu hoped that this would ensure a coalition government dominated by the powerful lords of the *kōbu-gattai* party, but because of lack of agreement among the participants, the body disbanded and Hisamitsu returned to Satsuma.

In the period following 1864, Hisamitsu looked on with dissatisfaction as the *kōbu-gattai* movement faltered and the expedition to punish Chōshū gave way to an armed effort to overthrow the shogunate, developments which saw the sudden rise to prominence of such lower ranking samurai as Saigō Takamori and Ōkubo Toshimichi. He remained in retirement in Kagoshima, the chief city of Satsuma, after the formation of the new Meiji government, and was reported to have been considerably dissatisfied with the order issued in 1871 abolishing the feudal domains and replacing them with a system of prefectures. But he continued as before to be a staunch supporter of the principle of imperial rule, and in 1873, when the central government had been weakened by a split over Korean policy, he took up a position as an advisor to the cabinet. In 1874 he became minister of the left, but because of his proposals to outlaw Western dress and other moves indicative of his antiforeign sentiments, he was not entrusted with any appreciable degree of responsibility. He resigned the post in 1876 and returned to the former domain of Satsuma, where he spent the remainder of his life in retirement. For a time in the late Edo period Hisamitsu had wielded great power because of the support that he enjoyed from his own and other important domains, but after the establishment of the Meiji government he tended to be treated respectfully but coldly because of his extreme conservatism.

Shimazu Nariakira 島津齊彬 (1809–1858)

Daimyo of the late Edo period and lord of the domain of Satsuma in Kyushu. He was born in the domain residence in Edo. Under the influence of his great-grandfather Shimazu Shigehide, he took an interest in the material culture of the West and favored the opening of the country to foreign contacts. In 1844, when a French warship appeared in the Ryūkyū Islands, which were under the jurisdiction of the domain of Satsuma, and requested to engage in trade, the *rōjū* (senior councilor) Abe Masahiro, who was friendly with Nariakira, left the matter up to Nariakira to handle. He accordingly adopted a policy of opening the Ryūkyūs to trade.

In spite of opposition within the domain, Nariakira, supported by members of the reform faction such as Saigō Takamori and Ōkubo Toshimichi, in 1851 succeeded his father Narioki as lord of the domain and set about to reform the domain administration. He set up a refinery, manufactured chemicals, and succeeded in constructing five warships propelled by sail and one steamship. He proposed to the shogunate that a flag with a rising sun on a white background be used by such ships, and this in time became the origin of the Japanese national flag. In 1853 in the grounds of his residence in Kagoshima he had a reverberatory furnace built. He built a Western style factory called the Shūseikan in which cannon, gun powder, ceramics, colored glass, and telegraphic instruments were manufactured. He also introduced the use of spinning machines and tried his own hand at photography. He was one of the most enlightened and progressive daimyo of the time and worked assiduously to encourage production and industrialization within his domain.

On the political scene, he joined with Tokugawa Nariaki and Matsudaira Yoshinaga in supporting Hitotsubashi Yoshinobu as a candidate for succession to the shogunate. But with the appointment of Ii Naosuke, leader of the opposing faction, to the position of *tairō* (chief councilor) in 1858, his hopes on this score were disappointed, and he died shortly afterward. Shimazu Hisamitsu, who played an important role in politics at the end of the Edo period, was his younger brother by a different mother.

Soejima Taneomi 副島種臣 (1828–1905)

Meiji period statesman; he held the title of count; his common name was Jirō. He was born in the domain of Saga in Kyushu, the son of Edayoshi Nangō, but was later adopted into the Soejima family. His elder brother Edayoshi Shin'yō was a teacher in the official school of the domain and trained such important Meiji period leaders as Ōkuma Shigenobu, Ōki Takatō, and Etō Shimpei; Soejima himself was very much influenced by his brother in his scholarship and ways of thinking. During the late years of the Edo period, Soejima traveled to Kyoto and Edo and made many friends among the courtiers and samurai who were active in the movement to restore power to the emperor and expel the foreigners. When his elder brother died, however, he returned to Saga to take his brother's place as a teacher in the domain school. From 1864 on, he studied English in Nagasaki and, along with Ōkuma Shigenobu, received instruction in Western studies from Guido Herman Fridolin Verbeck, a missionary and schoolteacher.

At the time of the Meiji Restoration in 1868, he took part in drafting the *Seitaisho*, the regulations defining the organs of the new government and their functions. He was given the position of *san'yo* (junior councilor), and in 1869 advanced to the more important post of councilor of state. In 1871, when Iwakura Tomomi embarked on his mission to Europe and America, Soejima succeeded him as foreign minister. On the counsel of his American advisor, he embarked on a course of independent or national prestige diplomacy. Thus, in 1872 he dealt firmly with the problem of the Ryūkyū castaways who were murdered by Taiwan aborigines and freed the Chinese coolies who were being held aboard the Peruvian ship *Maria Luz*. The following year, when he went as ambassador extraordinary and plenipotentiary to China to discuss the Taiwan question, he was able to obtain a private audience with the Chinese emperor before any of the ministers of the European powers had been received in audience. In his negotiations with Russia concerning the island of Sakhalin, he attempted to arrange for Japanese purchase of the entire island, but failed in this attempt.

After the Iwakura mission returned to Japan in 1873, a controversy broke out among the government leaders concerning the proposal to launch a military expedition against Korea. Iwakura opposed the idea, and Soejima, Itagaki Taisuke, and the others who favored it accordingly resigned. The following year, Soejima joined Itagaki Taisuke and others in petitioning the government for the creation of an elected assembly, but he was never a member of the people's rights movement. He refused all offers of government posts and for a time was completely removed from political affairs, at one period touring China. In 1879, however, he was summoned to be a lecturer to Emperor Meiji and later he served as advisor in the Imperial Household Ministry and to the Privy Council, posts that he held until his death from illness in the midst of the Russo-Japanese War. In 1892, he served for three months as home minister in the Matsukata cabinet.

He had his own distinctive ideas as to what Japan's policy should be on the Asian continent and favored a belligerent approach. In 1891 he set up a research organization called the Tōhō Kyōkai with himself as director and devoted himself with great enthusiasm to its direction. He had a profound knowledge of Chinese literature and culture, and his erudition and personality were said to have won him high respect among Chinese. He was skilled at composing poetry in Chinese and was noted for his distinctive style of calligraphy.

Sugiura Shigetake (Jūgō) 杉浦重剛 (1855–1924)

Educator of the Meiji and Taishō eras; he went by the literary names Baisō and Tendai Dōshi. He was born in the domain of Zeze in the province of Ōmi, the second son of a Confucian scholar; his childhood name was Jōjirō. In 1865 he began study under Takahashi Tandō, a Confucian scholar of the domain, but the same year the domain took measures to repress those who favored restoration of power to the emperor, and his teacher was put to death. Following this, he studied under Kuroda Kikuro, a scholar of the domain who specialized in Western learning and who produced the first Japanese translation of *Robinson Crusoe*; under him, Sugiura commenced the study of Western science and languages. For a time he attended a school in Kyoto operated by Iwagaki Gesshū, but later returned to Zeze and assisted in the operation of the official school of the domain.

In 1870 he was chosen by the leaders of the domain to be sent to Tokyo for study. There he entered the Daigaku Nankō, the forerunner of Tokyo Imperial University. When the school was renamed the Kaisei Gakkō, he was selected to lecture on science in the presence of the emperor. In 1876 he went to England, where he studied agricultural chemistry, and later attended Owens College (present-day University of Manchester), studying under the well-known chemistry scholar Roscoe.

Illness obliged him to return to Japan in 1880, but after a period of recuperation, he took up a position in the museum of Tokyo Imperial University. In 1881, he and his colleagues began publication of a scientific journal titled *Tōyō Gakugei Zasshi*, which was comparable in character to the British scientific journal *Nature*. From 1882 to 1885 he served as director of Tokyo University Preparatory School, later known as the First High School. In 1888 he became a councilor in the Ministry of Education and in 1897 a member of the Council on Higher Education, taking part in government educational activities. But the real focus of his activities was rather private education and the formation of public opinion. To this end, he wrote editorials for the *Yomiuri Shimbun* and *Tokyo Asahi Shimbun*. In 1888, with the formation of the society known as the Seikyōsha, he joined with Miyake Setsurei and others in founding a magazine called *Nihonjin* to express the views of the society and he also assisted Kuga Minoru (Katsunan) in starting the newspaper called *Nihon*. The purpose of these various measures was to combat the tide of Westernization in Japan and to encourage nationalism.

He interested himself in the question of the revision of Japan's treaties with the foreign powers, gaining a knowledge of the subject through his friend Komura Jutarō. He regarded Foreign Minister Ōkuma Shigenobu's conduct of the matter as injurious to the national prestige and joined with friends in forming the Nihon Kurabu, an organization that bitterly opposed Ōkuma's position. In 1890 he became the first representative from Shiga Prefecture to the Lower House of the Diet, but resigned shortly after and retired from political activity.

In the field of education, in 1892 he reorganized the Tokyo English School, founded in 1885, renaming it Nihon Chūgakkō and acting as its director; it graduated many outstanding students, among them the prominent postwar political leader Yoshida Shigeru. He also acted as head of Kokugakuin (present-day Kokugakuin University) and of the Tōa Dōbun Shoin and opened a private school in his own home, called the Shōkōjuku, in which he trained students. In his late years, he devoted all his time to the education of members of the imperial family. In 1914 he became an educational official in the household of the crown prince (the present Emperor Hirohito) and for the following seven years instructed the prince in ethics. He also lectured to the present Empress Nagako on ethics.

Suzuki Bunji 鈴木文治 (1885–1946)

Leader of the labor movement in the Taishō and Shōwa periods; he was born in Miyagi Prefecture, the son of a saké maker. In spite of financial difficulties, he succeeded in graduating from the political course of Tokyo Imperial University. While a student, he joined the Hongō Church of the well-known educator and Christian leader Ebina Danjō, and under the influence of the political thinkers Yoshino Sakuzō and Abe Isoo developed a deep interest in social problems. After working for a printing company called Shūeisha and the Tokyo *Asahi Shimbun*, in 1911 he became secretary of the Unitarian Church in Japan. In the factory area near Mita in Tokyo, he began devoting his time to social education for the workers.

In 1912 he and a group of associates, fifteen persons in all, formed a labor organization called the Yūaikai, which advocated cooperation between labor and management. It rapidly grew in size until it incorporated a number of labor unions throughout the country. In 1921 the name was changed to Nihon Rōdō Sōdōmei (Japan General Labor Federation). Suzuki headed the organization until 1930, advocating social reformism of a Christian nature and opposing communist principles. During this period, he took part in the formation of the Shakai Minshūtō (Social Popular Party) in 1926 and, in the first universal suffrage election in 1928, he was elected to the Lower House of the Diet.

As representative of the Yūaikai, he attended the general convention of the American Federation of Labor and four times went abroad to participate in international labor meetings. In the first general election after the end of the Pacific War, he ran as a candidate on the Socialist Party ticket, but collapsed while on a campaign tour to Sendai.

Suzuki Daisetsu (Daisetz) 鈴木大拙 (1870–1966)

Thinker and scholar of religion of the Meiji, Taishō, and Shōwa periods; his personal name was Teitarō. He was born in Ishikawa Prefecture, the son of a doctor. He attended the Fourth High School in the area, where he was friendly with Nishida Kitarō and Fujioka Sakutarō, both eminent scholars in later years. He also received instruction in Zen meditation from Setsumon, priest of a temple in the area called Kokutai-ji. In 1887 he withdrew from high school and for a time served as a substitute teacher in elementary school. In 1891 he went to Tokyo and entered Tokyo Semmon Gakkō (present-day Waseda University). At the same time he received Zen instruction from the Zen master Imakita Kōsen of the Rinzai Zen temple Engaku-ji in Kamakura. The following year he entered Tokyo Imperial University as a special student. After the death of Imakita Kōsen, he continued Zen study under Shaku Sōen.

In 1897, on the recommendation of Shaku Sōen, he went to America to become assistant to the philosopher Paul Carus in La Salle, Illinois. He remained there until 1908, translating works of Taoism into English and helping to edit a scholarly journal. At the same time he published various works on Buddhism such as an English translation of Aśvaghoṣa's *Discourse on the Awakening of Faith in Mahayana Buddhism* (1901) and *Outline of Mahayana Buddhism* (1907). He went to London in 1908, where he studied the thought of Swedenborg, and returned to Japan the following year. During the period 1910 to 1921 he served as a professor at the Peers' School in Tokyo, and from 1921 on as professor of Ōtani University in Kyoto. In 1927 he published *Essays in Zen Buddhism,* a collection of articles in English, and this was followed by a number of subsequent works on Zen in English.

In time he became known as the person most responsible for introducing Zen Buddhism to Europe and America. He was not a mere popularizer of the subject, however, nor did he treat it simply from an academic point of view. Rather he wrote in the light of his own profound experience and thinking on the subject, presenting Zen in a manner that possessed a wide intellectual appeal. For this reason, he holds a place of importance in Japanese philosophical circles as well as those abroad. The core of his thinking is the so-called *sokuhi no ronri* or "logic of identity through difference," which transcends formal logic and is the basis of Zen thought. It can be summed up in the formula: To say that A is A means that A is not A; therefore A is A; in other words, any truth must include its opposite. This type of thinking had a great influence on Suzuki's friend, the philosopher Nishida Kitarō. Suzuki also published a study of the important Sanskrit work, *Lankāvatāra Sūtra,* and helped to draw attention to the Edo period Zen leader Bankei and the commoner devotees of *nembutsu* practice known as *myōkōnin.* Thus, although somewhat removed for formal academic circles, he produced works that display a very high level of scholarship. In 1949 he received a Cultural Medal.

Suzuki Kantarō 鈴木貫太郎 (1868–1948)

Naval leader and statesman of the Meiji, Taishō, and Shōwa eras; he held the title of baron. He was the son of a magistrate of the domain of Sekiyado in present-day Chiba Prefecture and was born in the official residence in Izumi (present-day Osaka Prefecture) of the Kuze family, the lords of Sekiyado. His younger brother Suzuki Takao (1869–1964) became a general of the army.

After attending Gumma Middle School for a time, he went to Tokyo, where he entered a school headed by Kondō Makoto, an expert on navigation and naval affairs. Later he attended the Naval Academy and graduated from the Naval Staff College. In 1889 he was commissioned an ensign in the navy. He was active in the Sino-Japanese War as commander of a torpedo boat and in 1895 played an important part in the attack on Wei-hai-wei. In 1898 he was promoted to the rank of lieutenant commander; the following year, as a staff member of the Naval Ministry, he became an instructor in the Naval Staff College, at the same time teaching at the Military (Army) Staff College.

During the period from 1901 to 1904 he was a military officer in residence in Germany and later, as commander of the *Kasuga*, a warship purchased from England, he returned to Japan immediately after the outbreak of the Russo-Japanese War. He was active during the war as commander of a destroyer flotilla. After the war he continued to serve as an instructor in the Naval Staff College and later headed a torpedo school and commanded various types of warships. In 1913 he was promoted to the rank of rear admiral and at the same time became commander of the torpedo force at Maizuru, becoming known in naval circles as an expert on torpedo warfare.

The same year he became head of the Personnel Section of the Naval Ministry and, in 1914, having attracted the notice of Yashiro Rokurō, minister of the navy in the Ōkuma cabinet, he was appointed vice-minister. In 1917 he advanced to the rank of vice-admiral and was made commander of the training fleet. Following this, he served as head of the Naval Academy, commander of the Second Fleet, of the Third Fleet, and of the Kure Naval Yard. In 1924 he became commander of the Combined Fleet and in 1925 assumed the important post of chief of the naval general staff. In 1929 he entered the reserve and was appointed to serve at court as grand chamberlain and advisor to the Privy Council. During the following seven years or more, he served close to the emperor. He was attacked and seriously wounded during the young army officers' uprising on February 26, 1936, but managed to escape with his life. In 1940 he became vice-president of the Privy Council and in 1944, president.

In 1945, when Japan was suffering grave losses in the Pacific War, he was unanimously recommended by the high officials in the government and at court for the post of prime minister and replaced Koiso Kuniaki in that post, forming a new cabinet. Though outwardly advocating that Japan continue its struggle even on home soil, he secretly held hopes that peace could be arranged through the intervention of the Soviet Union and worked toward that end. In July of the same year, he announced that Japan would ignore the Potsdam Declaration issued by Britain, America, and China calling for Japan's unconditional surrender. August brought the atomic bombings of

Hiroshima and Nagasaki and the Soviet Union's entry into the war. On August 14, Suzuki, following the decision of the emperor, agreed to accept the terms of the Potsdam Declaration, and on August 15, after the emperor had announced the conclusion of the war over the radio, he and his cabinet resigned. For half a year in 1946 he once more served as president of the Privy Council.

Suzuki Mosaburō 鈴木茂三郎 (1893–1970).

Politician and leader of the socialist movement in the Taishō and Shōwa eras; he was born in Aichi Prefecture. In 1915 he graduated from the political and economic course of Waseda University and for a time worked as a reporter for the *Hōchi Shimbun* and *Tokyo Nichinichi Shimbun.* He later traveled about America, Europe, and the Soviet Union and on his return to Japan devoted his energies to the study and encouragement of socialism, founding an organization known as the Seiji Kenkyūkai (Political Study Society) toward the close of the Taishō era. He took part in the socialist movement to the extent that such activities were permitted by the laws of the time, helping to found the Nōmin Rōdōtō (Farmer Labor Party) in 1925 and the Rōdō Nōminto (Labor Farmer Party) in 1926. In 1927 he became a member of the staff of the magazine *Rōdō,* helping to formulate the system of thought associated with the so-called Labor-Farmer faction within the socialist movement.

In 1928, after the government had ordered the dissolution of the Rōdō Nōmintō, he became chief secretary of the Musan Taishūtō (Proletarian Popular Party). When the latter party split apart, he became a member of the standing committee of the Nihon Taishūtō (Japan Popular Party). In 1930 he became a member of the central executive committee of the Zenkoku Taishūtō (National Popular Party) and also served as chief secretary of the Nihon Musantō (Japan Proletarian Party) and director of the Nihon Keizai Kenkyūkai (Japan Economic Study Society), working in the early thirties to combat the growing trend toward fascism in Japan. In 1937 he was arrested along with a number of other left-wing leaders when the government carried out the first of its so-called *jimmin sensen* (popular front) actions. His appeal was pending when the Pacific War came to an end.

In the postwar period he was active in the Nihon Shakaitō (Japan Socialist Party) from the time of its founding, being associated with the left-wing faction of the party. In 1947, when the left wing cooperated with the more conservative forces to bring about the formation of a socialist cabinet headed by Katayama Tetsu, he joined with the labor unions in opposing the government. In 1949 he became chief secretary of the Socialist Party and, in 1951, after the party had split, he became chairman of the Saha Shakaitō (Leftist Socialist Party). He resigned this post in 1960 but continued to be an advisor to the party. During the period preceding his resignation he was active on the international scene as well, in 1951 attending the Socialist Internationale in Berlin, East Germany, and later becoming a secretary of the organization. In 1952 he proposed the holding of a congress of Asian socialist parties, traveling to many countries in Asia to implement the plan and later becoming honorary president of the congress. During the period from 1946 to 1966, he was elected nine times as a member of the Lower House of the Diet. He compiled a collection of materials dealing with social problems and the socialist movement that was made public under the title *Shakai bunko.*

Suzuki Umetarō 鈴木梅太郎 (1874–1943)

Agricultural chemist of the Meiji, Taishō, and Shōwa eras; he was born in Shizuoka Prefecture. In 1896 he graduated from the agricultural chemistry course of Tokyo Imperial University. In 1901 he went to Europe and, under the guidance of Emil Fischer of Berlin University, a specialist in organic chemistry, devoted himself to studies of protein. On his return to Japan in 1906 he became a teacher of the Morioka Agricultural and Forestry College and the following year was appointed a professor of Tokyo Imperial University. In 1910 he succeeded in extracting vitamin B_1 from rice bran, giving it the name oryzanin. This discovery became the foundation for the science of vitaminology. In addition to his studies of vitamins and nutritional science, he also devoted himself to the development of insecticides and a preservative for saké and other wines.

In 1916 he participated as one of the founders of the Institute of Physical and Chemical Research and in his capacity as chief researcher discovered a method for making synthetic saké and contributed in other ways to the advancement of science. His achievements were important not only in terms of pure research, but in their applicability to daily life, and as a pioneer in the fields of agricultural and biological chemistry he played an important role in improving the level of Japanese chemical research. In 1943 he received a Cultural Medal.

TAGUCHI UKICHI 田口卯吉 (1855–1905)

Meiji period economist and cultural historian; he held the degree of Doctor of Law. He was born in Edo, the son of a minor official in the shogunate; his personal name was Gen and his literary name Teiken. After the collapse of the shogunate, he moved to Shizuoka, where the Tokugawa family had retired, and studied medicine in a hospital there. He went to Tokyo in 1871 and studied in the Kyōritsu Gakusha school operated by Seki Shimpachi, a scholar of English. When Seki took a position in the Finance Ministry, Taguchi became a student attached to the Translation Bureau of the ministry, applying himself to the study of economics and English. He completed the course of study in 1874 and until 1878 did translation work in the Currency Bureau of the ministry.

During the period 1877–82 he published a work called *Nihon kaika shōshi*, a systematic history of Japanese culture that was influenced by the writings of Guizot and Buckle and stressed matters of production and the living conditions of the common people. Because of these features and the fact that it attempts to define the principles of social evolution, it has proved to be a pioneer work in its field. In 1879, Taguchi founded a journal devoted to economic matters entitled *Tokyo Keizai Zasshi* and modeled after the English journal, *The Economist*. In it, he attacked protectionist theories and advocated the principles of a free economy, criticizing the government's economic policies and winning for himself the name "the Japanese Adam Smith."

In addition to this publication, which he continued to edit for the remainder of his life, he also founded a historical journal called *Shikai* and, in order to further the study of Japanese history, edited and published a series of Japanese historical texts known as *Kokushi taikei* (32 volumes). He also took part in the preparation of the biographical dictionary, *Daijimmei jiten*. In addition to his writing and editorial activities, he was active in the business and political worlds as well, interesting himself in the stock market, banks, and private railways, and serving as a representative in the Tokyo prefectural assembly and the Lower House of the Diet.

TAKAHASHI KOREKIYO 高橋是清 (1854–1936)

Statesman and financier of the Taishō and Shōwa eras; he held the title of viscount. He was born in Edo, the son of a painter named Kawamura, but became the adopted son of a samurai of the domain of Sendai named Takahashi. At the age of eleven he was employed as a houseboy to a foreigner in

Yokohama and learned English. In 1867 he was sent to America at the expense of his domain to continue his studies, but in time left the country and returned to Japan. He then became a houseboy in the service of Mori Arinori, an official in charge of foreign affairs, and in 1869 entered a school in Tokyo known as the Daigaku Nankō. After serving for a time as English instructor in the former domain of Karatsu and employee in the Ministry of Finance, he entered Kaisei Gakkō, the forerunner of Tokyo Imperial University, but left before completing the course. In 1875 he founded a school known as Kyōritsu Gakkō and at the same time was active as a speculator.

In 1881 he became a commissioner in the Ministry of Education and later was transferred to the Ministry of Agriculture and Commerce. In 1885 he was sent to America to study the setting up of a monopoly trademark protection system and in 1887 became the first chief of the Patent Office. In 1889 he was also assigned to the position of director of the Agriculture and Forestry School, an assignment in which he displayed great skill. Filled with ambitions of opening a silver mine in Peru, he journeyed to South America, but fell victim to fraud and failed in the venture.

For a time he was in dire financial straits, but eventually his abilities were recognized by Kawata Koichirō, the president of the Bank of Japan, and in 1892 he was taken into the bank's employ. Thereafter, he had an opportunity to display his unusual ability in financial affairs. As manager of the Shōkin Bank of Yokohama, he advised Prime Minister Matsukata Masayoshi to put Japan on the gold standard. He continued to advance until in 1898 he reached the position of vice-president of the Bank of Japan. During and immediately after the Russo-Japanese War he succeeded in floating foreign loans amounting to around 1.25 billion yen. After serving as president of the Shōkin Bank and the Bank of Japan, in 1913 he became finance minister in the cabinet of Yamamoto Gombei and at the same time joined the political party known as the Rikken Seiyūkai. In 1918 he served as finance minister in the cabinet of Hara Takashi, a leader in the Seiyūkai, and worked to expand Japan's naval power through the establishment of an eight-battleship eight-cruiser fleet and also devoted himself to putting the government's financial affairs in order in the post-World War One period.

In 1921, when Prime Minister Hara was assassinated, Takahashi became prime minister and formed a cabinet of his own. He also became president of the Seiyūkai, but resigned when he found he lacked the necessary competence. In 1924, when the Seiyūkai split over the question of support for the Kiyoura Keigo cabinet, Takahashi led the party in the movement to protect the constitution. When Katō Takaaki formed a new cabinet from the members of the three parties who had joined the movement, Takahashi was chosen to serve as minister of agriculture and commerce and later as minister of commerce and industry. For a time following this, he withdrew from the political scene, but as the financial situation worsened and developed into a panic in 1927, he assumed the post of finance minister in the cabinet of Tanaka Giichi. He attempted to bring the situation under control through an emergency declaration of a moratorium. Later he served as finance minister in the Inukai, Saitō, and Okada cabinets, pursuing a positive fiscal policy that included the reimposition of the embargo on gold, the issuing of deficit bonds, and munitions spending, and attempting to promote harmony between the military and the financial world. In the end, however, he was unable to keep up with the continuing demands of the military, and in the uprising of young army officers on February 26 of 1936, he was shot and killed.

Takakusu Junjirō 高楠順次郎 (1866–1945)

Scholar of Buddhism; he was born in the area that later became Hiroshima Prefecture; his family name was originally Sawai. After serving as a primary school teacher in his native place, he entered a school called Bungakuryō operated by Nishi Hongan-ji, one of the main temples of the Jōdo Shin sect. There he formed a society for ethical culture called the Hanseikai. The *Hanseikai Zasshi*, a magazine representing the views of the society, later evolved into a general magazine called *Chūō Kōron*, which continues in existence today. In 1887, he was adopted into the Takakusu family of Kobe. He spent the years from 1888 to 1896 in Europe, studying at Oxford under Max Müller, the eminent Indologist, and at other universities in France and Germany. During this period he published an English translation of the Amitāyurdyāna Sutra (*Kammuryōju-kyō*), one of the most important sutras of Pure Land Buddhism, and wrote various works designed to introduce a knowledge of Buddhism to the West.

In 1899 he became a professor of Tokyo Imperial University. In 1900 he received the Ph.D. degree and the same year also became president of Tokyo Gaikokugo Gakkō. In 1912 he became a member of the Japan Academy. Earlier, in 1904, he had been sent to London by the Japanese government to carry on negotiations with the British government in connection with the Russo-Japanese War and was thus active in many spheres other than the academic. In 1927, after his retirement from Tokyo Imperial University, he became president of Tōyō University. His most important achievement was that carried out in cooperation with Watanabe Kaikyoku, the editing and publication of the *Taishō shinshū daizōkyō*, a 100-volume edition of the Tripitaka containing Chinese translations of works of Indian Buddhism, as well as important writings of Chinese and Japanese Buddhism. The work continues today to be regarded as the finest edition of the Tripitaka and constitutes a basic source for the study of Buddhism. Takakusu also acted as editor of a 65-volume collection of Japanese translations from the scriptures of Theravada Buddhism entitled *Nanden daizōkyō*. In 1944 he received a Cultural Medal. His disciples include Kimura Taiken and Ui Hakuju, both men who have helped to raise Japanese Buddhist studies to a level comparable to those anywhere in the world.

TAKAMINE JŌKICHI 高峰譲吉 (1854–1922)

Specialist in applied chemistry in the Meiji and Taishō eras; he was born in what later became Ishikawa Prefecture. In 1879 he completed the applied chemistry course of the College of Public Works in Tokyo and the following year went to Britain for further study. On his return to Japan in 1883, he was appointed to a post in the Engineering Bureau of the Ministry of Agriculture and Commerce and the following year was sent to America to attend an international industrial exposition. In 1890 he went to America once more at the invitation of a brewing company. There he established the Takamine Research Center and in 1897 discovered a digestive medicine that he called Taka-Diastase and that won worldwide recognition. At this time scientists throughout the world were attempting to obtain a crystalline extract of the hormone known as *Nebennierenmarkhormon*. In 1901 Takamine succeeded in doing so, giving the extract the name Adrenalin. This was the first hormone to be extracted in pure form. Because of these achievements, he won a lasting place in the history of science and also played a large role in the development of various chemical industries in Japan. He worked vigorously to bring about the establishment of the Institute of Physical and Chemical Research in Japan and, because of his long residence in the United States, contributed greatly to the promotion of cultural exchange between Japan and America.

TAKANO FUSATARŌ 高野房太郎 (1864–1904)

Social reformer and leader of the labor movement in the Meiji period. (His younger brother Takano Iwasaburō was a statistician and professor of

Tokyo Imperial University.) He was born in Nagasaki Prefecture and moved to Tokyo in 1877. He graduated from Yokohama Commercial School and in 1886 went to America. He remained there for ten years, supporting himself by operating a small general store in San Francisco and by doing various other types of jobs, and pursuing his studies, often under very difficult conditions. During this period, he organized the Japanese immigrant workers in the region into an association known as the Shokkō Giyūkai, the aim of which was to work for the formation of a labor union. He also contributed articles on Japanese labor problems to American magazines.

Upon returning to Japan in 1896, he became a reporter for the *Japan Advertiser*. In 1897 he joined with Katayama Sen, Jō Tsunetarō, Sawada Hannosuke, and others in setting up an organization called the Rōdōkumiai Kiseikai as a preliminary step toward the formation of labor unions. He also participated in the operation of the Iron Workers Union, playing an important role as one of the first organizers of the modern labor movement in Japan. In 1899 he took the initiative in the management of the Consumers Cooperative Union, a workers' organization. In 1900, when the government set up a system of security police and outlawed strikes, the labor movement went into decline. Takano, apparently out of despair for the future of the movement, went to Tsingtao in China and died there in 1904.

TAKIGAWA YUKITOKI 瀧川幸辰 (1891–1962)

Scholar of criminal law and Doctor of Law of the Shōwa era; he was born in the city of Okayama. In 1915 he graduated from Kyoto Imperial University. After serving as a judge in the Kyoto District Court, he became an assistant professor in the law department of Kyoto Imperial University in 1918. In 1924 he advanced to the rank of full professor, lecturing on criminal law and emphasizing a liberal approach to the subject. The government, however, claimed that his writings and lectures were communist in outlook and banned the sale of his work on criminal law, *Keihō kōgi*, published in 1926, and a similar work, *Keihō dokuhon*, published in 1932. Following these moves, Hatoyama Ichirō, the minister of education at the time, began to press the president of Kyoto University, Konishi Shigenao, to relieve Takigawa of his teaching position. A meeting of the faculty of the law department rejected the government's request on the grounds that it represented an invasion of academic freedom and autonomy. When in 1933, the government nevertheless dismissed Takigawa, the members of the faculty committee of the law department submitted their resignations en masse as a gesture of protest, and the student body demonstrated their support of the faculty. The government thereupon accepted the resignations of Sasaki Sōichi, Suekawa Hiroshi, and a few other professors, while rejecting the others, thus succeeding in disrupting the unity of the faculty and bringing about a split of opinion. The incident, which caused much comment at the time, was known as the Kyoto University affair or the Takigawa affair. After leaving his position at Kyoto University, Takigawa opened a private law practice and also became a professor of Ritsumeikan University in Kyoto.

After the war, he returned to his post at Kyoto University in 1946 and later served as head of the law department and president of the university. In 1953 he was made a member of the Japan Academy. In addition to the works already mentioned, he wrote *Hanzaigaku josetsu* and other works.

Tanaka Chigaku 田中智學 (1861–1939)

Religious leader and exponent of Nichiren thought in the Meiji, Taishō, and Shōwa periods; he was born in Edo and lost both parents at an early age. In 1870 he became a disciple of Nisshin of the Nichiren sect of Buddhism. In 1871 he entered a school called Iidaka Gakurin in the province of Shimōsa and later transferred to Nichirenshū Daigakurin in Tokyo, studying under Arai Nissatsu. He withdrew from school in 1876 due to illness and, while convalescing in Yokohama, devoted himself to the study of Nichiren's writings. He became increasingly nationalistic in his thinking. Though previously a member of the clergy, he renounced his clerical status in 1879 and thereafter worked as a lay Buddhist leader to spread the teachings of Nichiren as he interpreted them.

In 1880 he founded a religious society in Yokohama called Rengekai. In 1884 he moved his activities to Tokyo, changing the name of his organization to Risshō Ankokukai. He gained great notoriety in 1901 when he announced in *Shūmon no ishin* the slogan, "The Lotus Sutra is a sword," strongly emphasizing the militaristic nature of the type of Nichiren Buddhism that he favored. This attitude continued to characterize his thinking throughout the remainder of his life and allied him with the militaristic and expansionist elements of the time.

In 1914 he renamed the Risshō Ankokukai the Kokuchūkai, expanding its social activities in a number of areas. His thinking exercised great influence upon Inoue Nisshō, an agrarian nationalist and leader of the right-wing Ketsumeidan group, and upon the poet Miyazawa Kenji. He also contributed to the study of Nichiren Buddhism, cooperating with his followers in publishing a reference work entitled *Honge seiten daijirin*. Yamakawa Chiō was his principal disciple.

TANAKADATE AIKITSU 田中館愛橘 (1856–1952)

Physicist of the Meiji, Taishō, and Shōwa eras; he was born in the area of modern Iwate Prefecture. In 1882 he completed the physics course of Tokyo Imperial University, where he studied under the American scholar Thomas Corwin Mendenhall and the British scholar James Alfred Ewing. In 1889 he went to the University of Glasgow, where he studied under Lord Kelvin, and the following year to the University of Berlin. Upon his return to Japan in 1891 he became a professor of Tokyo Imperial University. As a result of the Nōbi earthquake in the same year, he worked to set up the Seismological Investigation Committee, which as the basis of its investigations carried out studies of terrestrial magnetism throughout Japan. He also guided Kimura Hisashi and others in establishing the International Latitude Observatory of Mizusawa in Iwate Prefecture.

He was very active in pioneer researches in the field of aviation, set up an aviation research center, and helped to lay the foundations for civil aviation in Japan. He thus played a leading role in the promotion of geophysics and the physics of aerial navigation in Japan. As a member of the Imperial Academy and the Science Research Council, he did much to encourage the advancement of science and technology and was also active in the international exchange of scientific information. In addition to these activities, he worked to bring about the spread of the metric system in Japan and promoted the development and adoption of the Nihonshiki system of romanization for the Japanese language. He received a Cultural Award in 1944.

TANAKA GIICHI 田中義一 (1863–1929)

Army leader and statesman of the Meiji, Taishō, and Shōwa eras; he held the rank of general and the title of baron. He was born in the domain of Chōshū. After the abolishment of the feudal domains, he suffered considerable hardship, but in 1883 joined the army and, after completing the Military Academy, entered the Military Staff College in 1889. He took part in the Sino-Japanese War and later was attached to the General Staff Office.

In 1898 he was chosen by Kawakami Sōroku, the chief of the General Staff, to go to Russia, where he spent four years studying the military and social situation there. He was able to make good use of his experience at the time of the Russo-Japanese War, when he served as a member of the staff of the Japanese army in Manchuria and urged an early cessation of hostilities.

In 1907 he volunteered to become commander of the Third Infantry Regiment and in 1909 became head of the military section in the War Ministry, working to reorganize Japanese military forces. In 1911, as head of the Bureau of Military Affairs, he advocated the establishment of two new army divisions. In 1913 he went to Europe and America in order to inspect the armaments in those areas. After his return to Japan in 1914, he became a member of the General Staff and in 1915 vice-chief of the General Staff. While holding such key positions in the army, he at the same time devoted his energies to organizing the Imperial Army Veterans' Association in 1910 and the Greater Japan Young Men's Organization in 1917, working to spread militaristic ideals throughout the country.

In 1918 he became minister of war in the cabinet of Hara Takashi, embarking on a political career; he presided over the dispatch of Japanese forces to Siberia and urged that Japan increase its expenditures for national defense. In 1921 he reached the rank of full general of the army and in 1923 became minister of war in the Yamamoto Gombei cabinet. After his retirement from active military service, he entered the reserve in 1925 and became president of the political party known as the Seiyūkai. In 1927, after financial crisis had brought about the fall of the Wakatsuki Reijirō cabinet, Tanaka formed his own cabinet, serving simultaneously as prime minister, foreign minister, and minister of colonization.

After the death of Yamagata Aritomo in 1922, Tanaka had replaced him as leader of the Chōshū faction within the bureaucracy and was highly critical of the conciliatory foreign policy of his predecessor, Foreign Minister Shidehara Kijūrō. He himself, by contrast, pursued a highly active foreign policy, dispatching Japanese troops to Shantung, calling a conference of Chinese leaders in Tokyo, interfering in the Chinese revolution, and doing all he could to secure Japanese rights in Manchuria and Mongolia. On the internal scene he appointed Takahashi Korekiyo as his finance minister and worked to allay the agitation brought about by the financial crisis.

In 1928, on urgent imperial order, he put through changes in the Peace Preservation Act that allowed him to take stern measures to suppress the Japanese Communist Party, as seen in the mass arrests of party members on March 15, 1928, and April 16, 1929. But he came under attack because of his forceful policies at home and abroad, and problems arising out of the signing of the Paris Antiwar Pact and the assassination of the Chinese warlord Chang Tso-lin by Japanese army officers in Manchuria forced him to resign in July 1929. He died abruptly not long after.

Tanaka Shōzō 田中正造 (1841–1913)

Meiji period statesman and leader of the movement to assist the Ashio Mine pollution victims. He was born in Aso District of the province of Shimotsuke in present-day Tochigi Prefecture, the son of a *nanushi* (village head). At the age of sixteen he succeeded his father as village head and continued in that post for the following twelve years. But he and his father joined in censuring the lord of the domain for the harshness of his rule and as a result were imprisoned and later expelled from the domain. In 1870 Tanaka became a minor official in the government of Esashi Prefecture, later a part of Iwate Prefecture. When one of his superior officials was assassinated, he was suspected of having a hand in the affair and was imprisoned for over three years.

In 1878 he determined to devote all his efforts to governmental reform and in 1879 founded a newspaper called the *Tochigi Shimbun*, in which he discussed the issues of the times. He participated in the democratic rights movement, in 1880 became a member of the prefectural assembly, and in 1886 became president of the assembly. During this period he also took part in the movement to establish a national Diet. In 1884 he was put in prison for opposing an engineering project ordered by Mishima Michitsune, the prefectural governor, which he felt would be too much of a burden on the people of the prefecture.

In the first general election, held in 1890, he was elected to the Lower House of the Diet. In 1891, at the second session of the Diet, he appealed to the government to take measures to combat the pollution caused by the Ashio Mine and thereafter devoted his full energies to this problem. The Ashio Mine, situated in Tochigi Prefecture, was owned and operated by Furukawa Ichibei, the founder of the Furukawa *zaibatsu*. Poisonous wastes from the mine were dumped into the Watarase River, killing the fish in the river and rendering the farmland in the area unfit for use.

In 1900, a number of the farmers who were victims of the pollution went in a group to Tokyo to appeal their case and in the process clashed with the police. The following year, Tanaka resigned his seat in the Diet, and, when Emperor Meiji was returning from the opening ceremony of the Diet session, he presented a direct appeal to the emperor, the text of which had been written at his request by Kōtoku Shūsui. To solve the problem, the government proposed to buy up the farmland of the village of Yanaka and convert the area into an artificial lake, but Tanaka opposed this plan, took up residence in the village, and joined the farmers who were resisting it. The farmers, however, were split in their reaction to the government's proposal, and in the end the resistance movement failed and the plan was put into effect. Though ill at the time, Tanaka set about conducting an investigation of the river, but collapsed on his way home to Yanaka and died a month later.

Tani Kanjō 谷干城 (1837–1911)

Army leader and statesman of the Meiji period; he held the title of viscount. His common name was Moribe, and his literary name Waizan. Born in the fief of Tosa in Shikoku, he went to Edo in 1856 and studied Confucianism and military science. Later he became associated with the group in Tosa that favored restoration of power to the emperor. In 1866 he was ordered by his domain to make an inspection tour of Nagasaki and Shanghai. In 1868, after his return to Japan, he served as a commander in the Boshin civil war, which took place between the imperial forces and those that remained loyal to the shogunate, fighting in a number of engagements. In 1869 he served in the central government, but later returned to Tosa and devoted himself to reforms in the administration of the domain.

In 1871 he resumed service in the central government, holding the post of chief assistant in the Ministry of Military Affairs. Later he served as head of the military court, commander of the Kumamoto Garrison, and in other posts. In 1874 he was active in suppressing the rebellion in Saga and dispatching troops to Taiwan. In 1876 he once more became commander of the Kumamoto Garrison, and in the Seinan War of 1877 won fame for his brilliant defense of Kumamoto Castle against the attacks of the rebels. In 1878, he advanced to the rank of lieutenant general and, as Eastern Army Supervisor, he took his place among the military leaders of the nation. He later held the posts of head of the Military Academy and Army Supervisor.

Because of disagreement with Yamagata Aritomo, the outstanding army leader of the time, he resigned from service. After his resignation he entered political life and in 1881 formed a political party known as the Chūseitō to oppose the popular rights movement of the time. In 1885 he became minister of agriculture and commerce in the first Itō cabinet, but because of his opposition to Westernization and to Foreign Minister Inoue's handling of treaty revision, he resigned in 1887. Thereafter he became an exponent of nationalism, forming a new conservative party and in 1890 becoming a member of the Upper House of the Diet. Because of his conservative principles, he opposed clan factionalism in the government and the Russo-Japanese War and advocated measures to aid and protect the lot of the farmers. He also served as head of the Peers' School and of the Peeresses' School.

TERAJIMA MUNENORI 寺島宗則 (1833–1893)

Diplomat active in the early and middle part of the Meiji period; he held the title of baron. Born in the fief of Satsuma in Kyushu, he studied Western medicine; at this time he went by the name Matsumoto Hiroyasu. Shimazu Nariakira, lord of the fief of Satsuma, believing that the time had come for Japan to open its doors to the world, summoned him and questioned him on his knowledge of foreign affairs and the countries of the West. With the outbreak of hostilities between Satsuma and the British in 1863, Terajima, because of his knowledge of English, was ordered by the lord of the fief, along with Godai Saisuke, to attempt to negotiate a settlement, but they were taken prisoner, put aboard a British gunboat, and taken to England. Terajima was allowed to return to Japan two years later, but he was unable to go to his home in Satsuma because of the strong antiforeign sentiment that prevailed there. Instead he became an assistant and later a professor in the Bansho Shirabesho (later renamed the Kaiseisho), an institution set up by the shogunate in Edo for the teaching of Western subjects and the translation of Western writings.

With the establishment of the Meiji government in 1868, he became a councilor and officer in charge of foreign affairs in the new government and was assigned to duty in Hyōgo. Under the imperial envoy Higashikuze Michitomi, he had his first opportunity to deal directly with the foreign ministers as an official of the government. In the same year he was appointed a judge of Kanagawa Prefecture and a judge in the Bureau of Foreign Affairs. In 1869 he was made vice-governor of the Foreign Office and later chief assistant of foreign affairs. In 1872 he was assigned a high post in the Japanese embassy in Britain and then promoted to the post of envoy extraordinary and minister plenipotentiary. In 1873 he became a councilor of state and foreign minister and, in these capacities, played an important role in negotiations involved in the incident over the Peruvian ship *Maria Luz*, the treaty that gave Russia Karafuto in exchange for the Chishima (Kurile) Islands, the Kanghwa Treaty on trade between Japan and Korea, and the recognition of Japanese sovereignty over the Ogasawara Islands.

At the same time he was very active in efforts to carry out treaty revisions and restore tariff autonomy to Japan. In 1878 he succeeded in negotiating an agreement by which the United States recognized tariff autonomy for Japan (the so-called Yoshida-Everts Convention), but it was never put into effect because of opposition from the British ambassador Sir Harry Smith-Parkes and others. He was transferred to the post of minister of education and later, after serving as chief of the Bureau of Legislation and president of the Genrōin (Senate), in 1882, as envoy extraordinary and minister plenipotentiary, he was assigned to duty in the United States. In 1884 he was assigned to a post in the Imperial Household Ministry, in 1886 became an advisor to the Privy Council, and in 1891 became president of the Privy Council.

TERAUCHI MASAKATA 寺内正毅 (1852–1919)

Military leader and statesman of the Meiji and Taishō periods; he held the rank of general of the army and the title of count. He was born in the domain of Chōshū and at the age of twelve entered one of the military forces of the domain, where he came under the guidance of such important leaders as Yamada Akiyoshi and Shinagawa Yajirō. In 1869 in the Boshin civil war he served as a member of the maintenance corps in the attack on the forces remaining loyal to the shogunate at Hakodate. His ability was recognized by Ōmura Masujirō, the leader of the imperial forces, and he was enrolled in the army training school in Osaka. In 1871 he was commissioned as a second lieutenant. While serving as a captain of the Imperial Guards in the Seinan civil war in 1877, he was wounded in the battle of Tabaruzaka and lost the use of his right hand, but because his talent in military matters was highly esteemed, he was retained on active duty and thereafter assigned to administrative posts.

In 1883 he served as military attaché to the Japanese legation in Paris. After returning to Japan, he became undersecretary to the war minister and in 1887 became head of the Military Academy and chief of staff of the First Division. In 1892 he was transferred to the post of first bureau chief of the General Staff Office, where he worked to build up the strength of the army. During the Sino-Japanese War in 1894, he served as Chief of Transport and Communications. In 1896 he took over the administrative duties of the chief of the bureau of military affairs and went to Europe in order to study the military situation there. His next assignment was that of commander of the

Third Division. In 1898 he became the first inspector-general of military education, organizing a system of education within the army. In 1900, as vice-chief of the General Staff, he helped to plan the dispatch of Japanese troops to Peking to combat the forces of the Boxer Rebellion. In 1902, while serving as head of the Military Staff College, he was appointed war minister in the first Katsura Tarō cabinet, a post that he retained for the following ten years until the time of the second Katsura cabinet.

During this interval, he participated in drawing up the articles pertaining to military affairs for the Anglo-Japanese alliance of 1902. After the Russo-Japanese War, he became chairman of the committee for the establishment of the South Manchuria Railway Company. In 1910, after the annexation of Korea, he served as the first governor-general of Korea, in this and other ways acting as a leader in Japan's expansion on the continent. In 1916, when pressure from the elder statesmen and military leaders had brought about the fall of the Ōkuma Shigenobu cabinet, Terauchi formed a cabinet of his own made up of former bureaucrats, expounding the principle of nonparty government and insisting that the conduct of public affairs should not be conditioned by the whims of political parties. He did, however, cooperate with the Rikken Seiyūkai party of Hara Takashi and the Rikken Kokumintō of Inukai Tsuyoki.

In the field of foreign affairs, he concluded, in the midst of World War One, the Ishii-Lansing agreement of 1917, in which Japan and the United States sought a reconciliation in their views regarding China. In 1918, when a number of foreign powers were sending troops to Russia in an attempt to change the course of the Russian revolution, Terauchi followed their example by dispatching Japanese troops to Siberia. On the home front, he was criticized for failing to stabilize the postwar economy and allowing inflation to become rampant and was looked upon as a spokesman for the military clique that was intent upon forcing military expansion upon the country. The economic distress and unease that resulted from these conditions erupted in the form of rice riots in many of the cities, which, in turn, brought about the downfall of the Terauchi cabinet.

Tōgō Heihachirō 東郷平八郎 (1847–1934)

Naval leader of the Meiji and Taishō eras and fleet admiral; he held the title of marquis. As a samurai of the domain of Satsuma in Kyushu, he took part in his youth in the war between Satsuma and the British in 1863 and the Boshin civil war in 1868. During the period from 1870 to 1878 he was a student in England engaged in the study of naval affairs. On his return to Japan he was made a lieutenant junior grade and gradually advanced until, by 1894, he had reached the rank of captain. He participated in the Sino-Japanese War as commander of the warship *Naniwa.* He attacked and sank a merchant vessel that was flying the British flag and carrying Chinese soldiers and weapons, but the attack was recognized as legal under international law and brought him considerable fame. After holding various positions such as head of the Naval Staff College and commander of the headquarters of the regular fleet, he served as commander of the combined fleet in the Russo-Japanese War.

In 1904, the first year of the war, he carried out the blockade of Port Arthur and the following year attacked Russia's Baltic Fleet in the Tsushima Straits. With his flagship *Mikasa,* he led the fleet in a daring shift of direction in the face of the enemy, which came to be referred to as a Tōgō turn, and succeeded in all but annihilating the enemy, an accomplishment that won him fame at home and abroad. After the war, he served as chief of the Naval General Staff. In 1911 he went to England to attend the coronation of George V. In 1913 he was promoted to the rank of fleet admiral. From 1914 to 1921 he served as president of the Tōgū Gogakumonjo, an organ charged with the education of the crown prince. In 1930 he strongly opposed the ratification of the agreement signed at the London Disarmament Conference and in other ways played an important role as an elder naval leader. Among the people in general he was looked up to as a hero and ranked beside Nogi Maresuke, the distinguished army leader. Upon his death in 1934 he was given a state funeral and is deified at the Tōgō Shrine in Harajuku in Tokyo.

Tōjō Hideki 東條英機 (1884–1948)

Shōwa period military and political leader; he held the rank of general of the army. His father, Tōjō Hidenori, was the son of a samurai of the domain of Nambu; he attended the Military Staff College, where he studied under the German military instructor Major Klemens Meckel and in time advanced to the rank of lieutenant general.

Tōjō Hideki was born in Tokyo and, after attending lower schools maintained by the army, graduated from the Military Academy. In 1905 he was commissioned as a second lieutenant. He graduated from the Military Staff College in 1915 and thereafter advanced until he reached the rank of lieutenant general in 1936. During this period, he was assigned to posts in Germany and Switzerland. In 1922 he became an instructor in the military

Staff College. In 1929 he joined with Colonel Nagata Tetsuzan and others in leading the principal reform group within the army, which became known as the Tōsei (Control) faction. But they were at this time largely eclipsed by a rival group known as the Kōdō (Imperial Way) faction. In 1931 Tōjō became a section chief in the General Staff Office and in 1934 he was appointed commander of an infantry brigade. He was sent to Manchuria in 1935 as commander of the military police of the Kwantung Army. In 1937 he became chief of staff of the Kwantung Army. In 1938 he was made vice-minister of war, serving under Minister of War Itagaki Seishirō. He quickly demonstrated his administrative ability and came to be known as "Razor Tōjō."

After serving as Commissioner of Aviation, in 1940 he took the post of minister of war in the second Konoe cabinet and continued in that post in the third Konoe cabinet. He led the faction in the army that supported an uncompromising approach in the negotiations between Japan and the United States. In 1941, after the mass resignation of the Konoe cabinet, he was appointed prime minister on the recommendation of Lord Keeper of the Privy Seal Kido Kōichi, who had called a conference of high officials to discuss the matter.

As head of the government, Tōjō continued to carry on negotiations with the United States, but in the face of the latter's adamant attitude, decided to commence hostilities. In the initial stage, his conduct of the war proved successful and he took measures to tighten control over the civilian population. In the general election in 1942, he instituted a system of government "recommendation" of candidates, which insured that the Lower House of the Diet would fully support his policies, and after the election he established a single-party government that amounted to a military dictatorship. In the same year, he set up the Daitōa-shō (Greater East Asia Ministry) to deal with representatives of China, Manchuria, Thailand, Burma, and the Philippines, all areas that by this time were largely under Japanese control, as well as with representatives from adjacent countries such as India, though Tōgō Shigenori, the foreign minister, resigned in protest over the move.

In 1943 he held a Greater East Asia Congress in Tokyo, which adopted a joint declaration calling upon the participants to work for mutual benefit and to respect one another's independence. As a wartime prime minister he simultaneously held the post of minister of war, and at times also those of foreign minister, minister of home affairs, minister of education, and minister of commerce and industry. In 1943 he established a new post called minister of munitions and assumed that as well. In 1944, he also took on the position of chief of the General Staff, thus assuring that complete control over all political and military decisions would rest in his hands.

He strengthened the power of the militrary police to make certain that there would be no criticisms of his policies. But with the worsening of the military situation and the fall of Saipan, a group of high officials led by Admiral Okada Keisuke began a movement to overthrow him, and in the same year, 1944, they succeeded in bringing about the resignation of his entire cabinet. He was removed from active military service and placed on the reserve list.

In 1945, after the surrender, when he was facing arrest by the Occupation authorities, he attempted to take his life with a pistol, but failed in the attempt. He was brought before the International Military Tribunal for the Far East as an A-class war criminal, where he was charged with the highest degree of responsibility for the war. In 1948 he was put to death by hanging along with Itagaki Seishirō and five others who had been similarly charged.

Tokuda Kyūichi 徳田球一 (1894–1953)

Taishō and Shōwa period political figure, leader of the socialist movement and the Japan Communist Party; he was born in Okinawa. He attended the Seventh High School in Kagoshima but withdrew in protest over the insulting treatment accorded natives of Okinawa by the people of Kagoshima Prefecture. He went to Tokyo, where he managed, after considerably difficulty, to graduate from the evening school law course of Nihon University. After graduation, he began a career as a lawyer. In 1920 he joined Sakai Toshihiko and Yamakawa Hitoshi in forming the Japan Socialist League. In 1922 he and Katayama Sen went to Moscow as Japanese representatives to the Congress of Far Eastern Peoples.

After his return to Japan, he participated in the formation of the Japan Communist Party in 1922 and was arrested in the first government move to suppress the party in 1923. He opposed the action taken to disband the party and in 1924 worked to reestablish it. In 1926 he succeeded in holding a general meeting of the party. He went to the Soviet Union again in 1927 and took part in the drafting of the 1927 *Thèse*. He was a candidate in the first general election in 1928, but failed to gain election. He was arrested the same year along with many other members of the party and spent the following eighteen years in jail. Though many of the others renounced their political beliefs and were released, he refused to do so. He was freed after the end of the Pacific War in 1945 and joined Shiga Yoshio in reestablishing the Japan Communist Party, with himself as chief secretary.

In 1946 he was elected to the Lower House of the Diet, but was purged by order of General MacArthur in 1950 along with other leaders of the Communist Party. He turned to underground activity, laying down a strongly militant policy for the party, which caused it to decline rapidly in strength and influence. He died of illness in 1953 while a refugee in Communist China, though his death was not formally announced by the party until two years later. He was outstanding less as a theorist than as a vigorous and decisive leader. He and Shiga Yoshio collaborated in writing an account of their period of emprisonment entitled *Gokuchū jūhachinen.*

Tokutomi Sohō 徳富蘇峰 (1863–1957)

Critic, journalist, and historian of the Meiji, Taishō, and Shōwa periods; he was born in present-day Kumamoto Prefecture in Kyushu; his personal name was Iichirō. After studying Chinese, he entered the Yōgakkō (School of Western Learning) in Kumamoto, where he was converted to Christianity by a teacher, a retired American army officer named Lieutenant Janes, and received baptism. He studied under Niijima Jō at Dōshisha College in Kyoto, but left school before completing his degree. In 1881 he returned to Kumamoto and opened a private school. The publication of a work entitled *Shōrai no Nihon* in 1886 brought him rapid literary fame, and the following year he went to Tokyo, where he founded a publishing company called the Min'yūsha. With such men as Yamaji Aizan and Takekoshi Yosaburō on his staff, he also began publication of a magazine called *Kokumin no Tomo.* In 1890 he founded a newspaper called *Kokumin Shimbun* and until 1929 continued to act as both president and chief editor of the paper.

At first he advocated a liberal form of democracy, but after the Triple Intervention of Russia, Germany, and France following the conclusion of the Sino-Japanese War in 1895, he became increasingly nationalistic in outlook. In 1896 he accepted an appointment as a councilor to the minister of the interior, but in doing so incurred popular criticism for betraying his earlier democratic principles. In 1898 he suspended publication of *Kokumin no Tomo.* Meanwhile, the newspaper *Kokumin Shimbun* had become little more than a voice for the old domain cliques that dominated the government, and its offices were twice attacked and burned by angry mobs of citizens, in 1905 because it supported the government's moderate demands with regard to the Portsmouth Treaty and again in 1913 when popular sentiment was aroused against the Katsura cabinet. The same year, with the death of Katsura Tarō, the statesman to whom he had been so closely tied, he withdrew from political life and devoted all his time to writing, particularly works of history.

His fifty-volume work entitled *Kinsei Nihon kokumin-shi* received a Japan Academy prize, and his thinking, which focussed upon loyalty to the imperial house, assured him a position of prominence in intellectual circles in the early Shōwa and wartime periods. He was given a Cultural Medal in 1943. After the war, he was purged from public life, and renounced all his previous honors and positions, including the seat in the Upper House of the Diet, which he had held since 1911. He was a member of the Japan Art Academy and the author of works running to over three hundred volumes. His younger brother was the novelist Tokutomi Roka.

TOMONAGA SHIN'ICHIRŌ 朝永振一郎 (1906–)

Theoretical physicist of the Shōwa period. He was born in Tokyo and in 1929 graduated from Kyoto University. In 1932 he entered the Institute of Physical and Chemical Research, studying under Nishina Yoshio, and later went to Germany, where he studied under Werner Carl Heisenberg. In 1941 he became a professor of the Tokyo University of Science and Literature, later known as the Tokyo University of Education. He made important contributions to the study of the atomic nucleus, elementary particles, cosmic rays, electrical engineering, and the many-body problem, the last a problem lying on the borderline between nuclear physics and solid state physics. In 1943 he advanced the so-called super-many-time theory and in the years 1946 and 1947 set forth an expansion of it known as the renormalization theory. From 1956 to 1962 he acted as president of the Tokyo University of Education and from 1963 to 1969 as head of the Science Council of Japan. In 1948 he received a Japan Academy prize, in 1952 a Cultural Award, and in 1965 the Nobel Prize in physics. He has been active not only in research and education, but helped to establish joint research centers for nuclear and cosmic ray studies and, as a member of the Pugwash Conference and the Seven Man Committee for World Peace, has continually spoken out on problems of society and international peace.

TŌYAMA MITSURU 頭山満 (1855–1944)

Nationalistic thinker of the Meiji, Taishō, and Shōwa periods; he was born into a samurai family of the domain of Fukuoka named Tsutsui; he was later adopted into his mother's family and took the name Tōyama. He sympathized with Saigō Takamori's call for an expedition against Korea and, in 1876, after the government had rejected Saigō's policies, took part in antigovernment activities in Fukuoka carried out by discontented members of the former samurai class. As a result, he was put in prison. After the so-called Seinan War, Saigo's unsuccessful attempt to defy the government, he was released from prison and took part in the popular rights movement. In 1879 he joined Hakoda Rokusuke and Hiraoka Kōtarō in forming a political organization called the Kōyōsha, which supported the movement to set up a national assembly. In 1881 the Kōyōsha was renamed the Gen'yōsha and, with Hiraoka Kōtarō as president, called upon Japan to play a greater role in Asian affairs and advocated Japanese expansion on the continent.

After the establishment of the Diet, Tōyama and his associates cooperated with the government and assisted in the government interference in the second general election in 1892. He lent his support to Uchida Ryōhei and others in 1901 in their founding of a nationalistic organization called the Kokuryūkai (the Black Dragon or Amur River Society), and also participated in the Tai-Ro Dōshikai, an organization calling for a firmer foreign policy towards Russia. He gave assistance to patriotic leaders of various Asian nations who had taken refuge in Japan such as the Korean political reformer Kim Ok-kyun, the leader of the Chinese revolution Sun Yat-sen, and B. Bose, the head of the Indian independence movement. He remained a private citizen all his life, but as a powerful leader of right-wing factions in Japanese society, he exerted a large measure of covert influence in the political world.

Tsuda Masamichi 津田眞道 (1829–1903)

Scholar and official of the Meiji period; he was the son of a samurai of the domain of Tsuyama in present-day Okayama Prefecture. His childhood name was Kikuji and his common name Shin'ichirō; after the Meiji Restoration, he changed his name to Masamichi. At first he studied Chinese and military science, but after arranging for his younger brother to replace him as family heir, he went to Edo in 1850, where he studied Dutch learning under Mitsukuri Gempo and Western style military techniques under Sakuma Shōzan. From 1857 on, he served in the Bansho Shirabesho, an organization for the study and teaching of Western learning set up by the shogunate. In 1862 he was ordered by the shogunate to go to Holland for further study and, along with Nishi Amane, attended Leyden University, concentrating upon the study of law. He returned to Japan in 1865 and the following year became a teacher-official in the Kaiseijo, a school that had grown out of the Bansho Shirabesho and the forerunner of Tokyo Imperial University. In 1868 he advanced to the office of *metsuke* (overseer) in the shogunate bureaucracy. The same year, he published a work entitled *Taisei kokuhōron*, a work on legal theory based on the lectures of one Professor Vissering of Leyden University and the first work of its kind to appear in Japan.

At the time of the Meiji Restoration, he accompanied the Tokugawa shogunate family when it moved from Edo to Shizuoka, but the following year, 1869, returned to Tokyo, where he was ordered to act as a penal official and to conduct a survey of different types of deliberative bodies. In 1870 he was summoned to join the newly formed Meiji government, being appointed an official in the Ministry of Justice. He participated in the drawing up of a new legal code. From 1871 on, he also worked for the Ministry of Foreign Affairs, being dispatched to China in connection with his duties in that capacity. From 1873, he took on duties related to the army as well, participating in the drawing up of a criminal code for the army. While carrying out these activities as an official and investigator of legal matters, he was also active as a scholar. In 1873 he joined with Mori Arinori, Nishimura Shigeki, and other intellectual leaders to form the Meirokusha, an organization designed to promote the spread of culture and Westernization, and helped to found the magazine *Meiroku Zasshi*, which served as its mouthpiece.

In 1874 he published the *Hyōki teikō*, one of the first works on the science of statistics to appear in Japan, which was translated from a work by Vissering. In 1876 he was appointed a member of the Genrōin (Senate). In 1890 he was elected a member of the Lower House of the Diet and served as its first vice-president. In 1896 he became a member of the Upper House and in 1900 received the title of baron. He was awarded the degree of Doctor of Law in 1903 and died the same year. Although he did not publish many book-length works, a number of articles by him appeared in *Meiroku Zasshi* and *Tōkyō Gakushi Kaiin Zasshi*.

Tsuda Sōkichi 津田左右吉 (1873–1961)

Historian and Doctor of Literature of the Taishō and Shōwa periods; he was born in Gifu Prefecture. He attended Tokyo Semmon Gakkō, the forerunner of Waseda University, and after graduation served as a middle school teacher in various areas. In 1906 he joined a group headed by Shiratori Kurakichi of the South Manchurian Railway, a scholar of Chinese history, in carrying out historical and geographical surveys in Manchuria and Korea. Beginning with a work entitled *Jindaishi no atarashii kenkyū* in 1913, he published a series of philological studies of the *Kojiki* and *Nihon Shoki*, in which he argued that the accounts of the mythical period contained in these ancient works of Japanese history were in fact fabricated at a later period to lend legitimacy to the imperial line. As a result, he came under attack from the nationalists, and in 1940 four of his major works were banned. In 1942 he was accused of violating the publication laws. He was found guilty of having profaned the dignity of the imperial house and was sentenced to three months in jail, but was acquitted in 1944.

During the prewar period, he served as a professor of Waseda University from 1920 to 1940 and lectured in the law department of Tokyo Imperial University in 1939; he was also a member of the Tōyō Bunko from 1920 until the time of his death. In addition to his studies of Japanese history and thought, he also published works on Chinese Taoism, Confucianism, and Buddhism. He became a member of the Japan Academy in 1947 and received a Cultural Medal in 1949. In the years following the end of the war he took up an anti-Marxist position in his writings and activities.

Tsuda Umeko 津田梅子 (1864–1929)

Educator of the Meiji and Taishō eras; she was born in Edo, the daughter of a retainer of the shogunate named Tsuda Sen. Her father was very progressive in his ideas and had at an early period ceased to wear his hair in the old-fashioned style and had taken up the study of English. In 1871, when Kuroda Kiyotaka, the head of the agency for colonization of Hokkaido, proposed that girl students be sent abroad for study, Tsuda Sen arranged for his daughter Umeko, who was seven at the time, to be sent to America. She boarded with the family of one Charles Lanman in the suburbs of Washington, where she attended primary school and was baptized a Christian. On completion of primary school, she attended a school for girls.

In 1882 she returned to Japan and in 1885 became an instructor in the Kazoku Girls' School, the forerunner of the Peeresses' School. She found herself unable to adjust to Japanese customs and institutions, however, and in 1889 went to America once more, where she studied biology and education. Upon returning to Japan in 1892, she held positions as an instructor in the Kazoku Girls' School and the Women's Higher Normal School, the forerunner of Ochanomizu Women's College. She resigned these positions in 1900 and established a women's school in Kōjimachi in Tokyo called

Joshi Eigakujuku (now known as Tsuda College). The school was designed to train women to be teachers of English and was the first professional school for women to be established in Japan. In 1904 the school received official recognition as a professional school, and in 1905 its graduates were permitted to become English teachers without taking a qualifying examination.

While continuing to direct the school, Tsuda also published an English language newspaper called *Eibun Shimpō* and in other ways worked to encourage the spread of English studies. She made a tour of Europe and America in 1907 and went to America again in 1913 to attend the International Christian Student Conference. Poor health forced her to curtail her numerous activities in her later years. She relinquished the direction of the school in 1919 and died ten years later.

Uchimura Kanzō 内村鑑三 (1861–1930)

Thinker and Christian leader of the Meiji and Taishō eras; he was born in Edo, the son of a samurai of the domain of Takasaki in present-day Gumma Prefecture. In 1874 he entered Tokyo Foreign Language School and studied English. In 1878 he entered Sapporo Agricultural College in Hokkaido and became a Christian convert. After graduating from college, he worked for a time in the Fisheries Section of the Ministry of Agriculture and Commerce, but in 1884 went to America and entered Amherst College. After graduating from Amherst, he entered Hartford Theological Seminary, but withdrew shortly afterward and returned to Japan in 1888. In 1890 he became an instructor in the First Higher Middle School. The following year, however, he caused an uproar by refusing to pay reverence to the recently issued Imperial Rescript on Education. He was severely criticized, and resigned from his position. The incident aroused widespread opposition to Christianity on the grounds that it was incompatible with the Japanese theory of the state.

After retiring from teaching, Uchimura moved about to Osaka, Kumamoto, Kyoto, Nagoya, and other cities, devoting his time to the writing of various religious works such as *Kirisutokyō shinto no nagusame*, *Kyūanroku*, and *How I Became a Christian*. In 1897 he joined the staff of a newspaper called *Yorozu Chōhō* and, with Kōtoku Shūsui and other socialists, was active in opposing the growing sentiment in favor of a war with Russia. His opinions, however, clashed with those of the head of the newspaper, and he resigned. In 1900 he founded a magazine called *Seisho no Kenkyū* (Bible Study), which he continued to publish throughout his life.

In his late years, he became convinced that the Second Coming of Christ was at hand and worked avidly to spread his beliefs. His thought was characterized by his advocacy of *mukyōkai* (the nonchurch movement), which emphasized the prime importance of the Bible and paid little attention to church ceremonies or institutions. As he frequently declared, his aim was to serve the "two J's," Japan and Jesus. He is also noteworthy for his rejection of all guidance and financial assistance offered by foreign Christian missions.

UEKI EMORI 植木枝盛 (1857–1892)

Political leader and popular rights thinker of the Meiji period; he was the son of a samurai of the domain of Tosa in Shikoku. After attending the Chidōkan, the official school of the domain, he went to Tokyo in 1873. There he attended the Kainan, a private school, but withdrew and returned to Kōchi, as the former domain of Tosa was now called. There he attended lectures given by the political leader Itagaki Taisuke and determined to enter the world of politics himself. He went to Tokyo again in 1875, where he was greatly influenced by the lectures and writings of the members of the Meirokusha, an organization of intellectuals devoted to the advancement of culture and Westernization. In 1877 he joined the Risshisha, a political organization founded in Kōchi in 1874 by Itagaki Taisuke for the promotion of the people's rights movement, in time becoming one of its leading figures. He also participated in the revival of the Aikokusha, another organization designed to promote democracy, and the formation of the Jiyūtō (Liberal Party). In 1882 he organized a meeting known as the Saké Sellers' Conference, which demanded a reduction in the tax on saké.

In the first general election, held in 1890, he was elected a member of the Diet, where he served as a leading exponent of the theories underlying the popular rights movement. In this capacity he wrote articles for party newspapers, went on lecture tours throughout the country, and participated in the drafting of petitions submitted to the government by the Risshisha and in drawing up a proposal plan for a constitution, as well as writing a number of books such as *Minken jiyūron* and others. In his writings and speeches, he asserted the premise of the sovereignty of the people and on this basis argued on behalf of the natural rights of man, the right to resist, a unicameral legislature, universal suffrage, women's liberation, and the modernization of the family system.

Uemura Masahisa 植村正久 (1858–1925)

Theologian and Christian leader of the Meiji and Taishō periods; he was born in Edo, the son of a samurai in the service of the shogun. In order to revive the family fortunes, which had been dealt a severe blow by the Meiji Restoration, he determined to take up the study of English and Western affairs and in 1871 entered a school in Yokohama called the Shūbunkan. In 1873 he transferred to a school operated by an American missionary named James Ballagh and later to a school headed by another American missionary, Samuel Brown. At the same time, in 1873, he was baptized and determined to devote his life to the preaching of Christianity in Japan. In 1877 he entered Tokyo Itchi Theological Seminary and graduated the following year. He began his preaching activities in the Shitaya area of Tokyo, but in 1887 founded the Tokyo Ichibanchō Itchi Church, serving as its pastor until the time of his death. He was determined to build up a Japanese Christian church that was wholly independent of foreign missionary activities and for that purpose in 1904 founded a theological school called Tokyo Shingakusha, with himself as head. He also founded the magazines *Fukuin Shimpō* and *Nihon Hyōron* in which to set forth the views of the Japanese Christian church. Throughout his life he was a strict upholder of orthodox belief and opposed those who advocated materialism, liberal theology, or the type of Christianity that was strongly colored by Japanese nationalism.

Ugaki Kazushige 宇垣一成 (1868–1956)

Statesman and military leader of the Taishō and Shōwa eras. He was the son of a farming family in Okayama Prefecture and in his youth went by the name Mokuji. He became a member of the first class to attend the Military Academy and later graduated from the Military Staff College. In 1902 he joined the General Staff Office and was assigned to duty in Germany to pursue military studies. With the outbreak of the Russo-Japanese War he returned to Japan and served as a staff officer at the front. After the war, he was once more assigned to duty in Germany (1906–08) and in 1910 advanced to the rank of colonel. In 1911 he became a section chief in the Bureau of Military Affairs in the War Ministry and, under the direction of Chief of the Bureau of Military Affairs Tanaka Giichi (later war minister and prime minister), was active in setting up two new army divisions, attracting attention as a figure of importance in military circles.

In 1913, when the Yamamoto Gombei cabinet abolished the practice of filling the posts of minister of war and navy with officers on active duty, Ugaki opposed the move and distributed an anonymous pamphlet expressing his views. As a result he was for a time demoted to the post of regimental commander in Nagoya, but in 1915 was reassigned to duty as a section chief in the Bureau of Military Affairs. He advanced to the rank of major general, and in 1916, on the recommendation of Vice-Chief of the General Staff Tanaka, he became chief of the strategy division of the General Staff Office. In 1919 he became head of the Military Staff College and a lieutenant general and in 1921 became division commander in Himeji. The following year he became head of the main office of the Department of Military Education, in 1923 he became vice-minister of war (under Tanaka as minister of war), and in 1924 was appointed minister of war in the cabinet of Kiyoura Keigo, a post that he continued to hold in the Katō Takaaki and Wakatsuki Reijirō cabinets as well. During this period, in response to demands both within Japan and abroad for reductions in military strength, he abolished four divisions in a move known as the "Ugaki military reductions." At the same time, however, he worked to modernize and mechanize the remaining divisions and established military training in all schools, public or private, above the primary school level.

In 1929 he became minister of war in the Hamaguchi Osachi cabinet and gradually organized his own clique within the army, and in 1931 a coup d'état was actually planned for the purpose of putting Ugaki in power, though it was called off before the date for execution (the so-called March incident). The same year, he was appointed governor-general of Chōsen (Korea) and entered the reserve. In his capacity as governor-general of Korea, he worked to improve the lot of the farmers. He resigned the post in 1936 and in 1937 was ordered to form his own cabinet, but he met with violent opposition from the principal leaders of the army, and the plan came to nothing.

Following the outbreak of hostilities between China and Japan, he was appointed foreign minister after the reorganization of the Konoe Fumimaro cabinet in 1938, as well as minister of overseas affairs, and attempted to restore peace with China, but his efforts proved unsuccessful. Because of his opposition to the establishment of the Kōain, he resigned after little more than four months in office. Thereafter, he retired from political life. At the conclusion of the Pacific War, he was barred from public office. In 1953, when the ban was ended, he ran for a seat in the Upper House of the Diet and received the largest number of votes of any candidate in the country. He was eighty-five at the time, but his health was failing, and he died three years later.

Ui Hakuju 宇井伯壽 (1882–1963)

Buddhist scholar of the Shōwa period; he was born in Aichi Prefecture and in childhood went by the name Moshichi. In 1893 he entered the clergy under the direction of Katsuzan Manju of Tōzen-ji, a temple of the Sōtō branch of the Zen sect; he changed his name to Hakuju and went by the literary name Katsuō. After finishing Aichi Middle School and the First High School, he entered the literature department of Tokyo Imperial University, where he studied Indian philosophy under Takakusu Junjirō. He was a fellow student of Kimura Taiken (1881–1930), who likewise in time became a distinguished scholar. He graduated in 1909 and during the years from 1913 to 1917 studied in Germany and England.

Upon his return to Japan he successively held posts as lecturer of Sōtōshū University (present-day Komazawa University) and of Tokyo Imperial University; in 1923 he became a professor of Tōhoku Imperial University. In 1930, with the sudden death of Kimura Taiken, he replaced Kimura as a professor of Tokyo Imperial University. In 1931 he received a Japan Academy prize for his six-volume study of Indian philosophy, *Indo tetsugaku kenkyū.* He retired from teaching in 1943 and in 1945 became a member of the Japan Academy. In 1953 he received a Cultural Medal. His other writings include *Bukkyō hanron*, *Indo tetsugaku-shi*, and many others. In contrast to Kimura Taiken, whose scholarship was marked by boldness and freedom of speculation, Ui's work was based upon meticulous examination of the sources. He produced numerous basic studies covering a wide range of topics in Indian philosophy and Buddhist history and thought and exercised an important influence upon younger scholars in the field.

Wakatsuki Reijirō 若槻禮次郎 (1866–1949)

Bureaucrat and statesman of the Meiji, Taishō, and Shōwa eras; he held the title of baron. He was born in the domain of Matsue; his family name was Okumura, but he was adopted into the Wakatsuki family. In 1892 he graduated from Tokyo Imperial University, having specializing in French law, and entered the Ministry of Finance. After serving as chief of the Bureau of Revenue, in 1906 he advanced to the post of vice-minister of finance. In 1912 he became finance minister in the third Katsura Tarō cabinet and also joined the political party known as the Rikken Dōshikai. In 1914, after control of the government had been removed from the hands of the old clan leaders, he became finance minister in the second Ōkuma Shigenobu cabinet and joined Katō Takaaki in becoming a member of the Kenseikai. In 1924, when Kiyoura Keigo formed a cabinet made up principally of members of the Upper House of the Diet, he became active in the Constitution Protection Movement, which advocated the formation of a party cabinet.

He served as minister of home affairs in the Katō Takaaki cabinet, which was formed from the three political parties participating in the Constitution Protection Movement, and helped to put through the universal male suffrage law and the peace preservation law. With Kato's death in 1926, Wakatsuki succeeded him as president of the Kenseikai and, as prime minister, formed a cabinet of his own. Working principally through his foreign minister, Shidehara Kijūrō, he sought to promote international cooperation, but it was a time of financial panic, and when the Privy Council refused a proposal to save the Bank of Taiwan from ruin through imperial intervention, he and his cabinet resigned en masse in 1927.

For a time he withdrew from political life, but in 1930 served as head of the Japanese delegation to the London Disarmament Conference and, despite the opposition of naval circles in Japan, signed the agreement that resulted from it. Shortly after the conference, the prime minister at the time, Hamaguchi Osachi, was attacked and wounded by a right-wing fanatic. When his condition worsened, Wakatsuki replaced him as president of the Rikken Minseitō (an outgrowth of the Kenseikai) and became prime minister in April of 1931, forming his second cabinet. He attempted to reduce expenditures and restore order to the government, as well as supporting Foreign Minister Shidehara in a conciliatory policy abroad, but he faced strong opposition from the military and the Seiyūkai. Following the outbreak of the Manchurian Incident in September of the same year, he found himself unable to curb the willful activities of the army. Meanwhile his Minister of Home Affairs Adachi Kenzō began calling for cooperation in the cabinet among the political, military, and bureaucrat members. This resulted, instead, in dissent among the members, and the cabinet collapsed in December of 1931.

Thereafter, Wakatsuki served as a member of the Upper House of the Diet and enjoyed considerable respect as a senior statesman. He was never able to overcome his bureaucratic background and devote himself wholeheartedly to party affairs, however, and in 1934 he resigned his position as president of the Minseitō. He has been looked upon as a supporter of liberal principles, but in the debates that preceded the outbreak and the conclusion of the Pacific War, his ability to speak out effectively and to influence the course of events was highly limited in spite of his senior standing.

YAMAGATA ARITOMO 山縣有朋 (1838–1922)

Military leader and statesman of the late Edo, Meiji, and Taishō periods; he held the rank of general of the army and field marshal, the title of duke, and was a *genrō* (elder statesman). He was born in the domain of Chōshū, the son of a samurai of the lowest rank; in his youth he went by the name Kyōsuke. He served as an errand boy in the Meirinkan, the official school of the domain, and at the same time studied the marshal arts. Later, while serving as a lesser official of the domain, he entered the Shōka Sonjuku, a private school operated by the Confucian scholar Yoshida Shōin. As a result, he became an ardent supporter of his teacher's call for restoration of power to the emperor and expulsion of the foreigners. In 1862 he journeyed to Kyoto and Edo for the purpose of meeting with other patriot-reformers who shared the same view.

In 1863 he became an officer in the Kiheitai, a military unit organized by Takasugi Shinsaku for the defense of the Shimonoseki Straits. The following year, when a joint force of British, Dutch, French, and American ships bombarded and occupied Shimonoseki, Yamagata was wounded in the fighting. Thereafter he took part in struggles for power within his domain, leading a special military unit and attempting to put down his opponents, and he also fought valiantly against the shogunate forces that were sent to punish Chōshū for its acts of insubordination. In order to bring to an end the rivalry and bitter relations that existed between the domains of Chōshū and Satsuma, he helped to plan an alliance of friendship, which, through the mediation of Sakamoto Ryōma, was successfully concluded in 1866. At this time, Yamagata first demonstrated his aptitude for political affairs.

During the Boshin civil war, he served as a staff officer in command of the imperial forces that were dispatched to put down resistance in Aizu and other areas of northern Honshu, taking part in a number of engagements. In 1869 he joined Saigō Tsugumichi in making a tour of inspection of England, France, and other countries of Europe. In 1870, after returning to Japan by way of America, he became assistant vice-minister of military affairs and carried on the task of organizing the nation's military forces, an undertaking interrupted in the previous year by the sudden death of Ōmura Masujirō. In 1872 he became vice-minister of war and, after the reorganization of the bureaucracy, lieutenant general and commander of the Imperial Guards. In 1873 he also assumed the position of war minister. During this period he worked to lay the foundations for the modern Japanese army and sought to insure its maintenance and improvement through a system of military conscription. In 1874 he also became a councilor of state. At this time there were frequent outbreaks of rioting and resistance among the farmers and disaffected samurai, which Yamagata showed great skill in putting down. He also took a leading role in putting down the rebel forces in the Seinan civil war. He worked vigorously to inculcate a proper military spirit in the newly organized conscript army, increasing his efforts in order to counteract any deleterious effects that the rising popular rights movement might have upon the discipline and resolve of the armed forces. These efforts culminated in the promulgation of the Imperial Rescript on the Military in 1882.

Meanwhile, in 1878 he became chief of the General Staff Office, in 1882 head of the Sanjiin, a legal organ, and in 1883 assumed the post of home minister as well. He served as home minister once more in the first Itō Hirobumi cabinet formed in 1885, devoting his attention to reorganizing the police system and setting up effective agencies of local government under the supervision of the central administration. In 1888 he made a trip to Europe to study systems of local government. In 1889 he formed his own cabinet for the first time, serving simultaneously as prime minister and home minister and playing an important role in the establishment of the Japanese Diet, the setting up of a new system of prefectures and subprefectures, and the promulgation of the Imperial Rescript on Education.

In 1892 he served as minister of justice in the second Itō Hirobumi cabinet and in 1893 became head of the Privy Council. With the outbreak of the Sino-Japanese War in 1894, he took part in the hostilities as commander of the First Army, engaging the enemy at a number of different points in Korea. He was recalled to Japan because of illness and, thereafter, at the time of the restoration of peace, presided over the withdrawal of Japanese troops as commander of the armed forces and war minister. Later, as Japanese and Russian interests in Korea came to be increasingly at odds with each other, he worked to repair the worsening relations between the two countries by signing the Yamagata-Lobanov Agreement of 1896.

In 1898 he became general of the army and formed his second cabinet. Cooperating closely with the Kenseitō (Constitution Party), he labored to rebuild the economy after the effects of the Sino-Japanese War and instituted changes in the Civil Service Appointment Regulations designed to prevent political parties from interfering with the political influence of the old domain cliques in government circles. He also put through the Security Police Law and took other measures to suppress popular political parties. In 1900 he dispatched troops to Peking to combat the Boxers and help relieve the seige on the foreign legations. With the outbreak of the Russo-Japanese War in 1904, he was made commander-in-chief of the General Staff and commissary general and took an active part in the hostilities. After the conclusion of the peace treaty, he became head of the Privy Council.

He had a deep dislike of political parties and endeavored to promote the interests of the bureaucracy, placing various bureaucrats and military men who belonged to his faction such as Hirata Tōsuke, Kiyoura Keigo, and Katsura Tarō in key government positions and, in his role as a *genrō* (elder statesman), through them exercising great influence over the political scene. In 1921, however, he was discovered to have been plotting to interfere in the selection of a consort for the crown prince and, as a result, fell from power. He retired from public life and died the following year at his villa in Odawara. He was a skilled writer of Japanese poetry and also submitted many memorials to the government.

YAMAJI AIZAN 山路愛山 (1864–1917)

Historian and critic of the Meiji and early Taishō periods; he was born in Edo, the son of a retainer of the shogunate; his personal name was Yakichi. The Restoration reduced his family to poverty, and he was obliged to educate himself. He became an assistant teacher in a primary school in Shizuoka and at the same time studied English at a Christian church, eventually receiving baptism. In 1889 he went to Tokyo, where he studied at the Tōyō Eiwa Gakkō. In 1891 he became chief editor of *Gokyō*, a magazine put out by the Methodist League. In 1892 he became acquainted with Tokutomi Sohō and joined the Min'yūsha, the publishing company founded by Tokutomi. Thereafter he began to publish distinctive articles on history and literature in *Kokumin no Tomo*, the magazine put out by the Min'yūsha, and elsewhere, and carried on literary debates with Takayama Chogyū and Kitamura Tōkoku.

In 1899, on the recommendation of Tokutomi Sohō, he was made chief editor of the *Shinano Mainichi Shimbun* in Nagano Prefecture. He returned to Tokyo in 1903 and founded a private magazine called *Dokuritsu Hyōron*. At the time of the Russo-Japanese War, he came out in favor of the war and even changed the name of his magazine to *Nichi-Ro Sensō Jikki*, or "Authentic Record of the Russo-Japanese War," though he changed back to the original name after the conclusion of the war. From around this time, he began to advocate national socialism as an antidote to the socialism preached by the Marxists and in 1905 he formed the Kokka Shakaitō (National Socialist Party).

He published works on history and biography in *Kokumin Zasshi*, a magazine that he founded in 1910, as well as in other magazines such as *Chūō Kōron* and *Taiyō*, and made a reputation for himself as an independent scholar of history. Though associated with no academic institution, he lectured on occasion at Waseda, Keiō, and Dōshisha universities. In his late years, he worked on a history of the Japanese people, though it never reached the publication stage. Among his numerous works are *Gendai kinken-shi*, *Ashikaga Takauji*, and *Gendai Nihon kyōkai shiron*.

YAMAKAWA HITOSHI 山川均 (1880–1958)

Socialist leader of the Meiji, Taishō, and Shōwa periods; he was born in Kurashiki in Okayama Prefecture, the son of a merchant. After attending Dōshisha University in Kyoto for a time, he withdrew in 1897 and went to Tokyo. In 1900 he was accused of lèse-majesté because of a magazine published by himself and a friend and was sentenced to three years in prison. In 1906 he participated in the formation of the Japan Socialist Party. He also acted as editor and writer for the daily newspaper *Heimin Shimbun*. In 1908 he was among those sent to prison for displaying anarchist slogans at a gathering in Kanda in Tokyo. In 1916 he joined the Baibunsha, an advertising and publishing company founded by Sakai Toshihiko and, along with Sakai and Takabatake Motoyuki, edited a magazine called *Shinshakai*. He soon distinguished himself as a leading writer on Marxist theory. In 1922, at the time of the founding of the Japan Communist Party, he published articles in the magazine *Zen'ei* in which he called upon socialism in Japan to become a truly popular-based and law-abiding proletariat party. In 1928, he severed his connections with the Communist Party.

From around this time, he became active as a spokesman for a group known as the Rōnōha, or Labor Farmer Faction. In 1937 he was among the left-wing leaders arrested in connection with the antifascist movement known as the *jimmin sensen*. After the war, when the Communist leader Nosaka Sanzō returned to Japan in 1946, he attempted to start a new movement called the *minshu jimmin sensen*, but met with no success. From 1951 on, he was active as a leading theorist of the left-wing faction of the Socialist Party. His wife, Yamakawa Kikue, (1890–) was a leader in the socialist women's movement and the first head of the Women and Minors Bureau of the Ministry of Labor.

Yamakawa Kenjirō 山川健次郎 (1854–1931)

Physicist of the Meiji, Taishō, and early Shōwa eras; he held the title of baron. He was born in what later became Fukushima Prefecture, the son of a samurai of the domain of Aizu. In 1871 he went to the United State and studied at Yale University. He returned to Japan in 1875 and the following year became a professorial assistant in Tokyo Kaisei Gakkō, which later became Tokyo Imperial University. In 1886 he was appointed a professor in the Science College of Tokyo University and in time was put in charge of the subject of physics. In 1888 he received the degree of Doctor of Science. In 1893 he became head of the Science College and in 1901 was appointed president of Tokyo Imperial University. He left the position in 1905, after which he served as president of Kyushu Imperial University, as head of Tokyo University once more, and as head of Kyoto Imperial University. Thus, in addition to laying the foundations for the study of physics in Japan, he also contributed to the establishment of higher education through his various academic posts, acting as a leader in the educational field.

In addition to the posts in national universities mentioned above, he also contributed to the advancement of private educational institutions and special schools, heading such private schools as the Meiji Professional School in Tobata in Kyushu and the Musashi High School. He was also very active in the administrative end of scientific affairs, helping to found the Institute of Physical and Chemical Research and the Aviation Research Center.

In 1923 he became an advisor to the Privy Council. In his late years he became associated with the Central United Organization of Social Education and the political body known as the Kokuhonsha, working to advance the movement for nationalistic education.

Yamamoto Gombei 山本權兵衞 (1852–1933)

Naval leader and statesman of the Meiji and Taishō periods; he held the rank of full admiral and the title of count. He was born in the domain of Satsuma in Kyushu. He served in the forces loyal to the throne at the time of the Boshin civil war in 1868, taking part in the actions at Toba and Fushimi and later in northern Honshu and Hakodate. In 1870 he was assigned to the Naval Training Station and later to the Naval Training Barracks. On graduating from the course of instruction, in 1874 he became a candidate for the rank of ensign. In 1877, in order to study navigation and logging, he was assigned to German warships. After his return to Japan in

1878, his career as a navy man began in earnest. He was appointed to the position of the commander of the *Takachiho* and in 1891 became chief secretary of the Naval Ministry.

With the outbreak of the Sino-Japanese War in 1894, he was made adjutant to the naval minister at Imperial Headquarters. The following year he advanced to the rank of rear admiral and, in his capacity as chief of the Bureau of Naval Affairs, member of the council of generals and admirals, and staff officer of Imperial Headquarters, exercised virtual control over the navy's role in the war, displaying great talent in the task of leadership. In 1898 he advanced to the rank of vice-admiral and was appointed naval minister in the second Yamagata Aritomo cabinet. From that time until 1906, when he became a military councilor of state, he continued to serve as naval minister in succeeding cabinets. Prior to the Russo-Japanese War, he joined with Terauchi Masakata in drawing up the articles for the Anglo-Japanese Military alliance of 1902. With regard to the sending of Japanese troops to Korea, he opposed Yamagata Aritomo and others like him who favored military intervention, but at the same time he appointed Tōgō Heihachirō as commander-in-chief of the standing fleet and took other steps on his own to make certain that Japan would be prepared in the event of an outbreak of hostilities with Russia.

In 1913, when the first movement to preserve the constitution brought about the fall of the Katsura Tarō cabinet, Yamamoto formed his own cabinet in cooperation with the Rikken Seiyūkai. He established the principle that the posts of minister of war and minister of the navy should be held by officers on active duty, carried out changes in the civil service appointment system, took steps to improve the financial administration of the government, and introduced other political reforms. But because of the Siemens affair, in which a German company named Siemens was found to have given bribes to affect the assignment of naval contracts, and because of the failure to arrive at a budget due to cuts in naval expenditures, Yamamoto and his cabinet were obliged to resign in 1914. Yamamoto at the same time retired from military service.

In 1923, Yamamoto became prime minister once more and formed a second cabinet, appointing Inukai Tsuyoki, a member of the Kakushin Kurabu, as minister of communications and minister of education. The first major task that confronted the new cabinet was that of guiding the country through the aftermath of the Great Kantō Earthquake of September 1. Yamamoto declared a state of marshal law throughout the Tokyo area and issued orders designed to maintain order and security. But rumors of riots and uprisings bred by the social unrest soon spread, resulting in a reign of terror in which Koreans and persons of socialist or anarchist beliefs were massacred, while the government stood by in silence. In order to alleviate the economic situation, Yamamoto put through a moratory law and worked to rebuild Tokyo. But in December of 1923, an anarchist made an attempt on the life of the crown prince, who at this time was acting as regent, at Toranomon in Tokyo. The following year, the Yamamoto cabinet, accepting responsibility for the incident, resigned en masse. Yamamoto is remembered chiefly for his achievements in building up the Japanese navy and also showed remarkable ability in selecting and advancing men of talent.

Yamamoto Isoroku 山本五十六 (1884–1943)

Naval leader of the Taishō and Shōwa eras who rose to the rank of fleet admiral. He was born into the Takano family, samurai of the former domain of Nagaoka in present-day Niigata Prefecture, but was later adopted as heir to the Yamamoto family. He graduated from Nagaoka Middle School, the Naval Academy, and the Naval Staff College. He saw action in the Russo-Japanese War and in 1905 was wounded in the battle of the Japan Sea. The same year he was commissioned as an ensign. During the years from 1919 to 1921 he was stationed in the United States and studied at Harvard. After his return to Japan, he became an instructor in the Naval Staff College. In 1924 he was made executive officer of the Kasumigaura Naval Air Squadron. He went once more to America, spending the years 1925–28 as naval attaché to the Japanese Embassy.

In 1929 he went to England as a member of the Japanese delegation to the London Disarmament Conference and advanced to the rank of rear admiral. In 1931 he became commander of the air squadron and in 1934 went to England as Japan's representative to negotiate preparations for an arms reduction agreement. He advanced to the rank of vice-admiral and in 1935 became commander of the air force headquarters. In 1936 he became vice-minister of the navy and the following year joined with Navy Minister Yonai Mitsumasa in attempting to block the conclusion of a military pact between Japan and Germany. In 1939 he was shifted to the post of commander of the Combined Fleet. Though personally opposed to the idea of war with Britain and the United States, he was obliged to lay plans for such a war. Emphasizing the prime importance of air power, he drew up the strategies for the Pearl Harbor and Midway attacks and directed their execution, but, while on an inspection tour of the front line bases in 1943, he was killed in an enemy air attack. He was given a state funeral.

YAMAMOTO SENJI 山本宣治 (1889–1929)

Biologist of the Taishō and Shōwa periods and the first Diet member to be elected from a proletarian party; he was born in Kyoto. He went to America as a boy and spent five years from 1907 studying under difficult circumstances in Canada. During this period he became a Unitarian and developed an interest in socialism. After returning to Japan, he attended the Third High School and Tokyo Imperial University. Upon completing the zoology course of the latter, he became a lecturer in Dōshisha and Kyoto universities and devoted himself to sexology. In 1922, when Margaret Sanger visited Japan, he became interested in the birth-control movement and worked to promote it. He conducted a survey of the sexual activities of Japanese students in various colleges, which was highly praised by specialists in the field. These activities brought him into contact with members of the working class, and in 1924 he became head of the Kyoto Workers' School.

In 1925–26, when steps were taken to suppress left-wing students in the Kyoto schools, Yamamoto became implicated and was deprived of his university teaching positions. He later became active in the Japan Farmers' Union. In 1927 he was made chairman of the Kyoto Prefecture branch of the Rōdō Nōmintō (Labor Farmer Party). In 1928, in the first election carried out under the universal manhood suffrage law, he was elected to the Diet as a member of the same party, thus becoming the sole Diet member representative of a communist type party. In the 56th session of the Diet in 1929, he vigorously attacked the Peace Preservation Law, which was being utilized by the police for the harrassment of left-wing activities. As a result, he was attacked the same year at an inn in the Kanda section of Tokyo by a member of a right-wing organization called Shichishō Gidan and stabbed to death. The Central Committee of the Japan Communist Party posthumously conferred membership in the party on him. His writings include *Musansha seibutsugaku*, *Seikyōiku*, and other works.

YANAGIDA KUNIO 柳田國男 (1875–1962)

Folklorist of the Meiji, Taishō, and Shōwa periods; he was born in Hyōgo Prefecture. His elder brother was Inoue Michiyasu, a doctor, poet, and scholar of Japanese literature; his younger brother Matsuoka Shizuo was a scholar of linguistics, while another younger brother, Matsuoka Eikyū, was a Japanese style painter. Yanagida graduated from the political course of Tokyo Imperial University in 1900 and took a position in the Agricultural

Affairs Bureau of the Ministry of Agriculture and Commerce. In 1901 he was adopted into the Yanagida family. In 1902 he transferred to the Cabinet Legislation Bureau and later to the Department of the Imperial Household. In 1914 he became chief secretary of the Upper House of the Diet, but retired from this post in 1919. He went to Europe to participate in the League of Nations mandatory rule committee, residing in Switzerland during the period 1921–22. In 1924 he became an editorial writer for the *Asahi Shimbun*, a position that he resigned in 1932. In 1946 he became an advisor to the Privy Council, in 1947 a member of the Japan Art Academy, and in 1948 a member of the Japan Academy.

In his youth he was friendly with such literary figures as Shimazaki Tōson, Tayama Katai, and Kunikida Doppo and became known as a writer of modern style poetry. He also was instrumental in introducing new works of foreign literature to Japan. Later he ceased to be active in the literary world, and his scholarly interests turned from his specialty, agricultural policy, to the field of folklore. He traveled extensively around the country, making walking tours of remote mountain areas and gathering data. In 1909 he published a collection of such data entitled *Nochi-no-kari kotoba-no-ki*, a work that marked the beginning of Japanese folklore studies. The following year he brought out a second collection entitled *Tōno monogatari*. In 1913 he and a friend founded a magazine devoted to folklore studies entitled *Kyōdo Kenkyū*. He published further works on the subject such as *Minzoku* in 1925 and *Minkan denshō* in 1935. In addition to his numerous works on folklore, he also wrote a number of articles on Japanese language, in particular local dialects. He lectured on folklore at Keiō University and many other prominent schools, acted as leader of the Japan Folklore Society, and set up an Institute of Folklore Studies at Seijō in Tokyo. In recognition of his many contributions over the years to the establishment and promotion of Japanese folklore studies, he was awarded an Asahi Cultural Prize in 1941 and a Cultural Award in 1951. His library, known as the Yanagida Collection, is preserved in Seijō University.

Yanaihara Tadao 矢内原忠雄 (1893–1961)

Economist and Doctor of Economics of the Taishō and Shōwa periods; he was born in Ehime Prefecture. From the time he was a student in the First High School, he came under the influence of such Christian intellectual leaders as Uchimura Kanzō and Nitobe Inazō. While a student in the law course of Tokyo Imperial University, he was also influenced in his thinking by Nitobe's views on colonial policy and Yoshino Sakuzō's lectures on political history. After graduating from Tokyo University, he worked for a time for a mining company, Sumitomo Besshi Kōzan, but in 1920 became an assistant professor in the economics department of Tokyo University. After a period of study in Europe and America, he became a full professor in 1923, lecturing on colonial policy.

In 1929 he published a work entitled *Teikokushugi-ka no Taiwan* ("Taiwan under Imperialism") that was translated into Chinese and Russian. In 1937, shortly after the outbreak of war between China and Japan, he published an article entitled *Kokka no risō* ("Ideals of the State") in the magazine *Chūō Kōron*, which was attacked by the militarists and right-wing elements because of its antiwar sentiment. The incident led to his resignation from Tokyo University. Throughout the war period, he continued to publish a private magazine entitled *Kashin*, which embodied Christian ideals, and opened a private school in his home on Saturdays to teach pacificist principles based upon religious faith. With the conclusion of the war in 1945, he returned to his teaching position at Tokyo University. In 1949 he became a member of the Japan Academy.

At Tokyo University he served as head of the Social Science Institute, head of the economics department, and head of the department of liberal arts, and in 1951 succeeded Nambara Shigeru as president of the university. He retired in 1957 to become a professor emeritus. During these postwar years in Tokyo University he worked consistently to guard the principles of academic freedom.

Yasuda Zenjirō 安田善次郎 (1838–1921)

Financier of the Meiji and Taishō periods and founder of the Yasuda *zaibatsu*. He was born in the province of Etchū in present-day Toyama Prefecture. As a young man he made his way to Edo where, after serving as an apprentice, in 1864 he set up a money exchange shop at Nihonbashi. In the period immediately after the Meiji Restoration, when the currency situation was in considerable confusion, he made huge profits by cornering the paper money issued by the government and similar activities. He founded and managed a number of banks, beginning with the Third National Bank in 1876, and in 1880 set up the Yasuda Bank, the forerunner of the present Fuji Bank. He gradually merged a number of local banks and in the course of his lifetime built up a *zaibatsu*, or business empire, that was strongly family oriented and centered mainly on finance. In 1912 he set up the Yasuda Hozensha, a company that grew out of a property management system, thus giving final shape to his *zaibatsu* activities. He was also a founding member of the Bank of Japan and later a director.

In the political field, he was elected a member of the first Tokyo Prefectural Council in 1879 and a member of the Tokyo City Council in 1889. He took a very active part in public affairs as well, building at his own expense Hibiya Public Hall in Hibiya Park and Yasuda Hall in Tokyo University. He was killed at his country home in Ōiso by a right-wing thug named Asahi Heigo.

Yokoi Shōnan 横井小楠 (1809–1869)

Political leader and thinker of the late Edo period; he was born in Kumamoto, the son of a samurai of the province of Higo; his personal name was Tokihiro, his common name Heishirō, and his literary names were Shōnan and Shōzan. He attended the school operated by the domain of Kumamoto and in 1839 was sent to Edo by his domain for further study. There he became friendly with Fujita Tōko, a samurai of the domain of Mito, and the shogunate official Kawaji Toshiakira. The following year he returned to Higo, where he opened a private school and formed a group known as the Jitsugakutō (Practical Party). His aim was to bring about reforms in the domain by emphasizing knowledge that was of practical application, but his efforts failed, and he set off upon a tour through various other parts of the country.

At this time he became acquainted with Hashimoto Sanai, a physician of Echizen. From 1855 on, as he learned more about the Western world, he became an advocate of the opening of the country. At the invitation of Matsudaira Yoshinaga (Shungaku), the lord of the domain of Echizen, he went to Echizen in 1858 to act as an advisor on political affairs. In 1860 he wrote a work entitled *Kokuze sanron* in which he advocated the opening of Japan to foreign trade and the adoption of measures to enrich the country and strengthen its military position. After the death of Hashimoto Sanai in 1859, he acted as leader of the reform group in Echizen. In 1862, when Matsudaira Yoshinaga was given a high advisory post in the shogunate, Yokoi played an important role as his political planner, working for reform in the shogunate and a policy of cooperation between the shogunate and the imperial court. A sudden shift in the political situation in Echizen in 1863 led him to return to Kumamoto, where he was looked upon as an advocate of dangerous ideas, was deprived of his samurai status, and placed under house confinement. While living in retirement, he was visited by such important young leaders of the time as Sakamoto Ryōma.

At the time of the Meiji Restoration, he was summoned by the new government and appointed as a *sanyo* (junior councilor), being treated with great respect because of his age. But he was attacked and assassinated in Kyoto by a party of six conservative samurai, who suspected him of being a Christian and of favoring republican thinking. One of his disciples was Yuri Kimimasa, a samurai of Echizen who took part in the drafting of the five article Charter Oath that laid down the principles of the new government, and the document reflects Yokoi's thinking. Yokoi's eldest son, Yokoi Tokio (1857–1928), was a Christian minister and president of Dōshisha University in Kyoto. He edited a volume of his father's posthumous works, which was published in 1889 under the title *Shōnan ikō*.

Yonai Mitsumasa 米内光政 (1880–1948)

Naval leader of the Taishō and Shōwa eras; he was born in Iwate Prefecture. He graduated from Morioka Middle School, the Naval Academy, and the Naval Staff College, and in 1903 was commissioned as an ensign. An expert in gunnery, he was stationed in Russia during the years 1915–17, in Berlin during 1920–22, and held other posts, among them commander of a warship. By 1925 he had advanced to the rank of rear admiral and in 1930 became a vice-admiral. After serving as commander of various naval yards, he in 1936 became commander of the Combined Fleet. From 1937 to 1939 he served as minister of the navy in the Hayashi, Konoe, and Hiranuma cabinets, and in 1940 entered the reserve. The same year, he formed a cabinet of his own, but he faced opposition from the army leaders who favored the concluding of a Tripartite Military Pact with Germany and Italy. When he dismissed from office War Minister Hata Shunroku, who had urged cooperation with the "New Order," the army refused to put forward any successor to the post of war minister and thus brought about the downfall of the cabinet.

In 1944, toward the close of the Pacific War, he and Koiso Kuniaki were ordered to form a cabinet, and he became minister of the navy in the cabinet headed by Koiso. He continued in that post in the Suzuki cabinet that succeeded it. Yonai, as a result of his years of residence abroad, had a sound understanding of the international scene and could foresee that the war would end in Japan's defeat. During his period of service in the Suzuki cabinet, he accordingly advocated surrender. After the conclusion of the war, he continued to serve in the Higashikuni-no-miya and Shidehara cabinets, functioning as chief of the naval funeral committee. He appeared before the International Military Tribunal for the Far East as a witness for the defense at the trial of Hata Shunroku.

Yoshida Shigeru 吉田茂 (1878–1967)

Diplomat and statesman of the Shōwa period. He was born in Tokyo, the fifth son of Takeuchi Tsuna, a noted leader of the Jiyūtō (Liberal Party) from Kōchi, but later was adopted by a trading merchant named Yoshida Kenzō. In 1906 he graduated from the political science course of Tokyo Imperial University and entered the Foreign Ministry. He was assigned to positions in the consulates in England, Italy, and China and in 1925 was appointed Japanese consul in Mukden. He played an active role in the Tōhō Kaigi, a meeting called to discuss Japan's China policy, and advocated strong measures in dealing with the Chinese warlord Chang Tso-lin. In 1928 he became vice-minister of foreign affairs in the Tanaka Giichi cabinet and later served as ambassador to England and Italy. During this period, he was considered as a candidate for the post of foreign minister in the cabinet of Hirota Kōki, but he was rejected by the militarists because he was married to the eldest daughter of the statesman Makino Nobuaki and was considered too liberal and pro-British and American in his views. Toward the end of the Pacific War, he joined with the former prime minister Konoe Fumimaro in attempts to arrange a peace settlement, but these ended in failure, and Yoshida was for a time taken into custody by the military police.

In 1945, after the conclusion of the war, he was appointed foreign minister in the Higashikuni-no-miya Naruhiko cabinet and remained in that post in the Shidehara Kijūrō cabinet that followed shortly after. In 1946 the Liberal Party emerged as the victor in the general elections, but its leader, Hatoyama Ichirō, was ordered by the Occupation authorities to be purged from political activities. Yoshida thereupon succeeded him as president of the Liberal Party and formed his first cabinet. In matters of foreign policy he was obliged to negotiate all matters with General MacArthur and the other Occupation authorities, while in internal affairs he was threatened by the growing power of the Socialist and Communist parties. Although he did his best to strengthen and unify the conservative forces, he was often overridden by left-wing elements. When the Socialists emerged victor in the 1947 elections, he declared his intention of leading a healthy opposition party and stepped down from power. In 1948, after the fall of the Ashida Hitoshi cabinet, he returned to office, forming his second cabinet with himself in the post of prime minister and foreign minister. He remained as head of the government until 1953, forming five cabinets in all.

In his third cabinet, formed in 1949, he appointed Ikeda Hayato as finance minister and, by adopting the policies recommended by the American economic advisor to General Headquaters Joseph Dodge, he succeeded in curbing the inflation that had plagued Japan in the postwar period. He also strengthened his ties with the conservative faction in General Headquarters and in 1951 at San Francisco signed the peace treaty between Japan and most of the countries that had fought in the Pacific War, as well as the Japan-American Security Protection Treaty. Thus, while he succeeded in ending the Occupation and securing Japan's independence, he at the same time set up the Police Reserve Force, the forerunner of the Self-Defense Forces. Meanwhile, a fierce struggle for the presidency of the Liberal Party developed between him and Hatoyama Ichirō, who had been depurged.

In 1953, the anti-Yoshida faction in the Liberal Party succeeded in putting through a motion to enforce disciplinary measures against him, and he was obliged to relinquish the post of prime minister. He thereafter withdrew from the political arena, but continued to maintain close connections with the political leaders of the time. His pronouncements on foreign and domestic affairs carried great weight and, as an elder statesman, he wielded a strong influence over conservative circles in Japan. After promising, in a memorandum to the United States Secretary of State John Foster Dulles in 1951, that Japan would sign a peace treaty with the Chinese government in Taiwan, he laid the foundations for Japan's policy of cooperating with America on matters pertaining to Taiwan and the People's Republic of China. He was noted for his humor and skill in conversation, though his dictatorial ways as prime minister aroused resentment in many quarters. On his death in 1967 he was given a state funeral.

Yoshino Sakuzō 吉野作造 (1878–1933)

Political scientist and Doctor of Law of the Meiji, Taishō, and Shōwa periods; he was born in Miyagi Prefecture. He became a Christian while still a high school student in Sendai. When he entered the law course of Tokyo Imperial University, he joined the Hongō Church headed by Ebina Danjō and became friendly with such exponents of Christian socialism as Abe Isoo and Kinoshita Naoe. In 1906, after his graduation, he was invited to go to Tientsin by the Chinese political and military leader Yuan Shih-k'ai, where he taught at a school specializing in legal and political education. He returned to Japan in 1909 and became an assistant professor at Tokyo University.

After spending the years 1910–13 studying in Europe and America, he advanced to the rank of professor in 1914, lecturing on political history and political science. At the same time, breaking away from the stereotyped academicism typical of the national universities, he began to publish articles in the magazine called *Chūō Kōron* that were written in simple style and dealt with political topics or the issues of the times. Those published in 1916 dealing with the establishment of constitutional government, which called upon the political leaders to take into consideration the wishes of the populace as a whole in formulating government policy, were particularly influential, and helped to lay the theoretical foundations for the so-called era of Taishō democracy. Such views brought him under attack from right-wing groups such as the ultranationalistic Rōninkai, a branch of the Gen'yōsha, but he was able to defend himself successfully. At the same time, he gained support among students and intellectuals, and in 1918 played a central role in the formation of the Shinjinkai, an ideological organization made up of Tokyo University students who were members of the Study Group on Universal Suffrage. He thereafter exercised considerable influence on the student social movement.

In the same year, he also founded the Reimeikai, a society for the advancement of enlightened democratic thought, and from the following year began to hold lecture meetings along with another leader of the movement, Ōyama Ikuo. He continued to be very active in journalistic circles, calling for reduction of the powers entrusted to the Upper House of the Diet and the Privy Council and the immediate establishment of universal suffrage, and criticizing the militarists.

In 1924 he resigned his position as professor of Tokyo University and joined the *Asahi Shimbun*, writing editorials on political affairs, but he was forced to resign when the newspaper incurred government censorship. He thereafter served as a lecturer at Tokyo University. In the same year as these events, he set up the Meiji Bunka Kenkyūkai, an association for the study of Meiji period culture and, with a number of associates, succeeded in editing and publishing a twenty-four-volume work entitled *Meiji bunka zenshū* (1927–30) containing basic sources for the study of Meiji culture. In 1926 he assisted in the formation of the Shakai Minshutō (Social Popular Party). Earlier, in 1919, he had established a consumers' cooperative union called the Katei Kōbai Kumiai, and had devoted much effort to hospital work. His numerous works include *Nisshi kōshō-ron*, *Shina kakumei shōshi*, *Futsū senkyo-ron*, and *Gendai kensei no un'yō*.

YOSHIOKA YAYOI 吉岡彌生 (1871–1959)

Pioneer in medical education for women in modern Japan and founder of the only women's medical college. She was born in Shizuoka, the second daughter of Washiyama Yōsai, a doctor of Chinese style medicine. At the age of seventeen she determined to make a career of medicine and went to Tokyo to enter a school called the Saisei Gakusha. In 1892 she passed the national examination for medical practitioners and returned to Shizuoka to set up her own practice. In 1895 she went to Tokyo once more and opened a practice in Hongō. Shortly after, she married Yoshioka Arata (the marriage was not registered until 1908).

In 1900 she was given one room in the Shisei Hospital in Iida-machi, which she used for medical education, founding the Tokyo Women's Medical School and embarking on her project to provide medical education for women. Amid opposition from the government and society at large, she worked vigorously to raise the status of the school to that of a regular medical college. In time she set up the Tokyo Women's Medical College, which in 1920 received full accreditation and established its position as the headquarters for women's medical education in Japan. While continuing to operate the school and the hospital attached to it, she served as chairman of the Tokyo Federation of Women's Societies and held a number of other important positions of leadership in various women's organizations. In 1928 she represented Japan at the First Pan-Pacific Women's Conference in Hawaii, and in 1939 made an inspection tour of Europe and America.

As head of the National Federation of Women's Educators, she worked to set up a system of women's colleges and in 1937 became the first woman member of the Educational Council. In 1946 she became an advisor to the Welfare Ministry. In 1947, as a result of the purge law promulgated by the Occupation Forces, she was banned from public and educational activities, but the ban was lifted in 1951, and the following year she became head of the Tokyo Women's Medical College.

YUKAWA HIDEKI 湯川秀樹 (1907–)

Theoretical physicist of the Shōwa period; he was born in Tokyo. He graduated from Kyoto Imperial University in 1929 and in 1932 became a lecturer at the same university. In 1933 he became a lecturer at Osaka Imperial University and began his studies of the atomic nucleus and the quantum theory of fields. In 1934 he published his theory of interaction of elementary particles and posited the existence of a new elementary particle (the meson), which, as a new quantum field, would serve as a medium for nuclear force and B-decay. In 1937, when the existence of meson particles in cosmic rays was unmistakably observed, he cooperated with Sakata Shōichi, Taketani Mitsuo, Kobayashi Minoru, and others in developing the meson field theory, in this way making a major contribution to the world of international theoretical physics.

In 1940 he became a professor of Kyoto University, serving as head of the Kyoto University Institute of Basic Physics until his retirement in 1970. In 1940 he received an Imperial Award of the Japan Academy, in 1943 a Cultural Medal, and in 1949 he became the first Japanese to receive a Nobel prize, the award in physics. He is also known for his writings and pronouncements on Japanese culture and the future of mankind and, as a member of the World Peace Appeal, World Association of World Federists, and Pugwash Conference, has devoted great effort to the achievement of international peace.

Yuri Kimimasa 由利公正 (1829–1909)

Statesman of the late Edo and Meiji periods; he held the title of viscount. He was born in the domain of Fukui, the son of a lower-ranking samurai. His family name was originally Mitsuoka, and he went by the common name Ishigorō and later Hachirō. In 1847 he studied with the Confucian thinker Yokoi Shōnan, who was visiting the domain of Fukui, and carried out a survey of the domain's finances. He set up a place for the manufacture of guns and gunpowder in Fukui and worked to improve the military system of the domain. In 1859, Hashimoto Sanai, a samurai of Fukui who had worked in cooperation with Yuri to carry out reforms in the domain, was put to death in the purge of political opponents carried out by Ii Naosuke. Yuri, however, was ordered to carry out a general survey of the shogunate's finances in Edo. He was active as an exponent of mercantilism.

For a time his fortunes did not prosper, but with the formation of the new imperial government in 1867, he was taken into service as a councilor and put in charge of the handling of money and grain. He worked to raise funds for the military expenses of the new government and, in 1868, in his capacity as an official in the Bureau of Accounts, supervised the printing of Japan's first paper currency. In these and other ways, he played a central role in the fiscal affairs of the government in the early Meiji period. He is also famous for having drafted the proposal that in time was promulgated as the five-article Charter Oath, a statement issued in 1868 that defined the principles of the new government.

In 1869 he returned to Fukui, where he was active in the movement to abolish the feudal domains and return their lands to the direct control of the central government. In 1871 he became governor of Tokyo Prefecture and in 1872 accompanied Iwakura Tomomi on his tour of Europe. In 1874 he joined Itagaki Taisuke and others in petitioning the government for the creation of an elected assembly. In 1875 he became a member of the Genrōin and in 1890 a member of the Upper House of the Diet.

APPENDICES

Imperial Family Lineage
(rulers indicated by number)

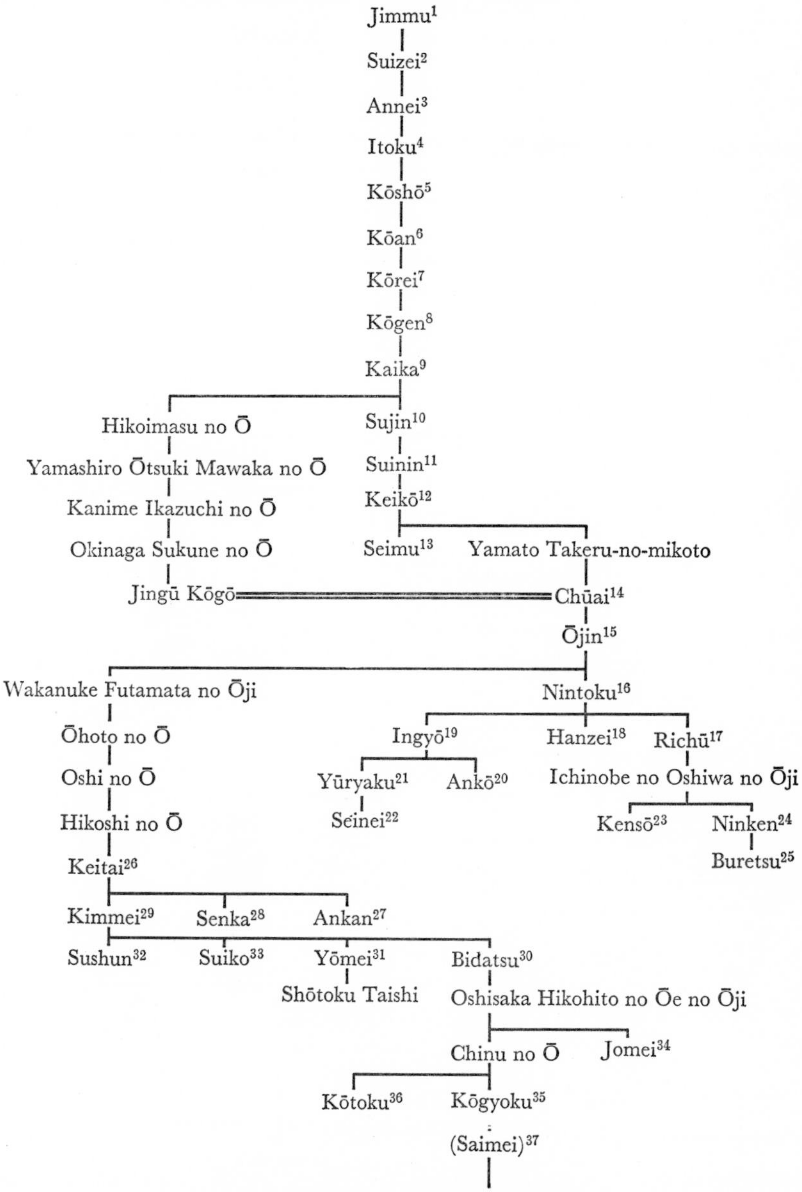

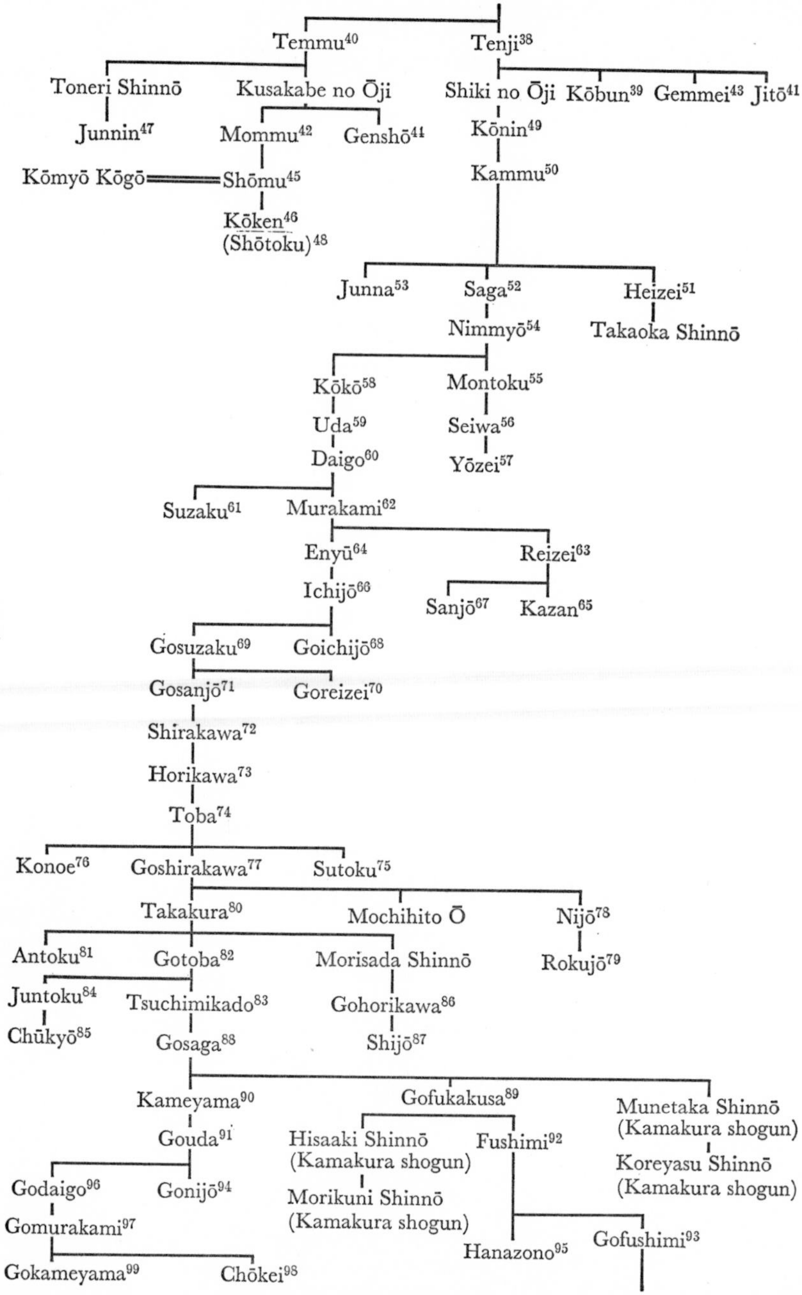

Temmu[40]
Tenji[38]
Toneri Shinnō
Kusakabe no Ōji
Shiki no Ōji
Kōbun[39]
Gemmei[43]
Jitō[41]
Junnin[47]
Mommu[42]
Genshō[44]
Kōnin[49]
Kōmyō Kōgō
Shōmu[45]
Kammu[50]
Kōken[46]
(Shōtoku)[48]
Junna[53]
Saga[52]
Heizei[51]
Nimmyō[54]
Takaoka Shinnō
Kōkō[58]
Montoku[55]
Uda[59]
Seiwa[56]
Daigo[60]
Yōzei[57]
Suzaku[61]
Murakami[62]
Enyū[64]
Reizei[63]
Ichijō[66]
Sanjō[67]
Kazan[65]
Gosuzaku[69]
Goichijō[68]
Gosanjō[71]
Goreizei[70]
Shirakawa[72]
Horikawa[73]
Toba[74]
Konoe[76]
Goshirakawa[77]
Sutoku[75]
Takakura[80]
Mochihito Ō
Nijō[78]
Antoku[81]
Gotoba[82]
Morisada Shinnō
Rokujō[79]
Juntoku[84]
Tsuchimikado[83]
Gohorikawa[86]
Chūkyō[85]
Gosaga[88]
Shijō[87]
Kameyama[90]
Gofukakusa[89]
Munetaka Shinnō
(Kamakura shogun)
Gouda[91]
Hisaaki Shinnō
(Kamakura shogun)
Fushimi[92]
Koreyasu Shinnō
(Kamakura shogun)
Godaigo[96]
Gonijō[94]
Morikuni Shinnō
(Kamakura shogun)
Gomurakami[97]
Gofushimi[93]
Hanazono[95]
Gokameyama[99]
Chōkei[98]

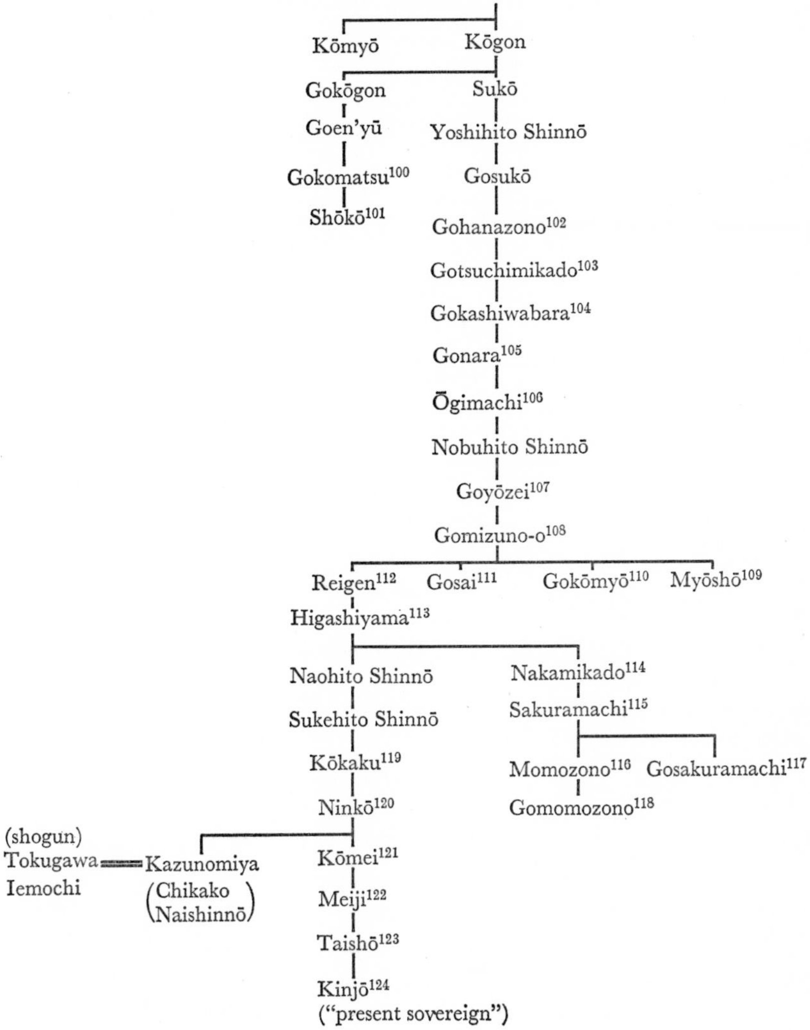
Kōmyō
Kōgon
Gokōgon
Sukō
Goen'yū
Yoshihito Shinnō
Gokomatsu100
Gosukō
Shōkō101
Gohanazono102
Gotsuchimikado103
Gokashiwabara104
Gonara105
Ōgimachi106
Nobuhito Shinnō
Goyōzei107
Gomizuno-o108
Reigen112
Gosai111
Gokōmyō110
Myōshō109
Higashiyama113
Naohito Shinnō
Nakamikado114
Sukehito Shinnō
Sakuramachi115
Kōkaku119
Momozono116
Gosakuramachi117
Ninkō120
Gomomozono118
(shogun) Tokugawa Iemochi
Kazunomiya (Chikako Naishinnō)
Kōmei121
Meiji122
Taishō123
Kinjō124 ("present sovereign")

Fujiwara Family Lineage

(rulers indicated by number
= link by marriage)

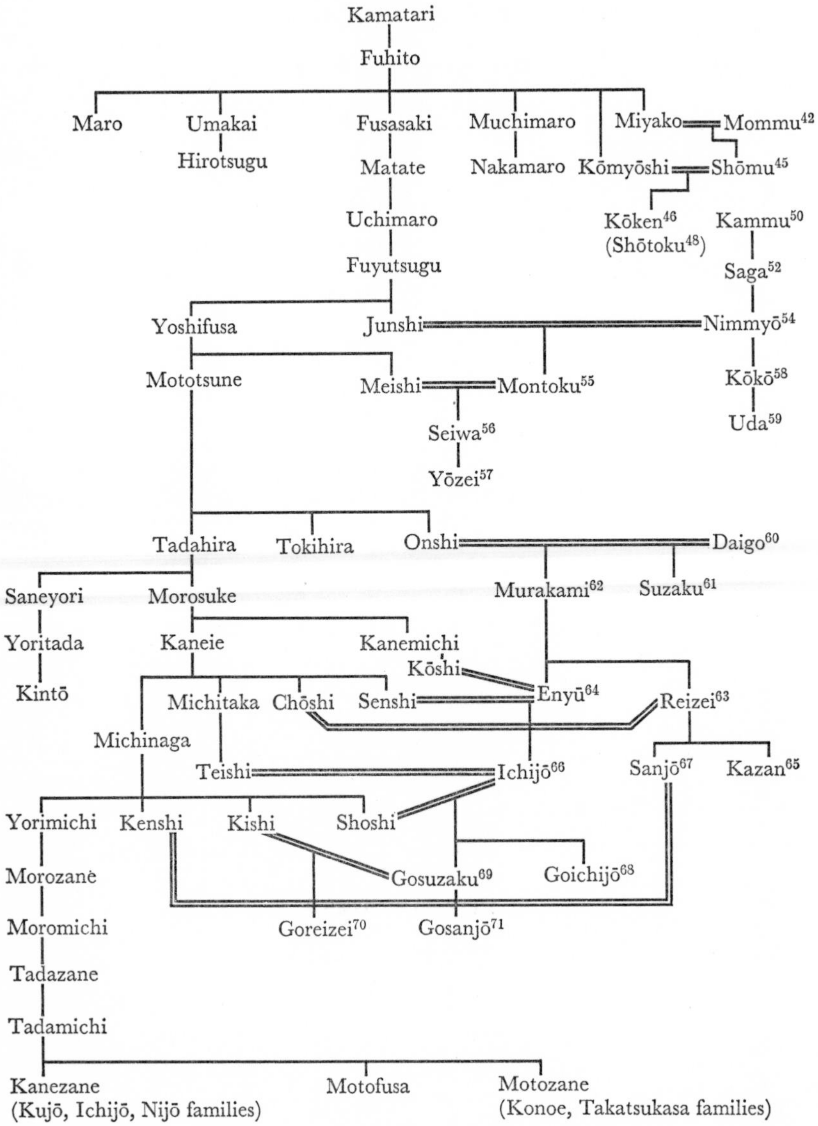

Minamoto Family (Genji Clan) Lineage

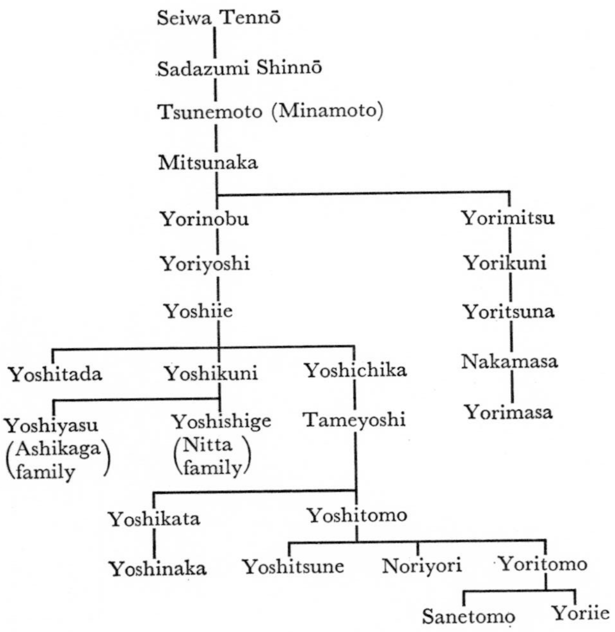

Taira Family (Heike) Lineage

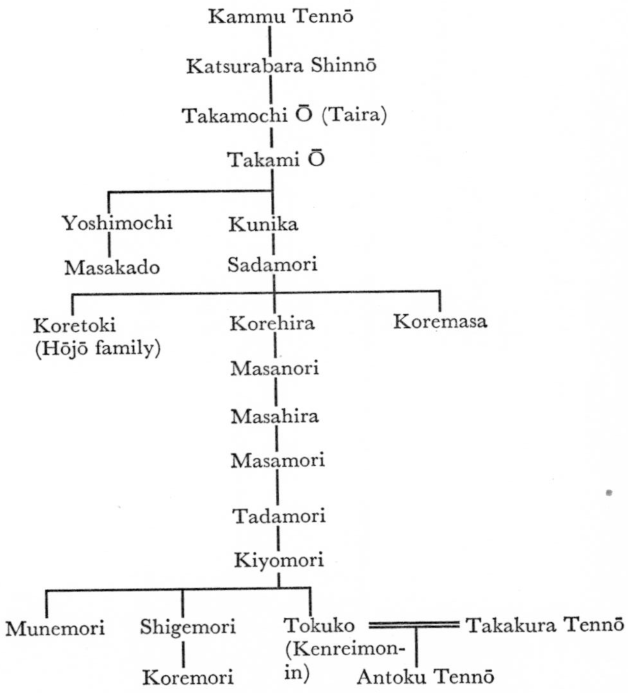

Lineage of the Hōjō Regents
(regents indicated by number)

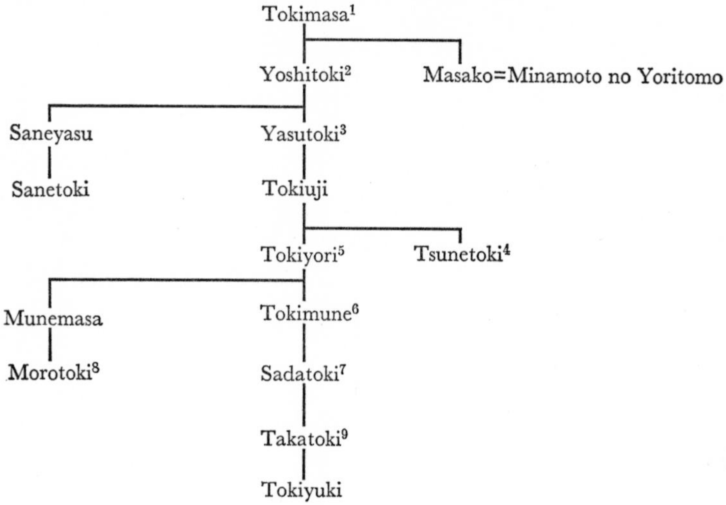

Lineage of the Ashikaga Shoguns
(shoguns indicated by number)

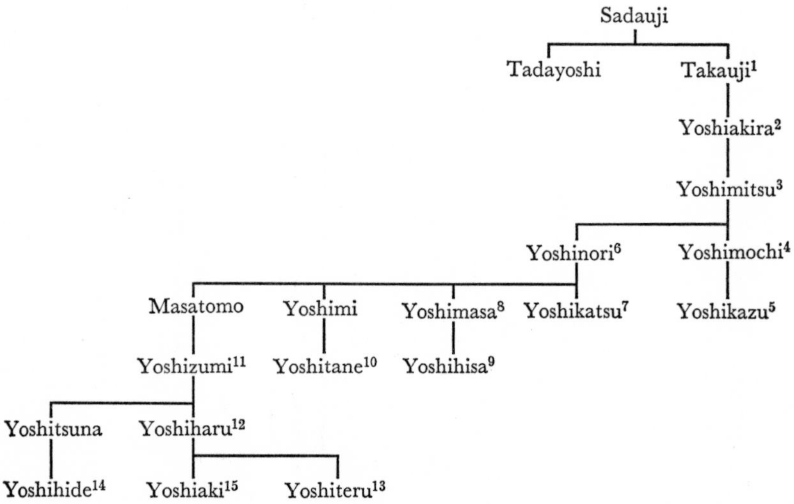

Lineage of the Tokugawa Shoguns
(shoguns indicated by number)

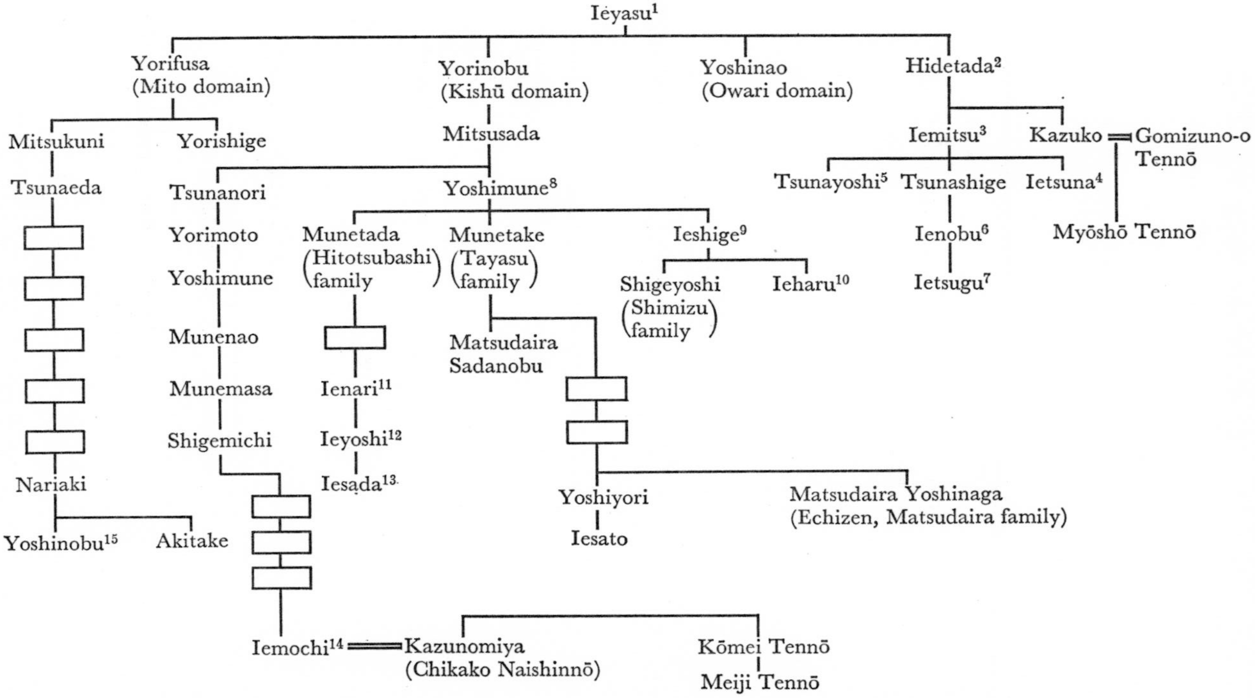

Buddhist Sects

Sanron Sect

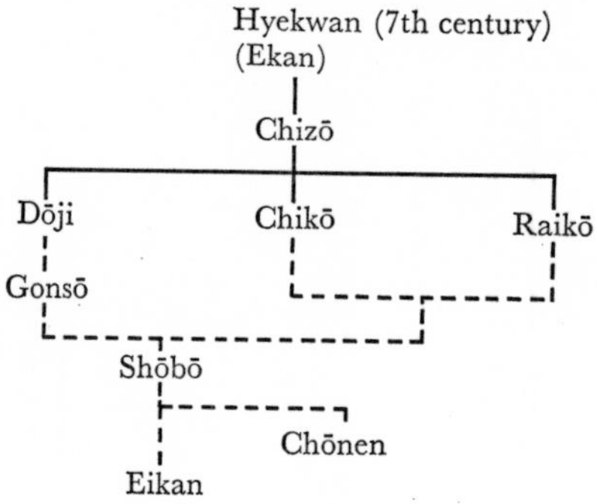

Hossō Sect

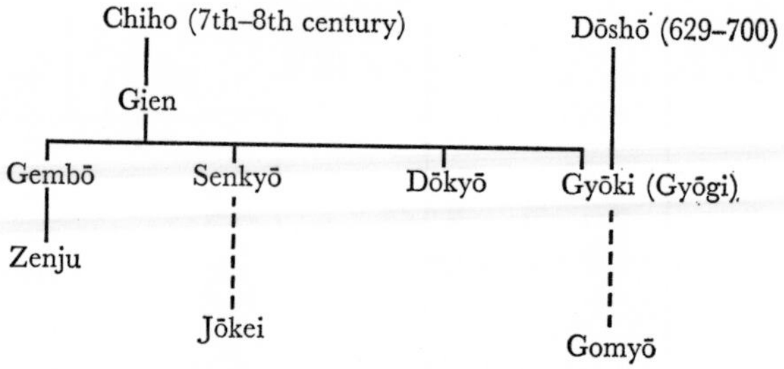

Ritsu Sect

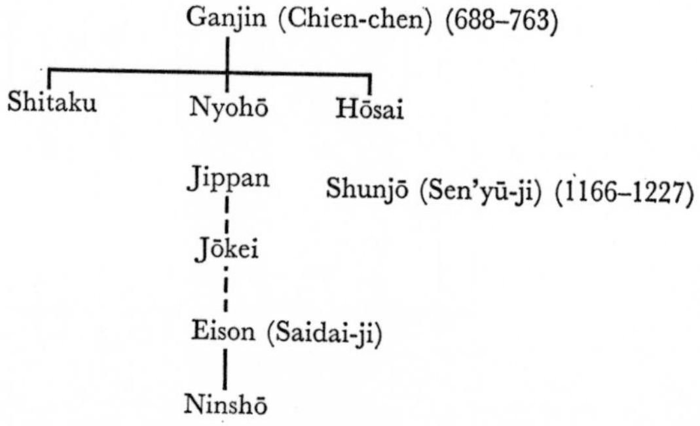

Kegon Sect

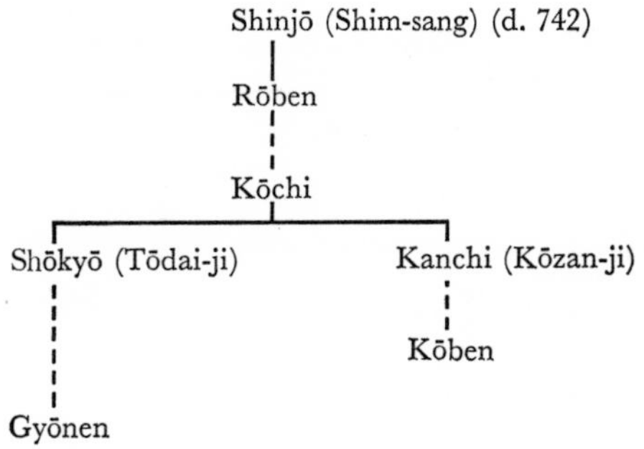
Shinjō (Shim-sang) (d. 742)
Rōben
Kōchi
Shōkyō (Tōdai-ji)
Kanchi (Kōzan-ji)
Kōben
Gyōnen

Tendai Sect

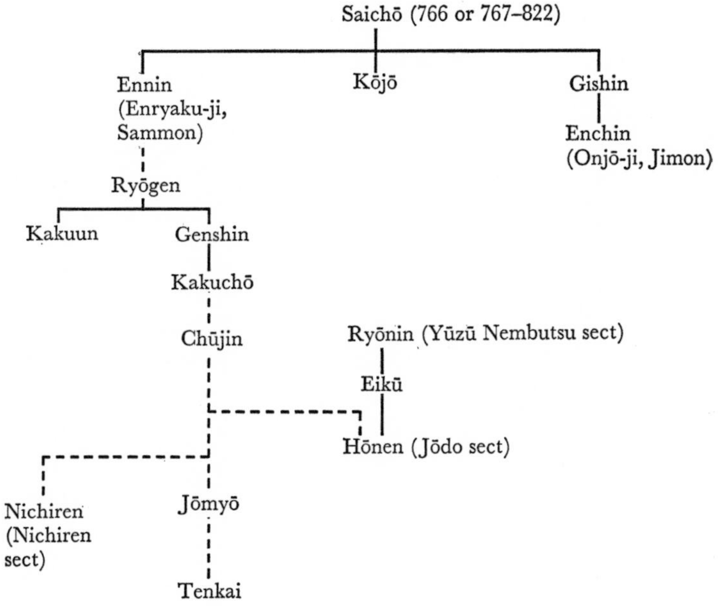
Saichō (766 or 767–822)
Ennin (Enryaku-ji, Sammon)
Kōjō
Gishin
Enchin (Onjō-ji, Jimon)
Ryōgen
Kakuun
Genshin
Kakuchō
Chūjin
Ryōnin (Yūzū Nembutsu sect)
Eikū
Hōnen (Jōdo sect)
Nichiren (Nichiren sect)
Jōmyō
Tenkai

Shingon Sect

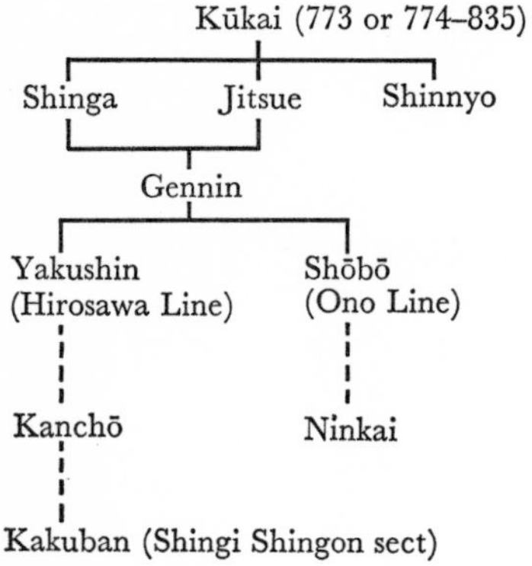
Kūkai (773 or 774–835)
Shinga
Jitsue
Shinnyo
Gennin
Yakushin (Hirosawa Line)
Shōbō (Ono Line)
Kanchō
Ninkai
Kakuban (Shingi Shingon sect)

Jōdo Shin Sect

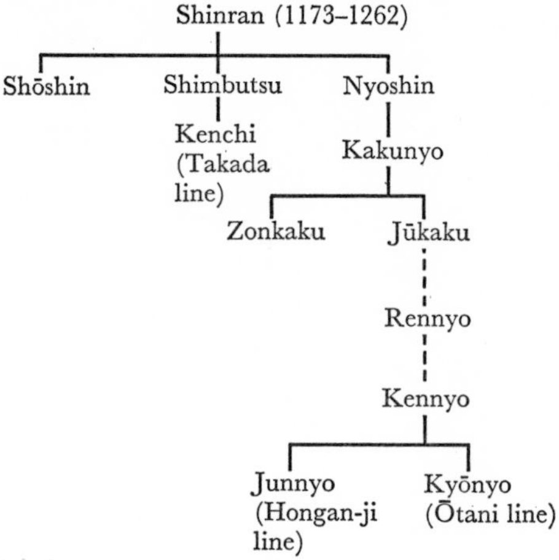
Shinran (1173–1262)
Shōshin
Shimbutsu
Nyoshin
Kenchi (Takada line)
Kakunyo
Zonkaku
Jūkaku
Rennyo
Kennyo
Junnyo (Hongan-ji line)
Kyōnyo (Ōtani line)

Jōdo Sect, Ji Sect

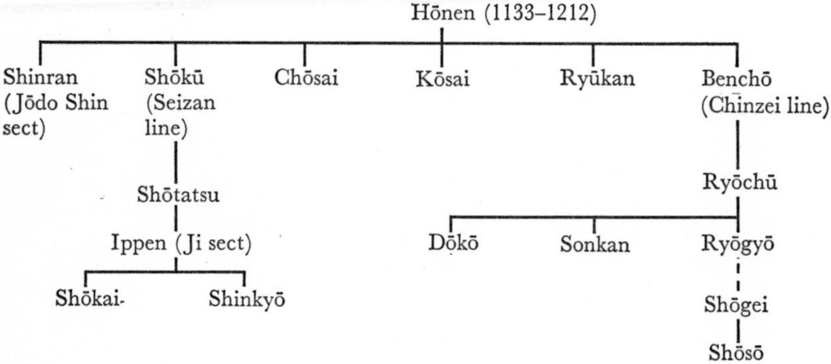
Hōnen (1133–1212)
Shinran (Jōdo Shin sect)
Shōkū (Seizan line)
Chōsai
Kōsai
Ryūkan
Benchō (Chinzei line)
Shōtatsu
Ippen (Ji sect)
Shōkai
Shinkyō
Ryōchū
Dōkō
Sonkan
Ryōgyō
Shōgei
Shōsō

Nichiren Sect

Nichiren (1222–82)
- Nisshō
- Nichirō
  - Nichiō (Fuju Fuse line)
- Nikkō (Fuji-mon line)
- Nikkō (Minobu-mon line)
- Nitchō
- Nichiji
- Nichijō (Nakayama-mon line)
  - Nisshin

Sōtō Zen Sect

Dōgen (1200–53)
- Koun Ejō
  - Tettsū Gikai
    - Keizan Jōkin
      - Gazan Jōseki

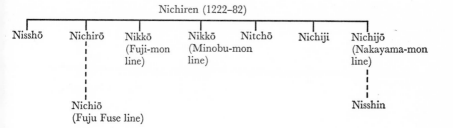

Rinzai Zen Sect

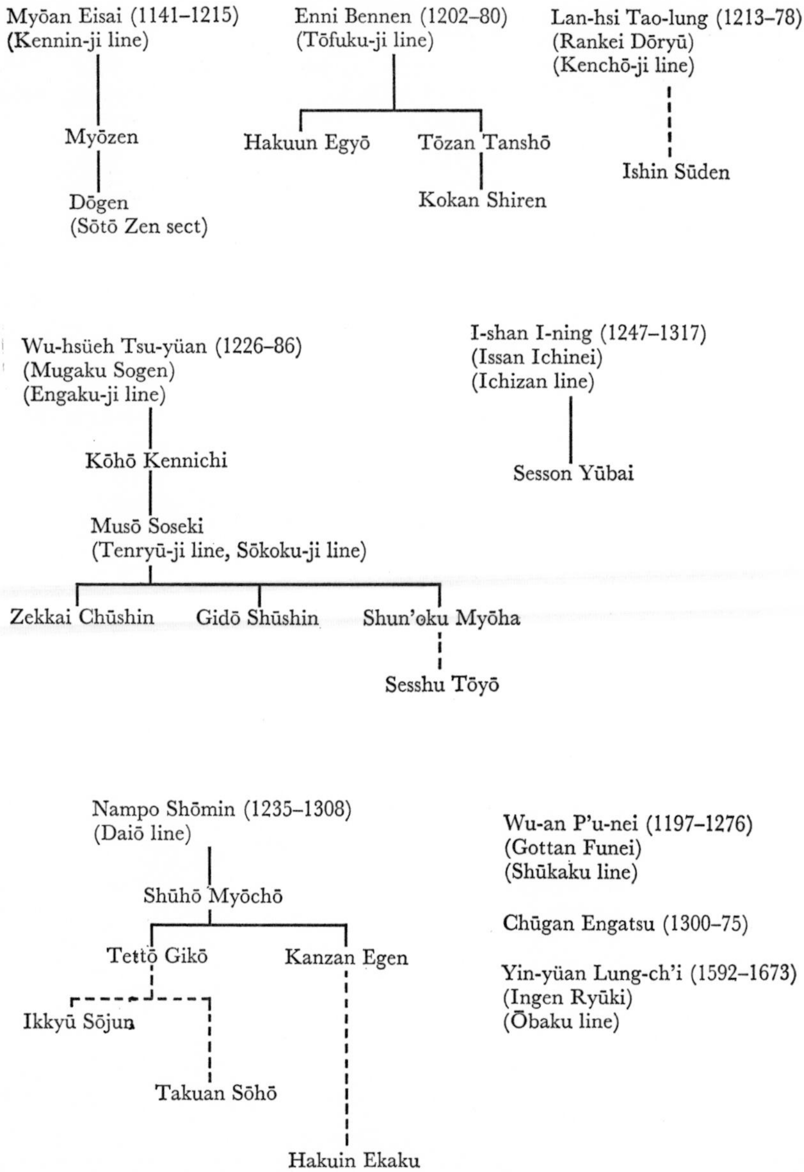

Myōan Eisai (1141–1215)
(Kennin-ji line)
Myōzen
Dōgen
(Sōtō Zen sect)
Enni Bennen (1202–80)
(Tōfuku-ji line)
Hakuun Egyō
Tōzan Tanshō
Kokan Shiren
Lan-hsi Tao-lung (1213–78)
(Rankei Dōryū)
(Kenchō-ji line)
Ishin Sūden
Wu-hsüeh Tsu-yüan (1226–86)
(Mugaku Sogen)
(Engaku-ji line)
Kōhō Kennichi
Musō Soseki
(Tenryū-ji line, Sōkoku-ji line)
Zekkai Chūshin
Gidō Shūshin
Shun'oku Myōha
Sesshu Tōyō
I-shan I-ning (1247–1317)
(Issan Ichinei)
(Ichizan line)
Sesson Yūbai
Nampo Shōmin (1235–1308)
(Daiō line)
Shūhō Myōchō
Tettō Gikō
Kanzan Egen
Ikkyū Sōjun
Takuan Sōhō
Hakuin Ekaku
Wu-an P'u-nei (1197–1276)
(Gottan Funei)
(Shūkaku line)
Chūgan Engatsu (1300–75)
Yin-yüan Lung-ch'i (1592–1673)
(Ingen Ryūki)
(Ōbaku line)

Organization of the *Ritsuryō* Bureaucracy

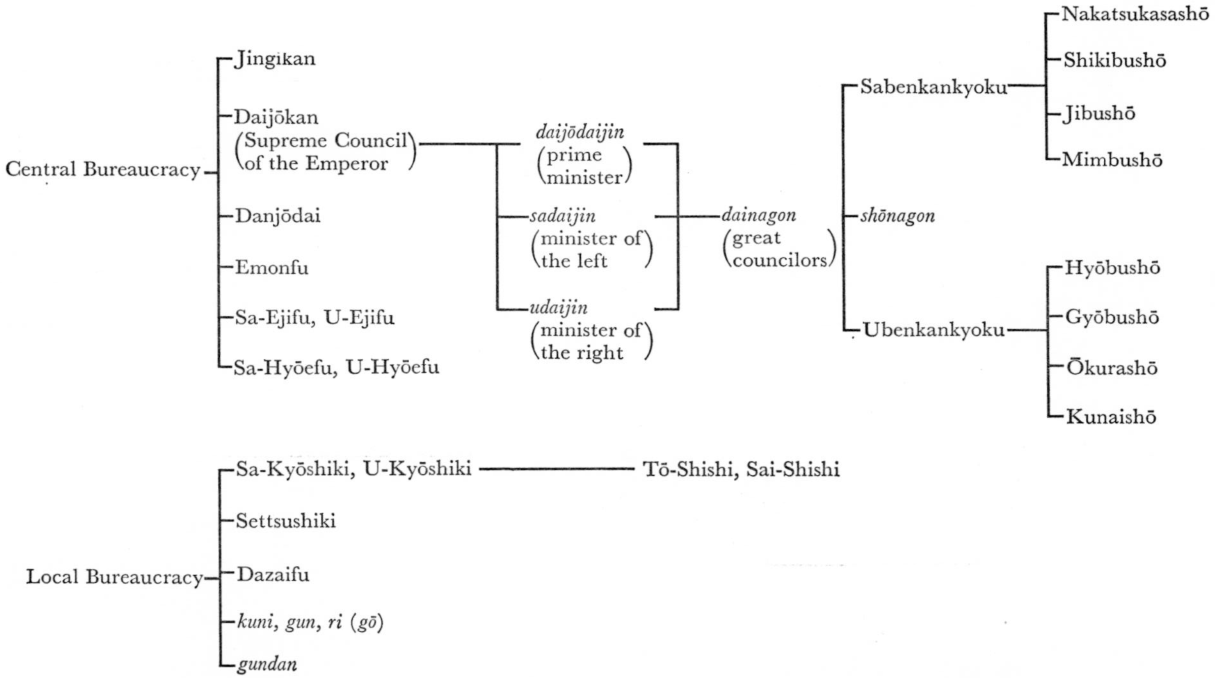

Central Bureaucracy
Jingikan
Daijōkan (Supreme Council of the Emperor)
Danjōdai
Emonfu
Sa-Ejifu, U-Ejifu
Sa-Hyōefu, U-Hyōefu
daijōdaijin (prime minister)
sadaijin (minister of the left)
udaijin (minister of the right)
dainagon (great councilors)
Sabenkankyoku
shōnagon
Ubenkankyoku
Nakatsukasashō
Shikibushō
Jibushō
Mimbushō
Hyōbushō
Gyōbushō
Ōkurashō
Kunaishō
Local Bureaucracy
Sa-Kyōshiki, U-Kyōshiki
Tō-Shishi, Sai-Shishi
Settsushiki
Dazaifu
kuni, gun, ri (gō)
gundan

Organization of the Kamakura Shogunate

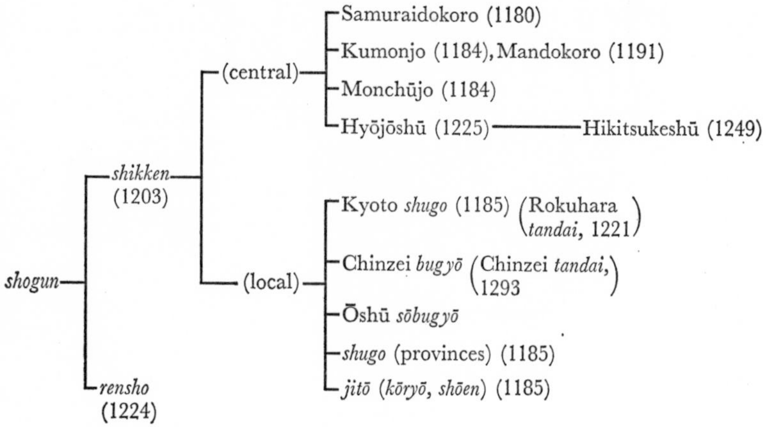

Organization of the Muromachi Shogunate

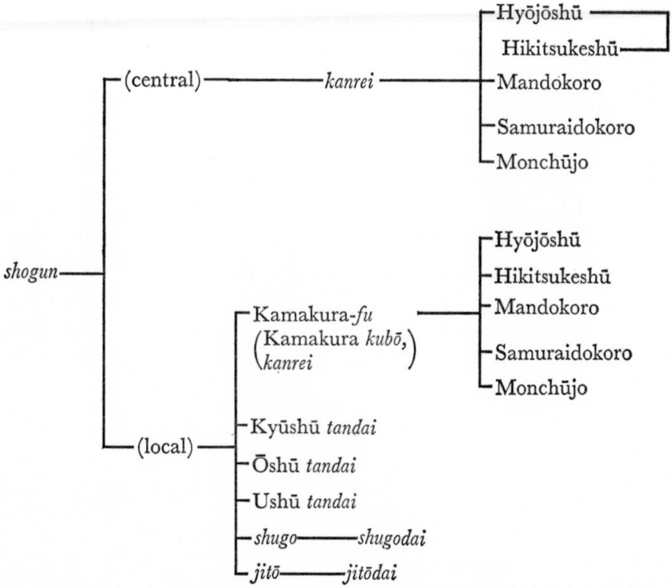

Organization of the Tokugawa (Edo) Shogunate

- _shogun_
  - _tairō_
  - _rōjū_*
    - _ōmetsuke_*
    - _kanjō bugyō_*
      - _gundai, daikan_
      - _Kinza, Ginza_
    - _machi bugyō_ (Edo)*
    - _shoshidai_ (Kyoto)
    - _jōdai_ (Sumpu, Osaka)
    - _ongoku bugyō_ (Nagasaki, Yamada, Nikkō, Sado, etc.)
  - _jisha bugyō_*
  - _sobayōnin_
  - _wakadoshiyori_
    - _metsuke_*
  - _daimyō_ (approximately 260–270 families)

*member of Hyōjōijo

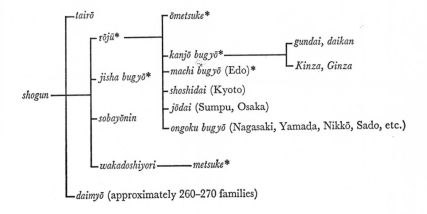

Organization of the Dajōkan Bureaucracy
(excluding 1869–71)

Dajōkan System (1868–1869)

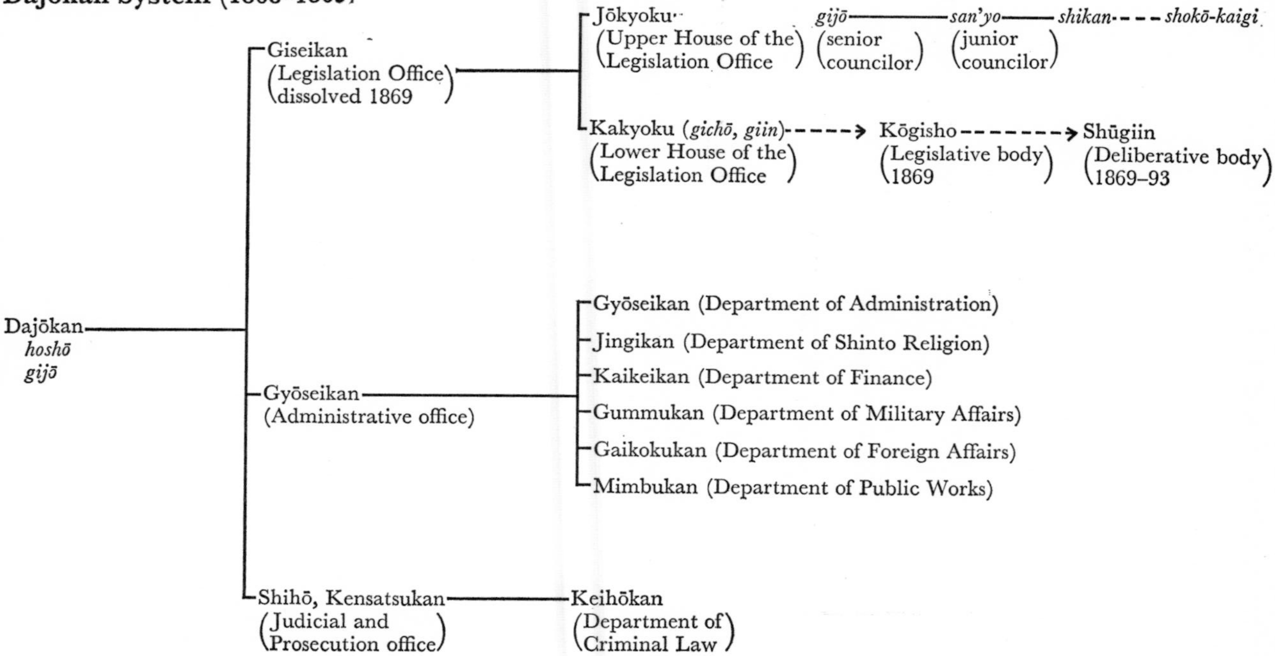

Dajōkan System (1871–1885)

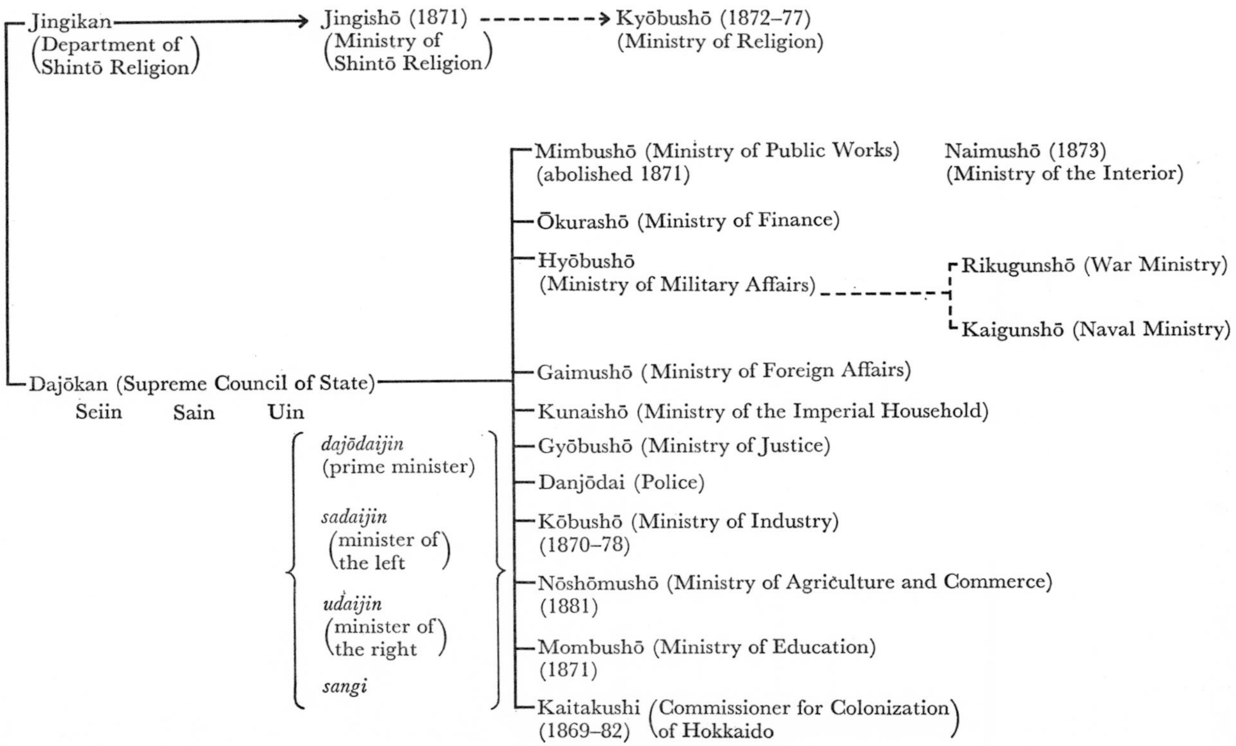
Jingikan
(Department of Shintō Religion)
Jingishō (1871)
(Ministry of Shintō Religion)
Kyōbushō (1872–77)
(Ministry of Religion)
Dajōkan (Supreme Council of State)
Seiin
Sain
Uin
dajōdaijin
(prime minister)
sadaijin
(minister of the left)
udaijin
(minister of the right)
sangi
Mimbushō (Ministry of Public Works)
(abolished 1871)
Naimushō (1873)
(Ministry of the Interior)
Ōkurashō (Ministry of Finance)
Hyōbushō
(Ministry of Military Affairs)
Rikugunshō (War Ministry)
Kaigunshō (Naval Ministry)
Gaimushō (Ministry of Foreign Affairs)
Kunaishō (Ministry of the Imperial Household)
Gyōbushō (Ministry of Justice)
Danjōdai (Police)
Kōbushō (Ministry of Industry)
(1870–78)
Nōshōmushō (Ministry of Agriculture and Commerce)
(1881)
Mombushō (Ministry of Education)
(1871)
Kaitakushi (Commissioner for Colonization of Hokkaido)
(1869–82)

Major Military Actions in Japanese History

Battle of Hakusuki-no-e (Paek Ch'on River); date: 663
Defeated: Japanese army under Kamitsukenu no Wakugo, Abe no Hirafu; army of the king of Paekche
Victor: Army of Silla; army of T'ang China
Site: Entrance to Paek Ch'on River, Ch'ung-ch'ŏng Province, Korea
Japanese army sent to aid king of Paekche defeated in naval battle, destruction of the state of Paekche.

Jinshin Uprising; date: 672
Defeated: Army of Prince Ōtomo, son of Emperor Tenji
Victor: Army of Prince Ōama, brother of Emperor Tenji
Sites: Ōmi, Mino, Ise, Yamato
Struggle for succession following death of Emperor Tenji.

Uprising of Taira no Masakado; date: 935–940
Defeated: Taira no Masakado
Victor: Taira no Sadamori, Fujiwara no Hidesato
Site: Kantō region
Major revolt headed by provincial military leader.

Uprising of Fujiwara no Sumitomo; date: 939–941
Defeated: Fujiwara no Sumitomo
Victor: Ono no Yoshifuru
Site: Areas bordering the Inland Sea
Major revolt headed by provincial military leader.

Uprising of Taira no Tadatsune; date: 1028–1031
Defeated: Taira no Tadatsune
Victor: Minamoto no Yorinobu
Site: Southern part of Kantō region
Major revolt headed by provincial military leader.

Earlier Nine Years' War; date: 1051–1066
Defeated: Abe no Yoritoki, Abe no Sadatō
Victor: Minamoto no Yoriyoshi, Minamoto no Yoshiie
Site: Area of present-day Iwate Prefecture
Uprising in area of northern Honshu. Minamoto family strengthens its power in that region.

Later Three Years' War; date 1083–1087
Defeated: Kiyohara no Iehira, Kiyohara no Takehira
Victor: Minamoto no Yoshiie
Site: Area of present-day Iwate Prefecture
Minamoto family strengthens its power in northern Honshu.

Hōgen Uprising; date: 1156
Defeated: Fujiwara no Yorinaga, Minamoto no Tameyoshi, Taira no Tadamasa, supporting Retired Emperor Sutoku
Victor: Minamoto no Yoshitomo, Taira no Kiyomori, supporting Emperor Goshirakawa
Site: Kyoto
Internal disputes among aristocracy settled by intervention of military leaders. Taira family gains in power.

Heiji Uprising; date: 1159
Defeated: Minamoto no Yoshitomo, Fujiwara no Nobuyori
Victor: Taira no Kiyomori, Fujiwara no Michinori (Shinzei)
Site: Kyoto
Taira family gains in power.

Gempei War; date: 1180–1185
Defeated: Taira no Munemori
Victor: (1) Minamoto no Yoshinaka; (2) Minamoto no Yoritomo, Minamoto no Noriyori, Minamoto no Yoshitsune
Sites: Fujigawa (Shizuoka), Ichinotani (Hyōgo), Yashima (Kagawa), Dan-no-ura (Yamaguchi)
Minamoto family seizes power of government from Taira family, Kamakura shogunate established.

Jōkyū Disturbance; date: 1221
Defeated: 60,000 men supporting Retired Emperor Gotoba
Victor: Hōjō Tokifusa, Hōjō Yasutoki and 190,000 men supporting the shogunate
Site: Kyoto region
Attempt by the court to overthrow the shogunate is defeated.

Bun'ei Campaign; date: 1274
Defeated: Mongol army (150,000 men), army of Korean Koryŏ dynasty (80,000 men)
Victor: Shogunate army
Sites: Islands of Tsushima, Iki, Hakata region of Kyushu
First Mongol attempt to invade Japan.

Kōan Campaign; date: 1281
Defeated: Army of Mongols, Koreans (40,000 men), former Southern Sung army (100,000 men)
Victor: Shogunate army
Sites: Islands of Tsushima, Iki, Hakata region of Kyushu
Second Mongol attempt to invade Japan.

Genkō Disturbance; date: 1331–1333
Defeated: Shogunate army
Victor: Kitabatake Chikafusa, Kitabatake Akiie, Kusunoki Masashige, Nitta Yoshisada, Ashikaga Takauji, supporting Emperor Godaigo
Site: Kyoto-Nara area

Effort by Emperor Godaigo to overthrow the Kamakura shogunate; resulted in the destruction of the shogunate, initiation of the Kemmu Restoration of imperial rule.

Ōnin War; date: 1467–1477
Contestants A: Western Camp headed by Yamana Sōzen and supporters
Contestants B: Eastern Camp headed by Hosokawa Katsumoto and supporters
Site: Kyoto and outlying regions
Result inconclusive. Major disturbance combining struggle for power among large daimyo and dispute over succession to the shogunate, resulting in destruction of Kyoto. Beginning of Age of Civil Wars (1467–1568).

Bunroku Campaign; date: 1592–1593
Contestants A: Army of Toyotomi Hideyoshi
Contestants B: Korean army, supporting army of Ming China
Site: Korean peninsula
Result inconclusive. First attempt by Toyotomi Hideyoshi to conquer Korea.

Keichō Campaign; date: 1597–1598
Contestants A: Army of Toyotomi Hideyoshi
Contestants B: Korean army, supporting army of Ming China
Site: Korean peninsula
Result inconclusive. Second attempt by Toyotomi Hideyoshi to conquer Korea.

Battle of Sekigahara; date: 1600
Defeated: Western Camp headed by Ishida Mitsunari, with support of Konishi Yukinaga, Shimazu Yoshihiro, Mōri Terumoto
Victor: Eastern Camp headed by Tokugawa Ieyasu with support of Asano Yukinaga, Ikeda Terumasa, Kuroda Nagamasa
Site: Sekigahara (Gifu)
Tokugawa Ieyasu establishes his supremacy, beginning of Edo (Tokugawa) shogunate.

Shimabara Uprising; date: 1637–1638
Defeated: Amakusa Shirō Tokisada and peasant army
Victor: Shogunate army (forces of neighboring domains of Kyushu) under leadership of Itakura Shigemasa (killed in battle), later Matsudaira Nobutsuna
Site: Shimabara Peninsula, Amakusa Islands
Large-scale peasant revolt in protest over excessive taxation and proscription of Christianity.

Satsuma-British War; date: 1863
Contestants A: British squadron (7 ships)
Contestants B: Domain of Satsuma, Shimazu family
Site: Kagoshima Bay
Result inconclusive. British ships seek satisfaction over murder of Englishman by Satsuma samurai at Namamugi (Kanagawa) in 1862.

First Punitive Expedition against Chōshū; date: 1864
Contestants A: Shogunate army under Tokugawa Yoshikatsu
Contestants B: Army of domain of Chōshū
Site: Chōshū (present Yamaguchi Prefecture)
Result inconclusive. Military clash between shogunate and Chōshū.

Second Punitive Expedition against Chōshū; date: 1866–1867
Defeated: Shogunate army
Victor: Army of domain of Chōshū
Site: Encounters over area of present-day Yamaguchi, Shimane, Hiroshima, Fukuoka prefectures
Military clash between shogunate and Chōshū, weakness of shogunate becomes apparent.

Toba and Fushimi Encounters; date: 1868
Defeated: Former shogunate forces led by shogunate officials, forces of domains of Aizu, Kuwana
Victor: Government forces, forces of domains of Satsuma, Chōshū, Tosa
Site: Toba and Fushimi south of Kyoto
Forces loyal to old shogunate government clash with those supporting new imperial government. Beginning of Boshin War.

Boshin War; date: 1868–1869
Defeated: Forces loyal to shogunate, Shōgitai in Ueno, Edo; Ōu-Etsu Reppan Dōmei in northern Honshu; army of Enomoto Takeaki at Goryōkaku in Hakodate, Hokkaido
Victor: Government forces
Sites: Edo, Kantō, Tōhoku, Hokuriku, Hokkaido
Clash between forces of new government and those loyal to shogunate.

Taiwan Expeditionary Force; date: 1874
Defeated: Aboriginal tribes of Taiwan
Victor: Japanese force of 3,600 men under Saigō Tsugumichi
Site: Taiwan
Military action in response to murder of Ryūkyū castaways by aboriginal tribesmen in 1871.

Seinan War; date: 1877
Defeated: Force of Kyushu samurai under Saigō Takamori
Victor: Government forces
Site: Kyushu
Large-scale uprising of discontented samurai in Kyushu.

Sino-Japanese War; date: 1894–1895
Defeated: Military forces of Chinese Ch'ing dynasty
Victor: Japanese military forces
Sites: Korean peninsula, Liaotung Peninsula, Yellow Sea
Struggle between China and Japan over control of Korea.

North China Incident; date: 1900
Defeated: Chinese government forces, Boxers
Victor: Allied forces of England, America, Russia, Germany, Italy, Austria, Japan
Site: North China
Dispatch of troops by treaty powers in response to the Boxer Rebellion.

Russo-Japanese War; date: 1904–1905
Defeated: Russian military forces
Victor: Japanese military forces
Sites: Northeast China (Manchuria), Tsushima Straits
Struggle between Russia and Japan over control of Korea.

World War I (Japan–German War); date: 1914
Defeated: German military forces
Victor: Japanese military forces
Sites: Shantung Peninsula, North Pacific
With Anglo-Japanese Alliance as an excuse, Japan attempts to eliminate German influence in East Asia.

Siberian Expeditionary Force; date: 1918–1925
Contestants A: Allied military forces (24,000), including 12,000 Japanese
Contestants B: Russian partisan forces
Sites: Eastern Siberia, northern Sakhalin
Attempt to intervene in Russian revolution with military force, ending in failure.

Manchurian Incident; date: 1931
Defeated: Chinese military forces
Victor: Japanese military forces
Site: Northeastern China (Manchuria)
Liu-t'iao-kou incident leading to Japanese invasion of Manchuria. Followed by founding of state of Manchukuo, Japan's withdrawal from League of Nations.

China Incident (Japan-China War); date: 1937–1945
Defeated: Japanese military forces
Victor: Forces of Kuomintang government, Red Army
Site: China
Full-scale hostilities between Japan and China beginning with Marco Polo Bridge incident.

Pacific War; date: 1941–1945
Defeated: Japanese military forces
Victor: Allied military forces
Sites: Southeast Asia, western Pacific
Difficulties arising from Japan's hostilities in China lead her to participate in World War II, resulting in defeat, democratization, and rebirth of Japan.

Japanese Army Cliques

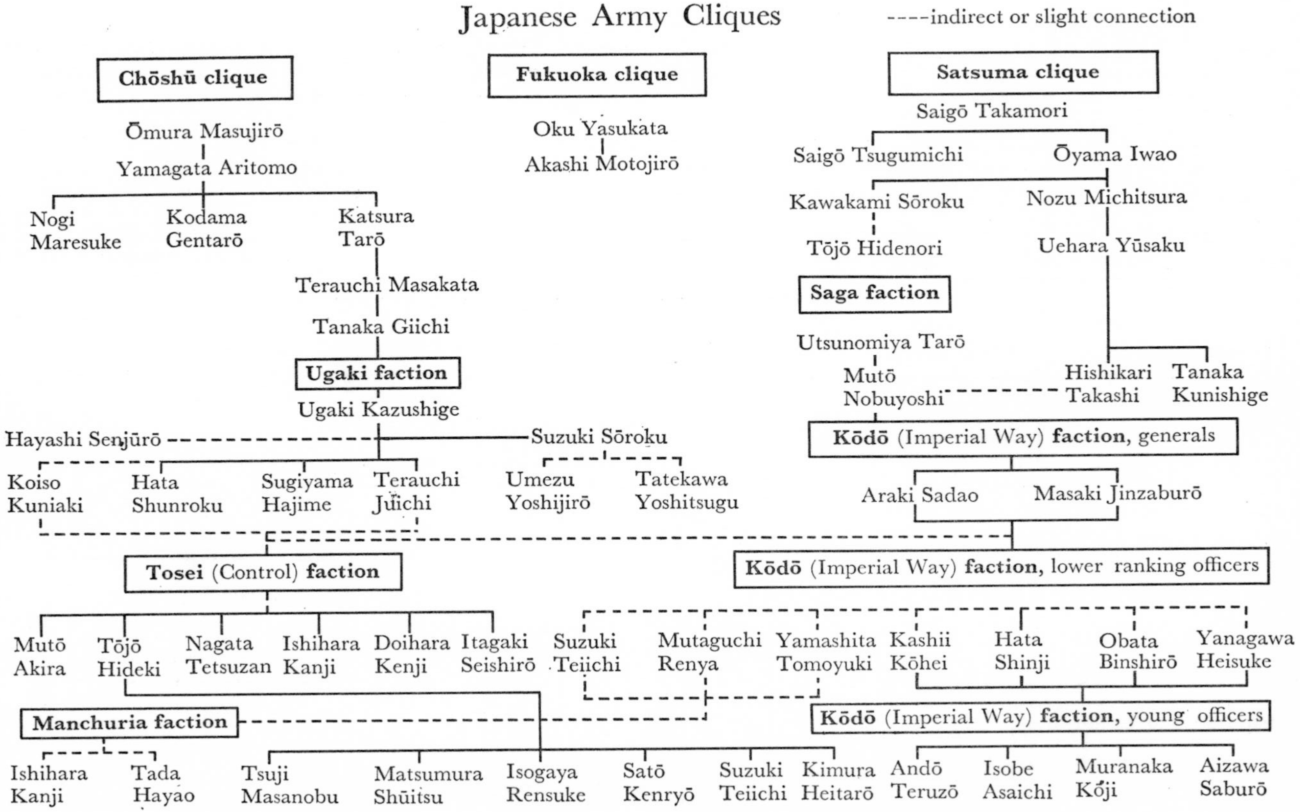

Japanese Navy Cliques

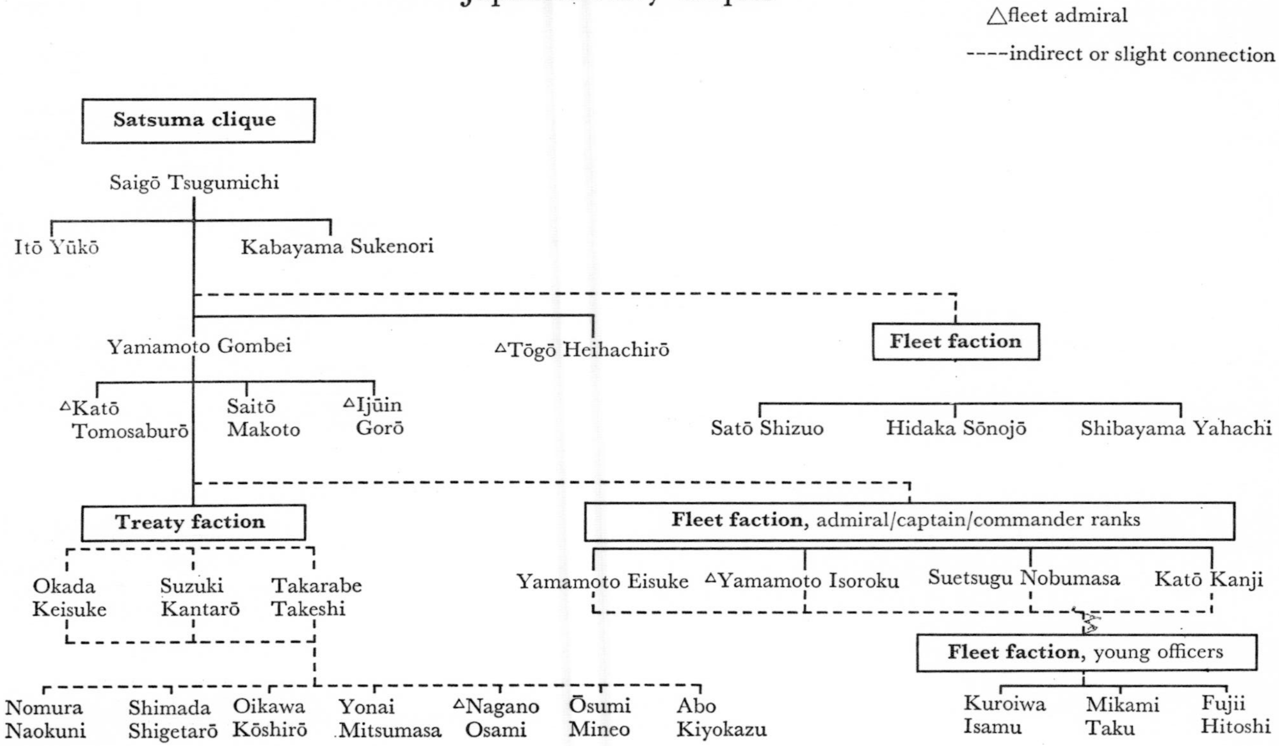
△fleet admiral
----indirect or slight connection
Satsuma clique
Saigō Tsugumichi
Itō Yūkō
Kabayama Sukenori
Yamamoto Gombei
△Tōgō Heihachirō
Fleet faction
△Katō Tomosaburō
Saitō Makoto
△Ijūin Gorō
Satō Shizuo
Hidaka Sōnojō
Shibayama Yahachi
Treaty faction
Fleet faction, admiral/captain/commander ranks
Okada Keisuke
Suzuki Kantarō
Takarabe Takeshi
Yamamoto Eisuke
△Yamamoto Isoroku
Suetsugu Nobumasa
Katō Kanji
Fleet faction, young officers
Nomura Naokuni
Shimada Shigetarō
Oikawa Kōshirō
Yonai Mitsumasa
△Nagano Osami
Ōsumi Mineo
Abo Kiyokazu
Kuroiwa Isamu
Mikami Taku
Fujii Hitoshi

Right-Wing Organizations I

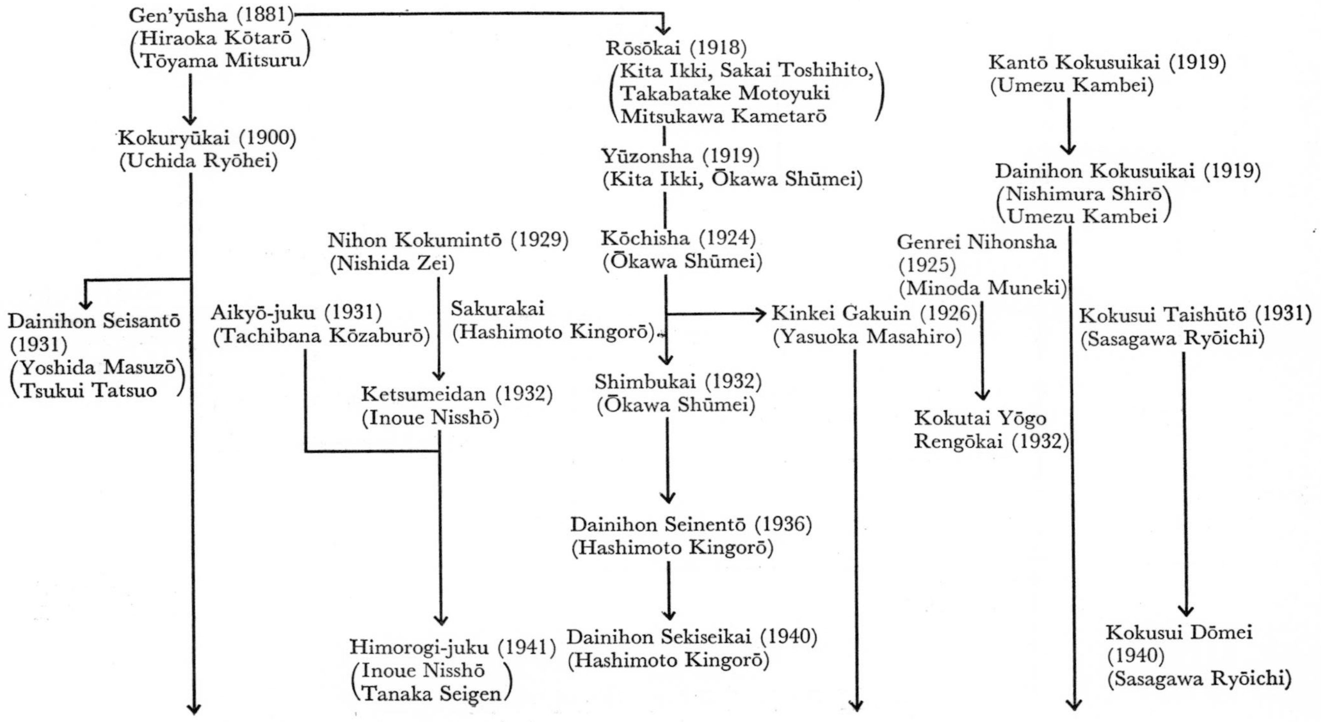

Gen'yūsha (1881)
(Hiraoka Kōtarō
Tōyama Mitsuru)
Kokuryūkai (1900)
(Uchida Ryōhei)
Dainihon Seisantō
(1931)
(Yoshida Masuzō
Tsukui Tatsuo)
Rōsōkai (1918)
(Kita Ikki, Sakai Toshihito,
Takabatake Motoyuki
Mitsukawa Kametarō)
Yūzonsha (1919)
(Kita Ikki, Ōkawa Shūmei)
Kōchisha (1924)
(Ōkawa Shūmei)
Nihon Kokumintō (1929)
(Nishida Zei)
Aikyō-juku (1931)
(Tachibana Kōzaburō)
Sakurakai
(Hashimoto Kingorō)
Ketsumeidan (1932)
(Inoue Nisshō)
Himorogi-juku (1941)
(Inoue Nisshō
Tanaka Seigen)
Shimbukai (1932)
(Ōkawa Shūmei)
Dainihon Seinentō (1936)
(Hashimoto Kingorō)
Dainihon Sekiseikai (1940)
(Hashimoto Kingorō)
Kinkei Gakuin (1926)
(Yasuoka Masahiro)
Genrei Nihonsha
(1925)
(Minoda Muneki)
Kokutai Yōgo
Rengōkai (1932)
Kantō Kokusuikai (1919)
(Umezu Kambei)
Dainihon Kokusuikai (1919)
(Nishimura Shirō
Umezu Kambei)
Kokusui Taishūtō (1931)
(Sasagawa Ryōichi)
Kokusui Dōmei
(1940)
(Sasagawa Ryōichi)

Right-Wing Organizations II

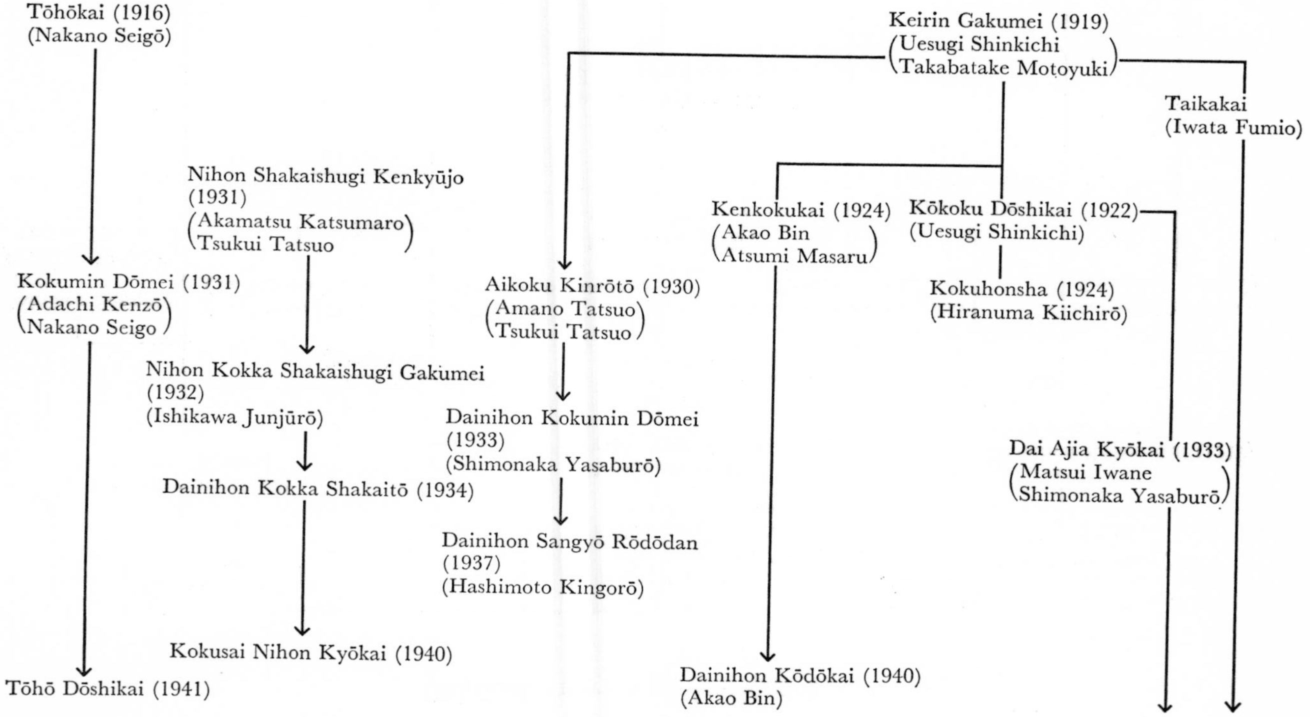

Political Parties

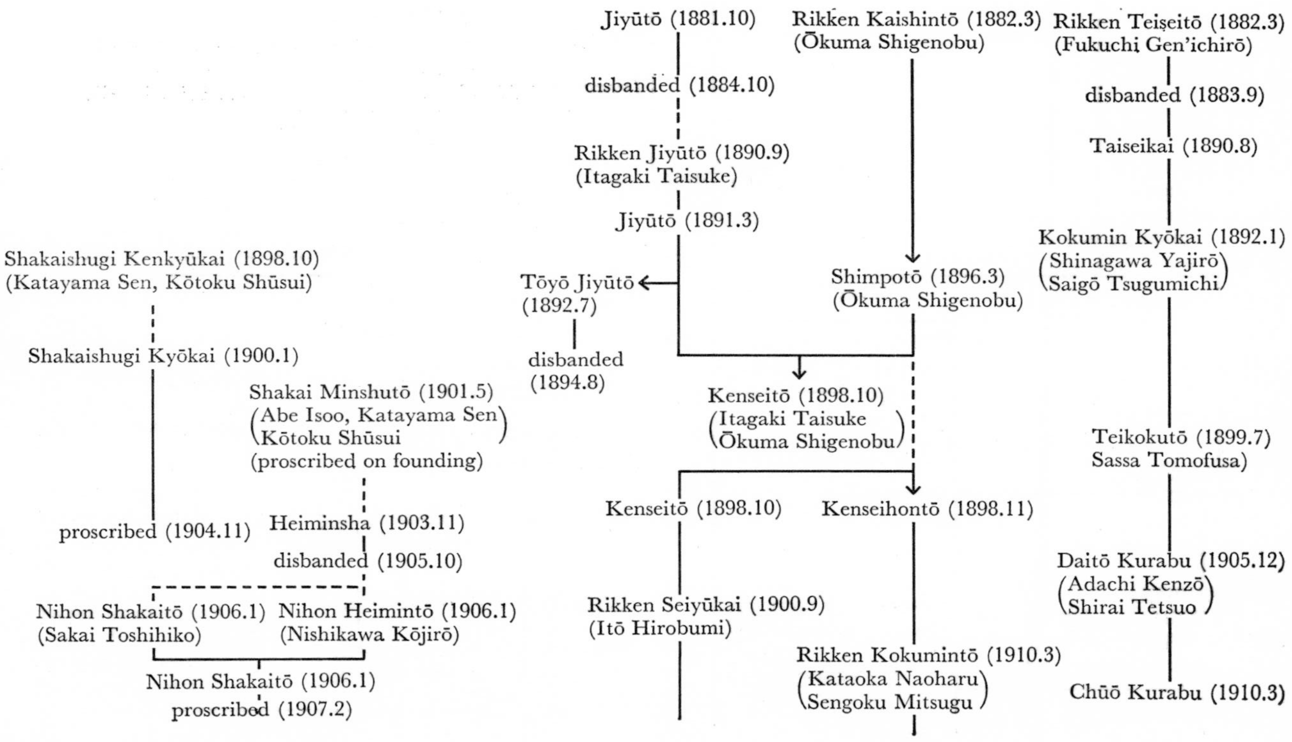

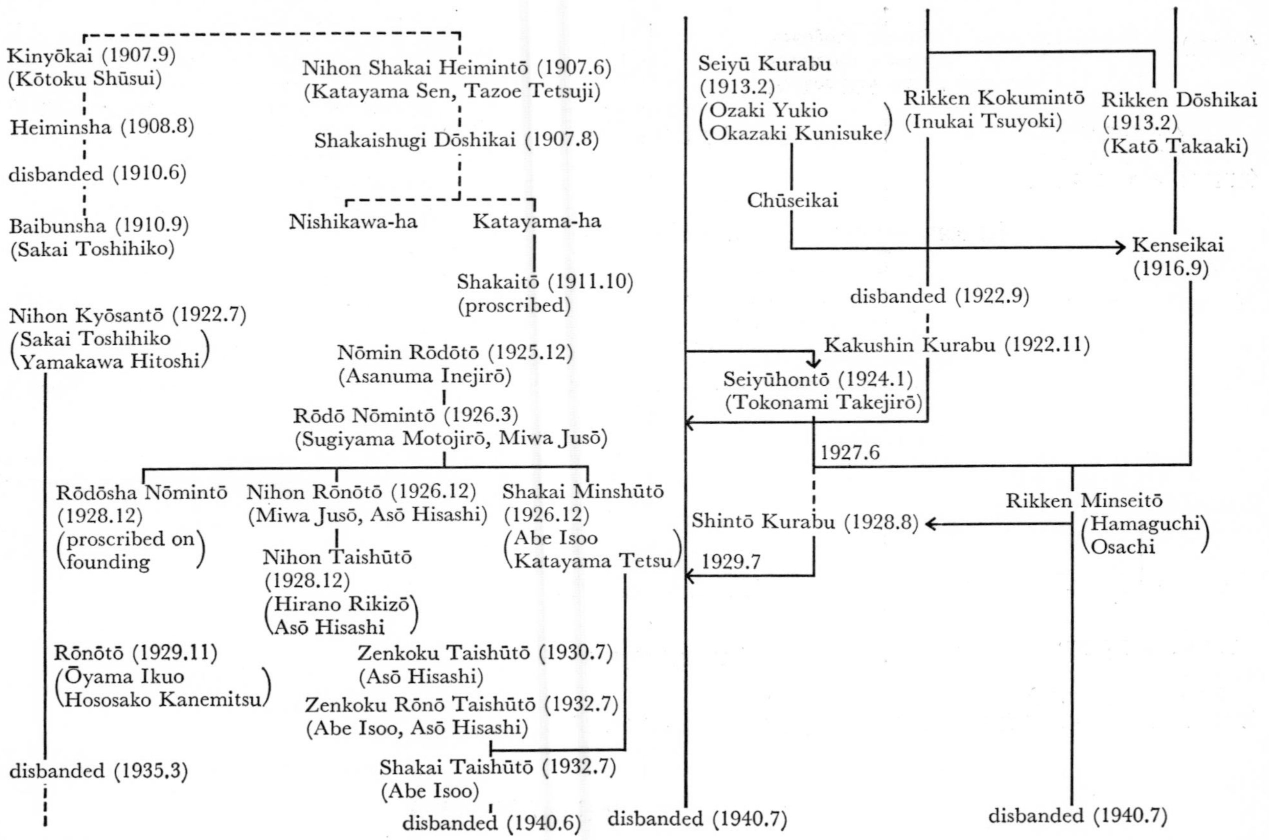
Kinyōkai (1907.9)
(Kōtoku Shūsui)
Heiminsha (1908.8)
disbanded (1910.6)
Baibunsha (1910.9)
(Sakai Toshihiko)
Nihon Kyōsantō (1922.7)
(Sakai Toshihiko
Yamakawa Hitoshi)
disbanded (1935.3)
Nihon Shakai Heimintō (1907.6)
(Katayama Sen, Tazoe Tetsuji)
Shakaishugi Dōshikai (1907.8)
Nishikawa-ha
Katayama-ha
Shakaitō (1911.10)
(proscribed)
Nōmin Rōdōtō (1925.12)
(Asanuma Inejirō)
Rōdō Nōmintō (1926.3)
(Sugiyama Motojirō, Miwa Jusō)
Rōdōsha Nōmintō
(1928.12)
(proscribed on
founding)
Nihon Rōnōtō (1926.12)
(Miwa Jusō, Asō Hisashi)
Nihon Taishūtō
(1928.12)
(Hirano Rikizō
Asō Hisashi)
Shakai Minshūtō
(1926.12)
(Abe Isoo
Katayama Tetsu)
Rōnōtō (1929.11)
(Ōyama Ikuo
Hososako Kanemitsu)
Zenkoku Taishūtō (1930.7)
(Asō Hisashi)
Zenkoku Rōnō Taishūtō (1932.7)
(Abe Isoo, Asō Hisashi)
Shakai Taishūtō (1932.7)
(Abe Isoo)
disbanded (1940.6)
Seiyū Kurabu
(1913.2)
(Ozaki Yukio
Okazaki Kunisuke)
Chūseikai
Rikken Kokumintō
(Inukai Tsuyoki)
Rikken Dōshikai
(1913.2)
(Katō Takaaki)
Kenseikai
(1916.9)
disbanded (1922.9)
Kakushin Kurabu (1922.11)
Seiyūhontō (1924.1)
(Tokonami Takejirō)
1927.6
Rikken Minseitō
(Hamaguchi
Osachi)
Shintō Kurabu (1928.8)
1929.7
disbanded (1940.7)
disbanded (1940.7)

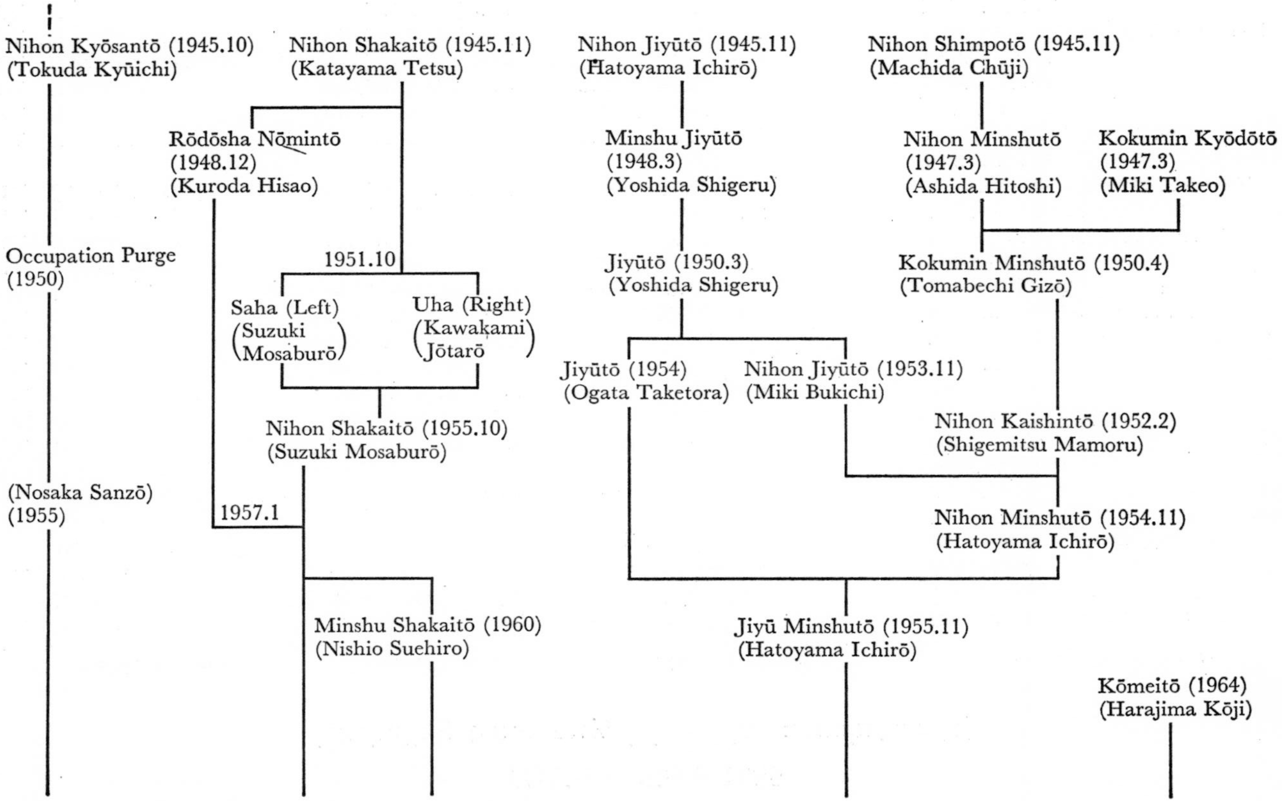
Nihon Kyōsantō (1945.10)
(Tokuda Kyūichi)
Nihon Shakaitō (1945.11)
(Katayama Tetsu)
Nihon Jiyūtō (1945.11)
(Hatoyama Ichirō)
Nihon Shimpotō (1945.11)
(Machida Chūji)
Rōdōsha Nōmintō
(1948.12)
(Kuroda Hisao)
Minshu Jiyūtō
(1948.3)
(Yoshida Shigeru)
Nihon Minshutō
(1947.3)
(Ashida Hitoshi)
Kokumin Kyōdōtō
(1947.3)
(Miki Takeo)
Occupation Purge
(1950)
1951.10
Jiyūtō (1950.3)
(Yoshida Shigeru)
Kokumin Minshutō (1950.4)
(Tomabechi Gizō)
Saha (Left)
(Suzuki Mosaburō)
Uha (Right)
(Kawakami Jōtarō)
Jiyūtō (1954)
(Ogata Taketora)
Nihon Jiyūtō (1953.11)
(Miki Bukichi)
Nihon Shakaitō (1955.10)
(Suzuki Mosaburō)
Nihon Kaishintō (1952.2)
(Shigemitsu Mamoru)
(Nosaka Sanzō)
(1955)
1957.1
Nihon Minshutō (1954.11)
(Hatoyama Ichirō)
Minshu Shakaitō (1960)
(Nishio Suehiro)
Jiyū Minshutō (1955.11)
(Hatoyama Ichirō)
Kōmeitō (1964)
(Harajima Kōji)

Cabinets Since 1885
(excluding temporary, joint-office appointments)

	Cabinet Name	Dates of Term	Prime Minister	Foreign Minister(s)
1.	Itō (1st)	1885.12,22–'88. 4,30	Itō Hirobumi	Inoue Kaoru, Ōkuma Shigenobu
2.	Kuroda	1888. 4,30–'89.12,24	Kuroda Kiyotaka	Ōkuma Shigenobu
3.	Yamagata (1st)	1889.12,24–'91. 5, 6	Yamagata Aritomo	Aoki Shūzō
4.	Matsukata (1st)	1891. 5, 6–'92, 8, 8	Matsukata Masayoshi	Aoki Shūzō, Enomoto Takeaki
5.	Itō (2nd)	1892. 8, 8–'96. 9,18	Itō Hirobumi	Mutsu Munemitsu, Saionji Kimmochi
6.	Matsukata (2nd)	1896. 9,18–'98. 1,12	Matsukata Masayoshi	Saionji Kimmochi, Ōkuma Shigenobu, Nishi Tokujirō
7.	Itō (3rd)	1898. 1,12–'98. 6,30	Itō Hirobumi	Nishi Tokujirō
8.	Ōkuma (1st)	1898. 6,30–'98.11, 8	Ōkuma Shigenobu	Ōkuma Shigenobu
9.	Yamagata (2nd)	1898.11, 8–1900.10,19	Yamagata Aritomo	Aoki Shūzō
10.	Itō (4th)	1900.10,19–'01. 6, 2	Itō Hirobumi	Katō Takaaki
11.	Katsura (1st)	1901. 6, 2–'06. 1, 7	Katsura Tarō	Terauchi Masakata, Komura Jutarō
12.	Sainoji (1st)	1906. 1, 7–'08. 7,14	Saionji Kimmochi	Katō Takaaki, Hayashi Tadasu
13.	Katsura (2nd)	1908. 7,14–'11. 8,30	Katsura Tarō	Komura Jutarō
14.	Saionji (2nd)	1911. 8,30–'12.12,21	Saionji Kimmochi	Uchida Kōsai
15.	Katsura (3rd)	1912.12,21–'13. 2,20	Katsura Tarō	Katsura Tarō, Katō Takaaki
16.	Yamamoto (1st)	1913. 2,20–'14. 4,16	Yamamoto Gombei	Makino Nobuaki
17.	Ōkuma (2nd)	1914. 4,16–'16.10, 9	Ōkuma Shigenobu	Katō Takaaki, Ōkuma Shigenobu, Ishii Kikujirō
18.	Terauchi	1916.10, 9–'18. 9,29	Terauchi Masakata	Motono Ichirō, Gotō Shimpei
19.	Hara	1918. 9,29–'21.11,13	Hara Takashi	Uchida Kōsai
20.	Takahashi	1921.11,13–'22, 6,12	Takahashi Korekiyo	Uchida Kōsai
21.	Katō (Tomosaburō)	1922. 6,12–'23. 9, 2	Katō Tomosaburō	Uchida Kōsai
22.	Yamamoto (2nd)	1923. 9, 2–'24. 1, 7	Yamamoto Gombei	Yamamoto Gombei, Ijūin Hikokichi
23.	Kiyoura	1924. 1, 7–'24. 6,11	Kiyoura Keigo	Matsui Keishirō

	Cabinet Name	Dates of Term	Prime Minister	Foreign Minister
24.	Katō (Takaaki) (1st)	1924. 6,11–'25. 8, 2	Katō Takaaki	Shidehara Kijūrō
25.	Katō (Takaaki) (2nd)	1925. 8, 2–'26, 1,30	Katō Takaaki	Shidehara Kijūrō
26.	Wakatsuki (1st)	1926. 1,30–'27, 4,20	Wakatsuki Reijirō	Shidehara Kijūrō
27.	Tanaka	1927. 4,20–'29, 7, 2	Tanaka Giichi	Tanaka Giichi
28.	Hamaguchi	1929. 7, 2–'31. 4,14	Hamaguchi Osachi	Shidehara Kijūrō
29.	Wakatsuki (2nd)	1931. 4,14–'31.12,13	Wakatsuki Reijirō	Shidehara Kijūrō
30.	Inukai	1931,12,13–'32. 5,36	Inukai Tsuyoki	Inukai Tsuyoki, Yoshizawa Kenkichi
31.	Saitō	1932. 5,26–'34. 7, 8	Saitō Makoto	Saitō Makoto, Uchida Kōsai, Hirota Kōki
32.	Okada	1934. 7, 8–'36. 3, 9	Okada Keisuke	Hirota Kōki
33.	Hirota	1936. 3, 9–'37. 2, 2	Hirota Kōki	Hirota Kōki, Arita Hachirō
34.	Hayashi	1937. 2,10–'37. 6, 4	Hayashi Senjūrō	Hayashi Senjūrō, Satō Naotake
35.	Konoe (1st)	1937. 6, 4–'39. 1, 5	Konoe Fumimaro	Hirota Kōki, Ugaki Kazushige, Konoe Fumimaro, Arita Hachirō
36.	Hiranuma	1939. 1, 5–'39. 8,30	Hiranuma Kiichirō	Arita Hachirō
37.	Abe	1939. 8,30–'40. 1,16	Abe Nobuyuki	Abe Nobuyuki, Nomura Kichisaburō
38.	Yonai	1940. 1,16–'40. 7,22	Yonai Mitsumasa	Arita Hachirō
39.	Konoe (2nd)	1940. 7,22–'41. 7,18	Konoe Fumimaro	Matsuoka Yōsuke
40.	Konoe (3rd)	1941. 7,18–'41.10,18	Konoe Fumimaro	Toyoda Teijirō
41.	Tōjō	1941.10,18–'44. 7,22	Tōjō Hideki	Tōgō Shigenori, Tōjō Hideki, Tani Masayuki, Shigemitsu Mamoru
42.	Koiso	1944. 7,22–'45. 4, 7	Koiso Kuniaki	Shigemitsu Mamoru
43.	Suzuki	1945. 4, 7–'45. 8,17	Suzuki Kantarō	Suzuki Kantarō, Tōgō Shigenori
44.	Higashikuninomiya	1945. 8,17–'45.10, 9	Higashikuninomiya Naruhiko	Shigemitsu Mamoru, Yoshida Shigeru
45.	Shidehara	1945.10, 9–'46, 5,22	Shidehara Kijūrō	Yoshida Shigeru
46.	Yoshida (1st)	1946. 5,22–'47. 5,24	Yoshida Shigeru	Yoshida Shigeru
47.	Katayama	1947. 5,24–'48. 3,10	Katayama Tetsu	Ashida Hitoshi
48.	Ashida	1948. 3,10–'48.10,15	Ashida Hitoshi	Ashida Hitoshi
49.	Yoshida (2nd)	1948.10,19–'49. 2,16	Yoshida Shigeru	Yoshida Shigeru
50.	Yoshida (3rd)	1949. 2,16–'52.10,30	Yoshida Shigeru	Yoshida Shigeru, Okazaki Katsuo

	Cabinet Name	Dates of Term	Prime Minister	Foreign Minister
51.	Yoshida (4th)	1952.10,30–'53. 5,21	Yoshida Shigeru	Okazaki Katsuo
52.	Yoshida (5th)	1953. 5,21–'54.12,10	Yoshida Shigeru	Okazaki Katsuo
53.	Hatoyama (1st)	1954,12,10–'55. 3,19	Hatoyama Ichirō	Shigemitsu Mamoru
54.	Hatoyama (2nd)	1955. 3,19–'55.11,22	Hatoyama Ichirō	Shigemitsu Mamoru
55.	Hatoyama (3rd)	1955.11,22–'56.12,23	Hatoyama Ichirō	Shigemitsu Mamoru
56.	Ishibashi	1956.12,23–'57. 2,25	Ishibashi Tanzan	Kishi Nobusuke
57.	Kishi (1st)	1957. 2,25–'58. 6,12	Kishi Nobusuke	Kishi Nobusuke, Fujiyama Aiichirō
58.	Kishi (2nd)	1958. 6,12–'60. 7,15	Kishi Nobusuke	Fujiyama Aiichirō
59.	Ikeda (1st)	1960. 7,19–'60.12, 8	Ikeda Hayato	Kosaka Zentarō
60.	Ikeda (2nd)	1960.12, 8–'63.12, 9	Ikeda Hayato	Kosaka Zentarō, Ōhira Masayoshi
61.	Ikeda (3rd)	1963.12, 9–'64.11, 9	Ikeda Hayato	Ōhira Masayoshi, Shiina Etsusaburō
62.	Satō (1st)	1964.11, 9–'67. 2,17	Satō Eisaku	Shiina Etsusaburō, Miki Takeo
63.	Satō (2nd)	1967. 2,17–'70. 1,14	Satō Eisaku	Miki Takeo, Aichi Kiichi
64.	Satō (3rd)	1970. 1,14–'72. 7, 7	Satō Eisaku	Aichi Kiichi, Fukuda Takeo
65.	Tanaka (1st)	1972. 7, 7–'72.12,22	Tanaka Kakuei	Ōhira Masayoshi
66.	Tanaka (2nd)	1972.12,22–'74.12, 9	Tanaka Kakuei	Ōhira Masayoshi, Kimura Toshio
67.	Miki	1974.12, 9–'76.12,24	Miki Takeo	Miyazawa Kiichi
68.	Fukuda	1976.12,24	Fukuda Takeo	Hatoyama Iichirō, Sonoda Sunao

Institutions and Terms

The Ritsuryō System

The term *ritsu* refers to criminal laws; *ryō* to ordinary laws and regulations. Together they form the designation of a bureaucratic form of government modeled on that of T'ang China and adapted to the conditions prevailing in Japan in early times.

Around the fourth and fifth centuries A.D., the Japanese islands were united under a single state centering about the Yamato court. During the regency of Crown Prince Shōtoku (593–622) and the period of the Taika Reforms, which began in 646, various steps were taken to increase the power of the central government and the prestige of the emperor who headed it. The Taika Reforms, in particular, instituted a bureaucratic system modeled on that of China, at this time under the rule the T'ang dynasty. Various laws were promulgated for the regulation of all areas and people of the country, and a system of government offices and officials set up to administer them.

This system of laws was put into final form in the *Taihō ritsuryō*, the penal and civil code completed in 701, the first year of the Taihō era. Certain revisions were made in the code in the following decade, the revised version being known as the *Yōrō ritsuryō*. The system of government set up by this code remained in nominal effect until 1885, when it was replaced by the cabinet system. In the latter part of this period, the system existed as a mere formality. But it functioned more or less effectively for the 550 years from the time of the Taika Reforms to the end of the Heian period in 1184, and it is customary to refer to this as the period of *ritsuryō* type government.

The government was headed by the emperor. Under him was a central bureaucracy presided over by two chief ministers, eight government bureaus or ministries, and various subordinate officials. A standardized system of local officials handled the administration of the various provinces, districts, and hamlets into which the country was divided, and military forces were stationed in the outlying areas to keep order. A law known as the *Handen shūju no hō*, promulgated in 652, mandated equal distribution of land to all farmers and fixed the taxes required of them. These taxes provided the fiscal basis for the government, while the members of the traditional aristocracy provided the personnel for the upper ranks of the bureaucracy.

ORGANIZATION OF THE RITSURYŌ *BUREAUCRACY*

Central Government

The central government was headed by two agencies. One was the Jingikan, which handled matters pertaining to the Shinto religion. The other was the Daijōkan, which had jurisdiction over the eight ministries and other organs of government and handled political affairs. The Daijōkan was headed by the *daijōdaijin*, *sadaijin*, and *udaijin*, who were known collectively as the Sankō, or Three Lords, as well as by *dainagon* and lesser officials, and had under its jurisdiction various offices and ministries.

Daijōdaijin: The *daijōdaijin*, or prime minister, was the highest government official and served as aide to the emperor. If there was no one who was regarded as suitable to fill the post, it was often left vacant. In the Heian period, it was seldom filled after the period in office of Fujiwara no Yoshifusa (804–872). Under certain special circumstances, the post was bestowed upon military leaders such as Taira no Kiyomori, Ashikaga Yoshimitsu, Toyotomi Hideyoshi, and Tokugawa Ieyasu.

Sadaijin: The *sadaijin*, minister of the left, also known as *ichi-no-kami*, acted as head of the Daijōkan when the office of *daijōdaijin* was vacant, and thus in many cases was the actual head of government.

Udaijin: The *udaijin*, or minister of the right, ranked directly below the minister of the left and, like him, served as an advisor to the emperor.

Dainagon: The *dainagon*, or great counselors, ranked below the Sankō, or Three Lords, described above, and handled affairs of state in their absence. The *Taihō ritsuryō* stipulated the there should be four persons in the post of *dainagon*, but the number was later increased.

The central government included the following eight ministries:

Nakatsukasashō: The Nakatsukasashō, or Ministry of Central Affairs, acted as attendant to the emperor and handled affairs within the palace such as the promulgation of imperial edicts and the presentation of memorials to the throne.

Shikibushō: The Shikibushō, or Ministry of Ceremony, handled matters pertaining to the promotion of civil officials and other personnel matters.

Jibushō: The Jibushō, or Ministry of Civil Administration, had charge of matters pertaining to the names, family succession, marriages, and funerals of officials of the fifth court rank or above, as well as matters pertaining to Buddhism and foreign affairs.

Mimbushō: The Mimbushō, or Ministry of the Interior, had charge of matters pertaining to cultivated lands, population registers, taxes, corvée labor, and other affairs pertaining to the populace in general.

Hyōbushō: The Hyōbushō, or Ministry of Military Affairs, handled the promotion of military officials and matters pertaining to troops, military installations, etc.

Gyōbushō: The Gyōbushō, or Ministry of Justice, handled judicial affairs.

Ōkurashō: The Ōkurashō, or Ministry of the Treasury, handled matters pertaining to tribute from the various provinces, government revenue and expenditure, currency, and weights and measures. This name is still used today for the Finance Ministry.

Kunaishō: The Kunaishō, or Ministry of the Imperial Household, handled general affairs pertaining to the court.

Other offices not originally provided for in the *ritsuryō* system were at later times added to the Daijōkan as the need arose. These included the offices of *chūnagon*, or middle counselor, *shōnagon*, or minor counselor, and *sangi*, or consultant. In the Heian period, two special offices developed out of that of *daijōdaijin*. One was that of *sesshō*, or regent, who handled affairs of state when the emperor was a minor. The other was that of *kampaku*, or chancellor, a chief official who reviewed state papers before they were presented to the emperor and acted as his assistant. These two posts were held for succeeding generations by members of the Fujiwara family, who in this way maintained control over the government.

In addition to the two government agencies described above, there was an agency called the Danjōdai, which was charged with the supervision of public morals and the maintenance of law and order, and various offices of palace guards such as the Emonfu, Sa- and U-Ejifu, and Sa-, and U-Hyōefu.

Local Government

The country as a whole was divided up into *kuni* (provinces), *gun* (districts), and *ri* (hamlets); the last were later renamed *gō*.

The provinces were headed by a *kokushi*, or governor, who was dispatched from the central government. The districts were headed by a *gunji*, or district head, who was selected from among the powerful families living in the district In addition, a special administrative area was set up in the capital, known as Kyōshiki, a second in the nearby province of Settsu known as Settsushiki, and a third in Kyushu known as the Dazaifu.

For military protection and the maintenance of order, one *gundan* (army unit) was usually set up for every four districts. Soldiers were recruited from among the peasant population by conscription.

Shogunate (*Bakufu*)

The term *bakufu* originally designated the curtained field headquarters of a military leader where the affairs of the army were conducted. Later, it came to refer to the administrations of the various military families that exercised de facto rule in Japan.

Seii-taishōgun (abbreviated to *shōgun*): The title *seii-taishōgun*, or Barbarian Subjugating Great General, was originally a temporary designation assigned to a military leader who was dispatched by the emperor to subjugate the Ezo people living in the northern region of the main island of Honshu. In 1192 the title was given to the military leader Minamoto no Yoritomo, who proceeded to set up a *bakufu*, or military headquarters, at Kamakura and establish a system of control over the various provinces. Thereafter, the term shogun came to designate the person who headed this military government. Yoritomo was succeeded as shogun by his sons Yoriie and Sanetomo, but thereafter the Minamoto line ended. Sanetomo, the third shogun of the Kamakura shogunate, was succeeded by two shoguns chosen from the Kujō branch of the Fujiwara family, members of the Kyoto aristocracy, and four shoguns chosen from the imperial family.

It became the custom to assign the title of shogun only to members of the Minamoto family. Thus the Ashikaga and Tokugawa families, who became shoguns in later centuries, were careful to trace their lineage back to some branch of the Minamoto family.

KAMAKURA SHOGUNATE

The system of military government established by Minamoto no Yoritomo is known as the Kamakura *bakufu* or shogunate and constitutes the beginning of the Japanese feudal system.

Yoritomo reserved to himself the right to appoint and dismiss *shugo* (constables) in all the provinces and *jitō* (stewards) in all public and private estates, and controlled all military and police power throughout the nation. In principle, these powers had been delegated to the shogun by the imperial court in Kyoto. The old *ritsuryō*, or bureaucratic, system of government centered around the Kyoto court remained nominally in existence, though actual power was wielded by the shogunate in Kamakura. Thus Japan at this time had two governments existing side by side.

The financial basis of the Kamakura shogunate was the Kantō Goryō—a large number of estates that had formerly belonged to the Taira clan but which were presented by the court to Yoritomo after his overthrow of the Tairas—and the Kantō Gobunkoku, a number of provinces over which Yoritomo had been given jurisdiction and to which, on his recommendation, various of his vassals were assigned as governors. Revenue from these estates and administrative areas supplied the funds needed by the shogunate, and the economic institutions in effect in the past were allowed to continue functioning as before.

In addition to its financial basis, the shogunate was supported and stabilized by the feudalistic ties that existed between the shogun and his *goke'nin* (vassals). The shogun confirmed his vassals in the possession of the domains that they had inherited from their forebears, and when they achieved victory in battle, he rewarded them by assigning them to posts as constables or stewards. They, in turn, were obligated to guard Kyoto and Kamakura and to carry out other duties in time of warfare or emergency.

ORGANIZATION OF THE KAMAKURA SHOGUNATE

Central Government

The most important organ in the shogunate administration was the Samuraidokoro, which handled all affairs pertaining to the *goke'nin* (vassals). Another office, the Kumonjo, later renamed the Mandokoro, handled the finances of the shogunate and ordinary matters of business. The Monchūjo handled law suits and other legal affairs. In 1249, however, a special office called the Hikitsukeshū was set up to handle law suits of the *goke'nin*, and the Monchūjo was thereafter limited to the handling of ordinary law suits and matters pertaining to debts.

Shikken: The highest official position in the shogunate under the shogun was that of *shikken* (regent). After the death of the first shogun, Yoritomo, the Hōjō family, the family of Yoritomo's wife and one of the most powerful retainer families, succeeded in overthrowing other important retainer families and assuming the directorship of both the Mandokoro and the Samuraidokoro. The members of the family took the official title of *shikken*, which became hereditary in the family, and thereafter wielded actual control over the shogunate. Yoritomo's line died out with the murder of the third shogun, Sanetomo, in 1219. Thereafter, youth of the Kujō branch of the Fujiwara family or of the imperial family were brought from Kyoto to fill the post of shogun, but all real power was in the hands of the members of the Hōjō family who held the office of *shikken*. In 1225 the regent Hōjō Yasutoki created the posts of *rensho* and *hyōjōshū*, and in 1249 the regent Hōjō Tokiyori created the office of Hikitsukeshū already mentioned above.

Rensho: The *rensho* acted as an assistant to the regent and, along with the regent, signed all documents issued by the shogunate. The post was always filled by an important member of the Hōjō family.

Hyōjōshū: The *hyōjōshū* was a group of officials that met with the regent to deliberate on legal and governmental matters and assist him in making decisions. Its members also served as the directors of the government offices already mentioned above, the Mandokoro, Monchūjo, and Hikitsukeshū.

LOCAL GOVERNMENT

Shugo: Minamoto no Yoritomo, having fallen out with his uncle Yukiie and his younger brother Yoshitsune, claimed that he needed special powers in order to search them out and arrest them. In 1185 he was accordingly granted special military and police powers by the emperor. These allowed him to appoint his vassals as *shugo* (constables) in the various provinces, to summon them together for the protection of Kyoto and Kamakura, and to take measures to arrest and punish those guilty of murder or treason. In theory, the *shugo* were not supposed to interfere with the powers of the *kokushi* (governors of the provinces) appointed by the court in Kyoto, but in fact the two authorities often conflicted.

Jitō: At the same time that he was granted permission to appoint *shugo* to the provinces, he was also permitted to appoint his vassals as *jitō* (stewards) to the various public and private estates throughout the country. These officials supervised the estates, collected taxes on behalf of the public or private owners, and carried out policing activities like the *shugo*. Toward the end of the Kamakura period, the vassals who held the position of *jitō* increasingly took illegal possession of the estates in their charge and added them to their own domains.

Kyoto *shugo:* The Kyoto *shugo* was an office created by the Kamakura shogunate and filled by a vassal of the shogunate. The official was charged with protecting and maintaining order in the city of Kyoto and overseeing communications between the shogunate and the imperial court. After the Jōkyū disturbance in 1221, the office was abolished and a new institution called the Rokuhara *tandai* set up in Kyoto to take over its functions.

Ōshū *sōbugyō:* In 1189, Minamoto no Yoritomo received imperial permission to lead a large force in an attack on the Fujiwaras living in the province of Mutsu (Ōshū) in the northern region of Honshu, ostensibly on the grounds that they had given shelter to Yoshitsune, his younger brother whom he was seeking to do away with. He succeeded in overthrowing the Fujiwaras and took possession of Mutsu and the neighboring province of Dewa. He thereupon created the office of Ōshū *sōbugyō* and appointed two of his vassals to head it. The office was charged with maintaining order in the area, handling law suits, and overseeing affairs pertaining to the vassals of the shogunate in the region.

Chinzei *bugyō:* Also called Chinzei *tandai*. Because the Taira clan had numerous connections in Kyushu, Minamoto no Yoritomo created the office of Chinzei *bugyō* in Kyushu in 1186, the year after defeating the Tairas. The office was situated at Dazaifu and exercised military and police power over Kyushu and supervised matters pertaining to the vassals of the shogunate in that area.

MUROMACHI SHOGUNATE

The Muromachi shogunate dates from 1338, when the military leader Ashikaga Takauji received the title of *seii-taishōgun* from the emperor of the Northern Court. For the following half century, the rivalry between the Northern Court in Kyoto and the Southern Court in the Yoshino area continued, but the dispute was finally resolved in 1392. In 1378, the third shogun, Ashikaga Yoshimitsu, established his residence at Muromachi in Kyoto and succeeded in strengthening the power of the shogun. As a result, the shogunate came to be referred to as the Muromachi *bakufu* or shogunate. The revenues that supported the shogunate came mainly from the lands under its direct control, though in times of need, it would also exact levies from the *shugo* and *jitō* of the various provinces. When its needs were particularly great, it imposed levies on the populace in general and it also derived funds from overseas trade and special taxes imposed upon wealthy merchants.

ORGANIZATION OF THE MUROMACHI SHOGUNATE

The administrative system of the Muromachi shogunate was modeled on that of the Kamakura shogunate and reached its final form around the time of the third shogun, Yoshimitsu.

Central Government

Kanrei: The office of *kanrei* (shogunal deputy) was the highest under that of shogun and in general corresponded to that of *shikken* in the Kamakura shogunate. The duties of the *kanrei* were to assist the shogun, but his powers were never as great as those exercised by the *shikken* in the Kamakura period. The *kanrei* was always chosen from one of the three branches of the Ashikaga clan, namely, the Shiba, Hatakeyama, and Hosokawa families.

Under the *kanrei's* jurisdiction were the offices of the Mandokoro, Monchūjo, and Samuraidokoro, but these bodies had far less power than their predecessors in the Kamakura period and were not consulted on matters of vital importance.

Mandokoro: The Mandokoro handled the finances of the shogunate, the household affairs of the shogun, and civil actions of a minor nature.

Monchūjo: The Monchūjo handled records and documents pertaining to the shogunate and legal disputes that arose over such documents.

Samuraidokoro: The Samuraidokoro was charged with maintaining order in Kyoto and its environs and handling promotions, punishments, and legal matters pertaining to the samurai or members of the warrior class. The office was the highest in the administration under the *kanrei* and was headed by an official chosen from one of four families, the Yamana, Akamatsu, Kyōgoku, and Isshiki.

In addition, other offices existed such as the *hyōjōshū* and Hikitsukeshū, but they had very little authority, the actual power being in the hands of the *bugyō*, or administrative offices.

Local Government

Kamakura-*fu:* Ashikaga Takauji, though he established his shogunate in Kyoto, fully realized the importance of maintaining control over the eastern region. For this reason he established his second son, Ashikaga Motouji, in Kamakura and gave him direct jurisdiction over ten provinces of the eastern region. The administrative system of the Kamakura-*fu*, as the office came to be known, was roughly the same as that of the shogunate in Kyoto, and the head of it constituted a kind of second shogun in the east. The position of head of the office passed down to Motouji's heirs, and the holder of the position was referred to as the Kamakura *kubō*.

Ōshū *tandai:* This office was charged with the supervision of military and civil affairs in the provinces of Mutsu and Dewa in northern Honshu.

Shugo, jitō: Shugo (constables) and *jitō* (stewards) were assigned to the various provinces and public and private estates as had been done in the Kamakura period. The *shugo*, however, had a much wider range of powers than they had possessed under the Kamakura shogunate. They officiated in disputes concerning stolen crops, and when the shogunate handed down a decision concerning a land dispute, they had the power to size the lands of the loser and turn them over to the winner.

In addition, in 1352 the shogunate granted permission to certain samurai, mainly those holding the position of *shugo*, to collect half the yearly revenue from estates owned by shrines and temples or members of the court aristocracy. This procedure was justified on the grounds that the crops were needed as provisions for fighting men in the event of an outbreak of war. It thereafter became customary for the *shugo* to collect revenues, a development that helped greatly to strengthen their economic position.

Thus the *shugo* gained increasing control over the lands in the province under their jurisdiction and came to treat the samurai living in the province as their personal retainers. Powerful figures known as *shugo* daimyo appeared, who gained control over large domains comprising a whole province or even a number of provinces, which they handed down to their heirs.

The *jitō* (stewards), as seen earlier, were members of the warrior class who managed to have themselves appointed as supervisors of public and private estates. Their task was to reside on the estate, oversee its management, collect revenues, and forward them to the absentee owner. But by taking advantage of the power that such duties gave them, they gradually came to set themselves up as rivals of the owners. Frequently, the owners, to avoid outright conflict with the *jitō*, would leave the management of the estate entirely to the latter, in return receiving from the *jitō* a fixed annual revenue. Thus, particularly during the troubled times of the conflict between the Northern and Southern Courts, the *jitō*, in effect, became the lords of small domains in the rural areas. This occurred at the time when the *shugo* were working to make themselves the lords of the provinces under their supervision, and the *jitō* therefore became the retainers of the *shugo* within whose jurisdiction their estates were situated.

EDO SHOGUNATE

The Edo shogunate, founded by Tokugawa Ieyasu, had its headquarters in the city of Edo, present-day Tokyo. It was officially founded in 1603, when Tokugawa Ieyasu received the title of *seii-taishōgun*. It lasted until 1867, or a period of 265 years, and was headed by a succession of fifteen shoguns. The shogun was the largest daimyo in the country, having a number of vassals or retainers known as *hatamoto* and *goke'nin* in his service. The lands under the direct control of the shogun brought in a revenue of approximately four million *koku* of rice a year, or seven million if the domains of the shogun's *hatamoto* retainers are included. This latter figure represents about one-fourth of the revenue of the country as a whole. The shoguns in the Edo period had far greater power than their predecessors in the Kamakura and Muromachi periods. These included the right to appoint or dismiss daimyo in the other domains, a monopoly over important mines, exclusive power to mint currency, direct jurisdiction over such important cities as Edo, Kyoto, Osaka, and Nagasaki, and exclusive control over the limited foreign trade carried out with the Chinese and Dutch via the port of Nagasaki.

Daimyo: During the Edo period, the term *daimyō* was commonly used to designate military leaders who were recognized by the shogun as possessors of domains with a revenue of ten thousand *koku* or more of rice and who had large numbers of retainers in their service. They were also referred to as *hanshu*, "domain lords," or *shokō*, "feudal lords."

The term *daimyō* dates back to the latter part of the Heian period. At that time the old system of land tenure was breaking down and large numbers of farmers were farming land that belonged to the great estates known as *shōen* or to branches of the government. The more powerful of these farmers, in order to assert ownership over the lands that they farmed and that were contracted to them, attached their names to the lands, referring to them as so-and-so's *myō* or "name." Lands that were designated by the name of the user-owner came to be known as *myōden*, or "name fields," and the owner as *myōshu*, or "name (field) lord." Those who possessed large land holdings were called *daimyōshu*, those who possessed small holdings, *shōmyōshu*.

Because of the troubled state of the times, the more powerful of these landowners and farmers were obliged to provide military protection for their estates, and thus many of them in time came to be important military leaders. In the Kamakura period, these military leaders came to be referred to as *daimyō*. The term continued in use in the Muromachi period that followed. In order to distinguish the *daimyō* of this period from those of the Edo period, Japanese historians customarily refer to them as *shugo daimyō* or *Sengoku daimyō*.

In the Edo period, when a new shogun was appointed or when a new daimyo became lord of a domain, he received from the shogun a register of the lands in his domain sealed with a vermilion seal, thus confirming his right to the domain. In return, he was obliged to reside in Edo for certain stipulated periods of time (usually six months) according to the system known as *sankin kōtai*, or "alternate attendance," and to provide funds and labor for various building and maintenance projects ordered by the shogunate. Within his own domain, the daimyo was granted the authority to control his retainers and direct the affairs of the domain as he saw fit.

In the early years of the Edo period, the shogunate frequently moved daimyo around from one domain to another, reduced their holdings, or deprived them of their domains outright. But from the time of the third shogun, Tokugawa Iemitsu, the position of the daimyo became much more stable. The total number ranged around 260 to 270.

The daimyo fell into three categories. First were the *shimpan*, or daimyo who were closely related to the family of the shogun. Next were the *fudai* daimyo, who constituted the most numerous class. The *fudai*, whose domains were of fifty thousand *koku* or less, consisted of those lords who had already become vassals of the Tokugawa family before the crucial battle of Sekigahara in 1600. Though their domains were small, they were a part of the shogunate administrative system and were often given the opportunity to participate in shogunal affairs.

The third and last category of daimyo were the *tozama*, consisting of such powerful families as the Maeda, the Shimazu of Kagoshima, and the Mōri of Nagato who had submitted to the Tokugawa family only after the battle of Sekigahara. Though many of them possessed large domains, they were on principle forbidden to hold office in the shogunate. However, in the late years of the Edo period, the arrival of foreign ships in Japanese waters gave the *tozama* lords the opportunity to increase their power, and in the end they led the movement that overthrew the shogunate in 1867.

ORGANIZATION OF THE EDO SHOGUNATE

Tairō: The office of *tairō* (regent) was the highest in the Edo shogunate. An appointment was made only in time of crisis, but when made, the *tairō* took precedence over the *rōjū* (councilors). The office was filled by a man chosen from among the *fudai* daimyo with a revenue of one hundred thousand *koku* or more, though in effect the office was monopolized by the four powerful daimyo families of Sakai, Doi, Ii, and Hotta. There were a total of ten *tairō* in the course of the Edo period. Particularly famous is the *tairō* Ii Naosuke, who in 1858 signed trade treaties with the United States, Holland, Russia, England, and France.

Rōjū: The *rōjū* (councilors of state), who usually numbered four or five, were in normal times the highest officials in the shogunate. They were selected from among *fudai* daimyo with a revenue of 25,000 *koku* or more. The *rōjū* performed their duties in turn, each one taking responsibility for a month at a time. The senior member among the *rōjū* was known as the *rōjū shuza*. Matsudaira Sadanobu, who was appointed to that position in 1787, succeeded in greatly increasing the powers of the office. Another famous holder of the office was Mizuno Tadakuni, who instituted a series of government measures known as the Tempō Reforms during the years 1841–43.

In 1866, the system of monthly rotation of duties was abandoned, and the *rōjū* were given specific assignments such as navy minister, army minister, minister of finance, minister of foreign affairs, etc. Katsu Kaishū was appointed army minister and as such persuaded Tokugawa Yoshinobu, the last shogun, to hand over Edo Castle without resistance when the shogunate came to an end in 1867.

Wakadoshiyori: The *wakadoshiyori* (assistant councilors of state) ranked below the *rōjū* in the shogunate administration. There were customarily three to five of them, chosen from among the *fudai* daimyo of moderate revenue. Like the *rōjū*, they took turns serving a month at a time.

Sobayōnin: The *sobayōnin* (chamberlain to the shogun) was an official who regularly attended the shogun and conveyed his orders to the *rōjū*. The *sobayōnin* was treated as a *rōjū*, though his actual rank was somewhere between that of *rōjū* and *wakadoshiyori*. Yanagisawa Yoshiyasu, who rose from a relatively humble position to become *sobayōnin* to the fifth shogun, Tokugawa Tsunayoshi, is famous for the ability and forcefulness that he displayed in that office.

Ōmetsuke: The *ōmetsuke* (major overseers) were officials responsible for supervision of the activities and personnel of the shogunate. Because they were also charged with supervision of the daimyo, they are often called daimyo *metsuke*. There were four or five persons appointed to the office.

Metsuke: The *metsuke* (overseers) acted as informants for the *wakadoshiyori*, supervising the *hatamoto* and *goke'nin* vassals of the shogun and making certain that officials assigned to the various branches of the shogunate administration were carrying out their duties properly. Because their special function was to ferret out maladministration, they wielded considerable power. There were ten *metsuke*, chosen from among the *hatamoto*.

Bugyō: The term *bugyō* originally meant to receive orders from a superior and carry them out, though in time it came to designate the person who bears chief responsibility for some activity. In the Kamakura shogunate and the shogunates that followed, various kinds of *bugyō* were appointed to carry out different activities. In the Edo shogunate, some twenty or thirty persons held this title, some assigned to positions in the central administration in Edo, others to posts in the provinces. The latter were known as *angoku bugyō*. The most important *bugyō* were the *jisha bugyō*, *kanjō bugyō*, and *machi bugyō*, referred to collectively as the "three *bugyō*."

Jisha bugyō: An office charged with the supervision of temples and shrines throught the country and the handling of affairs pertaining to their maintenance. The office had existed earlier in the Kamakura and Muromachi shogunates, but in the Edo shogunate it was made the highest of the three *bugyō* mentioned above and placed directly under the direction of the shogun. The office usually was held by four *fudai* daimyo, who took turns exercising responsibility for a month at a time.

Kanjō bugyō: The *kanjō bugyō* were the chief financial officials of the shogunate government, having charge of collecting taxes, managing the shogunate's finances, and handling law suits concerning the lands under its direct jurisdiction. They had under them a large number of local officials such as *gundai* and *daikan*, who handled financial and civil affairs in the shogun's domains. Four *hatamoto* were selected to hold the office, which was under the supervision of the *rōjū*. Particularly famous holders of the office include Ogiwara Shigehide, who served under the shogun Tokugawa Tsunayoshi and carried out currency reforms in 1695, and Oguri Tadamasa, who in the late years of the Edo period cooperated with the French minister Leon Roche in reforming the finances of the shogunate and planning the creation of a Western style army.

Kinza, Ginza: The Edo shogunate reserved to itself the sole right to mint gold and silver coins. The offices of Kinza and Ginza were established under the supervision of the *kanjō bugyō*, who contracted with them for the minting of gold and silver coins respectively. At first such offices were located in several places around the country, but soon after were restricted to the two offices in Edo. The Kinza in Edo was located on the site now occupied by the Bank of Japan in Tokyo.

Machi bugyō: The term *machi bugyō* by itself refers to the officials in charge of the government of the city of Edo. There were similar officials in some other cities such as Kyoto or Osaka, who were designated by the term *machi bugyō* prefixed by the name of the city. The *machi bugyō* of Edo were under the jurisdiction of the *rōjū* and had charge of civil, legal, and police administration within the city of Edo. Two men were selected from the *hatamoto* to hold the office, and they took turns exercising authority a month at a time. There were two administrative headquarters, one in the northern part of the city and the other in the southern part. The *machi bugyō* had under them various minor officials such as *yoriki* and *dōshin*. Most of the actual policing and management of the city was carried out by the townsmen themselves, who were appointed to such civic offices as *machi doshiyori* and *machi nanushi*. Ōoka Tadasuke, who became a *machi bugyō* of Edo in 1717, is particularly noted for his administrative skill and fairness in making legal decisions.

Shoshidai: The *shoshidai* was a shogunate official who was appointed to reside in Kyoto and supervise the city and the imperial court and aristocracy. He had control over the Kyoto *machi bugyō*, Fushimi *machi bugyō*, and Nara *machi bugyō*, and also handled legal matters pertaining to the shogun's domains in the eight provinces in the vicinity of Kyoto. In addition, he kept watch over the activities of the daimyo in western Honshu, Shikoku, and Kyushu. The holder of the office was chosen from among the *fudai* daimyo. Itakura Katsushige, who held the office from 1603 to 1620, and his son Shigemune, who held the office from 1620 to 1654, are well known as administrators.

Jōdai: The *jōdai* were officials appointed to guard various castles belonging to the shogun such as Osaka Castle, Nijō Castle in Kyoto, Fushimi Castle, Sumpu Castle, etc., and to supervise the officials attached to the castles. Because the *jōdai* were often in charge of very large and strategic fortifications such as Osaka Castle and because they were charged with the responsbility of keeping watch over the movements of the daimyo in western Japan, they were chosen from among the *fudai* daimyo with a revenue of sixty thousand *koku* or more.

The Dajōkan System

This was the form of organization used for the central government from the beginning of the Meiji Restoration in 1868 until the formation of a cabinet type government in 1885, or from the 21st day of the 4th intercalary month of Keiō 4 until December 22nd of Meiji 18. It was based on the *ritsuryō* system.

1. The first step in the establishment of this system took place in 1868 on the date mentioned above, when a statement on the form of government was promulgated. This stated in part, "In order to avoid the confusion that might arise if government ordinances issued from more than one source, all power shall be vested in the Dajōkan. The powers shall be divided into the three categories of administrative, legislative, and judicial, and three bodies shall be set up to execute these three powers respectively."

At this time the Dajōkan, or Supreme Council of State, presided over seven government bodies, which included the Giseikan, the legislative body; the Gyōseikan, the administrative body with is five departments of state; and the Kensatsukan, the judicial body. The changes in the Dajōkan system in the first years of Meiji were very rapid, making it difficult to present a clear picture of its structure.

2. As a second step, revisions in the bureaucratic system were carried out on the 8th day of the 7th month of Meiji 2, 1869. At that time, the Dajōkan was put in charge of six ministries, namely, the Ōkurashō (Finance Ministry), the Hyōbushō (Ministry of Military Affairs), the Gyōbushō (Ministry of Justice), the Kunaishō (Ministry of the Imperial Household), the Gaimushō (Foreign Ministry), and the Mimbushō (Ministry of Public Works). At this time, in keeping with the ancient Japanese concept of the unity of religious and governmental functions, the Department of the Shinto Religion was elevated to a position superior to the Dajōkan.

3. A third reorganization was carried out in 1871 with the official abolishment of feudalism. On the 29th day of the 7th month of Meiji 4, 1871, a three-chamber system was set up, the Dajōkan being organized into the Seiin, or Central Chamber, the Sain, or Chamber of the Left, and the Uin, or Chamber of the Right.

The Seiin was the highest organ within the Dajōkan, being made up of the *dajōdaijin* (prime minister), the *sadaijin* and *udaijin* (ministers of the left and right respectively), and the *sangi* (councilors). The emperor attended in person and presided over the making of decisions.

The Sain deliberated on legislative matters. It developed into the body known as the Genrōin (Senate), which lasted from 1875 to 1890.

The Uin was made up of the ministers (*kyō*) and vice-ministers (*taiyū*) of the various ministries and handled affairs pertaining to the ministries.

The Cabinet System

The system was established in December 1885 (Meiji 18) and made the cabinet the highest administrative organ of the state. Previously the Dajōkan system had been in effect, in which the government was headed by a *dajōdaijin* (prime minister) and ministers of the left and right, chosen from among the members of the imperial family and the peerage. With the promulgation of a constitution scheduled for 1889, it was felt that changes in the system of government should be made in order to insure faster and more efficient handling of state affairs. Hence the *naikaku,* or cabinet, system was introduced.

The cabinet consists of the *naikaku sōridaijin* or *shushō,* commonly referred to in English as prime minister, and the heads of the various government ministries. The system was modeled on that of Prussia and gives the prime minister, as head of the cabinet, a wide range of powers. The first cabinet was formed in 1885 with Itō Hirobumi as prime minister.

According to the Meiji Constitution promulgated in 1889, the cabinet was not in any way responsible to the Diet, which was set up by the constitution, and hence was entirely independent of Diet control. For a long time, the selection of the prime minister was carried out by the *genrō,* a group of elder statemen whose existence and functions were not recognized in the Constitution.

In actual practice, the cabinet, though the highest administrative organ, was rather restricted in its functions. This was because the war and navy ministers were military officials who could appeal directly to the emperor as supreme commander of military forces, and because the Privy Council, the highest advisory body to the emperor, often interferred with the cabinet in important matters of state.

In the early days of the system, the cabinet tended to be made up largely of men from the old domain cliques of Satsuma, Chōshū, Tosa, and Hizen. But with the establishment and growth of political parties, it became customary to choose party members for cabinet posts. The first true party cabinet was formed in 1898 when the Jiyūtō (Liberal Party) and Shimpotō (Progressive Party) combined to form the Kenseitō, or Constitution Party. It was headed by Ōkuma Shigenobu and is known as the first Ōkuma cabinet. Beginning with the first Katō Takaaki cabinet in 1924, the *giin naikaku* system was adopted, by which cabinet members were selected from the Diet.

After the fall of the Inukai Tsuyoshi cabinet as a result of the May 15 incident in 1932, party cabinets came to an end and were replaced by cabinets made up of military officers and bureaucrats. After the first Konoe Fumimaro cabinet in 1937, the selection of the prime minister was removed from the *genrō* and assigned to the Jūshin Kaigi, a body of senior statesmen headed by the *naidaijin,* or Lord Keeper of the Privy Seal, and made up of the president of the Privy Council and former prime ministers.

Under the new constitution promulgated after the conclusion of the Pacific War, the prime minister is appointed by the Diet, which is the elected representative of the people, and the cabinet he forms is collectively responsible to the Diet. Party cabinets have become the rule.

Political Parties

Japanese political parties fall into two main categories. First are those that derive from the popular rights movement of the 1870s, which called for the creation of a constitutional form of government and an elected legislature. Second are those that are anti-Establishment in nature, advocate socialism, and have their basis in the labor movement that came to sudden prominence in the 1890s.

The earliest nationwide parties in the first category were the Jiyūtō (Liberal Party) formed in 1881 and the Rikken Kaishintō (Progressive Party) founded in 1882. The Jiyūtō, headed by Itagaki Taisuke, advocated French style radicalism, argued that sovereignty resides in the people, and called for universal suffrage and the establishment of a unicameral legislature. It drew its support mainly from landowners, independent farmers, and *shizoku* (descendants of samurai). The Rikken Kaishintō was headed by Ōkuma Shigenobu, advocated English style gradualism, believed that sovereignty resided in the ruler and the populace as a whole, and called for the establishment of a bicameral legislature. It was supported mainly by wealthy businessmen in the cities.

Standing in opposition to these was the Rikken Teiseitō headed by Fukuchi Gen'ichirō, which supported the government and insisted that sovereignty resided in the ruler alone.

The Jiyūtō, which played a leading role in the popular rights movement, from the time of its formation showed great vigor in fighting for its principles. But it was weakened by appeasement and pressure from the government, and worsening economic conditions led the members of the landlord class to look with distrust upon the radicalism advocated by the party and to withdraw their support. As a result, the party was disbanded in 1884. Meanwhile, the Kaishintō, having lost Ōkuma as its leader, failed to attract widespread support.

When the first general election was held in 1890, the old Jiyūtō, reestablished under the name Rikken Jiyūtō, gained a number of seats in the Lower House of the Diet, where it worked to strengthen the rights of the people and reduce government expenditures. Along with the Kaishintō, which had also won seats in the election, it came to be known as the *mintō* or "people's party," standing in opposition to the bureaucratic faction and other groups that supported the government. In time, however, both parties became increasingly conciliatory in attitude, and after the conclusion of the Sino-Japanese War in 1895, they customarily supported the government. In 1898 the Jiyūtō combined with the Shimpotō, as the Kaishintō had been renamed, to form a new party called the Kenseitō (Constitution Party) headed by Ōkuma and Itagaki. Ōkuma proceeded to form the first party cabinet in Japanese history, but it quickly fell. The old Jiyūtō members reorganized the Kenseitō and joined the Seiyūkai (Association of Political Friends) organized by Itō Hirobumi in 1900. The group that had originally belonged to the Kaishintō reformed under the name Kenseihontō, and later under the name Kokumintō, playing an active role as an opposition party. But in 1913 the majority of the members joined the political party formed by Katsura Tarō, in time forming an association called the Rikken Dōshikai and headed by Katō Takaaki. The organization was later renamed Kenseikai, and still later, Rikken Minseitō, sharing political prominence with its rival, the Seiyūkai.

In 1918 Hara Takashi formed a cabinet made up mainly of members of the Seiyūkai. In 1924, Katō Takaaki of the Kenseikai formed a cabinet, and thereafter until the formation of the Inukai cabinet in 1932, it became customary to form cabinets made up of several political parties.

Turning now to political parties in the second category, one finds that the earliest was the Shakai Minshutō (Social Democratic Party) formed by Abe Isoo and others in May, 1901. It espoused socialism and democracy and firmly declared itself in opposition to capitalism, militarism, and the class system. On the very day of its formation it was ordered dissolved by the fourth Itō Hirobumi cabinet. In 1906 the Nihon Shakaitō (Japan Socialist Party) was formed but was outlawed the following year, and similar attempts met with severe government opposition, culminating in the lèse-majesté affair of 1910, when

Kōtoku Shūsui and other socialists were arrested on suspicion of plotting the assassination of the emperor and were condemned to death the following year.

The Nihon Kyōsantō (Japan Communist Party) was formed in 1922, though its existence was illegal. In 1925 the universal male suffrage law was promulgated, and the following year the socialists formed a legally recognized proletarian party known as the Rōdō Nōmintō (Labor Farmer Party). It quickly split apart because of ideological differences, the right-wing faction forming the Shakai Minshūtō (Social Democratic Party), the cental faction the Nihon Rōnōtō (Japan Labor Farmer Party), and the left-wing faction the Rōdō Nōmintō (Labor Farmer Party). These groups were subjected to increasingly severe government pressure and split apart and reformed a number of times.

In 1940, as the militarists gained increasing power, all political parties were ordered disbanded and their members were absorbed into an organization known as the Taisei Yokusankai, or Imperial Rule Assistance Association.

With the conclusion of the Pacific War in 1945, the old prewar political parties were revived. The most important parties to appear on the scene were the Nihon Jiyūtō (Liberal Party), the Nihon Shimpotō (Progressive Party), and the Nihon Shakaitō (Socialist Party); and the Nihon Kyōsantō (Communist Party) also resumed open political activity. In November, 1955, the Liberal and Progressive parties, along with other conservative parties, merged to form the Jiyū Minshutō (Liberal Democratic Party). In 1960 the Socialist Party split, the dissidents forming a new party called the Minshu Shakaitō (Democratic Socialist Party). Another new party, the Kōmeitō (Clean Government Party), was formed in 1964 by members of the Sōka Gakkai, a lay Buddhist organization associated with one of the branches of the Nichiren sect. Thus, in the postwar period, moderate parties have dominated the political scene, and there has been a tendency for the number of political parties to increase.

Right-Wing Groups *(Uyoku Dantai)*

The term *uyoku dantai* refers to groups active in political and social affairs that are reactionary, anti-Communist, and ultranationalist in nature. The first of such groups to appear in Meiji period Japan was the Gen'yōsha, founded in 1881. It was followed by the Kokuryūkai (the Amur River Society, more often called the Black Dragon Society), founded in 1900. These Meiji period groups were antiforeign in nature and urged a strong foreign policy and Japanese expansion in Asia.

The First World War was followed by the period of so-called Taishō democracy, when various democratic and socialist movements appeared. Reaction to these took shape under the slogan *kokusui hozon*, "preservation of the national essence." Two groups of this nature were founded in 1919, the Dai-Nihon Kokusuikai (Japan National Essence Society) and the Kantō Kokusuikai (Kantō National Essence Society), to be followed in 1921 by the Yamato Minrōkai. These groups increasingly used violence in an attempt to disrupt the labor movement and other popular movements.

In the early Shōwa period, particularly after the depression of the thirties set in, groups began to appear from the right wing that called for the establishment of national socialism and the carrying out of extensive government reforms. The forerunner of these fascist groups was the Keirin Dōmei founded in 1919 by Takabatake Motoyuki and Uesugi Shinkichi, which disappeared in time but was followed by a number of groups of a similar nature. Through organizations related to the earlier Gen'yōsha group such as the Yūsonsha (Society for Preservation of the National Essence) and the Shimbukai, right-wing thinkers such as Ōkawa Shūmei and Kita Ikki came to exert increasing influence. These groups linked up with national reform groups in the military such as the Sakurakai (Cherry Society), and planned and carried out such terrorist activities and attempts at a coup d'état as the March incident of 1931, the May 15 incident of 1932, and the February 26 incident of 1936. The same groups helped pave the way for the Pacific War.

After the Pacific War, the right-wing groups were disbanded on order of the Occupation authorities, but they reappeared following the conclusion of the peace treaties in 1952. During the sixties, they frequently engaged in brawls with groups demonstrating against the Japan–American Treaty of Mutual Security and Cooperation and were behind the assassination of the chairman of the Socialist Party Asanuma Inejirō in 1960. More recently, they have carried out attacks on radical student groups and have been active in opposing the growth of the Communist Party.

The right-wing groups in the period before the Pacific War belonged to two categories, the theorist groups, which expounded Japanese nationalism, and the reformist groups, which supported national socialism and highly organized right-wing activites. In the postwar period, they are classifiable only by the fact that some are prewar in origin and others are postwar.

Militarists (*Gumbatsu*)

The term *gumbatsu*, used to refer to groups of military men who employ their positions and power to seize political control, is usually translated in English as military cliques or militarists.

The government in the early Meiji period was dominated by the so-called clan clique, which was made up largely of men from the former clans or domains of Satsuma and Chōshū. Because the country at this time was pursuing a policy summed up in the slogan "enrich the nation and strengthen the military," the government tended to be militaristic in nature and the militarists emerged as a central force that dominated the government.

Up to the time of the First World War the militarists from Satsuma dominated the navy, and those from Chōshū dominated the army. The militarists were able to gain political power because of the fact that the emperor was the supreme commander of all military forces. Affairs pertaining to the military were handled separately from other matters of state, and the chief of the Army General Staff and chief of the Navy General Staff consulted with the emperor in making decisions on them. The war and navy ministers, who had charge of military administration, were both military officials, and they had the right to appeal directly to the emperor, the supreme commander, without referring the matter to a cabinet conference. As a result, militarists were often able to exercise life and death control over a cabinet and from time to time assumed the post of prime minister.

After the First World War, Japan embarked on a period of disarmament. The militarists became the target of considerable criticism, and for a time the influence of the men of Satsuma and Chōshū over the military forces was considerably lessened. During the twenties, however, Ugaki Kazushige, a general who served some seven years as war minister, set about reducing, improving, and modernizing the army, and in time became the leader of a new group known as the Ugaki Clique.

In March, 1931, a group of young army officers plotted to carry out a coup d'état to set up a military government headed by War Minister Ugaki, but the plan was called off. Ugaki was replaced as war minister by General Araki Sadao, who proceeded to remove all members of the Ugaki Clique, the most powerful clique up until this time, from positions of importance, and to replace them with members of his own group. This led to the formation of what came to be known as the Kōdō, or Imperial Way, faction. The group was dominated by the idealism of such men as Araki Sadao and Masaki Jinzaburō and was supported by a number of young officers who favored direct action, including attempts at a coup d'état, to carry out reforms in the government. In contrast to this group was another known as the Tōsei, or Control, faction, which rejected the approach of the Araki Clique and opposed any attempt at a coup.

After Araki retired from the post of war minister, the opposition between the two groups grew increasingly bitter. In 1935 Nagata Tetsuzan, a leader of the Tōsei Clique, was murdered by Lieutenant Colonel Aizawa Saburō of the Kōdō faction. On February 26 of the following year, a number of young officers of the Kōdō faction attempted to carry out a coup, attacking and killing high government officials. The leaders of the attack, however, were put to death as rebels and the group declined in influence. The Tōsei faction thereafter allied itself with leaders of the political and financial world and in time gained a position of leadership among all the military forces. In time Tōjō Hideki and the other leaders of the group succeeded in establishing a dictaorship of the military and led Japan into the Pacific War.

Tokyo University

Tokyo University was established in 1877, the first government university to be set up in Japan. It had its origin, however, in various educational institutions set up late in the Edo period by the Tokugawa shogunate for the study of Western science and culture.

In 1811 the shogunate selected a number of outstanding scholars of Dutch learning (*rangaku*), as Western studies were called at the time, and assigned them to the shogunate astronomical observatory in Edo to translate Dutch books. In 1854, treaties of friendship were signed between Japan and the United States and other foreign nations, and the country was opened for limited foreign trade. In 1855, the Temmongata Bansho Wage Goyō, as the office for the translation of Dutch books was known, was made into an independent organization, established in a place called the Yōgakusho (Office for Western Studies). In 1857 the name was changed to Bansho Shirabesho (Office for the Study of Foreign Books), and a school was initiated. The institution thus performed two functions, translating Western books and studying and teaching Western studies.

In 1862 the institution was moved to Hitotsubashi and renamed the Yōsho Shirabesho, and the following year the name was again changed, this time to Kaiseijo.

At first the only language studied and taught was Dutch, but later English, French, German, and Russian were added. The subjects of study were related to science and technology and included astronomy, geography, physics, chemistry, production methods, printing, etc.

With the Meiji Restoration in 1868, the institution was taken over by the new government and called the Daigaku Nankō. Outstanding students from the various domains were chosen to study there, and in time it became the core of Tokyo University.

In 1858, Itō Gemboku, a physician in attendance on the shogun, joined with some eight other physicians of Western style medicine in Edo to form an organization and set up a center for smallpox vaccination at Otamagaike in the Kanda area of Edo. The center was later taken over and operated by the shogunate, which renamed it Seiyō Igakusho (Center for Western Style Medicine) and broadened its activities.

In 1868 it was in turn taken over by the newly established Meiji government and for a time was known as the Daigaku Gōkō. In 1877 it became the Medical Department of Tokyo University.

In 1886, Tokyo Daigaku (University) was renamed Teikoku Daigaku (Imperial University), and took over an engineering school called the Kōbu Daigakkō, thus adding an engineering department. In 1890 it took over an agricultural school called the Tokyo Nōrin Gakkō, in the same way adding an agricultural department. In 1885 it was transferred to the jurisdiction of the Ministry of Education, and the following year was renamed the Teikoku Daigaku Kōka Daigaku (Imperial University Engineering University).

In 1897 a second imperial university was established in Kyoto, making it necessary to designate the institution in Tokyo the Tokyo Teikoku Daigaku, or Tokyo Imperial University. After the conclusion of the Pacific War, the name was once more changed in 1947 to Tokyo Daigaku, or Tokyo University, the name that it goes by today.

Map of Old Provinces

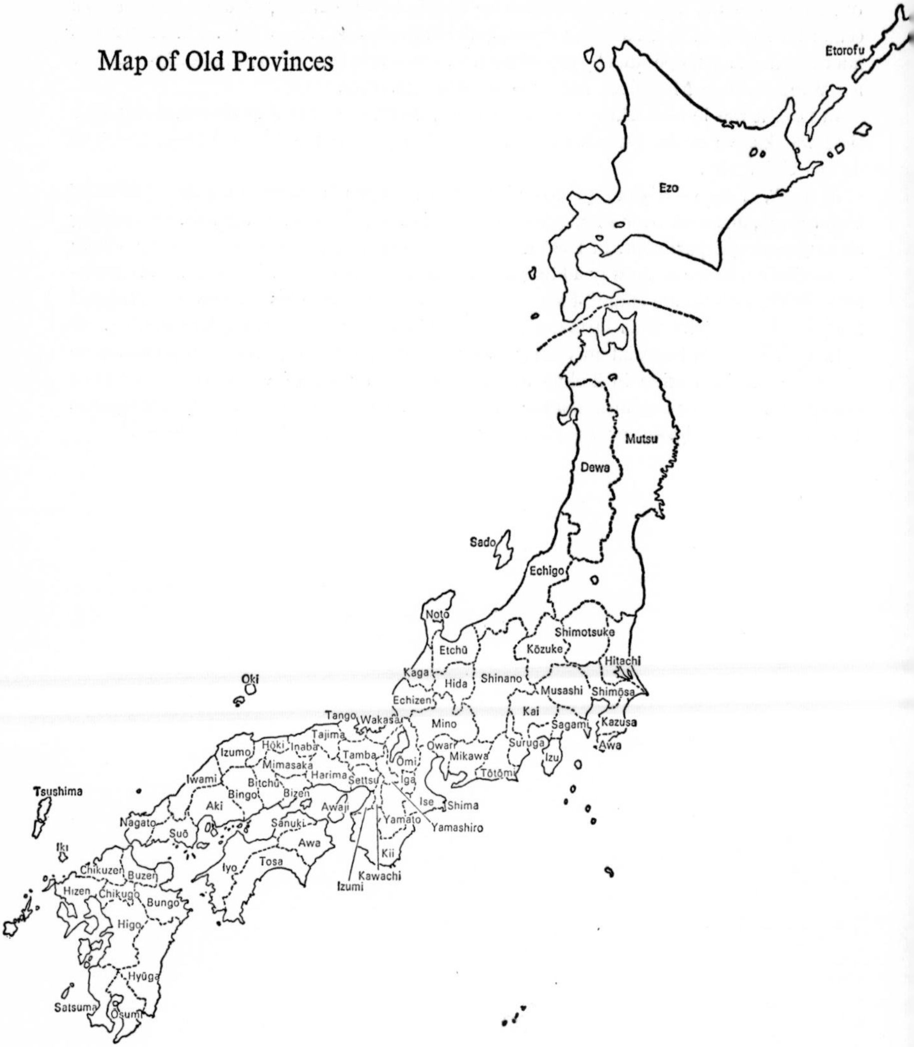

Map of Modern Prefectures

REGIONS

1. Hokkaido
2. Tōhoku
3. Kantō
4. Hokuriku
5. Tōsan
6. Tōkai
7. Kinki
8. Chūgoku
9. Shikoku
10. Kyūshū

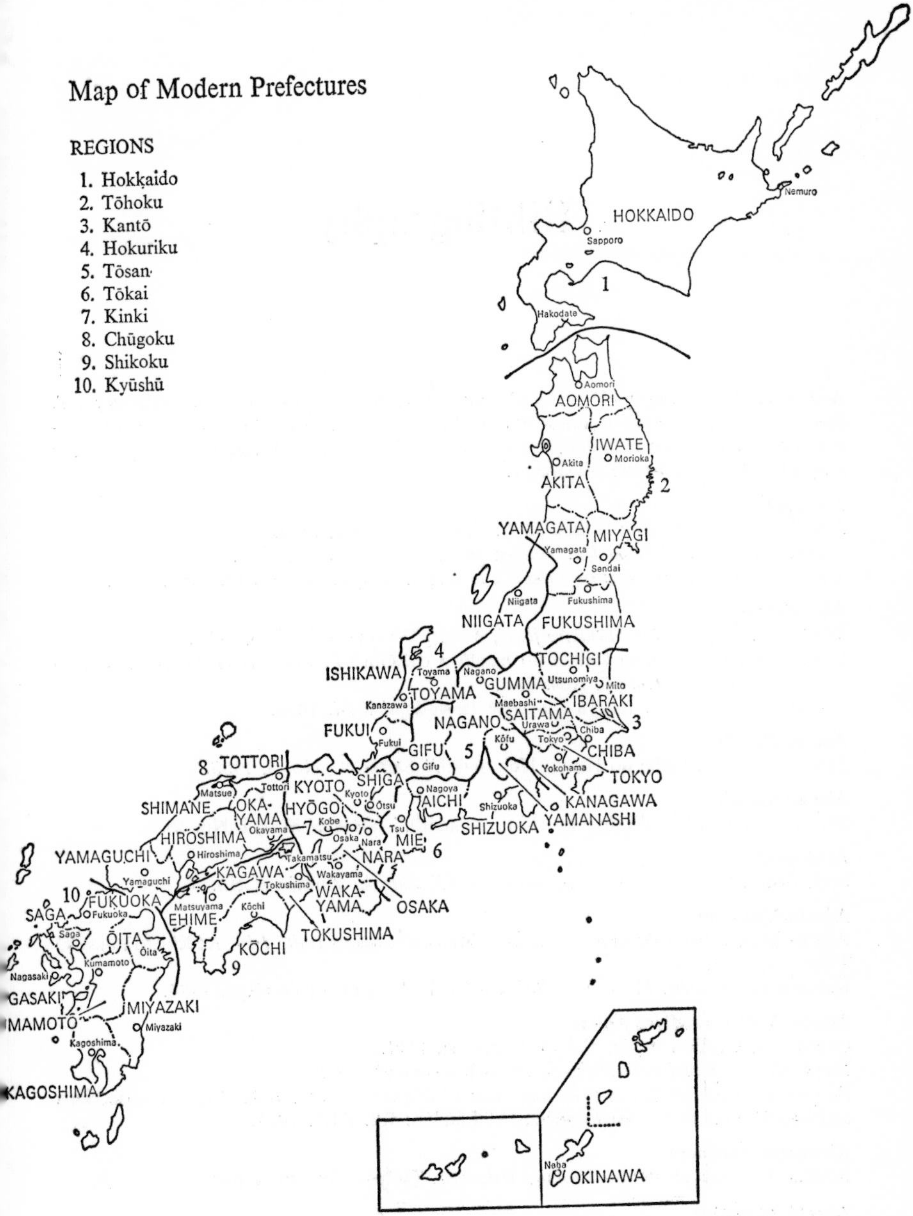

Bibliography

APOLOGY: All bibliographic material supplied by the compilers of this dictionary was checked in the files of the Japanese National Diet Library. In some cases complete bibliographic data were not avialible, but such material was retained here in the hope that it might be of service to the researcher.

Abe Isoo

Abe, Isoo. *Shakaishugisha to naru made*. Tokyo: Kaizōsha, 1932.
Katayama, Tetsu. *Abe Isoo den*. Tokyo: Mainichi Shimbunsha, 1958.
Takano, Zen'ichi. *Abe Isoo: sono chosaku to shōgai*. Tokyo: Waseda Daigaku, 1964.

Abe Masahiro

Watanabe, Shūjirō. *Abe Masahiro jiseki*, 2 vols. Watanabe, Shūjirō, 1910.
Ishii, Takashi. "Bakuhan kankei no hendō o chūshin to shitaru Kaei Ansei nenkan no seikyoku." *Nihonshi Kenkyū*, Nos. 7, 8.
Hamano, Shōkichi, ed. *Kaikyū kiji—Abe Ise-no-kami jiseki*. 1899.

Abe no Hirafu

Muroga, Nobuo. "Abe no Hirafu Hokuseikō." *Shirin* 39, No. 5, 1956.

Abe no Sadatō

Miyake, Chōhei. "Zen-kunen-no-eki no saikentō." *Nihonshi Kenkyū*, No. 43.

Achi no Omi

Seki, Akira. "Yamato no Ayauji no kenkyū." *Shigaku Zasshi* 62, No. 9.

Adachi Mineichirō

Adachi Mineichirō Tsuitōkai, ed. *Adachi Mineichirō hakase tsuitō roku*. Adachi Mineichirō Tsuitōkai, 1935.
Hammarskjöld, Dag. *Ko Adachi shochō*. Adachi Mineichirō Ki'nenkan, 1964.

Adams, William (Miura Anjin)

Okada, Akio. *Miura Anjin*. Tokyo: Sōgensha, 1944.
Mutō, Chōzō. *Kaitei zōho Nichi-Ei kōtsū-shi no kenkyū*. 1937.
Purnell, Christopher James. *The Log-Book of William Adams, 1614–1619*. Transactions and Proceedings of the Japan Society of London, vol. XIII. 1915.

Akamatsu Norimura

Kōsaka, Konomu. *Akamatsu Enshin, Mitsusuke*. Tokyo: Yoshikawa Kōbunkan, 1970.

Akechi Mitsuhide

Takayanagi, Mitsutoshi. *Akechi Mitsuhide*. Jimbutsu sōsho. Tokyo: Yoshikawa Kōbunkan, 1958.

Amakusa Tokisada
Okada, Akio. *Amakusa Tokisada.* Tokyo: Yoshikawa Kōbunkan, 1960.
Corea, Duarto. *Amakusa Shimabara Ikki Hōkokushi.* Translated by Kimura Ki. 1946.

Amaterasu Ōmikami
Ueda, Masaaki. *Nihon Shinwa.* Tokyo: Iwanami Shoten, 1970.

Andō Nobumasa
Fujisawa, Morihiko. *Kakurō Andō Tsushima no kami.* Heiyōsha, 1914.

Andō Shōeki
Kanō, Kōkichi. *Andō Shōeki, Kanō Kōkichi ibun-shū.* Tokyo: Iwanami Shoten, 1958.
Noda, Kenjirō, ed. *Hachinohe no rekishi,* vol. 1. Chihō Shunshūsha, 1961.
Bitō, Masahide, ed. and annotator. *Kinsei shisōka bunshū.* Nihon koten bungaku taikei. Tokyo: Iwanami Shoten, 1966.

Anezaki Masaharu
Anezaki, Masaharu. *Shimpen Waga shōgai* (autobiography). Anezaki Masaharu Sensei Seitan Hyakunen Ki'nenkai, 1974.
Anezaki Masaharu sensei no gyōseki. Anezaki Masaharu Sensei Seitan Hyakunen Ki'nenkai, 1974.

Antoku Tennō
Fujiwara, Toyoyasu. *Antoku Tennō hisseki.* 1934.

Aoki Kon'yō
Shimmura, Izuru. *Aoki Konyō den hotei, Zoku Namban kōki.* Tokyo: Iwanami Shoten, 1925.
Inomata, Entarō. *Aoki Konyō den.* Inomata Aya, 1909.

Aoki Shūzō
Sakane, Yoshihisa, ed. and annotator. *Aoki Shūzō jiden.* Tōyō bunko, 168. Tokyo: Heibonsha, 1975.

Arahata Kanson
Kanson jiden. Tokyo: Chikuma Shobō, 1965.
Arahata Kanson chosakushū, 10 vols. Tokyo: Heibonsha, 1976.

Arai Hakuseki
Kurita, Mototsugu. *Arai Hakuseki no bunchi seiji.* Tokyo: Ishizaki Shoten, 1952.
Hatano, Ken'ichi. *Arai Hakuseki zenshū.* Tokyo: Kokusho Kankōkai, 1905–07.
Miyazaki, Michio. *Arai Hakuseki no kenkyū.* Tokyo: Yoshikawa Kōbunkan, 1958.
Kamper, Ulrich. *Arai Hakuseki und seine Geschichtsauffasssung, ein Beitrag zur Historiographie Japans in der Tokugawa Zeit.* Wiesbaden: Harrassowitz, 1967.

Araki Sadao
Kikukawa, Manabu. *Hiroku rikugun rimenshi,* 2 vols. Araki Sadao Shōgun Denki Hensan Kankōkai, 1954–55.

Arima Harunobu
Hamada, Seiryō. *Tenshō ken'ō shisetsu.* Tokyo: Iwanami Shoten, 1931.
Steichen, Michael. *Les Daymyos Chrétiens ou siécle de l'histoire et politique du Japon 1549–1650.* Hong Kong: 1904.
Okamoto, Yoshitomo. *Kyūshū sankō ken'ō shisetsu kōki,* 2 vols. Tokyo: Tōkyōdō, 1947, 1949.

Arisugawa-no-miya Taruhito
Taruhito Shinnō gyōjitsu, 2 vols. Takamatsu-no-miya family, 1929.
Taruhito Shinnō nikki, 6 vols. Takamatsu-no-miya family, 1935–6.

Arita Hachirō
Arita, Hachirō. *Hito no me no chiri o miru.* Tokyo: Kōdansha, 1948.
———. *Baka Hachi to hito wa yuu.* Tokyo: Kōwadō, 1959.

Asada Gōryū
Kimura, Yasuyuki. "Nihon kagakushaden: Asada Gōryū." *Chūō Kōron* 70-11, 1941

Asai Nagamasa
Shiga-ken shi, 6 vols. Shiga Prefecture, 1927–28.

Asano Naganori
Watanabe, Yosuke. *Seishi Akō gishi*. Tokyo: Kōwadō, 1975.
Matsushima, Eiichi. *Chūshingura*. Tokyo: Iwanami Shoten, 1964.

Asanuma Inejirō
Asanuma, Inejirō. *Watakushi no rirekisho* 2. Tokyo: Nihon Keizai Shimbunsha, 1957.
Asanuma Tsuitō Shuppan Henshū Iinkai, ed. *Ningen kikansha Numa-san no kiroku*. Nihon Shakaitō Kikanshi Kyoku, 1961.

Ashida Hitoshi
Ishiyama, Kenkichi. *Ashida shushō o egaku*. Tokyo: Daiyamondosha, 1948.

Ashikaga Takauji
Takayanagi, Mitsutoshi. *Ashikaga Takauji*. Tokyo: Shunjūsha, 1955.

Ashikaga Yoshiaki
Okuno, Takahiro. *Ashikaga Yoshiaki*. Tokyo: Yoshikawa Kōbunkan, 1960.

Ashikaga Yoshimasa
Nagashima, Fukutarō. *Ōnin no ran*. Tokyo: Shibundō, 1967.
Varley, H. P. *The Ōnin War: History of its Origins and Background with a Selective Translation of the Chronicle of Ōnin*. New York: Columbia University Press, 1967.

Ashikaga Yoshimitsu
Usui, Nobuyoshi. *Ashikaga Yoshimitsu*. Tokyo: Yoshikawa Kōbunkan, 1960.

Ashikaga Yoshimochi
Uozumi, Sōgorō. *Muromachi bakufu seiji*. Tokyo: Iwanami Shoten, 1933.

Ashikaga Yoshinori
Satō, Shin'ichi. "Ashikaga Yoshinori shiritsuki no bakufu seiji." *Hōsei Shigaku*, No. 20.

Ashikaga Yoshiteru
Nagae, Shōichi. *Miyoshi Nagaharu*. Tokyo: Yoshikawa Kōbunkan, 1968.

Baba Tatsui
Yasunaga, Gorō. *Baba Tatsui*. Tokyo: Tōkyōdō, 1897.
Hagiwara, Nobutoshi. *Baba Tatsui*. Tokyo: Chūō Kōronsha, 1967.
Baba, Kochō. "Baba Tatsui jiden." *Kaizō* 6, nos. 7, 8, 11, 12 (1924).

Bankei Eitaku
Fujimoto, Tsuchishige. *Bankei kokushi no kenkyū*. Tokyo: Shunjūsha, 1971.
Terao, Ryūji, ed. *Bankei zenji zenshū*. Tokyo: Daizō Shuppan, 1976.
Suzuki, Daisetsu. *Bankei zen*. Zen shososhi kenkyū, vol. 1. Tokyo: Iwanami Shoten, 1933.

Benkei
Shimazu, Hisamoto. *Yoshitsune densetsu to bungaku*. Tokyo: Meiji Shoin, 1935.

Chaya Shirōjirō
Tsuji, Zennosuke. *Kaigai kōtsū shiwa*. Tokyo: Naigai Shoseki, 1930.
Iwao, Seiichi. *Shuinsen to Nihonmachi*. Tokyo: Shibundō, 1962.
Kitajima, Masamoto. *Edo bakufu sono jitsuryokushatachi*. Tokyo: Jimbutsu Ōraisha, 1964.

Cheng Ch'eng-kung (Tei Seikō)
Tsuji, Zennosuke. *Zōtei kaigai kōtsū shiwa*. Tokyo: Naigai Shoseki, 1942.
Ishihara, Michihiro. *Minmatsu Shinsho Nihon kisshi no kenkyū*. Tokyo: Fuzanbō, 1946.
———. *Tei Seikō*. Tokyo: Yoshikawa Kōbunkan, 1959.

Chōgen
Kobayashi, Takeshi, ed. *Shunjōbō Chōgen shiryō shūsei.* Tokyo: Yoshikawa Kōbunkan, 1965.

Chōnen
Tsuji, Zennosuke. *Nihon bukkyō-shi,* vol. 1. Tokyo: Iwanami Shoten, 1960.
Shin, Tung-ch'u. *Chung-jih fo-chiao chiao-t'ung shih.* Chung-hua ta-tien pien-yin-hui. Taiwan, 1970.

Daigo Tennō
Ryū, Susumu. "Engi no chi." *Heian jidai.* Tokyo: Shunjūsha, 1962.

Daikokuya Kōdayū
Shimmura, Izuru. *Ise hyōmin no jiseki.* Shimmura Izuru senshū, vol. 2. 1945.
Kamei, Kōkō. *Daikokuya Kōdayū.* Tokyo: Yoshikawa Kōbunkan 1964.

Dan Takuma
Ko Dan Danshaku Denki Hensan Iinkai, ed. and pub. *Danshaku Dan Takuma den,* 2 vols. 1938.
"Dan Takuma tsuitōgō." *Keizai remmei,* vol. 2, no. 3. Nihon Keizai Remmeikai, 1932.

Date Masamune
Kobayashi, Seiji. *Date Masamune.* Tokyo: Yoshikawa Kōbunkan, 1959.
Tokutomi, Sohō. *Nihon rekishijō ni okeru Date Masamune kō no ichi.* Sohōkai Miyagi Shibu 1935.

Dazai Shundai
Azuma, Shintarō. *Dazai Shundai no keizai shisō.* Shōbunkan 1929.
Maezawa, Masao. *Dazai Shundai.* Shinano Kyōdo Bunka Fukyūkai, 1943.
Nomura, Kentarō. "Dazai Shundai no keizairon." *Mita Gakkai Zasshi* 26–2, 1932.

Deguchi Onisaburō
Inui, Takashi, Oguchi, Iichi, Saki, Akio; and Matsushima, Eiichi. *Kyōso—shomin no kamigami.* Tokyo: Aoki Shoten, 1955.
Deguchi, Kyōtarō. *Kyojin Deguchi Onisaburō.* Tokyo: Kōdansha, 1975.

Dōgen
Okubo, Dōshū, ed. *Dōgen zenji zenshū,* 2 vols. Tokyo: Chikuma Shobō, 1969–70.
Terada, Tōru, and Mizuno, Yahoko. *Dōgen* 2 vols., Nihon shisō taikei. Tokyo: Iwanami Shoten, 1970–72.
Takasaki, Jikodō, and Umehara, Takeshi. *Kobutsu no manebi (Dōgen).* Tokyo: Kadokawa Shoten, 1969.

Dōkyō
Yokota, Ken'ichi. *Dōkyō.* Tokyo: Yoshikawa Kōbunkan, 1959.

Dōshō
Fukihara, Shōshin. *Nihon yuishiki shisō-shi.* Taigadō, 1944.
Nakai, Shinkō. *Nihon kodai no bukkyō to minshū.* Tokyo: Hyōronsha, 1973.
Tamura, Enchō. *Asuka hakuhō bukkyō-ron.* Tokyo: Yūzankaku, 1975.

Ebina Danjō
Watarase, Tsunekichi. *Ebina Danjō sensei.* Ryūginsha, 1938.
Takeda, Kiyoko. "Ebina Danjō sensei hyōden." *Shinjin no sōzō.* Tokyo: Kyōbunkan, 1960.
Oshimo, Aya. *Chichi Ebina Danjō.* Tokyo: Shufu no Tomosha, 1975.

Egawa Tarōzaemon Hidetatsu
Sakamoto, Keisuke. *Egawa Tan'an.* Kōa Bunka Kyōkai, 1937.
Furumi, Kazuo. *Bakumatsu ijin Egawa Tarōzaemon.* 1933.
———. *Egawa Tarōzaemon.* Tokyo: Kokumin Bungakusha, 1930.

Eikan
Inoue, Mitsusada. *Nihon jōdokyō seiritsu-shi no kenkyū.* Tokyo: Yamakawa Shuppansha, 1956.
Inoue, Mitsusada, and Ōsone, Shōsuke. *Ōjōden, Hokke genki.* Tokyo: Iwanami Shoten, 1974.

Eison
Wajima, Yoshio. *Eison, Ninshō.* Tokyo: Yoshikawa Kōbunkan, 1959.

Enchin
Onjō-ji, ed. *Chishō Daishi.* Shiga: Onjō-ji, 1927.

Engetsu
Tsuji, Zennosuke. *Nihon bukkyōshi.* Tokyo: Iwanami Shoten, 1949.
Tamamura, Takeji, ed. *Chūgan Engetsu shū.* Gozan bungaku shinshū, vol. 4. Tokyo: Tokyo Daigaku Shuppankai, 1970.

Enni Bennen
Tsuji, Zennosuke. *Nihon bukkyō-shi,* vol. 3. 2nd ed. Tokyo: Iwanami Shoten, 1960.
Imaeda, Aishin. *Zenshū no rekishi.* Tokyo: Shibundō, 1960.

Ennin
Fukui, Kōjun ed. *Jikaku Daishi kenkyū.* Taishō Daigakunai Tendai Gakkai, 1964.
Reichauer, Edwin O. *Ennin's Travels in T'ang China.* New York: Donald Press, 1955.

En no Ozunu
Wakamori, Tarō. *Shugendō-shi kenkyū.* Tokyo: Heibonsha, 1973.
Tamamuro, Taijō. *Nihon bukkyō-shi gaisetsu.* Gendai Bukkyō meicho zenshū, vol. 1. Tokyo: Ryūbunkan, 1960.
Murayama, Shūichi. *Yamabushi no rekishi.* Haniya Shobō, 1970.

Enomoto Takeaki
Enomoto, Takeaki. *Shiberia nikki.* Tokyo: Kaigun Yūshūkai, 1935.
Kamo, Giichi. *Enomoto Takeaki.* Tokyo: Chūō Kōronsha, 1960.
Iguro, Yatarō. *Enomoto Takeaki den.* Sapporo: Miyama Shobō, 1968.

Etō Shimpei
Matono, Hansuke. *Etō Nampaku,* 2 vols. Nampaku Kenshōkai, 1914.
Sugitani, Akira. *Etō Shimpei.* Tokyo: Yoshikawa Kōbunkan, 1962.

Fujii Nittatsu
Yoshida, Kyūichi, ed. *Bukkyō.* Gendai Nihon shisō taikei. Tokyo: Chikuma Shobō, 1965.
Tokoro, Shigemoto. *Kindai Nihon no shūkyō to nashonarizumu.* Tokyo: Fuzambō, 1966.
———. *Kindai shakai to Nichiren shugi.* Tokyo: Hyōronsha, 1972.

Fujita Tōko
Kikuchi, Kenjirō. *Fujita Tōko-den.* Kinkōdo, 1899.
Sugihara, Sansei, ed. *Fujita Tōko genkōroku.* Naigai Shuppan Kyōkai, 1909.
Takasu, Yoshijirō, ed. *Fujita Tōko zenshū,* 6 vols. Shōkasha, 1935–36.

Fujiwara no Fuhito
Fujiwara no Fuhito. Jimbutsu Nihon no rekishi, vol. 2. Tokyo: Yomiuri Shimbunsha, 1966.

Fujiwara no Fuyutsugu
Hayashi, Rikurō. "Fujiwara no Otsugu to Fujiwara no Fuyutsugu." *Rekishi Kyōiku,* vol. 10, No. 5.

Fujiwara no Hirotsugu
Kitayama, Shigeo. "Nanahyaku yonjūnen no Fujiwara no Hirotsugu no hanran." *Nihon kodai seijishi no kenkyū.* Tokyo: Iwanami Shoten, 1959.

Fujiwara (Nakatomi) no Kamatari
Tamura, Enchō. *Fujiwara no Kamatari*. Tokyo: Hanawa Shobō, 1966.

Fujiwara no Michinaga
Akagi, Shizuko. *Midō Kampaku Fujiwara no Michinaga*. Tokyo: Shūei Shuppan, 1969.

Fujiwara no Mototsune
Sakamoto, Tarō. *Fujiwara no Yoshifusa*. Rekishi to jimbutsu. Tokyo: Yoshikawa Kōbunkan, 1964.

Fujiwara no Nakamaro
Kishi, Toshio. *Fujiwara no Nakamaro*. Tokyo: Yoshikawa Kōbunkan, 1969.

Fujiwara no Shōshi
Akagi, Shizuko. *Heian kizoku no seikatsu to bunka*. Tokyo: Kōdansha, 1964.

Fujiwara no Sumitomo
Uwayokote, Masataka. "Shōhei-Tengyō no ran no rekishiteki igi." *Nihonshi Kenkyū*, No. 23, 1954.

Fujiwara no Yorimichi
Yamanaka, Yutaka. "Fujiwara no Michinaga, Yorimichi fushi." *Heian ōchō—sono jitsuryokushatachi*. Tokyo: Jimbutsu Ōraisha, 1965.

Fujiwara no Yoshifusa
Uehara, Eiko. "Fujiwara no Yoshifusa to Tomo no Yoshio." *Heian ōchō—sono jitsuryokushatachi*. Tokyo: Jimbutsu Ōraisha, 1965.

Fukanzai Fabian
Cieslik, Hubert. *Fukan Fabian den nōto*. Kirishitan bunka kenkyū kaihō 15th yr., vol. 9, 1973.
Shimmura, Izuru. *Hayashi Razan oyobi Matsunaga Teitoku to Yasosha Fukan Fabian*. Namban kōki. Tokyo: Iwanami Shoten, 1924.
Elison, George. *Deus Destroyed, The Image of Christianity in Early Modern Japan*. Cambridge: Harvard University Press, 1973.

Fukuda (Kageyama) Hideko
Murata, Shizuko. *Fukuda Hideko*. Tokyo: Iwanami Shoten, 1959.

Fukuoka Takachika
Ishin Shiryō Hensankai. *Shishaku Fukuoka Takachika danwa hikki*. 1912.

Fukuzawa Yukichi
Fukuzawa, Yukichi. *Fukuō jiden*. Tokyo: Iwanami Shoten, 1954.
Ishikawa, Mikiaki. *Fukuzawa Yukichi den*, 4 vols Tokyo: Iwanami Shoten, 1932.
Keiō Gijuku, ed. *Fukuzawa Yukichi zenshū*, 21 vols. Tokyo: Iwanami Shoten, 1958–64.

Ganjin
Andō, Nobuo. *Ganjin*. Tokyo: Yoshikawa Kōbunkan 1958.

Gembō
Tsuji, Zennosuke. *Nihon bukkyōshi*, ch. 1. 1944.

Gemmei Tennō
Kishi, Toshio. "Gemmei Taijō Tennō no hōgyo." *Kodaishi kōza*, ch. 12. Tokyo: Gakuseisha, 1965.

Genshin
Minamoto, Hironobu. *Genshin*. Kyoto: Hōzōkan, 1934.
Sakata, Yoshihiro. *Eshin Sōzu no kenkyū*. 1938.
Eshin Sōzu zenshū. Shibunkaku, 1971.

Gidō Shūshin
Tamamura, Takeji. *Gozan bungaku*. Tokyo: Shibundō, 1957.

Godaigo Tennō
Kuroita, Katsumi. *Godaigo Tennō gojiseki*. Yoshino Jingū Hōsankai, 1932.
Godaigo Tennō shinkan-shū. Tokyo: Kokumin Seishin Bunka Kenkyūjo, 1937.

Godai Tomoatsu
Nihon Keieishi Kenkyūjo, ed. *Godai Tomoatsu denki shiryō*, 4 vols. Tokyo: Tōyō Keizai Shimpōsha, 1971–74.

Gokameyama Tennō
Nakamura, Naokatsu. *Nanchō no kenkyū*. Kyoto: Hoshino Shoten, 1927.

Gokomatsu Tennō
Satō, Shin'ichi. *Nambokuchō no dōran*. Nihon no rekishi, vol. 9. Tokyo: Chūō Kōronsha, 1965.

Gomizuno-o Tennō
Tsuji, Zennosuke. "Gomizuno-o Tennō no Zenshū Goshinkō." *Zenshū* 403–404, 1928.
Kitakōji, Isamitsu. *Hana no yukue: Gomizuno-o Tennō no jidai*. Kyoto: Shishindo, 1973.

Gomurakami Tennō
Kimura, Takeo. *Gomurakami Tennō no seiseki*. Kyoto: Yanagihara Shoten, 1943.

Gosanjō Tennō
Takeuchi, Rizō. *Nihon no rekishi*, ch. 6. Tokyo: Chūō Kōronsha, 1965.

Goshirakawa Tennō
Watanabe, Tamotsu, *Genji to Heishi*. Tokyo: Shibundō, 1955.
Yoshimura, Shigeki. *Insei*. Tokyo: Shibundō, 1958.
Yasuda, Motohisa. *Insei to Heishi*. Nihon no rekishi, 7. Tokyo: Shōgakkan, 1974.

Gotō Mitsutsugu
Kobata, Atsushi. *Nihon no kahei*. Tokyo: Shibundō, 1958.

Gotō Shimpei
Tsurumi, Yūsuke. *Gotō Shimpei*, 4 vols. Gotō Shimpei Haku Denki Hensankai, 1937–38.
———. *Gotō Shimpei den*, 11 vols. Tokyo: Taiheiyō Kyōkai Shuppankai, 1943–47.

Gotō Shōjirō
Ōmachi, Keigetsu. *Hakushaku Gotō Shōjirō*. Tokyo: Fuzambō, 1914.

Gouda Tennō
Ryō, Susumu. *Kamakura jidai*, vol. 2. Tokyo: Shunjūsha, 1957.

Gyōki
Inoue, Kaoru. *Gyōki*. Tokyo: Yoshikawa Kōbunkan, 1959.

Gyōnen
Shimaji, Daitō. *Nihon bukkyō kyōgaku-shi*. Nakayama Shobō, 1976 (reprint).
Kamata, Shigeo, and Tanaka, Hisao. *Kamakura kyūbukkyō*. Tokyo: Iwanami Shoten, 1971.
Kamata, Shigeo. "Nihon kegon ni okeru seitō to itan." *Shisō* 593, 1973.

Hakuin Ekaku
Hakuin Oshō Hensankai, ed. *Hakuin oshō zenshū*. 8 vols. Ryūginsha, 1935.
Rikukawa, Taiun. *Hakuin oshō shōden*. Tokyo: Sankibō Busshorin, 1963.
Tsuyama, Sōkaku. *Hakuin*. Kōza: Zen, vol. 4. Tokyo: Chikuma Shobō, 1967.

Hamada Hikozō
Amerika Hikozō-den. Japanese translation of *The Narrative of a Japanese*. Translated by Nakagawa, Tsutomu, and Yamaguchi, Osamu. 2 vols. Tokyo: Heibonsha, 1964.
Chikamori, Haruyoshi. *Josefu Hiko*. Tokyo: Yoshikawa Kōbunkan, 1963.

Hamada Yahyōe
Nachod, Oskar. *Die Beziehungen der Niederlandischen Ostindischen Kompagnie zu Japan im ziebzehnten Jahrhundert*. Leipzig, 1897.

Tsuji, Zennosuke. *Zōtei Kaigai kōtsū shiwa*. Tokyo: Naigai Shoseki Shuppan Kaisha, 1930.
Iwao, Seiichi. *Shuinsen bōeki-shi no kenkyū*. Kyoto: Kōbundō, 1956.

Hamaguchi Osachi
Hamaguchi, Osachi. *Zuikanroku*. Tokyo: Sanseidō, 1931.
Kitada, Teiko. *Chichi Hamaguchi Osachi*. Tokyo: Hibiya Shobō, 1932.
Sekine, Minoru. *Hamaguchi Osachi den*. Hamaguchi Osachi Den Kankōkai, 1931.

Hanaoka Seishū
Kure, Shūzō. *Hanaoka Seishū sensei oyobi sono geka*. Tohōdō, 1923.
Mori, Keizō, ed. *Hanaoka Seishū nempu*. Nanki Shidankai, 1962.
———. ed. *Isei Hanaoka Seishū*. Hanaoka Seishū Sensei Kenshōkai, 1964.

Hanawa Hokiichi
Watanabe, Tomosaburō. *Kūzen zetsugo mōjin no ō Hanawa kengyō den*. 1892.
Ichimura, Hiroshi. *Hanawa Hokiichi no shōgai*. Tokyo: Nihon Shoin, 1946.
Ota, Zemmaro. *Hanawa Hokiichi*. Tokyo: Yoshikawa Kōbunkan, 1966.

Harada Kiemon
Murakami, Naojirō. *Ikoku ōfuku shokan-shū, Ikoku sōsho*. Tokyo: Yūshōdō, 1967.
Takayanagi, Mitsuyoshi, and Matsudaira, Nen'ichi. *Sengoku jimmei jiten*. Tokyo: Yoshikawa Kōbunkan 1959.
Colin Francisco. *Lavor Evangelica de los Obreros de la Compañia de Iesus en las Islas Filipinas, por el Padre Pablo Pastells*, 3 vols. Barcelona, 1900–04.
San Antonio, Francisco de. *Chronicas de la Apostolica Provincia de S. Gregorio de Religiosos descalzos de N.S.P.S. Francisco en las Islas Philippinas, China, Japan*, vol. III. Manila, 1744.

Hara Takashi
Hara Takashi Zenshū Kankōkai, ed. & pub. *Hara Takashi zenshū*, 2 vols. 1929.
Hara, Keiichirō, ed. *Hara Takashi nikki*, 6 vols. Tokyo: Fukumura Shoten, 1965–69.
Tetsuo, Najita. *Hara Kei in the Politics of Compromise: 1905–15*. Harvard University Press, 1967.

Hasegawa Sahyōe Fujihiro
Shintei Kansei jūshū shokafu, 13 vols. Tokyo: Yoshikawa Kōbunkan, 1965.
Gesshū. *Jijitsu bunhen*, 5 vols. Hasegawa Fujihiro den. Tokyo: Kokusho Kankōkai, 1910.
Pagés, Léon. *Histoire de la Religion Chrétiènne au Japon, depuis 1598 jusqu'à 1651*. Paris, 1869.
Boxer, Charles Ralph. "The Affair of the *Madre de Deus*, A Chapter in the History of the Portuguese in Japan," Transactions of the Japan Society of London, vol. XXVI. London, 1929.

Hasekura Tsunenaga
Suzuki, Shōzō. *Hasekura Tsunenaga denki*. 1928.
Nakame, Satoru. *Hasekura Rokuemon*. Hakureikai, 1957.
Ogura, Hiroshi. *Date Masamune no Namban kenshi to shisetsu Hasekura Rokuemon*. 1938.

Hashimoto Sanai
Keigakukai, ed. *Hashimoto Keigaku zenshū*. Sebō Shobō, 1939.
Nishimura, Fuminori. *Hashimoto Sanai*. Shōbundō, 1909.
Yamaguchi, Muneyuki. *Hashimoto Sanai*. Jimbutsu sōsho. Tokyo: Yoshikawa Kōbunkan, 1962.

Hatoyama Ichirō
Hatoyama, Ichirō. *Hatoyama Ichirō kaikoroku*. Tokyo: Bungei Shunjūsha, 1957.
———. *Watakushi no rirekisho* 7. Tokyo: Nihon Keizai Shimbunsha, 1959.

Hayashi Shihei
Suzuki, Shōzō. *Hayashi Shihei denki*. Rokumukai, 1928.
Matsuo, Akira. *Hayashi Shihei-den*. Okugawa Shobō, 1932.
Otsuki, Shūzō. *Rokumusai zenshū*, 4 vols. Dōkyūsha, 1882.

Higashikuni (Higashikuni-no-miya) Naruhiko
Higashikuni, Naruhiko. *Ichikōzoku no sensō nikki*. Tokyo: Nihon Shūhōsha, 1957.

Himiko
Shiratori, Kurakichi. *Wa no joō Himiko kō*. Shiratori Kurakichi zenshū, vol. 1. Tokyo: Iwanami Shoten 1969.

Hino Tomiko
Katsuno, Ryūshin. "Hino Tomiko." *Muromachi bakufu*. Tokyo: Jimbutsu Ōraisha, 1965.

Hiraga Gennai
Irita, Seizō, ed. *Hiraga Gennai zenshū*. Hiraga Gennai Sensei Kenshōkai, 1932.
Jōfuku, Isamu. *Hiraga Gennai*. Tokyo: Yoshikawa Kōbunkan, 1971.
Maes, Hubert. *Hiraga Gennai et son temps*. École Française d'Extrême-Orient, vol. LXXII. Paris, 1970.

Hiranuma Kiichirō
Iwasaki, Sakae. *Hiranuma Kiichirō den*. Tokyo: Kaiseisha, 1939.
Hiranuma Kiichirō Kaiko Roku Hensan Iinkai, ed. & pub. *Hiranuma Kiichirō kaiko roku*. 1955.

Hirata Atsutane
Muromatsu, Iwao, ed. *Hirata Atsutane zenshū*, 15 vols. Hōbunkan, 1911–18.
Sagara, Tōru. *Hirata Atsutane*, Nihon no meicho. Tokyo: Chūō Kōronsha, 1972.
Tawara, Tsuguo; Seki, Akira; Saeki, Arikiyo; and Haga, Noboru. *Hirata Atsutane, Ban Nobutomo, Ōkuni Takamasa*. Nihon shisō taikei. Tokyo: Iwanami Shoten, 1973.

Hiratsuka Raichō
Hiratsuka, Raichō. *Watakushi no aruita michi*. Tokyo: Shinhyōronsha, 1955.
———. *Hiratsuka Raichō jiden, Genshi josei wa taiyō de atta*, 4 vols. Tokyo: Otsuki Shoten, 1971–72.
Kobayashi, Tomie. *Hiratsuka Raichō*. Tokyo: Ōtsuki Shoten 1977.

Hirota Kōki
Hirota Kōki Denki Kankōkai, ed. *Hirota Kōki*. Tokyo: 1966.

Hōjō (Taira) Masako
Watanabe, Tamotsu. *Hōjō Masako*. Tokyo: Yoshikawa Kōbunkan 1961.

Hōjō Sanetoki
Nakamura, Mitsu and Seki Yasushi. *Hōjō Yasutoki, Hōjō Sanetoki*. Hokkai Shuppansha, 1937.

Hōjō Sōun
Inagaki, Yasuhiko. "Hōjō Sōun." *Nihon jimbutsushi taikei*, vol. 2. Tokyo: Asakura Shoten, 1959.

Hōjō Takatoki
Kuroda, Toshio. *Nihon no rekishi*, vol. 8. Tokyo: Chūō Kōronsha, 1965.

Hōjō Tokimasa
Takayanagi, Mitsutoshi. *Nihon bushōden*. Tokyo: Dai-Nihon Shuppan, 1945.

Hōjō Tokimune
Seki, Yasushi. *Shiwa Hōjō Tokimune*. Tokyo: Asahi Shimbunsha, 1944.

Hōjō Yasutoki
Uwayokote, Masataka. *Hōjō Yasutoki*. Tokyo: Yoshikawa Kōbunkan, 1958.

Hōjō Yoshitoki
Yasuda, Motohisa. *Hōjō Yoshitoki*. Tokyo: Yoshikawa Kōbunkan, 1961.

Honda Kōtarō
Honda Kōtarō Kinenkai, ed. *Honda Kōtarō sensei no omoide*. Tokyo: Seibundō Shinkōsha, 1955.
Ishikawa, Teijirō. *Honda Kōtarō den*. Tokyo: Nikkan Kōgyō Shimbunsha, 1963.

Honda Masanobu
Kitajima, Masamoto. *Edo bakufu sono jitsuryokusha-tachi*, vol. 1. Tokyo: Jimbutsu Ōraisha, 1964.

Honda Toshiaki
Uchida, Ginzō. *Honda Toshiaki*. Tokyo: Fuzanbō, 1929.
Keene, Donald. *The Japanese Discovery of Europe, Honda Toshiaki and other Discoverers 1720–1789*. Rev. ed. Stanford Univ. Press, 1969.
Honjō, Eijirō, ed. *Honda Toshiaki-shū*. Kinsei shakai keizai gakusetsu taikei, vol. 1. Tokyo: Seibundō Shinkōsha, 1935.

Hōnen
Shunjō, Hōnen, the Buddhist Saint, his life and teaching. Translated by Harper Havelock Coates and Ishizuka Ryūgaku, Kyoto; Society for the Publication of Sacred Books of the World, 1925 and 1949.
Ishii, Kyōdō, and Ohashi, Shunnō, eds. *Shōwa shinshū Hōnen shōnin zenshū*. Kyoto: Heiraku-ji Shoten, 1955.
Ōhashi, Shunnō. *Hōnen, Ippen*. Nihon shisō taikei. Tokyo: Iwanami Shoten, 1971.
Kajimura, Noboru. *Hōnen*. Tokyo: Kadokawa Shoten, 1970.

Hoshi Tōru
Nakamura Kikuo. *Hoshi Tōru*. Jimbutsu sōsho. Tokyo: Yoshikawa Kōbunkan 1963.

Hosokawa Gracia
Mitsue, Iwao. *Hosokawa Garasha fujin*. Tokyo: Tōkō Shoin 1937.
Laures, Johannes. *Hosokawa Garasha fujin*. Translated by Yanagiya Takeo. Tokyo: Chūō Shuppansha, 1958.

Hosokawa Katsumoto
Ogawa, Makoto. *Yamana Sōzen to Hosokawa Katsumoto*. Tokyo: Jimbutsu Ōraisha 1966.

Hosokawa Tadaoki
Ashida, Kan. "Hosokawa Tadaoki." *Fukuchiyama* 142. 1964.
Tamura, Shunsō. "Chasen Hosokawa Sansai shōden." *Jōmō oyobi Jōmōjin* 143.
Laures, Johannes. "Hosokawa-ke no kirishitan." Translated by Yanagiya Takeo. *Kirishitan Kenkyū* 4.

Hotta Masayoshi
Fukuchi, Gen'ichirō. *Bakumatsu seijika*. 1900.
Chiba-ken, Imba-gun Yakusho, ed. *Hotta Masayoshi-kō iseki ippan*. 1913.
Hotta Masayoshi jitsuden. Bōsō kyōdo kenkyū, vol. 8/2-4. 1941.

Hozumi Nobushige
Hozumi, Shigetō, ed. *Hozumi Nobushige ibunshū*. Tokyo: Iwanami Shoten, 1932–34.

Hozumi Yatsuka
Uesugi, Shinkichi, ed. *Hozumi Yatsuka hakase rombunshū*. Tokyo: Yūhikaku. 1943.
Hozumi, Shigeyuki. "Meiji jūnendai ni okeru Doitsu hōgaku no juyō." *Meiji kokka no hō to shisō*. Tokyo: Ochanomizu Shobō, 1966.

Hyekwan
Hashikawa, Tadashi. *Sōgō Nihon bukkyō-shi*. Tokyo: Meguro Shoten, 1932.

Ichijō Tennō
Tsuchida, Naoshige. "Ichijō Tennō no kyūtei. *Ōchō no kizoku*. Nihon no rekishi. Tokyo: Chūō Kōronsha.

Ii Naosuke
Shimada, Saburō. *Kaikoku Shimatsu Ii Naosuke den*. Kōronsha, 1888.
Yoshida, Tsunekichi. *Ii Naosuke*. Tokyo: Yoshikawa Kōbunkan, 1963.
Nakamura, Matsumaro. *Lord Ii Naosuke and New Japan*. Translated and adapted by Shunkichi Akimoto. Tokyo: Japan Times, 1909.

Ikeda Shigeaki
Ikeda Shigeaki Denki Kankōkai, ed. and pub. *Ikeda Shigeaki*. 1962.

Imagawa Yoshimoto
Kojima, Hirotsugi. *Imagawa Yoshimoto*. Tokyo: Jimbutsu Ōraisha, 1966.

Imamura Eisei
Imamura, Akitsune. *Rangaku no so: Imamura Eisei*. Tokyo: Asahi Shimbunsha, 1942.

Inatomi Ichimu
Tōdaiki. Shiseki zassan, vol. II. Tokyo: Kokusho Kankōkai, 1911.
Dai-Nihon shiryō, 12-7, under Keichō 16th year, 2nd month, 6th day. Tokyo: Tōkyō Daigaku Shiryō Hensangakari, 1905.

Inō Tadataka
Ōtani, Ryōkichi. *Inō Tadataka*. Tokyo: Iwanami Shoten, 1917.
Hoyanagi, Mutsumi. *Inō Tadataka no Kagakuteki gyōseki*. Tokyo: Kokon Shoin, 1975.

Inoue Enryō
Miwa, Masaichi. *Inoue Enryō sensei*. Tokyo: Tōyō Daigaku Kōyūkai, 1919.
Funayama, Shin ichi. *Meiji tetsugakushi kenkyū*. Kyoto: Mineruba Shobō, 1965.

Inoue Junnosuke
Inoue Junnosuke Ronsō Hensankai, ed. and pub. *Inoue Junnosuke ronsō*, 4 vols. 1935.
———. *Inoue Junnosuke*. 1935.
Yoshino, Toshihiko. *Rekidai Nihon ginkō sōsai-ron*. Tokyo: Mainichi Shimbunsha, 1976.

Inoue Kaoru
Inoue Kaoru Kō Denki Hensankai, ed. *Seigai Inoue Kō den*, 5 vols. Tokyo: Hara Shobō, 1968.

Inoue Kowashi
Inoue Kowashi Denki Hensan Iinkai, eds. *Inoue Kowashi den, shiryō-hen*, 5 vols. Tokyo: Kokugakuin Daigaku Toshokan, 1966–75.
Pittau Joseph. *Inoue Kowashi to gendai Nihon no keisei*. Tokyo: Jiji Tsūshinsha, 1967.
Kaigo, Tokiomi, ed. *Inoue Kowashi no Kyōiku seisaku*. Tokyo: Tokyo Daigaku Shuppankai, 1968.

Inoue Tetsujirō
Senken rombushū, 2 vols. Tokyo: Fuzambō, 1899–1901.
Kouhara, Issei. *Inoue Tetsujirō*. Nihon rekishi, 78. 1954.

Inukai Tsuyoki
Bokudō sensei denki kankōkai. *Inukai Bokudō den*, 3 vols. Tokyo: Tōyō Keizai Shimpōsha, 1938–39.
Iwabuchi, Tatsuo. *Inukai Tsuyoki*. Sandai saishō retsuden. Tokyo: Jiji Tsūshinsha, 1958.

Ippen
Yanagi, Sōetsu. *Namu amida butsu*. Tokyo: Daihōrin-kaku, 1955.
Karaki, Junzō. *Muyōsha no keifu*. Tokyo: Chikuma Shobō, 1960.
Ōhashi, Shunnō. *Hōnen, Ippen*. Tokyo: Iwanami Shoten, 1971.
———. *Ippen—sono kōdō to shisō*. Tokyo: Hyōronsha, 1971.

I-shan I-ning
Tsuji, Zennosuke. *Nihon Bukkyō-shi*, vol. 3. Tokyo: Iwanami Shoten, 1960.
Imaeda, Aishin. *Zenshū no rekishi.* Tokyo: Shibundō, 1966.

Ishibashi Tanzan
Ishibashi, Tanzan. *Tanzan kaisō.* Tokyo: Mainichi Shimbunsha, 1951.
Ishibashi Tanzan Zenshū Hensan Iinkai, ed. *Ishibashi Tanzan zenshū*, 15 vols. Tokyo: Tōyō Keizai Shimpōsha, 1972.
Chō, Yukio, ed. *Ishibashi Tanzan—hito to shisō.* Tokyo: Tōyō Keizai Shimpōsha, 1973.

Ishida Baigan
Ishikawa, Ken. *Ishida Baigan.* Nihon Kyōiku Sentetsu Sōsho, vol. 15. Tokyo: Bunkyō Shoin, 1943.
Iwauchi, Seiichi. *Kyōikusha to shite no Ishida Baigan.* Kyoto: Ritsumeikan Shuppanbu, 1934.
Shibata, Minoru, ed. *Ishida Baigan zenshū.* 2 vols. Sekiman Shingakkai, 1956–57.

Ishida Mitsunari
Watanabe, Yosuke. *Kōhon Ishida Mitsunari.* Tokyo: Yūzankaku, 1929.
Imai, Rintarō. *Ishida Mitsunari.* Tokyo: Yoshikawa Kōbunkan, 1961.
Ikezaki, Tadataka. *Gaisetsu Ishida Mitsunari.* Okakura Shobō, 1942.

Ishihara Kanji
Ishihara Kanji zenshū, 8 vols. Ishihara Kanji Zenshū Kankōkai, 1976.
Kakuta, Jun. *Ishihara Kanji shiryō.* Tokyo: Hara Shobō, 1967–68.
Yokoyama, Shimpei. *Hiroku: Ishihara Kanji.* Tokyo: Fuyō Shobō, 1971.

Ishii Kikujirō
Ishii, Kikujirō. *Gaikō yoroku.* Tokyo: Iwanami Shoten 1930.

Itagaki Taisuke
Itagaki, Morimasa, ed. *Itagaki Taisuke zenshū.* Tokyo: Shunjūsha, 1933; Tokyo: Hara Shobō, 1969.
Toyabe, Shuntei. *Hakushaku Itagaki Taisuke.* Shuntei zenshū. Tokyo: Hakubunkan, 1909.
Hirao, Michio. *Mukei Itagaki Taisuke.* Kōchi: Kōchi Shimbunsha, 1974.

Itakura Katsushige
Kokubu, Taneyuki, ed. *Gyosui jitsuroku.* Kyū Takahashihan Shinbokukai, 1911.
Tamura, Eitarō. *Itakura Iga no kami.* Tokyo: Tōkyō Sangensha, 1941.

Itakura Shigemasa
Takayanagi, Mitsutoshi, and Matsudaira, Nen'ichi. *Sengoku jimmei jiten*, 1962.

Itō Gemboku
Itō, Sakae. *Itō Gemboku den.* 1916.
Itazawa, Takeo. *Nichi-Ran bunka kōshōshi no kenkyū.* Tokyo: Yoshikawa Kōbunkan, 1959.

Itō Hirobumi
Itō Hirobumi Kankei Monjo Kenkyūkai, ed. *Itō Hirobumi kankei monjo.* Tokyo: Hanawa Shobō, 1973.
Shumpo Kō Tsuishōkai, ed., and pub. *Itō Hirobumi den*, 3 vols. Tokyo: 1940, (reprinted. Tokyo: Hara Shobō, 1965.)

Itō Mansho
Hidaka, Shigetaka. "Rōma Shisetsu Itō Mansho ni tsuite." *Shigaku Zasshi*, 39-5, 1928.

Itō Miyoji
Shinteikai, ed. and pub *Hakushaku Itō Miyoji*, 2 vols. Tokyo: 1938.
Kobayashi, Tatsuo, ed. *Suiusō nikki.* Tokyo: Hara Shobō, 1966.
Akita, George. "The Other Itō: A Political Failure." In *Personality in Japanese History.* Edited by A. M. Craig and D. H. Shively. Berkeley: University of California Press, 1970.

Itō Tōgai
Shimmura, Izuru. *Tōgai Sensei to sono Monka.* Nihon Bunka, 22, 1943.
Katō, Jimpei. *Itō Tōgai ni okeru Jinsaigaku no hatten.* Tokyo: Oka Shoin, 1929.

Iwakura Tomomi
Iwakurakō Kyūseki Hozonkai, ed. and pub. *Iwakura kō jikki,* 3 vols. Tokyo: Hara Shobō, 1968.
Iwakura Tomomi kankei monjo, 8 vols. Tokyo: Nihon Shiseki Kyōkai, 1927–35.
Ōkubo, Toshiaki. *Iwakura Tomomi,* Chūkō shinsho. Tokyo: Chūō Kōronsha, 1973.

Iwasaki Yatarō
Irimajiri, Yoshinaga. *Iwasaki Yatarō.* Jimbutsu sōsho. Tokyo: Yoshikawa Kōbunkan, 1960.
Iwasaki Yatarō, Iwasaki Yanosuke Denki Hensankai, ed. and pub. *Iwasaki Yatarō den,* 2 vols. Tokyo, 1967.

Izawa Shūji
Shinano Kyōikukai, ed. *Izawa Shūji senshū.* Nagano: Shinano Kyōikukai, 1958.
Kaminuma, Hachirō. *Izawa Shūji.* Jimbutsu sōsho. Tokyo: Yoshikawa Kōbunkan, 1962.

Jimmu Tennō
Kadowaki, Teiji. *Jimmu Tennō.* Tokyo: San'ichi Shobō, 1957.
Uemura, Seiji. *Jimmu Tennō.* Tokyo: Shibundō, 1957.
Nakayama, Kyūshirō. *Jimmu Tennō to Nihon no rekishi.* Tokyo: Ogawa Shoten, 1961.

Jingū Kōgō
Jingū Kōgō. Mie: Kōgakukan Daigaku Shuppanbu, 1972.

Jiun Onkō
Kinami, Takuichi. *Jiun sonja—shōgai to sono kotoba.* Kyoto: Sammitsudō Shoten, 1961.
———. *Jiun sonja hōgoshū.* Kyoto: Sammitsudō Shoten 1971.
Miyasaka, Yūshō. *Kana hōgoshū.* Nihon koten bungaku taikei. Tokyo: Iwanami Shoten, 1964.

Jōkei
Kamata, Shigeo, and Tanaka, Hisao. *Kamakura kyūbukkyō.* Tokyo: Iwanami Shoten, 1971.
Fukihara, Shōshin. *Nihon chūsei yuishiki Bukkyō-shi.* Tokyo: Daitō Shuppansha, 1975.

Joosten van Lodensteijn, Jan
Iwao, Seiichi. *Jan Joosten van Lodensteijn; the Forerunner of the Dutch-Japanese Relation.* Bulletin of the Japan-Netherlands Society, No. 1. Tokyo: Japan-Netherlands Society, 1958.

Kagawa Toyohiko
Kagawa Toyohiko chosakushū, 24 vols. Tokyo: Kirisuto-kyō Shimbunsha, 1962–64.
Yokoyama, Shun'ichi. *Kagawa Toyohiko den.* Tokyo: Keiseisha, 1959.

Kaibara Ekiken
Ban, Kōkei. *Kaibara Ekiken den.* Shuyōbunko Kankōkai, 1919.
Irizawa, Munehisa. *Kaibara Ekiken.* Tokyo: Bunkyō Shoin, 1948.
Inoue, Tadashi. *Kaibara Ekiken.* Tokyo: Yoshikawa Kōbunkan, 1968.
Graf, Olaf. *Kaibara Ekiken, ein Beitrag zur japanischen Geistesgeschichte des 17 Jahrunderts und zur chinesische Sung Philosophie.* Leiden: E. J. Brill, 1942.

Kakuban
Nakano, Tatsue. *Kōkyō Daishi seiden.* Tokyo: Seishōken, 1934.

Kakunyo
Shigematsu, Akihisa. *Kakunyo.* Tokyo: Yoshikawa Kōbunkan, 1964.

Kamiya Sōtan
Kawashima, Genjirō. *Shuinsen bōekishi.* 1921.
Haga, Kōshirō. *Sōtan nikki,* Sadō koten zenshū, vol. 6. 1958.

Kammu Tennō
Murao, Jirō. *Kammu Tennō.* Tokyo: Yoshikawa Kōbunkan, 1963.

Kanchō
Toganoo, Shōun. *Mikkyō Bukkyō-shi.* Gendai Bukkyō meicho zenshū, vol. 9. Tokyo: Ryūbunkan 1964.

Kaneko Kentarō
Fujii, Shin'ichi. *Teikoku kempō to Kaneko haku.* Tokyo: Kōdansha, 1942.
Kaneko, Kentarō. "Jijoden 1-2." *Kaizō* 24-2, 24-3, 1942.

Kanō Jigorō
Kanō Jigorō Sensei Denki Hensankai, ed. *Kanō Jigorō.* Tokyo: Kōdōkan, 1964.

Kataoka Kenkichi
Kawada, Mizuho. *Kataoka Kenkichi sensei den.* Kyoto: Ritsumeikan Shuppanbu, 1940.
Kataoka, Kenkichi. *Kataoka Kenkichi nikki.* Kōchi: Kōchi Shimin Toshokan 1974.

Katayama Sen
Katayama Sen chosakushū, 3 vols. Tokyo: Kawade Shobō Shinsha, 1959–60.
Kishimoto, Eitarō, et. al. *Katayama Sen,* 2 vols Tokyo: Miraisha, 1959–60.
Kublin, Hyman. "Katayama Sen, ichi borishebiki no seitan." *Shakai Kagaku Kenkyū* 1/2, 1956.

Katayama Tetsu
Katayama, Tetsu *Watakushi no rirekisho.* Tokyo: Nihon Keizai Shimbunsha, 1958.

Katō Hiroyuki
Katō, Hiroyuki, ed. and pub. *Katō Hiroyuki jijoden.* 1913.
Tabata, Shinobu. *Katō Hiroyuki.* Jimbutsu sōsho. Tokyo: Yoshikawa Kōbunkan, 1959.
Yoshida, Kōji. *Katō Hiroyuki no kenkyū.* Tokyo: Ōhara Shinseisha, 1976.

Katō Kiyomasa
Yamaji, Aizan. *Katō Kiyomasa.* Minyūsha, 1909.
Nakano, Katarō. *Katō Kiyomasa seiden.* Tokyo: Ryūbunkan, 1909.
Wada, Masao. *Katō Kiyomasa.* Chōbunkaku, 1943.

Katō Takaaki
Itō, Masanori. *Katō Takaaki,* 2 vols. Tokyo: Hara Shobō, 1965.
Hosoya, Chihiro. "Taishō gaikō ni okeru seitō to itan: Katō Takaaki to Gotō Shimpei." *Nihon oyobi Nihonjin* 16/2, 1965.

Katō Tomosaburō
Gensui Katō Tomosaburō den. Tokyo: Miyata Mitsuo, 1928.
Arai, Tatsuo. *Katō Tomosaburō.* Tokyo: Jiji Tsūshinsha, 1958.

Katsu Kaishū
Katsu, Awa. *Kaishū zenshū,* 10 vols. Tokyo: Kaizōsha, 1927–29.
Katsube, Mitake, et al. *Katsu Kaishū zenshū,* 12 vols. Keisō Shobō, 1970.
Ishii, Takashi. *Katsu Kaishū.* Jimbutsu sōsho. Tokyo: Yoshikawa Kōbunkan 1974.

Katsuragawa Hoshū
Imaizumi, Genkichi. *Rangaku no ie Katsuragawa no hitobito,* 3 vols 1965, 1968, 1969.
Meiji-zen Nihon igaku-shi. Nihon gakushiin, 1955–64.

Katsura Tarō
Tokutomi, Iichirō. *Kōshaku Katsura Tarō den,* 2 vols. Ko Katsura Kōshaku Ki'nen Jigyōkai, 1917.
Kawahara, Jikichirō *Katsura Tarō.* Sandai saishō retsuden. Tokyo: Jiji Tsūshinsha, 1959.

Kawai Eijirō
Shakai Shisō Kenkyūkai, ed. and pub. *Kawai Eijirō zenshū,* 24 vols. Tokyo, 1967–69.
———. *Kawai Eijirō, denki to tsuioku.* Tokyo, 1948.

Kawaji Toshiakira
Kawaji, Kandō. *Kawaji Toshiakira no shōgai.* Tokyo: Yoshikawa Kōbunkan, 1903.
Tamura, Eitarō. *Kawaji Toshiakira* Nihon Dempō Tsūshinsha Shuppanbu, 1942.
Satō, Seisaburō. *Kindai Nihon no seiji shidō.* Seijika kenkyū, vol. II. 1965.
Nagasaki nikki, Shimoda nikki. Tōyō bunko, 124. Tokyo: Heibonsha, 1968.

Kawakami Hajime
Kawakami Hajime chosakushū, 12 vols. Tokyo: Chikuma Shobō, 1964–65.
Kawakami, Hajime. *Jijoden,* 4 vols., Sekai Hyōronsha, 1947–48; 5 vols., Tokyo: Iwanami Shoten, 1949.
Amano, Keitarō, and Noguchi, Tsutomu, eds. *Kawakami Hajime no ningenzō.* Tokyo: Tosho Shimbunsha, 1968.

Kawamura Zuiken
Furuta, Ryōichi. *Kawamura Zuiken,* Jimbutsu sōsho, #121. Tokyo: Yoshikawa Kōbunkan, 1967.
———. "Higashi-mawari kaiun oyobi nishi-mawari kaiun no kenkyū." Tōhoku teikoku daigaku hō/bungakubu Ōu shiryō chōsa hōkoku. 1942 (summary in French).
———. *Kaiun no rekishi.* Nihon rekishi shinsho. Tokyo: Shibundō 1961.

Kawate Bunjirō
Murakami, Shigeyoshi. *Kindai minshū shūkyō-shi no kenkyū.* Kyoto: Hōzōkan, 1957.
Murakami, Shigeyoshi, and Yasumaru, Yoshio. *Minshū shūkyō no shisō.* Nihon shisō taikei. Tokyo: Iwanami Shoten, 1971.

Kazunomiya
Seikan'in-no-miya gonikki, 1927; reprinted by Tokyo Daigaku Shuppankai, 1976.
Takebe Toshio. *Kazunomiya.* Jimbutsu sōsho. Tokyo: Yoshikawa Kōbunkan, 1965.

Keian Genju
Ashikaga, Enjutsu. *Kamakura, Muromachi jidai no jukyō.* 1932.

Keizan Jōkin
Kagamishima Genryū. *Nihon zenshū-shi—Sōtōshū.* Kōza: Zen, vol. 4. Tokyo: Chikuma Shobō, 1967.

Kibi no Makibi
Miyata, Toshihiko. *Kibi no Makibi.* Tokyo: Yoshikawa Kōbunkan, 1961.

Kido Kōichi
Kido Nikki Kenkyūkai, ed. *Kido Kōichi kankei monjo.* Tokyo: Tokyo Daigaku Shuppankai, 1966.
———. *Kido Kōichi nikki,* 2 vols. Tokyo: Tokyo Daigaku Shuppankai, 1974.

Kido Takayoshi
Kido-kō Denki Hensanjo. *Shōkiku Kido-kō den,* 2 vols. Tokyo: Meiji Shoin, 1927.
Tsumagi, Chūta, ed. *Kido Takayoshi monjo,* 8 vols. Tokyo: Nihon Shiseki Kyōkai, 1931.
———. *Kido Takayoshi nikki,* 3 vols. Tokyo: Nihon Shiseki Kyōkai, 1932.

Kimmei Tennō
Hayashiya, Tatsusaburō. "Keitai, Kimmeichō nairan no shiteki bunseki." *Kodai kokka no kaitai.* Tokyo: Tokyo Daigaku Shuppankai, 1955.

Kimura Hisashi
Ikeda, Tetsurō. "Kimura Hisashi sensei no gyōseki." *Kagaku,* vol. 14, no. 2. Tokyo: Iwanami Shoten, 1944.

Kinokuniya Bunzaemon
Kamiyama, Kantarō. *Jitsuden Kinokuniya Bunzaemon.* Tokyo: Meiji Shoin, 1939.

Kinoshita Jun'an
Inoue, Tetsujirō. *Nihon Shushi gakuha no tetsugaku.* Tokyo: Kokusho Kankōkai, 1919.

Sawada Fusakiyo. *Kinoshita Jun'an to Arai Hakuseki*. Kinsei Nihon no Jugaku. Tokyo: Iwanami Shoten, 1939.

Kinoshita Naoe

Kinoshita Naoe chosakushū, 19 vols. Tokyo: Meiji Bunken, 1968–73.

Yamagiwa, Keiji. *Kinoshita Naoe*. Tokyo: Rironsha, 1955.

Takeda Kiyoko, ed. *Kinoshita Naoe shū*. Kindai Nihon shisō taikei, 10. Tokyo: Chikuma Shobō, 1975.

Kishi Nobusuke

Yoshimoto, Shigeyoshi, *Kishi Nobusuke*. Tokyo: Tōyō Shokan, 1957.

Kishi, Nobusuke. *Watakushi no rirekisho*, No. 8. Tokyo: Nihon Keizai Shimbunsha, 1959.

Kitabatake Akiie

Nakamura, Takaya. *Kitabatake Akiie Kyō*. Zenkoku Hōsankai, 1938.

Kitabatake Chikafusa

Hiraizumi, Kiyoshi. *Kitabatake Chikafusa-kō no kenkyū*. Tokyo: Nihon-gaku Kenkyūjo, 1954.

Nakamura, Naokatsu. *Kitabatake Chikafusa-kō keiden*. Kyoto: Hoshino Shoten, 1943.

Nagahara, Keiji. *Kitabatake Chikafusa*. Nihon jimbutsushi taikei, 2. Tokyo: Asakura Shoten 1959.

Kita Ikki

Kita Ikki chosaku shū, 3 vols. Tokyo: Misuzu Shobō, 1959–72.

Tanaka, Sōgorō. *Kita Ikki*. Tokyo: San'ichi Shobō, 1971.

Wilson, G. M. *Radical Nationalist in Japan: Kita Ikki, 1883–1937*. Cambridge: Harvard University Press, 1969.

Kitazato Shibasaburō

Miyajima Mikinosuke, ed. *Kitazato Shibasaburō den*. Tokyo: Kitazato Kenkyūjo, 1932.

Takano, Rokurō. *Kitazato Shibasaburō*, Gendai denki zenshū, vol. 3. Tokyo: Nihon Shobō, 1960.

Kiyoura Keigo

Inoue, Masaaki, ed. *Hakushaku Kiyoura Keigo den*, 2 vols. Tokyo: Hakushaku Kiyoura Keigo Den Kankōkai, 1935.

Kiyozawa Manshi

Kiyozawa Manshi zenshū, 8 vols. Kyoto: Hōzōkan, 1953.

Yoshida, Kyūichi. *Kiyozawa Manshi*. Jimbutsu sōsho. Tokyo: Yoshikawa Kōbunkan, 1961.

———, ed. *Bukkyō*. Gendai Nihon Shisō taikei, vol. 7. Tokyo: Chikuma Shobō, 1965.

Hashimoto Mineo, ed. *Kiyozawa Manshi, Suzuki Daisetsu*. Nihon no meicho, vol. 43. Tokyo: Chūō Kōronsha, 1970.

Kodama Gentarō

Sukuri, Shigeichi. *Kodama taishō den*. Tokyo: Taikyōsha, 1938.

Koiso Kuniaki

Katsuzan Kōsō. Koiso Kuniaki Jijoden Kankōkai, 1963.

Kojima Korekata (Iken)

Harada, Mitsusaburō. *Kojima Korekata den*. Shōkikudō, 1961.

Kojima, Korekata. *Ōtsu jiken nisshi*. Edited and annotated by Ienaga Saburō. Tōyō bunko, No. 187. Tokyo: Heibonsha, 1971.

Taoka, Ryōichi. *Ōtsu jiken no saihyōka*. Tokyo: Yūhikaku, 1976.

Kokan Shiren

Okada, Masayuki. *Nihon kambungaku-shi*. Rev. ed. Tokyo: Yoshikawa Kōbunkan, 1954.

Imaeda, Aishin. *Zenshū no rekishi*. Tokyo: Shibundō, 1966.

Kōken Tennō
Nakagawa, Osamu. "Shōtoku Kōken Tennō." *Hokkaido shigaku kyōiku kenkyū kyōkai kenkyū kiyō*, No. 15.

Komura Jutarō
Gaimushō, ed. *Komura gaikōshi*. Tokyo: Hara Shobō, 1966.
Kuroki, Yūkichi. *Komura Jutarō*. Tokyo: Kōdansha, 1968.

Kōmyō Kōgō
Hayashi, Rikurō. *Kōmyō Kōgō*. Tokyo: Yoshikawa Kōbunkan, 1961.
Kobayashi, Tsuyoshi. *Tōdai-ji*. Tokyo: Mainichi Shimbunsha, 1952.

Kondō Morishige
Kondō Seisai zenshū, 3 vols. Tokyo: Kokusho Kankōkai, 1905–06.
Ono, Kinjirō. *Kondō Jūzō*. Kyōzaisha, 1941.

Konishi Yukinaga
Mitsue, Iwao. *Kirishitan daimyō Konishi Yukinaga*. Kirisutokyō Shuppansha, 1943.
Takayanagi, Kōju, and Matsudaira, Nen'ichi. *Sengoku daimyō jiten*. 1962.
Ikeda, Akira. *Konishi Yukinaga*. 1936.
Steichen, Michael. *Les Daimyos Chrétiens ou un siècle de l'histoire et politique du Japon 1549–1650*. 1904.

Konoe Fumimaro
Asahi Shimbunsha, ed. and pub. *Ushinawareshi seiji*. 1946.
Yabe, Teiji. *Konoe Fumimaro*, 2 vols. Kyoto: Kōbundō, 1952; Yomiuri Shimbunsha, 1976.
Oka, Yoshitake. *Konoe Fumimaro*. Tokyo: Iwanami Shoten, 1972.

Kōtoku Shūsui
Kōtoku Shūsui zenshū, 11 vols. Tokyo: Meiji Bunken, 1968–73.
Itoya, Toshio. *Kōtoku Shūsui kenkyū*. Tokyo: Aoki Shoten, 1967.
Kanzaki, Kiyoshi. *Jitsuroku Kōtoku Shūsui*. Tokyo: Yomiuri Shimbunsha, 1971.

Kōtoku Tennō
Ienaga, Saburō. "Kōtokuki no shiryōgakuteki kenkyū," *Nihon kodaishi ronshū*, vol. 1. Tokyo: Yoshikawa Kōbunkan, 1962.

Kozeki San'ei
Sugimoto, Tsutomu. *Kozeki San'ei den*. 1972.

Kudō Heisuke
Kōno Tsuneyoshi. "Aka Ezo fūsetsukō no chosha Kudō Heisuke," *Shigaku Zasshi* 26–5.
Tsuji, Zennosuke. *Zōtei Kaigai kōtsū shiwa*. 1930.
Satō, Shōsuke. *Yōgakushi kenkyū josetsu*. 1964.

Kujō Kanezane
Taga, Munehaya. "Fujiwara no Kanezane ni tsuite." *Nihon Rekishi*, Nos. 246, 247, 249.

Kūkai
Kōbō daishi zenshū, 8 vols.
Watanabe, Shōkō, and Miyasaka Yūshō, ed. and annotator. *Sangō shiiki, Shōryō-shū*. Nihon koten bungaku taikei. Tokyo: Iwanami Shoten, 1965.
———. *Shamon Kūkai*. Tokyo: Chikuma Shobō, 1967.
Kawasaki, Tsuneyuki. *Kūkai*. Nihon shisō taikei. Tokyo: Iwanami Shoten, 1975.
Miyasaka, *Yūshō*, and Umehara, Takeshi. *Seimei no umi, Kūkai*. Tokyo: Kadokawa Shoten, 1968.

Kumazawa Banzan
Gotō, Saburō. *Kumazawa Banzan*. Nihon kyōiku sentetsu sōsho, vol. 6. Tokyo: Bunkyō Shoin, 1942.

Shibata, Kanzaburō. "Tōju to Banzan." *Kinsei Nihon no jugaku.* Tokyo: Iwanami Shoten, 1939.
Aira, Kyō. "Kumazawa Banzan." *Kinsei Nihon no jukyō shisō.* Hanawa Shoten, 1966.

Kuroda Kiyotaka
Kuroda, Kiyotaka. *Kan'yū nikki,* 3 vols. 1887.
Iguro, Yatarō. *Kuroda Kiyotaka.* Jimbutsu sōsho. Tokyo: Yoshikawa Kōbunkan, 1976.

Kurozumi Munetada
Hara, Keigo. *Kurozumi Munetada.* Tokyo: Yoshikawa Kōbunkan, 1960.
Murakami, Shigeyoshi, and Yasumaru, Yoshio. *Minshū shūkyō no shisō.* Nihon shisō taikei. Tokyo: Iwanami Shoten, 1971.

Kusunoki Masashige
Uemura, Seiji. *Kusunoki Masashige.* Tokyo: Shibundō, 1962.

Kūya
Tsuji, Zennosuke. *Nihon Bukkyō-shi,* vol. 1. Tokyo: Iwanami Shoten, 1944.
Hori, Ichirō. *Kūya.* Tokyo: Yoshikawa Kōbunkan, 1963.
———. *Waga kuni minkan shinkō-shi no kenkyū,* vol. 2. Tokyo: Sōgensha, 1954.

Kyōshin
Inoue, Mitsusada, and Ōsone, Shōsuke. *Ōjōden, Hokke genki.* Tokyo: Iwanami Shoten, 1974.

Lan-hsi Tao-lung
Tsuji, Zennosuke. *Nihon Bukkyō-shi,* vol. 3. 2nd ed. Tokyo: Iwanami Shoten, 1960.
Imaeda, Aishin. *Zenshū no rekishi.* Tokyo: Shibundō, 1960.

Maeda Eun
Maeda Eun zenshū, 8 vols. Maeda Eun Zenshu Kankōkai, 1931–32.
Tsunemitsu, Kōnen. *Meiji no Bukkyōsha,* vol. 2. Tokyo: Shunjūsha, 1969.

Maejima Hisoka
Teishin Kyōkai, ed. and pub. *Yūbin sōgyōdan.* 1936.
Maejima Hisoka jijoden. Kanagawa: Maejima Hisoka Denki Kankōkai, 1956.
Oda, Takeo. *Maejima Hisoka.* Niigata: Maejima Hisoka Kenshōkai, 1958.

Maeno Ryōtaku
Kurashige, Jisaku, ed. *Ranka sensei nempu to shōden.* Kuroshige Jisaku, 1894.
Iwasaki, Katsumi, ed. *Maeno Ranka.* Iwasaki Katsumi, 1938.
Ogawa, Teizō. *Kaitai shinsho—Rangaku wo okoshita hitobito.* Tokyo: Chūō Kōronsha, 1968.

Makiguchi Tsunesaburō
Makiguchi Tsunesaburō zenshū, 5 vols. Tokyo: Tōzai Tetsugaku Shoin, 1965.
Higuma, Takenori. *Sōka gakkai.* Kōza Nichiren, vol. 4. Tokyo: Shunjūsha, 1972.

Makino Nobuaki
Makino, Nobuaki. *Kaikoroku,* 3 vols. Tokyo: Bungei Shunjū Shinsha, 1948–49; 2 vols. Tokyo: Chūō Kōronsha, 1977–78.
———. *Shōtō kandan.* Tokyo: Sōgensha, 1940.
Shimozono, Sakichi. *Makino Nobuaki haku.* Jimbunkaku, 1930.

Makino Tomitarō
Makino, Tomitarō. *Makino Tomitarō jiden.* Nagashima Shobō, 1957.
Kamimura, Noboru. *Makino Tomitarō den.* Rokugatsusha, 1955.

Mamiya Rinzō
Abe, Makoto. "Edo makki ni okeru Karafuto tanken." *Rekishi Chiri,* 63–3, 1934.
Hora, Tomio. *Mamiya Rinzō.* Tokyo: Yoshikawa Kōbunkan, 1960.
Yoshida, Yoshio. *Mamiya Rinzō.* Tokyo: Kaiseisha, 1955.

Mansai Jugō
Mansai Jugō nikki. Tokyo: Zoku-gunshoruijū Kanseikai, 1928.

Matsudaira Nobutsuna
Kitajima, Masamoto. *Edo bakufu; sono jitsuryokusha-tachi,* vol. 1. Tokyo: Jinbutsu Ōraisha, 1964.
Nakano, Reishirō. "Matsudaira Izu-no-kami Nobutsuna," *Taiyō* 3/9–12, 1897.

Matsudaira Sadanobu
Shibusawa, Eiichi. *Rakuō-kō den.* Tokyo: Iwanami Shoten, 1937.
Mikami, Sanji. *Shirakawa Rakuō to Tokugawa jidai.* 1940.
Satō, Tahei. *Rakuō Matsudaira Sadanobu.* Miyakoshi Taiyōdō, 1942.

Matsukata Masayoshi
Tokutomi, Iichirō. *Kōshaku Matsukata Masayoshi den,* 2 vols. Kōshaku Matsukata Masayoshi Denki Hakkōsho, 1935. (Reprinted by Meiji Bunken, 1976.)

Matsuoka Yōsuke
Matsuoka Yōsuke Denki Kankōkai, ed. *Matsuoka Yōsuke.* Tokyo: Kōdansha, 1974.
Miwa, Kimitada. *Matsuoka Yōsuke.* Chūkō shinsho. Tokyo: Chūō Kōronsha, 1971.
Kase, Toshikazu. "Shirarezaru Matsuoka Yōsuke." *Bungei Shunjū* 43/2, 1965.

Matsuura Shigenobu
Matsuura, Atsushi, ed. *Matsuura Hōin seikan nikkishō.* Tokyo: Yoshikawa Hanshichi, 1894.
Matsuura-ke Bunko, Rakusaidō, ed. and pub. *Zō-Jusammi Shikibukyō Hōin Shigenobukyō ryakuden.* 1924.
Nagasaki Kenshi Henshū Iinkai, ed. *Nagasaki kenshi: Hanseihen.* Tokyo: Yoshikawa Kōbunkan, 1973.

Meiji Tennō
Kunai-shō, ed. *Meiji Tennō-ki,* 13 vols. Tokyo: Yoshikawa Kōbunkan, 1968–77.
Mochizuki, Kotarō. *Sekai ni okeru Meiji Tennō.* Eibun Tsūshinsha, 1913.
Watanabe, Ikujirō. *Meiji Tennō no seitoku,* 5 vols. Tokyo: Chikura Shobō, 1941–42.

Min (Bin)
Seki, Akira. *Kikajin.* Tokyo: Shibundō, 1956.

Minamoto no Yoriie
Ryō, Susumu. *Minamoto no Yoriie den no hihan.* Kamakura jidai no kenkyū. Tokyo: Shunjūsha, 1944.

Minamoto no Yoritomo
Nagahara, Keiji. *Minamoto no Yoritomo.* Tokyo: Iwanami Shoten, 1958.
Tokutomi, Iichirō. *Minamoto no Yoritomo,* 3 vols. Tokyo: Kōdansha, 1953–54.

Minamoto no Yoshiie
Yasuda, Motohisa. *Minamoto no Yoshiie.* Tokyo: Yoshikawa Kōbunkan, 1966.

Minamoto no Yoshitomo
Takayanagi, Mitsutoshi. *Nihon bushō hyōden,* vol. 1. Dai-Nihon Shuppan, 1945.

Minamoto no Yoshitsune
Watanabe, Tamotsu. *Minamoto no Yoshitsune.* Tokyo: Yoshikawa Kōbunkan, 1966.

Minobe Tatsukichi
Ienaga, Saburō. *Minobe Tatsukichi no shisōshi-teki kenkyū.* Tokyo: Iwanami Shoten, 1964.
Minobe, Ryōkichi. *Kumon suru demokurashī.* Tokyo: Bungei Shunjūshinsha, 1959.

Mitsui Takatoshi
Nakata, Yasunao. *Mitsui Takatoshi.* Tokyo: Yoshikawa Kōbunkan, 1959.
Kita, Takeroku. *Mitsui ganso: Takatoshi shugyō-ki.* Tokyo: Kokubunsha, 1942.
Nakagawa, Akeshi, ed. *Sōju daikoji gyōjō.* Tokyo: Yoshikawa Kōbunkan, 1943.

Miura Baien

Taguchi, Masaji. *Miura Baien.* Tokyo: Yoshikawa Kōbunkan, 1967.

Saegusa, Hiroto. *Baien tetsugaku nyūmon.* Tokyo: Daiichi Shobō, 1943.

———. *Miura Baien shū.* Tokyo: Iwanami Shoten, 1953.

Miyake Setsurei

Yanagida, Izumi. *Tetsujin Miyake Setsurei sensei.* Tokyo: Jitsugyō no Sekai-sha, 1956.

———, ed. *Miyake Setsurei shū.* Meiji bungaku zenshū, vol. 33. Tokyo: Chikuma Shobō, 1967.

Miyazaki Yasusada

Tohiro, Kazō. "Nōgaku no sōshō to Miyazaki Yasusada." *Rekishi Kagaku* 4–6, 1935.

Tamura, Gentarō. *Nihon no nōgyō shidōsha.* Kokumin Toshokankōkai, 1944.

Tsuchiya, Takao. *Nōgyō zensho.* Tokyo: Iwanami Shoten, 1949.

Ogawa, Jūichi. *Miyazaki Yasusada no nōgyō zensho no kekyū* 1, *tokuni bunkengaku, shoshigaku teki kenkyū.* Osaka sangyō daigakukiyō, 12, 1966.

Mizuno Tadakuni

Kitajima, Masamoto. *Mizuno Tadakuni.* Tokyo: Yoshikawa Kōbunkan, 1969.

Okamoto, Ryōichi. *Tempō kaikaku.* Nihon rekishi kōza, Kinsei 5. Tokyo: Iwanami Shoten, 1969.

Mogami Tokunai

Minagawa, Shinsaku. *Hokuhen no senkakusha Mogami Tokunai.* Tokyo: Dentsū Shuppanbu, 1943.

Tanaka, Iwao. *Mogami Tokunai.* Ten'yū Shobō, 1943.

Mononobe no Okoshi

Noda, Reishi. "Mononobeshi ni kansuru kisoteki kōsatsu," *Shirin*, vol. 51, No. 2.

Mori Arinori

Ōkubo, Toshiaki, ed. *Mori Arinori zenshū*, 3 vols. Tokyo: Sembundō Shoten, 1972.

———. *Mori Arinori.* Nihon kyōiku sentetsu sōsho, #18. Tokyo: Bunkyō Shoin, 1944.

Hall, Ivan. *Mori Arinori.* Cambridge: Harvard University Press, 1973.

Mōri Motonari

Ichinohe, Ōgai. *Mōri Motonari.* Ōkura Kōbundō, 1908.

Oikawa, Giemon. *Mōri Motonari.* Kyoto: Hoshino Shoten, 1942.

Segawa, Hideo. *Mōri Motonari.* Tokyo: Sōgensha, 1942.

Sankyō-den Hensan Jimusho, ed. *Mōri Motonari-kyō den.* Rokumeikan, 1944.

Mōri Terumoto

Taki, Yahachi. *Tenju kō ryaku fu.* Chōshū sōsho 10. Inagaki Tsunesaburō, 1892.

Ōta, Yūseki. "Mōri Terumoto-kyō onjiseki." *Bōchō Shidankai Zasshi* 16–18, 20, 28–31, 1910–12.

Motoda Eifu

Motoda, Takehiko, and Kaigo, Tokiomi, eds. *Motoda Eifu monjo*, 6 vols. Motoda Monjo Kenkyūkai, 1969—.

Kaigo, Tokiomi. *Motoda Eifu.* Nihon kyōiku sentetsu sōsho, #19. Tokyo: Bunkyō Shoin, 1942.

Shively, Donald H. "Motoda Eifu: Confucian Lecturer to the Meiji Emperor." In David S. Nivison and Arthur F. Wright, eds., *Confucianism in Action.* pp. 302–333. Stanford, 1959.

Motoki Einoshin

Koga Jūjirō. *Nagasaki yōgakushi*, vol. 1. Nagasaki: Nagasaki Bunkensha, 1966.

Kuwaki, Hayao. "Motoki Jindayū Yoshinaga no jiseki." *Kagaku chishiki* 6/11, 12, 1926.

Motoki Shōzō

Magata, Sei, ed. *Nihon kappan seizō shiso ko Motoki sensei shōden.* Tokyo: Tōkyō Tsukiji Kappan Seizōjo, 1894.

Shibata, Shirō. *Insatsu bunka no reimei, Motoki Shōzō no shōgai.* Nihon Insatsu Shimbunsha, 1954.

Mukai Genshō

Mukai, Genshō. *Kenkon bensetsu.* Edited by Tosho Kankōkai. Bummei genryū sōsho, vol. 2. 1914.

Ebizawa, Arimichi. *Namban gakutō no kenkyū.* Tokyo: Sōbunsha, 1958.

Itō, Tasaburō. "Kinsho ni kan sura shomondai." *Rekishi Chiri* 68/4, 5.

Uemura, Kandō. "Tenryū-ji no Korin to Mukai Genshō." *Zenshū* 209, 1912.

Murakami Senjō

Tsunemitsu, Kōnen. *Meiji no Bukkyōsha,* vol. 1. Tokyo: Shunjūsha, 1968.

Yoshida Kyūichi, ed. *Bukkyō.* Gendai Nihon shisō taikei. Tokyo: Chikuma Shobō, 1965.

Musō Soseki

Tamamura, Takeji. *Musō kokushi.* Kyoto: Heiraku-ji Shoten, 1958.

Hirata, Takashi. *Musō,* Kōza: Zen, vol. 4. Tokyo: Chikuma Shobō, 1967.

Imaeda, Aishin. *Zenshū no rekishi.* Tokyo: Shibundō, 1966.

Mutsu Munemitsu

Hakushaku Mutsu Munemitsu ikō. Tokyo: Iwanami Shoten, 1929.

Watanabe, Ikujirō. *Mutsu Munemitsu den.* Tokyo: Kaizōsha, 1934.

Shinobu, Seizaburō. *Mutsu Munemitsu.* Tokyo: Hakuyōsha, 1936.

Myōan Eisai

Taga, Munehaya. *Eisai.* Tokyo: Yoshikawa Kōbunkan, 1965.

Ichikawa, Hakugen; Iriya, Yoshitaka; and Yanagida Seizan. *Chūsei zenka no shisō.* Tokyo: Iwanami Shoten 1972.

Nagaoka Hantarō

Nagaoka, Hantarō. *Kaikodan.* Nihon butsuri gakkai shi, vol. 5, No. 6. 1950.

Itakura, Kiyonobu; Kimura, Tōsaku; and Yagi, Eri. *Nagaoka Hantarō den.* Tokyo: Asahi Shimbunsha, 1973.

Nakae Chōmin

Kaji, Ryūichi, ed. *Chōmin senshū.* Tokyo: Iwanami Shoten, 1936.

Kōtoku, Shūsui. *Chōmin sensei, Chōmin sensei gyōjōki.* Tokyo: Iwanami Shoten, 1960.

Kuwabara, Takeo, ed. *Nakae Chōmin no kenkyū.* Tokyo: Iwanami Shoten, 1966.

Nakae Tōju

Takahashi, Toshinori. *Nakae Tōju.* Tokyo: Kōbundō, 1942.

Imabori, Bun'ichirō. *Nakae Tōju.* Tokyo: Airyūdō, 1959.

Fisher, Galen M. *The Life and Teaching of Nakae Tōju.* TASJ 36, 1, (1908), pp. 24–94.

Nakagawa Jun'an

Wada, Shinjirō. *Nakagawa Jun'an sensei.* Kyoto: Ritsumeikan Shuppanbu, 1941.

Nakahama Manjirō

Nakahama, Tōichirō. *Nakahama Manjirō-den.* Tokyo: Fuzambō, 1936.

Warinner, E. V., and Tanaka, Itaru, tr. *Shin Jon Manjirō-den.* Tokyo: Shuppan Kyōdōsha, 1966.

Nakamura Masanao

Ishii, Kendō. *Nakamura Masanao den.* Tokyo: Seikō Zasshisha, 1907.

Takahashi, Masao. *Nakamura Keiu.* Jimbutsu sōsho. Tokyo: Yoshikawa Kōbunkan, 1966.

Nakayama Miki

Kasahara, Kazuo. *Tenkanki no shūkyō.* Tokyo: Nihon Hōsō Shuppan Kyōkai, 1966.

Oguri, Junko. *Nakayama Miki—Tenrikyō.* Tokyo: Shinjimbutsu Ōraisha, 1970.

Murakami, Shigeyoshi, and Yasumaru, Yoshio. *Minshū shūkyō no shisō.* Nihon shisō taikei. Tokyo: Iwanami Shoten, 1971.

Nanjō Bunyū
Tsunemitsu, Kōnen. *Meiji no Bukkyōsha*, vol. 1. Tokyo: Shunjūsha, 1968.

Nichiō
Miyazaki, Eishū. *Kinsei Fuju-fuse ha no kenkyū*. Kyoto: Heiraku-ji Shoten, 1959.
———. *Fuju-fuse ha no genryū to tenkai*. Kyoto: Heiraku-ji Shoten, 1969.
Tamamuro, Fumio, et al. *Kinsei no chika shinkō*. Tokyo: Hyōronsha, 1974.

Nichiren
Risshō Daigaku Nichiren Kyōgaku Kenkyūsho, ed. *Shōwa teihon Nichiren shōnin ibun*, 4 vols. 1952–59.
Tokoro, Shigemoto, and Takagi, Yutaka. *Nichiren*. Nihon shisō taikei. Tokyo: Iwanami Shoten, 1970.
Sakamoto Nisshin, ed. *Kōza Nichiren*, 5 vols. Tokyo: Shunjūsha, 1972–73.
Takagi, Yutaka. *Nichiren—sono kōdō to shisō*. Tokyo: Hyōronsha, 1970.
Anesaki, Masaharu. *Nichiren, the Buddhist Prophet*. Gloucester, Mass.: Peter Smith, 1966.

Niijima Jō
Davis, J. P.; Murata, Tsutomu; Matsuura, Seihō, trs. *Niijima Jō sensei den*. Fukuinsha, 1891.
Watanabe, Minoru. *Niijima Jō*. Jimbutsu sōsho. Tokyo: Yoshikawa Kōbunkan, 1959.
Dōshisha, ed. *Niijima Jō shokanshū*. Tokyo: Iwanami Shoten, 1954.

Nimmyō Tennō
Shoku Nihon kōki. Tokyo: Yoshikawa Kōbunkan, 1964.

Ninkai
Toganoo, Shōun. *Mikkyō Bukkyō-shi*. Gendai Bukkyō meicho zenshū, vol. 9. Tokyo: Ryūbunkan, 1964.

Ninomiya Sontoku
Ninomiya Sontoku zenshū, 36 vols. Ninomiya Sontoku Igyō Senyōkai, 1927–32.
Naramoto, Tatsuya. *Ninomiya Sontoku*. Tokyo: Iwanami Shoten, 1959.
A Peasamt Sage of Japan, the Life and Works of Sontoku Ninomiya, Translated by Yoshimoto Tadasu from the *Hōtokuki*. London: Longmans Green, 1912.
Tadaatsu, Ishiguro, ed. *Ninomiya Sontoku, His Life and Evening Talks*. Tokyo: Kenkyūsha, 1955.

Ninshō
Wajima, Yoshio. *Eison, Ninshō*. Tokyo: Yoshikawa Kōbunkan, 1959.

Nintoku Tennō
Tōma, Seita. *Wa no Goō*. Tokyo: Iwanami Shoten, 1968.

Nishi Amane
Okubo, Toshiaki, ed. *Nishi Amane zenshū*, 3 vols. Tokyo: Munetaka Shobō, 1960–63.
Mori, Ōgai, ed. and pub. *Nishi Amane den*. Ōgai zenshū. Tokyo: Iwanami Shoten, 1898.

Nishida Kitarō
Nishida Kitarō zenshū, 19 vols. Tokyo: Iwanami Shoten, 1965–66.
Shimomura, Toratarō. *Nishida Kitarō*. Tokyo: Tōkai Daigaku Shuppankai, 1965.
Takeuchi, Yoshitomo. *Nishida Kitarō*. Tokyo: Tokyo Daigaku Shuppankai, 1966.

Nishi Gempo
Itasawa, Takeo. *Nichiran bunka kōshōshi no kenkyū*. Tokyo: Yoshikawa Kōbunkan, 1973.
Koga, Jūjirō. *Seiyō igaku denraishi*. Nisshinshoin, 1944.

Nishikawa Joken
Hosokawa, Junjirō. *Nishikawa Joken den*, Nishikawa Joken isho, vol. 1. 1899.
Iijima, Tadao. *Nihon suidokō, Kai tsūshōkō jo*. Tokyo: Iwanami Shoten, 1944.

Nishimura Katsuzō
Inobe, Shigeo. *Nishimura Katsuzō-ō den*. Tokyo: Nishimura Denki Hensankai, 1921.
Horie, Yasuzō. "Jitsugyōkai no senkaku Nishimura Katsuzō-ō," *Keizaishi Kenkyū* 25–4, 1941.

Nishimura Shigeki
Nihon Kōdōkai, ed. *Hakuō sōsho*, 2 vols. Tokyo: Hakubunkan, 1909, 1912.
Nishimura Sensei Denki Hensankai, ed. *Hakuō Nishimura Shigeki den*, 2 vols. Tokyo: Nihon Kōdōkai, 1933.

Nisshin
Nakao, Takashi. *Nisshin—sono kōdō to shisō*. Tokyo: Hyōronsha, 1971.
Nakamura, Hajime; Kasahara, Kazuo; and Kanaoka, Shūyū, eds. *Nihon-hen*. Ajia Bukkyōshi, 6. Tokyo: Kōsei Shuppankai, 1972.

Nitobe Inazō
Nitobe Inazō zenshū, 16 vols. Tokyo: Kyōbunkan, 1969.
Ishii, Mitsuru. *Nitobe Inazō den*. Tokyo: Sekiya Shoten, 1934.
Matsukuma, Toshiko. *Nitobe Inazō*. Tokyo: Misuzu Shobō, 1969.

Nitta Yoshisada
Chijiwa, Minoru, ed. *Nitta Yoshisada Kō kompon shiryō*. Gumma Prefecture: Gumma-ken Kyōikukai, 1942.

Nogi Maresuke
Matsushita, Yoshio. *Nogi Maresuke*. Tokyo: Yoshikawa Kōbunkan, 1960.

Noguchi Hideyo
Okumura, Tsurukichi, ed. *Noguchi Hideyo*. Tokyo: Iwanami Shoten, 1933.
Eckstein, Gustav, and Uchida, Kiyonosuke, tr. *Noguchi Hideyo den*. Tokyo: Sōgensha, 1931.

Nomi no Sukune
"Nomi no Sukune," *Jimbutsu: Nihon no rekishi*, vol. 1. Tokyo: Yomiuri Shimbunsha, 1966.

Nomura Kichisaburō
Nomura, Kichisaburō. *Beikoku ni tsukai shite*. Tokyo: Iwanami Shoten, 1946.
Koba, Kōsuke, et al. *Nomura Kichisaburō*. Nomura Kichisaburō Denki Kankōkai, 1961.

Noro Eitarō
Noro Eitarō zenshū, 2 vols. Tokyo: Shin-Nihon Shuppansha, 1965.
Shiozawa, Tomiko. *Noro Eitarō no omoide*. Tokyo: Shin-Nihon Shuppansha, 1976.

Nosaka Sanzō
Nosaka Sanzō senshū, 2 vols. Tokyo: Nihon Kyōsantō Shuppanbu, 1966.
Nosaka, Sanzō. *Bōmei jūrokunen*. Tokyo: Jiji Tsūshinsha, 1946.
———. *Fūsetsu no ayumi*, 3 vols. Tokyo: Shin-Nihon Shuppansha, 1971–75.

Oda Nobunaga
Ōta, Gyūichi. *Nobunaga-kō ki*. Tokyo: Kadokawa Shoten, 1969.
Suzuki, Ryōichi. *Oda Nobunaga*. Tokyo: Iwanami Shoten, 1967.
Okuno, Takahiro. *Nobunaga to Hideyoshi*. Tokyo: Shibundō, 1955.
Kuwada, Tadachika. *Oda Nobunaga*. Tokyo: Kadokawa Shoten, 1964.
Laures, Johannes. *Nobunaga und das Christentum*. Tokyo: Monumenta Nipponica, 1950.

Oda Nobuo
Ōta, Gyūchi. *Nobunaga-kō-ki*. Tokyo: Kadokawa Shoten, 1969.
Hanami, Sakumi. *Azuchi Momoyama jidai-shi*. Tokyo: Naigai Shoten, 1939.
Okuno, Takahiro. *Nobunaga to Hideyoshi*. Tokyo: Shibundō, 1955.

Oda Nobutada
Ōta, Gyūichi. *Nobunaga-kō ki.* Tokyo: Kadokawa Shoten, 1969.
Hanami, Sakumi. *Azuchi Momoyama jidai-shi.* Tokyo: Naigai Shoseki, 1939.
Abe, Einosuke. *Oda Nobunaga, Nobutada fushi byōsho.* Shiseki meishō-hō, 7. 1938.

Ōe no Hiromoto
Nitta, Eiji. "Ōe no Hiromoto." *Nihon jimbutsushi taikei,* vol. 2. Tokyo: Asakura Shoten, 1959.

Ogata Kōan
Ogata, Tomio. *Ogata Kōan.* Tokyo: Kōbunsha, 1942.
Ogata Kōan Zōi Shukugakai, ed. *Kōan sensei ryakuden.* 1909.
Ogata, Keijirō. *Ogata Kōan to Ashimori.* 1927.

Ōgimachi Tennō
Hayashiya, Tatsusaburō. *Tenka ittō.* Nihon no rekishi, No. 12. Tokyo: Chūō Kōronsha, 1966.

Ogiwara Shigehide
Arai, Hakuseki. *Oritakushiba-no-ki.*
Kyūshōroku (shahon)
Kaganroku, Zoku-enseki jisshu, vol. 1. 1908.

Ōgo (Mokujiki Shōnin)
Hosokawa, Kameichi. "Kinsei shoki no Kōyasan to Mokujiki shōnin," *Rekishi Kyōiku,* vol. 6, No. 2, 1932.

Ōi Kentarō
Ōi, Kentarō. *Bajō Ōi Kentarō den.* Edited by Hirano Yoshitarō and Fukushima Shingo, Nagoya: Fūbaisha, 1968. (supplementary volume, *Ōi Kentarō no kenkyū*)

Ōishi Yoshio
Matsushima, Eiichi. *Chūshingura.* Tokyo: Iwanami Shoten, 1964.
Fukumoto, Nichinan. *Ōishi Kuranosuke.* Tokyo: Yōkendō, 1914.
Shinshi, Yoshimoto. *Ōishi Yoshio to sono ittō.* Nihon jimbutsu taikei 3. Tokyo: Asakura Shoten, 1959.

Ōjin Tennō
Mizuno, Hiroshi. *Nihon kodai ōchō shiron josetsu.* Tokyo: Komiyama Shoten, 1952.

Okada Keisuke
Okada Keisuke kaikoroku. Tokyo: Mainichi Shimbunsha, 1950.
Okada Keisuke. Ōkada Taishō Kiroku Hensankai, 1956.

Ōkawa Shūmei
Ōkawa Shūmei zenshū. Tokyo: Iwasaki Shoten, 1961–63.
Aochi, Shin. "Okawa Shūmei to Ajia kaihō." *Chūō Kōron* 80/3, 1965.

Ōkubo Toshimichi
Nihon Shiseki Kyōkai. *Ōkubo Toshimichi monjo* (1927–29), 10 vols. Tokyo: Tokyo Daigaku Shuppankai, 1967–69.
Rikkyō Daigaku Nihonshi Kenkyūshitsu. *Ōkubo Toshimichi kankei monjo,* 5 vols. Tokyo: Yoshikawa Kōbunkan, 1965–71.
Katsuta, Magoya. *Ōkubo Toshimichi den,* 3 vols. Tokyo: Dōbunkan, 1911.

Ōkuma Shigenobu
Watanabe, Ikujirō. *Ōkuma Shigenobu.* Ōkuma Shigenobu Kankōkai, 1952.
———, ed. *Ōkuma Shigenobu kankei monjo,* 6 vols. Nihon Shiseki Kyōkai, 1932–35.
Enjōji, Kiyoshi, ed. *Ōkuma haku sekijitsu dan.* 1st pub., 1895; Tokyo: Fuzambō, 1938.
Ichijima, Kenkichi, and Nakano, Reishirō, ed. *Ōkuma kō hachijūgo-nen shi,* 4 vols., Okumakō Hachijūgonen Shi Kankōkai, 1926.

Okumura Ioko
Ogasawara, Naganari. *Seiden Okumura Ioko*. Nampō Shuppansha, 1942.

Ōkura Nagatsune
Hayakawa, Kōtarō. *Ōkura Nagatsune*. Yamaoka Shoten, 1938.
Mihashi, Tokio. "Ōkura Nagatsune." *Keizaishi Kenkyū* 35, No. 3, 1941.
Tamura, Eitarō. *Sangyō shidōsha: Ōkura Nagatsune*. Tokyo: Tosho Shuppan, 1944.

Ōmi no Mifune
Sakamoto, Tarō. "Ressei Kampū shigō no senshū ni tsuite," *Shigaku Zasshi* 43, No. 7.

Ōmura Masujirō
Ōmura Masujirō. Ōmura Masujirō Sensei Denki Kankōkai, 1944.
Itoya, Toshio. *Ōmura Masujirō*. Tokyo: Chūō Kōronsha, 1971.
Uchida, Shin, ed. *Ōmura Masujirō monjo*. Yamaguchi (Tokuyama): Matsuno Shoten, 1977.

Ōmura Sumitada
Matsuda, Kiichi. *Ōmura Sumitada den*. Ōmura: Ōmura Sumitada Denki Kankōkai, 1955.

Ono Azusa
Nishimura, Shinji. *Ono Azusa den*. Tokyo: Fuzambō, 1935.
———, ed. *Ono Azusa zenshū*, 2 vols. Tokyo: Fuzambō, 1936.

Ono no Imoko
Mori, Katsumi. *Kentōshi*. Tokyo: Shibundō, 1941.

Ono Ranzan
Meijizen Nihon seibutsugakushi, 2 vols. Tokyo: Nihon Gakushi-in, 1960–63.
Meijizen Nihon igakushi, 5 vols. Tokyo: Nihon Gakushi-in, 1955–64.
Meijizen Nihon yakubutsugakushi, 2 vols. Tokyo: Nihon Gakushi-in, 1957–58.

Ōoka Tadasuke
Numada, Yorisuke. *Ōoka Echizen no Kami*. Tokyo: Meiji Shoin, 1929.
Tsuji, Tatsuya. *Ōoka Echizen no Kami*. Tokyo: Chūō Kōronsha, 1964.
Oishi, Shinsaburō, ed. *Ōoka Echizen no Kami Tadasuke nikki*, 3 vols. Tokyo: San'ichi Shobō, 1972–75.

Osakabe Shinnō
Takikawa, Masajirō. *Ritsuryō no kenkyū*. Tokyo: Tōkō Shoin, 1966.

Ōsen Keisen
Tamamura, Takeji, ed. *Ōsen Keisen shū*. Gozan bungaku shinshū, vol. 1. Tokyo: Tokyo Daigaku Shuppankai, 1967.

Ōshio Heihachirō
Kōda, Shigetomo. *Ōshio Heihachirō*. Tokyo: Sōgensha, 1943.
Okamoto, Ryōichi. *Ōshio Heihachirō*. Tokyo: Sōgensha, 1956.

Ōsugi Sakae
Ōsugi Sakae zenshū, 11 vols. Tokyo: Sekai Bunko, 1963–64.
Ōsugi Sakae Kenkyūkai, ed. *Ōsugi Sakae shokenshū*. Tokyo: Kaien Shobō, 1975.
Ōsawa, Masamichi. *Ōsugi Sakae kenkyū*. Tokyo: Dōseisha, 1968.

Ōtani Kōzui
Tsunemitsu, Kōnen. *Meiji no Bukkyōsha*, vol. 2. Tokyo: Shunjūsha, 1969.
Ōtani Kōzui zenshū, 13 vols. Tokyo: Daijōsha, 1934–36.

Ōtomo no Kanamura
Yagi, Atsuru. *Ōtomo no Kanamura no shikkyaku*. Nihon shoki kenkyū, vol. 1. Tokyo: Hanawa Shobō, 1964.

Ōtomo Sōrin
Hakusui, Kōji. *Ōtomo Sōrin*. Tokyo: Shunjūsha, 1970.
Akutagawa, Tatsuo. *Bungo-Ōtomo-shi*. Sengokushi-sōsho, No. 9. Tokyo: Shin Jimbutsu Ōraisha, 1972.

Ōtsuki Gentaku
Ōtsuki, Joden. *Ōtsuki Bansui*. Tokyo: Hakubunkan, 1902.
Sugi, Yasusaburō. "Nihon no kagaku o sodateta hitotachi, 14." *Kagaku Asahi* 2–12, 1942.

Ōuchi Yoshitaka
Fukuo, Mōichirō. *Ōuchi Yoshitaka*. Tokyo: Yoshikawa Kōbunkan, 1959.

Ōyama Ikuo
Ōyama Ikuo zenshū, 5 vols. Tokyo: Chūō Kōronsha, 1947–49.
Ōyama Ikuo Kinen Jigyōkai, ed. *Ōyama Ikuo-den*, 2 vols. Tokyo: Chūō Kōronsha, 1956.

Ōyama Iwao
Ono Minobu, ed. *Gensui kōshaku Ōyama Iwao*, 3 vols. Ōyama Gensui Den Kankōkai, 1932.

Ozaki Yukio
Ozaki Yukio zenshū, 12 vols. Tokyo: Kōronsha, 1955–56.
Isa, Hideo. *Ozaki Yukio*. Jimbutsu sōsho. Tokyo: Yoshikawa Kōbunkan, 1960.
Gakudō kaisōroku, 2 vols. Tokyo: Ondorisha, 1951–52.

Rennyo
Kasahara, Kazuo. *Rennyo*. Tokyo: Yoshikawa Kōbunkan, 1963.

Rōben
Inoue, Kaoru. *Narachō Bukkyōshi no kenkyū*. Tokyo: Yoshikawa Kōbunkan, 1966.

Ryōgen
Hirabayashi, Moritoku. "Ryōgen to Eizan no chūkō." *Rekishi Kyōiku*, vol. 12, No. 6, 1964.

Ryōnin
Inoue, Mitsusada. *Nihon jōdokyō seiritsu-shi no kenkyū*. Tokyo: Yamakawa Shuppansha, 1956.
———. *Nihon kodai no kokka to bukkyō*. Tokyo: Iwanami Shoten, 1971.
Ishida, Mizumaro. *Jōdokyō no tenkai*. Tokyo: Shunjūsha, 1967.

Saga Tennō
Kitayama, Shigeo. *Nihon no rekishi*, vol. 4. Tokyo: Chūō Kōronsha, 1965.

Saichō
Andō, Toshio, and Sonoda, Kōyū. *Saichō*. Nihon shisō taikei. Tokyo: Iwanami Shoten, 1974.
Fukunaga, Kōji, ed. *Saichō, Kūkai*. Nihon no meicho. Tokyo: Chūō Kōronsha, 1977.
Shioiri, Ryōchū. *Dengyō daishi*. Tokyo: Nihon Hyōronsha, 1937.
Kiuchi, Hiroshi. *Dengyō daishi no shōgai to shisō*. Tokyo: Daisan Bummeisha, 1976.

Saigō Takamori
Dai Saigō Zenshū Kankōkai. *Dai Saigō zenshū*, 3 vols. Tokyo: Heibonsha, 1926–27.
Katsuda, Magoya. *Saigō Takamori den*, 5 vols. Saigō Takamori Den Hakkōjo, 1894.
Saigō Takamori zenshū, 6 vols. Tokyo: Daiwa Shobō, 1976.
Tanaka, Sōgorō. *Saigō Takamori*. Tokyo: Yoshikawa Kōbunkan, 1957.

Saigō Tsugumichi
Saigō totoku to Kabayama sōtoku. Saigō Totoku Kabayama Sōtoku Ki'nen Jigyō Shuppan Iinkai, 1936.
Tokutomi, Iichirō. *Saigō Tsugumichi kō: Sohō bunsen*. Tokyo: Min'yūsha, 1915.

Saionji Kimmochi
Harada, Kumao. *Saionji Kō to seikyoku*, 9 vols. Tokyo: Iwanami Shoten, 1950–56.

Takekoshi, Yosaburō. *Tōan kō Saionji Kimmochi kō den*. Tokyo: Sōbunkaku, 1930.
Saionji Kimmochi jiden. Recorded by Koizumi Sakutarō; edited by Kimura Ki. Tokyo: Kōdansha, 1949.
Kimura, Ki. *Saionji Kimmochi*. Sandai saishō retsuden. Tokyo: Jiji Tsūshinsha, 1958.

Saitō Makoto
Saitō Shishaku Ki'nenkai, ed. and pub., *Shishaku Saitō Makoto den*, 4 vols. 1941–42.
Aritake, Shuji. *Saitō Makoto*. Sandai saishō retsuden. Tokyo: Jiji Tsūshinsha, 1958.

Sakai Tadakiyo
Kitajima, Masamoto. *Edo Bakufu: sono jitsuryokushatachi*, vol. 1. Tokyo: Jimbutsu Ōraisha, 1964.

Sakai Toshihiko
Sakai Toshihiko zenshū, 6 vols. Tokyo: Hōritsu Bunkasha, 1970–71.
"Sakai Kosen" (transcript of a discussion by Yamakawa Hitoshi, Arahata Kanson, and others). *Sekai* 118, 119, 1955.

Sakamoto Ryōma
Ikeda, Satoshi. *Sakamoto Ryōma*. Tokyo: Daiwa Shobō, 1864.
Ikeda, Yukimasa. *Sakamoto Ryōma*. Tokyo: Chūō Kōronsha, 1965.
Jansen, Marius. *Sakamoto Ryōma and the Meiji Restoration*. Princeton University Press, 1961.

Sakanoue no Tamuramaro
Takahashi, Takashi. *Sakanoue no Tamuramaro*. Tokyo: Yoshikawa Kōbunkan, 1959.

Sakuma Shōzan
Miyamoto, Chū. *Sakuma Shōzan*. Tokyo: Iwanami Shoten, 1932.
Shōzan zenshū, 5 vols. Nagano: Shinano Mainichi Shimbunsha, 1934–35.
Ōhira, Kimata. *Sakuma Shōzan*. Tokyo: Yoshikawa Kōbunkan, 1959.

Sakura Sōgorō
Kodama, Kōta. *Sakura Sōgorō*. Tokyo: Yoshikawa Kōbunkan.

Sanjōnishi Sanetaka
Hara, Katsurō. *Higashiyama jidai ni okeru ichi shinshin no seikatsu*. Tokyo: Sōgensha, 1941.
Haga, Kōshirō. *Sanjōnishi Sanetaka*. Tokyo: Yoshikawa Kōbunkan, 1960.
———. *Sanetaka nikki*, 6 vols. Tokyo: Gunsho Ruijū Kanseikai, 1956.

Sanjō Sanetomi
Sanjō Sanetomi kō nempu, 30 vols. Tokyo: Kunaishō Zushoryō, 1901.
Tokutomi, Iichirō. *Sanjō Sanetsumu kō, Sanjō Sanetomi kō*. Kyoto: Nashinoki Jinja Chinza Gojūnen Ki'nensai Hōsankai, 1935.

Sano Manabu
Sano Manabu Chosakushū Kankōkai, ed. *Sano Manabu chosakushū*, 5 vols. Sano Manabu Chosakushū Kankōkai, 1957–58.
Takabatake, Michitoshi. *Ikkoku shakaishugisha—Sano Manabu, Nabeyama Sadachika: Tenkō*. Tokyo: Heibonsha, 1959.

Sano Tsunetami
Kitajima, Kishū, and Nonaka, Mantarō. *Nihon sekijūjisha no sōritsusha Sano Tsunetami den*. 1928.
Iwasaki, Komatarō. *Nihon sekijūjishachō Hakushaku Sano Tsunetami den*. Nihon Sekijūji, ed., 1912.

Satō Eisaku
Ōya Sōichi. "Gen'ei no naka no seijika, Satō Eisaku." *Chūō Kōron* 80–2, 1965.

Satō Issai
Takase, Daijirō. *Satō Issai to sono monjin.* Tokyo: Manyōdō, 1922.
Kamei, Kazuo. *Daiju Satō Issai.* Tokyo: Kinkei Gakuin, 1931.

Satō Nobuhiro
Ono, Takeo. *Satō Nobuhiro.* Shin ijinden zenshū, vol. 30. Tokyo: Chōbunkaku, 1943.
Takimoto, Seiichi, ed. *Satō Nobuhiro kagaku zenshū,* 3 vols. Tokyo: Iwanami Shoten, 1924–32.
Hani, Gorō. *Satō Nobuhiro ni kansuru kisoteki kenkyū.* Tokyo: Iwanami Shoten, 1929.

Seiwa Tennō
Ōta, Ryō. *Nihon shinbunkashi: Heianchō shoki.* Tokyo: Naigai Shoseki, 1941.

Seki Takakazu
Mikami, Yoshio. "Seki Takakazu no gyōseki to Keihan no sanka narabi ni Shina no sampō to no kankei oyobi hikaku." *Tōyō gakuhō* 20–22.
Ogura Kinnosuke. *Sūgakushi no kenkyū,* 2. 1948.
Hirayama, Akira. *Seki Takakazu.* Tokyo: Kōseisha, 1959.

Senoo Girō
Inagaki, Masami. *Budda o seoite gaitō e.* Tokyo: Iwanami Shoten, 1974.
———, ed. *Senoo Girō nikki,* 7 vols. Tokyo: Kokusho Kankōkai, 1974.
Hayashi, Reihō. *Senoo Girō to shinkō Bukkyō seinen dōmei.* Kyoto: Hyakkaen, 1976.

Sesson Yūbai
Tamamura, Takeji, ed. *Sesson Yūbaishū.* Gozan bungaku shinshū, vol. 3. Tokyo: Tokyo Daigaku Shuppankai, 1969.

Shaku Sōen
Tsunemitsu, Kōnen. *Meiji no Bukkyōsha,* vol. 1. Tokyo: Shunjūsha, 1968.
Shaku Sōen zenshū, 10 vols. Tokyo: Heibonsha, 1929–30.

Shibata Kyūō
Ishikawa, Ken. *Shibata Kyūō no shōgai to sono shingaku shisō.* Nihon seishinshi ronsan, #2. Tokyo: Iwanami Shoten, 1935.
Ototake Iwazō. *Kyūō dōwa no kōzō oyobi seikaku.* Nihon kyōikushi kenkyū, #2. Tokyo: Meguro Shoten, 1939.

Shibukawa Shunkai
Nishiuchi, Masaru. *Shibukawa Shunkai no kenkyū.* Tokyo: Shibundō, 1940.

Shibusawa Eiichi
Shibusawa Eiichi denki shiryō, 58 vols. Tokyo: Ryūmonsha, 1955–66.
Seien kaikoroku, 2 vols. Tokyo: Ryūmonsha, 1927.
Tsuchiya, Takao. *Shibusawa Eiichi den.* Tokyo: Tōyō Shokan, 1955.

Shidehara Kijūrō
Shidehara Heiwa Zaidan, ed. *Shidehara Kijūrō.* Shidehara Heiwa Zaidan, 1955.
Shidehara, Kijūrō. *Gaikō gōjū nen.* Tokyo: Yomiuri Shimbunsha, 1951.

Shiga Kiyoshi
Shiga Kiyoshi. *Aru saikingakusha no kaisō.* Tokyo: Sekkasha, 1966.
Takahashi, Isao. *Shiga Kiyoshi.* Tokyo: Hōsei Daigaku Shuppankyoku, 1957.

Shiga Shigetaka
Shiga Shigetaka Zenshū Kankōkai, ed. *Shiga Shigetaka zenshū,* 8 vols. Shiga Shigetaka Zenshū Kankōkai, 1927–29.
Iwai, Tadakuma. "Shiga Shigetaka-ron." Pts. 1, 2, 3. *Ritsumeikan Bungaku* 186, 194, 198, 1960–61.

Shiga Yoshio
Tokuda, Kyūichi, and Shiga, Yoshio. *Gokuchū jūhachinen.* Tokyo: Jiji Tsūshinsha, 1947. (reprinted by Ōtsuki Shoten, 1955.)

Shigemitsu Mamoru
Shigemitsu, Mamoru. *Shōwa no dōran*, 2 vols. Tokyo: Chūō Kōronsha, 1952.

Shimaji Mokurai
Shimaji Mokurai zenshū, 5 vols. Kyoto: Hongan-ji Shuppan Kyōkai, 1973.
Yoshida, Kyūichi. *Nihon no kindai shakai to Bukkyō*. Tokyo: Hyōronsha, 1970.
Ikeda, Hidetoshi. *Meiji no Bukkyō—sono kōdō to shisō*. Tokyo: Hyōronsha, 1976.

Shimazu Hisamitsu
Shimazu Kōshaku-ke Hensansho. *Shimazu Hisamitsu-kō jikki*, 8 vols. Tokyo: Kokubunsha, 1910.
Tsukuba, Hisaharu. *Shimazu Hisamitsu ron*. Kyōdo kenkyū Meijiishin, Shisō no kagaku kenkyūkai. Tokyo: Tokuma Shoten, 1967.

Shimazu Nariakira
Shimazu Nariakira genkōroku. Tokyo: Iwanami Shoten, 1944.
Shimazu Nariakira monjo, 4 vols. Tokyo: Yoshikawa Kōbunkan, 1959–63.

Shinjō
Takamine, Ryōshū. *Kegon shisō-shi*. Hyakkaen, 1942.
Gyōnen. "Hokkai gikyō." *Kamakura kyūbukkyō*. Nihon shisō taikei, 15. Tokyo: Iwanami Shoten, 1971.

Shinran
Teihon Shinran shōnin zenshū, 9 vols. Kyoto: Hōzōkan.
Akamatsu, Toshihide. *Shinran*. Tokyo: Yoshikawa Kōbunkan, 1961.
Furuta, Takehiko. *Shinran shisō*. Tokyo: Fuzambō, 1975.
"The Life of Shinran Shōnin." Translated by Daisetz Suzuki. In *Collected Writings on Shin Buddhism*, pp. 165–93. Kyoto: Shinshū Otaniha, 1974.
The Private Letters of Shinran Shōnin. Translated by Yamamoto Kōshō. Tokyo: Okasakiya Shoten, 1946.

Shizuki Tadao
Kimura, Yasuyuki. "Shizuki Tadao." *Chūō Kōron*, vol. 56, no. 9, 1941.
Numata, Jirō. *Shizuki Tadao to sono jidai*. Rekishi to Jimbutsu. Tokyo: Yoshikawa Kōbunkan, 1964.

Shōbō
Sawa, Ryūken. *Daigo-ji*. Kyoto: Tōyō bunkasha, 1976.
Toganoo, Shōun. *Mikkyō Bukkyō-shi*, Gendai Bukkyō meicho zenshū, vol. 9. Tokyo: Ryūbunkan, 1964.
Hatta, Yukio. "Shugen Ein hōryū no giki to mikkyō (1)." *Nihon Bukkyō*, No. 40, 1977.

Shōmu Tennō
Tōdai-ji, ed. *Shōmu Tennō gyoden*. Nara: Tōdai-ji, 1956.
Kawasaki, Tsuneyuki. *Shōmu Tennō to sono jidai*. Nanto bukkyō, #2. 1955.

Shōtoku Taishi
Ogura, Toyofumi. *Shōtoku taishi to Shōtoku taishi shinkō*. Kyoto: Sōgeisha, 1963.
Ono, Tatsunosuke. *Shōtoku taishi no kenkyū*. Tokyo: Yoshikawa Kōbunkan, 1970.
Ienaga Saburō, et. al., ed. *Shōtoku taishi shū*. Nihon shisō taikei 2. Tokyo: Iwanami Shoten, 1975.
Anesaki, Masaharu. *Prince Shōtoku, the Sage Statesman*. Tokyo: Shōtoku Taishi Hōsankai, the Boonjudō Publishing House, 1948.
Bohner, Hermann. *Shōtoku-taishi*. Tokyo: Deutsche Gesellschaft für Natür und Völkerkunde Ostasiens, 1940.

Shūhō Myōchō
Ogisu, Jundō. *Daitō* Kōza: Zen, vol. 4. Tokyo: Chikuma Shobō, 1967.
Karaki, Junzō, ed. *Zenka goroku-shū*. Tokyo: Chikuma Shobō, 1969.

Shunjō
Ishida, Mitsuyuki, ed. *Kamakura Bukkyō no seiritsu, Shunjō risshi.* Kyoto: Hōzōkan, 1972.

Shun'oku Myōha
Tsuji Zennosuke. *Nihon Bukkyō-shi,* vol. 4. 2nd ed. Tokyo: Iwanami Shoten, 1960.
Imaeda, Aishin. *Zenshū no rekishi.* Tokyo: Shibundō, 1966.

Soejima Taneomi
Maruyama, Kanji. *Soejima Taneomi haku.* Tokyo: Dainichisha, 1936.
Soejima taishi teki-shin gairyaku, 1873. Meiji bunka zenshū, Gaikōhen. Tokyo: Nihon Hyōronsha, 1928.

Soga no Iname
Masuda, Takashi. "Kimmei Tennō jūsannen Bukkyō tokaisetsu no seiritsu." *Nihon kodaishi ronshū,* vol. 1. Tokyo: Yoshikawa Kōbunkan, 1962.

Soga no Iruka
Seki, Akira. "Taika kaishin." *Iwanami kōza Nihon rekishi,* ch. 2. Tokyo: Iwanami Shoten, 1962.

Soga no Umako
Naoki, Kōjirō. *Nihon no rekishi,* vol. 3. Tokyo: Chūō Kōronsha, 1965.

Sūden
Tsuji, Zennosuke. *Nihon Bukkyōshi,* 8 vols. Tokyo: Iwanami Shoten, 1961.

Sugawara no Michizane
Nakada, Norinobu. *Kan-kō jireki oyobi keifu, Kan-kō jireki tsuika.* Kōko ruisan, vol. 1. Kōkosha, 1900.
Takayanagi, Mitsuhisa. "Kan-kō ni kan suru bunken," *Kobijitsu Kenkyū* 163.
Sakamoto, Tarō. *Sugawara no Michizane.* Tokyo: Yoshikawa Kōbunkan, 1962.

Sugita Gempaku
Katagiri, Kazuo. *Sugita Gempaku.* Tokyo: Yoshikawa Kōbunkan, 1971.

Sugiura Shigetake
Sugiura, Shigetake. *Rinri goshinkō sōan.* 1936.
Sugiura Shigetake zadanroku. Tokyo: Iwanami Shoten, 1941.
Ikari, Shizan. *Sugiura Shigetake.* Tokyo: Shinchōsha, 1941.

Suiko Tennō
Mayuzumi, Hiromichi. "Suiko-chō no igi." *Iwanami koza—Nihon rekishi,* ch. 2. Tokyo: Iwanami Shoten, 1962.

Sujin Tennō
Inoue, Mitsusada. *Nihon rekishi,* vol. 1. Tokyo: Chūō Kōronsha, 1965.
Kojiki. Translated by Donald L. Philippi. Tokyo: University of Tokyo Press, 1968.

Suminokura Ryōi
Hayashiya, Tatsusaburō. *Suminokura Ryōi to sono ko.* Kyoto: Hoshino Shoten, 1944.
Iwao, Seiichi. *Shuinsen bōekishi no kenkyū.* Kyoto: Kōbundō, 1958.
Tsuji, Zennosuke. "Suminokura Ryōi to Biwako sosui keikaku." *Rekishi Chiri,* Sept., 1907.

Suzuki Bunji
Suzuki, Bunji. *Rōdō undō nijūnen.* Tokyo: Ichigensha, 1931.
Nakamura, Katsunori. "Suzuki Bunji to Taishō rōdō undō," *Hōgaku Kenkyū,* vol. 32, Nos. 2, 3, 6, 1959.

Suzuki Daisetsu
Suzuki Daisetsu zenshū, 30 vols. Tokyo: Iwanami Shoten, 1968.
Matsutani, Fumio, ed. *Suzuki Daisetsu.* Gendai Nihon shisō taikei. Tokyo: Chikuma Shobō, 1964.

Hisamatsu Shin'ichi; Yamaguchi, Susumu; and Furuta Shōkin, eds. *Suzuki Daisetsu—hito to shisō*. Tokyo: Iwanami Shoten, 1971.

Suzuki Kantarō

Suzuki, Hajime, ed. *Suzuki Kantarō jiden*. Ōkikukai Publication Division, 1949.

Suzuki Kantarō den. Suzuki Kantarō Denki Hensan Iinkai, 1960.

Suzuki Mosaburō

Suzuki, Mosaburō. *Watakushi no rirekisho*. Tokyo: Nihon Keizai Shimbunsha, 1957.

———. *Fashizumu hantai o tsuranuku, jimmin sensen jiken*. Ekonomisuto, 1965.

Suzuki Mosaburō senshū, vol. 1. Tokyo: Rōdō Daigaku, 1971.

Suzuki Shōsan

Nakamura, Hajime. *Kinsei Nihon ni okeru hihan-teki seishin no ichi kōsatsu*. Tokyo: Shunjūsha, 1965.

Karaki, Junzō, ed. *Zenka goroku-shū*. Tokyo: Chikuma Shobō, 1969.

Suzuki Shōsan dōjin zenshū. Tokyo: Sankibō Busshorin, 1962.

Suzuki Umetarō

Suzuki, Umetarō. *Kenkyū no kaiko*. Tokyo: Kibundō, 1943.

Suzuki, Umetarō Hakase Kenshōkai, ed. *Suzuki Umetaro sensei den*. Tokyo: Asakura Shoten, 1976.

Tachibana no Moroe

Kawasaki, Tsuneyuki "Tachibana no Moroe." *Ōrui Noburu hakase kiju kinen shigaku rombunshū*. Tokyo: Yamakawa Shuppan, 1962.

Taguchi Ukichi

Shiojima, Nikichi. *Teiken Taguchi sensei-den*. Tokyo: Keizai Zasshisha, 1912.

Teiken Taguchi Ukichi Zenshū Kankōkai, ed. and pub. *Teiken Taguchi Ukichi zenshū*, 8 vols. 1927–29.

Taira no Kiyomori

Tsuji, Zennosuke. "Taira no Kiyomori." *Nihon bunkashi betsuroku, 1*. Tokyo: Shunjūsha, 1953.

Taira no Masakado

Miyake, Chōbei. "Masakado no ran no shiteki zentei." *Ritsumeikan Bungaku*, No. 112.

Taira no Tadamori

Watanabe, Tamotsu, ed. *Heike ichimon*. Tokyo: Jimbutsu Ōraisha, 1964.

Takadaya Kahei

Takada, Keiichi. *Takadaya Kaheiō den*. Tokyo: Tokyo Hōbunkan, 1933.

Segawa, Kameyuki, and Oka, Ijō. *Takadaya Kahei*. Osaka: Hori Shoten, 1940.

Goshikimachi Kyōiku Iinkai, ed. *Takadaya Kahei*. Kobe: Hyōgo-ken Kyōiku Iinkai, 1960.

Takahashi Korekiyo

Uetsuka, Tsukasa, ed. *Takahashi Korekiyo jiden*. Tokyo: Chikura Shobō, 1936; reprinted, Tokyo: Chūō Kōronsha, 1976 (2 vols.).

Imamura, Takeo. *Takahashi Korekiyo*. Tokyo: Jiji Tsūshinsha, 1958.

Ōshima, Kiyoshi. *Takahashi Korekiyo*. Tokyo: Chūō Kōronsha, 1969.

Takahashi Yoshitoki

Tanaka, Yoshinaru. "Takahashi Sakuzaemon fushi no jiseki ni tsuite." *Shigaku Zasshi*, 6–4, 1896.

"Takahashi Yoshitoki." *Bunka* 7–7. Tokyo: Iwanami Shoten.

Takakusu Junjirō

Takakusu Junjirō zenshū, 12 vols. Tokyo: Kyōiku Shinchōsha, 1976.

Shūkyō zōkan: Takakusu Junjirō hakase tokubetsugō. Tokyo: Kyōiku Shinchōsha, 1976.
Tsunemitsu, Kōnen. *Meiji no Bukkyōsha,* vol. 2. Tokyo: Shunjūsha, 1969.

Takamine Jōkichi
Hashizume, Megumu, ed. *Kyojin Takamine hakase.* Tokyo: Sankyō, 1931.

Takano Chōei
Takano, Chōun. *Takano Chōei den.* Tokyo: Iwanami Shoten, 1939.
———, ed. *Takano Chōei zenshū.* Iwate Prefecture: Takano Chōei Zenshū Kankōkai, 1930–31.

Takano Fusatarō
Ōshima, Kiyoshi. "Takano Fusatarō to rōdōkumiai no tanjō." *Chūō Kōron* 80/6, 1965.
Kublin, Hyman, ed. *Meiji rōdō undōshi no hitokoma—Takano Fusatarō no shōgai to shisō.* Tokyo: Yūhikaku, 1959.

Takaoka Shinnō
Sugimoto, Naojirō. *Shinnyo Shinnōden kenkyū.* Tokyo: Yoshikawa Kōbunkan, 1965.

Takashima Shūhan
Arima, Seiho. *Takashima Shūhan.* Tokyo: Yoshikawa Kōbunkan, 1958.

Takasugi Shinsaku
Naramoto, Tatsuya, and Hori Tetsusaburō, ed. *Takasugi Shinsaku zenshū.* Tokyo: Shin Jimbutsu Ōraisha, 1974.
Naramoto, Tatsuya. *Takasugi Shinsaku.* Tokyo: Chūō Kōronsha, 1965.
Tōgyō Takasugi Shinsaku. Takasugi Tōgyō Sensei Hyakunensai Hōsankai, 1966.

Takayama Ukon
Ebisawa, Arimichi. *Takayama Ukon.* Tokyo: Yoshikawa Kōbunkan, 1958.
Laures, Johannes. *Takayama Ukon und die Anfänge der Kirche in Japan.* Munster, 1954.

Takeda Shingen
Okuno, Takahiro. *Takeda Shingen.* Tokyo: Yoshikawa Kōbunkan, 1959.
Inoue, Toshio. *Kenshin to Shingen.* Tokyo: Shibundō, 1964.

Takigawa Yukitoki
Dantō, Shigemitsu. "Takigawa Yukitoki no hito to gyōseki." *Jurisuto,* No. 264, 1962.
Takigawa, Haruo, ed. *Aru shōgai: Takigawa Yukitoki bun to hito.* Tokyo: Sekai Bunkasha, 1965.

Takuan
Furuta, Shōkin. *Takuan.* Tokyo: Koyama Shoin, 1949.
Fuji, Naomoto. *Takuan.* Tokyo: San'ichi Shobō, 1957.

Tanaka Chigaku
Satomi, Kishio, ed. *Tanaka Chigaku.* Tokyo: Kinseisha, 1968.
Watanabe, Hōyō. *Tanaka Chigaku.* Kōza Nichiren, vol. 4. Tokyo: Shunjūsha, 1972.
Tokoro, Shigemoto. *Kindai shakai to Nichiren shugi.* Tokyo: Hyōronsha, 1972.

Tanakadate Aikitsu
Nakamura, Seiji. *Tanakadate Aikitsu sensei.* Tokyo: Chūō Kōronsha, 1943.

Tanaka Giichi
Tanaka Giichi denki, 3 vols. Tanaka Giichi Denki Kankōkai, 1958–60.
Hosokawa, Ryūgen. *Tanaka Giichi.* Sandai saishō retsuden. Tokyo: Jiji Tsūshinsha, 1958.

Tanaka Kyūgu
Ishii, Kōtarō. *Tanaka Kyūgu-den no kenkyū.* Kanagawaken shiseki meishō tennen kinenbutsu chōsa hōkoku, No. 17. 1950.
Murakami, Tadashi. *Tanaka Kyūgu Yoshihiko.* Edo bakufu no daikan. Tokyo: Shin Jimbutsu Ōraisha, 1970.

Tanaka Shōzō
Kinoshita, Naoe. *Tanaka Shōzō ō*. Tokyo: Shinchōsha, 1921.
Shimada, Sōzō. *Tanaka Shōzō ō yoroku*, 2 vols. Tokyo: San'ichi Shobō, 1972.
Hayashi, Takeji. *Tanaka Shōzō no shōgai*. Tokyo: Kōdansha, 1976.
Tanaka Shōzō Zenshū Hensankai, ed. *Tanaka Shōzō zenshū*, 18 vols. Tokyo: Iwanami Shoten, 1977.

Tani Kanjō
Hirao, Michio. *Shishaku Tani Kanjō*. Tokyo: Fuzambō, 1935.
Shimauchi, Toshie, ed. *Tani Kanjō ikō*, 2 vols. Seikensha 1912; 4 vols. Tokyo: Tokyo Daigaku Shuppankai, 1975–76.

Tanuma Okitsugu
Doi, Noritaka. *Tanuma Okitsugu Okitomo fushi*. Edited by Kitajima, Masamoto. *Edo bakufu* (II): *sono jitsuryokusha-tachi shoshū*. Tokyo: Jimbutsu Ōraisha, 1964.
Hall, John W. *Tanuma Okitsugu (1719–1788): Forerunner of Modern Japan*. Harvard-Yenching Institute Monograph Series XIV. Cambridge, Harvard Univ. Press, 1955.

Tenji Tennō
Nakamura, Naokatsu. *Tenji Tennō*. Ōmi Jingū Hōsankai, 1938.
Sakamoto, Tarō. *Taika kaishin no kenkyū*. Tokyo: Shibundō, 1938.
Inoue, Mitsusada. *Taika kaishin*. Tokyo: Kaname Shobō, 1954.
Kitayama, Shigeo. *Man'yō no jidai*. Tokyo: Iwanami Shoten, 1954.

Tenkai
Sudō, Mitsuteru. *Daisōjō Tenkai*. Tokyo: Fuzambō, 1916.
Furuya, Kiyoshi. "Tenkai Daisōjō shūshū no Shina shiseki ni tsuite." *Shigaku Zasshi* 27–8.
Okuno, Yamabito. "Tenkai Oshō no yōji." *Rekishi Chiri* 8–1.

Terajima Munenori
"Terajima Munenori jijyoden," 1–3. *Denki*, vol. 4–6, 1936.

Terauchi Masakata
Kuroda, Kōshirō, ed. *Gensui Terauchi hakushaku den*. Gensui Terauchi Hakushaku Den Hensansho, 1920.
Katakura, Tōjirō. *Gensui Terauchi fushi*. Ajia Seinensha, 1935.

Toba Tennō
Hashimoto, Yoshihiko. "Hōgen no ran zenshi shōkō." *Nihon Rekishi*, No. 174.

Tōgō Heihachirō
Tōgō Heihachirō zenshū, 3 vols. Tokyo: Heibonsha, 1930.
Ogasawara, Naganari. *Tōgō gensui shōden*. Tokyo: Shun'yōdō, 1926.

Tōjō Hideki
Butow, Robert J. C. *Tōjō and the Coming of the War*. Princeton, N. J.: Princeton University Press, 1961.
Jōhō, Yoshio. *Tōjō Hideki*. Tokyo: Fuyō Shoten, 1974.

Tokiwa Gozen
Kasahara, Kazuo, ed. *Gekidō no yo to onna no aikan*. Nihon joseishi, vol. 2. Tokyo: Hyōron-sha, 1972.

Tokuda Kyūichi
Sugimori, Hisahide. *Tokuda Kyūichi*. Tokyo: Bungei Shunjū Shinsha, 1964.
Shiga, Yoshio. "Ningen Tokuda Kyūichi." *Chūō Kōron* 70/9, 1955.

Tokugawa Hidetada
Ikeda, Kōen. "Tokugawa Hidetada." *Shigakkai Zasshi* 15.
Fujino, Tamotsu. *Bakuhan taisei-shi no kenkyū*. Tokyo: Yoshikawa Kōbunkan, 1961.

Tokugawa Iemitsu

Tokugawa Iemitsu-kō-den. Nikkō Tōshōgū Shamusho, 1961.

Iwao, Seiichi. *Sakoku*. Tokyo: Chūō Kōronsha, 1966.

Fujino, Tamotsu. *Bakuhan taiseishi no kenkyū*. Tokyo: Yoshikawa Kōbunkan, 1961.

Tokugawa Iemochi

Horiuchi, Makoto. "Shōtoku-kō onki." *Kyū Bakufu*, vol. 2, nos., 1–2, 1898.

Juge, Kaijun. "Tokugawa Iemochi." *Chūō Shidan*, vol. 12, no. 9, 1917.

Tokugawa Ienari

Kitajima, Masamoto. *Bakuhansei no kumon*. Nihon no rekishi, 18. Tokyo: Chūō Kōronsha, 1966.

Hibata, Sekko. "Tokugawa Ienari no kyōyu sanshō to Bunsei no Kantōmuke torishimari." *Shirin* 13–3, July 1, 1928.

Tokugawa Ieyasu

Kitajima, Masamoto. *Edo bakufu no kenryoku kōzō*. Tokyo: Iwanami Shoten, 1964.

Nakamura, Kōya. *Tokugawa Ieyasu monjo no kenkyū*, vols. 1, 2, 3-A, 3-B. Tokyo: Nihon Gakujutsu Shinkōkai.

———. *Tokugawa Ieyasu-kō den*, Nikkō Tōshōgū Sambyaku Gojū Nensai Hōsaikai, 1940.

Kuwada, Tadachika. *Tokugawa Ieyasu*. Tokyo: Kadokawa Shoten, 1941.

Tokugawa Tsunayoshi

Kodama, Kōta. *Genroku jidai*. Nihon no rekishi, 16. Tokyo: Chūō Kōronsha, 1966.

Kurita, Mototsugu. "Tokugawa Tsunayoshi." *Chūō Shidan* 1/3–5.

Tokugawa Yoshimune

Tokugawa Yoshimune-kō den. Nikkō Tōshōgū Shamusho, 1962.

Tsuji, Tatsuya. *Tokugawa Yoshimune*. Tokyo: Yoshikawa Kōbunkan, 1958.

Tokugawa Yoshinobu

Shibusawa, Eiichi. *Tokugawa Yoshinobu-kō den*, 8 vols. Tokyo: Ryūmonsha, 1917; reprinted, Tokyo: Heibonsha, 1968 (2 vols).

Tanaka, Sōgorō. *Saigo no shōgun Tokugawa Yoshinobu*. Tokyo: Chikura Shobō, 1939.

Tokutomi Sohō

Sohō jiden. Tokyo: Chūō Kōronsha, 1935.

Shinobu, Seizaburō. "Tokutomi Sohō—sono shichijūnen no shisōteki henten." *Kaizō* 34/12, 1953.

Tominaga Nakamoto

Ishihama, Juntarō. *Tominaga Nakamoto*. Tokyo: Sōgen Shinsha, 1940.

Uchiyama, Toshihiko. "Tominaga Nakamoto ni okeru rekishi ninshiki no hōhō." *Tōhōgaku* 24, 1962.

Ienaga, Saburō. *Kindai Nihon no shisōka*. Tokyo: Yūshindō, 1962.

Tomonaga Shin'ichirō

Tomonaga Shin'ichirō rombunshū. Tokyo: Misuzu Shobō, 1970.

Toneri Shinnō

Tsuda, Sōkichi. *Nihon koten no kenkyū*, 2 vols. Tokyo: Iwanami Shoten, 1948, 1950.

Nihonshoki: Chronicles of Japan from the Earliest Times to A.D. 697. Translated by W. G. Aston. London: Allen and Unwin, 1954.

Tōyama Mitsuru

Fujimoto, Naonori. *Kyojin Tōyama Mitsuru*. Seikyōsha, 1922.

Hanzawa, Hiroshi. "Tōyama Mitsuru to Gen'yōsha." *Chūō Kōron* 80/6, 1965.

Toyotomi Hideyori

Suzuki, Ryōichi. *Toyotomi Hideyoshi*. Tokyo: Iwanami Shoten, 1954.

Watanabe, Yosuke. *Hō Taikō to sono kazoku*. Tokyo: Nippon Gakujutsu Fukyūkai, 1933.

Toyotomi Hideyoshi
Suzuki, Ryōichi. *Toyotomi Hideyoshi*. Tokyo: Iwanami Shoten, 1954.
Watanabe, Yosuke. *Hō Taikō no shiteki seikatsu*. Nihon bunka meichosen. Tokyo: Sōgensha, 1939.
101 Letters of Hideyoshi. Translated and edited by Adriana Boscaro. Tokyo: Sophia University, 1975.
Dening, Walter. *The Life of Toyotomi Hideyoshi*. Tokyo: Hokuseidō, 1955.

Tsuda Masamichi
Tsuda, Michiharu. *Tsuda Masamichi*. Tokyo: Tōkyōkaku, 1940.
Ōkubo, Toshiaki. *Tsuda Masamichi no chosaku ni tsuite*. Nihon gakushiin kiyō, 3–3, 4–1, 7–1, 1944, 1946, 1949.

Tsuda Sōkichi
Tsuda Sōkichi zenshū, 33 vols. Tokyo: Iwanami Shoten, 1963–66.
Ienaga, Saburō. *Tsuda Sōkichi no shisōshi-teki kenkyū*. Tokyo: Iwanami Shoten, 1972.
Kurita, Naomi. "Tsuda Sōkichi sensei no gakumon to hito." *Sekai* 195, 1962.

Tsuda Umeko
Yamazaki, Takako. *Tsuda Umeko*. Jimbutsu sōsho. Tokyo: Yoshikawa Kōbunkan, 1962.
Tsuda Eigakujuku, ed. *Tsuda Eigakujuku yonjūnenshi*. Tokyo: Tsuda Eigakujuku, 1941.

Uchimura Kanzō
Yamamoto, Taijirō. *Uchimura Kanzō shinkō chosaku zenshū*, 25 vols. Tokyo: Kyōbunkan, 1962–66.
Uchimura, Kanzō. *Uchimura Kanzō chosakushū*, 2 vols. Tokyo: Iwanami Shoten, 1953–55.
Suzuki, Toshirō, ed. *Kaisō no Uchimura Kanzō*. Tokyo: Iwanami Shoten, 1956.

Udagawa Genzui
Fujikawa, Yutaka. *Nihon igakushi*. Tokyo: Nisshin Shoin, 1941.
Itazawa, Takeo. *Nichi-Ran bunka kōshōshi no kenkyū*. Tokyo: Yoshikawa Kōbunkan, 1959.

Udagawa Yōan
Yoshikawa, Yoshiaki. *Nihon kagaku no senkaku Udagawa Yōan*. 1932.
Itazawa, Takeo. *Nichi-Ran bunka kōshōshi no kenkyū*. Tokyo: Yoshikawa Kōbunkan, 1959.

Ueki Emori
Ienaga, Saburō. *Ueki Emori kenkyū*. Tokyo: Iwanami Shoten, 1960.
Sotozaki, Mitsuhiro, ed. *Ueki Emori—katei kaikaku fujin kaihō ronshū*. Tokyo: Hōsei Daigaku Shuppankyoku, 1971.

Uemura Masahisa
Uemura Masahisa zenshū, 8 vols. Uemura Masahisa Zenshū Kankōkai, 1931–34.
Sawa, Wataru. *Uemura Masahisa to sono jidai*, 6 vols. 1937–41; reprinted by Kyōbunkan, 1966.
Kyōgoku, Jun'ichi. *Uemura Masahisa—sono hito to shisō*. Tokyo: Shinkyō Shuppansha, 1966.

Uesugi Kenshin
Inoue, Toshio. *Kenshin to Shingen*. Tokyo: Shibundō, 1964.
———. *Uesugi Kenshin*. Tokyo: Jimbutsu Ōraisha, 1966.

Uesugi Norizane
Yūki, Mitsurō. *Kanazawa bunko to Ashikaga gakkō*. Tokyo: Shibundō, 1959.

Ugaki Kazushige
Ugaki Kazushige nikki, 3 vols. Tokyo: Misuzu Shobō, 1968–71.
Inoue, Kiyoshi. *Ugaki Kazushige*. Tokyo: Asahi Shimbunsha, 1975.

Ui Hakuju
Ui Hakuju chosaku senshū, 7 vols. Tokyo: Daitō Shuppansha, 1967.
Tsunemitsu, Kōnen. *Meiji no Bukkyōsha*, vol. 2. Tokyo: Shunjūsha, 1969

Wada Yoshimori
Kuroita, Katsumi, and Kokushi Taikei Henshūkai, eds. *Azuma kagami*. Kokushi taikei. Tokyo: Yoshikawa Kōbunkan, 1964.

Wakatsuki Reijirō
Wakatsuki, Reijirō. *Kofūan kaikoroku*. Tokyo: Yomiuri Shimbunsha, 1950; rev. ed., 1975.
Amako, Todomu. *Heimin saishō Wakatsuki Reijirō*. Tokyo: Monasu Edition, 1926.

Wake no Kiyomaro
Hirano, Kunio. *Wake no Kiyomaro*. Tokyo: Yoshikawa Kōbunkan, 1964.

Wani
Inoue, Mitsusada. "Wani no kōei shizoku no Bukkyō." *Shigaku Zasshi* 54, No. 9.

Watanabe Kazan
Mori, Senzō. *Watanabe Kazan*, Sōgen Sensho. Osaka: Sōgensha, 1941.
Suganuma, Teizō. *Kazan no kenkyū*. Tokyo: Tokyo Mokujisha, 1947.
Yoshizawa, Tadashi. *Watanabe Kazan*. Tokyo: Tokyo Daigaku Shuppankai, 1956.

Watarai Ieyuki
Ōnishi, Gen'ichi. *Zō-shōsammi Watarai Ieyuki Kannushi jiseki*. Mie: Chōkokan Nōgyōkan, 1929.
Nishigaki, Seiji. "Minami-Ise ni okeru Nambokuchō dōran: Watarai Ieyuki to Yamada Ikkishū o megutte." *Rekishi Hyōron* No. 108, 1959.

Watarai Nobuyoshi
Muraoka, Tsunetsugu. *Shintō-shi*. Tokyo: Sōbunsha, 1956.
Taira, Shigemichi, and Abe, Akio. *Kinsei shintōron, Zenki kokugaku*. Nihon shisō taikei. Tokyo: Iwanami Shoten, 1972.
Ishida, Ichirō, ed. *Shintō shisōshū*. Nihon no shisō. Tokyo: Chikuma Shobō, 1970.

Wu-an P'u-ning
Tsuji, Zennosuke. *Nippon Bukkyōshi*. 2nd ed. Tokyo: Iwanami Shoten, 1960.
Imaeda, Aishin. *Zenshū no rekishi*. Tokyo: Shibundō, 1960.

Wu-hsüeh Tsu-yüan
Tamamura, Takeji, and Inoue, Zenjō. *Engakushi*. Tokyo: Shunjūsha, 1964.
Tsuji, Zennosuke. *Nippon Bukkyōshi*. 2nd ed. Tokyo: Iwanami Shoten, 1960.
Imaeda, Aishin. *Zenshū no rekishi*. Tokyo: Shibundō, 1960.

Yamada Nagamasa
Miki, Sakae. *Yamada Nagamasa*. Tokyo: Kokon Shoin, 1936.
Murakami, Naojirō. *Rokkon-ō Yamada Nagamasa*. Tokyo: Asahi Shimbunsha, 1942.
Iwao, Seiichi. *Historiael Verhael van Siam door Jeremias van Vliet, 1640*. Tōyō Bunko, 2 vols. 1956–58.
Satow, Ernest Mason. *Notes on the Intercourse between Japan and Siam in the Seventeenth Century*. Transactions of the Asiatic Society of Japan, vol. XIII, Part 2, 1885.

Yamaga Sokō
Kokumin Seishin Bunka Kenkyūjo, ed. and pub., *Yamaga Sokō shū*, 8 vols. Tokyo, 1936–43.
Hori, Isao. *Yamaga Sokō*. Tokyo: Yoshikawa Kōbunkan, 1959.
Tawara, Shirō, and Morimoto Jun'ichirō. *Yamaga Sokō*. Nihon shisō taikei, 32. Tokyo: Iwanami Shoten, 1970.
Yamaga Sokō zenshū, shisōhen, 15 vols. Tokyo: Iwanami Shoten, 1940–41.

Yamagata Aritomo
Tokutomi, Iichirō. *Kōshaku Yamagata Aritomo den*, 3 vols. Tokyo: Hara Shobō, 1969.
Oka, Yoshitake. *Yamagata Aritomo*. Tokyo: Iwanami Shoten, 1958.
Ōyama, Azusa, ed. *Yamagata Aritomo ikensho*. Tokyo: Hara Shobō, 1966.

Yamagata Bantō
Arisaka, Takamichi. *Yamagata Bantō no hito to shisō.* Nihon jimbutsushi taikei, vol. 4. Tokyo: Asakura Shoten, 1959.
Suenaka, Tetsuo. *Yamagata Bantō no kenkyū, Yume no shiro hen.* Osaka: Seibundō Shuppan, 1968.

Yamaji Aizan
Yamaji Aizan shū. Meiji bungaku zenshū, 35. Tokyo: Chikuma Shobō, 1965.
Kindai bungaku kenkyū sōsho, 16. Tokyo: Shōwa Joshi Daigaku, 1961.

Yamakawa Hitoshi
Yamakawa Hitoshi zenshū, 20 vols. Tokyo: Keisō Shobō, 1966.
Koyama, Hirotake, and Kishimoto, Eitarō. *Nihon no hi-kyōsantō marukusu-shugisha—Yamakawa Hitoshi no shōgai to shisō.* Tokyo: San'ichi Shobō, 1962.

Yamakawa Kenjirō
Hanami, Sakumi, ed. *Danshaku Yamakawa sensei den.* Ko Yamakawa Danshaku Ki'nenkai, 1940.
Nakamura, Seiji. "Yamakawa Kenjirō sensei no koto." *Nihon Butsuri Gakkai Shi,* vol. 14, No. 10, 1959.

Yamamoto Gombei
Kaigunshō Kaigun Daijin Kambō, ed. *Yamamoto Gombei to kaigun.* Tokyo: Hara Shobō, 1966.
Yamamoto, Eisuke. *Yamamoto Gombei.* Sandai saishō retsuden. Tokyo: Jiji Tsūshinsha, 1958.
Etō Jun. *Umi wa yomigaeru.* Tokyo: Bungei Shunjū, 1976.

Yamamoto Isoroku
Takagi, Sōkichi. *Yamamoto Isoroku to Yonai Mitsumasa.* Tokyo: Bungei Shunjū Shinsha, 1950.
Sorimachi, Eiichi. *Ningen Yamamoto Isoroku,* 2 vols. Tokyo: Kōwadō, 1956–57.

Yamamoto Senji
Yamamoto Senji zenshū, 8 vols. Tokyo: Rogosu Shoin, 1929–30.
Nishiguchi, Katsumi. *Yamasen.* Tokyo: Chūō Kōronsha, 1959.
Sasaki, Binji. *Yamamoto Senji,* 2 vols. Chōbunsha, 1974–76.

Yamamura Saisuke
Iwasaki, Katsumi. "Yamamura Saisuke den." *Nihon Ishigaku Zasshi* 1288, 1941.
Ayusawa, Shintarō. "Yamamura Masanaga no Kai ichiran zu ni tsuite. *Rekishi Chiri* 81–1, 1943.
———. *Yamamura Saisuke.* Jimbutsu sōsho. Tokyo: Yoshikawa Kōbunkan, 1959.

Yamana Sōzen
Ogawa, Makoto. *Yamana Sōzen to Hosokawa Katsumoto.* Tokyo: Jimbutsu Ōraisha, 1966.

Yamato Takeru-no-mikoto
Tōma, Seita. *Yamato Takeru-no-Mikoto.* Osaka: Sōgensha, 1953.
———. *Yamato Takeru—kodai gōzoku no botsuraku to banka.* Tokyo: Kadokawa Shoten, 1958.
Ueda, Masaaki. *Yamato Takeru-no-Mikoto.* Tokyo: Yoshikawa Kōbunkan, 1960.

Yamawaki Tōyō
Takiura, Bunya. "Yamawaki Tōyō ni oyoboseru Sorai no eikyō," *Nihon Ishigaku Zasshi* 1296, 1941.

Yamazaki Ansai
Yamazaki Ansai zenshū, 2 vols. Nihon Koten Gakkai, 1935.
Taira, Shigenao, and Abe, Akio. *Kinsei Shintō-ron, zenki kokugaku.* Nihon shisō taikei. Tokyo: Iwanami Shoten, 1972.

Nishida, Taichirō. *Fujiwara Seika, Nakae Tōju, Kumazawa Banzan, Yamazaki Ansai, Yamaga Sokō, Yamagata Daini shū.* Nihon no shisō, 17. Tokyo: Chikuma Shobō, 1970.
Denki Gakkai, ed. *Yamazaki Ansai to sono monryū.* Tokyo: Meiji Shoin, 1943.

Yanagida Kunio
Yanagida, Kunio. *Kokyō shichijūnen.* Kobe: Nojigiku Bunko, 1958.
Teihon Yanagida Kunio zenshū, 36 vols. Tokyo: Chikuma Shobō, 1962–65.
Nihon Bungaku Kenkyū Shiryō Kankōkai, ed. *Yanagida Kunio.* Yūseidō, 1975.

Yanagisawa Yoshiyasu
Kudō, Takeshige. *Yanagisawa Yoshiyasu.* Tokyo: Shōkabō, 1896.
Hayashi, Yawara. *Yanagisawa Yoshiyasu.* Tokyo: Jitsugyō no Nihonsha, 1921.
Tsuji, Zennosuke. *Yanagisawa Yoshiyasu no ichimen.* Nihon bunkashi betsuroku, 3. Tokyo: Shunjūsha, 1953.

Yanaihara Tadao
Yanaihara Tadao zenshū, 27 vols. Tokyo: Iwanami Shoten, 1963–65.
Yanaihara, Tadao. *Watakushi no ayunde kita michi.* Tokyo: Tokyo Daigaku Shuppankai, 1975.

Yasuda Zenjirō
Yano, Fumio. *Yasuda Zenjirō den.* Tokyo: Yasuda Hozensha, 1925.
Katō, Toshihiko. "Yasuda ginkō to Yasuda Zenjirō." *Shakai Kagaku Kenkyū* vol. 2, No. 3, 1950.

Yin-yüan
Takahashi, Chikumei. *Ingen, Mokuan, Sokuhi.* Zenmon sōsho, 4. Heigo Shuppansha, 1916.
Hirakubo, Akira. *Ingen.* Tokyo: Yoshikawa Kōbunkan, 1965.

Yodogimi
Kuwada, Tadachika. *Yodogimi.* Tokyo: Yoshikawa Kōbunkan, 1958.
Watanabe, Yosuke. *Hō taikō to sono kazoku.* Tokyo: Nippon Gakujutsu Fukyūkai, 1933.

Yodoya Tatsugorō
Takanashi, Kōji. "Yodoya ikka ni tsuite." *Kamigata,* 105. *Nihon shōninshi.* Nihon Rekishi Chiri Gakkai, 1925.

Yokoi Shōnan
Yamazaki, Masatada. *Yokoi Shōnan,* 2 vols. Tokyo: Meiji Shoin, 1938.
Tamamuro, Taijō. *Yokoi Shōnan.* Jimbutsu sōsho. Tokyo: Yoshikawa Kōbunkan, 1967.

Yonai Mitsumasa
Ogata, Taketora. *Ichigunjin no shōgai—kaisō no Yonai Mitsumasa.* Tokyo: Bungei Shunjū Shinsha, 1955.
Sanematsu, Yuzuru. *Yonai Mitsumasa.* Tokyo: Kōjinsha, 1966.

Yoshida Kanetomo
Naramoto, Tatsuya, ed. *Nihon no shisōka.* Tokyo: Mainichi Shimbunsha, 1954.
Ogasawara, Haruo. "Kami no sonzai to ninshiki: Yoshida Kanetomo yori Yoshikawa Koretari ni itaru." *Nihon bunka kenkyūjo kiyō,* No. 4, Tokyo: Kokugakuin Daigaku, 1959.

Yoshida Shigeru
Yoshida, Shigeru. *Kaisō jūnen,* 4 vols. Tokyo: Shinchōsha, 1957.
Fujiwara, Hirotatsu. *Yoshida Shigeru, sono hito sono seiji.* Tokyo: Yomiuri Shimbunsha, 1964.
Kōsaka, Masataka. *Saishō: Yoshida Shigeru.* Tokyo: Chūō Kōronsha, 1965.

Yoshida Shōin
Yamaguchi-ken Kyōikukai, ed. *Yoshida Shōin zenshū.* Tokyo: Iwanami Shoten, 1938–40.
Naramoto, Tatsuya. *Yoshida Shōin.* Tokyo: Iwanami Shoten, 1951.
Oka, Fukashi. *Yoshida Shōin.* Tokyo: Kadokawa Shoten, 1959.

Yoshikawa Koretari
Muraoka, Tsunetsugu. *Shintō-shi*. Tokyo: Sōbunsha, 1956.
Taira, Shigemichi. *Yoshikawa Shintō no kiso-teki kenkyū*. Tokyo: Yoshikawa Kōbunkan, 1966.
Taira, Shigemichi, and Abe, Akio. *Kinsei Shintōron*. Nihon shisō taikei. Tokyo: Iwanami Shoten, 1972.

Yoshino Sakuzō
Yoshino Sakuzō minshu-shugi ronshū, 8 vols. Tokyo: Shinkigensha, 1946.
Tanaka, Sōgorō. *Yoshino Sakuzō*. Tokyo: Miraisha, 1958; Tokyo: San'ichi Shobō, 1971.
"Tokushū: Toshino Sakuzō o shinobu." *Chūō Kōron* 48/5, 1933.

Yoshioka Yayoi
Yoshioka Yayoi den. Tokyo Rengō Fujinkai Shuppanbu, 1941; rev. ed., Tokyo Joshi Ika Daigaku Shiryōshitsu, 1967.
Yoshioka Yayoi. *Kono jū'nenkan—Zoku Yoshioka Yayoi den*. Tokyo: Gakufū Shoin, 1952.
Yoshioka, Hiroto. *Yoshioka Yayoi*. Tokyo: Tokyo Joshi Ika Daigaku Shiryōshitsu, 1969.

Yoshio Kōsaku
Koga, Jūjirō. *Seiyō igaku denrai-shi*. Tokyo: Nisshin Shoin, 1944.

Yoshishige no Yasutane
Inoue, Mitsusada. *Nihon jōdokyō seiritsu-shi no kenkyū*. Tokyo: Yamakawa Shuppansha, 1956.
Inoue, Mitsusada and Ōsone, Shōsuke. *Ōjōden, Hokke genki*. Tokyo: Iwanami Shoten, 1974.

Yui Shōsetsu
Shinshi, Yoshimoto. *Yui Shōsetsu*. Tokyo: Yoshikawa Kōbunkan, 1961.
Koizumi, Sanshin. *Yui Shōsetsu*, 1896, Koizumi Sanshin zenshū, vol. 2. Tokyo: Iwanami Shoten, 1941.
Keian taiheiki. Kinsei jitsuroku zensho, vol. 12. Tokyo: Waseda Daigaku, 1929.

Yukawa Hideki
Yukawa, Hideki. *Yukawa Hideki jisenshū*. Tokyo: Asahi Shimbunsha, 1971.
———. *Creativity and Intuition*. Tokyo: Kodansha International, 1973.

Yuri Kimimasa
Haga, Hachiya. *Yuri Kimimasa*. Yao Shoten, 1902.
Yuri, Masamichi, ed. *Shishaku Yuri Kimimasa den*. Tokyo: Iwanami Shoten, 1930.

Zekkai Chūshin
Okada, Masayuki. *Nippon kanbungakushi*. Tokyo: Yoshikawa Kōbunkan, 1954.
Tamamura, Takeji. *Gozan bungaku*. Tokyo: Shibundō, 1955.

Zeniya Gohei
Wakabayashi, Kisaburō. *Zeniya Gohei*. Tokyo: Sōgensha, 1957.
Tamura, Eitarō. "Zeniya Gohei-den." *Rekishi Kagaku* 3–9, 1934.

Zusho Hirosato
Zusho, Shōzaemon. "Zusho Hirosato kun jireki." *Shidankai Sokkiroku* No. 285, 1916.

Index

A

Abe Isoo (安部磯雄), **313-14**, 329, 373, 402, 476, 521
Abe Masahiro (阿部正弘), **161-62**, 378, 422, 472
Abe Masakiyo (阿部正精), 161
Abe Masayasu (阿部正寧), 161
Abe Nobuyuki (阿部信行), 434
Abe no Hirafu (阿部比羅夫), **17**
Abe no Sadatō (安倍貞任), **17-18**
Abe no Yoritoki (安倍賴時), 17, 48
Aburana roku (油菜錄), 233
Achi no Omi (阿知使主), **18**, 52, 72
Acollas, Emile, 453
Adachi Kenzō (安達謙藏), 507
Adachi Mineichirō (安達峰一郎), **314**
Adachi Shintō (足立信頭), 170
Adams, William (Miura Anjin) (三浦按針), **162**, 199
Adrenalin, 484
Agama sutras, 395
Agoin Shōshichi (安居院庄七), 224
Aikoku Fujinkai (愛國婦人會), 444
Aikoku Kōtō (愛國公黨), 335, 359, 372
Aikokusha (愛國社), 360, 372, 503
Ainu, 216
Aka Ezo Fūsetsukō (赤蝦夷風說考), 208
Akahata (赤旗), 468
Akamatsu Enshin (赤松圓心), 135
Akamatsu Mitsusuke (赤松滿祐), 91, 144
Akamatsu Norimura (赤松則村), **85**
Akamatsu Renjō (赤松連城), 469
Ākāśagarbha (虛空藏), 45
Akashi Ryūei (明石龍映), 165
Akechi Mitsuhide (明智光秀), **163**, 189, 190, 201, 227, 229, 252, 260, 267
Akegarasu Haya (曉烏敏), 395
Akita Nippō (秋田日報), 355
akunin shōki (惡人正機), 133
Amakasu Masahiko (甘粕正彥), 446
Amako family (尼子氏), 122, 217
Amakusa Tokisada (天草時貞), **164**
Amaterasu Ōmikami (天照大御神), **18-19**, 38, 66, 73, 141, 404
Amatomi Sugaichi (雨富須賀一), 181
Ame-no-minakanushi-no-kami (天之御中主神), 187
Amenomori Hōshū (雨森芳洲), 206
Ame-no-murakumo-no-tsurugi (天叢雲劍), 73
Amherst College, 426, 502
Amida (阿彌陀佛), 22, 47, 55, 74, 107, 109, 112, 133, 136
Amida-ji (阿彌陀寺), 200
Amitayur-dhyana Sutra (*Kammuryōju-kyō*) (觀無量壽經), 483
Amoghavajra (Fukū) (不空), 45
Amur River Society, *see* Kokuryūkai
Anahobe-no-hashibito, Empress (穴穗部間人皇女), 61
Analects, Confucian, 72, 198, 464
anarcho-syndicalisme, 317
Anatomische Tabellen, 209
An Chung-gun (安重根), 363
Andō Nobumasa (安藤信正), **164-65**
Andō Nobuyoshi (安藤信由), 164
Andō Shōeki (安藤昌益), **165-66**
Andō Tōno (安藤東野), 175
Andover Theological Seminary, 426
Anegakōji Kintomo (姉小路公知), 457
Anegawa, battle of (姉川の戰), 86, 260
Anezaki Masaharu (姉崎正治), **314-15**
Anglo-Japanese Alliance (日英同盟), 352, 376, 380, 399, 493, 513
Ankan, Emperor (安閑天皇), 42, 54
Ankokuji Ekei (安國寺惠瓊), 196
Annam, 246
Anō Zensei (阿野全成), 119
Anrakuju-in (安樂壽院), 70
Ansei earthquake, 177
Antoku, Emperor (安德天皇), **19**, 138
An'yō-in (安養院), 93
An'yō-ji (安養寺), 124
Aoki Kenzō (青木研造), 197, 315
Aoki Kon'yō (青木昆陽), **166-67**, 198, 208,

209
Aoki Shūzō (青木周藏), **315-16**, 326
Aoshima Toshizō (青島俊藏), 216
Appeal to Youth (青年に訴ふ), 445
Arahata Kanson (荒畑寒村), **316-17**, 445
Arai Hakuseki (新井白石), **167-68**, 192, 204, 206, 230, 275
Arai Hakuseki nikki (新井白石日記), 168
Arai Masanari (新井正濟), 167
Arai Nissatsu (新居日薩), 486
Araki Murashige (荒木村重), 163, 252
Araki Sadao (荒木貞夫), **317-18**, 381, 396
Arima Harunobu (有馬晴信), 130, **169**, 182, 198, 234
Arima Yoshinao (有馬義直), 169
Arima Yoshizumi (有馬義純), 169
Arisugawa-no-miya Taruhito (有栖川宮熾仁), **318-19**, 384
Arita Hachirō (有田八郎), **319**, 344
Army Staff College, 478
Asabuki Eiji (朝吹英二), 354
Asada Gōryū (麻田剛立), **169-70**, 248, 274
Asahi Heigo (朝日平吾), 518
Asahi Shimbun (朝日新聞), 516, 522
Asai Hisamasa (淺井久政), 85
Asai Nagamasa (淺井長政), **85-86**, 226, 228, 256, 267, 279
Asaka Gonsai (安積艮齋), 366
Asakura Toshikage (朝倉敏景), 226
Asakura Yoshikage (朝倉義景), 86, 260
Asami Keisai (淺見絅齋), 277
Asanga, 22
Asano Nagahiro (淺野長廣), 170
Asano Naganao (淺野長直), 273
Asano Naganori (淺野長矩), **170**, 231
Asano Nagashige (淺野長重), 231
Asano Nagatomo (淺野長友), 170
Asanuma Inejirō (淺沼稻次郎), **320**
Ashida Hitoshi (蘆田均), 317, **320-21**, 374, 520
Ashikaga Gakkō (School) (足利學校), 140, 256
Ashikaga Masatomo (足利政知), 103
Ashikaga Mochiuji (足利持氏), 91, 140
Ashikaga Motouji (足利基氏), 96
Ashikaga Naoyoshi (足利直義), 85
Ashikaga shogunate, 217, 226, 244, *see also* Muromachi shogunate
Ashikaga Tadayoshi (足利直義), 87, 123
Ashikaga Takauji (足利尊氏), 85, **87-88**, 89, 97-99, 108, 113-15, 117, 123, 128, 142, 143, 511
Ashikaga Yoshiaki (足利義昭), **86**, 128, 217, 226
Ashikaga Yoshiakira (足利義詮), 89
Ashikaga Yoshiharu (足利義晴), 86, 91
Ashikaga Yoshihide (足利義榮), 86
Ashikaga Yoshihisa (足利義尙), 88, 101
Ahikaga Yoshikatsu (足利義勝), 88
Ashikaga Yoshikazu (足利義量), 91
Ashikaga Yoshimasa (足利義政), **88-89**, 101, 108, 144, 178
Ashikaga Yoshimi (足利義視), 101, 108
Ashikaga Yoshimitsu (足利義滿), 88, **89-90**, 91, 96, 98, 101, 108, 118, 137, 145
Ashikaga Yoshimochi (足利義持), **90-91**, 101, 119
Ashikaga Yoshinobu (足利義宣), 91
Ashikaga Yoshinori (足利義教), 88, **91**, 101, 127, 140, 144
Ashikaga Yoshiteru (足利義輝), 86, **91-92**, 140, 217
Ashikaga Yoshitsugu (足利義嗣), 90
Ashina Yoshihiro (蘆名義廣), 174
Ashio Copper Mines (足尾鑛山), 320, 326, 389, 402, 489
Asuka-dera (飛鳥寺), 64
Aśvaghosha (馬鳴), 477
Ataka-no-seki no kanjinchō (安宅の關の勸進帳), 122
Ato no Ōtari (阿刀大足), 45
Atsuta Shrine (熱田神宮), 73
Atsuzane, Imperial Prince (敦實親王), 41
Australia, 467
Austria, 316, 319, 335, 408, 419, 433, 454
Aviation Research Center (航空研究所), 512
Ayabe Keisai (綾部絅齋), 170, 214
Ayuthia, 271
Azuma Ebisu people, 73

B

Baba Kokuri (馬場轂里), 269
Baba Tatsui (馬場辰猪), **321-22**
Baibunsha (賣文社), 511
Baishōron (梅松論), 88
Ballagh, James, 504
Bälz, Erwin, 366
Bammin tokuyō (萬民德用), 247
Bankei (盤珪), 477
Bankei Eitaku (盤珪永琢), **171**
Bank of Japan, 349, 350, 410, 482, 518
Bank of Taiwan, 342, 507
Bank of Tokyo, 350
Bankoku kōhō (萬國公報), 427
Bankoku shiryaku (萬國史略), 430
Bankoku zusetsu (萬國圖說), 203
Bansha imprisonment (蠻社の獄), 208, 250, 270
Banshokō (蕃藷考), 167
Bansho Shirabesho (蕃書調所), 162, 374, 426, 491, 499
Banshū hōgo-shū (播州法語集), 110
Bansui sonkyō (磐水存響), 236
Baō (馬翁), 179
Batavia, 272
Behring, Emile von, 392
Bekki Shōzaemon (別木庄左衞門), 211
Belgium, 314, 316, 319
Bell, Alexander Graham, 368
Bendōsho (辨道書), 187
Bengiroku (辨疑錄), 198

Benkei (辨慶), **92**, 122
Bentham, Jeremy, 419
Berlin, East, 480
Berlin, University of, 347, 487
bettō (別當), 22
Bidatsu, Emperor (敏達天皇), 64, 65, 67
Bimbō monogatari (貧乏物語), 382
Bin (旻), 48 *see also* Min
Bingashū (峨嵋集), 133
Black Dragon Society, *see* Kokuryūkai
Bōchō kaitenshi (防長回天史), 456
Bodai-ji (菩提寺), 107
Boissonade, Gustave Emile, 348, 352, 393
Bōkaisaku (防海策), 241
Bokuō Sogyū (牧翁祖牛), 171
Bonaparuto senki (卜那把盧的戰記), 208
Bongaku shinryō (梵學津梁), 199
Book of Changes, 116
Bose, R. B., 356, 499
Boshin War (戊辰戰爭), 318, 359, 372, 380, 395, 403, 431, 444, 447, 451, 452, 490, 492, 493, 508, 512
Boston Museum of Fine Arts, 49
Botanka Shōhaku (牡丹花肖柏), 132
Bowes, James L., 376
Boxer Rebellion, 316, 358, 380, 398, 444, 493, 509
Britain, 177, 251, 331, 399, 401, 409, 410, 420, 429, 457, 465, 469, 478, 491, 508, 514, *see also* England
British East India Company, 213
Brown, Samuel, 504
Buckle, Henry Thomas, 481
Buke jiki (武家事記), 273
Buke myōmokushō (武家名目抄), 182
Buke shohatto (武家諸法度), 168, 244, 257
Bukkaron (物價論), 212
Bukkō-ha (佛光派), 143
Bukkyō hanron (佛教汎論), 506
Bukkyō katsuron (佛教活論), 350
Bukkyō Kōwasho (佛教講話所), 418
Bukkyō Shakai Dōmei (佛教社會同盟), 462
Bukkyō shirin (佛教史林), 418
Bukkyō tōitsu-ron (佛教統一論), 418
Bukyō shōgaku (武教小學), 273
Bukyō yōroku (武教要錄), 273
Bummei Kyōkai (文明協會), 443
Bummeiron no gairyaku (文明論の概略), 331
Bun'ei campaign (文永の役), 105
Bungakuryō (文學寮), 483
Bunkyō hifuron (文鏡秘府論), 46
Bunron (文論), 175
Buretsu, Emperor (武烈天皇), 54
Burma, 328, 495
Bushidō, the Soul of Japan, 430
Butoku taiseiki (武德大成記), 206
Butsugo shinron (佛語心論), 116
Butsurui hinshitsu (物類品隲), 186
Byōdō-in (平等院), 31
Byōgaku tsūron (病學通論), 229

C
Cambodia, 272
Canada, 430, 515
Capron, Horace, 325, 403
Carlyle, Thomas, 430
Carus, Paul, 476
Catalogue of the Chinese Translation of the Buddhist Tripitaka by Bunyū Nanjō, 425
Catherine II, 174
Central Asia, 446
Ceylon, 462
Champa kingdom, 169
Ch'an, *see* Zen Buddhism
Chang Tso-lin (張作霖), 489, 520
Charter Oath(御誓文), 329, 386, 413, 519, 525
Chaya Kiyonobu (茶屋清延), 171
Chaya Kiyotada (茶屋清忠), 172
Chaya Munekiyo (茶屋宗清), 172
Chaya Shirōjirō (茶屋四郎次郎), **171-72**
Cheng Ch'eng-kung (Tei Seikō) (鄭成功), **172-73**
Cheng Chih-lung (鄭芝龍), 172
Cheng Ching (鄭經), 173
Cheng Jen-te (鄭仁德), 20
Ch'en Ho-ch'ing (陳和卿), 93
Ch'en Jen-shuang (陳仁爽), 20
Chiang Kai-shek (蔣介石), 400
Chiba Shūsaku (千葉周作), 237
Chidōkan (致道館), 503
Chienkan (致遠館), 441
Chien-yüan (鑑源), 278
Chigusa Tadaaki (千種忠顯), 85
Chih-chou (知周), 32
Chih-i (智顗), 57
Chijiwa Miguel (千々石ミイゲル), 234
Chikaku Fumyō Kokushi (智覺普明國師), 136
Chikamatsu Monzaemon (近松門左衞門), 173
Chikō (智光), 38
Chikurin-ji (竹林寺), 37
Chikyō yōroku (治教要錄), 273
Chikyū zenzu (地球全圖), 203
China, People's Republic of, 357, 374, 521
Chin dynasty, 275
Chinda Sutemi (珍田捨己), 454
Chinese Eastern Railway, 344
Chinese Revolution, 390, 400, 488
Ch'ing dynasty, 173, 298, 396
Ch'ing-lung-ssu, 45
Ching-te ch'uan-teng lu, 134
Chion-in (知恩院), 107
Chisen-in (智泉院), 161
Chishiki gammon (智識願文), 50
Chishima (Kurile) Islands (千島列島), 206, 210, 216, 248, 325, 403, 491
Chishima Toan (手島堵庵), 195
Chi-t'an Tsung-le, 145
Chiteiki (池亭記), 74
Chitose Maru (千歳丸), 331
Chi-tsang, 38
Chizō (智藏), 38

Chōei-ji (長榮寺), 199
Chōfu (長府), 431
Chōgen (重源), **92-93**
Chōkei, Emperor (長慶天皇), 98
Chōkiron (長器論), 189
Chokugo engi (勅語衍義), 354
Chomel, N. Noel, 269
Chōnen (奝然), **19-20**
chōningaku (町人學), 195
Chōsai (長西), 100
Chōshū (長州), 219, 233, 238, 251, 259, 264, 281, 315, 318, 329, 351, 359, 360, 364, 379, 380, 385, 387, 403, 409, 419, 439, 441, 443, 448, 450, 456, 458, 471, 487, 488, 492, 508
Chōsokabe Motochika (長曾我部元親), 267
Chōya Shimbun (朝野新聞), 355
chōzen-shugi (超然主義), 404
Christianity, 130, 164, 169, 172, 177, 182, 184, 187, 190, 197, 198, 207, 220, 233, 244, 252, 258, 268, 315, 324, 338, 350, 354, 368, 369, 372, 373, 389, 410, 416, 424-26, 430, 441, 475, 497, 501, 502, 504, 510, 516, 519, 521
Chūai, Emperor (仲哀天皇), 39, 52
Chu-an Ch'an-shih, 145
Ch'üan-shih Ch'an-shih, 145
Chūchō jijitsu (中朝事實), 273
Chūgū-ji (中宮寺), 62
Chu Hsi Neo-Confucianism (朱子學), 112, 136, 167, 175, 198, 200, 206, 212, 221, 235, 238, 240, 243, 262, 272, 273, 276, 441
Chung-chu-ssu, 145
Chung-t'ang Chüan (鐘堂學園), 143
Chung-yu Tsu-ch'an, 137
Chūō Hōritsu Shimpōsha (中央法律新報社), 373
Chuo Hsing-ssu, 72
Chūō Kōron (中央公論), 416, 483, 511, 517, 522
Chūō Shimbun (中央新聞), 402
Chūseitō (中正黨), 490
Civil Service Appointment Regulations, 509
Clemenceau, Georges, 453
Cobos, Juan, 101
Coen, Jan Pieterszoon, 272
Collegio (Nagasaki), 178
Comintern, 435
communism, 317, 382, 434, 435, 457, 459, 462, 468, 485, 488, 496, 511, 515, 520
Communist Party, Japan (日本共產黨), 317, 382, 434, 435, 457, 459, 462, 468, 488, 496, 511, 515
Conference on International Law, 370
Confucianism (儒學), 45, 61, 62, 111, 112, 116, 136, 142, 166-68, 171, 175, 176, 178, 185, 187, 194, 198, 199, 205, 208, 209, 211, 212, 214, 215, 220, 225, 232, 235, 240, 243, 254, 256, 262, 265, 271, 272, 274, 276, 278, 283, 354, 366, 401, 405, 429, 450, 463, 474, 490, 501, 508, 524
Congress of Far Eastern Peoples (極東民族會議), 496
Connaught, Prince Arthur, 414
Constitution Party, *see* Kenseitō
Constitution Protection Movement, 377, 394, 482, 507
Contrat social, 421

D

Daibutsu-ji (大佛寺), 94
Daidempō-in (Negoro-dera) (根來寺), 40
Daidō-danketsu (大同團結), 355
Daigaku Nankō (大學南校), 347, 367, 421, 436, 474, 482
Daigaku shōku (大學章句), 112
Daigaku wakumon (大學惑問), 209
Daigo-emmei-in (醍醐延明院), 50
Daigo, Emperor (醍醐天皇), **20-21**, 65, 98
Daigo-ji (醍醐寺), 59, 92, 116, 118
Daijimmei jiten (大人名辭典), 481
Daijō Bukkyō shiron (大乘佛教史論), 405
Daijō-ji (大乘寺), 113
Daikaku-ha (大覺派), 118
Daikaku-ji line (大覺寺統), 97, 114
daikan (代官), 254
daikanjin (大勸進), 96
Daiki Hōkin (大喜法忻), 145
Daikokuya Kōdayū (大黑屋幸太夫), **173-74**, 202, 217
Daikōmyō-ji (大光明寺), 137
Daikōryō (大綱領), 353
Daimai Zenji (大梅禪師), 199
Dainichi Nōnin (大日能忍), 124
Dai-Nihon Nichiren Shugi Seinendan (大日本日蓮主義青年團), 461
Dai-Nihon shi (大日本史), 277
Dai-Nihonteikoku Kempō (大日本帝國憲法), 353
Dai-Nippon Zokuzōkyō (大日本續藏經), 405
Daiō Kokushi (大應國師), 134
Daisen (大山), 124
Daishin-in (Supreme Court) (大審院), 387, 397
daisōjō (大僧正), 41, 256
Daitōa shin chitsujo no rekishiteki seikaku (大東新秩序の歷史的性格), 438
Daitō Kokushi (大燈國師), 124, 134
Daitō kokushi goroku (大燈國師語錄), 135
Daitoku-ji (大德寺), 135, 201, 253
Daitō Nippō (大東日報), 338
Daizōkyō (Tripitaka) (大藏經), 256, 425
dajōdaijin (太政大臣), 28, 35, 89
Dan-no-ura, battle of (壇の浦), 19, 36, 120, 121
Dan Takuma (團琢磨), **322-23**, 349
Daruma Zen (達磨宗), 124
Date family (伊達家(藩)) 185, 237, 274
Date Masamune (伊達政宗), **174-75**, 183
Date Muneharu (伊達宗春), 170
Date Munenari (伊達宗城), 471
Date Terumune (伊達輝宗), 174
Davis, Jerome Dean, 426
Dazaifu (太宰府), 25, 26, 65, 136, 458
Dazai Shundai (太宰春臺), **175**, 187

Deguchi Nao (出口ナオ), 323
Deguchi Onisaburō (出口王仁三郎), **323**
Democratic Party, *see* Minshutō
Democratic Socialist Party, *see* Minshu Shakaitō
Dengyō Daishi (傳教大師), *see* Saichō
Denju-shū (傳授集), 51
Denkōroku (傳光錄), 113
Denmark, 325, 432
Deussen, P, 315
Dirckz, Arnold, 225
Dodge, Joseph, 521
Dōetsu (道悅), 141
Dōgen (道元), **93-94**, 113, 125
Dōji (道慈), 38
Dōjidai-kan (*Dōjidai-shi*) (同時代觀(同時代史)), 416
Dōjima rice exchange (堂島米市場), 281
Dōjinsai (同仁齋), 89
Dōjinsha (同人社), 423
Dokuritsu Hyōron (獨立評論), 510
Dokushi yoron (讀史餘論), 168
Dokushōshū (獨嘯集), 214
Dōkyō (道鏡), **21**, 29, 43, 71
Dōkyō Etan (道鏡惠端), 179
Doryōkō settō (度量衡說統), 217
Dōsen, *see* Tao-hsüan
Dōshisha University (同志社), 313, 324, 426, 497, 511, 515, 517
Dōshō (道昭), **21-22**
Dōzenbō (道善房), 125
Dulles, John Foster, 521
Dutch, 162, 166, 173, 180, 181, 184-86, 191, 192, 197, 199, 202, 207-09, 213, 223, 225, 229, 233, 236, 239, 244, 245, 249, 250, 263, 268-70, 274, 284, 325, 330, 331, 351, 359, 378, 386, 423, 425, 429, 441, 499, 508

E

East Asia Economic Research Bureau (東亜經濟調査局), 437, 459
Ebina Danjō (海老名彈正), **324**, 475, 521
Echigoya (越後屋), 213
Echū (惠中), 247
Edayoshi Nangō (枝吉南濠), 473
Edayoshi Shin'yō (枝吉神陽), 326, 473
Edinburgh, Duke of, 414
Edo shogunate, 54, 106, 109, 196, 238, 246, 281, *see also* Tokugawa shogunate
Egawa Hidetake (江川英毅), 176
Egawa Tarōzaemon Hidetatsu (江川太郎左衛門英龍), 162, **176**, 239, 250, 386, 403, 422
Ehi, *see* Hyeja
Ei-Bei hon'i no heiwa shugi o haisu (英米本位の平和主義を排す), 399
Eibun Shimpō (英文新報), 502
Eichō (榮朝), 96, 125
Eiei (榮叡), 32
Eifuku-ji (永福寺), 127
Eihei-ji (永平寺), 94, 113
Eihei kōroku (永平廣錄), 94
Eikan (Yōkan) (永觀), **22**, 47
Eikan-dō (永觀堂), 22
Eikō-ji (永光寺), 113
Eikū (叡空), 107
Eikyō uprising (永享の亂), 140
Eisai (榮西), *see* Myōan Eisai
Eison (叡尊), **94-95**, 126
Ejō (懷弉), 94
Ekiken jukkun (益軒十訓), 200
Elements of Experimental Chemistry, 269
Elkinton, Mary P., 430
Ema Ransai (江馬蘭齋), 210
Emi no Oshikatsu, *see* Fujiwara no Nakamaro
Emi no Oshikatsu uprising (惠美押勝の亂), 58
Emishi (蝦夷), 69
Enchin (圓珍), **23**, 24, 58
Engaku-ji (圓覺寺), 95, 96, 111, 123, 143, 462, 476
Engetsu (圓月), **95**
Engi-Tenryaku peace (延喜・天曆の治), 21
England, 161, 162, 315, 316, 321, 322, 330, 332, 336, 343, 346, 347, 350, 351, 361, 376, 377, 381, 398, 414, 417, 423, 425, 432, 435, 474, 494, 506, 520, *see also* Britain
Enkan Bonsō (圓鑑梵相), 137
Enni Bennen (圓爾辨圓), **96**, 115, 142
Ennin (圓仁), **23-24**, 58
Ennin's Travels in T'ang China, 23
En no Gyōja (役行者), 24
En no Ozunu (役小角), **24**, 60
En no Ubasoku (役優婆塞), 24
Enomoto Takeaki (榎本武揚), **325-26**, 403
Enryaku-ji (延曆寺), 20, 23, 55, 58, 86, 131, 256
Ensai meibutsukō (遠西名物考), 269
Ensai sōmokuryaku (遠西草木略), 269
Enshō (圓證), 59
Enshō (圓照), 100
Enshō (延昌), 47
En'yū, Emperor (圓融天皇), 38, 41
erekiteru (エレキテル), 186
Erin-ji (惠林寺), 123, 145
Erlich, Paul, 466
Eshin-ni (惠信尼), 133
Eshin-ni monjo (惠信尼文書), 134
Eshin Sōzu (惠心僧都), 34
Esopu monogatari (*Aesop's Fables*), 177
Esoteric Buddhism (密教), 19, 41, 45, 50, 57, 59, 94, 95, 111, 113, 116, 118, 124, 136
Esperanto, 323
Essays in Zen Buddhism, 477
Etō Shimpei (江藤新平), **326-27**, 353, 359, 375, 440, 443, 473
Europe, 319, 322, 333, 335, 348, 361, 363, 365, 366, 375, 380, 382, 387, 395, 396, 406, 408, 419, 423, 426, 429, 430, 440, 446-48, 451, 452, 454, 463, 468, 470, 473, 477, 479, 480, 483, 488, 492, 502, 508, 517, 522, 523, 525

Ewing, James Alfred, 487
Ezawa Yōju (江澤養樹), 269
Ezochi (蝦夷地), 189, 194, 208, 210, 216, 241, 248, 285
Ezo dōchihen (蝦夷道知邊), 189
Ezo people (蝦夷), 17, 41, 58, 68
Ezo sōshi (蝦夷草紙), 217

F

Fabian Society, 313
Fa-chi Ta-shin (Hōsai Daishi) (法濟大師), 20
Fashizumu hihan (ファシズム批判), 381
Fa-tsang (法藏), 59
Faxecura, Don Fillipo Francesco, 183
February 26 incident (二・二六事件), 318, 319, 344, 381, 391, 400, 409, 437, 456, 478, 483
Federation of Japanese Women's Organizations (日本婦人團體連合會), 343
Fenollosa, Ernest, 394
Ferreira, Christovão (Sawano Chūan) (澤野忠庵), 221, 225
Fifteenth National Bank (第十五國立銀行), 366
First National Bank (第一國立銀行), 464
Fischer, Emil, 480
Five Classics of Shinto (神道五部書), 271
Flexner, Simon, 432
Formosa, 180
Four Books (四書大全), 178, 221
France, 251, 314, 320, 330, 336, 340, 343, 353, 358, 410, 420, 421, 435, 445, 447, 452, 453, 455, 460, 483, 508
Franco-Prussian War, 423, 447
French, 219, 380, 410, 421, 436, 445, 472, 508
fudai daimyo (譜代大名), 237
fudoki (風土記), 33
Fuji Bank (富士銀行), 517
Fujii Nittatsu (藤井日達), **327-28**
Fujioka Sakutarō (藤岡作太郎), 476
Fujita Keisho (藤田敬所), 214
Fujita Tōko (藤田東湖), **176-77**, 184, 518
Fujita Yūkoku (藤田幽谷), 177
Fujitsuka Shikibu (藤塚式部), 185
Fujiwara family (藤原氏), 27, 31, 34, 44, 50, 59, 61, 64, 67, 71, 121, 144, 399
Fujiwara Ginjirō (藤原銀次郎), 348
Fujiwara no Fuhito (藤原不比等), **24-25**, 31, 43, 60, 71
Fujiwara no Fuyutsugu (藤原冬嗣), **25**, 50, 56
Fujiwara no Gemmyō (藤原玄明), 68
Fujiwara no Hidehira (藤原秀衡), 121, 122
Fujiwara no Hirotsugu (藤原廣嗣), **25-26**, 33, 42, 61, 67
Fujiwara no Junshi (藤原順子), 31
Fujiwara (Nakatomi) no Kamatari (藤原鎌足), 24, **26-27**, 43, 63, 70
Fujiwara no Kaneie (藤原兼家), 38
Fujiwara no Kanshi (藤原寛子), 30
Fujiwara no Kenshi (藤原研子), 28
Fujiwara no Kinzane (藤原公實), 35
Fujiwara no Kiyohira (藤原清衡), 48
Fujiwara no Korechika (藤原伊周), 28
Fujiwara no Kusuko (藤原藥子), 56, 68
Fujiwara no Kuzunomaro (藤原葛野麻呂), 45
Fujiwara no Masatsura (藤原眞連), 19
Fujiwara no Michifusa (藤原通房), 30
Fujiwara no Michikane (藤原道兼), 28
Fujiwara no Michinaga (藤原道長), **27-28**, 29, 31, 34, 38, 50
Fujiwara no Michitaka (藤原道隆), 28
Fujiwara no Morosuke (藤原師輔), 55
Fujiwara no Motofusa (藤原基房), 93
Fujiwara no Mototsune (藤原基經), 27, **28**, 58, 64
Fujiwara no Muchimaro (藤原武智麻呂), 60
Fujiwara no Naganari (藤原長成), 121, 139
Fujiwara no Nagayoshi (藤原長良), 28
Fujiwara no Nakamaro (Emi no Oshikatsu) (藤原仲麻呂(恵美押勝)), 21, 24, 29, 33, 42-44, 52, 67, 71
Fujiwara no Otsugu (藤原緒嗣), 41
Fujiwara no Sadanori (藤原貞憲), 111
Fujiwara no Shōshi (藤原彰子), 28, **29**
Fujiwara no Sumitomo (藤原純友), 29-30, 116
Fujiwara no Tanetsugu (藤原種繼), 40, 72
Fujiwara no Teishi, (藤原定子), 29
Fujiwara no Tokihira (藤原時平), 20, 64, 65
Fujiwara no Umakai (藤原宇合), 25
Fujiwara no Yasuhira (藤原泰衡), 122
Fujiwara no Yorimichi (藤原頼通), 28, **30-31**, 34
Fujiwara no Yoritsune (藤原頼經), 102
Fujiwara no Yoshifusa (藤原良房), 27, 28, **31**, 58
Fujiyama Raita (藤山雷太), 348
Fuju-fuse branch of Nichiren Buddhism (日蓮宗不受不施派), 223
Fukanzai Fabian (不干齋ファビアン), **177-78**
Fukan zazengi (普勸坐禪儀), 93
Fukkohō gaigen (復古法概言), 241
Fukuchi Gen'ichirō (福地源一郎), 421
Fukuda Hankō (福田半香), 271
Fukuda (Kageyama) Hideko (福田 (景山) 英子), **328-29**
Fukuda Tomosaku (福田友作), 328
Fukuin Shimpō (福音新報), 504
Fukuoka Takachika (福岡孝弟), **329**, 334
Fukuryō (福亮), 38
Fukusai-ji (福濟寺), 279
Fukushima incident (福島事件), 436
Fukuuchi Kigai (福内鬼外), 185
Fukuzawa Yukichi (福澤諭吉), 229, **330-31**, 348, 392, 417, 423, 448
Fumon-ji (普門寺), 279
Fumoto no kusawake (麓草分), 247
Funado, Prince (道祖王), 43
Furukawa Ichibei (古河市兵衛), 489
Furukawa *zaibatsu* (古河財閥), 489
fusan (賦算), 109

Fushimi, Emperor (伏見天皇), 100
Fūshinchō (風信帖), 46
Fushō (普照), 32
Fushō kokushi kōroku (普照國師廣錄), 279
Fushō-zen (不生禪), 171
Futari bikuni (二人比丘尼), 247
Futsugaku-juku (佛學塾), 421
Futsū senkyo-ron (普通選擧論), 522

G
Gaiki seigokō (外紀西語考), 275
Gaikokugo Gakkō (外國語學校), 421
Gakan (我觀), 416
Gakudō yōjinshū (學道用心集), 94
Gakumon no susume (學問のすすめ), 331
Gamble, William, 220
Gandhi, Mahatma, 328
Ganjin (鑑眞), **32**, 53
Gankō-ji (元興寺), 22, 38
Gashin (雅眞), 50
Gautier, Judith, 455
Gazan Jitō (峨山慈棹), 180
Gazan Shōseki (峨山韶碩), 113
geba shogun (下馬將軍), 237
Geka taisei (外科大成), 203
Gekizetsu wakumon (鴃舌惑問), 270
gekokujō (下剋上), 92
Gembō (玄昉), 25, **32-33**, 42, 60, 67
gembun itchi (言文一致), 456
Gemmei, Empress (元明天皇), 24, **33**, 60, 71
Gempei seisuiki (源平盛衰記), 182
Gempo Reisan (玄圃靈山), 244
Gendai kensei no un'yō (現代憲政の運用), 522
Gendai kinken-shi (現代金權史), 511
Gendai Nihon kyōkai shiron (現代日本教會史論), 511
Gendō (言當), 281
General Staff Office (參謀本部), 319, 395, 396
Geneva Disarmament Conference, 358, 456
Genghis Khan, 105
Gengō (元杲), 19, 50
Gengo (玄語), 214
Genji, *see* Minamoto family
Genkō (源光), 107
Genkō disturbance (元弘の亂), 97
Genkō shakusho (元亨釋書), 116
Gennai ware (源内燒), 186
Gennin (源仁), 59
Genrōin (Senate) (元老院), 319, 329, 335, 352, 370, 375, 387, 406, 419, 421, 424, 427, 436, 445, 460, 492, 500
Genshin (源信), **33-34**, 74
Genshinbutsu to Hosshinbutsu (現身佛と法身佛), 315
Genshiroku (言志錄), 240
Genshō, Empress (元正天皇), 33, 60
Gen'yōsha (玄洋社), 343, 442, 499, 522
George V, King, 432, 494
Germany, 315, 330, 332, 333, 343, 347, 353, 354, 357, 359, 362, 375, 380, 381, 391, 412, 413, 415, 420, 430, 431, 433, 435, 443, 446, 452, 454, 478, 483, 495, 498, 504, 506, 512, 514
Gesshō (月照), 450
Giakushū Nihonjin (僞惡醜日本人), 416
Gidō Shūshin (義堂周信), **96-97**, 123, 145, 146
Gien (義淵), 21, 54
Gikeiki (義經記), 92
Ginkaku-ji (銀閣寺), 89
Ginza (銀座), 179
Gion Nankai (祇園南海), 206
Giō Shōnin, *see* I-weng Shao-jen
Gishin (義眞), 57
Glasgow, University of, 487
Goa, 130
Godaigo, Emperor (後醍醐天皇), 85, 87, 88, 95, **97-98**, 99, 100, 104, 113-17, 123, 124, 128, 135, 142
Godai Saisuke (五代戈助), 491
Godai Tomoatsu (五代友厚), **331-32**, 404
Goen'yū, Emperor (後圓融天皇), 98
Gofukakusa, Emperor (後深草天皇), 96, 100
Gofushimi, Emperor (後伏見天皇), 112
Gohanazono, Emperor (後花園天皇), 132
Go-Hōjōshi (後北條氏), 104
Goichijō, Emperor (後一條天皇), 28-30
Gōkai (豪海), 256
Gokameyama, Emperor (後龜山天皇), **98**
Gokashiwabara, Emperor (後柏原天皇), 132
Gokōgon, Emperor (後光嚴天皇), 137
Gokomatsu, Emperor (後小松天皇), 89, **98-99**
Gokōmyō, Emperor (後光明天皇), 116
Gokuchū jūhachinen (獄中十八年), 497
Gokui (極意), 193
Gokū Keinen (悟空敬念), 142
Gokuraku-ji (極樂寺), 93, 127
Gokyō (護教), 510
Gold and Silver Assay Office (金銀分析所), 332
Golovnin, Vasili Mikhailovi, 248
Gomizuno-o, Emperor (後水尾天皇), **178**, 253, 279
Gomurakami, Emperor (後村上天皇), 98, **99**, 115, 116
Gonara, Emperor (後奈良天皇), 132, 230
Gonchi (嚴智), 59
Go'ningumi seidoron (五人組制度論), 347
gon-negi (權禰宜), 271
Gonroku Fujimasa (權六藤正), 183
Goreizei, Emperor (後冷泉天皇), 30, 31, 34
Gorter, Johannes de, 203, 269
Gosaga, Emperor (後嵯峨天皇), 96, 100, 118
Gosanjō, Emperor (後三條天皇), 30, **34-35**
Goshirakawa, Emperor (後白河天皇), **35-36**, 49, 71, 117, 120, 121, 137
Gosuzaku, Emperor (後朱雀天皇), 28-30, 34
Gotoba, Emperor (後鳥羽天皇), 40, 117

Gotō Kōjō (後藤光乘), 179
Gotō Konzan (後藤艮山), 275
Gotō Mitsutsugu (後藤光次), **178-79**
Gotō Shimpei (後藤新平), **332-34**, 336, 455
Gotō Shōjirō (後藤象二郎), 238, 329, **334-35**, 355, 359, 360, 366, 421, 439, 440
Gotō Tokujō (後藤德乘), 179
Gotō Yūjō (後藤祐乘), 178
Gotsuchimikado, Emperor (後土御門天皇), 132
Gottan Funei, *see* Wu-an P'u-ning
Gouda, Emperor (後宇多天皇), 97, **99-100**, 111
Goyōzei, Emperor (後陽成天皇), 178, 230
Gozan (五山), 90
Gozan bungaku (五山文學), 95, 96, 111, 116, 123, 129, 133, 137, 145, 146
Grant, General, 414
Great Buddha of Tōdai-ji (東大寺の大佛), 37, 61, 67, 93
Greater East Asia Congress (大東亞交會議), 495
Greater East Asia Coprosperity Sphere (大東亞共榮圈), 412
Greater Japan Young Men's Organization, 488
Great Fire of Meireki era (明曆の大火), 204
Great Kantō Earthquake (關東大震災), 350, 513
Great Learning (大學), 171
"Greetings to Comrade Nosaka", 383
Grew, U.S. Ambassador, 434
Grey, Edward, 376
Gudō (愚堂), 247
Guizot, François Pierre Guillaume, 481
gunnery, 251, 351, 406, 429
Gunsho ruijū (群書類從), 182
Gutoku-shō (愚禿鈔), 134
Gyōhyō (行表), 56
Gyōki (行基), **36-37**, 55, 61
Gyokuyō (玉葉), 117
Gyōnen (凝念), 59, **100**
Gyōyū (行勇), 96

H

Ha Daiusu (破提宇子), 178
Hagiwara Kaneyori (萩原兼從), 283
Hagiwara Sōko (萩原宗固), 181
Hakka (Kakuka) (覺哥), 61
Hakoda Rokusuke (箱田六輔), 499
Hakuaisha (博愛社), 460
Hakuin Ekaku (白隱慧鶴), 135, **179-80**
Hakusuki-no-e (白村江), 70
Hakuun Egyō (白雲慧曉), 96, 113
Hamada Hikozō (濱田彥藏), **335-36**
Hamada Kunimatsu (濱田國松), 344
Hamada Yahyōe (濱田彌兵衞), **180**
Hamaguchi Osachi (濱口雄幸), 323, **336-37**, 351, 415, 505, 507
Hamaguri Gate incident, 318
Hanaoka Seishū (華岡靑洲), **181**
Hanawa Hokiichi (塙保己一), **181-82**
Hanazono, Emperor (花園天皇), 135
Handō-ji (飯道寺), 231
Han dynasty, 18
haniwa (埴輪), 52
Hankampu (藩翰譜), 168
Hanseikai (反省會), 483
Hanseikai Zasshi (反省會雜誌), 483
Hanzaigaku josetsu (犯罪學序說), 486
Harada Kiemon (原田喜右衞門), **100-101**
Harada Kumao (原田熊雄), 385
Harada Magoshichirō (原田孫七郎), 100
Hara Takashi (原敬), **337-39**, 377, 454, 482, 488, 493
Hartmann, Eduard von, 354
Harvard University, 368, 370, 398, 514
Hasegawa Fujihiro (長谷川藤廣), 172
Hasegawa Kohei (長谷川小兵衞), 274
Hasegawa Nyozekan (長谷川如是閑), 447
Hasegawa Sayhōe Fujihiro (長谷川左兵衞藤廣), **182-83**
Hasegawa Sōjin (長谷川宗仁), 100
Hasekura Tsunenaga (支倉常長), 175, **183-84**
Hashiba Hideyoshi (羽柴秀吉), 227, 229
Hashimoto Chōkō (橋本長綱), 184
Hashimoto Kingorō (橋本欣五郎), 438
Hashimoto Sanai (橋本左內), 176, **184**, 229, 239, 518, 524
Hashimoto Sōkichi (橋本宗吉), 236
Hasshū kōyō (八宗綱要), 100
Hatakeyama Mochikuni (畠山持國), 88
Hatakeyama Yoshitsugu (畠山義繼), 174
Hatano Hideharu (波多野秀治), 163
Hatano Yoshishige (波多野義重), 94
Hataraku mono kara miru mono e (働くものから見るものへ), 428
Hata Shunroku (畑俊六), 519, 520
Hatoyama Haruko (鳩山春子), 339
Hatoyama Ichirō (鳩山一郎), 321, **339-40**, 357, 469, 485, 520
Hatoyama Kazuo (鳩山和夫), 339
Hatsubisampō (發微算法), 202
Hatsu-kuni-shirasu-sumera-mikoto (始馭天下之天皇), 39
Hattori Chūyō (服部中庸), 187
Hattori Nankaku (服部南郭), 208
Hawaii, 346
Hayashi (Matsudaira) Jussai (林 (松平) 述齋), 235, 240
Hayashi Nobuatsu (林信篤), 206, 240, 262
Hayashi Razan (林羅山), 178, 272
Hayashi Senjūrō (林銑十郎), 400, 519
Hayashi Shihei (林子平), **185**, 208
Hayashi Tadasu (林董), 358
Hayashi Yūzō (林有造), 372, 401, 419
Hazama Shigetomi (間重富), 170, 249
Heco, Joseph, 336
Hegel, 375, 394
Heguri no Matori (平群眞鳥), 54
Heian-kyō (平安京), 41, 72

Heiji monogatari emaki (平治物語繪卷), 49
Heiji uprising (平治の亂), 35, 49, 104, 119, 121, 137
Heijō-kyō (平城京), 33, 41, 72
Heike, *see* Taira family
Heike monogatari (平家物語), 92, 138, 177
Heiminsha (平民社), 316, 328, 389, 390, 402, 445, 457
Heiminsha jidai (平民社時代), 317
Heimin Shimbun (平民新聞), 389, 402, 445, 511
Heisenberg, Werner Carl, 498
Heizei, Emperor (平城天皇), 56, 68
Henjō-ji (遍照寺), 41
Henry, William, 269
Heusken, Henry C. J., 164
Hiden-in (悲田院), 44
Hiei, Mt. (比叡山), 23, 34, 47, 55-57, 86, 93, 94, 96, 107, 124, 125, 133, 226, 256, 276
Higashi Hongan-ji (東本願寺), 394, 418, 443, 444
Higashikuni (Higashikuni-no-miya) Naruhiko(東久邇 (東久邇宮) 稔彥), **340-41**, 369, 401, 465, 469, 520
Higashikuze Michitomi (東久世通禧), 458, 491
higashi-mawari (東廻り), 204
Higashiyama culture (東山文化), 89
Hijikata Hisamoto (土方久元), 404, 458
Hijikata Shigeyoshi (土方成美), 381
Hiki Yoshikazu (比企能員), 102, 119
Hikonagisatake-ugayafukiaezu-no-mikoto (彥波瀲武鸕鷀草葺不合尊), 38
Himiko (卑彌呼), **37**
Himitsu mandara jūjūshinron (秘密曼荼羅十住心論), 46
Himorogi iwasaka no den (神籬磐境傳), 283
Hinayana Buddhism, 57
Hino Arinori (日野有範), 133
Hi no hashira (火の柱), 389
Hino Katsumitsu (日野勝光), 101
Hino Suketomo (日野資朝), 97
Hino Tomiko (日野富子), 88, **101**, 108, 144
Hino Toshimoto (日野俊基), 97
Hiraga Gennai (平賀源內), **185-86**, 222, 245
Hiraga Yuzuru (平賀讓), 381
Hiranuma Kiichirō (平沼騏一郎), 319, **341-42**, 385, 396, 400, 519
Hiraoka Kōtarō (平岡浩太郎), 499
Hirata Atsutane (平田篤胤), **187-88**, 241
Hirata Tōsuke (平田東助), 510
Hiratsuka Raichō (平塚らいてう), **342-43**
Hirosawa branch of Shingon Buddhism (眞言の廣澤流), 41
Hirose Tansō (廣瀨淡窓), 233, 393
Hirota Kōki (廣田弘毅), 319, **343-44**, 469, 520
Hishinuma Gorō (菱沼五郎), 323
History of the Kingdom of Wei, 37
Hitachi-obi (常陸帶), 177
Hito to naru michi (人となる道), 200
Hitotsubashi family (一橋家), 264
Hitotsubashi Haruzumi (一橋春濟), 259
Hitotsubashi Yoshinobu (一橋慶喜), 184, 191, 258, 463, 471, 472
Hizō hōyaku (秘藏寶鑰), 46
Hōchi Shimbun (報知新聞), 479
Hōchū biyō wamyō honzō (庖廚備用倭名本草), 221
Hōgen uprising (保元の亂), 35, 49, 71, 137
Hōhiron (放屁論), 186
Hōjō family (北條氏), 85, 102-04, 106, 123, 140, 141, 261, 268
Hōjō-ji (法成寺), 28
Hōjō (Taira) Masako (北條 (平) 政子), **102-03**, 104, 106, 119, 120, 125
Hōjō Naritoki (北條業時), 127
Hōjō Sadatoki (北條貞時), 111
Hōjō Sanetoki (北條實時), 95, **103**
Hōjō Saneyasu (北條實泰), 103
Hōjō Shigetoki (北條重時), 127
Hōjō Sōun (北條早雲), **103-04**
Hōjō Takatoki (北條高時), **104**
Hōjō Tokimasa (北條時政), 41, 102, **104-05**, 106, 119, 120, 141
Hōjō Tokimune (北條時宗), **105-06**, 118, 143
Hōjō Tokiyori (北條時賴), 94, 96, 105, 118, 126, 142
Hōjō Yasutoki (北條泰時), 103, **106**
Hōjō Yoshitoki (北條義時), 102, 103, **106-07**
Hōju-ji (法住寺), 36
Hōkan-ji (寶冠寺), 145
Hokekyō, *see* Lotus Sutra
Hokekyō-ji (法華經寺), 127, 161
Hokekyō no gyōja Nichiren (法華教の行者日蓮), 315
Hokkaido, *see* Ezochi
Hokke shūku (法華秀句), 57
Hōkō-ji (方廣寺), 223, 245
Hokui kōshō (北夷考證), 211
Hokumon Shimpō (北門新報), 422
Hokusa bunryaku (北槎聞略), 203
Hōkyōki (寶慶記), 93
Holland, 161, 251, 325, 332, 336, 343, 426, 465, 499, *see also* Dutch
Hompō-ji (本法寺), 128
Honda Kōtarō (本多光太郎), **345**
Honda Masanobu (本田正信), **188**
Honda Masazumi (本多正純), 188
Honda Nisshō (本多日生), 461
Honda Tadatoki (本多忠刻), 280
Honda Toshiaki (本多利明), **188-89**, 216
Hōnen (法然), 22, 34, 92, **107-08**, 112, 117, 133
Hongaku-ji (本覺寺), 116
Hongan-ji (本願寺), 60, 112, 131, 134, 217, 405, 469
Hongan-ji-ha gakuji-shi (本願寺派學事史), 406
Honge seiten daijirin (本化聖典大辭林), 487
Honkō kokushi nikki (本光國師日記), 245
Honkyō gaihen (本教外篇), 187
Honnō-ji (本能寺), 171, 189, 190, 218, 227, 229, 252, 260, 267

Honsaroku (本佐錄), 188
Honzō kōmoku bemmoku bengo (本草綱目辨目辨誤), 234
Honzō kōmoku keimō (本草綱目啓蒙), 234
Honzō kōmoku keimō kōsansetsu (本草綱目啓蒙廣參說), 234
Hōonkō-shiki (報恩講式), 112
Horikawa, Emperor (堀河天皇), 70
Horikawa Yasuchika (堀河康親), 364
Hōritsu shinkaron (法律進化論), 347
Hōryū-ji (法隆寺), 53, 62
Hōsai Daishi, *see* Fa-chi Ta-shin
Hoshina Masayuki (保科正之), 276, 283
Hōshi sōdan (報四叢談), 470
Hoshi Taijun (星泰順), 345
Hoshi Tōru (星亨), 339, **345-46**
Hosoi Heishū (細井平州), 278
Hosokawa family (細川家), 108, 130, 164, 196
Hosokawa Gracia (細川ガラシア), **189-90**, 193
Hosokawa Harumoto (細川晴元), 91, 92
Hosokawa Junjirō (細川潤次郎), 421
Hosokawa Katsumoto (細川勝元), 88, 101, **108**, 144
Hosokawa Morihisa (細川護久), 417
Hosokawa Okiaki (細川興秋), 189
Hosokawa Tadaoki (細川忠興), 189, **190-91**, 193
Hosokawa Tadataka (細川忠隆), 189
Hosokawa Tadatoshi (細川忠利), 189
Hosokawa Terutsune (細川輝經), 190
Hosokawa Tsunatoshi (細川綱利), 232
Hosokawa Yoriyuki (細川頼之), 108, 145
Hossō Buddhism (法相宗), 21, 57, 59, 111
Hōtokuki (報德記), 225
Hōtokusha (報德社), 224
Hotta Masachika (堀田正愛), 191
Hotta Masanobu (堀田正信), 239
Hotta Masatoshi (堀田正俊), 167, 262
Hotta Masayoshi (堀田正睦), 161, **191**, 364
Hōwa-shū (法話集), 123
How I Became a Christian, 502
Hozumi Nobushige (穗積陳重), **347**
Hozumi Shigetō (穗積重遠), 347
Hozumi Yatsuka (穗積八束), **347-48**
Hsi-chien Tsu-t'an (西磵子曇), 110
Hsing-man, 57
Hsü Ang, 243
Hsü-an Huai-ch'ang (虛菴懷敞), 124
Hsüan-tsang, 22
Hsü Fu, 145
Hsü Jen-man (徐仁滿), 20
Hsü-t'ang Chih-yü (虛堂智愚), 134
Huang-lung line, 124
Huang-po, (黃檗), 278, 425
Huan-hsi Wei-i (環溪惟一), 143
Hua-yen, *see* Kegon Buddhism
Hui-kuo (惠果), 45
Hyakugaku renkan (百學連關), 427
Hyeja (Ehi) (慧慈), 61
Hyekwan (Ekan) (慧灌), **37-38**
hyōbu-tayū (兵部大輔), 233
Hyōki teikō (表記提綱), 500
Hyōryūmin goranki (漂流民御覽記), 203

I

Iba Sōtarō (伊庭想太郎), 346
Ibuki, Mt. (伊吹山), 73
Ichijō, Emperor (一條天皇), 28, 29, **38**, 50
Ichijō-in (一條院), 86
Ichijō Kanera (一條兼良), 132
Ichijō Tadaka (一條忠香), 413
Ichijō Yoshiko (一條美子), 413
Ichikawa Beian (市川米庵), 271
Ichikawa Fusae (市川房枝), 343
Ichikawa Kansai (市河寬齋), 275
Ichikawa Shōichi (市川正一), 459
Ichimai kishōmon (一枚起請文), 107
Ichiman (一幡), 102, 119
Ichinen yūhan (一年有半), 422
Ichiryū ippen no sho (一流一返之書), 193
Igakkan (醫學館), 202
Iidaka Gakurin (飯高學林), 486
Ii Naoaki (井伊直亮), 192
Ii Naonaka (井伊直中), 192
Ii Naosuke (井伊直弼), 164, 165, 184, 191, **192-93**, 203, 258, 264, 384, 450, 457, 472, 524
Iio Sōgi (飯尾宗祇), 132
Ijichi Shigesada (伊地知重貞), 112
Ikeda Hayato (池田勇人), 461, 521
Ikeda Mitsumasa (池田光政), 208, 209, 222, 285
Ikeda Narimasa (池田齊政), 405
Ikeda Shigeaki (池田成彬), 323, **348-49**, 391
Ikeda Shōi (池田昌意), 243
Ike no Zenni (池禪尼), 120
Ikensho (意見書), 353
ikkō ikki (一向一揆), 227, 228, 260
Ikō Dōnen (葦航道然), 118
Ikoku nikki (異國日記), 245
Ikoma, Mt. (生駒山), 199
Ikuei Kyōkō (育英教校), 394
Imagawa Ujichika (今川氏親), 103, 109
Imagawa Yoshimoto (今川義元), **109**, 226, 260
Imagawa Yoshitada (今川義忠), 103
Imakita Kōsen (今北洪川), 462, 476
Imakōji Morofuyu (今小路師冬), 118
Imamura Eisei (今村英生), **192-93**
Imamura Ichizaemon (今村市左衛門), 192
Imawaka (今若), 139
Imbe Shintō (忌部神道), 273
Imna, *see* Mimana
Imperial House Law (皇室典範), 353, 362
Imperial Rescript on Education (教育勅語), 353, 354, 414, 417, 502, 509
Imperial Rescript on the Military (軍人勅諭), 509
Imperial Rule Assistance Association, *see* Taisei Yokusankai

Imperial Way faction, *see* Kōdō faction
Inamura Sampaku (稻村三伯), 236
Inatomi Ichimu (稻富一夢), **193**
Inatomi Naotoki (稻富直時), 193
Inayama Yukinori (稻山行教), 182
India, 187, 328, 446, 495
Indian Buddhism, 484
Indian independence movement, 356, 499
Indian philosophy, 315, 349, 437, 506
Indo tetsugaku kenkyū (印度哲學研究), 506
Indo tetsugaku-shi (印度哲學史), 506
Industry and Labor Research Center (產業勞働調查所), 434
Infectious Disease Research Center (傳染病研究所), 392
Inkyoron (隱居論), 347
Inleiding tot de waare Natuuren sterrekunde of de Natuur en Sterrekundige Lessen, 244
Inō Kagetaka (伊能景敬), 194
Inomata Denjiemon (猪股傳次右衞門), 197
Inō Nagayoshi (伊能長由), 193
Inō Tadataka (伊能忠敬), **193-94**, 210, 249
Inoue Enryō (井上圓了), **349-50**, 416
Inoue Junnosuke (井上準之助), **350-51**
Inoue Kaoru (井上馨), 316, 338, **351-52**, 361, 403, 464, 490
Inoue Kowashi (井上毅), **353**, 362, 365, 370
Inoue Masatoshi (井上正利), 276
Inoue Michiyasu (井上通泰), 515
Inoue Naokiyo (井上直清), 203
Inoue Nisshō (井上日召), 486
Inoue Tetsujirō (井上哲次郎), 314, **354**
insei (院政), 35, 70, 97
Institut de Droit International, 314
Institute for Research in Infectious Diseases (傳染病研究所), 466
Institute of Folklore Studies (民俗學研究所), 516
Institute of Pacific Relations, 411, 430
Institute of Physical and Chemical Research (理化學研究所), 480, 484, 498, 512
Institut für Experimentelle Therapie, 466
International Economic Conference, 359
International Latitude Observatory (緯度觀測所), 388, 487
International Military Tribunal for the Far East, 318, 342, 344, 358, 385, 397, 409, 412, 438, 496, 520
International Olympic Committee, 371
Introduction to the Principle of Morals and Legislation, An, 419
Inukai Tsuyoki (犬養毅), 317, 318, 340, 351, **354-56**, 449, 456, 461, 483, 493, 513
Inzentekiyō (飲膳摘要), 234
Ippanjin no jikakuteki hansei (一般人の自覺的反省), 428
Ippen (一遍), 47, **109-10**
Ippen hijirie (一遍聖繪), 110
Ippen shōnin ekotoba-den (一遍上人繪詞傳), 110
Ippen shōnin goroku (一遍上人語錄), 110
Iryō seishi (醫療正始), 197
Ise Grand Shrines (伊勢神宮), 18, 141, 144, 271, 276
Ise Hei (伊勢平), 428
Ise Katsu (伊勢勝), 428
Ise Shinkurō Nagauji (伊勢新九郎長氏), 103
Ise Shintō (伊勢神道), 66, 142, 271
I-shan I-ning (Issan Ichinei) (一山一寧), **110-11**, 116, 123, 132
Ishibashi Tanzan (石橋湛山), **356-57**, 390
Ishida Baigan (石田梅巖), 171, **194-95**, 243
Ishida Mitsunari (石田三成), 190, **195-96**, 202, 207, 256, 261, 266, 280
Ishida sensei goroku (石田先生語錄), 195
Ishida sensei ikō (石田先生遺稿), 195
Ishihara Kanji (石原莞爾), **357-58**, 411
Ishihara Masaaki (石原正明), 182
Ishii Kikujirō (石井菊次郎), **358-59**
Ishii-Lansing agreement, 358, 493
Ishii Tsuneemon (石井恒 (常) 右衞門), 269
Ishikawa no Natari (石川名足), 53
Ishikawa Sanshirō (石川三四郎), 313, 328, 389
Ishi to genshiki to shite no sekai (意志と現識としての世界), 315
Ishiwata Sōtarō (石渡莊太郎), 356
Ishiyama Hongan-ji (石山本願寺), 131, 227
Isonokami no Yakatsugu (石上宅嗣), 52
Issan Ichinei, *see* I-shan I-ning
Isshiki Hidekatsu (一色秀勝), 244
Itagaki Seishirō (板垣征四郎), 495, 496
Itagaki Taisuke (板垣退助), 322, 329, 333-35, **359-60**, 367, 375, 440, 442, 451, 473, 503, 525
Itakura Katsushige (板倉勝重), **196**
Itakura Shigemasa (板倉重昌), **196-97**, 211
Itakura Shigemune (板倉重宗), 196
Itakura Yoshishige (板倉好重), 196
Italy, 359, 408, 412, 520
Itō Gemboku (伊東玄朴), **197**
Itō Hirobumi (伊藤博文), 282, 326, 329, 336, 338, 339, 346, 351-53, **360-63**, 365, 366, 370, 376, 380, 395, 404, 408, 410, 419, 420, 442, 448, 449, 452, 454, 458, 490, 509
Itō Jinsai (伊藤仁齋), 198
Itō Keisuke (伊藤圭介), 269
Itō Mansho (Mancio) (伊藤滿所), **197-98**
Itō Miyoji (伊藤巳代治), 353, 362, **363-64**, 370
Itō Noe (伊藤野枝), 446
Itō Shūrinosuke (伊藤修理亮), 197
Itō Tōgai (伊藤東涯), 166, **198**, 199
Itō Yūshō (伊東祐章), 197
Itsukushima Shrine (嚴島神社), 19
Itsuzen (逸然), 278
Iwagaki Gesshū (岩垣月洲), 474
Iwakura Tomomi (岩倉具視), 327, 353, 361, **364-66**, 384, 387, 408, 418, 421, 426, 439, 444, 451, 453, 458, 471, 473, 525
Iwakura Tomosada (岩倉具定), 366
Iwamoto Masatoshi (岩本正利), 259
Iwasaki Yatarō (岩崎彌太郎), **366-67**, 376, 442

Iwase Tadanari (岩瀬忠震), 162, 191
Iwashimizu Hachiman Shrine (石清水八幡神社), 48
I-weng Shao-jen (Giō Shōnin) (義翁紹仁), 118
Izanagi (伊弉諾), 18
Izanami (伊弉冉), 18
Izawa Shūji (伊澤修二), **367-68**
Izawa Takio (伊澤多喜男), 367
Izumi Shikibu (和泉式部), 29
Izumi Shikibu Diary (和泉式部日記), 29

J

Jakushin (Ōe no Sadamoto) (寂心(大江定基)), 74
Japan Advertiser, 484
Japan-China Cultural Exchange Association (日中文化交流協會), 374
Japan Economic League (日本經濟聯盟會), 323
Japan Economic Study Society, *see* Nihon Keizai Kenkyūkai
Japanese Federation of Labor (日本勞働總同盟), 373, 434
Japan Farmers' Union (日本農民組合), 320, 369, 373, 515
Japan Fine Arts Association (日本美術工藝協會), 460
Japan Folklore Society (日本民俗學會), 516
Japan General Labor Federation, *see* Nihon Rōdō Sōdōmei
Japan-German Anti-Comintern Pact, 319, 344
Japan Miners' Union (日本鑛夫組合), 320
Japan Missionary Society (日本傳道協會), 324
Japan Popular Party, *see* Nihon Taishūtō
Japan Proletarian Party, *see* Nihon Musantō
Japan Railway Company (日本鐵道會社), 366
Japan Red Cross, 459, 460
Japan Sea, battle of, 514
Japan Socialist League (日本社會主義同盟), 496
Japan Socialist Party (日本社會黨), 313, 320, 369, 374, 389, 402, 479, 511
Japan-Soviet treaty, 334
Japan-Soviet Union Society, 357
Japan Times, The, 321
Japan-United Stated Security Treaty, 320, 390, 461, 521
Japan Women's University (日本女子大學), 342
Jesuit order, 130, 177, 198, 221, 234, 268
Ji Buddhism (時宗), 109, 110
Jien (慈圓), 133
Jigaku shōsei (字學小成), 210
Jiin-hatto (寺院法度), 244
Jiji Shimpō (時事新報), 331, 348
Jikaku Daishi (慈覺大師), 23
Jikaku ni okeru chokkan to hansei (自覺に於ける直觀と反省), 428
Jiki jūjō (寺規十條), 135
Jikin (慈訓), 59
Jimmin Sensen (人民戰線), 479, 511
Jimmu, Emperor (神武天皇), **38-39**
Jimmukai (神武會), 438
Jimon (Onjō-ji) faction of Tendai Buddhism (寺門(園城寺)派), 23, 24
Jimpo Toshizaemon Sadatsune (神保利左衛門貞恒), 193
Jimpūren (神風連), 395
Jimyō-in line (持明院統), 97, 114
Jindaishi no atarashii kenkyū (神代史の新しい研究), 501
Jinen shin'eidō (自然眞營道), 165
Jingen shisetsu (仁言私說), 210
Jingū, Empress (神功皇后), 37, **39-40**, 52
Jingū hiden mondō (神宮秘傳問答), 271
Jinkan (深觀), 22
Jinken shinsetsu (人權新說), 375
Jinnō shōtōki (神皇正統記), 114, 115, 142
Jinsei chiri-gaku (人生地理學), 407
Jinshin uprising (壬申の亂), 53, 70
Jinzen (尋禪), 55
Jishūkan (時習館), 391
jitō (地頭), 36, 105, 120, 128
Jitō, Empress (持統天皇), 71
Jitsugakutō (Practical Party) (實學黨), 518
Jitsunyo (實如), 131
Jiun Onkō (慈雲飲光), **199-200**
Jiun Shinto (慈雲神道), 200
Jiyū Minshutō (Liberal Democratic Party) (自由民主黨), 321, 340, 357
Jiyū shimbun (自由新聞), 322, 346, 402
Jiyū shisō (自由思想), 402
Jiyūtō (Liberal Party) (自由黨), 322, 329, 335, 346, 355, 356, 359, 360, 436, 442, 460, 503, 520
Jizō-dō (地藏堂), 171
Jōchirei (上知令), 216
Jōdo (Pure Land) Buddhism (淨土宗), 34, 107, 108, 110, 111, 117, 133, *see also* Pure Land Buddhism
Jōdo hōmon genryū-shō (淨土法門源流章), 100
Jōdo monrui jushō (淨土文類聚鈔), 134
Jōdo Shin Buddhism (淨土眞宗), 34, 112, 131, 133, 134, 394, 405, 418, 425, 443, 446, 469, 483
Jōdo wasan (淨土和讚), 134
Jōe (定惠), 27
Jōei-shikimoku (貞永式目), 106
Jōge fuyū no gi (上下富有の議), 177
Jōgyō-zammai-dō (常行三昧堂), 133
Johns Hopkins University, 430
Jōkei (貞慶), **111-12**
Jōkyō calendar (貞享暦書), 243
Jōkyū disturbance (承久の亂), 102, 106, 107, 129
Jomei, Emperor (舒明天皇), 63, 69
Jōmon period (縄文時代), 39
Joosten van Lodensteijn, Jan, 162, **199**
Jōraku-ji (常樂寺), 135
Jōri (條理), 214
Jōruri (淨瑠璃), 185, 186
Jōsan (盛算), 19, 20

Joshi Eigakujuku (女子英學塾), 502
Jōshin (靜心), 124
Jōtōmon-in (上東門院), 29
Jō Tsunetarō (城常太郎), 485
Jōwa disturbance (承和の變), 31, 50
Ju-ching, 93
Jufuku-ji (壽福寺), 118, 125
jūji (住持), 253
Juji calendar, 243
Junna, Emperor (淳和天皇), 25, 50, 56
Junnin, Emperor (淳仁天皇), 29, 43, 71
Jūtei katai shinsho (重訂解體新書), 236
Juzan (壽山), 284
Jūzen hōgo (十善法語), 200
Jūzenkai (十善戒), 200
Jūzen shiroku (十禪支錄), 116

K

kabuki (歌舞伎), 232
Kachio-dera (勝尾寺) 47
kachi sōzō (價值創造), 408
Kagawa Toyohiko (賀川豐彥), **368-70**
Kagen (價原), 214
Kagetsu sōshi (花月草紙), 212
Kageyama Hideko, *see* **Fukuda Hideko**
Kaian kokugo (槐安國語), 135, 180
Kaibara Ekiken (貝原益軒), **200**
Kaibara Rakuken (貝原樂軒), 215
Kai, battle of (甲斐國の戰), 229
Kaientai (海援隊), 238, 418
Kaigai Shimbun (海外新聞), 336
Kaigen (快元), 140
Kaigun Denshūjo (海軍傳習所), 425
Kaijō biyōhō gaishōmon (海上備要方外傷門), 203
Kaijūsen-ji (海住山寺), 111
Kaikei (快慶), 93
Kaikoku heidan (海國兵談), 185
Kaikoku zushi (海國圖誌), 203
Kaimokushō (開目抄), 126
Kainan Gisha (海南義社), 372
K'ai-pao-ssu (開寶寺), 20
Kaiseijo (開成所), 334, 375, 406, 416, 427, 436, 491, 500
Kaiseikan (開成館), 334, 366
Kaisei Gakkō (開成學校), 375, 415, 423, 474, 482
Kaishin (戒信), 134
Kaishintō (Progressive Party) (改進黨), 469
Kaitai shinsho (解體新書), 202, 219, 222, 236, 246, 284
Kaitai yakuzu (解體約圖), 246
Kaitei ritsurei (改定律例), 327
Kaiten shishi (回天詩史), 177
Kaitokudō (懷德堂), 265, 274
Kai tsūshōkō (華夷通商考), 225
Kaiyō Maru (開陽丸), 325
K'ai-yüan-ssu, 20
Kaizō-in (海藏院), 116
Kakampu (火浣布), 186, 222
Kakuban (覺鑁), **40**
Kakuka, *see* Hakka
Kakumei zenya no Roshia (革命前夜のロシア), 321
Kakunyo (覺如), **112**, 134
Kakushinkai (革新會), 394
Kakushin Kurabu (Reform Club)(革新倶樂部), 355, 513
Kakushin-ni (覺信尼), 133
Kakushintō (革新黨), 377
Kamakura shogunate (鎌倉幕府), 41, 87, 97, 102-06, 113, 117, 119, 121, 125, 128, 138, 141
Kameyama, Emperor (龜山天皇), 95, 96, 99, 111, 116
Kamiya Jutei (神屋壽貞), 200
Kamiyama Sen'an (神山仙庵), 165
Kamiyama Shigeo (神山茂夫), 468
Kamiya Sōtan (神屋宗湛(紙屋宗且)), **200-01**
Kammu Heishi (桓武平氏), 41
Kammuryōju-kyō, see Amitayur-dhyana Sutra
Kammu, Emperor (桓武天皇), **40-41**, 56, 58, 70, 72
Kamo no Mabuchi (賀茂眞淵), 181
Kamo no Tadayuki (賀茂忠行), 74
Kamōsho (呵妄書), 187
kampaku (關白), 28, 30, 31
Kamsatsu kashi (柬察加志), 210
Kanadehon Chūshingura (假名手本忠臣藏), 232
Kana hōgo (假名法語), 96, 135
Kanamori Tsūrin (金森通倫), 324
Kanazawa (Kanezawa) Bunko (金澤文庫), 310
Kanchō (寬朝), **41-42**, 51
Kanda Takahira (神田孝平), 197, 327, 363
Kan'ei-ji (寬永寺), 205, 255
Kaneko Jūsuke (金子重輔), 282
Kaneko Kentarō (金子堅太郎), 322, 353, **370-71**
Kaneko Kinryō (金子金陵), 270
Kaneko Taiei (金子大榮), 395
Kangaku (觀覺), 107
Kangaku-in (勸學院), 25
Kanghwa Incident (江華島事件), 352, 367, 403
Kanghawa Treaty (日鮮修好條規), 352
Kangien (咸宜園), 393
Kango (敢語), 214
Kanjin gakushō-ki (感身學生記), 95
Kanjin honzonshō (觀心本尊抄), 126
Kanjō (灌頂), 41
Kanjōdokoro (勘定所), 263
Kankai ibun (環海異聞), 236
Kanke bunsō (菅家文草), 65
Kanke kōshū (菅家後集), 65
Kanken (觀賢), 60
Kankū (寬空), 41
Kanno Suga (管野スガ), 402
Kanō Jigorō (嘉納治五郎), **371**
Kanō Kōkichi (狩野亨吉), 165
kanrei (管領), 65
Kanrei higen (管蠡秘言), 210
Kanri (觀理), 19
Kanrin Maru (咸臨丸), 330, 379, 423
Kansai Workers' League (關西勞働同盟), 369

Kansei prohibition (寛政異學の禁), 212
Kansei reforms (寛政改革), 212
Kansei-reki (寛政暦), 249
kanshi (漢詩), 56
Kanshin-ji (觀心寺), 99
Kantō earthquake (關東大震災), 315, 333, 446
Kantō-goseibai-shikimoku (關東御成敗式目), 106
Kantō *kanrei* (關東管領), 96
Kantō-ōkan-ki (關東往還記), 95
Kan'yū dōhōki (勸誘同法記), 111
Kanzan Egen (關山慧玄), 135
Kanzeon-ji (觀世音寺), 33, 136
Karakhan, Lev Mikailvich, 343
Karakuni-no-muraji Hirotari (韓國連廣足), 24
Karafuto, *see* Sakhalin
Karu, Prince (輕皇子), 44
Kasagi, Mt. (笠置山), 97, 111
Kasanui-no-mura (笠縫村), 66
Kashin (嘉信), 517
Kasuga (春日), 478
Kasuga-no-tsubone (春日局), 257
Kasuga Shrine (春日神社), 54
katanagari (刀狩り), 268
Kataoka Kenkichi (片岡健吉), 346, 359, **371-72**
Katayama Sen (片山潜), 313, **372-73**, 402, 485
Katayama Tetsu (片山哲), 321, **373-74**, 480
Katei Kōbai Kumiai (家庭購買組合), 522
Katei Zasshi (家庭雜誌), 456
Katō Hiroyuki (加藤弘之), 331, 350, **374-75**, 413
Katō Kiyomasa (加藤清正), **201-02**
Katō Takaaki (加藤高明), 355, 358, **375-77**, 465, 466, 505, 507
Katō Tomosaburō (加藤友三郎), **377-78**
Katō Yasuyoshi (加藤泰宣), 276
Katsu Kaishū (勝海舟), 238, 239, **378-79**, 386, 418, 451
Katsuo-dera (勝尾寺), 107
Katsuragawa Hoshū (桂川甫周), **202-03**, 210, 222, 268
Katsuragawa Kunioki (桂川國興), 203
Katsuragi, Mt. (葛城山), 24, 200
Katsura Harimann Memo (桂ハリマン覺書), 399
Katsura Tarō (桂太郎), 333, 352, 355, 376, **380-81**, 393, 395, 398, 448, 449, 454, 493, 497, 506, 510, 513
Katsuyō-sampō (括要算法), 242
Katsuzan Manju (活山卍壽), 506
Kawada Shōryū (河田小龍), 237
Kawai Eijirō (河合榮治郎), **381-82**
Kawaji Sanzaemon (川路三左衞門), 203
Kawaji Toshiakira (川路聖謨), 162, 176, 191, **203**, 518
Kawaji Toshiyoshi (川路利良), 327
Kawakami Hajime (河上肇), **382-83**, 385, 399, 447
Kawakami Jōtarō (河上丈太郎), 374
Kawakami Sōroku (川上操六), 431
Kawamura Zuiken (河村瑞賢), 167, **204**, 205
Kawashima Kirin (川島貴林), 181
Kawata Koichirō (川田小一郎), 482
Kawate Bunjirō (川手文治郎), **383**
Kayōkai (Tuesday Society) (火曜會), 400
Kazunomiya, Princess (和宮), 165, 258, 364, **384**
Kedai (華臺), 109
Kegon (Hua-yen) Buddhism (華嚴宗), 59, 100
Kegon hokkai gikyō (華嚴法界義鏡), 100
Kegon kinshin kangyō hōmon (華嚴起信觀行法門), 59
Keian disturbance (慶安の變), 285
Keian Genju (桂庵玄樹), **112-13**
Keiei yawa (形影夜話), 246
Keien shinkōroku (經延進講錄), 417
Keihō dokuhon (刑法讀本), 485
Keihō kōgi (刑法講義), 485
Keijō Imperial University (京城帝國大學), 466
Keijser, H. J., 193
Keikashū (京華集), 129
Keikō, Emperor (景行天皇), 72
Keikoku-shū (經國集), 46
Keiō Gijuku (慶應義塾), 321, 330, 348, 354, 435, 448, 462
Keiō University (慶應義塾大學), 321, 330, 392, 434, 516
Keill, John 244
Keisei hisaku (經世秘策), 189
Keitai, Emperor (繼體天皇), 42, 54
Keizairoku (經濟錄), 175
Keizairoku shūi (經濟錄拾遺), 175
Keizai yōroku (經濟要錄), 241
Keizan Jōkin (瑩山祝瑾), **113**
Keizan shingi (瑩山清規), 113
Kellogg-Briand Peace Pact, 314
Kelvin, Lord, 487
Kempō Taii (憲法大意), 348
Kemmu Restoration (建武中興), 85, 87, 97, 114, 128
Kemmu shikimoku (建武式目), 87
Kenchō-ji (建長寺), 95, 111, 118, 132, 134, 142, 143, 145, 244, 462
Ken'i (顯意), 124
Kenkairon (顯戒論), 57
Kenkenroku (蹇蹇錄), 420
Kenkon bensetsu (乾坤辨說), 221, 225
Kennin-ji (建仁寺), 93, 118, 125, 145
Kenreimon-in Tokuko (建禮門院德子), 19
Kensaku-in (羂索院), 55
Kenseihontō (憲政本黨), 443
Kenseikai (憲政會), 337, 376, 377, 394, 507
Kensei Kinenkan (憲政記念館), 449
Kenseitō (Constitution Party) (憲政黨), 346, 355, 362, 372, 442, 509
Kentōshi (遣唐使), 32
Ketsumeidan (血盟團), 323, 349, 351, 486
Kian Soen (規菴祖圓), 111, 115, 143
Kibi no Makibi (吉備眞備), 25, 33, **42**, 60, 65, 67

Kido Kōichi (木戸幸一), **384-85**, 495
Kido Takayoshi (木戸孝允), 336, 360, 361, 365, 384, **385-87**, 419, 439, 440, 451
Kigensetsu (紀元節), 39
Kiheitai (奇兵隊), 251, 380, 508
Kikkawa Koretari, *see* **Yoshikawa Koretari**
Kikkawa Motoharu (吉川元春), 217
Kikō (基好), 124
Kimbu, Mt. (金峰山), 60
Kimmei, Emperor (欽明天皇), **42-43**, 49, 54, 63, 65
Kim Ok-kyun (金玉均), 331, 335, 355, 499
Kimura Hisashi (木村榮), 387, **388**
Kimura Settsu-no-Kami (木村攝津守), 330
Kimura's Z-term (木村Z項), 388
Kimura Taiken (木村泰賢), 484, 506
Kindai Shisō (近代思想), 317, 445
Kinkaku-ji (金閣寺), 90
Kinkushū (金句集), 178
Kinokuniya Bunzaemon (紀國屋文左衛門), **204-05**
Kinoshita Jun'an (木下順庵), 167, **205-06**
Kinoshita Naoe (木下尙江), **388-89**, 402, 521
Kinoshita Yaemon (木下彌右衛門), 267
Ki no Tsurayuki (紀貫行), 21
Ki no Yoshito (紀淑人), 30
Kinri bunshū (錦里文集), 206
Kinsei Nihon kokumin-shi (近世日本國民史), 498
Kinsei Yōroppa shokuminshi (近世歐羅巴の殖民史), 439
Kinshiroku (近思錄), 240
Kinza (金座), 179
Kira Yoshinaka (吉良義央), 170, 231
Kirishitan shūmon no hakugai to sempuku (切支丹宗門の迫害と潜伏), 315
Kirisutokyō shinto no nagusame (基督教信徒の慰め), 502
kirokujo (記錄所), 34
Kishida Toshiko (Nakajima Shōen) (岸田俊子(中島湘煙)), 328
Kishimoto Nobuta (岸本能武太), 314
Kishi Nobusuke (岸信介), 357, **389-90**, 412, 460, 461
Kiso Yoshinaka (木曾義仲), 120
Kissa yōjō-ki (喫茶養生記), 125
Kitabatake Akiie (北畠顯家), 98, 99, **113-14**, 115
Kitabatake Akinobu (北畠顯信), 114, 115
Kitabatake Chikafusa (北畠親房), 97, 99, 113, **114-15**, 142
Kitabatake Moroshige (北畠師重), 114
Kitabatake Tomonori (北畠具教), 227
Kita Ezo zusetsu (北蝦夷圖說), 211
Kitahama Bank (北濱銀行), 339
Kita Ikki (北一輝), **390**, 438
Kita-in (喜多院), 256
Kitajima San'yata (北島三彌太), 219
Kitamura Kigin (北村季吟), 278
Kitamura Tōkoku (北村透谷), 510
Kita-no-Mitsui (北の三井), 214
Kitayama culture (北山文化), 90
Kitayama Jūhachikendo (北山十八間戸), 126
Kitazato Shibasaburō (北里柴三郎), **391-92**, 432, 466
Kitazato Institute (北里硏究所), 392, 466
Kitenkan (徽典館), 423
Kiuchi Taizō (木內泰藏), 241
Kiyohara no Iehira (淸原家衡), 48
Kiyomizu-dera (淸水寺), 58
Kiyoura Keigo (淸浦奎吾), 337, 355, **392-94**, 482, 505, 507, 510
Kiyozawa Manshi (淸澤滿之), **394-95**
Kiyozawa Yasuko (淸澤やす子), 394
kō (講), 131
Kōan campaign (弘安の役), 105
Kobayakawa Takakage (小早川隆景), 217
Kobayashi Ichizō (小林一三), 348
Kobayashi Minoru (小林稔), 524
Kōbō Daishi (弘法大師), 45, 46
Kobori Enshū (小堀遠州), 281
Kōbe Theological School (神戸神學校), 368
Kōbu-gattai (公武合體), 165, 264, 329, 364, 386, 410, 439, 458, 470, 471
Kōbujō (講武場), 162
Kōbusho (講武所), 162, 233
Kōchi (廣智), 23
Kōchisha (行地社), 438
Kōchi Shimbunsha (高知新聞社), 372
Koch, Robert, 392
Kodama Gentarō (兒玉源太郎), 333, **395-96**, 431, 432
Kōdō (Imperial Way) faction (皇道派), 318, 495
Kōdōkan (講道館), 371
Kōdōkan (弘道館), 264, 374, 441
Kodō taii (古道大意), 187
Koeber, Raphael, 314
Kōeki kokusan kō (廣益國產考), 233
Kōen (皇圓), 93, 107
Kōfuku-ji (興福寺), 22, 86, 111, 112, 256, 278
Kōfuku-ji sōjō (興福寺奏狀), 112
kogaku (古學), 214
kogakuha (古學派), 198, 272, 273
Kogaku shiyō (古學指要), 198
Kōgen, Emperor (光嚴天皇), 124
kogidō (古義堂), 198
kōgō (皇后), 44
Kōgonenjaku (庚午年籍), 70
Koguryŏ, 37, 40, 61
Kōgyoku, Emperor (皇極天皇), 26, 44, 69
Kōhō Kennichi (高峰顯日), 111, 123, 134, 143
koihō (古醫方), 181
Kōin (公胤), 93
Koiso Kuniaki (小磯國昭), **396-97**, 469, 478, 519
Kojiki (古事記), 18, 33, 38, 39, 66, 72, 187, 200, 501
Kojima Korekata (Iken) (兒島惟謙), **397-98**
Kokan Shiren (虎關師鍊), 111, **115-16**
Kōken, Empress (孝謙天皇), 21, 29, 42, **43**,

44, 61, 71
Kokin denju (古今傳授), 132, 278
Kokinshū (古今集), 21, 132, 178, 278
Kokka dōtokuron (國家道德論), 430
Kokken hanron (國憲汎論), 445
Kokkai Kisei Dōmei (國會期成同盟), 360, 372
Kokka no risō (國家の理想), 517
Kokka Shakaitō (National Socialist Party) (國家社會黨), 510
Kōkōdō (浩々洞), 395
Kōkō, Emperor (光孝天皇), 28
kokubun-ji (國分寺), 60
kokubun-niji (國分尼寺), 60
Kokuchūkai (國柱會), 486
kokugaku (國學), 241
Kokugakuin University (國學院大學), 475
Kokuhonsha (國本社), 342, 512
kokuji-goyōgakari (國事御用掛), 318
Koku-ki (國記), 62
Kokukyō-shū (谷響集), 123
Kokumin Dōmei (國民同盟), 422
Kokumin Eigakkai (國民英學會), 402
Kokumin Kyōdō (National Alliance) (國民協同), 321
Kokumin Kyōdōtō (Peoples' Cooperative Party) (國民協同黨), 374
Kokumin Kyōkai (國民協會), 453
Kokumin no Tomo (國民之友), 497, 510
Kokumin Shimbun (國民新聞), 497
Kokumintō (國民黨), 355, 422
Kokumin Zasshi (國民雜誌), 510
Kokuryūkai (黒龍會), 499
Kokusaihō oyobi kokusai seiji yori mitaru kokkai narabi ni Kumpu Kaikyō no chii (國際法および國際政治より見たる黒海ならびに君府海峡の地位), 321
Kokusenya kassen (國姓爺合戰), 172, 173
Kokushi goroku (國師語錄), 123
Kokushi taikei (國史大系), 481
Kokutai-ji (國泰寺), 496
Kokutai oyobi junsei shakai shugi (國體及び純正社會主義), 390
Kokutai shinron (國體新論), 375
Kokuze sanron (國是三論), 518
Kōkyō Daishi (興教大師), 40
Komaki, battle of (小牧の戰い), 190, 228
Komazawa University (駒澤大學), 506
Kōmei, Emperor (孝明天皇), 165, 258, 364, 384, 412, 471
Kompon bukkyō (根本佛教), 315
Komponchū-dō (根本中堂), 205
Kompon sōsei (根本僧制), 199
Komura Jutarō (小村壽太郎), 314, **398-99**, 475
Komura-Weber Agreement (Russo-Japanese Agreement) (小村・ウエーバー協定), 398
Kōmyō, Emperor (光明天皇), 97-99, 114, 124
Kōmyō, Empress (光明皇后), 25, 29, **43-44**, 60, 67
Kōmyō, Mt. (光明山), 22
Konchi-in (金地院), 205, 244
Kondō Jūzō (Morishige) (近藤重藏), 217
Kondō Makoto (近藤眞琴), 477
Kondō Morishige (近藤守重), **206**
Kongōbu-ji (金剛峯寺), 46
Konjin (金神), 383
Konkō-kyō (金光教), 383
Konkō daijin-kaku (金光大神覺), 383
Kōnin, Emperor (光仁天皇), 40, 70, 72
Konishi Ryūsa (小西隆佐), 206
Konish Shigenao (小西重直), 485
Konishi Yukinaga (小西行長), 164, 169, 196, 202, **206-07**, 252
Konoe Atsumaro (近衞篤麿), 399, 422
Konoe Fumimaro (近衞文麿), 27, 318, 319, 341, 342, 344, 349, 385, **399-401**, 412, 444, 455, 495, 505, 519, 520
Konoe Motozane (近衞基實), 116
Kōnō Ichirō (河野一郎), 357
Kōno Michihiro (河野通廣), 109
Konshō-ji (金鐘寺), 59
Koran (コーラン), 439
Korean independence movement (朝鮮獨立運動), 436
Korean Independence Party (朝鮮獨立黨), 331, 335, 355
Kōrin-ji (光林寺), 171
Koromogawa, battle of (衣川の戰), 92
Korori chijun (虎狼痢治準), 229
Koryŏ, 105
Kōryū-ji (廣隆寺), 62
kōsan-kata (興產方), 232
Kōsei shimpen (厚生新編), 269
Kose no Notari (巨勢野足), 25, 56
Kōsen Sōun (Imakita Kōsen) (洪川宗溫(今北洪川)), 462
Kose Rokuzaemon (巨勢六左衞門), 263
Koshichō (古史徵), 187
Koshiden (古史傳), 187
Koshitsū (古史通), 168
Kōshitsu tempan (皇室典範), *see* Imperial House Law
Kōshō Bosatsu (興正菩薩), 94
Kōshō Hōrin-ji (興聖寶林寺), 93
Kōshō-ji (光勝寺), 127
Kōshū school of military science (甲州流の兵學), 272
Kosugi Genteki (小杉玄適), 275
Kōtoku Denjirō (幸德傳次郎), *see* Kōtoku Shūsui
Kōtoku, Emperor (孝德天皇), 26, **44-45**, 69
Kōtoku-ji (高德寺), 443
Kōtoku Shūsui (幸德秋水), 313, 372, 389, 390, **401-03**, 422, 445, 457, 490, 502
Koun Ejō (孤雲懷讓), 113
Kōya, Mt. (高野山), 36, 40, 46, 50, 92, 109, 231
Kōya rui (空也誄), 47
Kōyōsha (向陽社), 499
Kōzan-ji (高山寺), 106
Kozeki San'ei (小關三英), **207-08**, 249

Kōzen gokoku-ron (興禪護國論), 124
Kōzuki Gyūzan (香月牛山), 200
Kozaki Hiromichi (小崎弘道), 324
Kropotkin, 445
KS steel (KS 鋼), 345
Kubilai Khan (忽必烈汗), 105, 110
Kudenshō (口傳抄), 112
Kūdō Heisuke (工藤平助), 185, **208**, 210
Kudō Jōan (工藤丈庵), 208
K'uei-chi (基), 22
Kuga Minoru (Katsunan) (陸實 (羯南)), 475
Kuga no Michichika (久我通親), 93
Kūge Dōjin (空華道人), 96
Kūge nikkushū (空華日工集), 97
Kuge-shohatto (公家諸法度), 178, 244
Kūgeshū (空華集), 97
Kugyō (公曉), 102
Kuhara Fusanosuke (久原房之助), 391
Kujikata osadamegaki (公事方御定書), 263
Kujō Hisatada (九條尙忠), 364
Kujō Kanezane (九條兼實), 107, **116-17**
Kujō Michiie (九條道家), 96
Kujō Michitaka (九條道孝), 446
Kūkai (空海), 40, **45-46**, 56, 57, 59, 68
Kulmus, Johann Adam, 210, 222
Kumamoto Band (熊本バンド), 324
Kumamoto Medical School (熊本醫學校), 391
Kumano (熊野), 36, 109
Kumashiro Naoto (神代直人), 233
Kumaso people (熊襲), 39, 73
Kumazawa Banzan (熊澤蕃山), **208-09**, 222
Kumazawa Morihisa (熊澤守久), 208
kumonjo (公文所), 120
kuni-hakase (國博士), 48
Kunikida Doppo (國木田獨步), 516
Kuninomiya Asahiko, Prince (久邇宮朝彥親王), 340
Kunitokotachi-no-kami (國常立神), 271
Kunitokotachi-no-mikoto (國常立尊), 283
Kunō, Mt. (久能山), 256
Kunitomo cloth (國倫織), 186
Kuon-ji (久遠寺), 223, 356
Kurenai Manjikai (紅卍字會), 323
Kurile Islands, *see* Chishima Islands
Kurimoto Joun (栗本鋤雲), 354
Kuroda Kikuro (黑田麴廬), 474
Kuroda Kiyotaka (黑田淸隆), 325, 352, **403-04**, 442, 458, 501
Kuroda Nagatomo (黑田長知), 370
Kurodani shōnin gotō-roku (黑谷上人語燈錄), 108
Kurōdodokoro (藏人所), 25, 56, 64
Kurozumi-kyō (黑住教), 404, 405
Kurozumi Munenobu (黑住宗信), 405
Kurozumi Munetada (黑住宗忠), **404-05**
Kurusu Saburō (來栖三郞), 434
Kusakabe, Prince (草壁親王), 33
Kusaka Genzui (久坂元瑞), 282
Kusanagi-no-tsurugi (草薙劍), 73
Kusunoki (楠木), 87
Kusunoki Fuden (楠不傳), 285
Kusunoki Masashige (楠木正成), 85, 97, 114, **117-18**, 284
Kusunoki Masatsura (楠木正行), 115
Kūya (空也), **46-47**
Kyodo Kakuen, *see* Chung-t'and Chüan
Kyōdo Kenkyū (鄕土硏究), 516
Kyōdō Un'yu Kaisha (共同運輸會社), 367
Kyōgoku Takatsugu (京極高次), 279
Kyōgyo shinshō (教行信證), 133
Kyōi no ben (狂醫之辨), 246
Kyōkai jigen (教界時言), 394
Kyōkaku-ji (教覺寺), 418
Kyōkan gijuku (共慣義塾), 338
Kyōō-gokoku-ji (教王護國寺), 46
Kyōritsu Gakkō (共立學校), 482
Kyōritsu Gakusha (共立學舍), 481
Kyōshin (教信), **47**
Kyoto Imperial University (京都帝國大學), 340, 382, 384, 399, 427, 430, 485, 498, 512, 515, 523
Kyoto University affair (京大事件), 486
Kyoto University Institute of Basic Physics (京都大學基礎物理學硏究所), 524
Kyoto Workers' School (京都勞働學校), 515
Kyōzon Dōshū (共存同衆), 322, 444
Kyūanroku (求安錄), 502
Kyūkō-ji (吸江寺), 276
Kyūkyodō (鳩居堂), 233
Kyūō dōwa (鳩翁道話), 243
Kyushu Imperial University (九州帝國大學), 512

L

Laband, P., 347
Labor Farmer Party, *see* Rōdō Nōmintō
Lalande, Joseph Jerôme Le Français de, 249
Lan-hsi Tao-lung (Rankei Dōryū) (蘭溪道隆), **118**
Lankāvatāra Sūtra (楞伽經), 116, 477
Lanman, Charles, 501
Laxman, Adam, 174, 217
League of Common Alliance (民衆同盟), 390
League of Nations, 314, 344, 357, 411, 430, 456, 516
League of University Professors (大學教授連盟), 340
Leftist Socialist Party, *see* Saha Shakaitō
Leyden University, 499
Liang dynasty, 51
Liberal Democratic Party, *see* Jiyū Minshutō
Liberal Party, *see* Jiyūtō
Liberal Party of Japan, *see* Nihon Jiyūtō
Li Hung-chang (李鴻章), 338, 362
Lin-chi Zen, *see* Rinzai Zen
Lincoln, Abraham, 336
Ling, Emperor, 18
Ling-yin-ssu, 145
Li Po, 374
London Disarmament Conference, 337, 342, 363, 415, 437, 465, 494, 507, 514

Lotus Sutra (法華經), 57, 62, 74, 125, 126, 328, 425
Louvain, University of, 314, 427
Lung-chiang Ying-hsüan (Ryūkō Ōsen) (龍江應宣), 118
Lung-hsiang-ssu, 142
Lun yü, see *Analects*, Confucian

M

Macao, 169, 182
MacArthur, General Douglas, 401, 435, 466, 468, 497, 520
Machino Yukiyori (町野ユキヨリ), 272
Madenokōji Nobufusa (萬里小路宣房), 114
Madre de Deus, 169, 183
Maeda Eun (前田慧雲), **405-06**
Maeda Toshiie (前田利家), 252
Maeda Tsunanori (前田綱紀), 205, 206
Maejima Hisoka (前島密), **406-07**
Maeno Ryōtaku (前野良澤), **209-10**, 222, 236, 246, 284
Maeno Tōgen (前野東元), 209
Mahayana Buddhism (大乘佛教), 57, 62, 418
Mainichi Shimbun (毎日新聞), 389
Makiguchi Tsunesaburō (牧口常三郎), **407-08**
Makino Nobuaki (牧野伸顯), **408-09**, 454, 520
Makino Tomitarō (牧野富太郎), **409**
Malacca, 272
Malik, Y.A., 344
Mamiya Rinzō (間宮林藏), **210-11**
Mampuku-ji (萬福寺), 265, 279
Manabe Akifusa (間部詮房), 167
Manabe Akikatsu (間部詮勝), 282
Manchurian Incident, 321, 357, 447, 465, 507
Manchurian Railway, 459
Mandara-ji (曼荼羅寺), 50
Mandokoro (政所), 120
Manjirō, John 422
Manju-ji (萬壽寺), 134
Mansai Jugō (滿濟准后), 90, **118-19**
Mansvert, C.G. van, 319
Mappō (末法), 30, 108
Marco Polo Bridge incident (蘆溝橋事件), 400
Maria Lux, 473, 491
Maruhashi Chūya (丸橋忠彌), 285
Marukusu-shugi (マルクス主義), 468
Marxism, 381, 382, 385, 437, 456, 468, 501, 510, 511
Masaki Jinzaburō (眞崎甚三郎), 318
Mason, L. W., 368
Massachusetts Institute of Technology, 322
Masuda Jimbei Yoshitsugu (益田甚兵衞好次), 164
Masuda Takashi (益田孝), 323
Masuya Heiemon (升屋平右衞門), 274
Masuya Kyūbei (升屋久兵衞), 274
Matsuda Denjūrō (松田傳十郎), 211
Matsudaira Hirotada (松平廣忠), 260
Matsudaira Jussai, *see* Hayashi Jussai
Matsudaira Masatsuna (松平正綱), 211
Matsudaira Nobuaki (松平信明), 259
Matsudaira Nobutsuna (松平信綱), 196, **211**
Matsudaira Sadakuni (松平定邦), 212
Matsudaira Sadanobu (松平定信), 189, **211-12**, 259
Matsudaira Shungaku, *see* Matsudaira Yoshinaga
Matsudaira Tadanori (松平忠德), 175
Matsudaira Yoshinaga (松平慶永), 258, 471, 472, 518
Matsuda Masahisa (松田正久), 453
Matsukata Masayoshi (松方正義), 326, 355, 362, 397, **409-10**, 419, 442, 452, 474, 482
Matsumae Ezochi (松前蝦夷地), 206
Matsumae shiryaku (松前史略), 217
Matsumura Kaiseki (松村介石), 437
Matsunaga Hisahide (松永久秀), 86, 92, 228
Matsunaga Hisamichi (松永久通), 228
Matsunaga Shakugo (松永尺五), 205
Matsuo Bashō (松尾芭蕉), 221
Matsuoka Eikyū (松岡映丘), 515
Matsuoka Joan (松岡如庵), 234
Matsuoka Shizuo (松岡靜雄), 515
Matsuoka Tokikata (松岡辰方), 182
Matsuoka Yoshikazu (松岡能一), 248
Matsuoka Yōsuke (松岡洋右), 319, 401, **411-12**
Matsushima Zenjō (松島善讓), 405
Matsushita Kahei (松下嘉兵衞), 267
Matsuura Shigenobu (松浦鎭信), **213**
Matsuura Takanobu (松浦隆信), 213
Matsuzaki Jikei (松崎自圭), 198
Matsuzaki Kōdō (松崎慊堂), 270
Matsuzaki Kyūtarō (松崎久太郎), 461
Mattō-shō (末燈鈔), 134
May 15th incident (五・一五事件), 355, 438
May Fourth Movement (五・四運動), 391
Meckel, Klemens Wilhelm Jakob, 380, 395, 494
Meidōkan (明道館), 184
Meihō Sotetsu (明峰素哲), 113
Meiji Bunka Kenkyūkai (明治文化研究會), 522
Meiji bunka zenshū (明治文化全集), 522
Meiji Civil Code (明治民法), 347
Meiji Constitution (*Nihonteikoku Kempō*) (明治憲法(日本帝國憲法)), 327, 346, 353, 362, 363, 365, 370, 404, 414, 417, 422, 448, 452
Meiji, Emperor (明治天皇), 265, 340, 363, 364, 366, 379, 396, 402, **412-14**, 417, 429, 432, 440, 448, 453, 454, 474, 489
Meiji Gakuin (明治學院), 368
Meiji Gijuku (明治義塾), 322
Meiji government (明治政府), 329, 330, 332, 334, 336, 351, 354, 359, 361, 379, 387, 403, 407, 410, 417, 420, 424, 426-28, 460, 463, 471, 491, 500
Meiji Hōritsu Gakkō (明治法律學校), 453
Meiji Jingū (明治神宮), 414
Meiji Professional School (明治專門學校), 512

Meiji Restoration (明治維新), 27, 45, 220, 233, 239, 265, 273, 282, 286, 321, 326, 345, 364, 370, 371, 379, 386, 395, 397, 406, 416, 418, 423, 425, 426, 429, 431, 436, 439, 441, 444, 452, 456, 458, 469, 473, 499, 504, 510, 517, 519
Meirinkan (明倫館), 251, 347, 431, 508
Meirinsha (明倫社), 243
Meirokusha (明六社), 331, 375, 417, 423, 427, 429, 500, 503
Meiroku Zasshi (明六雜誌), 331, 375, 424, 427, 429, 500
Meishō, Empress (明正女帝), 178
Mencius, 198
Mendenhall, Thomas Corwin, 487
Mexico, 183, 314, 419
Michi (道), 437
Michiyasu, Prince (道康親王), 31, 50
Middle Temple, 346, 347
Midō Kampaku ki (御堂關白記), 28
Miidera (三井寺), see Onjō-ji
Miike Mines (三池鑛山), 322
Mikagura-uta (みかぐらうた), 424
Mikasa (三笠), 377, 494
Miki Takeo (三木武夫), 374
Military Academy (陸軍士官學校), 317, 340, 357, 487, 494
Military Staff College (陸軍大學校), 317, 340, 357, 380, 395, 396, 487, 493, 494, 499, 504
Mill, John Stuart, 423, 427
Mimana (Imna) (任那), 43, 54, 62
Mimpō no hone (民法の骨), 445
Mimpō sōan (民法草案), 327
Mimura-ji (三村寺), 127
Min (Bin) (旻), 26, **48**
Min, Queen (閔妃), 398
Minabuchi no Shōan (南淵請安), 69
Minakawa Kien (皆川淇園), 240
Minamoto family (Genji) (源氏), 19, 35, 48, 49, 59, 87, 92, 93, 102, 104, 117, 119, 120, 128, 138
Minamoto no Arifusa (源有房), 116
Minamoto no Michichika (源通親), 117
Minamoto no Munetō (源宗任), 48
Minamoto no Sadatō (源貞任), 48
Minamoto no Sanetomo (源實朝), 102, 105, 106, 119
Minamoto no Tamekane (源爲憲), 47
Minamoto no Tameyoshi (源爲義), 49
Minamoto no Tsunekuni (源經國), 22
Minamoto no Yoriie (源賴家), 102, **119**, 125, 141
Minamoto no Yoritomo (源賴朝), 27, 36, 45, 92, 102, 104, 106, 117, **119-21**, 128, 138, 141
Minamoto no Yoriyoshi (源賴義), 18, 48
Minamoto no Yoshiie (源義家), 18, **48**
Minamoto no Yoshinaka (源義仲), 36, 120, 121
Minamoto no Yoshitoki (源義時), 102
Minamoto no Yoshitomo (源義朝), 35, **49**, 71, 102, 104, 119, 121, 137-39
Minamoto no Yoshitsune (源義經), 92, 120, **121-22**, 139, 141, 284
Minatogawa, battle of (湊川の戰), 85
Mine Shuntai (嶺春泰), 210
Ming dynasty, 90, 91, 112, 130, 137, 145, 172, 180, 187, 195, 201, 209, 221, 235, 265, 278
Minkan denshō (民間傳承), 516
Minkan seiyō (民間省要), 254
Minken jiyūron (民權自由論), 503
Minobe Ryōkichi (美濃部亮吉), 415
Minobe Tatsukichi (美濃部達吉), 348, **415**, 437
Minobu, Mt. (身延山), 126, 223
Minseitō (民政黨), 351, 357, 374, 437, 465, 469
Minshū (民衆), 511
Minshu Shakaitō (Democratic Socialist Party) (民主社會黨), 374
Minshutō (Democratic Party) (民主黨), 321, 357, 374, 465, 469
Minu, Prince (美努王), 43, 67
Min'yūsha (民友社), 497, 510
Minzoku (民族), 516
Miroku (Maitreya) (彌勒), 112
Mishihase (Su-shen) (肅愼), 17
Mishima Michitsune (三島通庸), 489
Mishima Tokushichi (三島德七), 345
Mishima Yatarō (三島彌太郎), 350
Mishima Yukio (三島由紀夫), 319
Missouri, USS, 469
Mitani Sokei (三谷素啓), 407
Mita Social Science Studies Society (三田社會科學研究會), 434
Mitsubishi companies (三菱會社), 367, 376, 442, 449
Mitsubishi *zaibatsu* (三菱財閥), 323, 349, 366, 442
Mitsui Bank (三井銀行), 348
Mitsui family (三井家), 213, 322
Mitsui Mining Company (三井鑛山株式會社), 322
Mitsui Partnership Company (三井合名會社), 322, 349
Mitsui Takatoshi (三井高利), **213-14**
Mitsukawa Kametarō (滿川龜太郎), 438
Mitsukuri Gempo (箕作阮甫), 499
Mitsukuri Rinshō (箕作麟祥), 421
Mitsuoka Hachirō (Yuri Kimimasa) (三岡八郎(由利公正)), 329
Miura Anjin (三浦按針), *see* Adams, William
Miura Baien (三浦梅園), **214**
Miura Giichi (三浦義一), 214
Miura Yoshiaki (三浦義明), 141
Miura Yoshimura (三浦義村), 141
Miyake Kanran (三宅觀瀾), 277
Miyake Setsurei (三宅雪嶺), **415-16**, 467, 470, 475
Miyake Shōsai (三宅尙齋), 277
Miyake Yūjirō (三宅雄二郎), 350
Miyako (宮子), 60
Miyamoto Kenji (宮本顯治), 434,435

Miyase Ryūmon (宮瀨龍門), 245
Miyata Zentaku (宮田全澤), 209
Miyazaki Giuemon (宮崎儀右衞門), 215
Miyazaki Yasusada (宮崎安貞), **215**
Miyazawa Kenji (宮澤賢治), 486
Miyoshi Nagaharu (三好長慶), 91, 92
Mizuno Tadakuni (水野忠邦), **215-16**, 232, 241
Mizuno Tadamasa (水野忠政), 260
Mizuno Tadamitsu (水野忠光), 215
Mizusawa Observatory (水澤觀測所), 388
Mōanjō (盲安杖), 247
Mochihito, Prince (以仁王), 102, 120
Mogami Tokunai (最上德内), 189, **216-17**
Mokujiki Shōnin, *see* **Ōgo**
Momijiyama Bunko (紅葉山文庫), 166, 206
Mommu, Emperor (文武天皇), 24, 33, 53, 60
Monchūjo (問注所), 120
Mongol attack (蒙古襲來), 95, 105, 126, 127, 132, 143
Mongolia, 396, 411, 488
Mononobe no Moriya (物部守屋), 49, 64
Mononobe no Okoshi (物部尾輿), **49**, 54, 63, 64
Montoku, Emperor (文德天皇), 31, 50, 58
Mori Arinori (森有禮), 326, 327, 375, **416-17**, 423, 427, 429, 482, 500
Mōri family (毛利氏), 122, 201, 206, 267, 431, 456
Mōri Hidenari (毛利秀就), 218
Mōri Hiromoto (毛利弘元), 122
Mori Kaku (森恪), 400
Mōri Motonari (毛利元就), **122**, 217, 230
Morinaga, Prince (護良親王), 85
Morioka Agricultural and Forestry College (盛岡高等農林學校), 480
Mōri Okimoto (毛利興元), 122
Mōri Takachika (毛利敬親), 386
Mōri Takamoto (毛利隆元), 122, 217
Mōri Terumoto (毛利輝元), **217-19**, 227
Mōri Yukimatsumaru (毛利幸松丸), 122
Motoda Eifu (Nagazane) (元田永孚), 353, 413, **417**
Motoi, Prince (基皇子), 44
Motoki Einoshin (本木榮之進), **219**
Motoki Shōdayū (本木庄太夫), 219
Motoki Shōzaemon (本木庄左衞門), 219
Motoki Shōzō (本木昌造), **219-20**
Motoki Yoshinaga (本木良永), 244
Motoori Norinaga (本居宣長), 187
Movement to Protect the Constitution (憲政擁護運動), 355, 376, 381, 449
Muchū mondō (夢中問答), 123
Mugan Soō (夢岩祖應), 116
Mugonshō (無言抄), 231
Muhon Kakushin (無本覺心), 113
Mujū Dōgyō (無住道曉), 96
Mukai Genshō (向井元升), **220-21**, 225
Mukai Kaneyoshi (向井兼義), 220
Mukai Kyorai (向井去來), 221
Mukai Rochō (向井魯町), 221
Mukan Fumon (無關普門), 96
mukyōkai (無教會), 503
Mukyoku Shigen (無極志玄), 123
Mukyū Tokusen (無及德詮), 118
Müller, Max, 425, 483
Mumyō Eshō, *see* Wu-ming Hui-hsing
Munenaga, Prince (宗良親王), 114
Mung, John 422
Murai Sadakatsu (村井貞勝), 163
Murakami, Emperor (村上天皇), 21
Murakami Hidetoshi (村上英俊), 421
Murakami Senjō (村上專精), **418**
Murakami Yoshiharu (村上義晴), 140
Murasaki Shikibu (紫式部), 29, 38
Murata Zōroku (Ōmura Masujirō) (村田藏六 (大村益次郎)), 229
Muro Kyūsō (室鳩巣), 206
Muromachi shogunate (室町幕府), 86-89, 98, 108, 140, *see also* Ashikaga shogunate
Muryōju-ji (無量壽寺), 256
Musansha seibutsugaku (無產者生物學), 515
Musansha Shimbun (無產者新聞), 459
Musan Taishūtō (Proletarian Popular Party) (無產大衆黨), 479
Musō Soseki (夢窓疎石), 88, 96, 111, **123-24**, 134, 136, 143, 145
Mutō Sanji (武藤山治), 248
Mutsu Munemitsu (陸奧宗光), 338, 345, **418-20**, 421
Myōan Eisai (明庵榮西), 93, **124-25**
Myōe (明惠), 106
Myōkaku-ji (妙覺寺), 223
myōkōnin (妙好人), 477
Myōman (明滿), 231
Myōsei-ji (妙誓寺), 469
Myōshin-ji (妙心寺), 135, 171, 179, 276
Myōtei mondō (妙貞問答), 178
Myōzen (明全), 93, 125

N

Nabeshima family (鍋島家), 196
Nabeshima Kansō (鍋島閑叟), 197
Nabeyama Sadachika (鍋山貞親), 459
Nagai Naomune (永井尚志), 162
Nagai Seigai (永井青崖), 378
Nagai Taiun (長井太雲), 208
Nagakute, battle of (長久手の戰), 228
Nagaoka Fujitaka (長岡藤孝), 190
Nagao Kagetora (長尾景虎), 140
Nagaoka Hantarō (長岡半太郎), 345, **420**
Nagaoka-kyō (長岡京), 41, 72
Nagao Tamekage (長尾爲景), 140
Nāgārjuna, 38
Nagasaki Kaigun Denshūjo (長崎海軍傳習所), 220
Nagasaki Takatsuna (長崎高綱), 104
Nagasaki yawagusa (長崎夜話草), 225
Nagasune-hiko (長髓彥), 39
Nagata Tetsuzan (永田鐵山), 495

Nagaya, Prince (長屋王), 44, 60, 71
Nagayo Sensai (長與專齋), 229
Naika senyō (内科選要) 203
Nakae Chōmin (中江兆民), 402, **421-22**, 453
Nakae Tōju (中江藤樹), 209, **221-22**
Nakagawa Jun'an (中川淳庵), 208, 210, **222-23**, 245, 246
Nakahama Manjirō (中濱萬次郎), 237, **422-23**
Nakai Chikuzan (中井竹山), 240, 274
Nakai Riken (中井履軒), 274
Nakajima Shōen (中島湘煙), 328
Nakamigawa Hikojirō (中上川彦次郎), 348
Nakamura Masanao (中村正直), 331, **423-24**
Nakano Kiken (中野撝軒), 175
Naka no Ōe, Prince (中大兄皇子), 24, 26, 27, 44, 48, 63, 69
Nakano Seigō (中野正剛), 416
Nakaoka Shintarō (中岡愼太郎), 238
Naka Ten'yū (中天遊), 229
Nakatomi no harai mizuho-shō (中臣祓瑞穂鈔), 271
Nakatomi no Kamatari (中臣鎌足), 44 63, 69, 70
Nakayama Miki (中山みき), **424**
Nakayama Tadayasu (中山忠能), 413
Nakayama Yoshiko (中山慶子), 412
Nakayama Zembei (中山善兵衞), 424
Nambara Shigeru (南原繁), 517
Nambu Nanzan (南部南山), 206
Nambu Sōju (南部艸壽), 225
Nampo Jōmyō (南浦紹明), 134
Namu Amida Butsu (南無阿彌陀佛), 22, 107, 110
Namu-Amidabutsu sazenshū (南無阿彌陀佛作善集), 93
Namu Myōhō Rengekyō (南無妙法蓮華經), 125
Nanden daizōkyō (南傳大藏經), 484
Naniwa (浪速), 494
Nanjō Bun'yū (南條文雄), **425**
nanushi (名主), 254
Nan'yō jiji (南洋時事), 467
Nanzen-ji (南禪寺), 96, 111, 112, 115, 116, 123, 129, 137, 244
Naraya Mozaemon (奈良屋茂左衞門), 205
Narrative of a Japanese, The, 336
Narushima Dōchiku (成島道筑), 254
Narutakijuku (鳴瀧塾), 249
National Alliance, *see* Kokumin Kyōdō
National Federation of Women's Educators, 523
National Labor Farmer Populace Party, *see* Zenkoku Rōnō Taishūtō
National League for the Protection of the Constitution (憲法擁護國民連合), 374
National Popular Party, *see* Zenkoku Taishūtō
National Socialist Party, *see* Kokka Shakaitō
Natsume Sōseki (夏目漱石), 462
Naval Academy (海軍兵學校), 377, 433, 436, 455, 478, 514, 519
Naval Affairs, Bureau of (海軍省軍務局), 433
Naval General Staff (海軍參謀本部員), 433, 455
Naval Staff College (海軍兵學校), 377, 433, 436, 478, 494, 514, 519
Naval Treaty, 415
Navy, Japanese Imperial (海軍操練所), 379
Nebennierenmarkhormon, 484
Negorodera, *see* Daidempō-in
nembutsu (念佛), 22, 47, 74, 107, 111, 133, 136, 477
Nembutsu zōshi (念佛草紙), 247
Nenashigusa (根無草), 186
Neo-Confucianism, 112, 115, 136, 167, 175, 198, 200, 206, 209, 212, 221, 222, 235, 238, 240, 243, 262, 265, 272, 273, 276, 366, 441, 450
Neo-Kantian philosophers (新カント派), 407
New Women's Society (新婦人協會), 343
Nichiei (日英), 127
Nichigetsukei wage (日月圭和解), 219
Nichiju (日樹), 223
Nichinichi kanai kokoroe no koto (日日家内心得の事), 405
Nichiō (日奥), **223**
Nichiren (日蓮), **125-26**, 127
Nichiren Buddhism (日蓮宗), 125, 127, 223, 315, 356, 358, 407, 461, 486
Nichiren Daigaku (日蓮宗大學), 327
Nichirenshū Daigakurin (日蓮宗大學林), 486
Nichi-Ro Sensō Jikki (日露戰爭實紀), 510
Niemann, Johannes Erdewin, 229
Nihon (日本), 475
Nihon chōreki (日本長暦), 243
Nihon Chūgakkō (日本中學校), 475
Nihon dōtokuron (日本道德論), 430
Nihon fūkei-ron (日本風景論), 467
Nihon Hyōron (日本評論), 504
Nihonjin (日本人), 350, 416, 419, 438, 467, 475
Nihon Jiyūtō (Liberal Party of Japan) (日本自由黨), 340
Nihon kaika shōshi (日本開化小史), 481
Nihon Keizai Kenkyūkai (Japan Economic Study Society) (日本經濟研究會), 479
Nihon Keizai Zasshi (日本經濟雜誌), 382
Nihon kodai shiron (日本古代史論), 459
Nihon Kōdōkai (日本講道會(日本弘道會)), 429
Nihon kogakuha no tetsugaku (日本古學派の哲學), 354
Nihon Kōgyō Kurabu (Industry Club of Japan) (日本工業倶樂部), 323
Nihon Kurabu (日本倶樂部), 475
Nihon Minshutō (Democratic Party of Japan) (日本民主黨), 340
Nihon Musantō (Japan Proletarian Party) (日本無產黨), 479
Nihon no Koe (日本のこえ), 468
Nihon no rōdō undō (日本の勞働運動), 373
Nihon ōjō gokuraku-ki (日本往生極樂記), 47, 74
Nihon oyobi Nihonjin (日本及日本人), 399, 416
Nihon Rōdō Sōdōmei (Japan General Labor Federation (日本勞働總同盟), 476
Nihon Seiji Keizai Kenkyūjo (日本政治經濟研

究所), 459
Nihon shihon shugi hattatsu shi (日本資本主義發達史), 434
Nihon Shoki (日本書紀), 18, 37-39, 51, 71, 72, 501
Nihon shokubutsu shi zuhen (日本植物志圖篇), 409
Nihon Shushi gakuha no tetsugaku (日本朱子學派之哲學), 354
Nihon Taishūtō (Japan Popular Party) (日本大衆黨), 479
Nihonteikoku kempō, see Meiji Constitution
Nihon University (日本大學), 342, 496
Nihon Yōmei gakuha no tetsugaku (日本陽明學派之哲學), 354
Nihon Yūsen Kaisha (NYK) (日本郵船會社), 367
Nihonzan Myōhō-ji (日本山妙法寺), 327
Niigata Shimbun (新潟新聞), 448
Niijima Jō (新島襄), 313, 324, **425-26**, 497
Niitabe, Prince (新田部親王), 32, 71
Nijō, Emperor (二條天皇), 35
Nijusseiki no kaibutsu teikoku shugi (二十世紀の怪物帝國主義), 403
Nikkei (日啓), 161
Nikkō (日興), 407
Nikkō-san (日光山), 256
Nikolai Alexandrovitch, Russian Crown Prince, 316, 326, 397, 414, 453
Nimmyō, Emperor (仁明天皇), 31, **50**
Nine Years' War, Earlier (前九年役), 18, 48
Ninigi-no-mikoto (瓊瓊杵命), 38
Ninkai (仁海), 42, **50-51**
Ninkō, Emperor (仁孝天皇), 384
Ninkō Teiki (忍綱貞紀), 199
Ninna-ji (仁和寺), 40, 41, 116
Ninomiya Sontoku (二宮尊德), **224-25**
Ninshō (忍性), 95, **126-27**
Nintoku, Emperor (仁德天皇), **51**, 52
Nippon (日本), 217
Nishi Amane (西周), 331, **426-27**, 499
Nishida Kitarō (西田幾太郎), 399, **427-28**, 476, 477
Nishi Gempo (西玄甫), **225**
Nishi Gentetsu (西玄哲), 245
Nishi Hongan-ji (西本願寺), 446, 483
Nishikawa Joken (西川如見), **225-26**
Nishikawa Joken isho (西川如見遺書), 226
nishi-mawari (西廻り), 204
Nishimura Katsuzō (西村勝三), **428-29**
Nishimura Shigeki (西村茂樹), 375, 417, 423, 427, 428, **429-30**, 500
Nishina Yoshio (仁科芳雄), 498
Nishio Suehiro (西尾末廣), 321, 374
Nishi Zenzaburō (西善三郎), 219
Nissatsu (日薩), 127
Nissen (日暹), 127
Nisshi kōshō-ron (日支交涉論), 522
Nisshin (日親), **127-28**
Nisshin (日進), 486
Nissō nikki (入宋日記), 20
Nitchō Kyōkai (日朝協會), 462
Nitchū Yūkō Kyōkai (日中友好協會), 462
Nitobe Inazō (新渡戸稲造), 411, **430**, 516
Nitta Yoshisada (新田義貞), 87, 98, 104, 114, **128**
Nitten (日典), 223
Nittō guhō junrei kōki (入唐求法巡禮行記), 23
NKS (New KS steel), 345
Nobel Peace Prize, 461
Nobel Prize in physics, 498, 524
Nochi-no-kari kotoba-no-ki (後狩詞記), 516
Nō drama (能), 89, 90
Nogi Maresuke (乃木希典), **431-32**, 494
Nogi Maretsugu (乃木希次), 431
Nogi Shizuko (乃木靜子), 432
Nogi Shrine (乃木神社), 432
Nōgu benri ron (農具便利論), 233
Noguchi Hideyo (野口英世), **432-33**
Nōgyō honron (農業本論), 430
Nōgyō zensho (農業全書), 215
Nōhei no gi (農兵の議), 176
Nōkaeki (農家益), 233
Nōkakun (農家訓), 204
Nomi no Sukune (野見宿禰), **51-52**
Nōmin Rōdōtō (Farmer Labor Party) (農民勞働黨), 320, 479
Nomura Bōtō (野村望東), 443
Nomura Kichisaburō (野村吉三郎), **433-34**
Nonaka Kenzan (野中兼山), 276
Norinaga, Prince (義良親王), 115
Noro Eitarō (野呂榮太郎), **434-45**
Noro Genjō (野呂元丈), 166, 208
Noronha, Dom Alfonso de, 130
Northern and Southern Courts (南北朝), 87, 89, 98-101, 114, 117, 123
North Manchuria Railway (北滿州鐵道), 344
Norway, 316
Nosaka Sanzō (野坂參三), 434, **435**, 511
Nōsei honron (農政本論), 241
Numazu Naval Academy (沼津兵學校), 427
Nuyts, Pieter, 180
Nyohō-ji (如法寺), 171
Nyoirin Kannon (如意輪觀音), 60
Nyorin Ryōsa (如霖良佐), 145
Nyoshin (如信), 112
Nyoshin Chūjo (如心中恕), 145
Nyūgan-ben (乳癌辨), 181

O

Ōama, Prince (大海人皇子), 50, 70
Ōbaku goroku (黃檗語錄), 279
Ōbaku (Huang-po) Zen (黃檗派), 278, 279, 425
Obata Kagenori (小幡景憲), 272
Occupation, American, 321, 340-42, 357, 369 415, 466, 496, 520, 523
Ochanomizu Women's College (お茶の水女子大學), 501
Odani-no-kata (小谷の方), 266, 279
Oda Nobuhide (織田信秀), 109, 226
Oda Nobunaga (織田信長), 85, 86, 139, 163,

171, 188-90, 206, 217, **226-27**, 228, 230, 252, 260, 267, 279
Oda Nobuo (織田信雄), **227-28**
Oda Nobutada (織田信忠), **228-29**
Oda Nobutaka (織田信孝), 228
Ōe no Hiromoto (大江廣元), **128-29**
Ōe no Sadamoto, *see* Jakushin
Ōe Taku (大江卓), 419
Ofudesaki (おふでさき), 424
ofumi (御文), 131
Ogasawara (Bonin) Islands (小笠原島), 423, 492
Ogasawara Shōsai (小笠原少齋), 190
Ogata Iin (緒方惟因), 229
Ogata Kōan (緒方洪庵), 184, 197, **229**, 233, 330
Ogata Taketora (緒方竹虎), 341
Ōgimachi, Emperor (正親町天皇), **230**
Ogiwara Shigehide (荻原重秀), **230**, 262
Ōgo (Mokujiki Shōnin) (應其), **231**
Oguri Ryōun (小栗了雲) 194
Ogyū Sorai (荻生徂徠), 175, 198, 254, 265, 278
Ogyū Yuzuru (大給恒), 460
Ōhara Shigetomi (大原重德), 471
Ōhiru Memuchi (大日靈貴), 18
Oichi-no-kata (お市の方), see Odani-no-kata
Ōi Kentarō (大井憲太郎), 328, **436**
Ōi, Prince (大炊王), 43, 71
Ōishi Susumu (大石進), 334
Ōishi Yoshikatsu (大石良勝), 231
Ōishi Yoshio (大石良雄), 170, **231-32**, 273
Ōjin, Emperor (應神天皇), 18, 39, **52**, 72
Ōjō jūin (往生拾因), 22
Ōjō kōshiki (往生講式), 22
Ōjō yōshū (往生要集), 34
Okada Keisuke (岡田啓介), **436-37**, 483, 496
Okada Mokichi (岡田茂吉), 324
Okamoto Shūki (岡本秋暉), 271
Okamura Gengohyōe Yoshimichi (岡村源五兵衞良通), 185
Okamura Shun'eki (岡村春益), 234
Okanoi Gentei (岡野井玄貞), 243
Ōkawa Shūmei (大川周明), 391, **437-39**
Okina mondō (翁問答), 221
Ōki Takatō (大木喬任), 473
Ōkōchi Hisatsuna (大河內久綱), 211
Ōkubo Ryōshi (大久保了思), 393
Ōkubo Tadahiro (大久保忠寬), 378
Ōkubo Tadasuke (大久保忠佐), 271
Ōkubo Toshimichi (大久保利通), 327, 335, 353, 361, 364, 367, 386, 387, 404, 406, 408, 409, 421, **439-41**, 451, 452, 471, 472
Okudaira Masashika (奥平昌鹿), 209
Okuda Sankaku (奥田三角), 198
Ōkuma Shigenobu (大隈重信), 337, 352, 354, 355, 358, 361, 365, 367, 376, 377, 404, 407, **441-43**, 445, 448, 449, 473, 475, 478, 493, 506
Okumura Hidezane (奥村榮實), 286
Okumura Hiroshi (奥村博史), 342
Okumura Ioko (奥村五百子), **443-44**
Okunen-ji (憶念寺), 425
Ōkuninushi-no-kami (大國主神), 187
Ōkura Nagatsune (大藏永常), **232-33**
Okuyama Seishuku (奥山靜叔), 233
Oldenberg, H., 315
Ōmi no Mifune (淡海三船), **52-53**
Ōmi ryō (近江令), 70
Ōmori Fujiyori (大森藤賴), 103
Ōmoto-kyō (大本敎), 323
Ōmura Masujirō (大村益次郎), 229, **233**, 386, 428, 492, 508
Ōmura Sumitada (大村純忠), 130, 169, 198, **233-34**
Ōnin War (應仁の亂), 88, 89, 101, 108, 112, 129, 132, 144
Ōnishi Hajime (大西祝), 314
Onjō-ji (Miidera) (園城寺(三井寺)), 23, 93, 256, 405
Onkodō (溫故堂), 429
On Liberty, 423
Ono Azusa (小野梓), 322, 370, **444-45**
Ono branch of Shingon Buddhism (眞言小野流), 50
Ono no Imoko (小野妹子), 48, **53**
Ono no Yoshifuru (小野好古), 30
Ono Ranzan (小野蘭山), **234**
Ono rokujō (小野六帖), 51
Onshin-ji (恩眞寺), 247
Onuma Shō (小沼正), 351
on'yō (陰陽), 144
Ōoka Tadasuke (大岡忠助), 166, **234-36**
Oranda chikujō-sho (和蘭築城書), 210
Oranda eizoku koyomi wage (和蘭陀永續曆和解), 219
Oranda honzō (和蘭陀本草), 219
Oranda Iji mondō (和蘭醫事問答), 246
Oranda kaheikō (和蘭貨幣考), 167
Oranda moji ryakkō (和蘭文字略考), 167
Oranda yakusen (和蘭藥選), 203
Oranda yakusen (和蘭譯筌), 210
Orategama (遠羅天釜), 180
Organtino, Gnecchi-Soldo, 252
Oritaku shibanoki (折りたく柴の記), 168
Osaka Asahi Shimbun (大阪朝日新聞), 382, 446
Osakabe Shinnō (刑部親王), 24, **53-54**
Osaka Castle, campaigns against, 175, 183, 196, 228, 231, 247, 257, 261, 266, 280
Osaka Commercial Training School (大阪商業講習所), 332
Osaka Conference (大阪會議), 352
Osaka Imperial University (大阪帝國大學), 420, 523
Osaka Incident (大阪事件), 328
Osaka Mainichi Shimbun (大阪每日新聞), 338
Osaka mint (大阪造幣廠), 332
Osaka Stock Exchange and Commercial Meeting Hall (大阪株式取引所商工會議所), 332
Ōsen Keisan (橫川景三), **129**
Ōshio Heihachirō (大鹽平八郎), **235-36**
Ōshio Kakunosuke (大鹽格之助), 235

Ōshio Yukitaka (大鹽敬高), 235
Ōsōshū (歐巢集), 178
Ōsugi Sakae (大杉榮), 316, **445-46**
Ōsu Tetsunen (大洲鐵然), 470
Otafuku jorō konahiki-uta (おたふく女郎粉引歌), 180
Ōtani branch of Jōdo Shin Buddhism (淨土眞宗大谷派), 394, 418, 425
Ōtani Kōson (大谷光尊), 446
Ōtani Kōzui (大谷光瑞), **446**
Ōtani University (大谷大學), 418, 425, 477
Ōten Gate disturbance (應天門の變), 31
Ōtomo family (大友氏), 54, 122, 129, 201
Ōtomo no Kanamura (大伴金村), 42, 49, **54**
Ōtomo, Prince (大友皇子), 53, 70
Ōtomo Sōrin (大友宗麟), **129-30**, 198, 234
Ōtomo Yoshiaki (大友義鑑), 129
Ōtomo Yoshishige (大友義鎭), 169
Ōtori Keisuke (大鳥圭介), 229, 334
Otowaka (乙若), 139
Ōtsu Incident (大津事件), 316, 326, 397, 414, 453
Ōtsuka Takayasu (大塚孝綽), 212
Ōtsuki Gentaku (大槻玄澤), 208, 210, **236**, 246, 275
Ōuchi Seiran (大內青巒), 405, 470
Ōuchi Yoshihiro (大內義弘), 90
Ōuchi Yoshioki (大內義興), 130
Ōuchi Yoshitaka (大內義隆), 122, **130**
Outline of Mahayana Buddhism, 477
Ōyama Ikuo (大山郁夫), 382, **446-47**, 522
Ōyama Iwao (大山巖), 380, 423, **447-48**
Ozaki Yukio (尾崎行雄), 354, 355, **448-49**

P

Pacific Steamship Company (太平洋汽船會社), 367
Pacific War, 224, 313, 318, 319, 340, 342, 356, 359, 369, 374, 382, 383, 385, 396, 408, 415, 434, 437, 438, 449, 462, 465, 468, 476, 478, 479, 496, 505, 507, 519, 520
Paekche kingdom, 17, 18, 27, 40, 42, 49, 54, 63, 69, 72
Paek Ch'on River (Haku River) (白村江), 17
Pan-Pacific Women's Conference, 523
Paris Antiwar Pact, 489
Paris Exhibition, 460, 463
Parkes, Sir Harry Smith-, 334, 418, 492
Peace Preservation Laws (治安警察法), 343, 346, 372, 377, 393, 401, 448, 488, 515
Pearl Harbor, 434, 514
Peers' School (學習院), 371, 384, 399, 427, 432, 434, 446, 477, 491
Peeresses's School (華族女學校), 429, 444, 491, 501
P'ei Shih-ch'ing (裴世淸), 48
Pennsylvania, University of, 432
Peoples' Cooperative Party, *see* Kokumin Kyōdōtō
Perry, Commodore, 161, 176, 203, 237, 239, 282
Pessoa, Andre, 183
Philip III, King, 183
Philippines, 100, 396, 495
Pillow Book (枕草子), 29, 38
P & O Steamship Line, 367
Pohai, 64
Police Reserve Force (警察豫備隊), 521
Political Study Society, *see* Seiji Kenkyūkai
Pope, 130, 169, 175, 183, 198, 234
Pope Paul V, 183
popular rights movement (自由民權運動), 328, 331, 335, 346, 355, 359, 360, 365, 372, 401, 436, 440, 442, 462, 473, 479, 490, 499, 503
Portsmouth Treaty, 314, 380, 399, 497
Portuguese, 129, 169, 221, 225, 233, 252, 258, 268
Potsdam Declaration, 478
Practical Party, *see* Jitsugakutō
prefectural system (廢藩置縣), 440
Privy Council, *see* Sūmitsuin
Progressive Party, see Kaishintō
Progressive Party, *see* Rikken Kaishintō
Progressive Party, see Shimpotō
Proletarian Popular Party, *see* Musan Taishūtō
Proletarian Science Research Center (プロレタリア科學研究所), 434
Proletarian Women's Art Alliance (無產婦人藝術聯盟), 343
Prussia, 164, 325
Pure Land Buddhism, 22, 46, 47, 50, 56, 92, 100, 109, 163, 483, *see also* Jōdo Buddhism
purple robe affair (紫衣事件), 245, 253

R

Raikō (禮光), 38
Rakusekisha (樂石社), 368
Rangaku kaitei (蘭學楷梯), 236
Rangaku kotohajime (蘭學事始), 246
Rangakuryō (蘭學寮), 441
rangakusha (蘭學者), 241
Rankei Dōryū, *see* Lan-hsi Tao-lung
Rarande rekisho kanken (ラランド曆書管見), 249
"red banner" incident (赤旗事件), 402
Reform Club, *see* Kakushin Kurabu
Reikai monogatari (靈界物語), 324
Reimeikai (黎明會), 447, 522
Reischauer, Edwin O., 23
"Religious Freedom in Japan," 417
renga (連歌), 132, 231, 281
Rengekai (蓮華會), 486
Rennyo (蓮如), **131**
Research Center for Infectious Diseases (傳染病研究所), 432
Research Institute for Iron, Steel, and Other Metals (金屬材料研究所), 345
Rhys-Davids, T. W., 315
Rigaku seisō (利學正宗), 419
Rigen Taishi (理源大師), 59
Rikken Dōshikai (立憲同志會), 336, 376, 443,

506
Rikken Jiyūtō (立憲自由黨), 360
Rikken Kaishintō (Progressive Party) (立憲改進黨), 346, 355, 407, 442, 445, 448
Rikken Kokumintō (立憲國民黨), 355, 493
Rikken Minseitō (立憲民政黨), 337, 507
Rikken seitairyaku (立憲政體略), 375
Rikken Seiyūkai (立憲政友會), 346, 362, 372, 449, 454, 482, 493, 513
Rikkokushi (六國史), 50, 181
Rikkyōkan (立教館), 212
Rikkyō Shinden (立教神傳), 383
Rinsen-ji (臨川寺), 123
Rinshō-ji (麟祥寺), 279
Rinzai (Lin-chi) Zen (臨濟宗), 93, 96, 110, 112, 113, 115, 118, 123, 124, 134-37, 142, 143, 145, 171, 179, 244, 253, 278, 462, 476
Risshisha (立志社), 359, 372, 503
Risshō ankoku (立正安國), 327
Risshō Ankokukai (立正安國會), 486
Risshō ankoku-ron (立正安國論), 126
Risshō chikoku-ron (立正治國論), 127
Risshō University (立正大學), 327, 357
Ritsu (Vinaya) Buddhism (律宗), 32, 57, 94, 95, 110, 124, 126, 135, 136
Ritsumeikan College (立命館大學), 358, 486
ritsuryō (律令), 21, 24, 26, 33, 41, 48, 53
Roankyō (驢鞍橋), 247
Rōben (良辨), **54-55**, 59
Robinson Crusoe, 474
Rōdōkumiai Kiseikai (勞働組合期成會), 485
Rōdō Nōmintō (Labor Farmer Party), 320, 369, 382, 447, 479, 515
Rōdō sekai (勞働世界), 372
Rōdō Zasshi (勞働雜誌), 462
Roesler, Karl Friedrich Hermann, 353
rōjū (老中), 232, 237
Rokkaku-no-Mitsui (六角の三井), 214
Rokkaku Yoshikata (六角義賢), 85
Rokoku jijitsu-shō (魯國事實鈔), 203
Rokuharamitsu-ji (六波羅蜜寺), 47
Rokujō engi (六條緣起), 110
Rome, 130, 169, 175, 183, 234
rōnin (浪人), 232, 262
Rōninkai (浪人會), 522
Rōnō (勞農), 317, 457, 479
Rōnō chawa (老農茶話), 233
Rōnōha (Labor Farmer Faction) (勞農派), 511
Rōnōtō (Labor Farmer Party) (勞農黨), 382
Rōnō Zen'eitō (勞農前衞黨), 459
Roosevelt, Franklin D., 401, 433
Roshia-shi (魯西亞誌), 203
Roscoe, Sir Henry Enfield, 474
Roshia hongi (魯西亞本紀), 210
Roshia keizai-shi (ロシア經濟史), 459
Roshia kokushi (魯西亞國誌), 275
Rousseau, Jean-Jacques, 421
Ruijū jingi hongen (類聚神祇本源), 142
Ruijū kokushi (類聚國史), 65
Ruiseikō (累世校), 469
Russia, 161, 164, 174, 184, 185, 203, 208, 212, 217, 248, 275, 282, 317, 319, 320, 325, 330, 336, 343, 352, 362, 376, 398, 403, 406, 411, 412, 420, 446, 452, 467, 473, 488, 491, 493, 494, 499, 502, 509, 513, 517, 519
Russo-German Nonaggression Pact (ドイツ・ソ聯不可侵條約), 342
Russo-Japanese agreement, 358, 398
Russo-Japanese War, 313, 314, 316, 317, 362, 370, 373, 377, 380, 389, 396, 399, 402, 414, 431, 444, 454-56, 467, 474, 478, 482, 483, 488, 491, 493, 494, 504, 509, 510, 513, 514
ryō (令), 24
Ryōbu Shintō (兩部神道), 273
Ryōfū Maru (凌風丸), 189
Ryōga (良賀), 56
Ryōgen (良源), 33, **55**
Ryōjin hishō (梁塵秘抄), 36
Ryōjin no jihaku (良人の自白), 389
Ryōkan (了寬), 443
Ryōnin (良忍), **55-56**
Ryōunshū (凌雲集), 56
Ryūchikai (龍池會), 460
Ryūkō-ji (龍興寺), 256
Ryūkoku University (龍谷大學), 405
Ryūkō Ōsen, *see* Lung-chiang Ying-hsüan
Ryūkyū Islands (琉球諸島), 286, 472,473
Ryūmon-ji (龍門寺), 171
Ryūshō-ji (龍翔寺), 135
Ryūtaku-ji (龍澤寺), 180
Ryūzan Tokken (龍山德見), 145

S

sabi (寂), 89
sadaijin (左大臣), 25
Sadasumi, Prince (貞純親王), 59
Saddharmapundarika, *see* Lotus Sutra
Saga, Emperor (嵯峨天皇), 25, 46, 50, **56**, 68
Saga Rebellion (佐賀の亂), 326
Saha Shakaitō (Leftist Socialist Party((左派社會黨), 480
Saichō (最澄), 23, 45, **56-58**, 57
Saidai-ji (西大寺), 95, 126
Saidai-jiryū (西大寺流), 95
Saifuku-ji (西福寺), 405
Saigō Takamori (西鄉隆盛), 327, 359, 361, 365, 372, 379, 386, 395, 404, 413, 439, 447, **449-52**, 471, 472, 499
Saigō Tsugumichi (西鄉從道), 450, **452-53**, 508
Saihō-ji (Kokedera) (西芳寺(苔寺)), 123, 394
Saihoku-an (濟北庵), 116
Saihokushū (濟北集), 116
Saihō shinan-shō (西方指南抄), 108
Saiiki monogatari (西域物語), 189
Saijukan (躋壽館), 234
Saikaron (齊家論), 195
Saikin sekai gaikōshi (最近世界外交史), 321
Saikō-ji (西光寺), 47
Saimei, Empress (齊明天皇), 17, 69

Sain (左院), 327, 335, 375
Saionji (西園寺), 381
Saionji Kimmochi (西園寺公望), 339, 376, 385, 400, 408, 421, 437, **453-55**, 456
Sairan igen (采覽異言), 168, 275
Sairyō (細領), 353
Saisei Gakusha (濟生學舍), 432, 523
Saiseikai (濟生會), 392
Saisei yogen (濟生餘言), 276
Saishin (濟信), 42
Saitō Makoto (齋藤實), 340, 344, 378, 437, 483, **455-56**
Saitō Takao (齋藤隆夫), 374
Saitō Tatsuoki (齋藤龍興), 226
Saitō Yakurō (齋藤彌九郎), 385
Saitō Zemmon (齋藤全門), 195
Sakabe Hironao (坂部廣胖), 189
Sakaino Kōyō (境野黃洋), 418
Sakai Tadakiyo (酒井忠淸), **237**, 262
Sakai Toshihiko (堺利彥), 316, 317, 390, 402, 445, **456-57**, 496, 511
Sakakibara Kōshū (榊原篁洲), 206
Saka Kōō (坂江鷗), 209
Sakamoto Ryōma (坂本龍馬), **237-38**, 239, 334, 361, 386, 418, 439, 508, 519
Sakanoue no Tamuramaro (坂上田村麻呂), 41, 56, **58**
Sakata Shōichi (坂田昌一), 524
Sakhalin (Karafuto) (樺太), 211, 216, 325, 403, 467, 473, 491
sakimori (防人), 27
Sakuma Kuniyoshi (佐久間國善), 238
Sakuma Shōzan (佐久間象山), 176, **238-39**, 240, 281, 374, 378, 499
Sakurakai (櫻會), 438
Sakura Sōgorō (佐倉宗五郎), **239-40**
Sammon (山門), 23
Sampitsu (Three Masters of Calligraphy) (三筆), 46, 56
Samuraidokoro (侍所), 120, 141
Sanada Masayuki (眞田昌幸), 257
Sanada Yukitsura (眞田幸貫), 239
Sandai jitsuroku (三代實錄), 65
Sandaikō (三大考), 187
Sanetaka-kō ki (實隆公記), 132
Sangatsu-dō (三月堂), 55
Sangen-in (三玄院), 253
Sanger, Margaret, 515
Sangoku bukkyō dentsū engi (三國佛教傳通緣起), 100
Sangoku tsūran zusetsu (三國通覽圖說), 185
Sangō shiiki (三教指歸), 45
Sangyō yōryaku (三教要略), 96
Sanjiin (參事院), 393
Sanjikarizumu Kenkyūkai (サンジカリズム研究會), 445
Sanjō, Emperor (三條天皇), 28
Sanjōnishi Kimiyasu (三條西公保), 131
Sanjōnishi Sanetaka (三條西實隆), **131-32**
Sanjō Sanetomi (三條實美), 365, **457-58**
Sanjō Sanetsumu (三條實萬), 457
Sanka sagen (產科鎖言), 181
sankin-kōtai (參勤交代), 257
San-kuo-chih (三國志), 37
Sano Manabu (佐野學), **459**
Sano Tsunetami (佐野常民), 197, 229, **459-60**
Sanron Buddhism (三論宗), 19, 22, 37, 59
Sansai hōtoku kimmō roku (三才報德金毛錄), 225
Sanshō-ji (三聖寺), 115, 116
Sansōshū (三草集), 212
Sansuijin keirin mondō (三醉人經綸問答), 421
Sanzen biken (三千備檢), 136
Sapporo Agricultural College (札幌農學校), 403, 430, 467, 502
Saris, John, 162, 213
Sartor Resartus, 430
Sasaki Gesshō (佐久木月樵), 395
Sasaki Sōichi (佐々木惣一), 486
Satō Eisaku (佐藤榮作), 389, 412, **460-61**
Satō Issai (佐藤一齋), 238, **240**, 270
Satomura Jōha (里村紹巴), 231
Satō Naokata (佐藤直方), 277
Satō Nobuhiro (佐藤信淵), **241**
Satow, Sir Ernest Mason, 334
Satsuma (薩摩), 238, 265, 286, 329, 331, 334, 350, 359, 361, 364, 386, 403, 404, 406, 408, 409, 416, 419, 422, 423, 439, 443, 447, 449, 452, 458, 470, 472, 491, 493, 508, 512
Satsuma-British War (薩英戰爭), 439
Satsunan gakuha (薩南學派), 113
Satta Tokuken (薩埵德軒), 242
Sawada Hannosuke (澤田半之助), 485
Sawamura Kinsho (澤村琴所), 198
Sawa Nobuyoshi (澤宣嘉), 458
Sawano Chūan, (澤野忠庵) *see* Ferreira, Christovão
Schopenhauer, 315
Second International, 373
Second Japanese-Korean agreement (第二次日韓協約), 363
Security Police Law, 509
Seichō no Ie (生長の家), 324
Seidotsū (制度通), 198
Seigaku mondō (聖學問答), 175
Seigan-ji (誓願寺), 124
Seigo (政語), 212
Seihen Gunsho ruijū (正編群書類從), 182
Seii gembyōryaku (西醫原病略), 208
seii-taishōgun (征夷大將軍), 58, 114, 117, 121
Seiji keizai-ron (政治經濟論), 177
Seiji Kenkyūkai (Political Study Society) (政治研究會), 479
Seijō University (成城大學), 516
Seijutsu taiyō kyūri ryōkai-setsu (星術太陽窮理了解說), 219
Seikatsuroku (製葛錄), 233
Seikyōiku (性教育), 515
Seikyōsha (政教社), 416, 467, 470, 475
Seikyō yōroku (聖教要錄), 273
Seimi kaisō (舎密開宗), 269

Seinan no bukkyō (西南の佛教), 462
Seinan War (西南戰爭), 354, 367, 372, 387, 404, 419, 431, 441, 442, 447, 451, 452, 460, 490, 492, 499, 509
Seirensha (精煉社), 460
Seirontō-shi (錫蘭島史), 462
Seisetsu botanikakyō (西說菩多尼訶經), 269
Seisetsu naika sen'yō (西說內科選要), 269
Seishinkai (精神界), 395
Seishin kōwa (精神講話), 395
Seishin shugi (精神主義), 395
Sei Shōnagon (清少納言), 29, 38
Seisho no Kenkyū (聖書の硏究), 502
Seishū zatsuwa (青州雜話), 181
Seismological Investigation Committee (震災豫防調査會), 487
Seitaisho (政體書), 473
Seitō (青鞜), 342
Seitō Kaishō Remmei (政黨解消連盟), 412
Seiyō jijō (西洋事情), 330
Seiyō jijō onkotaegaki (西洋事情御答書), 270
Seiyō kibun (西洋紀聞), 168, 193
Seiyō zakki (西洋雜記), 275
Seiyūhontō (政友本黨), 394
Seiyūkai (政友會), 321, 337, 339, 344, 351, 355, 360, 363, 377, 378, 394, 400, 411, 437, 440, 454, 465, 488, 507
Seiwa, Emperor (淸和天皇), 31, **58-59**
Seizan Jiei (青山慈永), 145
Seizan Kyōjukō (西山教授校), 405
Seizan line of Jōdo Buddhism (淨土宗西山派), 109
Sekai chishi (世界地誌), 207
Sekai Fujin (世界婦人), 328
Sekai heiwa-ron (世界平和論), 368
Sekai Meshiya-kyō (世界メシア教), 324
Sekai no Nihon (世界の日本), 420
Sekai sansui zusetsu (世界山水圖說), 467
Sekai Shūkyō Rengōkai (Federation of World Religions) (世界宗教連合會), 323
Sekigahara, battle of (關ヶ原の戰), 164, 169, 174, 188, 190, 193, 196, 202, 207, 213, 218, 228, 231, 237, 247, 257, 261, 266, 280
Sekijin mondō (赤人問答), 217
Seki school (關流), 242
Seki Shimpachi (尺振八), 481
Seki Takakazu (關孝和), **242**
Sekitokudō (積德堂), 273
sekkan (攝關), 31
Self-Defense Forces (自衛隊), 521
Self-Help (西國立志篇), 413, 423
Semman (千幡), 119
Senaphimuk, Okon, 272
Senate, *see* Genrōin
Senchaku hongan nembutsu-shū (選擇本願念佛集), 107, 133
Sengen Shinto Shrine (淺間神社), 272
Sengoku Jidai (戰國時代), *see* Warring States era
Sen-hime (千姫), 266, 280
Senka, Emperor (宣化天皇), 42, 54
Sen no Rikyū (千利休), 190, 201
Senoo Girō (妹尾義郎), **461-62**
Sen'yū-ji (泉涌寺), 136
Sen'yū-ji Fukaki hōshi-den (泉涌寺不可棄法師傳), 136
Seoul Incident (京城事變), 338, 352, 355, 362
Seoul Treaty (京城條約), 352
sesshō (攝政), 28, 30, 31
Sesson Yūbai (雪村友梅), 85, 111, **132-33**
Setsuhei (說蔽), 265
Setsumon (雪門), 476
Seventeen Article Constitution (十七條憲法), 62, 66
Seyaku-in (施藥院), 44
Shachū (社中), 238
Shakai bunko (社會文庫), 480
Shakai henkaku tojō no shinkō bukkyō (社會變革途上の新興佛教), 462
Shakai Kakumeitō (Social Revolution Party) (社會革命黨), 402
Shakai Minshutō (Social Democratic Party) (社會民主黨), 313, 373, 389, 402, 522
Shakai Minshūtō (Social Popular Party) (社會民衆黨), 373, 476
Shakai mondai kenkyū (社會問題硏究), 382, 434
Shakai shugi hyōron (社會主義評論), 382
Shakai Shugi Kyōkai (Socialist League) (社會主義協會), 373
Shakai shugi shinzui (社會主義神髓), 403
Shakai Taishūtō (Social Populace Party) (社會大衆黨), 313, 373
Shaku Sōen (釋宗演), **462**, 476
Shand, Alexander Allen, 336, 350
Shanghai Incident (上海事變), 411, 433, 469
Shang shu (尙書), 112
Shan-tao, 107
Shen Nam-p'in (沈南蘋), 270
Shibata Katsuie (柴田勝家), 267, 279
Shiba Takatsune (斯波高經), 128
Shibata Kyūō (柴田鳩翁), **242-43**
Shibukawa Shunkai (澁川春海), **243**
Shibusawa Eiichi (澁澤榮一), 336, 347, **463-64**
Shibusawa *zaibatsu* (澁澤財閥), 463
Shichishō Gidan (七生義團), 515
Shidehara diplomacy (幣原外交), 465
Shidehara Kijūrō (幣原喜重郞), 321, 337, 411, **464-66**, 488, 507, 520
Shidehara Taira (幣原坦), 464
Shien (芝園), 175
Shiga Kiyoshi (志賀潔), 392, **466-67**
Shiga Shigetaka (志賀重昂), 416, **467**
Shiga Yoshio (志賀義雄), 435, **468**, 496
Shigemitsu Mamoru (重光葵), 319, 396, 411, **468-69**
Shigi, Mt. (信貴山), 228
Shih-liang Jen-kung (石梁仁恭), 110
Shikai (史海), 481
Shikan taza (只管打坐), 94

Shikigenshō (職原抄), 115
Shimada Ichirō (島田一郎), 441
Shimaji Daitō (島地大等), 470
Shimaji Mokurai (島地默雷), **469-70**
Shimamoto Ryōjun (島本良順), 197
Shima Yoshitake (島義勇), 327, 413
Shimazaki Tōson (島崎藤村), 516
Shimazu Hisamitsu (島津久光), 409, 439, 450, **470-72**, 472
Shimazu Nariakira (島津齊彬), 250, 379, 422, 439, 450, 470, **472**, 491
Shimazu Narioki (島津齊興), 470, 472
Shimazu Nisshin (島津日新), 450
Shimazu Shigehide (島津重豪), 286, 472
Shimazu Tadamasa (島津忠昌), 112
Shimazu Tadayoshi (島津忠義), 470
Shimazu Yoshihisa (島津義久), 130
Shimbutsu Gappei Daikyō-in (神佛合併大教院), 470
Shimmi Buzen-no-kami Masaoki (新見豐前守正興), 379
Shimizu Ritsuan (清水立安), 275
Shimoda Utako (下田歌子), 444
Shimojō Yoshinosuke (下條吉之助), 210
Shimonoseki Treaty (下關條約), 420
Shimotsumichi Makibi (下道眞備), 42
Shimpotō (Progressive Party) (進歩黨), 346, 355, 442, 466, 467
Shim-sang, *see* Shinjō
Shinagawa Yajirō (品川彌二郎), 453, 492
Shina kakumei gaishi (支那革命外史), 390
Shina kakumei shōshi (支那革命小史), 522
Shinano Mainichi Shimbun (信濃每日新聞), 510
Shinchō shakai-shi (清朝社會史), 459
Shindai no maki kaden kikigaki (神代卷家傳聞書), 283
Shindai no maki kōjutsushō (神代卷講述鈔), 271
Shindai no maki Koretari shō (神代卷惟足抄), 283
Shinga (眞雅), 59
shingaku (心學), 171, 194, 242
Shingon (眞言), 46, 100, 127, 136
Shingon sect (眞言宗), 41, 45, 50, 59, 92, 123, 136, 199
Shinjin (新人), 324
Shinjinkai (新人會), 459, 468, 522
Shinjō (Shim-sang) (審祥), **59**
Shinkigen (新紀元), 313, 389
Shinkiron (愼機論), 270
Shinkō Bukkyō no Hata no Motoni (新興佛教の旗の下に), 462
Shinkō bukkyō no teishō (新興佛教の提唱), 462
Shinkō Bukkyō Seinen Dōmei (Shinkō Bussei) (新興佛教青年同盟(新興佛青)), 462
Shinkū (眞空), 100
Shinkyō (Tea) (眞教), 110
Shinnen (眞然), 59
Shin Nihon (新日本), 443
Shinonome Shimpō (東雲新報), 422
Shinran (親鸞), 34, 47, 108, 112, **133-34**
Shinrei yaguchi no watashi (神靈矢口渡), 186
Shinri kinshin (眞理金針), 350
Shinsai, *see* Udagawa Genshin
Shin sect (眞宗), 227, 228, 349
Shinsei taii (眞政大意), 375
Shinsen Tsukubashū (新撰菟玖波集), 132
Shinshakai (新社會), 511
Shinshiroku (愼思錄), 200
Shinshō Maru (神昌丸), 173
Shinshōryō-ji (新清涼寺), 95
Shinshun (眞俊), 135
Shinshū University (眞宗大學), 395, 425
Shinto (神道), 113, 115, 144, 181, 185, 187, 194, 241, 243, 265, 276, 283, 404, 470
Shintō daiichū (神道大意注), 283
Shintō gobusho (神道五部書), 141
Shintō kōdan (神道講談), 283
Shinto, Sectarian, 242, 383
Shin'yō wakashū (新葉和歌集), 99
Shinzembi Nihonjin (眞善美日本人), 416
Shinzui (信瑞), 136
Shiogama Shrine (鹽竈神社), 185
Shionoya Tōin (鹽谷宕陰), 184
Shirakawa, Emperor (白河天皇), 35, 70, 138
Shirakawa Shizan (白川芝山), 270
Shirandō (芝蘭堂), 236, 275
Shiratori Kurakichi (白鳥庫吉), 500
Shisen o Koete (死線を越えて), 369
Shitennō-ji (四天王寺), 62
Shizugatake, battle of (賤ケ嶽の戰), 190, 206, 267
Shizuki Tadao (志筑忠雄), 219, **244**
Shizu Teichū (志津貞中), 165
Shōbō (聖寶), **59-60**
Shōbō genzō (正法眼藏), 94
Shōbō genzō zuimonki (正法眼藏随聞記), 94
Shōbō line (聖寶の系統), 42
Shōchū disturbance (正中の變), 97
Shōchū no Shūron (正中の宗論), 135
Shōdaijōron (攝大乘論), 22
Shōen (莊園), 20, 34
Shōfuku-ji (聖福寺), 124, 142
Shōgon jikkyō (照權實鏡), 57
shogunate (幕府), 170, 174, 176, 178, 184, 186, 188, 191, 193, 194, 202, 204-08, 210, 214, 220, 232, 236, 239-43, 248, 250, 252-54, 263, 284-86, 325, 330, 359, 361, 364, 375, 378, 379, 384, 386, 406, 422, 423, 431, 436, 439, 444, 450, 453, 463, 470, 481, 499, 510, 518
Shōheikō (昌平校), 423, 444
Shōhei-Tengyō uprising (承平天慶の亂), 30
Shōhō-ji (正法寺), 136
Shōichi line (聖一派), 96, 115
Shōin-ji (松蔭寺), 179
Shōji jissō-gi (聲字實相義), 46
Shōjōkō-ji (清浄光寺), 110
Shōkai (聖戒), 110
Shōkai Reiken (性海靈見), 116, 145
Shōkan kōgi (傷寒講義), 181
Shōka sagen (傷科鎖言), 181
Shōkasonjuku (松下村塾), 251, 282, 361, 508

Shōken, Empress Dowager (昭憲皇太后), 413
Shōkenkō (蕉堅稿), 146
Shōkin Bank of Yokohama (横濱正金銀行), 482
Shokkō Giyūkai (職工義友會), 485
Shōkō (聖光), 108
Shōkōjuku (稱好塾), 475
Shōkōkan (彰考館), 177
Shōkoku-ji (相國寺), 145
Shokoku miyagesho (諸國土產書), 225
Shōkū (證空), 108, 109
Shokubutsu keigen (植物啓原), 269
Shoku Nihonkōki (續日本後紀), 50
Shokyō kōgi (書經講義), 417
Shōmu, Emperor (聖武天皇), 25, 32, 37, 42-44, 55, 59, **60-61**
shōmyō (聲明), 42, 56
Shōmyō-ji (稱名寺), 103
shōmyō nembutsu (稱名念佛), 22
Shōnan ikō (小楠遺稿), 519
Shōnyo (勝如), 47
Shōon Sōchi (正穩宗智), 253
Shōrai no Nihon (將來之日本), 497
Shōron (攝論), 22
Shōryō-ji (淸涼寺), 20, 127
Shōryō-shū (性靈集), 46
Shosha, Mt. (書寫), 134
Shōshikai (尙齒會), 207, 249, 270
Shōsō-in (正倉院), 44, 61
Shōtaku line (聖澤派), 171
Shōtatsu (聖達), 109
Shōten-ji (承天寺), 96
Shōtetsu (性徹), 179
Shōtoku, Empress (稱德天皇), 43, 71
shōtoku no chi (正德の治), 168
Shōtoku, Prince (聖德太子), 31, 53, **61-63**, 64, 66, 69
Shōzan shoin (象山書院), 238
Shūbunkan (修文館), 504
Shūeisha (秀英舍), 476
Shūgaku-in Detached Palace (修學院離宮), 178
Shūgaku Zenji, *see* Tsung-chüeh Ch'an-shih
Shugeishuchi-in (綜藝種智院), 46
Shugendō (修驗道), 24, 60
Shūgi gaisho (集義外書), 209
Shūgi washo (集義和書), 209
shugo (守護), 36, 105, 120, 128
Shugo kokkai-shō (守護國界章), 57
Shugo kokka-ron (守護國家論), 126
Shūhō Myōchō (宗峰妙超), 124, **134-35**
shuin (朱印), 172, 182, 199, 246
Shūi ōjōden (拾遺往生傳), 22
Shūko jisshu (集古十種), 212
Shūkyōgaku gairon (宗教學概論), 315
Shūkyō tetsugaku gaikotsu (宗教哲學骸骨), 394
Shūkyō yōroku (修教要錄), 273
Shūmon no ishin (宗門之維新), 486
Shun-hsiao, 57
Shunjō (俊芿), **135-36**
Shun'oku Myōha (春屋妙葩), 123, **136-37**, 145
Shūseikan (集成館), 472
Shūshinroku (修身錄), 212
Shūshō (宗性), 100
shūshō ittō (修證一等), 94
Shutsujō gogo (出定後語), 265
Shuzen-ji (修禪寺), 111, 119
Siam, 271
Sidotti, Giovanni Battista, 168, 192
Siebold, Philipp Franz von, 197, 207, 211, 217, 233, 249, 269
Siemens affair, 336, 455, 513
Silla dynasty (新羅國), 17, 39, 40, 43, 52, 59, 62, 66, 70
Sino-Japanese War (日淸戰爭), 319, 333, 338, 343, 346, 352, 362, 363, 377, 380, 395, 398, 414, 420, 431, 448, 460, 478, 487, 492, 494, 497, 509, 513
Sixth Comintern, 459
Smiles, Samuel, 413, 423
Sōchitsuryō (宗秩寮), 385
socialism, 313, 316, 320, 328, 372, 422, 436, 445, 456, 457, 459, 461, 468, 479, 496, 502, 510, 511, 514, 520
socialism, Christian, 313
Social Democratic Party, *see* Shakai Minshutō
Socialist International (社會主義インターナショナル), 480
Socialist League, *see* Shakai Shugi Kyōkai
Socialist Party (社會黨), 317, 321, 340, 476, 511
Socialist Party, American (アメリカ社會黨), 402
Socialist Party of Russia (ロシア社會黨), 402
Socialist Society (社會主義協會), 313
Socialist Study Society (社會主義研究會), 313 402
socialist women's movement (社會主義婦人運動家), 511
Social Populace Party, *see* Shakai Taishūtō
Social Revolution Party, *see* Shakai Kakumeitō
Society for the Preservation of the National Essence, *see* Yūzonsha
Soejima Taneomi (副島種臣), 326, 441, **473-74**
Sōfuku-ji (崇福寺), 279
Soga no Emishi (蘇我蝦夷), 63
Soga no Iname (蘇我稻目), 42, 49, **63**, 64, 65
Soga no Iruka (蘇我入鹿), 26, 44, **63**, 69
Soga no Umako (蘇我馬子), 49, 61, 63, **64**, 66
Soga Ryōshin (曽我量深), 395
Sōji-ji (總持寺), 113
sōjō (僧正), 38
Sōka Gakkai (創價學會), 408
Sōka Kyōiku Gakkai (創價教育學會), 408
Sōka kyōikugaku taikei (創價教育學大系), 407
Sōkoku-ji (相國寺), 129, 137
Sokuhi no ronri (卽非の論理), 477
sokushin jōbutsu (卽身成佛), 46
Sokushin jōbutsu-gi (卽身成佛義), 46

Sōkyō-ji (宗鏡寺), 253
Sōma, Viscount (相馬子爵), 333
Sonnō Hōbutsu Daidōdan (尊王奉佛大同團), 405
sonnō-jōi movement (尊皇攘夷), 192, 251, 282, 351, 361, 385, 441, 457, 458
Sonnyo (存如), 131
Sōryū-an (雙龍庵), 199
Sōtan nikki (宗湛日記), 201
Sotelo, Luis (ルイス・ソテロ), 175, 183
Sōtōshū University (曹洞宗大學), 418, 506
Sōtō (Ts'ao-tung) Zen (曹洞宗), 93
Southern Sung dynasty (南宋), 105, 142, 143
South Manchuria Railway (南滿州鐵道), 333, 396, 399, 411, 412, 437, 493, 500
Soviet Union (ソ連), 317, 340, 343, 357, 373, 401, 412, 435, 459, 468, 469, 478, 479, 496
Spain, 175, 183, 198
Spencer, Edmund, 375
Śrīmālā, Queen, sutra of, 62
Staatens Serum Institut, 432
Steel Research Center (鐵鋼研究所), 345
Stein, Lorenz von, 335, 419
Stockholm Olympics, 371
Student Alliance (學生聯合會), 468
Study Group on Universal Suffrage, 522
Sūden (崇傳), **244-45**
Sue Harukata (陶晴賢), 122, 130
Suekawa Hiroshi (末川博), 486
Suetsugu Heizō (末次平藏), 180
Sūfuku-ji (崇福寺), 96
Sugawara no Arisuke (菅原在輔), 116
Sugawara no Fumitoki (菅原文時), 74
Sugawara no Koreyoshi (菅原是善), 64
Sugawara no Michizane (菅原道眞), 20, **64-65**
Sugita Gempaku (杉田玄白), 210, 222, 236, **245-46**, 284
Sugita Hakugen (杉田伯元), 249
Sugita Seikei (杉田成卿), 184
Sugita Teishin (杉田定信), 245
Sugiura Shigetake (杉浦重剛), 416, **474-75**
Sugiura Shisai (杉浦止齋), 195
Sugiyama Motojirō (杉山元治郎), 369
Sugi Yurinosuke Tsunemichi (杉百合之助常道), 281
Sui dynasty (隋國), 27, 38, 48, 53, 62, 66
Suika Shintō (垂加神道), 276
Suiko, Empress (推古天皇), 31, 53, 61, 63, 64, **65-66**
Suinin, Emperor (垂仁天皇), 51
Suiriku sempōroku (水陸戰法錄), 241
Sujin, Emperor (崇神天皇), 39, **66-67**
Sukagawa Medical School (須賀川醫學校), 333
Sukhavati-vyuha (*Muryōju-kyō*) (無量壽經), 425
Suminokura Ryōi (角倉了以), **246-47**
Sumitomo Kichizaemon (住友吉左衞門), 453
Sūmitsuin (Privy Council) (樞密院), 362
Sung dynasty (宋), 19, 51, 110, 112, 118, 124, 136, 142, 146
Sung Chiao-jen (宋教仁), 390
Sun Yat-sen (孫逸仙(孫文)), 356, 400, 499
Supreme Court, *see* Daishin-in
Susano-o (素戔嗚), 19
Su-shen, *see* Mishihase
Sushun, Emperor (崇峻天皇), 61, 64, 66
Sutoku, Emperor (崇德天皇), 35, 70, 71, 137
Su Yin-kao (蘇因高), 53
Suzuki Bunji (鈴木文治), 369, 435, **475-76**
Suzuki Daisetsu (鈴木大拙), 462, **476-77**
Suzuki Kantarō (鈴木貫太郎), 341, **477-79**, 519
Suzuki Mosaburō (鈴木茂三郎), **479-80**
Suzuki Shigenari (鈴木重成), 247
Suzuki Shōsan (鈴木正三), **247**
Suzuki Shunzan (鈴木春山), 207
Suzuki Takao (鈴木孝雄), 477
Suzuki Umetarō (鈴木梅太郎), **480**
Sweden, 398
Swedenborg, Emanuel, 477
Switzerland, 495, 516
Syŏngmyŏng, King (聖明王), 42, 49, 63

T
Tabarazaka, battle of (田原坂の戰), 492
Tachibana no Hayanari (橘逸勢), 45, 46, 50, 56
Tachibana no Michiyo (橘三千代), 43, 67
Tachibana no Moroe (橘諸兄), 33, 42, 43, 60, **67**
Tachibana no Naramaro (橘奈良麻呂), 67
Tada Kanae (多田鼎), 395
Tagawa Daikichirō (田川大吉郎), 449
Taguchi Ukichi (田口卯吉), 382, **481**
Tahara clan (田原藩), 232
Ta-hsüeh chang-chü (*Daigaku shōku*) (大學章句), 112
Taian-ji (大安寺), 59
Taichiben (大知辨), 274
Taidō Ichii (大道一以), 116
Taigu (大愚), 247
Taiheishō (太平頌), 205
Taihoku Imperial University (臺北帝國大學), 464
Taihō Risshi (大寶律師), 405
Taihō ritsuryō (大寶律令), 24, 53
Taika Reforms (大化改新), 24, 26, 43, 45, 48, 62, 69
Taikan zakki (退閑雜記), 212
Taikenmon-in Shōshi (待賢門院璋子), 35
Taima no Kehaya (當麻蹶速), 51
Taiping Rebellion (大平天國の亂), 251
Taira family (Heike) (平氏), 19, 35, 41, 68, 87, 92, 93, 102, 104, 106, 117, 119, 120, 121, 138, 141
Taira no Kiyomori (平清盛), 19, 35, 41, 49, 71, 89, 102, 117, 120, 121, **137-38**, 139
Taira no Kunika (平國香), 68
Taira no Masakado (平將門), 30, 41, **68**
Taira no Masamori (平正盛), 138
Taira no Shigehira (平重衡), 93

Taira no Tadamori (平忠盛), 137, **138**
Taira no Yoshikado (平良將), 68
Tai-Ro Dōshikai (對露同志會), 499
Taisei kokuhōron (泰西國法論), 500
Taisei naika shūsei (泰西內科集成), 208
Taisei shikan (泰西史鑑), 430
Taisei Yokusankai (Imperial Rule Assistance Association) (大政翼賛會), 401
Taishō, Emperor (大正天皇), 446, 454
Taishōin (待詔院), 387
Taishō shinshū daizōkyō (大正新脩大藏經), 484
T'ai-tsung, Emperor (太宗皇帝), 20
Taiwan (臺灣), 101, 333, 367, 368, 380, 387, 390, 395, 430, 431, 440, 442, 452, 465, 473, 490, 521
Taiyō (太陽), 314, 511
Takabatake Motoyuki (高畠素之), 511
Takachiho (高千穗), 513
Takadaya Kahei (高田屋嘉兵衞), **248**
Taka-Diastase (タカジアスターゼ), 484
Takahara Yoshitsugu (高原吉繼), 242
Takahashi Kageyasu (高橋景保), 211, 249
Takahashi Korekiyo (高橋是清), 337, 351, 378, **481-83**, 488
Takahashi Tandō (高橋擔堂), 474
Takahashi Tokujirō (高橋德次郎), 248
Takahashi Yoshitoki (高橋至時), 170, 194, **248-49**
Takahito, Prince (尊仁親王), 30
Takakura, Emperor (高倉天皇), 138
Takakura Gakuryō (高倉學寮), 425
Takakusu Junjirō (高楠順次郎), **483-84**, 506
Takamatsu Hambei (高松半兵衞), 284
Takamine Jōkichi (高峰讓吉), **484**
Takamine Research Center (高峰研究所), 484
Takami Senseki (鷹見泉石), 271
Takamuku no Kuromaro (高向玄理), 48
Takamure Itsue (高群逸枝), 343
Takano Chōei (高野長英), 207, 241, **249-50**, 270
Takano family (高野家), 249, 514
Takano Fusatarō (高野房太郎), **484-85**
Takano Iwasaburō (高野岩三郎), 484
Takaoka Shinnō (高岳親王), **68**
Takarai Kikaku (寶井基角), 205
Takasaki Masakaze (高崎正風), 413
Takashima coalmines (高島炭抗), 335
Takashima Shirōbei (高島四郎兵衞), 250
Takashima Shūhan (高島秋帆), 176, **250-51**
Takashima Tomonosuke (高島鞆之助), 413
Takasugi Shinsaku (高杉晋作), **251-52**, 282, 351, 361, 380, 443, 508
Takatsukasa Masamichi (鷹司政通), 364
Takayama Chōgyū (高山樗牛), 314, 315, 510
Takayama (Tokyo) Dental College (高山齒科醫學院(東京齒科大學)), 432
Takayama Hikokurō (高山彥九郎), 210
Takayama Tomoteru (高山友照), 252
Takayama Ukon (高山右近), 190, **252-53**
Takechi Zuizan (武市瑞山), 238
Takeda Ayasaburō (武田斐三郎), 406
Takeda Gyōchū (武田行忠), 418
Takeda Katsuyori (武田勝頼), 226, 229, 260
Takeda Nobutora (武田信虎), 138
Takeda Shingen (武田信玄), **138-39**, 140, 260, 285
Takeda Shun'an (竹田春庵), 200
Takegoshi Yosaburō (竹越與三郎), 420, 497
Takenouchi Shikibu (竹內式部), 277
Taketani Mitsuo (武谷三男), 524
Takeuchi Tsuna (竹內綱), 520
Takigawa affair (瀧川事件), 486
Takigawa Yukitoki (瀧川幸辰), 340, **485-86**
Takikawa Kazumasu (瀧川一益), 163
Takimoto Shōjōbō (瀧本昭乘坊), 281
Takuan (澤庵), 178, **253**
Takuan oshō zenshū (澤庵和尙全集), 253
Takushoku University (拓殖大學), 438
Tale of Genji, The (源氏物語), 29, 38, 132
Tale of the Heike, The, see *Heike monogatari*
Tales of Ise (伊勢物語), 178
Tamadasuki (玉襷), 187
Tamaki Bunnoshin (玉木文之進), 281, 431
Tama-no-mahashira (靈の眞柱), 187
Tamayori-hime (玉依姬), 38
Ta-ming san-tsang sheng-chiao mu-lu (大明三藏聖教目錄), 425
Tamura, Prince (田村皇子), 63
Tamura Ransui (田村藍水), 185
Tanaka Chigaku (田中智學), **486-87**
Tanakadate Aikitsu (田中館愛橘), 388, **487**
Tanaka Fujimaro (田中不二麿), 426
Tanaka Giichi (田中義一), 337, 340, 355, 411, 437, 465, 483, **487-89**, 504, 520
Tanaka Hyōgo (田中兵庫), 254
Tanaka Kyūgu (田中邱愚), **254**
Tanaka Shōzō (田中正造), 316, 402, **489-90**
Tanaka Tōkō (田中桐江), 265
Tanegashima (種子島), 129
T'ang dynasty, 17, 21, 23, 27, 32, 42, 45, 48, 60, 65, 69, 70, 107, 243, 275
Tani Bunchō (谷文晁), 270
Taniguchi Masaharu (谷口雅春), 324
Taniguchi Shinsuke (谷口新介), 209
Tani Jichū (谷時沖), 276
Tani Kanjō (谷干城), 352, 490-91
Tanimori Yoshiomi (谷森善臣), 457
Tannishō (歎異抄), 134, 395
Tanuma Okitomo (田沼意知), 255
Tanuma Okitsugu (田沼意次), 186, 208, 212, **254-55**
Tanuma Okiyuki (田沼意行), 254
Tanrei (單嶺), 179
Tao-an, 32
Tao-hsüan (Dōsen) (道璿), 59
Taoism (道教), 45, 194, 221, 243, 476, 501
Tatebe Seian (建部淸庵), 236
Tatebe Takahiro (建部賢弘), 242
Tayama Katai (田山花袋), 516
Tayasu Munetake (田安宗武), 211

Tazoe Tetsuji (田添鐵二), 402
Teikoku Rayon Company (帝國人絹株式會社), 456
Teikokushugi-ka no Taiwan (帝國主義下の臺灣), 517
Teikoku Yūbin Jōkisen Kaisha (帝國郵便蒸汽船會社), 367
Tei Seikō, *see* Cheng Ch'eng-kung
Teisei zōyaku Sairan igen (訂正增譯采覽異言), 275
Teiyūkai (丁酉會), 315
Tejima Toan (手島堵庵), 171, 195
Tekitekisaijuku (Tekijuku) (適々齋塾), 184, 229
Temmangū shrine (天滿宮神社), 64, 65
Temmei famine (天明の大饑飢), 212
Temmei-jikiju (天命直授), 404
Temmon keitō (天文瓊統), 243
Temmon Seizō-zu, 243
Temmu, Emperor (天武天皇), 33, 53, 60, 70, 71
Tempō Reforms (天保の改革), 216
Tempyō era (天平), 60
Tenchi nikyū yōhō (天地二球用法), 219
Tendai (T'ien-t'ai) Buddhism (天臺宗), 23, 33, 55-57, 91, 93, 96, 107, 110, 112, 118, 123, 124-26, 134-37, 226, 255, 256
Tendaishū kōyō (天臺宗綱要), 406
tengen'jutsu (天元術), 242
Tenji, Emperor (天智天皇), 27, 33, 53, 63, **69-70**
tenjiku-yō (天竺樣), 93
Tenjin (天神), 20
Tenkai (天海), **255-56**
Tennō-ki (天皇記), 62
Tenri Kyōkai (天理教會), 424
Tenri Library (天理圖書館), 198
Tenriō-no-mikoto (天理生命), 424
Tenryaku (天曆), 21
Tenryū-ji, 88, 123, 136, 137, 145
Tenryū-ji bune (天龍寺船), 123
Tenryū-ji line (天龍寺派), 123
Tenshinrō Academy (天眞樓塾), 246
Ten'yūmaru (天祐丸), 331
Teppō chiryōsho (鐵砲治療書), 176
Teradaya incident (寺田屋事件), 409
Terajima Munenori (寺島宗則), 197, **491-92**
Teramura Sazen (寺村左膳), 334
Terauchi Hisaichi (寺內壽一), 344
Terauchi Masakata (寺內正毅), 333, 339, **492-93**, 513
Terazawa Katataka (寺澤堅高), 164
Tetsugakkan (Tōyō University) (哲學館), 350 418
Tetsugakkai (哲學會), 350
Tetsugaku no kompon mondai (哲學の根本問題), 428
Tetsugaku Zasshi (哲學雜誌), 314
Tettō Gikō (徹翁義亨), 135
Tettsū Gikai (徹通義介), 113
Thailand, 344, 495
Theravada Buddhism (南方佛教), 462, 484
These, 373, 382, 496
Third Japanese-Korean agreement (第三次日韓條約), 363
Third National Bank (第三國立銀行), 517
Three Years' War, Later (後三年役), 48
Thousand Character Classic (*Ch'ien-tzu-wen*) (千字文), 72
Thunberg, Carl Peter, 202, 222, 284
T'ien-t'ai, *see* Tendai Buddhism
T'ien-t'ai, Mt. (天臺山), 124
T'ien-tao su-yüan (天道溯源), 424
Tientsin Treaty (天津條約), 326, 338, 362
T'ien-t'ung, Mt., 93, 124, 143
Titsingh, Isaac, 223
Tōa Dōbunkai (東亞同文會), 400
Tōa Dōbun Shoin (東亞同文書院), 400, 475
Tōa-remmei (東亞聯盟), 358
Toba, Emperor (鳥羽天皇), 35, **70-71**
Tochigi Shimbun (栃木新聞), 489
Toda family (戸田氏), 165
Tōdai-ji (東大寺), 20, 22, 32, 44, 50, 51, 55, 56, 59, 61, 67, 93, 96, 100
Tōdaiwajō tōseiden (唐大和上東征傳), 53
Toda Jōsei (戸田城聖), 408
Tōdō shinden (統道眞傳), 165
Tōei-zan Kan'ei-ji (東叡山寛永寺), 256
Tōfuku-ji (東福寺), 96, 116, 142
Tōgan Ean (東巖慧安), 142
Tōgō Heihachirō (東鄉平八郎), 432, **493-94**, 513
Tōgō Shigenori (東鄉茂德), 344, 495
Tōgō Shrine (東鄉神社), 494
Tōgū Gogakumonjo (東宮御學問所), 494
Tohi mondō (都鄙問答), 195
Tōhō Kaigi (東方會議), 520
Tōhoku Imperial University (東北帝國大學), 345, 420, 506
Tōhō Kyōkai (東邦協會), 474
Tōitsu-kaku (統一閣), 461
Tō-ji (東寺), 41, 46, 50, 59
Tōji-ji (等持寺), 145
Tōjō Hideki (東條英機), 341, 358, 385, 389, 394, 396, 401, 437, 438, 449, 469, **494**
Tōjō Hidenori (東條英教), 494
Tōkai ichiōshū (東海一漚集), 95
Tōkai-ji (東海寺), 253
Tōkai Keizai Shimpō (東海經濟新報), 354
Tokai shimpō (渡海新法), 189
Tōkei Tokugo (桃溪德悟), 118
Tokiwa Gozen (常磐御前), 121, **139**
Tokudaiji Kin'ito (德大寺公純), 453
Tokudaiji Sanetsune (德大寺實則), 453
Tokuda Kyūichi (德田球一), 435, 468, **496-97**
Tokugawa Akitake (德川昭武), 463
Tokugawa family (德川家), 171, 191, 192, 238, 247, 257, 265, 278, 285, 384, 423, 463, 481, 500
Tokugawa Hidetada (德川秀忠), 162, 178,

188, 193, **256-57**, 261, 266, 279, 280
Tokugawa Ieharu (徳川家治), 255, 259
Tokugawa Iemitsu (徳川家光), 211, 253, 256, **257-58**, 261, 275, 285
Tokugawa Iemochi (徳川家茂), 165, 191, 192, **258-59**, 264, 364, 379, 384, 457
Tokugawa Ienari (徳川家齊), 216, **259**
Tokugawa Ienobu (徳川家宣), 167, 230
Tokugawa Iesada (徳川家定), 192, 264
Tokugawa Ieshige (徳川家重), 254
Tokugawa Ietsugu (徳川家繼), 168, 263
Tokugawa Ietsuna (徳川家綱), 237, 261, 279
Tokugawa Ieyasu (徳川家康), 109, 139, 162, 163, 169, 172, 174, 179, 182, 188-90, 193, 195, 196, 199, 201, 202, 206, 207, 213, 218, 223, 226, 228, 231, 237, 245, 252, 256, 258, 259, **260-61**, 266, 267, 280
Tokugawa Kazuko (徳川和子), 178
Tokugawa Mitsukuni (徳川光圀), 277
Tokugawa Mitsusada (徳川光貞), 263
Tokugawa Nariaki (徳川齊昭), 177, 264, 472
Tokugawa Saijun (徳川齊順), 258
Tokugawa shogunate (徳川幕府), 161, 170, 173, 178, 179, 184, 188, 202, 211, 215, 219, 224, 240, 242, 244, 245, 254-56, 259, 260, 272, 275, 277, 279, 282
Tokugawa Tsunatoyo (徳川綱豐), 242, 285
Tokugawa Tsunayoshi (徳川綱吉), 167, 168, 206, 230, 237, 242, **261-62**, 277
Tokugawa Yoshinao (徳川義直), 193
Tokugawa Yorinobu (徳川頼宣), 283, 285
Tokugawa Yoshimune (徳川吉宗), 166, 168, 193, 211, 225, 254, **263**
Tokugawa Yoshinobu (徳川慶喜), 239, **264-65**, 329, 334, 364, 379, 406, 413, 427
Tokuichi (徳一), 57
Tokuko (徳子), 138
Tokushima Mainichi Shimbun (徳島毎日新聞), 368
Tokutomi Roka (徳富蘆花), 498
Tokutomi Sohō (徳富蘇峰), **497-98**, 510
Tokyo Asahi Shimbun (東京朝日新聞), 475, 476
Tokyo College of Science (東京理科大學), 345
Tokyo English School (東京英語學校), 475
Tokyo Federation of Women's Societies (東京聯合婦人會), 523
Tokyo Gaikokugo Gakkō (Tokyo Foreign Language School) (東京外國語學校), 4, 45, 483, 502
Tokyo Gakushi Kaiin Zasshi (東京學士會院雜誌), 500
Tokyo Geographical Society (東京地學協會), 326
Tokyo Girls' Normal School (東京女子師範學校), 424
Tokyo Higher Normal School (東京高等師範學校), 368, 371
Tokyo Ichibanchō Itchi Church (東京一番町一致教會), 504
Tokyo Imperial University (東京帝國大學), 197, 314, 319, 320, 322, 339, 341, 343, 345, 347, 349, 350, 354, 358, 366, 368, 370, 371, 373, 375, 376, 381, 382, 388, 389, 391, 392, 398, 399, 405, 409, 415, 416, 418, 420, 421, 423-25, 427, 430, 436, 437, 459, 460, 465, 466, 468, 474-76, 480, 482, 483, 485, 487, 500, 501, 506, 512, 515, 516, 518, 520, 521
Tokyo Itchi Theological Seminary (東京一致神學校), 504
Tokyo Kaisei Gakkō (東京開成學校), 375, 512
Tokyo Keizai Zasshi (東京經濟雜誌), 481
Tokyo Mainichi Shimbun (東京毎日新聞), 356
Tokyo Medical School (東京醫學校), 391
Tokyo Nichinichi Shimbun (東京日日新聞), 363, 376, 479
Tokyo Normal School (東京師範學校), 368
Tokyo School for the Blind and Dumb (東京盲唖學校), 368
Tokyo Semmon Gakkō (Waseda University) (東京專門學校(早稲田大學)), 388, 407, 442, 445, 476, 500
Tokyo Shingakusha (東京神學社), 504
Tokyo Shūshin Gakusha (東京修身學者), 429
Tokyo University of Education (東京教育大學), 498
Tokyo University of the Arts (東京藝術大學), 368
Tokyo University Preparatory School (東京大學豫備門), 370
Tokyo Women's Medical College (東京女子醫學專門學校), 523
Tominaga Nakamoto (富永仲基), **265-66**
Tomioka Mochinao (富岡以直), 195
Tomita Takayoshi (富田高慶), 224
Tomonaga Shin'ichirō (朝永振一郎), **498**
Tomo no Kowamine (伴建岑), 50
Tōnan-in (東南院), 59
Toneri Shinnō (舎人親王), **71**
Tonkin, 246
Tōno monogatari (遠野物語), 516
Tōrei Enji (東嶺圓慈), 180
Tori no nakune (鳥の鳴音), 250
Tosa (土佐), 237, 276, 329, 334, 359, 366, 371, 419, 421, 423, 439, 440, 444, 457, 490, 503
Tosabō Shōshun (土佐坊昌俊), 121
Tōsan Tanshō (東山湛照), 96, 113, 115
Tosa Shōji (土佐商事), 366
Tōsei (Control) faction (統制派), 495
Tōshōdai-ji (唐招提寺), 32
Tōshō-gū (東照宮), 224, 261
Tōtatsu kikō (東韃紀行), 211
Totsuka Seikai (戸塚靜海), 269
Tōyama Mitsuru (頭山滿), **498-99**
Tōyō Bunko (東洋文庫), 501
Tōyō Eiwa Gakkō (東洋英和學校), 510
Tōyō Gakugei Zasshi (東洋學藝雜誌), 474
Tōyō Jiyū Shimbun (東洋自由新聞), 421, 453
Tōyō Jiyūtō (東洋自由黨), 436
Tōyōkan (東洋館), 445
Toyokawa Ryōhei (豐川良平), 354

Tōyō Keizai Shimpō (東洋經濟新報), 356
Toyomiyasaki Bunko (豐宮崎文庫), 271
Toyotomi family (豐臣氏), 183, 190, 202, 245, 257, 280
Toyotomi Hidetsugu (豐臣秀次), 266
Toyotomi Hideyori (豐臣秀頼), 196, 202, 218, 245, 257, 261, **266**, 279, 280
Toyotomi Hideyoshi (豐臣秀吉), 85, 86, 100, 104, 130, 163, 169, 174, 179, 190, 193, 195, 198, 201, 206, 213, 218, 223, 227, 230, 231, 246, 252, 256, 261, 266, **267-68**, 279, 280
Toyotomi Tsurumatsu (豐臣鶴松), 280
Toyouke Daijingū (豐受大神宮), 271
Toyouke no Ōkami (豐受大神), 141
Tōyō University (東洋大學), 405, 483
Tōzai byōkō (東西病考), 269
Treaty of Shimonoseki (下關講和條約), 362
Tripartite Pact (三國同盟), 401, 412, 519
Tripitaka (*Daizōkyō*) (大藏經), 20, 256, 405, 425, 484
Triple Intervention (三國干涉), 420, 497
Tsan kingdom, 51
Ts'ao-tung Zen, *see* Sōtō Zen
Tsubaki Chinzan (椿椿山), 271
Tsuboi Shindō (坪井信道), 229
Tsuchiya Toshisada (土屋利貞), 167
Tsuda College (津田塾大學), 502
Tsuda Masamichi (津田眞道), 331, 426, 427, **499-500**
Tsuda Sanzō (津田三藏), 397
Tsuda Sen (津田仙), 501
Tsuda Sōkichi (津田左右吉), **500-01**
Tsuda Sōkyū (津田宗及), 201
Tsuda Umeko (津田梅子), **501-02**
Tsugaru Nobumasa (津輕信政), 283
Tsukuba (筑波), 467
Tsukudaya Han'emon (佃屋半右衛門), 166
Tsukumo Company (九十九商會), 366
Tsukushi (筑紫), 377
Tsunesada, Prince (恒貞親王), 50
Tsuneyasu Yosaburō (常安與三郎), 280
Tsung-chüeh Ch'an-shih (Shūgaku Zenji) (宗覺禪師), 142
Tsutsui Masanori (筒井政憲), 162
Tungusic state, 17
Turkey, 320
Twenty-one Demands (21ケ條の要求), 376, 443

U

Uchida Kōsai (內田康哉), 344
Uchida Ryōhei (內田良平), 499
Uchimura Kanzō (內村鑑三), 402, 430, 457, **502-03**, 516
Uchiyama Shichibei (內山七兵衛), 242
Uda, Emperor (宇多天皇), 20, 21, 28, 41, 64
Udagawa Genshin (Shinsai) (宇田川玄眞(榛齋)), 229, 236, 269
Udagawa Genzui (宇田川玄隨), 203, 241, **268-69**
Udagawa Kōsai (宇田川興齋), 269
Udagawa Michinori (宇田川道紀), 268
Udagawa Shinsai, *see* Udagawa Genshin
Udagawa Yōan (宇田川榕庵), **269**
Ueki Emori (植木枝盛), **503**
Uemura Masahisa (植村正久), **504**
Ueno Sukeemon (上野助右衛門), 406
Uesugi Kagekatsu (上杉景勝), 174, 195, 256, 261
Uesugi Kenshin (上杉謙信), 139, **140**, 188
Uesugi Norimasa (上杉憲政), 140
Uesugi Norizane (上杉憲實), **140-41**
Uesugi Shinkichi (上杉愼吉), 348, 389, 415
Uesugi Zenshū (上杉禪秀), 90
Ugaki Kazushige (宇垣一成), 344, 357, **504-05**
Uge no hitokoto (宇下人言), 212
Ugoku Tera (動く寺), 461
Ui Hakuju (宇井伯壽), 484, **505-06**
Uji no chōja (氏長者), 28
Ukita Naoie (宇喜多直家), 206
ukiyo-e (浮世繪), 270
Umeda Umpin (梅田雲濱), 184, 277
Umeda Yūsai (梅田幽齋), 233
Ume Kenjirō (梅謙次郎), 347
Umezu Yoshijirō (梅津美治郎), 469
Ummon, *see* Yün-men
Ummon ikkyoku (雲門一曲), 137
Ummon-ji (雲門寺), 137
Umpo Zenshō (雲甫全祥), 171
Ungo-an (雲居庵), 134, 137, 145
Unkei (運慶), 93
Uruma no Tokikuni (漆間時國), 107
Uryū Tora (瓜生寅), 406
Usa Hachiman Shrine (宇佐八幡宮), 71
Utsunomiya Nobufusa (宇都宮信房), 136
U.S.A., 191, 237, 251, 258, 264, 313, 315, 316, 319, 322, 330, 333, 336, 341, 345, 346, 348, 350, 358, 361, 365, 368-70, 372, 375, 379, 387, 398, 399, 402, 403, 408, 411, 412, 416, 419-22, 426, 429, 430, 433-35, 440, 444, 447, 448, 451, 455, 462, 465, 468, 476-79, 482, 484, 485, 488, 493, 495, 501, 502, 508, 512, 514, 515, 517, 520, 522, 523
U.S.S.R., 333, 469

V

Vairocana, 46, 61
Vailgnano, Alessandro, 169
Vasubandhu, 22
Verbeck, Guido Herman Fridolin, 441, 473
vermilion-seal patent, see *shuin*
Versailles Peace Conference, 400, 411, 454, 469
Victoria, Queen, 334
Vietnam, 169
Vimalakīrti Sutra, 62
Vissering, Professor, 500
Vitte, Sergei Yulievich, 399

W

Wada Yoshimori (和田義盛), 106, 119, **141**

Wadō-kaichin (和銅開珎), 33
Wagaku Kōdansho (和學講談所), 182
Wakai Hito (若い人), 461
Wakatsuki Reijirō (若槻禮次郎), 337, 355, 363, 465, 488, 505, **506-07**
Wake no Kiyomaro (和氣清麻呂), 41, **71-72**
Wan-chi Hsing-mi (頑極行彌), 110
Wang Yang-ming Neo-Confucianism (Yōmei-gaku) (陽明學), 198, 209, 221, 222, 235, 240, 265, 366, 450
Wani, 52, **72**
Warawa no hanshōgai (妾の半生涯), 328
Warera (我等), 447
Warera no Ie (我等の家), 343
Warring States era (戰國時代), 89, 139, 267
Waseda University, 313, 320, 356, 357, 388, 390, 407, 442, 443, 445-47, 459, 467, 476, 479, 500, 501
Washington Conference, 378, 433
Washio Junkyō (鷲尾順敬), 418
Washiyama Yōsai (鷲山養齋), 523
Watanabe Kaikyoku (渡邊海旭), 483
Watanabe Kazan (渡邊崋山), 176, 207, 232, 240, 241, 249, **270-71**
Watanabe Sadamichi (渡邊定通), 270
Watarai Ieyuki (度會家行), **141-42**
Watarai Nobutsune (渡會延經), 271
Watarai Nobuyoshi (渡會延圭), **271-72**
Watarai Shintō (度會神道), 141, 271
Wei dynasty, 37
Welt als Wille und Vorstellung, Die, 315
Wen hsüan, 116
Wen-tsung, Emperor (文宗皇帝), 132
Wild Rover, 426
Women's Higher Normal School (女子高等師範學校), 501
Women's movement (婦人社會運動), 328, 342
World Mothers' Convention (世界母親大會), 343
World Religious Consference (世界宗教會議), 394
World War I, 317, 382, 445, 482, 493
Wu-an P'u-ning (Gottan Funei) (兀菴普寧), 118, **142**
Wu-chun Shin-fan, 96, 142, 143
Wu-hsi-ssu, 142
Wu-hsüeh Tsu-yüan (Mugaku Sogen) (無學祖元), 115, 134, **143**
Wu-i K'o-ch'in, 137
Wu-ming Hui-hsing (Mumyō Eshō) (無明慧性), 118
Wu-t'ai, Mt. (五臺山), 20
Wu-teng Hui-yung (無等惠融), 110

Y

Ya kingdom, 51
Yakuō Tokuken (約翁德儉), 118
Yakushi-ji (藥師寺), 21, 36
Yakushin (益信), 42
Yale University, 512
Yamada Akiyoshi (山田顯義), 492
Yamada Nagamasa (山田長政), **271-72**
Yamada Tonan (山田圖南), 216
Yamaga gorui (山鹿語類), 273
Yamaga school of military science (兵學の山鹿派), 272, 273, 281
Yamaga Sokō (山鹿素行), **272-73**
Yamagata Aritomo (山縣有朋), 282, 316, 339, 380, 393, 398, 419, 427, 431, 448, 452, 453, 458, 488, 490, **508-10**, 513
Yamagata Bantō (山片蟠桃), **274**
Yamagata Daini (山縣大貳), 277
Yamagata-Lobanov Agreement, 509
Yamaji Aizan (山路愛山), 497, **510-11**
Yamakawa Chiō (山川智應), 487
Yamakawa Hitoshi (山川均), 317, 457, 496, **511**
Yamakawa Kenjirō (山川健次郎), **512**
Yamakawa Kikue (山川菊榮), 511
Yamamoto Gombei (山本權兵衞), 333, 336, 339, 341, 350, 393, 408, 455, 482, 488, 504, **512-14**
Yamamoto Isoroku (山本五十六), **514**
Yamanoto Jōtarō (山本條太郎), 411
Yamamoto Kakuma (山本覺馬), 426
Yamamoto Senji (山本宣治), **515**
Yamamoto Teijirō (山本悌二郎), 319
Yamamura Saisuke (山村才助), **274-75**
Yamana Sōzen (山名宗全), 88, 91, 101, 108, **143-44**
Yamanouchi Toyokazu (山內豐策), 457
Yamanouchi Toyoshige (山內豐信), 471
Yamanouchi Yōdō (山內容堂), 238, 334
Yamaoka Matsuakira (山岡浚明), 181
Yamaoka Tesshū (Tetsutarō), 379, 413
Yamashiro no Ōe, Prince, (山背大兄王), 63
Yamatai (邪馬臺國), 37
Yamato court (大和朝廷), 8, 17
Yamato-hime-no mikoto (倭姬命), 73
Yamato Kenryū (大和見立), 181
Yamato no Ayauji (倭漢氏の東漢氏), 18
Yamato Takeru-no-mikoto (日本武尊), **72-73**
Yamawaki Genshū (山脇玄修), 275
Yamawaki Tōyō (山脇東洋), **275-76**
Yamaza Enjirō (山座圓次郎), 343
Yamazaki Ansai (山崎闇齋), 243, **276-77**
Yamazaki Ansai zenshū (山崎闇齋全集), 277
Yamazaki, battle of (山崎の合戰), 206, 267
Yamazaki Jōin (山崎淨因), 276
Yanagida Collection (柳田文庫), 516
Yanagida Kunio (柳田國男), **515-16**
Yanagisawa Yasusada (柳澤安貞), 278
Yanagisawa Yasutada (柳澤安忠), 277
Yanagisawa Yoshiyasu (柳澤吉保), 205, 262, **277-78**
Yanaihara Tadao (矢內原忠雄), **516-17**
Yanaka mura metsubō-shi (谷中村滅亡史), 316
Yang, Emperor, 53, 62
Yano Fumio (矢野文雄), 354, 448

Yasen kanwa (夜船閑話), 180
Yashiro Hirokata (屋代弘賢), 182
Yashiro Rokurō (矢代六郎), 478
Yasuda Bank (安田銀行), 517
Yasuda Hall (安田講堂), 518
Yasuda Hozensha (安田保善社), 517
Yasuda *zaibatsu* (安田財閥), 517
Yasuda Zenjirō (安田善次郎), **517-18**
Yasui Santetsu (安井算哲), 243
Yasuke cannon (彌助砲), 447
Yasutomi Kiseki (安富寄碩), 222
Yayoi culture (彌生文化), 39
Yin-yüan (Ingen) (隱元), 265, **278-79**
Yochishi (輿地誌), 208
Yodogimi (淀君), 85, 266, **279-80**
Yodoya Saburōemon (淀屋三郎右衞門), 281
Yodoya Tatsugorō (淀屋辰五郎), **280-81**
Yōfukuki (陽復記), 271
Yōgakkō (洋學校), 162, 497
Yōgaku kōyō (幼學綱要), 417
Yōjōkun (養生訓), 200
Yōjō-ryū (葉上流), 125
Yōjuin isoku (養壽院醫則), 276
Yōkai kōgiroku (妖怪講義錄), 350
Yokohama Mainichi Shimbun (橫濱每日新聞), 220
Yokohama Specie Bank (Bank of Tokyo) (橫濱正金銀行(東京銀行)), 350
Yokoi Shōnan (橫井小楠), 184, 240, **518-19**, 524
Yokoi Tokio (橫井時雄), 324, 519
Yōmei, Emperor (用明天皇), 61, 63, 64, 66
Yōmeigaku, *see* Wang Yang-ming Neo-Confucianism
Yomiuri Shimbun (讀賣新聞), 382, 475
Yonaga, Prince (世良親王), 114
Yonai Mitsumasa (米內光政), 319, 344, 385, 396, 412, 514, **519-20**
Yōrō ritsuryō (養老律令), 24
Yorozu Chōhō (萬朝報), 316, 402, 456, 502
Yosano Akiko (與謝野晶子), 342
Yoshida Chōshuku (吉田長叔), 249
Yoshida-Everts Convention, 492
Yoshida Kanetomo (吉田兼俱), **144-45**, 283
Yoshida Kenzō (吉田健三), 520
Yoshida Kukoku (吉田駒谷), 207
Yoshida, Mt. (吉田山), 144
Yoshida Sadafusa (吉田定房), 97, 114
Yoshida Shigeru (吉田茂), 340, 349, 357, 409, 460, 466, 475, **520-21**
Yoshida Shinto (吉田神道), 271, 283
Yoshida Shōin (吉田松陰), 239, 251, 273, **281-82**, 361, 385, 431, 508
Yoshida Shrine (吉田神社), 144
Yoshida Taisuke (吉田大助), 281
Yoshida Tōkō (吉田東篁), 184
Yoshida Tōyō (吉田東洋), 334, 366
Yoshii Tomozane (吉井友實), 413
Yoshikawa Genjūrō (吉川源十郎), 241
Yoshikawa Koretari (吉川惟足), 276, **283**
Yoshikawa Shigodō gyōjōki (吉川視吾堂行狀記), 283
Yoshikawa Shigodō kotogaki (吉川視吾堂事書), 283
Yoshimasu Nangai (吉益南涯), 181
Yoshinaga, Prince (義良親王), 113-15
Yoshinashikoto (よしなし言), 243
Yoshino (吉野), 377
Yoshino Sakuzō (吉野作造), 438, 447, 476, 517, **521-22**
Yoshioka Arata (吉岡荒太), 523
Yoshioka Yayoi (吉岡彌生), **523**
Yoshio Kōsaku (吉雄幸作), 209, **284**
Yoshio Kōzaemon (吉雄幸左衞門), 219
Yoshio school of surgery (吉雄流外科), 284
Yoshio Yūjirō (吉雄雄次郎), 284
Yoshishige no Yasutane (慶滋保胤), 47, **74**
Yoshitsune senbonzakura (義經千本櫻), 122
Yoshizaki Dōjō (吉崎道場), 131
Yōzei, Emperor (陽成天皇), 28
Yūaikai (友愛會), 369, 435, 476
Yüan dynasty, 105, 110, 132, 146
Yuan Shih-k'ai, 521
Yuasa Kurahei (湯淺倉平), 385
Yūbikan (有備館), 386
Yūbin Hōchi Shimbun (郵便報知新聞), 338, 354, 448
Yuge Dōkyō (弓削道鏡), 21
Yūgen (幽玄), 89
Yuien (唯圓), 134
yuishiki (唯識), 22
Yuishiki Buddhism (唯識學), 418
Yuishikiron dōgakushō (唯識論同學鈔), 111
Yui Shōsetsu (由井正雪), 211, **284-85**
Yuitsu (唯一), 144
Yūkan (融觀), 56
Yukawa Hideki (湯川秀樹), **523-24**
Yume-monogatari (夢物語), 249
Yume no shiro (夢の代), 274
Yün-men (Ummon) (雲門), 135
Yuri Kimimasa (由利公正), 329, 519, **524-25**
Yü-sang-shan (育王山), 110
Yushima Seidō (湯島聖堂), 262
Yūzonsha (Society for the Preservation of the National Essence) (猶存社), 391, 438
Yūzū Nembutsu sect (融通念佛宗), 56

Z

Zaikai Kaiko (財界回顧), 349
Zaisho zange-roku (在床懺悔錄), 394
Zange (懺悔), 389
Zazen yōjin-ki (坐禪用心記), 113
Zeami (世阿彌), 90
Zeigo (贅語), 214
Zekkai Chūshin (絕海中津), 123, **145-46**
Zen Buddhism (禪), 85, 88, 93-96, 110, 111, 113, 118, 123, 124, 129, 132, 135-37, 142, 143, 145, 179, 199, 201, 265, 276, 278, 427, 450, 476, 477, 506
Zen'ei (前衞), 511
Zengi gemonshū (禪儀外文集), 116

Zen-in (禪院), 22
Zeniya Gohei (錢屋五兵衛), **285-86**
Zenkō-ji (善光寺), 109
Zenkoku Rōnō Taishūtō (National Laber Farmer Populace Party) (全國勞農大衆黨), 320, 374, 457
Zenkoku Taishūtō (National Popular Party) (全國大衆黨), 479
Zen no kenkyū (善の研究), 427
Zenran (善鸞), 133
Zenrin-ji (禪林寺), 22
Zōho jūtei naika senyō (增補重訂內科選要), 269
Zoku Gunsho ruijū (續群書類從), 182
Zoku Ichinen yūhan (續一年有半), 422
Zola, Emile, 456
Zōshi (藏志), 275
Zōshikan (造士館), 416, 450
Zuiō-ji (隨鷗寺), 171
Zuisen-ji (瑞泉寺), 123
Zusho Hirosato (調所廣鄉), **286**
Zusho Kiyonobu (調所淸悅), 286